In the last century, a new way of looking at the Bible developed. Research into the ancient Near East and its texts recreated for us the civilizations out of which the Bible emerged. In this century, there has been a revival of Jewish biblical scholarship; Israeli and American scholars, in particular, concentrating in the fields of archaeology, biblical history, Semitic languages, and the religion of Israel, have opened exciting new vistas into the world of the Scriptures. For the first time in history, we have at our disposal information and methodological tools that enable us to explore the biblical text in a way that could never have been done before. This new world of knowledge, as seen through the eyes of contemporary Jewish scholars and utilizing at the same time the insights of over twenty centuries of traditional Jewish exegesis, is now available for the first time to a general audience in *The JPS Torah Commentary*.

The Commentary is published in five volumes, each by a single author who has devoted himself to the study of the text. Given the wide range of perspectives that now exist in biblical scholarship, the JPS has recognized the individual expertise of these authors and made no attempt to impose uniformity on the methodology or content of their work.

The Hebrew text is that of the Leningrad Codex B 19ᴬ, the oldest dated manuscript of the complete Hebrew Bible. Copied from a text written by the distinguished Masoretic scholar Aaron ben Moses ben Asher, who lived in the first half of the 10th century C.E., the manuscript was completed in 1009 C.E. In this edition it has been arranged according to the weekly synagogue Torah readings. The format has been adjusted to correspond to that adopted by the TANAKH, the new translation of the Hebrew Bible, published by the Jewish Publication Society and utilized in the present *Commentary*.

The Jewish Publication Society has completed this project with a full awareness of the great tradition of Jewish Bible commentary, with a profound sense of the sanctity of the biblical text and an understanding of the awe and love that our people has accorded its Bible. The voice of our new *Commentary* resounds with the spirit and concerns of our times—just as the Jewish spirit has always found its most sincere and heartfelt expression in its appreciation of the Bible; yet it acknowledges the intrinsic value of the tools of modern scholarship in helping to establish the original sense and setting of Scripture.

With all this fixed firmly in mind, the Jewish Publication Society commits its good name and its decades of pioneering in the world of English-language Jewish publishing to this *Torah Commentary* with the hope that it will serve as the contemporary addition to the classic commentaries created by Jews during past epochs in Jewish history.

Nahum M. Sarna, GENERAL EDITOR
Chaim Potok, LITERARY EDITOR

וְהַמַּשְׂכִּלִים יַזְהִרוּ כְּזֹהַר הָרָקִיעַ
וּמַצְדִּיקֵי הָרַבִּים כַּכּוֹכָבִים לְעוֹלָם וָעֶד

Sander H., Alan, and David C. Mendelson

Joseph and Rebecca Meyerhoff

Warren G. and Gay H. Miller

Mr. and Mrs. Hershel Muchnick
In memory of Max and Annie Sherman
and Lt. Louis O. Sherman

Joseph Muchnick
In memory of his wife, Mollie

Nancy and Morris W. Offit

Mr. and Mrs. Mitchell E. Panzer
In memory of their parents

Edith and Charles Pascal
In memory of their parents,
Harry and Lena Chidakel
Harry and Marion Pascal

Mr. and Mrs. Frank J. Pasquerilla

Leon J. Perelman

Mr. and Mrs. Ronald O. Perelman

Harry M. and Esther L. Plotkin

Anne and Henry S. Reich

Arleen and Robert S. Rifkind

Judy and Arthur Robbins
In honor of Sheila F. Segal

Mr. and Mrs. Daniel Rose

Sam Rothberg

Rabbi Stephen A. and Nina Berman Schafer
In memory of Joel Michael Schafer

Drs. Amiel and Chariklia-Tziraki Segal

Bernard G. Segal

Norma L. Shapiro
In memory of her parents,
Jane K. and Bert Levy

Lola and Gerald Sherman
In memory of Jean and Al Sherman
and Ada and Jack Kay

Jerome J. and Marciarose Shestack
In memory of Olga and Isadore Shestack
and Clara Ruth Schleifer

Jonathan and Jennifer Shestack
In memory of their great-grandfathers,
Rabbi Israel Shankman and
Rabbi Judah Shestack

Dr. and Mrs. Edward B. Shils

Charles E. Smith
In honor of Mr. and Mrs. Robert P. Kogod
and Mr. and Mrs. Robert H. Smith

Marian Scheuer Sofaer

William and Radine Spier

The Oscar and Lillian Stempler Foundation
In memory of Rose and Isadore Engel
and Lillian Stempler
In honor of Oscar Stempler

David B. Sykes
In memory of his wife, Shirley

Mr. and Mrs. Sylvan M. Tobin

Sami and Annie Totah
In honor of their parents

Adele and Bert M. Tracy
In memory of their parents

Elizabeth R. and Michael A. Varet

Edna and Charles Weiner

Simon and Trudy Weker
In honor of their children,
Laurie, Jonathan, and Robert

Morton H. Wilner

Mr. and Mrs. Seymour D. Wolf
In memory of their parents,
Abraham and Dora Wolf
Abraham and Sarah Krupsaw

Dr. Allen M. and Eleanor B. Wolpe

Ben Zevin

Benjamin Bernard Zucker
In honor of Lotty Gutwirth Zucker

PATRONS

And the knowledgeable will be radiant like the bright expanse of sky,
And those who lead the many to righteousness will be like the stars forever and ever.

DANIEL 12:3

Mr. and Mrs. Robert P. Abrams
    In memory of Peter Abrams

D.F. Antonelli, Jr.

Mr. and Mrs. Marvin Anzel and Sons
    In memory of Rose and Samuel Anzel

Stephen and Stephanie Axinn

Mr. and Mrs. Ronald S. Baron

Dr. Muriel M. Berman

Nancy Berman and Alan Bloch

Philip I. Berman

Steven M. Berman

Herbert and Nancy Bernhard

Mr. and Mrs. Arthur H. Bienenstock

Goldene and Herschel Blumberg
    In memory and in honor of their parents

Irvin J. Borowsky and Laurie Wagman

Elmer Cerin
    In memory of Sylvia S. Cerin

Dr. and Mrs. D. Walter Cohen
    In honor of their parents,
    Abram and Goldie Cohen
    Joseph and Bessie Axelrod

Melvin and Ryna Cohen

Rosalie and Joseph Cohen

Elsie B. and Martin D. Cohn
    In honor of their children and grandchildren

Mr. and Mrs. Charles M. Diker

Carole and Richard Eisner

Edward E. Elson

The Endowment Fund of the
    Greater Hartford Jewish Federation

Edith Brenner Everett and Henry Everett
    In memory of their father, Eli Brenner,
    and brother, Fred Brenner

Federation of Jewish Agencies
    of Greater Philadelphia

Peter I. Feinberg

Myer and Adrienne Arsht Feldman
    In honor of Bella Feldman

Mr. Joseph M. and Dr. Helen G. First

Libby and Alan Fishman

Selma and William Fishman

The Foundation for Conservative Judaism
    of Greater Philadelphia

Bernard and Muriel Frank

Aaron and Cecile Goldman

Evelyn and Seymour C. Graham

Dorothy Gitter Harman
    In memory of her parents,
    Morris and Maria Gitter

Irving B. Harris

Shirley and Stanley Hayman
    In memory of their parents

Evelyn and Sol Henkind

Erica and Ludwig Jesselson

Leonard Kapiloff

Sol and Rita Kimerling

Lillian and Sid Klemow

Mr. and Mrs. Ronald A. Krancer

William B. and Elaine Kremens

Mr. and Mrs. Harvey M. Krueger

Simon and Rosa Laupheimer

Fanney N. Litvin
    In memory of her husband, Philip Litvin

Ruth Meltzer
    In memory of her husband, Leon

Martha H. and Joseph L. Mendelson

Martha H. and Joseph L. Mendelson
    In memory of their parents,
    Alexander and Celia Holstein
    Abraham and Dora Mendelson

THE JPS TORAH COMMENTARY

EXODUS שמות

GENERAL EDITOR   *Nahum M. Sarna*
LITERARY EDITOR   *Chaim Potok*

GENESIS   *Nahum M. Sarna*
EXODUS   *Nahum M. Sarna*
LEVITICUS   *Baruch A. Levine*
NUMBERS   *Jacob Milgrom*
DEUTERONOMY   *Jeffrey H. Tigay*

THE JPS TORAH
COMMENTARY

EXODUS שמות

The Traditional Hebrew Text with the New JPS Translation

Commentary by NAHUM M. SARNA

THE JEWISH PUBLICATION SOCIETY

PHILADELPHIA · NEW YORK · JERUSALEM   5751 / 1991

Exodus Commentary © 1991 by The Jewish Publication Society

Masoretic Hebrew text, Codex Leningrad B19ᴬ, taken from
Biblia Hebraica Stuttgartensia (BHS) © 1967/77, 1983, by the Deutsche Bibelgesellschaft, Stuttgart
Synagogue adaptation and revised format © 1989 by The Jewish Publication Society

English translation of the Torah © 1962, 1985, 1989 by The Jewish Publication Society

All rights reserved   First edition
Manufactured in the United States of America
Composed by Polebridge Press in Galliard (English text) and Keter (Hebrew text).
Printed and bound by Arcata Graphics.

Library of Congress Cataloging-in-Publication Data
Sarna, Nahum M.
    Exodus : the traditional Hebrew text with the new JPS translation /
commentary by Nahum M. Sarna. — 1st ed.
        p.   cm. — (The JPS Torah commentary)
        English and Hebrew; commentary in English
        Includes bibliographical references.
        ISBN 0-8276-0327-4
        1. Bible. O.T. Exodus—Commentaries. I. Bible. O.T. Exodus.
Hebrew. 1991. II. Bible. O.T. Exodus. English. Jewish
Publication Society. 1991. III. Title. IV. Series.
BS1245.3.S27   1991   90-41773
222'.12077—dc20   CIP

GENESIS   *ISBN 0-8276-0326-6*
LEVITICUS   *ISBN 0-8276-0328-2*
NUMBERS   *ISBN 0-8276-0329-0*
DEUTERONOMY   *ISBN 0-8276-0330-4*
Five-volume set   ISBN 0-8276-0331-2

THE JPS TORAH COMMENTARY PROJECT
    JEROME J. SHESTACK *Chairman*
    JOSEPH L. MENDELSON *Vice Chairman*

Designed by ADRIANNE ONDERDONK DUDDEN

10   9   8   7   6   5   4   3   2

For my grandchildren
Ariel
  Leora
    Aaron
      Shira
        Leah

ACKNOWLEDGMENTS

While, of course, I take sole responsibility for the entire contents of this book, I must acknowledge my great indebtedness to several persons: to Chaim Potok for his skilled editorial labors and the innumerable improvements he made in my manuscript; to Sheila F. Segal, who also edited the book and much enhanced its style; to Marvin Fox, who was kind enough to read the entire *Commentary* with a critical, scholarly eye and who freely imparted of his learning and insights, from which I have greatly profited. Diane W. Zuckerman and Elissa Biren of the staff of The Jewish Publication Society, Ilene Cohen, the copy editor, and Adrianne Onderdonk Dudden, who designed the volume, have all rendered exemplary service in the production of *The Commentary*. I take this opportunity to thank Nehama Stampfer Glogower, who typed the entire manuscript and made several very helpful suggestions, Saul Isserow and Lee Mondshein, as well as my sons, David and Jonathan, for their contributions. I am grateful to Saul Leeman for his valuable comments and typographical corrections. I am indebted to the staffs of the libraries of Brandeis University, the Hebrew College, Boston, and the Library of Congress. Finally, I must express my deep appreciation, however inadequately, to my wife, Helen, for her patience, encouragement, and self-sacrifice, all of which enabled me to complete this book.

Nahum M. Sarna

CONTENTS

EXCURSUSES TO THE EXODUS COMMENTARY

WEEKLY TORAH READINGS FROM THE BOOK OF EXODUS

INTRODUCTION

The Title

The commonly known Hebrew title for the second book of the Torah is *Shemot*, shortened from the opening words *ve'elleh shemot*. This follows an ancient and widespread Near Eastern practice of naming a literary work by its initial word or words. In Genesis Rabba[1] we find the full title: *Sefer 'Elleh Shemot*, "The Book of 'These are the Names.'" The Hebrew name was transliterated in Greek as *oualesmoth*[2] and was used in Latin Bibles in the form of *Hebraica veelle semoth*.

Another ancient Hebrew name was *sefer yetsi'at mitsrayim*, "The Book of the Departure from Egypt," expressing its central theme. The Jews of Alexandria, Egypt, in pre–Christian times, rendered this title in Greek as *Exodos Aigyptou,* abbreviated simply as *Exodos,* which is how it appears in the Septuagint, the Jewish translation of the Torah into Greek. This was adopted for use in the Old Latin version of the Bible (pre–fourth century C.E.) in the form of *Exodus* and so passed into the Vulgate and through it into numerous European languages. Another Greek rendering of the Hebrew title was *Exagoge,* "The Leading Out/The Departure [from Egypt]." The Hellenistic Jewish philosopher Philo of Alexandria (ca. 20 B.C.E. to 50 C.E.) used this name and offered his belief that Moses himself had designated the Hebrew title behind it.[3] *Exagoge* must have been quite well known in Egypt, for the Hellenistic Jewish tragedian Ezekiel (latest date, mid first century B.C.E.) composed a drama by that name.

The Hebrew title *sefer yetsi'at mitsrayim* was still current in Palestine in the tenth century C.E., for it is cited in the *Dikdukei Ha-Te'amim* (§70) by the Masoretic scholar Aaron ben Moses ben Asher.[4]

Still a third Hebrew name for the book is mentioned in the Talmud:[5] *Ḥomesh Sheni,* "The Second Fifth [of the Torah]."

The Torah Readings

Present-day editions divide the Book of Exodus into forty chapters. This practice is not rooted in Jewish tradition but was borrowed from Christian Bibles. In the late Middle Ages, the Church forced Jews to engage in disputations, which usually focused upon the interpretation of scriptural passages. This necessitated a common, standardized system of reference, and so the Christian chapter and verse numberings were introduced into the Hebrew manuscript Bibles by Rabbi Solomon ben Ishmael (ca. 1330).[6]

This innovation displaced an earlier Jewish system based upon the weekly Torah readings. In Palestine and Egypt, the entire Pentateuch was originally completed in trien-

nial, or three-year, cycles. The Book of Exodus was variously divided into twenty-nine or thirty-three such *sedarim*, as the weekly Sabbath readings were called. Eventually, the Babylonian practice of completing the entire Torah in the course of a single year became universal. In this system, the Book of Exodus is divided into eleven sections, each known as a *parashah* (pl., *parashot* or *parshiyyot*) or *sidra(h)* (pl., *sedarot*).

The Contents and Character

Using the criterion of geographic location, one may divide Exodus into three parts. Chapters 1:1 to 15:21, which describe the oppression of Israel as well as the struggle for liberation and its final attainment, obviously have as their setting the land of Egypt. The events recorded in chapters 15:22 to 18:27 take place on the way from the Sea of Reeds to Sinai, although the location of chapter 18 is debatable. For the rest of the book, chapters 19 to 40, the scene of the action is Sinai.

Such a simple locational classification, however, obscures the richness and variety of the subject matter, which a glance at the Table of Contents given above will immediately reveal. The Book of Exodus is the great seminal text of biblical literature. Its central theme, God's redemption of His people from Egyptian bondage, is mentioned no less than one hundred and twenty times in the Hebrew Bible in a variety of contexts.[7] This event informed and shaped the future development of the culture and religion of Israel. Remarkably, it even profoundly influenced ethical and social consciousness, so that it is frequently invoked in the Torah as the motivation for protecting and promoting the interests and rights of the stranger and the disadvantaged of society.[8]

This pervasive and sustained impact of the Exodus drama is not limited to the period of the Bible itself. It continued throughout history down to the present time and in recent years has been a source of inspiration for the "theologies of liberation" movements.[9] If it has so profoundly affected peoples of widely different cultures, this is hardly because the biblical narrative is a straightforward account of an historical event; it is not. Rather, this influence is due to the special orientation and perspective of Exodus. It is a document of faith, not a dispassionate, secular report of the freeing of an oppressed people. The Book of Exodus possesses a character all its own and must be understood on its own terms.[10]

A close examination of the constituent elements of the Book of Exodus determines at once that we do not have a comprehensive, sequential narrative, only an episodic account. Moreover, the time frame in which the varied episodes are placed is extremely limited. The afore-cited passage from the *Dikdukei Ha-Te'amim* adduces a tradition that one hundred and forty years elapsed between the death of Joseph (1:4)—the first event recorded in the book—and the construction of the Tabernacle almost exactly one year after the Exodus, the last dated occurrence (40:2). Yet, the narrative is most sparing of detail relating to the period of the oppression. Neither the duration of the sufferings of the Israelites nor anything about their inner life and community existence is mentioned. Only incidentally do we learn that the period of Egyptian enslavement lasted at least eighty years. We are told that Moses, who was born after the king's genocidal decree, was eighty years old when he first presented himself before the pharaoh as the leader of the people. Further investigation reveals that the book really covers the events of just two years: the year-long diplomatic activity as well as the coercive measures taken against the Egyptians and a few incidents

from the year in the wilderness following the Exodus. This limitation, together with the paucity of historical data, suggests a high degree of deliberate selectivity. Both the selectivity and the disposition of the featured material stamp the Book of Exodus as falling into the category of historiosophy rather than historiography: Not the preservation and recording of the past for its own sake but the culling of certain historic events for didactic purposes is the intent.[11]

The entire narrative is God centered. Its focal points are God's mighty deeds on behalf of His people in times of oppression, in the act of liberation, and in the course of the wilderness wanderings. God is the sole actor, the only initiator of events. The various episodes, therefore, project Israelite concepts of God and of His relationship to the world; that is, they embody the fundamental tenets and crucial elements of the religion of Israel and of its world view.

The different aspects of the divine personality, as revealed in Exodus, express a conception of God that is poles apart from any pagan notions. There is but a single Deity, who demands exclusive service and fidelity. Being the Creator of all that exists, He is wholly independent of His creations, and totally beyond the constraints of the world of nature, which is irresistibly under His governance. This is illustrated by the phenomena of the burning bush, the ten plagues, and the dividing of the Sea of Reeds. As a consequence, any attempt to depict or represent God in material or pictorial form is inevitably a falsification and is strictly prohibited. The biblical polemic against idolatry appears here for the first time in the context of the Exodus.

Although the nature of God must be beyond the scope of the human imagination, the texts affirm, as one of their principal teachings, that He is nevertheless deeply involved in human affairs. History, therefore, is not a procession of causeless, undirected, meaningless happenings but is the deliberate, purposeful, unfolding plan of the divine intelligence. God chooses to enter into an eternally valid covenantal relationship with His people, Israel; this legal reality entails immutable and inescapable obligations on their part. The Decalogue and the legislative sections of Exodus thereby constitute divine law. They are not, as is the case with the Near Eastern law collections, the fruit of human wisdom or royal sagacity.

From this flows another credo, first explicated in Exodus, which thereafter animates all of biblical literature: that the welfare of society is conditional upon obedience to God's law. God is deemed to be absolutely moral, and He correspondingly demands moral standards of behavior from human beings. He delivers the faithful from injustice and oppression and ensures the ultimate and inevitable downfall of the wicked.

The religious calendar of Israel became transformed by the Exodus experience. Formerly tied to an expression of the rhythms of the seasons, the sacred times were reinterpreted in terms of that great historical event. They became commemorations of God's benefactions upon Israel in Egypt and in the wilderness and were emancipated from phenomena of nature.

Finally, two of the most important institutions of biblical Israel find their origins in this book. The account of the organization of the cult around a central place of worship with a hereditary priesthood occupies nearly one third of the entire book; thirteen of its forty chapters are concerned with this topic. And the prophetic office, of seminal importance for the national history and faith and later also for some of the world's other major religions, is initiated through the person of Moses. He is the archetypal prophet whose mission epitomizes the distinguishing features of later classical apostolic prophecy.

The Setting in Time

A clear distinction must be made between the special literary mold in which the narrative is cast—with its particular selectivity, emphases, and teachings—and the historical background of the Exodus. This last issue is complicated by the absence from the biblical accounts of certain data essential to establishing chronological parameters. The names of the reigning Egyptian kings are not given; we do not know how long after Joseph's death the reversal in the fortunes of the Israelites occurred; and we have no extra-biblical documentation that directly refers to Israel in Egypt, to the Exodus, or to the conquest of Canaan.

In addition to these matters, there is the problem that certain biblical texts have not yet yielded their secrets. For instance, Genesis 15:13 foretells that Abraham's offspring "shall be strangers in a land not theirs, and they shall be enslaved and oppressed for four hundred years." This time span is there coordinated with just four generations. Exodus 12:40–41 states that the Israelites resided in Egypt for four hundred and thirty years. We are not told when this period is thought to have commenced; hence one cannot work backward to the patriarchal era in order to fix the date of Israel's departure from Egypt, not to mention the fact that the dates of the patriarchs are still a matter of scholarly dispute.

The one apparently unambiguous chronological note is in 1 Kings 6:1, according to which four hundred and eighty years intervened between the building of Solomon's Temple and the Exodus. The king's project can be reliably dated to around 960 B.C.E. This would place the great event at about the middle of the fifteenth century B.C.E. Unfortunately, this dating cannot be reconciled with many other details of the biblical narrative. Thus Moses, who lived in the Nile Delta, is easily and frequently in touch with the ruling pharaoh, who must also have had his residence in the area. But in the fifteenth century B.C.E. the Egyptian capital and royal palace were located at Thebes, a distance of more than four hundred miles (ca. 650 km.) to the south of the Delta.

Moreover, commencing about 1550 B.C.E. and for the next few hundred years, energetic and powerful Egyptian monarchs maintained a tight grip on Canaan. This situation would hardly have been conducive to Israel's departure from Egypt and its conquest of Canaan in this period, especially as Egypt never figures in the biblical account of Joshua's campaigns.

On the other hand, a thirteenth century B.C.E. dating would seem to be far more satisfactory. It was then that the royal capital was situated in the Nile Delta; it was in this period that archaeological evidence shows the towns of Pithom and Ramses to have been built, and the Bible ascribes their erection to Israelite slaves. It was then that frenetic construction activity took place in the Nile Delta, which would have required the conscription of large numbers of laborers. The end of the thirteenth century was a period of Egypt's decline and loss of its Canaanite province. The invasion of the Sea Peoples and the Libyans occurred; there was a power vacuum in the East; and generally it was a period of turmoil and upheaval.

Although a mid–thirteenth-century B.C.E. dating for the Exodus presently appears to accommodate more facts than a dating two centuries earlier, it is not without its own difficulties. True, it is reinforced by the Stele of Merneptah, the inscribed monument set up in western Thebes by the pharaoh of that name (ca. 1224 to 1211 B.C.E.) to celebrate his victory over the invaders of Egypt. This stele mentions "Israel" as a people in Canaan but apparently not yet settled down within fixed borders. Nevertheless, the Exodus and con-

quest in the thirteenth century cannot be reconciled with the above-cited biblical chronology if it is to be taken literally. Moreover, the archaeological data collected from numerous sites in the area do not always fit in with the biblical reports of the towns in Transjordan that the Israelites encountered on their way to Canaan nor of the places that Joshua conquered and destroyed in the course of his campaigns inside Canaan, if a thirteenth century B.C.E. time frame be insisted on. Only future research will be able to solve the problem. In the meantime, it must always be remembered that the biblical narrative is a theological exposition—a document of faith, not a historiographical record.

Notes to the Introduction

1. J. Theodor and Ch. Albeck, eds. (Jerusalem: Wahrmann Books, 1965): 708, §64.

2. Used by Origen (3rd cent. C.E.), and by Eusebius (4th cent. C.E.) in his *Ecclesiastical History*, VI:25.

3. De Migratione Abrahami III. 14, Loeb, ed., p. 138.

4. S. Baer and H. L. Strack, eds. (Leipzig, 1879; [reprint] Jerusalem: Makor, 1970), 57.

5. Sotah 36b.

6. C. D. Ginsburg, *Introduction to the Massoretico-Critical Edition of the Hebrew Bible* ([Reprint] New York: Ktav, 1966), 25.

7. Y. Hoffman, *The Doctrine of the Exodus in the Bible* [Hebrew] (Tel Aviv: Tel Aviv University, 1983), 11.

8. Exod. 22:20–22; 23:9; Lev. 19:33–34; Deut. 5:12–15; 10:17–19; 15:12–15; 23:8; 24:17–18, 20–22.

9. Cf. W. Walzer, *Exodus and Revolution* (New York: Basic Books, 1985). On this subject, see J. Levenson, "Liberation Theology and the Exodus," *Midstream,* 35:7 (1989): 30–36.

10. See N. M. Sarna, *Exploring Exodus* (New York: Schocken Books, 1986), 1–9.

11. See I. Finkelstein, *The Archaeology of the Israelite Settlement* (Jerusalem: Israel Exploration Society, 1988); G. London, "A Comparison of Two Contemporaneous Lifestyles of the Late Second Millennium B.C.," BASOR 273 (1989): 37–55.

GLOSSARY

Abraham ben Maimonides (1186–1237)   Son of Moses Maimonides, religious philosopher. Egypt.

Abravanel, Isaac ben Judah (1437–1508)   Statesman, Bible commentator, and religious philosopher. Portugal, Spain, and Italy.

Aggadah   The nonhalakhic (nonlegal) homiletic side of rabbinic teaching, mostly anchored to the biblical text.

Akedat Yitshak   A compilation of sermons and philosophic discourses on the biblical text by Isaac ben Moses Arama (ca. 1420–1494). Spain.

Akkadian   An ancient Semitic language spoken in Mesopotamia; its chief dialects were Babylonian and Assyrian.

Aquila   A convert to Judaism from Pontus, Anatolia, and a disciple of Rabbi Akiba. He translated the standardized biblical Hebrew text into Greek in the 2nd century C.E.

Aramaic   A Semitic language closely related to biblical Hebrew and known in many dialects and phases, including Syriac. Aramaic flourished throughout the biblical period and thereafter, and is the language of the Targums, the Gemaras, and large sections of midrashic literature.

Avot de-Rabbi Nathan   An exposition of an early form of Mishnah Avot (Ethics of the Fathers), transmitted in two versions.

Baal ha-Turim   Commentary on the Torah by Jacob ben Asher (?1270–1340). Germany and Spain.

Bahya ben Asher (13th century)   Bible commentator and kabbalist. Saragossa, Spain.

Bekhor Shor   Commentary on the Torah by Joseph ben Isaac, 12th century. Northern France.

Dunash ben Labrat (mid-10th century)   Linguist, grammarian, and poet. Spain.

Exodus Rabba   Aggadic midrash on the Book of Exodus, originally two separate compositions, combined ca. 11th or 12th centuries.

Gemara   An exposition of the Mishnah in Aramaic and Hebrew.

Genesis Apocryphon   An elaboration of the Genesis narratives in Aramaic from 1st century B.C.E. or C.E., found in cave 1 at Qumran near the Dead Sea.

Genesis Rabba   Palestinian aggadic midrash on the Book of Genesis, edited ca. 425 C.E.

Genesis Rabbati   Midrash on the Book of Genesis ascribed to Rabbi Moses ha-Darshan of Narbonne, 11th century.

Gersonides   See Ralbag.

Halakhah   The individual and collective rabbinic legal rulings that regulate all aspects of Jewish life, both individual and corporate.

Ḥizkuni   Commentary on the Torah by Hezekiah ben Rabbi Manoah, mid-13th century. France.

Ibn Ezra, Abraham (1089–1164)   Poet, grammarian, and Bible commentator. Spain.

Ibn Janah, Jonah (first half of 11th century)   Grammarian and lexicographer. Spain.

Judah ben Samuel he-Hasid (the Pious) (ca. 1150–1217)   Ethical writer and mystic; authored a commentary on the Torah. Regensburg.

Judah Halevi (before 1075–1141)   Poet, philosopher, and author of *The Kuzari*. Spain.

Kara, Joseph (b. ca. 1060)   Bible commentator. Northern France.

Kere   The way the Masorah requires a word to be read, especially when it diverges from the *ketiv*.

Ketiv   The way a word, usually unvocalized, is written in the Bible; see *kere*.

Kimhi   See Radak.

Kimhi, Joseph (ca. 1105–1170)   Grammarian, Bible commentator, translator, and polemicist. Father of Radak.

Lekah Tov   A midrashic compilation on the Torah and the Five Megillot by Tobias ben Eliezer, 11th century. Balkans.

Maimonides, Moses ben Maimon, known as Rambam (1135–1204)   Halakhic codifier (*Yad Hazakah* = *Mishneh Torah*), philosopher (*Moreh Nevukhim, Guide of the Perplexed*), and commentator on the Mishnah. Spain and Egypt.

Malbim (1809–1879)   Acronym for Meir Loeb ben Yehiel Michael. Rabbi, preacher, and Bible commentator. Eastern Europe.

Masorah   The traditional, authoritative Hebrew text of the Bible with its consonants, vowels, and cantillation signs, as well as marginal notes that relate to orthographic, grammatical, and lexicographic oddities; developed by the school of Masoretes in Tiberias between the 6th and 9th centuries.

Mekhilta   Halakhic midrash on the Book of Exodus in two forms, the Mekhilta de-R. Ishmael and the Mekhilta de-R. Simeon ben Yohai, 1st and 2nd centuries C.E.

Menahem ben Jacob ibn Saruq (10th century)   Authored *Mahberet,* a dictionary of biblical Hebrew. Spain.

Midrash   Legal and homiletical expositions of the biblical text, and anthologies and compilations of such.

Mishnah   The written compilation of orally transmitted legal teachings covering all aspects of Jewish law, arranged in six orders that, in turn, are divided into tractates; executed by Judah ha-Nasi, ca. 200 C.E. Palestine.

Nahmanides   See Ramban.

Natziv (1817–1893)   Acronym for Naphtali Zevi Yehuda Berlin. Rabbinic scholar and head of yeshivah at Volozhin, Poland. Authored *Ha'amek Davar,* a commentary on the Torah.

Peshitta   A translation of the Bible into Syriac, parts of which are said to have been made in the first century C.E.

Pirkei de-Rabbi Eliezer   Aggadic work on scriptural narratives, 8th century. Palestine.

Pesikta de-Rav Kahana   Homilies on the synagogue lectionaries, (?)5th century C.E. Palestine.

Pesikta Rabbati   Medieval midrash on the festivals.

Qumran   The site of the caves overlooking the Dead Sea, where Bible manuscripts were found in 1949/50. The manuscripts are identified by such symbols as 4QSam^a (for manuscript *a* of Samuel, found in the fourth cave of Qumran); 1QIS^a (for manuscript *a* of Isaiah found in the first cave of Qumran).

Radak Acronym for Rabbi David ben Joseph Kimḥi (?1160–?1235) Grammarian, lexicographer, and Bible commentator. Narbonne, Provence.

Ralbag Acronym for Rabbi Levi ben Gershom, known as Gersonides (1248–1344) Mathematician, astronomer, philosopher, and Bible commentator. Southeastern France.

Rambam See Maimonides.

Ramban Acronym for Rabbi Moses ben Naḥman, known as Naḥmanides (1194–1270) Philosopher, halakhist, and Bible commentator. Spain.

Rashbam Acronym for Rabbi Samuel ben Meir (ca. 1080–1174) Grandson of Rashi. Commentator on the Bible and Talmud. Northern France.

Rashi Acronym for Rabbi Solomon ben Isaac (1040–1105) Commentator on the Bible and Talmud. Troyes, France.

Saadia ben Joseph (882–942) Philosopher, halakhist, liturgical poet, grammarian, and Bible commentator and translator. Gaon (head of academy) of Pumbedita, Babylonia.

Samuel ben Hofni (d. 1013) Talmudist and Bible commentator. Gaon of Sura, Babylonia.

Seder Olam (Rabba) Midrashic chronological work ascribed to Yose ben Ḥalafta, 2nd century C.E. Palestine.

Septuagint The Greek translation of the Torah made for the Jewish community of Alexandria, Egypt, 3rd century B.C.E.

Sforno, Obadiah ben Jacob (ca. 1470–ca. 1550) Bible commentator. Italy.

Shadal Acronym for Samuel David Luzzatto (1800–1865) Italian scholar, philosopher, Bible commentator, and translator.

Sherira ben Hanina (ca. 906–1006) Halakhist, author of numerous responsa. Gaon of Pumbedita, Babylonia.

Sifra = Torat Kohanim Tannaitic midrashic commentary to the Book of Leviticus, probably compiled about the end of the 4th century C.E. Palestine.

Sifrei Tannaitic halakhic midrash to the Books of Numbers and Deuteronomy, probably compiled at the end of the 4th century C.E.

Sumerian A non-Semitic language, written in cuneiform, spoken in the southern part of ancient Babylonia.

Symmachus (2nd century C.E.) Translator of the Bible into Greek.

Talmud The body of rabbinic law, dialectic, and lore comprising the Mishnah and Gemara, the latter being a commentary and elaboration on the former in Hebrew and Aramaic. Two separate talmudic compilations exist: the Babylonian Talmud and the Palestinian Talmud (also known as the Jerusalem Talmud).

Tanḥuma (Yelammedenu) Collection of homiletical midrashim on the Torah, arranged according to the triennial lectionary cycle. Attributed to Tanḥum bar Abba, Palestinian preacher, 4th century C.E.

Tanna(im) The Palestinian sages of the 1st and 2nd centuries C.E., whose rulings are cited in the Mishnah and Tosefta.

Targum Literally, "translation"; specifically of the Bible into Aramaic.

Targum Jonathan An unofficial Aramaic free translation of the Torah, erroneously ascribed to Jonathan ben Uzziel through misinterpretation of the initials "T.Y." (= Targum Yerushalmi). That scholar is the reputed author of the Targum to the Prophets.

Targum Onkelos The standard, official Aramaic translation of the Torah, made in the 2nd century C.E. and attributed to Onkelos, reputed nephew of the Roman emperor Hadrian and convert to Judaism. The name is probably a corruption of Aquila.

Theodotian (2nd century C.E.)   Reviser of the Septuagint.

Tosefta   A compilation of tannaitic rulings either omitted from the Mishnah or containing material parallel or supplementary to it. It is arranged according to the six orders of the Mishnah.

Tur   Short for *'Arba'ah Turim*, "the four rows"—a four-volumed, systematized compendium of Jewish law by Jacob ben Asher (?1270–1340).

Ugaritic   A Semitic language of inscriptions found at Ras Shamra, the site of the ancient city-state of Ugarit on the Syrian coast, in the second millennium B.C.E. Both the language and its literature have shed much light on the Hebrew Bible.

Vulgate   The Latin translation of the Bible made by the Church Father Jerome about 400 C.E. It became the official Bible of the Roman Catholic Church.

Yalkut Shimoni   Midrashic anthology on the Bible, attributed to a certain Simeon, 13th century.

Ziyyoni, Menahem (late 14th–early 15th century)   Kabbalist and Bible commentator. Cologne.

ABBREVIATIONS

AASOR	*Annual of the American Schools of Oriental Research*
AB	Anchor Bible
ABR	*Australian Biblical Review*
ADAJ	*Annual of the Department of Antiquities of Jordan*
AfO	*Archiv für Orientforschung*
AHW	W. von Soden, *Akkadisches Handwörterbuch*
AJSL	*American Journal of Semitic Languages and Literatures*
Akk.	Akkadian
ANEP	J. B. Pritchard, ed., *Ancient Near East in Pictures*
ANET	J. B. Pritchard, ed., *Ancient Near Eastern Texts*
Ant.	Josephus, *Antiquities*
AOAT	Alter Orient und Altes Testament
Aq.	Aquila
Ar.	Arakhin
Arab.	Arabic
Aram.	Aramaic
ARM	*Archives Royales de Mari*
ARN[1,2]	Avot de-Rabbi Nathan, versions 1 and 2, ed. S. Schechter (1887, reprinted 1967)
ASTI	*Annual of the Swedish Theological Institute,* Jerusalem
Av. Zar.	Avodah Zarah
BA	*Biblical Archeologist*
BAP	E. C. Kraeling, ed., *The Brooklyn Museum Aramaic Papyri*
BAR	*Biblical Archaeologist Reader*
BARev	*Biblical Archaeology Review*
BASOR	*Bulletin of the American Schools of Oriental Research*
BB	Bava Batra
BDB	F. Brown, S. R. Driver, and C. A. Briggs, *Hebrew and English Lexicon of the Old Testament*
Bek.	Bekhorot
Ber.	Berakhot
Bets.	Betsah
Bib.	*Biblica*
BIES	*Bulletin of the Israel Exploration Society (= Yediot)*
Bik.	Bikkurim
BJRL	*Bulletin of the John Rylands University Library of Manchester*
BK	Bava Kamma
BM	Bava Metsia
BO	*Bibliotheca Orientalis*

BR	*Biblical Research*
BTS	*Bible et Terre Sainte*
BZ	*Biblische Zeitschrift*
CAD	*The Assyrian Dictionary of the Oriental Institute of the University of Chicago*
CAP	A. Cowley, *Aramaic Papyri of the Fifth Century* B.C.
CBQ	*Catholic Biblical Quarterly*
CD	Damascus Document from the Cairo Genizah
CRAIBL	*Comptes Rendus de l'Académie des Inscriptions et Belles-Lettres*
Dem.	Demai
Deut. R.	Deuteronomy Rabba
DISO	C.-F. Jean and J. Hoftijzer, *Dictionnaire des Inscriptions Sémitiques de l'Ouest*
EB	*Encyclopaedia Biblica*
Eduy.	Eduyyot
EncJud	*Encyclopaedia Judaica* (1971)
Er.	Eruvin
EVT	*Evangelische Theologie*
Exod. R.	Exodus Rabba
ExpTim	*Expository Times*
Gen. Apoc.	Genesis Apocryphon
Gen. R.	Genesis Rabba
Git.	Gittin
Gk.	Greek
GKC	*Gesenius' Hebrew Grammar,* ed. E. Kautzsch and trans. A. E. Cowley
Ḥag.	Ḥagigah
Ḥal.	Ḥallah
HALAT	W. Baumgartner et al., *Hebräisches und aramäisches Lexicon zum Alten Testament*
Heb.	Hebrew
HKAT	*Handkommentar zum Alten Testament*
Hor.	Horayot
HTR	*Harvard Theological Review*
HUCA	*Hebrew Union College Annual*
Ḥul.	Ḥullin
IDB	*Interpreter's Dictionary of the Bible*
IEJ	*Israel Exploration Journal*
Int	*Interpretation*
JANES	*Journal of the Ancient Near Eastern Society of Columbia University*
JAOS	*Journal of the American Oriental Society*
JBL	*Journal of Biblical Literature*
JCS	*Journal of Cuneiform Studies*
JJS	*Journal of Jewish Studies*
JNES	*Journal of Near Eastern Studies*
JNSL	*Journal of Northwest Semitic Languages*
JPOS	*Journal of the Palestine Oriental Society*
JQR	*Jewish Quarterly Review*
JSJ	*Journal for the Study of Judaism in the Persian, Hellenistic, and Roman Periods*
JSOT	*Journal for the Study of the Old Testament*
JSOTSup	*Journal for the Study of the Old Testament: Supplement Series*

JSS	*Journal of Semitic Studies*
JTS	*Journal of Theological Studies*
KAI	H. Donner and W. Röllig, *Kanaanäische und aramäische Inschriften*
Ker.	Keritot
Ket.	Ketubbot
Kid.	Kiddushin
Kil.	Kilayim
Kin.	Kinnim
Lam. R.	Lamentations Rabba
Lev. R.	Leviticus Rabba
LXX	Septuagint
Maʿas.	Maʿaserot
Maʿas. Sh.	Maʿaser Sheni
Mak.	Makkot
Makhsh.	Makhshirin
Meg.	Megillah
Meʿil.	Meʿilah
MdRY	Mekhilta de-R. Ishmael
MdRSbY	Mekhilta de-R. Simeon bar Yoḥai
Men.	Menaḥot
Mid.	Midrash
Mid. Ag.	Midrash Aggadah
Mik.	Mikvaʾot
Mish.	Mishnah
MK	Moʿed Katan
Naz.	Nazir
Ned.	Nedarim
Neg.	Negaʿim
Nid.	Niddah
NJPS	New Jewish Publication Society translation
Num. R.	Numbers Rabba
OB	Old Babylonian
Oho.	Oholot
Or.	Orlah
OrAnt	*Oriens Antiquus*
OTS	*Oudtestamentische Studiën*
Par.	Parah
PdRE	Pesikta de-Rav Eliezer
PdRK	Pesikta de-Rav Kahana
PEQ	*Palestine Exploration Quarterly*
Pes.	Pesaḥim
Pesh.	Peshitta
Pesik.	Pesikta
Phoen.	Phoenician
PJ	*Palästina-Jahrbuch*
PRU	*Le Palais Royal d'Ugarit*
Q	Qumran

1QIsa^a	First copy of Isaiah from Qumran, cave 1
1QM	War Between the Children of Light and the Children of Darkness from Qumran, cave 1
1QS	Rule of the Congregation from Qumran, cave 1
4QDeut	Manuscript of Deuteronomy from Qumran, cave 4
4QGen	Manuscript of Genesis from Qumran, cave 4
11QTemple	Temple Scroll from Qumran, cave 11
RA	*Revue d'Assyriologie et d'Archéologie Orientale*
RB	*Revue Biblique*
RevQ	*Revue de Qumran*
RH	Rosh Ha-Shanah
Sam.	Samaritan
Sanh.	Sanhedrin
SANT	*Studien zum Alten und Neuen Testament*
SBT	*Studies in Biblical Theology*
Sem	*Semitica*
SER	Seder Eliyahu Rabba
Shab.	Shabbat
Shek.	Shekalim
Shev.	Shevi'it
Shevu.	Shevu'ot
Sif.	Sifrei
Sif. Zut.	Sifrei Zuta
Sifra	Sifra
Sof.	Soferim
SOR	Seder Olam Rabba
Sot.	Sotah
ST	*Studia Theologica*
Suk.	Sukkah
Sum.	Sumerian
Sym.	Symmachus
Syr.	Syriac
SyroP.	Syro-Palestinian
Ta'an.	Ta'anit
Tam.	Tamid
Tanh.	Tanhuma
Targ.	Onkelos
Targ. Jon.	Targum Jonathan
Targ. Neof.	Targum Neofiti
Targ. Yer.	Targum Yerushalmi
TDOT	G. J. Botterweck and H. Ringgren, eds., *Theological Dictionary of the Old Testament*
Tem.	Temurah
Ter.	Terumot
Theod.	Theodotian
TJ	Jerusalem Talmud
TLA	*Theologische Literaturzeitung*
Toh.	Tohorot
Tosaf.	Tosafot

Tosef.	Tosefta
TY	Tevul Yom
TUSR	*Trinity University Studies in Religion*
TynBul	Tyndale Bulletin
UF	*Ugarit-Forschungen*
Ugar.	Ugaritic
Uk.	Uktsin
UT	C. H. Gordon, *Ugaritic Textbook* (1965)
VT	*Vetus Testamentum*
VTSup	*Vetus Testamentum: Supplements*
Vulg.	Vulgate
WO	*Die Welt des Orients*
Yad.	Yadayim
Yal.	Yalkut
Yal. Reub.	Yalkut Reubeni
YD	Yoreh De'ah
Yev.	Yevamot
Zav.	Zavim
ZAW	*Zeitschrift für die alttestamentliche Wissenschaft*
ZDPV	*Zeitschrift des deutschen Palästina-Vereins*
Zev.	Zevahim

The editors have adopted a popular system for transliteration of Hebrew, except for the following letters, which have no English equivalent:

> ' = alef
> ' = ayin
> ḥ = ḥet (pronounced as the guttural "ch" in German)
> kh = khaf (pronounced as the guttural "ch" in German)

THE COMMENTARY TO EXODUS

1 These are the names of the sons of Israel who came to Egypt with Jacob, each coming with his household: [2]Reuben, Simeon, Levi, and Judah; [3]Issachar, Zebulun, and

שְׁמוֹת

א וְאֵלֶּה שְׁמוֹת בְּנֵי יִשְׂרָאֵל הַבָּאִים מִצְרָיְמָה אֵת יַעֲקֹב אִישׁ וּבֵיתוֹ בָּאוּ: 2 רְאוּבֵן שִׁמְעוֹן לֵוִי וִיהוּדָה: 3 יִשָּׂשכָר זְבוּלֻן וּבִנְיָמִן: 4 דָּן וְנַפְתָּלִי גָּד

CHAPTER 1

Reversal of Fortune   (vv. 1–22)

Shemot

The closing chapters of the Book of Genesis told of the settlement of the Israelites in Egypt. Joseph, through foresight and administrative skill, had saved Egypt from starvation during several years of famine, while at the same time shrewdly enhancing the wealth and landed estates of the crown. The Book of Exodus opens with a tale of base ingratitude on the part of a pharaoh and the Egyptian people, which precipitates a radical reversal of fortune for the tribes of Israel.

The text rests upon a knowledge of Genesis; it takes for granted that the reader knows the identity and experiences of Joseph, is aware of God's promises to the patriarchs, and is familiar with the account of the migration of Jacob and his family to Egypt.

"Strangers in a land not theirs," as Genesis 15:13 puts it, the Israelites are to be enslaved and oppressed for a long period of time. However, the Narrator of Exodus tells only briefly of the slavery and suffering, compressing it into a few verses. His account, rigorous and austere, offers only the barest of details. Attention is concentrated on the process of liberation. Here, by contrast, the narrative is generously expansive.

A singular tone of secularity seems to pervade the introductory saga of the Book of Exodus. There is no explicit mention of God directing events. Nevertheless, these developments were foretold in connection with God's covenant with Abraham in that pivotal passage, Genesis 15:13. As in the ostensibly secular story of Joseph, here too there is an unmistakable underlying sense of divine purposefulness.

AN INTRODUCTORY SUMMARY (vv. 1–7)

The sons—that is, the tribes of Israel—are listed within a formulaic framework (vv. 1,4) that is clearly adapted from Genesis 46:8,26–27; yet the order does not follow the one given in that chapter. Instead, it is based on Genesis 35:23–26. There is good reason for this seeming anomaly, for this latter chapter contains the divine blessing to Jacob: "Be fertile and increase; / A nation, yea an assembly of nations, / Shall descend from you" [v. 7]. Here, in this opening section of Exodus, the text affirms that the promise has been fulfilled.

1.   *These are* (Hebrew *ve-'elleh*)   The initial *vav*[1] acts as a connective with Genesis, thereby suggesting continuity with the preceding narrative.

Israel   As in verse 9, the use of this name denotes a national entity, not just the patriarch.

2–3.   Exactly as in Genesis 35:23–26, the sons/tribes are listed matrilineally, with those of the two wives mentioned first in order of seniority, followed by those of the two handmaids in reverse order to form a chiasm:

Benjamin; ⁴Dan and Naphtali, Gad and Asher. ⁵The total number of persons that were of Jacob's issue came to seventy, Joseph being already in Egypt. ⁶Joseph died, and all his brothers, and all that generation. ⁷But the Israelites were fertile and prolific; they multiplied and increased very greatly, so that the land was filled with them.

⁸A new king arose over Egypt who did not know Joseph.

וְאָשֵׁר: 5 וַיְהִי כָּל־נֶפֶשׁ יֹצְאֵי יֶרֶךְ־יַעֲקֹב שִׁבְעִים נָפֶשׁ וְיוֹסֵף הָיָה בְמִצְרָיִם: 6 וַיָּמָת יוֹסֵף וְכָל־אֶחָיו וְכֹל הַדּוֹר הַהוּא: 7 וּבְנֵי יִשְׂרָאֵל פָּרוּ וַיִּשְׁרְצוּ וַיִּרְבּוּ וַיַּעַצְמוּ בִּמְאֹד מְאֹד וַתִּמָּלֵא הָאָרֶץ אֹתָם: פ 8 וַיָּקָם מֶלֶךְ־חָדָשׁ עַל־מִצְרָיִם אֲשֶׁר לֹא־יָדַע אֶת־יוֹסֵף: 9 וַיֹּאמֶר אֶל־

1. Leah ——————— 2. Rachel
3. Bilhah ——————— 4. Zilpah
(Rachel's handmaid)   (Leah's handmaid)

Reuben Reuben is not termed the "first-born," as he was in Genesis 46:8. Jacob deprived him of that status in his dying testament.[2]

5. Jacob's issue Literally, "that came out of Jacob's loin." In the Bible, Hebrew *yerekh*, "thigh, loin," is the seat of procreative power. The singular form may be a euphemism for the reproductive organ, as in Genesis 24:2.

seventy This harks back to Genesis 46:8–27, which lists all the male descendants of Jacob through his wives and handmaids as follows: Leah 33 + Zilpah 16 + Rachel 14 + Bilhah 7 = 70. However, that total includes Judah's sons Er and Onan, who died in Canaan, as well as Joseph and his two sons, Manasseh and Ephraim, who were already in Egypt. The list there specifies that "all the persons belonging to Jacob who came to Egypt—his own issue, aside from the wives of Jacob's sons—all these persons numbered 66. . . . Thus the total of Jacob's household who came to Egypt was 70 persons." Clearly, seventy here is a round number. Deuteronomy 10:22 repeats the same figure: "Your ancestors went down to Egypt seventy persons in all." This context seems to include Jacob and Joseph but would certainly exclude Ephraim and Manasseh. It does not include Jacob's daughters-in-law and granddaughters.

The number seventy in the Bible is usually meant to be taken as typological, not literal; that is, it is used for the rhetorical effect of evoking the idea of totality, of comprehensiveness on a large scale. Thus, in Genesis 10 precisely seventy nations issue from the three sons of Noah, and these constitute the entire human family.[3]

6. The immigrant generation had wholly died out by the time the oppression began, but we are not told how long this took.[4]

7. This description of the extraordinary fertility of the Israelite population carries strong verbal echoes of the divine blessings of fertility bestowed on humankind at Creation and after the Flood.[5] It suggests a conception of the community of Israel in Egypt as a microcosm, a miniature universe, self-contained and apart from the larger Egyptian society—the nucleus, spiritually speaking, of a new humanity.

the land Not the whole of Egypt, but the area of Israelite settlement known as Goshen.[6]

THE OPPRESSION (vv. 8–14)

The Israelites find themselves undergoing a cataclysmic change. A new regime perceives them to be a potential threat to national security. "A new king" probably means a new dynasty, but the anonymity precludes the possibility of positive identification with a known pharaoh. The most reasonable explanation for the change in fortune lies in the policies adopted by the pharaohs of the Nineteenth Dynasty (ca. 1306–1200 B.C.E.), and especially by Ramses II (ca. 1290–1224 B.C.E.), who shifted Egypt's administrative and strategic center of gravity to the eastern Delta of the Nile, where he undertook vast building projects that required a huge local labor force.

⁹And he said to his people, "Look, the Israelite people are much too numerous for us. ¹⁰Let us deal shrewdly with them, so that they may not increase; otherwise in the event of war they may join our enemies in fighting against us and rise from the ground." ¹¹So they set taskmasters over them

עַמּוֹ הִנֵּה עַם בְּנֵי יִשְׂרָאֵל רַב וְעָצוּם מִמֶּנּוּ:
י הָבָה נִתְחַכְּמָה לוֹ פֶּן־יִרְבֶּה וְהָיָה כִּי־תִקְרֶאנָה
מִלְחָמָה וְנוֹסַף גַּם־הוּא עַל־שֹׂנְאֵינוּ וְנִלְחַם־
בָּנוּ וְעָלָה מִן־הָאָרֶץ: יא וַיָּשִׂימוּ עָלָיו שָׂרֵי מִסִּים

In fact, intimations of a deterioration in the Israelite situation are already discernible in the closing chapters of Genesis. Jacob, on his deathbed, feels the need to give his family the reassurance that "God will be with you and bring you back to the land of your fathers."[7] Joseph voices his anxiety for the future even more strongly. He tells his brothers, "God will surely take notice of you and bring you up from this land to the land that He promised on oath to Abraham, to Isaac, and to Jacob."[8] The dying statesman knows that his family will not wield the influence necessary to arrange for his burial in his ancestral land as he had been able to do for his father.

8. _arose_   Use of the Hebrew verb *k-w-m* rather than the usual *m-l-k*, "to reign," indicates the inauguration of a new era, not just a change in monarch.[9]

who did not know Joseph   He was oblivious of or indifferent to the benefactions that Joseph had bestowed on Egypt and the crown.[10]

know   This is the first appearance in Exodus of the verb *y-d-ʿ*. It is a key term in the Exodus narratives, occurring over twenty times in the first fourteen chapters.[11] The usual rendering, "to know," hardly does justice to the richness of its semantic range. In the biblical conception, knowledge is not essentially or even primarily rooted in the intellect and mental activity. Rather, it is more experiential and is embedded in the emotions, so that it may encompass such qualities as contact, intimacy, concern, relatedness, and mutuality. Conversely, not to know is synonymous with dissociation, indifference, alienation, and estrangement; it culminates in callous disregard for another's humanity.

9–10.   The initiative for the oppression comes from the king. The historical situation that prompted his fears may be plausibly reconstructed if it is assumed that the text refers to Ramses II. The eastern Delta of the Nile was vulnerable to penetration from Asia. In the middle of the eighteenth century B.C.E. it had been infiltrated by the Hyksos, an Egyptian term meaning "rulers of foreign lands." The Hyksos were a conglomeration of ethnic groups among whom Semites predominated. They gradually took over Lower Egypt and ruled it until their expulsion in the second half of the sixteenth century B.C.E.. After that, the Delta was neglected by the central government, although many Semites remained in the region. A revival of interest in that part of Egypt began with the reign of Haremheb (ca. 1330–1306 B.C.E.) and accelerated under his successors. It probably heightened sensitivity to the presence of a large body of foreigners in that strategic area. This population also constituted a sizeable pool of readily available manpower that could easily be drawn upon.

the Israelite people   Hebrew *ʿam benei yisraʾel* is a unique phrase. The familial term *ʿam*, as distinct from the political term *goy*, "nation," connotes a group bound by blood ties.[12] It is occasionally also used in the sense of a military force.[13] The coining of the present unparalleled combination may be an artful attempt to insinuate the idea of an alien ethnic group that is also a threat.

much too numerous   The use of Hebrew *rav* coupled with *ʿatsum* probably expresses both multitude and power.[14]

10. _deal shrewdly_   In order to control the growth of the Israelite population. Pharaoh now unwittingly challenges the will of God, for the divine promise to Abraham had pledged that his descendants would be as numerous as the stars of the heaven and the sands of the seashore.

in the event of war[15]

and rise from the ground   This Hebrew phrase, which recurs only in Hosea 2:2, is obscure. It is not likely to mean "shake off oppression" since the Israelites have not yet been oppressed.

to oppress them with forced labor; and they built garrison cities for Pharaoh: Pithom and Raamses. [12]But the more they were oppressed, the more they increased and spread out, so that the [Egyptians] came to dread the Israelites.

[13]The Egyptians ruthlessly imposed upon the Israelites [14]the various labors that they made them perform. Ruthlessly they made life bitter for them with harsh labor at mortar and bricks and with all sorts of tasks in the field.

[15]The king of Egypt spoke to the Hebrew midwives, one of whom was named Shiphrah and the other Puah, [16]say-

לְמַעַן עַנֹּתוֹ בְּסִבְלֹתָם וַיִּבֶן עָרֵי מִסְכְּנוֹת לְפַרְעֹה אֶת־פִּתֹם וְאֶת־רַעַמְסֵס: 12 וְכַאֲשֶׁר יְעַנּוּ אֹתוֹ כֵּן יִרְבֶּה וְכֵן יִפְרֹץ וַיָּקֻצוּ מִפְּנֵי בְּנֵי יִשְׂרָאֵל:

13 וַיַּעֲבִדוּ מִצְרַיִם אֶת־בְּנֵי יִשְׂרָאֵל בְּפָרֶךְ: 14 וַיְמָרְרוּ אֶת־חַיֵּיהֶם בַּעֲבֹדָה קָשָׁה בְּחֹמֶר וּבִלְבֵנִים וּבְכָל־עֲבֹדָה בַּשָּׂדֶה אֵת כָּל־עֲבֹדָתָם אֲשֶׁר־עָבְדוּ בָהֶם בְּפָרֶךְ:

15 וַיֹּאמֶר מֶלֶךְ מִצְרַיִם לַמְיַלְּדֹת הָעִבְרִיֹּת אֲשֶׁר שֵׁם הָאַחַת שִׁפְרָה וְשֵׁם הַשֵּׁנִית פּוּעָה:

Rashbam understands the phrase "go up out of the land" as expressing a fear of losing a potentially rich reserve of manpower. A rabbinic tradition has the king superstitiously substituting the third person ('alah) for the first person plural ('alinu) to avoid the disagreeable "We shall [be forced] to go up out of the land." We may be dealing here with a lost idiom that means "to gain ascendancy over."

11.   The Israelites are not pressed into private domestic slavery but are conscripted for compulsory unpaid labor on public works projects for indefinite periods. The two Hebrew verbs used to describe the subjugation of the people (vv. 11-13), '-n-h, "to oppress," and '-v-d, "to be a slave," hark back to the prediction of Genesis 15:13, "they shall be enslaved and oppressed."

forced labor[16]

they built   The Hebrew may connote the founding of new cities as well as the rebuilding of existing ones.[17]

garrison cities   This rendering of Hebrew 'arei miskenot, the latter word being of uncertain origin, is supported by the Septuagint tradition and by the other biblical usages of the term.[18]

Pharaoh   The title is formed by a combination of two Egyptian words, per-aa, literally, "the great house." The phrase originally applied to the royal palace and court; later, during the Nineteenth Dynasty (ca. 1306–1200 B.C.E.), it was employed as an honorific title for the reigning monarch. It is thus analogous to the present-day use of "the Palace" or "the White House."

Pithom and Raamses   Both names are well known in Egyptian sources, but their precise location has not been fixed. Pithom is never again mentioned in the Bible. The name derives from the Egyptian pr/pi-'tm, which means "the House of Atum," indicating the presence of a major temple dedicated to the primeval creator god of that name. Obviously, several localities could have borne such a designation, but the site of Tell el-Maskuta in Wadi Tumeilat in the northeastern Delta of the Nile is regarded by many authorities as being the most likely candidate for the city. Raamses can be none other than the famous Delta residence of the pharaoh Ramses II; its beauty and glory were extolled in poems still extant. The city was situated in "the region of Goshen," a phrase that is synonymous with "the region of Rameses," where the Israelites lived. This is described as being "the choicest part of the land of Egypt."[19] It was here that the Israelites assembled in preparation for the Exodus.[20] The precise site has not yet been located, but Egyptologists believe that it is the region of modern el-Khata'na and Qantur in the northeastern Delta.[21]

12.   The tyrant's efforts are inexplicably foiled. Mysteriously, the Israelite population has expanded even more. The lack of a natural explanation for the phenomenon has engendered a sense of disquiet and frustration that finds an outlet in the intensification of the oppression.

13-14.   The Israelite labor gangs are now exploited for exhausting toil in construction work and agriculture. This experience indelibly stamped Egypt as the "house of bondage" in the Israelite consciousness.[22]

14. ***mortar and bricks***   The prodigious building activity required a brickmaking industry of gargantuan proportions. On this subject, see Comment to 5:7–8.

ing, "When you deliver the Hebrew women, look at the birthstool: if it is a boy, kill him; if it is a girl, let her live." [17]The midwives, fearing God, did not do as the king of Egypt had told them; they let the boys live. [18]So the king of Egypt summoned the midwives and said to them, "Why have you done this thing, letting the boys live?" [19]The

16 וַיֹּאמֶר בְּיַלֶּדְכֶן אֶת־הָעִבְרִיּוֹת וּרְאִיתֶן עַל־
הָאָבְנָיִם אִם־בֵּן הוּא וַהֲמִתֶּן אֹתוֹ וְאִם־בַּת הִיא
וָחָיָה: 17 וַתִּירֶאןָ הַמְיַלְּדֹת אֶת־הָאֱלֹהִים וְלֹא
עָשׂוּ כַּאֲשֶׁר דִּבֶּר אֲלֵיהֶן מֶלֶךְ מִצְרָיִם וַתְּחַיֶּיןָ
אֶת־הַיְלָדִים: שני 18 וַיִּקְרָא מֶלֶךְ־מִצְרַיִם
לַמְיַלְּדֹת וַיֹּאמֶר לָהֶן מַדּוּעַ עֲשִׂיתֶן הַדָּבָר הַזֶּה

THE MIDWIVES (vv. 15–22)

In response to the failure of his scheme, the pharaoh resorts to unrestrained cruelty. In addition to the harsh burdens he imposes on the adult males, he now issues a decree of crushing barbarity: infanticide, in order to reduce the Israelite population.

15. Hebrew   The origin of Hebrew ʿivri is still a puzzle. It was first used in Genesis 14:13 to designate Abram. Genesis Rabba 42:18 suggests three explanations for the epithet: (1) It is connected with Eber, grandson of Noah;[23] (2) it is derived from Hebrew ʿever, "beyond," that is, the one who came from beyond the river Euphrates; and (3) it indicates Abraham's religious nonconformism —"All the world was on one side (ʿever) and he on the other side." Each of these interpretations is open to serious objections. Another line of investigation has been opened by the discovery of a class of people known as ʿapiru in a variety of Near Eastern texts. On this subject see Excursus 1.

midwives   Until as late as the sixteenth century of this era, midwifery was everywhere an exclusively female occupation. It was regarded as a violation of the code of modesty for a male, even a doctor, to be present at a birth.[24] Midwifery was thus one of the few occupations open to women; and it seems to have been a prestigious profession in ancient Egypt.

It is strange that there were only two midwives to service such a large population. Ibn Ezra suggests that these two were the overseers of the practitioners, directly responsible to the authorities for the many women under them. It is also possible that the two names may be those of guilds of midwives.[25]

The Hebrew phrase *ha-meyalledot ha-ʿivriyot* can mean either "Hebrew midwives" or "midwives to the Hebrews"; the latter is how it is understood by the Septuagint and by Josephus[26] as well as by Abravanel. Judah he-Ḥasid cites a tradition that they were Egyptians. However, the two names are Semitic.[27]

Shiphrah   The Semitic stem means "to be beautiful."[28] The name appears in a list of slaves attached to an Egyptian estate and is indicated as being Asiatic.

Puah   The daughter of the hero Danel in Ugaritic literature bears this name. Apparently it was originally a term for a fragrant blossom and came to connote "a girl."[29]

The names of the midwives are recorded but not those of the reigning pharaohs. In the biblical scale of values these lowly champions of morality assume far greater historic importance than do the all-powerful tyrants who ruled Egypt.

16. birthstool   Hebrew 'ovnayim, literally "two stones," probably refers to the two bricks on which women in labor crouched opposite the midwife during parturition.[30] The squatting position made for easier delivery.

17.   Faced with a conflict between the laws of God and those of the pharaoh, the midwives followed the dictates of conscience. Their defiance of tyranny constitutes history's first recorded act of civil disobedience in defense of a moral imperative. It is stated that they were actuated by "fear of God," a phrase frequently associated with moral and ethical behavior.[31] "Fear of God" connotes a conception of God as One who makes moral demands on humankind; it functions as the ultimate restraint on evil and the supreme stimulus for good.

let . . . live   The Hebrew verbal form can also denote sustaining life,[32] and a midrash sees the midwives actively providing the indigent mothers with food and shelter in addition to obstetric services.[33]

midwives said to Pharaoh, "Because the Hebrew women are not like the Egyptian women: they are vigorous. Before the midwife can come to them, they have given birth." ²⁰And God dealt well with the midwives; and the people multiplied and increased greatly. ²¹And because the midwives feared God, He established households for them. ²²Then Pharaoh charged all his people, saying, "Every boy that is born you shall throw into the Nile, but let every girl live."

19 וַתְּחַיֶּיןָ אֶת־הַיְלָדִים: וַתֹּאמַרְןָ הַמְיַלְּדֹת אֶל־
פַּרְעֹה כִּי לֹא כַנָּשִׁים הַמִּצְרִיֹּת הָעִבְרִיֹּת כִּי־חָיוֹת
הֵנָּה בְּטֶרֶם תָּבוֹא אֲלֵהֶן הַמְיַלֶּדֶת וְיָלָדוּ:
20 וַיֵּיטֶב אֱלֹהִים לַמְיַלְּדֹת וַיִּרֶב הָעָם וַיַּעַצְמוּ
מְאֹד: 21 וַיְהִי כִּי־יָרְאוּ הַמְיַלְּדֹת אֶת־הָאֱלֹהִים
וַיַּעַשׂ לָהֶם בָּתִּים: 22 וַיְצַו פַּרְעֹה לְכָל־עַמּוֹ
לֵאמֹר כָּל־הַבֵּן הַיִּלּוֹד הַיְאֹרָה תַּשְׁלִיכֻהוּ
וְכָל־הַבַּת תְּחַיּוּן: ס

2 A certain man of the house of Levi went and married a Levite woman. ²The woman conceived and bore a son; and

ב וַיֵּלֶךְ אִישׁ מִבֵּית לֵוִי וַיִּקַּח אֶת־בַּת־לֵוִי:
2 וַתַּהַר הָאִשָּׁה וַתֵּלֶד בֵּן וַתֵּרֶא אֹתוֹ כִּי־טוֹב הוּא

19. The evasiveness of the midwives in response to the charge of disobedience is motivated by a sense of self-preservation and by the desire to be able to continue to save lives. At the same time their excuse has a sardonic twist, for it unfavorably contrasts Egyptian women with their Israelite sisters.

vigorous   Hebrew *ḥayot*, literally "lively." The singular, *ḥayyah*, was used for "a midwife" in later Hebrew.[34] Here, the women appear to be acting as their own midwives.

20. multiplied and increased   The narrative closes on the same note with which it began (v. 7). The pharaoh's diabolical measures have not changed the situation because God has willed otherwise.

21. established households   The meaning of the Hebrew phrase is uncertain because of the unclarity of the subject of the verb and the masculine form of the dative (*lahem*). Shadal suggests that the midwives were drawn from among the childless women, and God rewarded their virtue by blessing them with families. Saadia and Radak take the phrase to be idiomatic for providing protection, whereas Rashbam, Tur, and Malbim think it means that the pharaoh put them under state control. This last seems the most probable explanation.

22.   All else having failed, the pharaoh promulgates one last genocidal decree. He mobilizes "all his people," the entire apparatus of the state, to annihilate the people of Israel. There is subtle irony in his decree, for the chosen instrument of destruction—water—will in the end become the agency of Egypt's punishment.[35]

the Nile   Hebrew *ye'or* is borrowed from Egyptian, where it is used for the Nile and its tributaries.

CHAPTER 2

The Birth and Youth of Moses   (vv. 1–25)

The oppressive acts of the pharaoh have built to a climax. Strangely, his third and most barbarous decree—infanticide—is never again referred to in the Bible. We are not told to what extent it was implemented or whether it was later rescinded. The primary function served by its narration is to set the stage for the story of the birth and survival of Moses. His arrival gives new direction to the life of the suffering people. The unseen hand of God is at work so that the king's crowning evil actually initiates a series of events that is to culminate in the humiliation of its perpetrator and the liberation of Israel.

when she saw how beautiful he was, she hid him for three months. [3]When she could hide him no longer, she got a wicker basket for him and caulked it with bitumen and pitch. She put the child into it and placed it among the reeds by the bank of the Nile. [4]And his sister stationed herself at a distance, to learn what would befall him.

[5]The daughter of Pharaoh came down to bathe in the Nile, while her maidens walked along the Nile. She spied the basket among the reeds and sent her slave girl to fetch it. [6]When she opened it, she saw that it was a child, a boy

וַתִּצְפְּנֵהוּ שְׁלֹשָׁה יְרָחִים: 3 וְלֹא־יָכְלָה עוֹד
הַצְּפִינוֹ וַתִּקַּח־לוֹ תֵּבַת גֹּמֶא וַתַּחְמְרָה בַחֵמָר
וּבַזָּפֶת וַתָּשֶׂם בָּהּ אֶת־הַיֶּלֶד וַתָּשֶׂם בַּסּוּף עַל־
שְׂפַת הַיְאֹר: 4 וַתֵּתַצַּב אֲחֹתוֹ מֵרָחֹק לְדֵעָה מַה־
יֵּעָשֶׂה לוֹ:

5 וַתֵּרֶד בַּת־פַּרְעֹה לִרְחֹץ עַל־הַיְאֹר וְנַעֲרֹתֶיהָ
הֹלְכֹת עַל־יַד הַיְאֹר וַתֵּרֶא אֶת־הַתֵּבָה בְּתוֹךְ
הַסּוּף וַתִּשְׁלַח אֶת־אֲמָתָהּ וַתִּקָּחֶהָ: 6 וַתִּפְתַּח
וַתִּרְאֵהוּ אֶת־הַיֶּלֶד וְהִנֵּה־נַעַר בֹּכֶה וַתַּחְמֹל

THE ABANDONMENT AND SALVATION OF MOSES   (vv. 1–10)

1. *man . . . woman*   Amram and Jochebed.[1]

married   The Hebrew stem *l-k-ḥ*, literally "to take," is frequently used of marriage.[2] The text is henceforth silent about the father. The narrative focuses entirely on the role of the mother.

2. *she saw how beautiful he was*   Hebrew *tov*, usually "good," might also here connote "robust, healthy." The entire clause stirs immediate association with a key phrase, seven times repeated in the Genesis Creation narrative, "God saw that . . . was good" (*tov*).[3] This parallel suggests that the birth of Moses is intended to be understood as the dawn of a new creative era.

Based on the use of *tov* here, a rabbinic comment suggests that Tobiah was the original Hebrew name that Moses received from his parents.[4]

3. The desperate mother must finally comply with the iniquitous decree. But she does so only in a formal way and actually takes every possible precaution to ensure the baby's safety. On the abandoned hero motif, see Excursus 2.

a wicker basket   The receptacle is called a *tevah*, a term that, in this sense, appears elsewhere in the Bible only as the ark in which Noah and his family were saved from the waters of the Flood.[5] Its use here underscores both the vulnerability of its occupant and its being under divine protection. Evocation of the Flood narrative also suggests, once again, that the birth of Moses signals a new era in history.

wicker   Hebrew *gome'* is the papyrus plant, once abundant in the marshlands of the Nile Delta. Its huge stems, often more than ten feet high, were used by the Egyptians for a variety of purposes, especially for the construction of light boats.[6]

she put . . . placed   Hebrew *s-y-m* implies gentle, loving action, as opposed to the harsh verb *hishlikh*, "to abandon," used in the decree of the pharaoh.[7]

the reeds   Hebrew *suf* is borrowed from Egyptian and means a reed thicket. Placing the basket in the reeds prevented its being carried downstream. This rare word is artfully allusive, prefiguring Israel's deliverance from the Egyptians at the Sea of Reeds (Heb. *yam suf*).

4. *his sister*   Miriam.[8]

at a distance   So as to be inconspicuous and not arouse suspicions that the child was not really abandoned.

5. *to bathe in the Nile*   An Egyptian princess would not bathe publicly in the mighty, crocodile-infested river itself. One of its innumerable rivulets, where privacy and safety could be enjoyed, is certainly intended.[9] This suggests that the mother deliberately selected the spot after observing the character and habits of this particular princess.

crying. She took pity on it and said, "This must be a Hebrew child." ⁷Then his sister said to Pharaoh's daughter, "Shall I go and get you a Hebrew nurse to suckle the child for you?" ⁸And Pharaoh's daughter answered, "Yes." So the girl went and called the child's mother. ⁹And Pharaoh's daughter said to her, "Take this child and nurse it for me, and I will pay your wages." So the woman took the child and nursed it. ¹⁰When the child grew up, she brought him to Pharaoh's daughter, who made him her son. She named him Moses, explaining, "I drew him out of the water."

עָלָיו וַתֹּאמֶר מִיַּלְדֵי הָעִבְרִים זֶה: 7 וַתֹּאמֶר אֲחֹתוֹ אֶל־בַּת־פַּרְעֹה הַאֵלֵךְ וְקָרָאתִי לָךְ אִשָּׁה מֵינֶקֶת מִן הָעִבְרִיֹּת וְתֵינִק לָךְ אֶת־הַיָּלֶד: 8 וַתֹּאמֶר־לָהּ בַּת־פַּרְעֹה לֵכִי וַתֵּלֶךְ הָעַלְמָה וַתִּקְרָא אֶת־אֵם הַיָּלֶד: 9 וַתֹּאמֶר לָהּ בַּת־פַּרְעֹה הֵילִיכִי אֶת־הַיֶּלֶד הַזֶּה וְהֵינִקִהוּ לִי וַאֲנִי אֶתֵּן אֶת־שְׂכָרֵךְ וַתִּקַּח הָאִשָּׁה הַיֶּלֶד וַתְּנִיקֵהוּ: 10 וַיִּגְדַּל הַיֶּלֶד וַתְּבִאֵהוּ לְבַת־פַּרְעֹה וַיְהִי־לָהּ לְבֵן וַתִּקְרָא שְׁמוֹ מֹשֶׁה וַתֹּאמֶר כִּי מִן־הַמַּיִם מְשִׁיתִהוּ:   שלישי

6.   This is the only biblical report of a baby crying. Otherwise, the verb *b-k-h* always has an adult as its subject.

7–10.   This fateful development is spiced with irony. The evil designs of the pharaoh are unwittingly thwarted by his own daughter. Not only does she save the future redeemer of the Israelites persecuted by her father but she actually pays the mother of the "foundling" to suckle her own baby.

The arrangements she makes follow a pattern found in Mesopotamian legal documents relating to the adoption of foundlings. These "wet nurse contracts" specify payment for the services of nursing and rearing the infant for a specified period; they stipulate that, following weaning, the child is returned to the finder, who adopts it.¹⁰

That the princess can personally execute such a contract accords with the relatively high social and legal position of women in ancient Egypt. She possessed rights of inheritance and disposal of property, and she enjoyed a fair measure of economic independence.

9.   *Take*   Hebrew *heilikhi*, a very unusual form, which may have been selected to intensify the ironic effect, since the play of language allows the word to signify "here, it is yours" (*hei likhi*), an unconscious acknowledgment of the true mother.¹¹

nurse it   The wet nurse is termed *meineket* in verse 7, a word that corresponds to the Akkadian *musheniqtum*, "the one who suckles." She frequently had the additional duties of *tarbitum*, rearing the child and acting as guardian. From Genesis 24:59 and 35:8 it is clear that Rebekah's *meineket* was an esteemed member of the household. Her position is reflected in the rendering of *meineket* by Targum Jonathan in those passages as *padgogtha*, from Greek *paidagogos*, "tutor." In the case of Moses, one can be sure that the mother nurtured his mind and character and instilled in him the values and traditions cherished by his people.

10.   The high infant mortality rate in the ancient world dictated that formal adoption and naming by the adoptive parent be postponed until after the weaning, which took place at a far later age than it would in modern societies.

Moses   The Hebrew name is of Egyptian origin. Its basic verbal stem *msy* means "to be born," and the noun *ms* means "a child, son." It is a frequent element in Egyptian personal names, usually but not always with the addition of a divine element, as illustrated by Ahmose, Ptahmose, Ramose, and Thotmose. Two papyri from the time of Ramses II mention officials named Mose.¹²

explaining   The Narrator puts a Hebrew origin for the name into the mouth of the Egyptian princess; unbeknown to her, it foreshadows the boy's destiny. By means of word play, the Egyptian Mose is connected with Hebrew *m-sh-h*, "to draw up/out (of water)."¹³ The princess explains the name as though the form is *mashui*, "the one drawn out," a passive participle, whereas it is actually an active participle, "he who draws out," and becomes an oblique reference to the future crossing of the Sea of Reeds. Isaiah 63:11 seems to reflect this inner biblical midrash: "Then they remembered the ancient days, Him, who pulled his people out [*mosheh*] [of the water]: Where is He who brought them up from the Sea. . . ."¹⁴

10

¹¹Some time after that, when Moses had grown up, he went out to his kinsfolk and witnessed their labors. He saw an Egyptian beating a Hebrew, one of his kinsmen. ¹²He turned this way and that and, seeing no one about, he struck down the Egyptian and hid him in the sand. ¹³When he went out the next day, he found two Hebrews fighting; so he said to the offender, "Why do you strike your fellow?" ¹⁴He retorted, "Who made you chief and ruler over us? Do you mean to kill me as you killed the Egyptian?" Moses was frightened, and thought: Then the matter is known! ¹⁵When Pharaoh learned of the matter, he sought to kill Moses; but Moses fled from Pharaoh. He arrived in the land of Midian, and sat down beside a well.

יא וַיְהִ֣י ׀ בַּיָּמִ֣ים הָהֵ֗ם וַיִּגְדַּ֤ל מֹשֶׁה֙ וַיֵּצֵ֣א אֶל־אֶחָ֔יו וַיַּ֖רְא בְּסִבְלֹתָ֑ם וַיַּ֙רְא֙ אִ֣ישׁ מִצְרִ֔י מַכֶּ֥ה אִישׁ־עִבְרִ֖י מֵאֶחָֽיו: יב וַיִּ֤פֶן כֹּה֙ וָכֹ֔ה וַיַּ֖רְא כִּ֣י אֵ֣ין אִ֑ישׁ וַיַּךְ֙ אֶת־הַמִּצְרִ֔י וַֽיִּטְמְנֵ֖הוּ בַּחֽוֹל: יג וַיֵּצֵא֙ בַּיּ֣וֹם הַשֵּׁנִ֔י וְהִנֵּ֛ה שְׁנֵֽי־אֲנָשִׁ֥ים עִבְרִ֖ים נִצִּ֑ים וַיֹּ֙אמֶר֙ לָֽרָשָׁ֔ע לָ֥מָּה תַכֶּ֖ה רֵעֶֽךָ: יד וַ֠יֹּאמֶר מִ֣י שָֽׂמְךָ֞ לְאִ֨ישׁ שַׂ֤ר וְשֹׁפֵט֙ עָלֵ֔ינוּ הַלְהָרְגֵ֙נִי֙ אַתָּ֣ה אֹמֵ֔ר כַּאֲשֶׁ֥ר הָרַ֖גְתָּ אֶת־הַמִּצְרִ֑י וַיִּירָ֤א מֹשֶׁה֙ וַיֹּאמַ֔ר אָכֵ֖ן נוֹדַ֥ע הַדָּבָֽר: טו וַיִּשְׁמַ֤ע פַּרְעֹה֙ אֶת־הַדָּבָ֣ר הַזֶּ֔ה וַיְבַקֵּ֖שׁ לַהֲרֹ֣ג אֶת־מֹשֶׁ֑ה וַיִּבְרַ֤ח מֹשֶׁה֙ מִפְּנֵ֣י פַרְעֹ֔ה וַיֵּ֥שֶׁב בְּאֶֽרֶץ־מִדְיָ֖ן וַיֵּ֥שֶׁב עַֽל־הַבְּאֵֽר:

THE CHARACTER OF MOSES   (vv. 11–15)

How long Moses remained in the royal palace and how his days were spent there are of no interest to the biblical Narrator. Evidence from the period of the Ramesides for the presence of foreigners, especially of Semites, in the royal schools suggests that, like other privileged boys in court and bureaucratic circles in Egypt, Moses' formal education would have commenced at an early age and lasted about twelve years. Concentrating largely on the three R's, it would have been conducted under a regimen of strict discipline, with drill and memorization as the principal pedagogic techniques.[15] Be that as it may, the Narrator is concerned with the character of Moses and the nature of his commitments. These are illustrated by three incidents that display his moral passion and his inability to tolerate injustice: 2:11–12, 13, and 16–17. It is these qualities that mark him as being worthy to lead the struggle for the liberation of Israel.

11. *his kinsfolk*   Literally, "his brethren." Repetition of the word emphasizes that the years spent in court circles did not alienate Moses from his people and his origins.

witnessed their labors   Not as a detached observer but with empathy, wholeheartedly identifying with their suffering.[16]

beating   In a life-threatening way.[17]

12.   Outraged, Moses at once goes to the aid of the victim. His initial caution is dictated by the knowledge that, in the eyes of Egyptian law, he is about to commit a mutinous act. With this act, he will also sever his ties to the aristocratic society in which he was raised.

he struck down   The Hebrew uses the same verb as employed in verse 11 for the action of the Egyptian assailant. A midrash actually has God questioning Moses' act.[18]

13. *he found*   Hebrew *ve-hinneh* introduces a totally unexpected development.

the offender   Hebrew *rasha'* is often a legal term meaning "the one in the wrong." According to a midrash, he is so identified because he resorts to the use of force.[19]

14.   Moses discovers that some of his own people can act insidiously as informers to the oppressive authorities.[20]

15.   Moses is now an outcast fleeing for his life. The "land of Midian," where he takes refuge, refers to an area under the control of one or more of the five seminomadic tribes that, according to biblical sources, made up the Midianite confederation.[21] The eponymous, or name-giving, ancestor Midian is said in Genesis to be a son of Abraham by Keturah.[22] This tradition reflects an early history of close and friendly relations between Israel and the Midianites. By the period of the judges, however, the two peoples had become thoroughly hostile to one another.[23]

The Midianites ranged over a wide area of the Near East, stretching from the eastern shore of the

16Now the priest of Midian had seven daughters. They came to draw water, and filled the troughs to water their father's flock; 17but shepherds came and drove them off. Moses rose to their defense, and he watered their flock. 18When they returned to their father Reuel, he said, "How is it that you have come back so soon today?" 19They answered, "An Egyptian rescued us from the shepherds; he even drew water for us and watered the flock." 20He said to his daughters, "Where is he then? Why did you leave the man? Ask him in to break bread." 21Moses consented to stay with the man, and he gave Moses his daughter Zipporah as wife. 22She bore a son whom he named Gershom, for he said, "I have been a stranger in a foreign land."

טז וּלְכֹהֵן מִדְיָן שֶׁבַע בָּנוֹת וַתָּבֹאנָה וַתִּדְלֶנָה וַתְּמַלֶּאנָה אֶת־הָרְהָטִים לְהַשְׁקוֹת צֹאן אֲבִיהֶן: יז וַיָּבֹאוּ הָרֹעִים וַיְגָרְשׁוּם וַיָּקָם מֹשֶׁה וַיּוֹשִׁעָן וַיַּשְׁקְ אֶת־צֹאנָם: יח וַתָּבֹאנָה אֶל־רְעוּאֵל אֲבִיהֶן וַיֹּאמֶר מַדּוּעַ מִהַרְתֶּן בֹּא הַיּוֹם: יט וַתֹּאמַרְןָ אִישׁ מִצְרִי הִצִּילָנוּ מִיַּד הָרֹעִים וְגַם־דָּלֹה דָלָה לָנוּ וַיַּשְׁקְ אֶת־הַצֹּאן: כ וַיֹּאמֶר אֶל־בְּנֹתָיו וְאַיּוֹ לָמָּה זֶּה עֲזַבְתֶּן אֶת־הָאִישׁ קִרְאֶן לוֹ וְיֹאכַל לָחֶם: כא וַיּוֹאֶל מֹשֶׁה לָשֶׁבֶת אֶת־הָאִישׁ וַיִּתֵּן אֶת־צִפֹּרָה בִתּוֹ לְמֹשֶׁה: כב וַתֵּלֶד בֵּן וַיִּקְרָא אֶת־שְׁמוֹ גֵּרְשֹׁם כִּי אָמַר גֵּר הָיִיתִי בְּאֶרֶץ נָכְרִיָּה: פ

Gulf of Akaba, up through the Syro-Arabian Desert, and into the borders of the Land of Israel, west and northwest of Elath.[24]

a well   Wells in the ancient Near East served as meeting places for shepherds, wayfarers, and townsfolk. It was the natural thing for a newcomer to gravitate toward them.[25]

MOSES IN MIDIAN[26]   (vv. 16–22)

Moses displays his instinctive intolerance of injustice a third time. Although himself a fugitive, utterly alone in a strange land, he spontaneously comes to the assistance of the weak and defenseless, this time foreign shepherd girls.

16. the priest   The high priest, named in verse 18.

to draw water   A common occupation of young women in that part of the world.[27]

18. their father Reuel   The name means "friend of God."[28] It is mentioned once again in Numbers 10:29—"Hobab son of Reuel the Midianite, Moses' father-in-law"—where it is uncertain which of the two is so designated. From Judges 4:11 it would appear that Hobab is the father-in-law, but in other texts this latter epithet is given to Jethro, who also bears the title "priest of Midian."[29] Rabbinic exegesis reconciles the discrepancies by assuming that Reuel was the grandfather of the girls and that the other names all refer to the same person, who bore several names.[30] Many modern scholars prefer to assign the variants to different strands of tradition.[31] However, it is to be noted that the title "priest of Midian" is only attached to Jethro. This raises the possibility that Hebrew *yitro* (*yeter*) is not a proper name but an honorific meaning "His Excellency."[32] In Akkadian *atru* (*watru*) means "preeminent, foremost," and several old Akkadian names begin with that element.[33] In Ugaritic several personal names are prefixed by the element *ytr*.[34]

How is it   The question suggests that the girls regularly experienced such maltreatment at the hands of the male shepherds.

19. an Egyptian   His garb so suggested.

21. he gave   The father had the power to make such decisions.[35]

Zipporah   The name means "a bird."

22. Gershom   Some intimately personal significance likely attaches to the name, for its stem *g-r-sh*, "to drive off/out," is the same used to describe the action of the shepherds in verse 17, which was the occasion for Moses to meet his future wife and to be received into Jethro's family. But Gershom also carries a wider, national allusiveness, for later in the narrative the stem is used three more times, to underscore the abject humiliation of the stubborn pharaoh as he is forced to reverse his refusal to let Israel go.[36] The folk etymology interprets the name as a composite of *ger sham*, "a stranger there" and is taken to signify being "a stranger in a foreign land"; this echoes God's covenant

²³A long time after that, the king of Egypt died. The Israelites were groaning under the bondage and cried out; and their cry for help from the bondage rose up to God. ²⁴God heard their moaning, and God remembered His covenant with Abraham and Isaac and Jacob. ²⁵God looked upon the Israelites, and God took notice of them.

כג וַיְהִי בַיָּמִים הָרַבִּים הָהֵם וַיָּמָת מֶלֶךְ מִצְרַיִם וַיֵּאָנְחוּ בְנֵי־יִשְׂרָאֵל מִן־הָעֲבֹדָה וַיִּזְעָקוּ וַתַּעַל שַׁוְעָתָם אֶל־הָאֱלֹהִים מִן־הָעֲבֹדָה: כד וַיִּשְׁמַע אֱלֹהִים אֶת־נַאֲקָתָם וַיִּזְכֹּר אֱלֹהִים אֶת־בְּרִיתוֹ אֶת־אַבְרָהָם אֶת־יִצְחָק וְאֶת־יַעֲקֹב: כה וַיַּרְא אֱלֹהִים אֶת־בְּנֵי יִשְׂרָאֵל וַיֵּדַע אֱלֹהִים: ס רביעי

with Abraham, which foretold: "Your offspring shall be strangers in a land not theirs."[37] The "land" is Egypt, not Midian, and Moses speaks of "there" not "here," as well as referring to the past. The fulfillment of the predicted slavery evokes the associated promise of liberation, so that the birth of the child may be seen as symbolic of the coming regeneration of downtrodden Israel.

A TRANSITIONAL POSTSCRIPT   (vv. 23–25)

These verses redirect attention to the miserable plight of the Israelites back in Egypt and so serve as a transition to the next development. God breaks His silence and directly intervenes in Israel's history. Divine causality, hitherto implicit, is now made emphatically explicit by the fivefold reference to God in just three verses.

23–25.   It was established practice in Egypt for a new king to celebrate his accession to the throne by granting amnesty to those guilty of crimes, by releasing prisoners, and by freeing slaves. An extant hymn composed in honor of the accession of Ramses IV illustrates the custom. It records "a happy day" for Egypt when "fugitives returned to their towns" and when "those in hiding emerged" and "those in prison were freed."[38] This being so, the Israelites had good reason to expect that the change in regime would bring with it some amelioration of their condition. But this was not to be. Hence the stress on the intensified misery of the enslaved Israelites. Moses, however, did benefit from the amnesty personally, as 4:19 confirms.

Four terms give voice to Israel's suffering: "groaning," "cried out," "cry for help," "moaning"; and four verbs express God's response: "heard," "remembered," "looked upon," "took notice."

24.   remembered   The Hebrew stem *z-k-r* connotes much more than the recall of things past. It means, rather, to be mindful, to pay heed, signifying a sharp focusing of attention upon someone or something. It embraces concern and involvement and is active not passive, so that it eventuates in action.[39] As Menaḥot 43b has it: "Looking upon leads to remembering, and remembering leads to action."

His covenant   The oft-repeated dual promises to the patriarchs of nationhood and national territory.[40]

25.   This concise sentence is fully elaborated in 3:7, which shows that the two verbs here mean, respectively, "to empathize" and "to identify with" suffering. On *y-d-ʿ*, see the Comment to 1:8.

CHAPTER 3

The Commissioning of Moses   (3:1–4:17)

God's "taking notice" of Israel's sufferings (2:25) foreshadows the action that is about to occur. The appointment of a leader to rally the demoralized people and represent them before the Egyptian authorities is the first stage in the process of liberation.

The account of the commissioning of Moses is divided into three main parts: (1) the theophany at the burning bush (vv. 1–6); (2) the divine call (vv. 7–10); and (3) Moses' dialogue with God (3:11–4:17).

3 Now Moses, tending the flock of his father-in-law Jethro, the priest of Midian, drove the flock into the wilderness, and came to Horeb, the mountain of God. ²An angel of the LORD appeared to him in a blazing fire out of a bush. He gazed, and there was a bush all aflame, yet the bush was not consumed. ³Moses said, "I must turn aside to look at this marvelous sight; why doesn't the bush burn up?" ⁴When the LORD saw that he had turned aside to look, God called to him out of the bush: "Moses! Moses!" He answered, "Here I am." ⁵And He said, "Do not come closer.

ג וּמֹשֶׁה הָיָה רֹעֶה אֶת־צֹאן יִתְרוֹ חֹתְנוֹ כֹּהֵן
מִדְיָן וַיִּנְהַג אֶת־הַצֹּאן אַחַר הַמִּדְבָּר וַיָּבֹא אֶל־הַר
הָאֱלֹהִים חֹרֵבָה: 2 וַיֵּרָא מַלְאַךְ יְהֹוָה אֵלָיו
בְּלַבַּת־אֵשׁ מִתּוֹךְ הַסְּנֶה וַיַּרְא וְהִנֵּה הַסְּנֶה בֹּעֵר
בָּאֵשׁ וְהַסְּנֶה אֵינֶנּוּ אֻכָּל: 3 וַיֹּאמֶר מֹשֶׁה אָסֻרָה־
נָּא וְאֶרְאֶה אֶת־הַמַּרְאֶה הַגָּדֹל הַזֶּה מַדּוּעַ לֹא־
יִבְעַר הַסְּנֶה: 4 וַיַּרְא יְהֹוָה כִּי סָר לִרְאוֹת וַיִּקְרָא
אֵלָיו אֱלֹהִים מִתּוֹךְ הַסְּנֶה וַיֹּאמֶר מֹשֶׁה מֹשֶׁה
וַיֹּאמֶר הִנֵּנִי: 5 וַיֹּאמֶר אַל־תִּקְרַב הֲלֹם שַׁל־

THE THEOPHANY AT THE BURNING BUSH　(vv. 1–6)

1.　into the wilderness　Hebrew 'aḥar here means westward, in the direction of Egypt from Midian.[1] The orientation to the rising sun gives "front" (*kedem*) the connotation of "east" and "behind" the meaning of "west." The "wilderness" (Heb. *midbar*) is a region of uninhabited and unirrigated pastureland.[2]

Horeb　Many texts seem to identify this location with Sinai, but there are also indications that they may not be identical. Thus, while Mount Sinai appears frequently, Mount Horeb is rare,[3] and there is no reference to the wilderness of Horeb as there is to that of Sinai. Further, an impression of some distance between the two is gained from the story of the water crisis at Rephidim as told in Exodus 17:1–7. The divine spirit is said to have been manifest before Moses, close by "on a rock at Horeb"; yet Rephidim was the last station of the Israelites before entering the wilderness of Sinai.[4] We may be dealing with different strands of tradition,[5] or Horeb may have been the name of a wider region in which Mount Sinai, a specific peak, was located; perhaps that peak eventually lent its name to the entire area. Horeb means "desolate, dry." Its location has not been identified.

the mountain of God　This description is traditionally taken as anticipating its later role as the site of the national covenant between God and Israel.[6] Even if it indicates a pre-Israelite history as a religious center for the seminomadic tribes of the wilderness,[7] the present narrative makes clear that Moses is quite unaware of any prior sanctity attaching to it.

2.　an angel of the LORD　The "angel" has no role in the entire theophany; it is the fire that attracts Moses' attention, and it is always God Himself who speaks. Most likely the angel is mentioned only to avoid what would be the gross anthropomorphism of localizing God in a bush.[8]

in a blazing fire　Fire, because of its nonmaterial, formless, mysterious, and luminous characteristics, is frequently used in descriptions of the external manifestation of the Divine Presence.[9]

a bush　Hebrew *seneh* occurs only here and in Deuteronomy 33:16, where God is poetically named "the Presence in the Bush." *Seneh* is most likely word play on Sinai, an intimation of the Sinaitic revelation foreshadowed in verse 12.[10]

The bush in question has been variously identified as the thorny desert plant *Rubus sanctus* that grows near wadis and in moist soil, and as the *cassia senna* shrub known in Arabic as *sene*.[11]

not consumed　The two elements of the spectacle suggest two levels of interpretation. The self-sustaining fire, requiring no substance for its existence or perpetuation, is a clear representation of the Divine Presence. The bush that remains intact in the face of the flames may be symbolic of the people of Israel surviving Egyptian oppression.[12]

3.　The startling suspension of nature's fixed laws arouses Moses' curiosity.

4.　Moses! Moses!　In the Bible, repetition of a name often characterizes a direct divine call.[13]

Here I am　Hebrew *hinneni* is the standard, spontaneous, unhesitating response to a call.[14]

Remove your sandals from your feet, for the place on which you stand is holy ground. ⁶I am," He said, "the God of your father, the God of Abraham, the God of Isaac, and the God of Jacob." And Moses hid his face, for he was afraid to look at God.

⁷And the LORD continued, "I have marked well the plight of My people in Egypt and have heeded their outcry because of their taskmasters; yes, I am mindful of their sufferings. ⁸I have come down to rescue them from the Egyptians and to bring them out of that land to a good and spacious land, a land flowing with milk and honey, the region of the Canaanites, the Hittites, the Amorites, the Perizzites, the Hivites, and the Jebusites. ⁹Now the cry of

נְעָלֶ֙יךָ֙ מֵעַ֣ל רַגְלֶ֔יךָ כִּ֣י הַמָּק֗וֹם אֲשֶׁ֤ר אַתָּה֙ עוֹמֵ֣ד עָלָ֔יו אַדְמַת־קֹ֖דֶשׁ ה֑וּא׃ 6 וַיֹּ֗אמֶר אָנֹכִי֙ אֱלֹהֵ֣י אָבִ֔יךָ אֱלֹהֵ֧י אַבְרָהָ֛ם אֱלֹהֵ֥י יִצְחָ֖ק וֵאלֹהֵ֣י יַעֲקֹ֑ב וַיַּסְתֵּ֤ר מֹשֶׁה֙ פָּנָ֔יו כִּ֣י יָרֵ֔א מֵהַבִּ֖יט אֶל־הָאֱלֹהִֽים׃ 7 וַיֹּ֣אמֶר יְהוָ֗ה רָאֹ֥ה רָאִ֛יתִי אֶת־עֳנִ֥י עַמִּ֖י אֲשֶׁ֣ר בְּמִצְרָ֑יִם וְאֶת־צַעֲקָתָ֤ם שָׁמַ֙עְתִּי֙ מִפְּנֵ֣י נֹֽגְשָׂ֔יו כִּ֥י יָדַ֖עְתִּי אֶת־מַכְאֹבָֽיו׃ 8 וָאֵרֵ֞ד לְהַצִּיל֣וֹ ׀ מִיַּ֣ד מִצְרַ֗יִם וּֽלְהַעֲלֹתוֹ֮ מִן־הָאָ֣רֶץ הַהִוא֒ אֶל־אֶ֤רֶץ טוֹבָה֙ וּרְחָבָ֔ה אֶל־אֶ֛רֶץ זָבַ֥ת חָלָ֖ב וּדְבָ֑שׁ אֶל־מְק֤וֹם הַֽכְּנַעֲנִי֙ וְהַ֣חִתִּ֔י וְהָֽאֱמֹרִי֙ וְהַפְּרִזִּ֔י וְהַחִוִּ֖י וְהַיְבוּסִֽי׃ 9 וְעַתָּ֕ה הִנֵּ֛ה צַעֲקַ֥ת בְּנֵי־יִשְׂרָאֵ֖ל בָּ֣אָה

5. The idea of explicitly sacred (Heb. *kadosh*) space is encountered here for the first time. No such concept exists in Genesis, which features only sacred time—the Sabbath.[15] The pagan mythological notion that certain areas are inherently holy does not exist in the Bible. It is solely the theophany that temporarily imparts sanctity to the site, rendering it inaccessible to man.

In the ancient Near East, removal of footwear, here probably sandals of papyrus or leather, was a sign of respect and displayed an attitude of humility. Priests officiated barefoot in the sanctuary;[16] and to this day they remove their footwear before pronouncing the priestly benediction in the synagogue service.

6. I am . . . This solemn, self-identifying mode of address frequently introduces royal proclamations and inscriptions in the ancient Near East.[17] It lends special weight to the ensuing announcement, which thereby becomes authoritative and unchallengeable. Since this formula is often used in divine communications with the patriarchs,[18] it is particularly meaningful in the present context.[19]

the God of your father This epithet, frequently used in the Book of Genesis, all but vanishes in Israel[20] during the period of the Exodus, to be replaced by "the God of the fathers," the plural form referring to the three patriarchs. In the present instance, the epithet identifies the God who is addressing Moses with the One who made promises of peoplehood and national territory to each of the patriarchs.[21] It gives voice to the unbroken continuity of the generations and puts the present plight of the Israelites and the imminent call to Moses into historical and theological perspective. On the "God of the Father," see Excursus 3.

Moses hid his face His initial encounter with God is a terrifying experience, a reaction shared by other biblical characters.[22] Later in the course of his career, by dint of his intimacy with God, Moses is so emboldened as to request a glimpse of the Divine Presence.[23]

THE DIVINE CALL (vv. 7–10)

The intimation of deliverance from bondage advanced in 2:24–25 is now elaborated in all its fullness as a clear message of hope and redemption.

7. outcry The Hebrew stem *ts-ʿ-k* is one of the most powerful words in the language. Pervaded by moral outrage and soul-stirring passion, it denotes the anguished cry of the oppressed, the agonized plea of the helpless victim.[24]

8. I have come down A common anthropomorphic figure of speech used to express God's decisive involvement in human affairs.[25]

a good and spacious land This depiction of the Land of Israel is drawn from the mental image of an oppressed seminomadic people confined to the limited area of Goshen. Deuteronomy's

the Israelites has reached Me; moreover, I have seen how the Egyptians oppress them. [10]Come, therefore, I will send you to Pharaoh, and you shall free My people, the Israelites, from Egypt."

אֵלָי וְגַם־רָאִ֫יתִי אֶת־הַלַּ֫חַץ אֲשֶׁ֣ר מִצְרַ֫יִם לֹחֲצִ֥ים אֹתָֽם׃ 10 וְעַתָּ֣ה לְכָ֔ה וְאֶֽשְׁלָחֲךָ֖ אֶל־פַּרְעֹ֑ה וְהוֹצֵ֛א אֶת־עַמִּ֥י בְנֵֽי־יִשְׂרָאֵ֖ל מִמִּצְרָֽיִם׃ 11 וַיֹּ֤אמֶר

description (8:7) does not include the sense of spaciousness found in Nehemiah's nostalgic review of past glories (Neh. 9:35).

flowing with milk and honey   A recurrent symbol of the land's fertility. The combination of the two products is also popular in classical literature. The phrase is never included in the divine promises made to the patriarchs,[26] for whom famine was frequently a grim reality. Besides, their faith did not need to be reinforced by stressing the attractiveness of the land. For the demoralized, enslaved masses of Israel, however, such an enticement would carry weight. As a matter of fact, ancient Egyptian sources testify to the richness of the land.[27]

Milk in the Bible is generally from the goat, "the little man's cow." A plentiful supply presupposes an abundance of goats, which in turn points to ample pasturage and the prospect of much meat, hide, and wool.

Honey in the Bible (Heb. *devash*) is predominantly the thick, sweet syrup produced from dates and known to the Arabs as *dibs*. Apiculture seems to have been unknown in Palestine; the few explicit references in the Bible to bees' honey pertain to the wild variety.[28] While the date itself is never mentioned, the inclusion of honey among the seven characteristic products of the land listed in Deuteronomy 8:8 indicates that, like all the others, it too derives from the soil.[29]

The combination of milk and honey provides a highly nutritious diet. Milk, widely regarded in the ancient world as a source of vitality, is rich in protein; the dried date is rich in carbohydrates. Ben Sira (39:26) declared milk and honey to be among the chief necessities of human life. Some Arab tribes are known to subsist for months at a time solely on milk and honey.

the region of the Canaanites...   The most comprehensive of the numerous biblical lists of the pre-Israelite inhabitants of the land is that of Genesis 15:19–21, which features ten peoples. Other lists register seven, six, five, or even three ethnic groups.[30] The origin of these rosters is obscure, as is the reason for the variations in number, order, and content. The fact that the Jebusites invariably appear in the final position may be an intimation of David's capture of Jebusite Jerusalem, which was the culmination of his conquests.[31]

The lists carry significance apart from their immediate context. The extraordinarily complex ethnic situation that they reflect is paralleled by the thirty-one city-states that Joshua encountered in this tiny country, as related in Joshua 12. The explanation lies in the centrifugal forces produced by the accidents of topography and climate. Within the narrow belt between the sea and the desert, about 100 miles (ca. 161 km.) in width and 160 miles (ca. 258 km.) in length from Dan to Beersheba, are to be found no fewer than four parallel longitudinal zones, each of which undergoes considerable internal modification. The coastal plain gives way to the central mountain region, which in turn yields abruptly to the Jordan Valley, only to be succeeded by the plateau of Transjordan. The extremes of altitude are astonishing. The mountains of Lebanon rise to a height of 8,800 feet (2,531.5 m.) above sea level, and the deepest point of the Dead Sea lies about 2,500 feet (762.5 m.) below the surface of the Mediterranean. The intensity and direction of the winds and air movements, the seasonal rainfalls, the deposits of dew, and the daily variations in temperature are all subject to wide-ranging regional fluctuations. In addition, the major overland routes of the ancient world passed through the land so that the internal disunity promoted by nature was further intensified by the powerful and diverse external cultural influences and strategic and political forces.

In light of all this, it is not surprising that in the long history of the country it was usually ruled by foreign powers, and its fate was never tied to the fortunes of any one people within it—with the sole and remarkable exception of the people of Israel during the biblical period, the Second Jewish Commonwealth, and today.

10. Come   This charge is the pivotal point of the theophany. Moses is elected to be the conscious agent of divine will, the human instrument by which the redemption of Israel is to be effectuated. The biblical institution of the messenger prophet is now initiated.

16

¹¹But Moses said to God, "Who am I that I should go to Pharaoh and free the Israelites from Egypt?" ¹²And He said, "I will be with you; that shall be your sign that it was I who sent you. And when you have freed the people from Egypt, you shall worship God at this mountain."

¹³Moses said to God, "When I come to the Israelites and say to them 'The God of your fathers has sent me to you,' and they ask me, 'What is His name?' what shall I say to them?" ¹⁴And God said to Moses, "Ehyeh-Asher-Ehyeh."

מֹשֶׁה אֶל־הָאֱלֹהִים מִי אָנֹכִי כִּי אֵלֵךְ אֶל־פַּרְעֹה וְכִי אוֹצִיא אֶת־בְּנֵי יִשְׂרָאֵל מִמִּצְרָיִם: ¹² וַיֹּאמֶר כִּי־אֶהְיֶה עִמָּךְ וְזֶה־לְּךָ הָאוֹת כִּי אָנֹכִי שְׁלַחְתִּיךָ בְּהוֹצִיאֲךָ אֶת־הָעָם מִמִּצְרַיִם תַּעַבְדוּן אֶת־הָאֱלֹהִים עַל הָהָר הַזֶּה: ¹³ וַיֹּאמֶר מֹשֶׁה אֶל־הָאֱלֹהִים הִנֵּה אָנֹכִי בָא אֶל־בְּנֵי יִשְׂרָאֵל וְאָמַרְתִּי לָהֶם אֱלֹהֵי אֲבוֹתֵיכֶם שְׁלָחַנִי אֲלֵיכֶם וְאָמְרוּ־לִי מַה־שְּׁמוֹ מָה אֹמַר אֲלֵהֶם:

you shall free In contrast to verse 8, entry into the land is omitted, perhaps because Moses is not destined to experience it.[32]

MOSES' DIALOGUE WITH GOD (3:11–4:17)

A lengthy dialogue between Moses and God now takes place. Moses instinctively shrinks from the task assigned him, raising three objections. His reluctance to accept the prophetic call would be characteristic of many later prophets.[33]

11. Who am I . . . The initial reaction is one of personal unworthiness.[34] This innate humility, mentioned in Numbers 12:3, must have been intensified by his understandable fear for his life and by the recollection of his previous experience with the two quarreling Hebrews.

12. This difficult verse has occasioned much exegesis. The first clause is clear enough. God's "being with" someone is an assurance of protection. This is usually given at critical moments of human fear and indecision.[35] In the present instance, Hebrew *'ehyeh,* "I shall be," also artfully connects with the next section of the dialogue (v. 14).

The next clause is unclear. Hebrew *'ot,* "a sign," is largely something that functions to corroborate either a promise or an appointment to office.[36] But to what does the Hebrew demonstrative *zeh,* "this, that," refer?[37] Is it the spectacle at the bush? This would mean that the phenomenon is the sign that affirms the divinely appointed nature of Moses' mission. Or is it his unique ability to negotiate freely and safely with the all-powerful pharaoh that will authenticate his calling? Either interpretation makes an independent statement of the last sentence of the verse, which begins with "when." More difficult and less likely is the possibility that *zeh* refers to the following clause, yielding the understanding that the worship of God in freedom at Sinai will retroactively legitimate Moses' role.

you shall worship Whether it be a prediction or a prescription, this phrase is a subtle hint to Moses on how to handle the negotiations with the Egyptian authorities. The motif of the worship of God as one of the objectives of the Exodus is reiterated time and again before Pharaoh.[38] Since the Hebraic stem *'-v-d* means both "to be in servitude" and "to worship," the phrase insinuates the idea that worship of God is incompatible with servitude to the pharaoh.

13. Moses' second objection is related to the inability to represent Israel without a mandate from the people and without even knowing the name of the God for whom he is now asked to speak. The title "God of your father" was a widely used Near Eastern epithet, also applicable to any of the pagan gods, as noted in Excursus 3. By asking for God's name, Moses implicitly denies knowledge of it, as Rashbam notes.

Ehyeh-Asher-Ehyeh This phrase has variously been translated, "I Am That I Am," "I Am Who I Am," and "I Will Be What I Will Be." It clearly evokes YHVH, the specific proper name of Israel's God, known in English as the Tetragrammaton, that is, "the four consonants." The phrase also indicates that the earliest recorded understanding of the divine name was as a verb derived from the stem *h-v-h,* taken as an earlier form of *h-y-h,* "to be." Either it expresses the quality of absolute Being, the eternal, unchanging, dynamic presence, or it means, "He causes to be." *YHVH* is the third

He continued, "Thus shall you say to the Israelites, 'Ehyeh sent me to you.'" ¹⁵And God said further to Moses, "Thus shall you speak to the Israelites: The LORD, the God of your fathers, the God of Abraham, the God of Isaac, and the God of Jacob, has sent me to you:

This shall be My name forever,

This My appellation for all eternity.

¹⁶"Go and assemble the elders of Israel and say to them: the LORD, the God of your fathers, the God of Abraham, Isaac, and Jacob, has appeared to me and said, 'I have taken note of you and of what is being done to you in Egypt, ¹⁷and I have declared: I will take you out of the misery of Egypt to the land of the Canaanites, the Hittites, the Amorites, the Perizzites, the Hivites, and the Jebusites, to a land flowing with milk and honey.' ¹⁸They will listen to you; then you shall go with the elders of Israel to the king of

וַיֹּ֤אמֶר אֱלֹהִים֙ אֶל־מֹשֶׁ֔ה אֶֽהְיֶ֖ה אֲשֶׁ֣ר אֶֽהְיֶ֑ה 14
וַיֹּ֗אמֶר כֹּ֤ה תֹאמַר֙ לִבְנֵ֣י יִשְׂרָאֵ֔ל אֶֽהְיֶ֖ה שְׁלָחַ֥נִי
אֲלֵיכֶֽם׃ 15 וַיֹּאמֶר֩ עוֹד֨ אֱלֹהִ֜ים אֶל־מֹשֶׁ֗ה
כֹּֽה־תֹאמַר֘ אֶל־בְּנֵ֣י יִשְׂרָאֵל֒ יְהֹוָ֞ה אֱלֹהֵ֣י אֲבֹֽתֵיכֶ֗ם
אֱלֹהֵ֨י אַבְרָהָ֜ם אֱלֹהֵ֧י יִצְחָ֛ק וֵֽאלֹהֵ֥י יַעֲקֹ֖ב
שְׁלָחַ֣נִי אֲלֵיכֶ֑ם
זֶה־שְּׁמִ֣י לְעֹלָ֔ם
וְזֶ֥ה זִכְרִ֖י לְדֹ֥ר דֹּֽר׃   חמישי
16 לֵ֣ךְ וְאָֽסַפְתָּ֞ אֶת־זִקְנֵ֣י יִשְׂרָאֵל֘ וְאָֽמַרְתָּ֣ אֲלֵהֶם֒
יְהֹוָ֞ה אֱלֹהֵ֤י אֲבֹֽתֵיכֶם֙ נִרְאָ֣ה אֵלַ֔י אֱלֹהֵ֧י אַבְרָהָ֛ם
יִצְחָ֥ק וְיַֽעֲקֹ֖ב לֵאמֹ֑ר פָּקֹ֤ד פָּקַ֙דְתִּי֙ אֶתְכֶ֔ם וְאֶת־
הֶֽעָשׂ֥וּי לָכֶ֖ם בְּמִצְרָֽיִם׃ 17 וָֽאֹמַ֗ר אַֽעֲלֶ֣ה אֶתְכֶם֮
מֵֽעֳנִ֣י מִצְרַ֒יִם֒ אֶל־אֶ֤רֶץ הַֽכְּנַֽעֲנִי֙ וְהַ֣חִתִּ֔י וְהָֽאֱמֹרִי֙
וְהַפְּרִזִּ֔י וְהַֽחִוִּ֖י וְהַיְבוּסִ֑י אֶל־אֶ֛רֶץ זָבַ֥ת חָלָ֖ב וּדְבָֽשׁ׃
18 וְשָׁמְע֖וּ לְקֹלֶ֑ךָ וּבָאתָ֡ אַתָּה֩ וְזִקְנֵ֨י יִשְׂרָאֵ֜ל

person masculine singular; *ehyeh* is the corresponding first person singular. This latter is used here because name-giving in the ancient world implied the wielding of power over the one named; hence, the divine name can only proceed from God Himself.³⁹

In the course of the Second Temple period the Tetragrammaton came to be regarded as charged with metaphysical potency and therefore ceased to be pronounced. It was replaced in speech by 'adonai, "Lord," rendered into Greek *Kyrios*. Often the vowels of 'adonai would later accompany *YHVH* in written texts. This gave rise to the mistaken form *Jehovah*. The original pronunciation was eventually lost; modern attempts at recovery are conjectural.

God's response to Moses' query cannot be the disclosure of a hitherto unknown name, for that would be unintelligible to the people and would not resolve Moses' dilemma. However, taken together with the statement in 6:3, the implication is that the name YHVH only came into prominence as the characteristic personal name of the God of Israel in the time of Moses. This tradition accords with the facts that the various divine names found in Genesis are no longer used, except occasionally in poetic texts; that of all the personal names listed hitherto, none is constructed of the prefixed *yeho-/yo-* or the suffixed *-yahu/-yah* contractions of YHVH; that the first name of this type is *yokheved* (Jochebed), that of Moses' mother.⁴⁰ Ibn Ezra points out that Moses, in his direct speech, invariably uses the name YHVH, not 'elohim, "God." Without doubt, the revelation of the divine name YHVH to Moses registers a new stage in the history of Israelite monotheism.

15. My name ... My appellation⁴¹   How I am addressed and referred to.

forever ... for all eternity   God's unvarying dependability provides assurance that His promises will be fulfilled.

16. the elders   Moses' first concern in his new role must be to win the confidence and support of the acknowledged leaders of the people. These are the elders (Heb. *zekenim*) who are frequently mentioned in the Exodus narratives, although little information about them is offered.⁴² The institution of elders is rooted in the tribal-patriarchal system that shaped the character of Israelite society in early times. The rich Mari archives dealing with Northwest Semitic tribes show that the council of elders was entrusted with considerable authority, judicial and political. Its members acted as the spokesmen and the delegates of the tribes in dealings with the urban administration.⁴³

I have taken note   This statement echoes the dying words of Joseph as recorded in Genesis 50:24: "God will surely take notice of you and bring you up from this land to the land that He promised on oath to Abraham, to Isaac, and to Jacob." This promise was handed down from generation to generation.

Egypt and you shall say to him, 'The LORD, the God of the Hebrews, manifested Himself to us. Now therefore, let us go a distance of three days into the wilderness to sacrifice to the LORD our God.' ¹⁹Yet I know that the king of Egypt will let you go only because of a greater might. ²⁰So I will stretch out My hand and smite Egypt with various wonders which I will work upon them; after that he shall let you go. ²¹And I will dispose the Egyptians favorably toward this people, so that when you go, you will not go away empty-handed. ²²Each woman shall borrow from her neighbor and the lodger in her house objects of silver and gold, and clothing, and you shall put these on your sons and daughters, thus stripping the Egyptians."

אֶל־מֶ֣לֶךְ מִצְרַ֔יִם וַאֲמַרְתֶּ֣ם אֵלָ֗יו יְהֹוָ֞ה אֱלֹהֵ֤י הָעִבְרִיִּים֙ נִקְרָ֣ה עָלֵ֔ינוּ וְעַתָּ֗ה נֵֽלְכָה־נָּ֞א דֶּ֣רֶךְ שְׁלֹ֤שֶׁת יָמִים֙ בַּמִּדְבָּ֔ר וְנִזְבְּחָ֖ה לַיהֹוָ֥ה אֱלֹהֵֽינוּ: ¹⁹וַאֲנִ֣י יָדַ֔עְתִּי כִּ֠י לֹֽא־יִתֵּ֥ן אֶתְכֶ֛ם מֶ֥לֶךְ מִצְרַ֖יִם לַהֲלֹ֑ךְ וְלֹ֖א בְּיָ֥ד חֲזָקָֽה: ²⁰וְשָׁלַחְתִּ֣י אֶת־יָדִ֗י וְהִכֵּיתִ֣י אֶת־מִצְרַ֔יִם בְּכֹל֙ נִפְלְאֹתַ֔י אֲשֶׁ֥ר אֶֽעֱשֶׂ֖ה בְּקִרְבּ֑וֹ וְאַחֲרֵי־כֵ֖ן יְשַׁלַּ֥ח אֶתְכֶֽם: ²¹וְנָתַתִּ֛י אֶת־חֵ֥ן הָֽעָם־הַזֶּ֖ה בְּעֵינֵ֣י מִצְרָ֑יִם וְהָיָה֙ כִּ֣י תֵֽלֵכ֔וּן לֹ֥א תֵלְכ֖וּ רֵיקָֽם: ²²וְשָׁאֲלָ֨ה אִשָּׁ֤ה מִשְּׁכֶנְתָּהּ֙ וּמִגָּרַ֣ת בֵּיתָ֔הּ כְּלֵי־כֶ֥סֶף וּכְלֵ֛י זָהָ֖ב וּשְׂמָלֹ֑ת וְשַׂמְתֶּ֗ם עַל־בְּנֵיכֶם֙ וְעַל־בְּנֹ֣תֵיכֶ֔ם וְנִצַּלְתֶּ֖ם אֶת־מִצְרָֽיִם:

18. The LORD, the God of the Hebrews This divine epithet appears exclusively in the Exodus stories,⁴⁴ invariably in connection with addressing the pharaoh and always coupled with a demand for permission to worship in the wilderness. Although this king does not know YHVH, he never claims to be ignorant of "the God of the Hebrews." This suggests that this epithet, like "the God of the father," belongs to a pre-Mosaic stage in the history of Israelite religion and was perhaps widely used among the pastoral nomads of the region.⁴⁵ For that reason, it is carefully identified with YHVH each time it is used by Moses.

manifested Himself Hebrew *nikrah*, as opposed to the usual *nir'ah*, "appeared," emphasizes the sudden and unexpected nature of the encounter with the divine;⁴⁶ and it explains to the pharaoh why no such demand had been made before.

three days In the biblical consciousness, this conventionally constitutes a significant segment of time, particularly in connection with travel.⁴⁷ In the present context, it may well indicate that the intended sacrifice, which would be anathema to the Egyptians,⁴⁸ as stated in Exodus 8:22, would take place well beyond the recognized range of Egyptian cultic holiness.⁴⁹

to sacrifice In terms of the corvée system, the state-organized forced labor gangs, this limited request was not exceptional, as is proved by entries in extant logs of their Egyptian supervisors.⁵⁰ There is also archaeological evidence for the custom among pastoral nomads of making periodic pilgrimages to sacred shrines in the wilderness.⁵¹ On both scores, therefore, the denial of these reasonable and basic demands of the Israelites exposes the true character of the pharaoh and the brutal nature of his tyrannical rule.

19. a greater might Hebrew *yad ḥazakah*, literally "a strong hand," meaning the "hand" of God, mentioned again in verse 20, as opposed to the oppressive "hand of Egypt" of verse 8.

20. wonders Hebrew *nifla'ot* is almost always used of God's timely, direct intervention in human affairs, which does not necessarily express itself through the suspension of the laws of nature.⁵²

stretch out . . . let you go There is a kind of word play here, for the first and last verbs in the sentence are formed from the same stem *sh-l-ḥ*. The one will effect the other.

21–22. Such a dignified departure from Egypt was foretold in the original covenant with Abraham: "I will execute judgment on the nation they shall serve, and in the end they shall go free with great wealth."⁵³ This promise was fulfilled at the time of the Exodus.⁵⁴ Early Jewish exegesis as reflected in Jubilees 48:18 and Philo of Alexandria,⁵⁵ as well as in the Talmud,⁵⁶ looked upon these spoils as well-deserved compensation to the Israelites for their long years of unpaid forced labor. It is also possible to interpret the development as being in accordance with the law of Deuteronomy 15:13 that requires the master to provision his slave liberally at the time of emancipation: "When you set him free, do not let him go empty-handed."⁵⁷

22. shall borrow Rather, "shall request," which is the usual meaning of the stem *sh-'-l*.⁵⁸

4 But Moses spoke up and said, "What if they do not believe me and do not listen to me, but say: The Lord did not appear to you?" ²The Lord said to him, "What is that in your hand?" And he replied, "A rod." ³He said, "Cast it on the ground." He cast it on the ground and it became a snake; and Moses recoiled from it. ⁴Then the Lord said to Moses, "Put out your hand and grasp it by the tail"—he put out his hand and seized it, and it became a rod in his hand—⁵"that they may believe that the Lord, the God of

ד וַיַּעַן מֹשֶׁה וַיֹּאמֶר וְהֵן לֹא־יַאֲמִינוּ לִי וְלֹא יִשְׁמְעוּ בְּקֹלִי כִּי יֹאמְרוּ לֹא־נִרְאָה אֵלֶיךָ יְהוָה: ² וַיֹּאמֶר אֵלָיו יְהוָה מזה בְיָדֶךָ וַיֹּאמֶר מַטֶּה: ³ וַיֹּאמֶר הַשְׁלִיכֵהוּ אַרְצָה וַיַּשְׁלִיכֵהוּ אַרְצָה וַיְהִי לְנָחָשׁ וַיָּנָס מֹשֶׁה מִפָּנָיו: ⁴ וַיֹּאמֶר יְהוָה אֶל־מֹשֶׁה שְׁלַח יָדְךָ וֶאֱחֹז בִּזְנָבוֹ וַיִּשְׁלַח יָדוֹ וַיַּחֲזֶק בּוֹ וַיְהִי לְמַטֶּה בְּכַפּוֹ: ⁵ לְמַעַן יַאֲמִינוּ כִּי

v. 2. מַה־זֶּה ק'

stripping　The same Hebrew term is used literally in 2 Chronicles 20:25, but here it should be taken as hyperbole.[59]

CHAPTER 4

1.　Moses presents his third objection: the possibility of being rejected by the Israelite masses. God, after all, had mentioned only the elders, not the people, in 3:18. Knowledge of the divine name does not of itself validate a claim to be divinely commissioned. Since the days of Jacob no Israelite had professed to receiving a theophany.

What if...[1]

2–9.　This time Moses' argument is not refuted. Instead, he is instructed how to dissipate popular skepticism should it materialize. Deuteronomy 13:2–6 discusses the role of the sign in the legitimation of a prophet in Israel. Here, the signs, which will be executed in Egypt, possess a distinctly Egyptian coloration. This is not surprising, for magic was a pervasive ingredient of everyday life in Egypt, deeply embedded in the culture. The signs taught to Moses are intended, first and foremost, to validate his claim to be the divinely chosen instrument for the redemption of Israel. On a secondary level, they also function to establish the superiority of Moses over the Egyptian magicians and, by extension, to affirm the superior might of Israel's God over those whom the Egyptians worshiped as gods.

Moses, however, is not a magician. He possesses no superhuman powers and no esoteric knowledge; he is unable to initiate or perform anything except by precise instructions from God; he pronounces no spells, observes no rituals, and employs no occult techniques, and often he does not know in advance the consequences of the actions he is told to perform.

THE FIRST SIGN (vv. 2–5)

2.　*What is that in your hand?*　The query serves to certify that the object is an ordinary shepherd's crook and is not invested with magical powers.[2]

3.　That Moses recoils before the transformed rod expresses his astonishment at the marvel; his act intimates that God, not he, is in command of the situation.

a snake　This creature probably serves a dual purpose here, practical and symbolic. As we learn from 7:8–11, the trick is later duplicated by the court magicians, which then enables Moses to demonstrate the superiority of Israel's God. The rod in ancient Egypt was a symbol of royal authority and power,[3] while the snake, the uraeus, represented the patron cobra-goddess of Lower Egypt. Worn over the forehead on the headdress of the pharaohs, it was emblematic of divinely protected sovereignty, and it served as a menacing symbol of death dealt to the enemies of the crown. See Comment to 7:8–12.

A midrash interprets the scene allegorically as a rebuke to Moses. He had misstated Israel's faithfulness, just as the serpent had misrepresented God's word to Eve.[4]

4.　*by the tail*　Normally a foolhardy act, it here manifests Moses' implicit faith in God.

their fathers, the God of Abraham, the God of Isaac, and the God of Jacob, did appear to you."

⁶The LORD said to him further, "Put your hand into your bosom." He put his hand into his bosom; and when he took it out, his hand was encrusted with snowy scales! ⁷And He said, "Put your hand back into your bosom."—He put his hand back into his bosom; and when he took it out of his bosom, there it was again like the rest of his body.— ⁸"And if they do not believe you or pay heed to the first sign, they will believe the second. ⁹And if they are not convinced by both these signs and still do not heed you, take some water from the Nile and pour it on the dry ground, and it—the water that you take from the Nile— will turn to blood on the dry ground."

¹⁰But Moses said to the LORD, "Please, O Lord, I have never been a man of words, either in times past or now that You have spoken to Your servant; I am slow of speech and slow of tongue." ¹¹And the LORD said to him, "Who gives man speech? Who makes him dumb or deaf, seeing or blind? Is it not I, the LORD? ¹²Now go, and I will be with you as you speak and will instruct you what to say." ¹³But he said, "Please, O Lord, make someone else Your agent."

נִרְאָה אֵלֶיךָ יְהוָה אֱלֹהֵי אֲבֹתָם אֱלֹהֵי אַבְרָהָם
אֱלֹהֵי יִצְחָק וֵאלֹהֵי יַעֲקֹב: ⁶וַיֹּאמֶר יְהוָה לוֹ עוֹד הָבֵא־נָא יָדְךָ
בְּחֵיקֶךָ וַיָּבֵא יָדוֹ בְּחֵיקוֹ וַיּוֹצִאָהּ וְהִנֵּה יָדוֹ
מְצֹרַעַת כַּשָּׁלֶג: ⁷וַיֹּאמֶר הָשֵׁב יָדְךָ אֶל־חֵיקֶךָ
וַיָּשֶׁב יָדוֹ אֶל־חֵיקוֹ וַיּוֹצִאָהּ מֵחֵיקוֹ וְהִנֵּה־שָׁבָה
כִבְשָׂרוֹ: ⁸וְהָיָה אִם־לֹא יַאֲמִינוּ לָךְ וְלֹא יִשְׁמְעוּ
לְקֹל הָאֹת הָרִאשׁוֹן וְהֶאֱמִינוּ לְקֹל הָאֹת הָאַחֲרוֹן:
⁹וְהָיָה אִם־לֹא יַאֲמִינוּ גַּם לִשְׁנֵי הָאֹתוֹת
הָאֵלֶּה וְלֹא יִשְׁמְעוּן לְקֹלֶךָ וְלָקַחְתָּ מִמֵּימֵי
הַיְאֹר וְשָׁפַכְתָּ הַיַּבָּשָׁה וְהָיוּ הַמַּיִם אֲשֶׁר תִּקַּח
מִן־הַיְאֹר וְהָיוּ לְדָם בַּיַּבָּשֶׁת: ¹⁰וַיֹּאמֶר מֹשֶׁה אֶל־יְהוָה בִּי אֲדֹנָי לֹא
אִישׁ דְּבָרִים אָנֹכִי גַּם מִתְּמוֹל גַּם מִשִּׁלְשֹׁם
גַּם מֵאָז דַּבֶּרְךָ אֶל־עַבְדֶּךָ כִּי כְבַד־פֶּה וּכְבַד
לָשׁוֹן אָנֹכִי: ¹¹וַיֹּאמֶר יְהוָה אֵלָיו מִי שָׂם פֶּה
לָאָדָם אוֹ מִי־יָשׂוּם אִלֵּם אוֹ חֵרֵשׁ אוֹ פִקֵּחַ אוֹ
עִוֵּר הֲלֹא אָנֹכִי יְהוָה: ¹²וְעַתָּה לֵךְ וְאָנֹכִי אֶהְיֶה
עִם־פִּיךָ וְהוֹרֵיתִיךָ אֲשֶׁר תְּדַבֵּר: ¹³וַיֹּאמֶר בִּי
אֲדֹנָי שְׁלַח־נָא בְּיַד־תִּשְׁלָח: ¹⁴וַיִּחַר־אַף יְהוָה

THE SECOND SIGN (vv. 6–7)

6. encrusted Hebrew *tsaraʿat*,⁵ usually mistranslated "leprosy," has none of the major symptoms of that malady, and the descriptions of *tsaraʿat* given in Leviticus 13–14 are incompatible with Hansen's disease. The comparison to snow is not in respect of its whiteness but of its flakiness. Apart from the startling phenomenon of the sudden appearance and disappearance of the encrustation, this particular sign has an ominous aspect to it in that it is seen in the Bible as a divine punishment for human misbehavior.⁶

THE THIRD SIGN (vv. 8–9)

8. pay heed to Literally, "listen to the voice of." The sign, as it were, "speaks"; it testifies to the divine commissioning.

9. The third sign. This can be performed only inside Egypt. It later becomes the first of the ten plagues.⁷

The Nile—the life-blood of Egypt—was deified; thus, this sign, like the first, signifies God's sovereign rule over nature and the subordination of Egypt and its so-called gods to YHVH.

10. Moses puts forth his final objection: his claim of inadequacy to the task of being God's spokesman before the Egyptian court. The precise nature of the deficiency is unclear as is the variant term "impeded speech" (literally "uncircumcised lips") used in 6:12,30. Most traditional commentators understood it as a speech defect, but some construed the phraseology as connoting a lack of eloquence or a loss of fluency in the Egyptian language. Whatever the circumstances, it is certain that the underlying idea is that prophetic eloquence is not a native talent but a divine endowment granted for a special purpose, the message originating with God and not with the prophet.⁸

13. Having exhausted his arguments, Moses makes one last desperate appeal.

¹⁴The Lᴏʀᴅ became angry with Moses, and He said, "There is your brother Aaron the Levite. He, I know, speaks readily. Even now he is setting out to meet you, and he will be happy to see you. ¹⁵You shall speak to him and put the words in his mouth—I will be with you and with him as you speak, and tell both of you what to do—¹⁶and he shall speak for you to the people. Thus he shall serve as your spokesman, with you playing the role of God to him, ¹⁷And take with you this rod, with which you shall perform the signs."

¹⁸Moses went back to his father-in-law Jether and said to him, "Let me go back to my kinsmen in Egypt and see how they are faring." And Jethro said to Moses, "Go in peace."

בְּמֹשֶׁה וַיֹּאמֶר הֲלֹא אַהֲרֹן אָחִיךָ הַלֵּוִי
יָדַעְתִּי כִּי־דַבֵּר יְדַבֵּר הוּא וְגַם הִנֵּה־הוּא יֹצֵא
לִקְרָאתֶךָ וְרָאֲךָ וְשָׂמַח בְּלִבּוֹ: ¹⁵ וְדִבַּרְתָּ אֵלָיו
וְשַׂמְתָּ אֶת־הַדְּבָרִים בְּפִיו וְאָנֹכִי אֶהְיֶה עִם־
פִּיךָ וְעִם־פִּיהוּ וְהוֹרֵיתִי אֶתְכֶם אֵת אֲשֶׁר
תַּעֲשׂוּן: ¹⁶ וְדִבֶּר־הוּא לְךָ אֶל־הָעָם וְהָיָה הוּא
יִהְיֶה־לְּךָ לְפֶה וְאַתָּה תִּהְיֶה־לּוֹ לֵאלֹהִים: ¹⁷ וְאֶת־
הַמַּטֶּה הַזֶּה תִּקַּח בְּיָדֶךָ אֲשֶׁר תַּעֲשֶׂה־בּוֹ אֶת־
הָאֹתֹת: פ ששי
¹⁸ וַיֵּלֶךְ מֹשֶׁה וַיָּשָׁב אֶל־יֶתֶר חֹתְנוֹ
וַיֹּאמֶר לוֹ אֵלְכָה נָּא וְאָשׁוּבָה אֶל־אַחַי אֲשֶׁר־
בְּמִצְרַיִם וְאֶרְאֶה הַעוֹדָם חַיִּים וַיֹּאמֶר יִתְרוֹ
לְמֹשֶׁה לֵךְ לְשָׁלוֹם:

14. *Aaron* Mentioned now for the first time, he is three years older than Moses.⁹

the Levite A strange designation, since Moses too was from the tribe of Levi. There may be an allusion to skill and accomplishment, for the Levites may have constituted an educated elite.¹⁰ Alternatively, the Hebrew can be translated as "your brother Levite."¹¹

setting out to meet you There must be some lost tradition behind this statement.

16. *your spokesman* Hebrew *peh*, literally "mouth," that is, mouthpiece. The parallel text in 7:1 has "your prophet," indicating the biblical understanding of the prophet as the spokesman for God.

17. The theophany comes to an end. Moses has nothing more to utter; he succumbs to his fate. Jeremiah (20:7,9) expresses his own, similar experience as follows: "You enticed me, O Lᴏʀᴅ, and I was enticed; / You overpowered me and You prevailed. . . . / I thought, 'I will not mention Him, / No more will I speak in His name'— / But [His word] was like a raging fire in my heart, / Shut up in my bones; / I could not hold it in, I was helpless."

The Challenge of Leadership: Initial Failure   (4:18–6:1)

This section covers the events between the two great theophanies of 3:1–4:17 and 6:2–8. It subdivides into four sections: (1) leave-taking and departure (4:18–23); (2) the night encounter and circumcision (4:24–26); (3) the acceptance of Moses' leadership (4:27–31); and (4) the first audience with Pharaoh (5:1–6:1).

LEAVE-TAKING AND DEPARTURE   (vv. 18–23)

18. Moses returns to Midian with the sheep. He needs to obtain his father-in-law's formal permission to leave his household.¹² He does not disclose the true reason for returning to Egypt, probably because Jethro might think the mission to be impossible and therefore withhold his consent.

my kinsmen The phrase links the return with the original flight, which was a consequence of his having gone out "to his kinsmen" (2:11).

how they are faring Literally, "whether they are still alive." The Hebrew idiom covers general welfare in a wider sense.¹³

22

¹⁹The LORD said to Moses in Midian, "Go back to Egypt, for all the men who sought to kill you are dead." ²⁰So Moses took his wife and sons, mounted them on an ass, and went back to the land of Egypt; and Moses took the rod of God with him.

²¹And the LORD said to Moses, "When you return to Egypt, see that you perform before Pharaoh all the marvels that I have put within your power. I, however, will stiffen his heart so that he will not let the people go. ²²Then you

19 וַיֹּאמֶר יְהוָה אֶל־מֹשֶׁה בְּמִדְיָן לֵךְ שֻׁב
מִצְרָיִם כִּי־מֵתוּ כָּל־הָאֲנָשִׁים הַמְבַקְשִׁים אֶת־
נַפְשֶׁךָ: 20 וַיִּקַּח מֹשֶׁה אֶת־אִשְׁתּוֹ וְאֶת־בָּנָיו
וַיַּרְכִּבֵם עַל־הַחֲמֹר וַיָּשָׁב אַרְצָה מִצְרָיִם וַיִּקַּח
מֹשֶׁה אֶת־מַטֵּה הָאֱלֹהִים בְּיָדוֹ:
21 וַיֹּאמֶר יְהוָה אֶל־מֹשֶׁה בְּלֶכְתְּךָ לָשׁוּב
מִצְרַיְמָה רְאֵה כָּל־הַמֹּפְתִים אֲשֶׁר־שַׂמְתִּי בְיָדֶךָ
וַעֲשִׂיתָם לִפְנֵי פַרְעֹה וַאֲנִי אֲחַזֵּק אֶת־לִבּוֹ וְלֹא
יְשַׁלַּח אֶת־הָעָם: 22 וְאָמַרְתָּ אֶל־פַּרְעֹה כֹּה אָמַר

19. Apparently still fearing for his personal safety, Moses tarries; hence the divine directive and reassurance.

are dead   See Comment to 2:23.

20. went back   This seems to contradict verse 21. Rashi observes that the biblical texts do not always follow strict chronological sequence. Perhaps the Hebrew verb expresses the process rather than its completion.

his wife and sons   According to 18:2–5, Jethro brought Zipporah and the two sons from Midian to Sinai after the Exodus. This shows that they were not in Egypt all the while. Possibly, a fuller version of the story behind the incident of verses 24–26 explained why the family returned to Midian. A midrash has Aaron convincing Moses not to subject his family to the rigors of life in Egypt.[14]

sons   Only Gershom has so far been mentioned (2:22). The ancient versions have a singular here.

the rod of God[15]   The shepherd's crook mentioned in verses 2–4. The designation has been variously explained: as stemming from its use in performing the divinely ordained miracles,[16] as being the subject of a divine command,[17] and as meaning "the rod now invested with divine potency."[18] The Septuagint rendering, "the rod that he had from God," recalls a widespread ancient Near Eastern artistic and literary convention, according to which gods carried rods as the symbol of authority and as emblems of supernatural power. Biblical poetic texts occasionally assign such a rod to God as a figure of speech.[19] This fanciful notion is elaborated in postbiblical midrashim, which take as one and the same Moses' rod, Aaron's rod (mentioned later), and God's rod.[20] Mishnah Avot 5:6(9) included the rod among ten apparently ordinary objects that play an extraordinary role in God's intervention in human affairs in the Bible. All were created at twilight on the eve of the original Sabbath. This is the rabbinic way of stating that what appears to be a miraculous suspension of the laws of nature was providentially integrated into the cosmic order at Creation.[21]

21.   The verse harks back to 3:19–20. The "marvels" are the forthcoming plagues. Moses is again warned of the obstacles that lie ahead on the road to liberation.

will stiffen his heart   The motif of the stiffening, or hardening, of Pharaoh's heart runs through the entire Exodus story; it appears exactly twenty times. Half of the references are to an essential attribute of the man's character,[22] half are attributed to divine causality.[23] In the biblical conception, the psychological faculties are considered to be concentrated in the heart. Regarded as the seat of the intellectual, moral, and spiritual life of the individual, this organ is the determinant of behavior. The "hardening of the heart" thus expresses a state of arrogant moral degeneracy, unresponsive to reason and incapable of compassion. Pharaoh's personal culpability is beyond question.

It is to be noted that in the first five plagues Pharaoh's obduracy is self-willed. It is only thereafter that it is attributed to divine causality. This is the biblical way of asserting that the king's intransigence has by then become habitual and irreversible; his character has become his destiny. He is deprived of the possibility of relenting and is irresistibly impelled to his self-wrought doom.[24]

shall say to Pharaoh, 'Thus says the LORD: Israel is My first-born son. [23]I have said to you, "Let My son go, that he may worship Me," yet you refuse to let him go. Now I will slay your first-born son.'"

[24]At a night encampment on the way, the LORD encountered him and sought to kill him. [25]So Zipporah took a flint

יְהוָֹה בְּנִי בְכֹרִי יִשְׂרָאֵל: 23 וָאֹמַר אֵלֶיךָ שַׁלַּח אֶת־בְּנִי וְיַעַבְדֵנִי וַתְּמָאֵן לְשַׁלְּחוֹ הִנֵּה אָנֹכִי הֹרֵג אֶת־בִּנְךָ בְּכֹרֶךָ:

24 וַיְהִי בַדֶּרֶךְ בַּמָּלוֹן וַיִּפְגְּשֵׁהוּ יְהוָֹה וַיְבַקֵּשׁ הֲמִיתוֹ: 25 וַתִּקַּח צִפֹּרָה צֹר וַתִּכְרֹת אֶת־

22. Thus says the LORD Hebrew *koh 'amar YHVH*. This is the first use of the regular formula introducing a prophetic address. Believed to be an adaptation of the conventional opening words of royal heralds,[25] it serves to secure audience attention while emphasizing the unimpeachable authority behind the ensuing proclamation. Moses is to approach the Egyptian king as the emissary of the sovereign Lord of the universe.[26]

My first-born son The relationship of Israel to God is expressed poetically, in filial terms.[27] All peoples are recognized as being under the universal fatherhood of God, but Israel has the singular status of being the first to acknowledge YHVH and to enter into a special relationship with Him. As such, Israel enjoys God's devoted care and protection.[28] Jeremiah 2:3 expresses the same thought: "Israel was holy to the LORD, / The first fruits of His harvest. / All who ate of it were held guilty; / Disaster befell them." The first-born son in Israel was regarded as being naturally dedicated to God[29] and in early times had certain cultic prerogatives and obligations. It is this that informs the concomitant demand of verse 23 that Israel be allowed to worship in the wilderness. Denial of this right on the part of Pharaoh will incur appropriate punishment.

23. your first-born son Pharaoh here stands for all Egyptians, in parallel with the collective "Israel." The threat alludes to the tenth plague, the one that finally breaks the tyrant's obstinacy.[30]

THE NIGHT ENCOUNTER AND CIRCUMCISION[31]　(vv. 24–26)

The account of Moses' return to Egypt is interrupted by a brief but thoroughly perplexing story. At first glance, the obscure, three-verse narrative seems to lack integration into the larger context of the chapter. Moses is not mentioned. If he is the afflicted person, one could well ask how God could want to kill him, the chosen instrument for the liberation of Israel, as he sets out in fulfillment of the divine command. To complicate matters further, the application of some of the verbs, personal pronouns, and pronominal suffixes is unclear. Finally, there is also uncertainty about the meaning of some of the language and about the person to whom it is directed.

These various obscurities arise primarily because the account here is only a truncated version of a larger, popular story that circulated orally in Israel. Its details were well known and were expected to be supplied by the audience. There are several such fragmentary narratives in the Book of Genesis: the marriage of Cain (4:17), the Song of Lamech (4:23–24), the celestial beings and terrestrial girls (6:1–3), the depravity of Canaan (9:18–29), the nocturnal assailant of Jacob (32:23–33), and Reuben's affair with his father's concubine (35:22).

In point of fact, the sketchy tale of the night incident in verses 24–26 is not as unconnected with the larger context as is often claimed. The introductory phrase, "It happened on the way," immediately establishes the chronological linkage with verse 20. Then there are several verbal tie-ins with both the foregoing and the following texts. Thus, the phrase "sought to kill" in verse 24 echoes "who sought to kill you" in verse 19; "her son" in verse 25 recalls "his sons," "My son," "your son" in verses 20,22,23, and the Hebrew for "encountered him" (*va-yifgeshehu*) in verse 24 is identical with that for "met him" in verse 27.

Aside from these shared expressions, there are other indications of careful design. The featuring of the circumcision episode following the reference to the first-born provides an artfully wrought

and cut off her son's foreskin, and touched his legs with it, saying, "You are truly a bridegroom of blood to me!" ²⁶And when He let him alone, she added, "A bridegroom of blood because of the circumcision."

עָרְלַת בְּנָהּ וַתַּגַּע לְרַגְלָיו וַתֹּאמֶר כִּי חֲתַן־דָּמִים אַתָּה לִי׃ 26 וַיִּרֶף מִמֶּנּוּ אָז אָמְרָה חֲתַן דָּמִים לַמּוּלֹת׃ פ

literary framework for the entire narrative, one that encompasses the struggle for liberation from Pharaoh's oppression. That struggle begins with Moses' setting out to return to Egypt (v. 20), and its successful conclusion is signaled by the death of the Egyptian first-born (12:29–36). This latter is followed immediately by the law requiring circumcision as the precondition for participation in the paschal sacrifice (12:43–49), which in turn is followed by the law of the first-born (13:1,11–15). The effect is a thematically arranged chiasm:

First-born (4:22–23) ——————————— Circumcision (12:43–49)

Circumcision (4:24–26) ——————————— First-born (13:1,11–15)

In addition to the literary structure, there is also a functional correspondence between the blood of circumcision and the visible sign of the blood on the paschal sacrifice. In both instances, evil is averted on account of it (4:26; 12:7,13,22–23). This inextricable tie between circumcision and the Passover, as plainly set forth in 12:43–49, is also unmistakably operative in chapter 5 of the Book of Joshua. It is related there that after crossing the Jordan into the promised land a mass circumcision ceremony was performed as a prelude to the first celebration of the Passover feast inside the country (vv. 2–11).

Rabbinic exegesis gave midrashic expression to this association in interpreting Ezekiel 16:6: "When I passed by you and saw you wallowing in your blood, I said to you: 'Live in spite of your blood.' Yea, I said to you: 'Live in spite of your blood.'" The Hebrew phrase *be-damayikh ḥayi*, emphatically reiterated, was interpreted by the rabbis to mean "survive through your blood [plural]"; that is, the survival and redemption of Israel was assured because of the two mitzvot—that of circumcision and that of paschal sacrifice.[32] Genesis 17:9–14, it should be noted, made circumcision the indispensable precondition for admittance to the community of Israel.

In sum, the brief narrative in verses 24–26 underscores the paramount importance of the institution of circumcision and the surpassing seriousness of its neglect.[33]

24. *a night encampment* Hebrew *malon* may be word play on the stem *m-w-l*, "to circumcise," used in verse 26.

encountered him Whereas polytheistic literature would attribute the experience to a demonic being, Israelite monotheism admits of no independent forces other than the one God. Hence, the action is directly ascribed to Him. In order to soften the anthropomorphism, rabbinic sources, as reflected in the Targums and medieval commentaries, introduce an angel as the instrument of affliction.

sought to Rather, "was on the verge of killing him." This is the force of the Hebrew phrase.[34] The victim was suddenly smitten with a deadly ailment.

kill him It would be wholly inconsistent with the drift of the preceding narrative to assume that Moses was the one stricken. The sequence of verses strongly suggests that it was Moses' first-born, Gershom, whose life was imperiled.[35]

25. *Zipporah* Knowledge of her identity is taken for granted (2:21). It is not to be wondered that she, a Midianite, was familiar with the rite of circumcision; the practice was widespread among the ancient Semites and was prevalent in Egypt.[36] The reason for the mother's attribution of her son's illness to uncircumcision must have some background that now eludes us. Moses may well have neglected this rite because of the danger of exposing a newly circumcised boy to the rigors of the journey through the wilderness. This widely held explanation receives some support from Joshua 5:5,7, which tells that the generation born in the course of the wilderness wanderings was not circumcised. Targum Jonathan reflects a tradition that Jethro had disallowed the operation.

²⁷The Lᴏʀᴅ said to Aaron, "Go to meet Moses in the wilderness." He went and met him at the mountain of God, and he kissed him. ²⁸Moses told Aaron about all the things that the Lᴏʀᴅ had committed to him and all the signs about

²⁷ וַיֹּאמֶר יְהוָה אֶל־אַהֲרֹן לֵךְ לִקְרַאת מֹשֶׁה הַמִּדְבָּרָה וַיֵּלֶךְ וַיִּפְגְּשֵׁהוּ בְּהַר הָאֱלֹהִים וַיִּשַּׁק־לוֹ: ²⁸ וַיַּגֵּד מֹשֶׁה לְאַהֲרֹן אֵת כָּל־דִּבְרֵי יְהוָה אֲשֶׁר

a flint   Rather than a metal knife, even though the events occurred in the Late Bronze Age.³⁷ A stone knife is still widely preferred in primitive societies that practice circumcision, a testimony to both the great antiquity of the rite and the inherent conservatism of religion.

cut off . . .   The unique use of the Hebrew *k-r-t* for this action rather than the otherwise invariable *m-w-l* may reflect Midianite terminology. But there may also be a double word play here, for *k-r-t berit* is the Hebrew term for making a covenant, and in Genesis 17:9–14 circumcision is called "the sign of the covenant." Further, in that same text (v. 14) it is stated that he who fails to fulfill the rite—the first command in the Torah specifically enjoined upon Abraham and his descendants— "shall be cut off from his kin; he has broken My covenant." The Hebrew term for the prescribed penalty is *karet*. An uncircumcised Israelite who thereby alienates himself from the community of Israel would be excluded from the Passover and from the redemption from Egypt. Joshua 5:5 explicitly records that all the males who came out of Egypt had undergone the rite. It would have been ironically paradoxical indeed had the son of the central figure in the story of the Exodus been an outsider.

touches his legs   Whose legs is unclear, as is the symbolism of the gesture. "Legs" may be a euphemism for the genital organs,³⁸ here of the child. The act might signify: See, the foreskin has been cut off; the requirement of circumcision has been fulfilled! Or it may well be a reference to placing a bloodstain on the child because the Hebrew verb used here (rendered "touched") is the same as that used for the daubing of the blood of the paschal lamb on the lintel and doorposts in 12:22 (rendered "apply"). In both cases, the purpose would be the same: The blood would act as a protective sign against plague; the Destroyer would not smite.³⁹

a bridegroom of blood   This is the traditional English rendering of the unique Hebrew phrase *ḥatan damim*, for which, so far, no parallel has been found in ancient Near Eastern literature. If *ḥatan* possesses its usual meaning of "groom," it would hardly be applicable to Moses, who by now has been married for some time. Conceivably, it might be a term of endearment addressed to the child, but the meager evidence for such a usage stems from rabbinic, not biblical, times.⁴⁰ *Ḥatan damim* may be a linguistic fossil, pre-Israelite or Midianite, the meaning of which has been lost. However, it can hardly be coincidental that in Arabic the stem *ḥ-t-n* denotes "to circumcise" as well as "to protect." This latter is also its meaning in Akkadian. Hence, the enigmatic phrase could convey, "You are now circumcised [and so] protected for me by means of the blood—the blood of circumcision." Curiously, *p-s-ḥ*, the Hebrew stem behind Passover, can also mean "to protect." See Comment to 12:11.

26. He let him alone   The subject is God. The crisis has passed.

she added   Literally, "then she said," perhaps invoking or coining a proverb that may mean "circumcision has been performed, and he is no longer liable to *karet*," the penalty of being "cut off" from one's kin.⁴¹

because of the circumcision   Hebrew *la-mulot* is another unique form, apparently an abstract noun.

MOSES' LEADERSHIP IS ACCEPTED   (vv. 27–31)

27. Aaron   See verse 14.

the mountain of God   See Comment to 3:1.

he kissed him   The standard biblical greeting between close relatives.⁴²

which He had instructed him. ²⁹Then Moses and Aaron went and assembled all the elders of the Israelites. ³⁰Aaron repeated all the words that the Lord had spoken to Moses, and he performed the signs in the sight of the people, ³¹and the people were convinced. When they heard that the Lord had taken note of the Israelites and that He had seen their plight, they bowed low in homage.

שְׁלָחֽוֹ וְאֵת כָּל־הָאֹתֹת אֲשֶׁר צִוָּֽהוּ: 29 וַיֵּ֫לֶךְ מֹשֶׁ֣ה
וְאַהֲרֹ֑ן וַיַּ֣אַסְפ֔וּ אֶת־כָּל־זִקְנֵ֖י בְּנֵ֥י יִשְׂרָאֵֽל:
30 וַיְדַבֵּ֣ר אַהֲרֹ֔ן אֵ֚ת כָּל־הַדְּבָרִ֔ים אֲשֶׁר־דִּבֶּ֥ר
יְהֹוָ֖ה אֶל־מֹשֶׁ֑ה וַיַּ֥עַשׂ הָאֹתֹ֖ת לְעֵינֵ֥י הָעָֽם:
31 וַֽיַּאֲמֵ֖ן הָעָ֑ם וַֽיִּשְׁמְע֡וּ כִּֽי־פָקַ֣ד יְהֹוָה֩ אֶת־בְּנֵ֨י
יִשְׂרָאֵ֜ל וְכִ֤י רָאָה֙ אֶת־עָנְיָ֔ם וַֽיִּקְּד֖וּ וַיִּֽשְׁתַּחֲוֽוּ:
שביעי

5 Afterward Moses and Aaron went and said to Pharaoh, "Thus says the Lord, the God of Israel: Let My people go that they may celebrate a festival for Me in the wilderness." ²But Pharaoh said, "Who is the Lord that I should heed Him and let Israel go? I do not know the Lord, nor will I let Israel go." ³They answered, "The God of the Hebrews

ה וְאַחַ֗ר בָּ֚אוּ מֹשֶׁ֣ה וְאַהֲרֹ֔ן וַיֹּאמְר֖וּ אֶל־פַּרְעֹ֑ה
כֹּֽה־אָמַ֤ר יְהֹוָה֙ אֱלֹהֵ֣י יִשְׂרָאֵ֔ל שַׁלַּח֙ אֶת־עַמִּ֔י
וְיָחֹ֥גּוּ לִ֖י בַּמִּדְבָּֽר: 2 וַיֹּ֣אמֶר פַּרְעֹ֔ה מִ֣י יְהֹוָה֒
אֲשֶׁ֤ר אֶשְׁמַע֙ בְּקֹל֔וֹ לְשַׁלַּ֖ח אֶת־יִשְׂרָאֵ֑ל לֹ֤א
יָדַ֙עְתִּי֙ אֶת־יְהֹוָ֔ה וְגַ֥ם אֶת־יִשְׂרָאֵ֖ל לֹ֥א אֲשַׁלֵּֽחַ:

29. The directive given in 3:16 is carried out.

31. As predicted (vv. 8–9), the signs are accepted as testimony to the reliability of Moses and to the veracity of his message.[43]

taken note   See Comment to 3:16.

bowed low . . .   Here a gesture of thanksgiving.

CHAPTER 5   THE FIRST AUDIENCE WITH PHARAOH   (5:1–6:1)

The narrative moves to a new phase in the tragic history of Israel in Egypt. The new Israelite leadership seizes the initiative with a diplomatic approach. It ends in failure, and the plight of the people becomes an issue in Egyptian public policy. It is now that the struggle for freedom begins in earnest. This chapter serves as an introduction to the narrative of the plagues.

THE FIRST CONFRONTATION WITH THE COURT (vv. 1–5)

1. Afterward   Upon meeting with popular acceptance.

Moses and Aaron   Contrary to the instruction in 3:18, the elders are not included. According to a midrash, they lost their nerve, and one by one they dropped off on the way to the palace.[1]

Thus says the Lord   See Comment to 4:22.

the God of Israel   This epithet more precisely defines the name YHVH.

celebrate a festival   Hebrew *ḥag* is basically a sacrificial feast associated with a pilgrimage to a sanctuary.[2] Arabic *ḥaj*, the Islamic pilgrimage to Mecca, derives from the same stem.

2. Who is the Lord?   A contemptuous retort that contrasts starkly with the humble response of Moses to the divine call: "Who am I?"[3] The pharaoh was the incarnation of a god in Egyptian doctrine. This divine status meant that his power was unlimited, that his will was incontestable law, and that his utterances possessed divine force. He regards himself as YHVH's superior.

I do not know   I do not acknowledge His authority. On the key word *y-d-ʿ* in Exodus, see Comment to 1:8.

has manifested Himself to us. Let us go, we pray, a distance of three days into the wilderness to sacrifice to the LORD our God, lest He strike us with pestilence or sword." ⁴But the king of Egypt said to them, "Moses and Aaron, why do you distract the people from their tasks? Get to your labors!" ⁵And Pharaoh continued, "The people of the land are already so numerous, and you would have them cease from their labors!"

⁶That same day Pharaoh charged the taskmasters and foremen of the people, saying, ⁷"You shall no longer pro-

3 וַיֹּאמְרוּ אֱלֹהֵי הָעִבְרִים נִקְרָא עָלֵינוּ נֵלֲכָה נָּא
דֶּרֶךְ שְׁלֹשֶׁת יָמִים בַּמִּדְבָּר וְנִזְבְּחָה לַיהוָה
אֱלֹהֵינוּ פֶּן־יִפְגָּעֵנוּ בַּדֶּבֶר אוֹ בֶחָרֶב: 4 וַיֹּאמֶר
אֲלֵהֶם מֶלֶךְ מִצְרַיִם לָמָּה מֹשֶׁה וְאַהֲרֹן תַּפְרִיעוּ
אֶת־הָעָם מִמַּעֲשָׂיו לְכוּ לְסִבְלֹתֵיכֶם: 5 וַיֹּאמֶר
פַּרְעֹה הֵן־רַבִּים עַתָּה עַם הָאָרֶץ וְהִשְׁבַּתֶּם אֹתָם
מִסִּבְלֹתָם:
6 וַיְצַו פַּרְעֹה בַּיּוֹם הַהוּא אֶת־הַנֹּגְשִׂים בָּעָם
וְאֶת־שֹׁטְרָיו לֵאמֹר: 7 לֹא תֹאסִפוּן לָתֵת תֶּבֶן

3. The reaction of Moses and Aaron is restrained. They seem to be surprised and cowed by the king's aggressive arrogance.

The God of the Hebrews They use the very language prescribed in 3:18, except that they omit "the LORD" because the monarch has already denied all knowledge of Him. On the "Hebrews," see Excursus 4.

manifested Himself See Comment to 3:18.[4]

lest He strike us For disregarding our obligation. The pharaoh should be concerned about this since he will lose our labor.[5] The "us" may also be a sly intimation that the Egyptians too will be stricken.[6]

pestilence or sword These are conventional symbols of divine judgment.[7]

4. Pharaoh treats the request for time out to worship as a ploy to shirk work.

5. This statement can be variously understood. It may explain the economic reasons for refusing the request. The Israelites are so numerous that any interruption of their labors would entail an enormous loss of productivity.[8] It might also take up the original theme of 1:7, 9–10 that the huge population would constitute a power to be reckoned with were they to quit working. Either way, the second half of the verse is exclamatory.

The people of the land Meaning the common laborers, perhaps a derisive term.[9]

A PEREMPTORY REFUSAL (vv. 6–9)

Moses and Aaron are silent. The disastrous audience with the king is abruptly terminated. The tyrant loses no time in issuing peremptory orders designed to drive home to the Israelites the futility of entertaining any hope of gaining relief.

6. *taskmasters and foremen* In the Egyptian corvée system the workers were organized into manageable gangs, each headed by a foreman from among their own. He, in turn, was directly responsible to his superior, the "taskmaster."[10] As verses 14 and 20–21 show, the foremen were Israelites, the taskmasters, Egyptian. The foremen kept careful logs of their wards and the activities of each. Several such logs are extant, some from the time of Ramses II.[11] Hebrew *shoter*, "foreman," in fact derives from a stem meaning "to write," a denotation reflected in the Septuagint rendering *grammateus*, "scribe, keeper of records."[12]

7–8. The new directive did not demand "bricks without straw," as the English saying goes. Rather, it ordered the brickmakers to collect their own straw; until then it had been supplied by the state. Chopped straw or stubble was a crucial ingredient in the manufacture of bricks. It was added to the mud from the Nile, then shaped in a mold and left to dry in the sun. The straw acted as a binder, and the acid released by the decay of the vegetable matter greatly enhanced the plastic and cohesive properties of the brick, thus preventing shrinking, cracking, and loss of shape.[13]

vide the people with straw for making bricks as heretofore; let them go and gather straw for themselves. [8]But impose upon them the same quota of bricks as they have been making heretofore; do not reduce it, for they are shirkers; that is why they cry, 'Let us go and sacrifice to our God!' [9]Let heavier work be laid upon the men; let them keep at it and not pay attention to deceitful promises."

[10]So the taskmasters and foremen of the people went out and said to the people, "Thus says Pharaoh: I will not give you any straw. [11]You must go and get the straw yourselves wherever you can find it; but there shall be no decrease whatever in your work." [12]Then the people scattered throughout the land of Egypt to gather stubble for straw. [13]And the taskmasters pressed them, saying, "You must complete the same work assignment each day as when you had straw." [14]And the foremen of the Israelites, whom Pharaoh's taskmasters had set over them, were beaten. "Why," they were asked, "did you not complete the prescribed amount of bricks, either yesterday or today, as you did before?"

[15]Then the foremen of the Israelites came to Pharaoh and cried: "Why do you deal thus with your servants? [16]No straw is issued to your servants, yet they demand of us: Make bricks! Thus your servants are being beaten, when the fault is with your own people." [17]He replied, "You are shirkers, shirkers! That is why you say, 'Let us go and

לָעָם לִלְבֹּן הַלְּבֵנִים כִּתְמוֹל שִׁלְשֹׁם הֵם יֵלְכוּ וְקֹשְׁשׁוּ לָהֶם תֶּבֶן: 8 וְאֶת־מַתְכֹּנֶת הַלְּבֵנִים אֲשֶׁר הֵם עֹשִׂים תְּמוֹל שִׁלְשֹׁם תָּשִׂימוּ עֲלֵיהֶם לֹא תִגְרְעוּ מִמֶּנּוּ כִּי־נִרְפִּים הֵם עַל־כֵּן הֵם צֹעֲקִים לֵאמֹר נֵלְכָה נִזְבְּחָה לֵאלֹהֵינוּ: 9 תִּכְבַּד הָעֲבֹדָה עַל־הָאֲנָשִׁים וְיַעֲשׂוּ־בָהּ וְאַל־יִשְׁעוּ בְּדִבְרֵי־שָׁקֶר:

10 וַיֵּצְאוּ נֹגְשֵׂי הָעָם וְשֹׁטְרָיו וַיֹּאמְרוּ אֶל־הָעָם לֵאמֹר כֹּה אָמַר פַּרְעֹה אֵינֶנִּי נֹתֵן לָכֶם תֶּבֶן: 11 אַתֶּם לְכוּ קְחוּ לָכֶם תֶּבֶן מֵאֲשֶׁר תִּמְצָאוּ כִּי אֵין נִגְרָע מֵעֲבֹדַתְכֶם דָּבָר: 12 וַיָּפֶץ הָעָם בְּכָל־אֶרֶץ מִצְרָיִם לְקֹשֵׁשׁ קַשׁ לַתֶּבֶן: 13 וְהַנֹּגְשִׂים אָצִים לֵאמֹר כַּלּוּ מַעֲשֵׂיכֶם דְּבַר־יוֹם בְּיוֹמוֹ כַּאֲשֶׁר בִּהְיוֹת הַתֶּבֶן: 14 וַיֻּכּוּ שֹׁטְרֵי בְּנֵי יִשְׂרָאֵל אֲשֶׁר־שָׂמוּ עֲלֵהֶם נֹגְשֵׂי פַרְעֹה לֵאמֹר מַדּוּעַ לֹא כִלִּיתֶם חָקְכֶם לִלְבֹּן כִּתְמוֹל שִׁלְשֹׁם גַּם־תְּמוֹל גַּם־הַיּוֹם:

15 וַיָּבֹאוּ שֹׁטְרֵי בְּנֵי יִשְׂרָאֵל וַיִּצְעֲקוּ אֶל־פַּרְעֹה לֵאמֹר לָמָּה תַעֲשֶׂה כֹה לַעֲבָדֶיךָ: 16 תֶּבֶן אֵין נִתָּן לַעֲבָדֶיךָ וּלְבֵנִים אֹמְרִים לָנוּ עֲשׂוּ וְהִנֵּה עֲבָדֶיךָ מֻכִּים וְחָטָאת עַמֶּךָ: 17 וַיֹּאמֶר נִרְפִּים אַתֶּם נִרְפִּים עַל־כֵּן אַתֶּם אֹמְרִים נֵלְכָה נִזְבְּחָה

8. **to our God**   Pharaoh does not recognize the Lord and therefore refrains from using the divine name.

9. **heavier work**   Hebrew *tikhbad ha-'avodah* is artfully allusive. The first word derives from the same Hebrew stem *k-v-d* that is soon to be used of Pharaoh's "hardening of the heart,"[14] and foreshadows that development. The noun can mean both "work, labor" and "worship."[15] The former meaning is Pharaoh's response to God's demand that Israel worship Him in the wilderness. See Comments to verse 18 below and to 3:12.

deceitful promises   This refers back to 4:29–31. Egyptian intelligence must have reported back about the promises of redemption.

THE OPPRESSION INTENSIFIES (vv. 10–14)

10. **Thus says Pharaoh**   As opposed to "Thus says the LORD" (4:22; 5:1). Pharaoh is now set on a collision course with the God of Israel.

13–14.   According to the chain of command, it would have been the Israelite foremen who were pressured. However, the inherent ambiguity in "them" allows a midrash to conclude that the Israelite foremen took pity on their toiling brethren and as a consequence were beaten.[16]

THE FOREMEN PROTEST (vv. 15–18)

16. **the fault is with your own people**   We are being treated unfairly.[17]

29

sacrifice to the Lord.' ¹⁸Be off now to your work! No straw shall be issued to you, but you must produce your quota of bricks!"

¹⁹Now the foremen of the Israelites found themselves in trouble because of the order, "You must not reduce your daily quantity of bricks." ²⁰As they left Pharaoh's presence, they came upon Moses and Aaron standing in their path, ²¹and they said to them, "May the Lord look upon you and punish you for making us loathsome to Pharaoh and his courtiers—putting a sword in their hands to slay us." ²²Then Moses returned to the Lord and said, "O Lord, why did You bring harm upon this people? Why did You send me? ²³Ever since I came to Pharaoh to speak in Your name, he has dealt worse with this people; and still You have not delivered Your people."

6 Then the Lord said to Moses, "You shall soon see what I will do to Pharaoh: he shall let them go because of a greater might; indeed, because of a greater might he shall drive them from his land."

לַיהוָֽה׃ 18 וְעַתָּה֙ לְכ֣וּ עִבְד֔וּ וְתֶ֖בֶן לֹא־יִנָּתֵ֣ן לָכֶ֑ם וְתֹ֥כֶן לְבֵנִ֖ים תִּתֵּֽנּוּ׃

19 וַיִּרְא֞וּ שֹֽׁטְרֵ֧י בְנֵֽי־יִשְׂרָאֵ֛ל אֹתָ֖ם בְּרָ֣ע לֵאמֹ֑ר לֹֽא־תִגְרְע֥וּ מִלִּבְנֵיכֶ֖ם דְּבַר־י֥וֹם בְּיוֹמֽוֹ׃ 20 וַֽיִּפְגְּע֞וּ אֶת־מֹשֶׁ֣ה וְאֶֽת־אַהֲרֹ֗ן נִצָּבִ֔ים לִקְרָאתָ֖ם בְּצֵאתָ֥ם מֵאֵ֣ת פַּרְעֹ֑ה׃ 21 וַיֹּאמְר֣וּ אֲלֵהֶ֔ם יֵ֧רֶא יְהוָ֛ה עֲלֵיכֶ֖ם וְיִשְׁפֹּ֑ט אֲשֶׁ֧ר הִבְאַשְׁתֶּ֣ם אֶת־רֵיחֵ֗נוּ בְּעֵינֵ֤י פַרְעֹה֙ וּבְעֵינֵ֣י עֲבָדָ֔יו לָֽתֶת־חֶ֥רֶב בְּיָדָ֖ם לְהָרְגֵֽנוּ׃ מפטיר 22 וַיָּ֧שָׁב מֹשֶׁ֛ה אֶל־יְהוָ֖ה וַיֹּאמַ֑ר אֲדֹנָ֗י לָמָ֤ה הֲרֵעֹ֙תָה֙ לָעָ֣ם הַזֶּ֔ה לָ֥מָּה זֶּ֖ה שְׁלַחְתָּֽנִי׃ 23 וּמֵאָ֞ז בָּ֤אתִי אֶל־פַּרְעֹה֙ לְדַבֵּ֣ר בִּשְׁמֶ֔ךָ הֵרַ֖ע לָעָ֣ם הַזֶּ֑ה וְהַצֵּ֥ל לֹֽא־הִצַּ֖לְתָּ אֶת־עַמֶּֽךָ׃

ו וַיֹּ֧אמֶר יְהוָ֛ה אֶל־מֹשֶׁ֖ה עַתָּ֣ה תִרְאֶ֑ה אֲשֶׁ֤ר אֶֽעֱשֶׂה֙ לְפַרְעֹ֔ה כִּ֣י בְיָ֤ד חֲזָקָה֙ יְשַׁלְּחֵ֔ם וּבְיָ֣ד חֲזָקָ֔ה יְגָרְשֵׁ֖ם מֵאַרְצֽוֹ׃ ס

---

18.   ***Be off now to your work!***   Hebrew *lekhu ʿivdu* is tinged with irony because later on Pharaoh will be constrained to use the identical phrase in the sense of "be off now to your worship!"[18]

DEMORALIZATION (5:19–6:1)

21.   ***for making us loathsome***   Literally, "for causing our breath to be malodorous in the eyes of . . ." The mixed metaphor means "brought us into contempt."

putting a sword   Imperiling our lives.

22–23.   Moses' deep disappointment at his initial failure shows he had unrealistic expectations of early success. The bitterness of his outburst traces back to his original reluctance to accept the divine commission.

22.   ***returned to the Lord***   He retreated into seclusion to commune with God.

CHAPTER 6   1.¹   ***a greater might***   See Comment to 3:19.

drive them from   See Comment to 2:22.

Divine Reaffirmation   (6:2–7:13)

Va-'Eraʾ   The preceding verses cite evidence of pervasive demoralization. In order to combat this despondent mood, God now amplifies His response to the complaint of 5:23. Moses lamented the deterioration in Israel's situation that followed his petition to Pharaoh in God's name. The divine Name and its significance in relation to the promises made to the patriarchs are now the topic of God's renewed theophany to Moses. Seven verbs, each in the first person with God as the subject, are employed

VA'ERA'

²God spoke to Moses and said to him, "I am the LORD. ³I appeared to Abraham, Isaac, and Jacob as El Shaddai, but I did not make myself known to them by My name יהוה. ⁴I also established My covenant with them, to give them the land of Canaan, the land in which they lived as sojourners. ⁵I have now heard the moaning of the Israelites because the Egyptians are holding them in bondage, and I have remembered My covenant. ⁶Say, therefore, to the Israelite people:

וַיְדַבֵּר אֱלֹהִים אֶל־מֹשֶׁה וַיֹּאמֶר אֵלָיו אֲנִי יְהוָה: ²
וָאֵרָא אֶל־אַבְרָהָם אֶל־יִצְחָק וְאֶל־יַעֲקֹב בְּאֵל ³
שַׁדָּי וּשְׁמִי יְהוָה לֹא נוֹדַעְתִּי לָהֶם: ⁴ וְגַם
הֲקִמֹתִי אֶת־בְּרִיתִי אִתָּם לָתֵת לָהֶם אֶת־אֶרֶץ
כְּנָעַן אֵת אֶרֶץ מְגֻרֵיהֶם אֲשֶׁר־גָּרוּ בָהּ: ⁵ וְגַם אֲנִי
שָׁמַעְתִּי אֶת־נַאֲקַת בְּנֵי יִשְׂרָאֵל אֲשֶׁר מִצְרַיִם
מַעֲבִדִים אֹתָם וָאֶזְכֹּר אֶת־בְּרִיתִי: ⁶ לָכֵן אֱמֹר

emphatically to reaffirm the certainty of redemption (vv. 6–8). Significantly, the theophany is framed by the authoritative royal formula of self-identification. For the origin of this formula, see Comment to 3:6.

3. Were this statement to mean that a previously unknown divine Name—YHVH—is now to be revealed for the first time, the effect of the "I am" formula would be vitiated. The credibility of a promise is undermined, not enhanced, if it is issued by one whose name is unfamiliar.[2] Furthermore, the phrase "I am YHVH" appears scores of times in the Bible and is widespread in corresponding form in Northwest Semitic royal inscriptions, such as "I am Mesha," "I am Shalmaneser," "I am Esarhaddon." It cannot, therefore, reflect the introduction of a new name. On the contrary, precisely because the bearer of the name is well known, and its mention evokes such emotions as awe, reverence, honor, and fear, its use as the source and sanction of a law or edict reinforces its authority and encourages compliance. In the present context the invocation of a hitherto unknown divine name would hardly serve to counteract the widespread demoralization— which is, after all, the very function of God's declaration.

In light of these considerations, the meaning of this verse needs to be reexamined. In the ancient Near Eastern world names in general, and the name of a god in particular, possessed a dynamic quality and were expressive of character, or attributes, and potency. The names of gods were immediately identified with their nature, status, and function, so that to say, "I did not make myself known to them by[3] My name YHVH," is to state that the patriarchs did not experience the essential power associated with the name YHVH. The promises made to them belonged to the distant future. The present reiteration of those promises exclusively in the name of YHVH means that their fulfillment is imminent. This, indeed, is how Rashi, Rashbam, Bekhor Shor, and others construed verses 2–3.

Support for the understanding that "knowing the name of YHVH" means witnessing or being made to experience the display of divine might is found in several biblical passages.[4] The two most illuminating are Isaiah 52:6 and Jeremiah 16:21. The first reads: "Assuredly, My people shall learn [Heb. *yedaʿ*] My name, / Assuredly [they shall learn] on that day / That I, the One who promised, / Am now at hand." The second passage states: "Assuredly, I will teach them [Heb. *modiʿam*], / Once and for all I will teach them [Heb. *'odiʿem*] / My power and My might. / And they shall learn [Heb. *ve-yadeʿu*] that My name is LORD [YHVH]."

El Shaddai   The reference is to Genesis 17:1–8 and 35:11–12.[5] Although this divine Name is usually translated "God Almighty," there are no convincing traditions as to its meaning and little etymological justification for that particular rendering. With the advent of Moses, El Shaddai became obsolete; it is preserved only in poetic texts. See Excursus 4.

4. *I also*   The emphatic Hebrew *ve-gam* underscores the unalterability of the divine commitment.[6]

to give them   The patriarchs received ownership of the land; their descendants would receive possession of it.

5. *I have now*   As before, Hebrew *ve-gam* is emphatic, with the sense of "indeed."

I have remembered   See Comment to 2:24.

I am the LORD. I will free you from the labors of the Egyptians and deliver you from their bondage. I will redeem you with an outstretched arm and through extraordinary chastisements. ⁷And I will take you to be My people, and I will be your God. And you shall know that I, the LORD, am your God who freed you from the labors of the Egyptians. ⁸I will bring you into the land which I swore to give to Abraham, Isaac, and Jacob, and I will give it to you for a possession, I the LORD." ⁹But when Moses told this to the Israelites, they would not listen to Moses, their spirits crushed by cruel bondage.

לִבְנֵי־יִשְׂרָאֵל֙ אֲנִ֣י יְהֹוָ֔ה וְהוֹצֵאתִ֣י אֶתְכֶ֗ם מִתַּ֙חַת֙ סִבְלֹ֣ת מִצְרַ֔יִם וְהִצַּלְתִּ֥י אֶתְכֶ֖ם מֵעֲבֹֽדָתָ֑ם וְגָאַלְתִּ֤י אֶתְכֶם֙ בִּזְר֣וֹעַ נְטוּיָ֔ה וּבִשְׁפָטִ֖ים גְּדֹלִֽים: 7 וְלָקַחְתִּ֨י אֶתְכֶ֥ם לִי֙ לְעָ֔ם וְהָיִ֥יתִי לָכֶ֖ם לֵאלֹהִ֑ים וִֽידַעְתֶּ֗ם כִּ֣י אֲנִ֤י יְהֹוָה֙ אֱלֹֽהֵיכֶ֔ם הַמּוֹצִ֣יא אֶתְכֶ֔ם מִתַּ֖חַת סִבְל֥וֹת מִצְרָֽיִם: 8 וְהֵבֵאתִ֤י אֶתְכֶם֙ אֶל־הָאָ֔רֶץ אֲשֶׁ֤ר נָשָׂ֙אתִי֙ אֶת־יָדִ֔י לָתֵ֣ת אֹתָ֔הּ לְאַבְרָהָ֥ם לְיִצְחָ֖ק וּֽלְיַעֲקֹ֑ב וְנָתַתִּ֨י אֹתָ֥הּ לָכֶ֛ם מֽוֹרָשָׁ֖ה אֲנִ֥י יְהֹוָֽה: 9 וַיְדַבֵּ֥ר מֹשֶׁ֛ה כֵּ֖ן אֶל־בְּנֵ֣י יִשְׂרָאֵ֑ל וְלֹ֤א שָֽׁמְעוּ֙ אֶל־מֹשֶׁ֔ה מִקֹּ֣צֶר ר֔וּחַ וּמֵעֲבֹדָ֖ה קָשָֽׁה: פ

My covenant With the patriarchs.

6. *therefore* Hebrew *lakhen* at the beginning of a verse frequently introduces a solemn declaration that has the force of an oath.[7]

I am the LORD See Comment to verse 2. According to several rabbinic sources,[8] it is on account of the following four verbs of redemption—"I will free . . . deliver . . . redeem . . . take you"—that there arose the obligation to drink four cups of wine at the Passover Seder.

free you Literally, "bring you out." The Hebrew verb *y-ts-'* is often used in the context of emancipation and liberation.[9]

redeem you The Hebrew stem *g-'-l* in its verbal and nominal form is a socio-legal term that belongs to the realm of kinship rights and obligations. The *go'el* was the near kin who had primary responsibility for protecting or regaining persons and property for the extended family.[10] The term came to be used figuratively, as here, with God as the subject.[11] In time, the abstract noun *ge'ulah* acquired messianic associations referring to God's ultimate redemption of Israel from exile.

outstretched arm . . . These phrases introduce the plague narrative that begins in the next chapter. The arm is the symbol of strength and power and thus is used metaphorically of God's mighty deeds, overwhelmingly in connection with the Exodus.[12]

7.   This declaration prefigures the covenant that is to be established at Sinai. The phraseology suggests the institution of marriage, a familiar biblical metaphor for the relationship between God and Israel.[13] The first two verbs, *l-k-ḥ*, "to take,"[14] and *h-y-h le-*, "to be (someone's),"[15] are both used in connection with matrimony; the second is also characteristic covenant language.[16] Similarly, the Hebrew term for a covenant, *berit*, is also used for the bond of marriage.[17]

you shall know On the verb *y-d-ʿ*, "to know," as a key word in the Exodus narratives, see Comment to 1:8.

8. *I swore* Literally, "I raised my hand," the phrase deriving from a symbolic gesture accompanying oath-taking,[18] a practice still in vogue. The Bible stresses innumerable times that the Land of Israel was pledged on oath to the patriarchs and their descendants.[19]

I the LORD See Comment to verse 2.

MOSES TRANSMITS THE DIVINE MESSAGE (v. 9)

they would not listen Moses' message did not succeed in strengthening their morale, in contrast to the experience recorded in 4:31.

their spirits crushed Literally, "from shortness of spirit." Hebrew *ruaḥ* is the spiritual and psychic energy that motivates action. Its absence or attenuation signifies atrophy of the will.

[10]The LORD spoke to Moses, saying, [11]"Go and tell Pharaoh king of Egypt to let the Israelites depart from his land." [12]But Moses appealed to the LORD, saying, "The Israelites would not listen to me; how then should Pharaoh heed me, a man of impeded speech!" [13]So the LORD spoke to both Moses and Aaron in regard to the Israelites and Pharaoh king of Egypt, instructing them to deliver the Israelites from the land of Egypt.

[14]The following are the heads of their respective clans.

The sons of Reuben, Israel's first-born: Enoch and Pallu, Hezron and Carmi; those are the families of Reuben. [15]The

י וַיְדַבֵּר יְהֹוָה אֶל־מֹשֶׁה לֵּאמֹר: יא בֹּא דַבֵּר
אֶל־פַּרְעֹה מֶלֶךְ מִצְרָיִם וִישַׁלַּח אֶת־בְּנֵי־יִשְׂרָאֵל
מֵאַרְצוֹ: יב וַיְדַבֵּר מֹשֶׁה לִפְנֵי יְהֹוָה לֵאמֹר הֵן
בְּנֵי־יִשְׂרָאֵל לֹא־שָׁמְעוּ אֵלַי וְאֵיךְ יִשְׁמָעֵנִי
פַרְעֹה וַאֲנִי עֲרַל שְׂפָתָיִם: פ יג וַיְדַבֵּר יְהֹוָה
אֶל־מֹשֶׁה וְאֶל־אַהֲרֹן וַיְצַוֵּם אֶל־בְּנֵי יִשְׂרָאֵל
וְאֶל־פַּרְעֹה מֶלֶךְ מִצְרָיִם לְהוֹצִיא אֶת־בְּנֵי־יִשְׂרָאֵל
מֵאֶרֶץ מִצְרָיִם: ס שני
יד אֵלֶּה רָאשֵׁי בֵית־אֲבֹתָם
בְּנֵי רְאוּבֵן בְּכֹר יִשְׂרָאֵל חֲנוֹךְ וּפַלּוּא
חֶצְרוֹן וְכַרְמִי אֵלֶּה מִשְׁפְּחֹת רְאוּבֵן: טו וּבְנֵי

A RENEWED CALL TO ACTION (vv. 10–13)

Failure to energize the people must not deter Moses from persevering in his mission.

11. Go The place is not specified, but the palace is understood.[20]

12. Moses employs a reasoned argument to justify resistance to the divine command. It is the type of logical inference known in later Hebrew as *kal va-ḥomer*.[21] The lack of response on the part of the Israelites (5:21; 6:9) will itself impair the effectiveness of Moses' petition to Pharaoh, and the unfortunate situation will be aggravated by Moses' own oratorical handicap.

impeded speech Literally, "uncircumcised of lips," a synonym of "slow of speech and slow of tongue" (4:10). "Uncircumcised" is also used metaphorically of the heart and ear,[22] the idea being that the organ involved is, so to speak, obstructed by a "foreskin" that blocks its proper functioning.

13. Ignoring Moses' objections, God orders him and his brother to resume their mission to both Israel and Pharaoh. Aaron is introduced here for two reasons. First, he is to act as spokesman and thereby offset Moses' impairment; second, he is the focus of the following genealogy. His name thus serves to smooth the transition to the next section.

A GENEALOGY (vv. 14–25)

The narrative breaks off at this low point in the wretched fortunes of Israel with the insertion of a genealogy. This interruption is not an interpolation but a literary device that definitively marks off the first stage in the process of liberation—the unavailing human efforts—from the coercive intervention of God that will ensue—the ten plagues. At the same time, it links the time of the Exodus with the patriarchal period. Because a genealogy inherently symbolizes vigor and continuity, its presence here also injects a reassuring note into the otherwise despondent mood.[23]

A detailed analysis of the content of the genealogy discloses careful design and purpose. The line of the Levites is framed by a separate introduction and conclusion (vv. 16,26); the lifespans of individuals are registered only in the list of Levites (vv. 16,18,20); and the descendants of Levi are traced to five generations in contrast to the single generation given for the Reubenites and Simeonites. Still more peculiarities appear in the Levitical listing: Aaron's name precedes that of Moses (v. 20); Moses' wife is not mentioned but Aaron's is (v. 23); only the fathers-in-law of Aaron and his son Eleazar are named (vv. 23–25); only Aaron's brother-in-law is recorded; only Aaron's descendants and not those of Moses are listed, and to three generations. To put it all another way, the Levites are here singled out from among the other tribes of Israel; the Aaronides are distinguished from among the other Levitical families; and there is a further differentiation within the Aaronide families themselves.

These special features undoubtedly anticipate later developments: the special status to be granted to the tribe of Levi, the appointment of the Aaronides to serve as priests, and the investment

sons of Simeon: Jemuel, Jamin, Ohad, Jachin, Zohar, and Saul the son of a Canaanite woman; those are the families of Simeon. [16]These are the names of Levi's sons by their lineage: Gershon, Kohath, and Merari; and the span of Levi's life was 137 years. [17]The sons of Gershon: Libni and Shimei, by their families. [18]The sons of Kohath: Amram, Izhar, Hebron, and Uzziel; and the span of Kohath's life was 133 years. [19]The sons of Merari: Mahli and Mushi. These are the families of the Levites by their lineage.

[20]Amram took to wife his father's sister Jochebed, and she bore him Aaron and Moses; and the span of Amram's life was 137 years. [21]The sons of Izhar: Korah, Nepheg, and Zichri. [22]The sons of Uzziel: Mishael, Elzaphan, and Sithri.

שִׁמְעוֹן יְמוּאֵל וְיָמִין וְאֹהַד וְיָכִין וְצֹחַר
וְשָׁאוּל בֶּן־הַכְּנַעֲנִית אֵלֶּה מִשְׁפְּחֹת שִׁמְעוֹן: [16] וְאֵלֶּה שְׁמוֹת בְּנֵי־לֵוִי לְתֹלְדֹתָם גֵּרְשׁוֹן
וּקְהָת וּמְרָרִי וּשְׁנֵי חַיֵּי לֵוִי שֶׁבַע וּשְׁלֹשִׁים וּמְאַת שָׁנָה: [17] בְּנֵי גֵרְשׁוֹן לִבְנִי וְשִׁמְעִי לְמִשְׁפְּחֹתָם:
[18] וּבְנֵי קְהָת עַמְרָם וְיִצְהָר וְחֶבְרוֹן וְעֻזִּיאֵל וּשְׁנֵי חַיֵּי קְהָת שָׁלֹשׁ וּשְׁלֹשִׁים וּמְאַת שָׁנָה: [19] וּבְנֵי
מְרָרִי מַחְלִי וּמוּשִׁי אֵלֶּה מִשְׁפְּחֹת הַלֵּוִי לְתֹלְדֹתָם:
[20] וַיִּקַּח עַמְרָם אֶת־יוֹכֶבֶד דֹּדָתוֹ לוֹ
לְאִשָּׁה וַתֵּלֶד לוֹ אֶת־אַהֲרֹן וְאֶת־מֹשֶׁה וּשְׁנֵי חַיֵּי עַמְרָם שֶׁבַע וּשְׁלֹשִׁים וּמְאַת שָׁנָה: [21] וּבְנֵי יִצְהָר
קֹרַח וָנֶפֶג וְזִכְרִי: [22] וּבְנֵי עֻזִּיאֵל מִישָׁאֵל וְאֶלְצָפָן וְסִתְרִי: [23] וַיִּקַּח אַהֲרֹן אֶת־אֱלִישֶׁבַע בַּת־

of Aaron as High Priest, with one specific line of his descendants exclusively designated to succeed him.[24] The exaltation of Aaron is enhanced even further by the note about his marriage in verse 23; his brother-in-law, Nahshon, and also presumably his father-in-law, Amminadab, was a chieftain of the tribe of Judah and an ancestor of King David.[25]

14–15.   The lists duplicate those of Genesis 46:8–10. Ramban suggests that the genealogy begins with the Reubenites and Simeonites, even though the primary focus is on Levi, in order to emphasize that the last named was not Jacob's first-born and that the Levites were elevated because of their own merit.[26]

14.   *their*   The antecedent is probably "Moses and Aaron."

15.   *Zohar*   In Numbers 26:13 and 1 Chronicles 4:24 this name is replaced by Zerah. Both names mean "shining, brightness."

a Caananite woman   This exceptional notice most likely reflects the disfavor with which intermarriage with the Canaanites was viewed.[27]

16.   These three are the heads of Levitical clans that later performed menial duties in connection with the wilderness Tabernacle. The names of the members of their families and the services assigned to them are listed in detail in Numbers 3:17–39.

18.   Of the four sons of Kohath, only Hebron's descendants are not listed, although Numbers 26:58 and 1 Chronicles 15:9 attest to his having had offspring. Rashbam suggests that the omission is because the Hebronites, unlike the others mentioned, play no role in the Torah narratives. According to Ḥizkuni, the same also governs the omission of the descendants of Moses and of Ithamar son of Aaron (v. 23).

20.   *his father's sister*   Marriage to a paternal aunt is prohibited in the legislation of Leviticus 18:12 and 20:19. Therefore, the present notice must preserve a very ancient tradition.[28]

Jochebed   She is the anonymous "Levite woman" of Exodus 2:1, the first biblical personage to bear a name composed of *yo-*, the shortened form of the divine Name YHVH.[29] Her name seems to mean "YHVH is Glory."

Aaron and Moses   The Septuagint, Syriac, and Samaritan texts add, "and their sister Miriam," just as in Numbers 26:59.[30]

21.   Ibn Ezra suggests that the sons of Izhar are recorded on account of Korah, who contended with Moses, as told in Numbers 16.

22.   According to Ibn Ezra, these are listed because Mishael and Elzaphan are later mentioned in connection with the death of Aaron's two sons, as told in Leviticus 10:4.

23Aaron took to wife Elisheba, daughter of Amminadab and sister of Nahshon, and she bore him Nadab and Abihu, Eleazar and Ithamar. 24The sons of Korah: Assir, Elkanah, and Abiasaph. Those are the families of the Korahites. 25And Aaron's son Eleazar took to wife one of Putiel's daughters, and she bore him Phinehas. Those are the heads of the fathers' houses of the Levites by their families.

26It is the same Aaron and Moses to whom the LORD said, "Bring forth the Israelites from the land of Egypt, troop by troop." 27It was they who spoke to Pharaoh king of Egypt

עֲמִּינָדָב אֲחוֹת נַחְשׁוֹן לוֹ לְאִשָּׁה וַתֵּלֶד לוֹ אֶת־
נָדָב וְאֶת־אֲבִיהוּא אֶת־אֶלְעָזָר וְאֶת־אִיתָמָר:
24 וּבְנֵי קֹרַח אַסִּיר וְאֶלְקָנָה וַאֲבִיאָסָף אֵלֶּה
מִשְׁפְּחֹת הַקָּרְחִי: 25 וְאֶלְעָזָר בֶּן־אַהֲרֹן לָקַח־
לוֹ מִבְּנוֹת פּוּטִיאֵל לוֹ לְאִשָּׁה וַתֵּלֶד לוֹ אֶת־
פִּינְחָס אֵלֶּה רָאשֵׁי אֲבוֹת הַלְוִיִּם לְמִשְׁפְּחֹתָם:
26 הוּא אַהֲרֹן וּמֹשֶׁה אֲשֶׁר אָמַר יְהוָה לָהֶם
הוֹצִיאוּ אֶת־בְּנֵי יִשְׂרָאֵל מֵאֶרֶץ מִצְרַיִם עַל־
צִבְאֹתָם: 27 הֵם הַמְדַבְּרִים אֶל־פַּרְעֹה מֶלֶךְ־

23. As noted by Lekah Tov, this marriage betokens the interrelationship of the priesthood and royalty, for Nahshon was the ancestor of King David. The two institutions respectively provided the ecclesiastical and secular leadership of later Israel.

Nadab and Abihu Exodus 24:1 introduces the sons of Aaron without any description, presupposing a knowledge of Aaronide genealogy.

24. The Korahites, observes Ibn Ezra, are mentioned on account of the statement in Numbers 26:11 that "the sons of Korah . . . did not die" in their father's rebellion against Moses and Aaron. The Korahite clan later became a guild of Temple singers to whom several psalms are attributed. They are also listed as having been "guards of the threshold of the Tabernacle" and as performing other tasks, such as baking and gatekeeping.[31] A bowl inscribed with "the sons of Korah" (*bny krḥ*) has been uncovered in an Israelite shrine at Arad deriving from the eighth century B.C.E.[32]

25. *Putiel's* The text assumes that he was well known although he is not otherwise mentioned. The name itself is a hybrid of Egyptian[33] and Hebrew, meaning "the one whom God has given."

Phinehas This name is also Egyptian and means "the Nubian/dark-skinned one."[34] It was fairly common in Egypt in the thirteenth century B.C.E.. By virtue of his zeal for the high moral standards of the religion of Israel, Phinehas was granted "a pact of priesthood for all time," as told in Numbers 25:1–18.[35]

A RECAPITULATION (vv. 26–30)

Following the digression this brief concluding summary acts as a resumptive repetition of verses 9–12.[36] It also encloses the genealogy in a literary frame and reconnects it with the account of the Exodus.

26. *It is the same* That is, the same as those mentioned in the genealogy.

Aaron and Moses The order reflects the focus of the lists, as explained above. It also makes for a chiastic arrangement with verse 13 and verse 27, as follows:

Moses	Aaron (v. 13)
Aaron	Moses (v. 26)
Moses	Aaron (v. 27)

troop by troop The narratives employ military terminology for the organization of the Israelites during the Exodus and the wilderness wanderings. Thus, in Numbers 1:52 it is prescribed that "the Israelites shall encamp troop by troop, each man with his division and each under his standard."[37]

to free the Israelites from the Egyptians; these are the same Moses and Aaron. 28For when the LORD spoke to Moses in the land of Egypt 29and the LORD said to Moses, "I am the LORD; speak to Pharaoh king of Egypt all that I will tell you," 30Moses appealed to the LORD, saying, "See, I am of impeded speech; how then should Pharaoh heed me!"

7 The LORD replied to Moses, "See, I place you in the role of God to Pharaoh, with your brother Aaron as your prophet. 2You shall repeat all that I command you, and your brother Aaron shall speak to Pharaoh to let the Israelites depart from his land. 3But I will harden Pharaoh's heart, that I may multiply My signs and marvels in the land of Egypt. 4When Pharaoh does not heed you, I will lay My hand upon Egypt and deliver My ranks, My people the Israelites, from the land of Egypt with extraordinary chastisements. 5And the Egyptians shall know that I am the LORD, when I stretch out My hand over Egypt and bring

מִצְרַ֔יִם לְהוֹצִ֥יא אֶת־בְּנֵֽי־יִשְׂרָאֵ֖ל מִמִּצְרָ֑יִם ה֥וּא מֹשֶׁ֖ה וְאַהֲרֹֽן׃ 28 וַיְהִ֗י בְּי֨וֹם דִּבֶּ֧ר יְהֹוָ֛ה אֶל־מֹשֶׁ֖ה בְּאֶ֥רֶץ מִצְרָֽיִם׃ פ 29 וַיְדַבֵּ֧ר יְהֹוָ֛ה אֶל־מֹשֶׁ֥ה לֵּאמֹ֖ר אֲנִ֣י יְהֹוָ֑ה דַּבֵּ֗ר אֶל־פַּרְעֹה֙ מֶ֣לֶךְ מִצְרַ֔יִם אֵ֛ת כׇּל־אֲשֶׁ֥ר אֲנִ֖י דֹּבֵ֥ר אֵלֶֽיךָ׃ 30 וַיֹּ֥אמֶר מֹשֶׁ֖ה לִפְנֵ֣י יְהֹוָ֑ה הֵ֤ן אֲנִי֙ עֲרַ֣ל שְׂפָתַ֔יִם וְאֵ֕יךְ יִשְׁמַ֥ע אֵלַ֖י פַּרְעֹֽה׃ פ

ז וַיֹּ֤אמֶר יְהֹוָה֙ אֶל־מֹשֶׁ֔ה רְאֵ֛ה נְתַתִּ֥יךָ אֱלֹהִ֖ים לְפַרְעֹ֑ה וְאַהֲרֹ֥ן אָחִ֖יךָ יִהְיֶ֥ה נְבִיאֶֽךָ׃ 2 אַתָּ֣ה תְדַבֵּ֔ר אֵ֖ת כׇּל־אֲשֶׁ֣ר אֲצַוֶּ֑ךָּ וְאַהֲרֹ֤ן אָחִ֙יךָ֙ יְדַבֵּ֣ר אֶל־פַּרְעֹ֔ה וְשִׁלַּ֥ח אֶת־בְּנֵֽי־יִשְׂרָאֵ֖ל מֵאַרְצֽוֹ׃ 3 וַאֲנִ֥י אַקְשֶׁ֖ה אֶת־לֵ֣ב פַּרְעֹ֑ה וְהִרְבֵּיתִ֧י אֶת־אֹתֹתַ֛י וְאֶת־מוֹפְתַ֖י בְּאֶ֥רֶץ מִצְרָֽיִם׃ 4 וְלֹֽא־יִשְׁמַ֤ע אֲלֵכֶם֙ פַּרְעֹ֔ה וְנָתַתִּ֥י אֶת־יָדִ֖י בְּמִצְרָ֑יִם וְהוֹצֵאתִ֨י אֶת־צִבְאֹתַ֜י אֶת־עַמִּ֤י בְנֵֽי־יִשְׂרָאֵל֙ מֵאֶ֣רֶץ מִצְרַ֔יִם בִּשְׁפָטִ֖ים גְּדֹלִֽים׃ 5 וְיָדְע֤וּ מִצְרַ֙יִם֙ כִּֽי־אֲנִ֣י יְהֹוָ֔ה בִּנְטֹתִ֥י אֶת־יָדִ֖י עַל־מִצְרָ֑יִם וְהוֹצֵאתִ֥י אֶת־בְּנֵֽי־

28. In some Hebrew texts the letter *samekh* follows this verse and signifies the closing of a section (Heb. *parashah setumah*). However, as Rashi and Ibn Ezra note, this division contradicts the syntax, which requires that the clause be attached to the next sentence. There is as yet no satisfactory solution to this anomaly.

CHAPTER 7   REAFFIRMATION AND RENEWAL OF MOSES' MISSION   (vv. 1–7)

1. This passage is more than simply a repetition or variant form of 4:16. The earlier verse concerned the functions of Moses and Aaron in their dealings with the people of Israel; here Moses is to fill the role of God in negotiations with Pharaoh, who claimed divinity for himself. Moses' divinely endowed power and authority will expose the hollowness of that claim.

your prophet   Your spokesman. Hebrew *navi'*, is derived from a stem meaning "to call, proclaim," that is, the divine word.

2. Moses and Aaron speak not on their own initiative but as agents of God's will.

3–4. These verses allude to the forthcoming plagues. At the same time, they constitute God's response to Moses' protestations in 6:30, as though to say, "Of course Pharaoh will not be easily swayed, but not on account of your inadequacy. Rather, it is because I utilize his stubbornness in order to demonstrate My active Presence." Indirectly, Moses is once more warned against harboring unrealistic optimism in the discharge of his mission,[1] for such may lead to demoralization.[2] On the "hardening of the heart,"[3] see Comment to 4:21.

4. ranks   See Comment to 6:26.[4]

chastisements   See Comment to 6:6.

5. the Egyptians shall know . . .   The ultimate response to Pharaoh's contemptuous declaration, "I do not know the LORD."[5] See Comment to 5:2.

6. A retrospective summation; the details are given in the subsequent chapters.[6]

out the Israelites from their midst." ⁶This Moses and Aaron did; as the LORD commanded them, so they did. ⁷Moses was eighty years old and Aaron eighty-three, when they made their demand on Pharaoh.

⁸The LORD said to Moses and Aaron, ⁹"When Pharaoh speaks to you and says, 'Produce your marvel,' you shall say to Aaron, 'Take your rod and cast it down before Pharaoh.' It shall turn into a serpent." ¹⁰So Moses and Aaron came before Pharaoh and did just as the LORD had commanded: Aaron cast down his rod in the presence of Pharaoh and his courtiers, and it turned into a serpent. ¹¹Then Pharaoh, for his part, summoned the wise men and the sorcerers; and the Egyptian magicians, in turn, did the same with their spells; ¹²each cast down his rod, and they turned into serpents. But Aaron's rod swallowed their rods. ¹³Yet Pharaoh's

יִשְׂרָאֵל מִתּוֹכָם: 6 וַיַּעַשׂ מֹשֶׁה וְאַהֲרֹן כַּאֲשֶׁר צִוָּה יְהוָה אֹתָם כֵּן עָשׂוּ: 7 וּמֹשֶׁה בֶּן־שְׁמֹנִים שָׁנָה וְאַהֲרֹן בֶּן־שָׁלֹשׁ וּשְׁמֹנִים שָׁנָה בְּדַבְּרָם אֶל־פַּרְעֹה: פ רביעי

8 וַיֹּאמֶר יְהוָה אֶל־מֹשֶׁה וְאֶל־אַהֲרֹן לֵאמֹר: 9 כִּי יְדַבֵּר אֲלֵכֶם פַּרְעֹה לֵאמֹר תְּנוּ לָכֶם מוֹפֵת וְאָמַרְתָּ אֶל־אַהֲרֹן קַח אֶת־מַטְּךָ וְהַשְׁלֵךְ לִפְנֵי־פַרְעֹה יְהִי לְתַנִּין: 10 וַיָּבֹא מֹשֶׁה וְאַהֲרֹן אֶל־פַּרְעֹה וַיַּעֲשׂוּ כֵן כַּאֲשֶׁר צִוָּה יְהוָה וַיַּשְׁלֵךְ אַהֲרֹן אֶת־מַטֵּהוּ לִפְנֵי פַרְעֹה וְלִפְנֵי עֲבָדָיו וַיְהִי לְתַנִּין: 11 וַיִּקְרָא גַּם־פַּרְעֹה לַחֲכָמִים וְלַמְכַשְּׁפִים וַיַּעֲשׂוּ גַם־הֵם חַרְטֻמֵּי מִצְרַיִם בְּלַהֲטֵיהֶם כֵּן: 12 וַיַּשְׁלִיכוּ אִישׁ מַטֵּהוּ וַיִּהְיוּ לְתַנִּינִם וַיִּבְלַע מַטֵּה־אַהֲרֹן אֶת־מַטֹּתָם:

7. eighty years old   Moses commences his career at an age that was taken in biblical times to be the completion of unusual longevity.[7]

SIGNS BEFORE PHARAOH (vv. 8–13)

In order to verify his authenticity as a divinely appointed emissary to Israel, Moses had earlier performed his corroborative signs before the people.[8] Now he must do the same before Pharaoh.

9. say to Aaron   Henceforth, Aaron performs the signs as long as the Egyptian magicians are present. This enables Moses to negotiate with the Egyptian king as an equal.

your rod   See Comments to 4:2–3.

a serpent   In 4:3 the Hebrew term is *naḥash*; here it is *tannin*, a more general term for a large reptile. Lekaḥ Tov and Bekhor Shor plausibly suggest that *tannin* has special relevance to Pharaoh, who is addressed as follows in Ezekiel 29:3: "Thus says the Lord GOD: / I am going to deal with you, O Pharaoh, king of Egypt, / Mighty monster [Heb. *ha-tannin ha-gadol*]."

11. for his part   Hebrew *gam* is used here as an emphasizing particle.[9]

magicians   Hebrew *ḥartumim* derives from an Egyptian title meaning "chief lector priest."[10] Its bearer was a learned scribe whose skills included expertise in magic and dream interpretation. Several postbiblical sources[11] identify Pharaoh's magicians as Jannes and Jambres,[12] said to have been the two sons of Balaam.[13]

with their spells   The Hebrew stem *l-w-t* means "to enwrap,"[14] so that the noun would mean "things kept under wraps," or closely guarded secrets. The use of "spells" contrasts strongly with the simplicity of Aaron's act, which is unaccompanied by any incantation or praxis. The term itself suggests that the wonder belonged to the magicians' conventional repertoire of tricks. In fact, to this day Egyptian snake charmers practice the deception of turning a rod into a serpent.[15] They are able to induce catatonic rigidity in the native cobra by exerting strong pressure on a nerve just below its head. In this state, the snake assumes a rodlike appearance and can even be handled by onlookers. The jolt it receives when thrown to the ground restores its mobility.

12–13.   In the present case, Aaron does nothing further, but the rod—a real one—appears to act on its own and should establish the superiority of the power of Aaron's God over that of the magicians'. Nevertheless, Pharaoh is unmoved.

heart stiffened and he did not heed them, as the LORD had said.

^{14}And the LORD said to Moses, "Pharaoh is stubborn; he refuses to let the people go. ^{15}Go to Pharaoh in the morning, as he is coming out to the water, and station yourself before him at the edge of the Nile, taking with you the rod that turned into a snake. ^{16}And say to him, 'The

יג וַיֶּחֱזַק לֵב פַּרְעֹה וְלֹא שָׁמַע אֲלֵהֶם כַּאֲשֶׁר
דִּבֶּר יְהוָה: פ

יד וַיֹּאמֶר יְהוָה אֶל־מֹשֶׁה כָּבֵד לֵב פַּרְעֹה
מֵאֵן לְשַׁלַּח הָעָם: טו לֵךְ אֶל־פַּרְעֹה בַּבֹּקֶר הִנֵּה
יֹצֵא הַמַּיְמָה וְנִצַּבְתָּ לִקְרָאתוֹ עַל־שְׂפַת הַיְאֹר
וְהַמַּטֶּה אֲשֶׁר־נֶהְפַּךְ לְנָחָשׁ תִּקַּח בְּיָדֶךָ:

The Plagues [16]　(7:14–11:10)

Pharaoh's intransigence—as foretold—sets off the "extraordinary chastisements" mentioned in verse 4. These take the form of ten disasters that strike Egypt in the course of a year.[17] They are popularly known as the "Ten Plagues," in Hebrew *'eser makkot*.

The Hebrew Bible features three accounts of the plagues. The longest and most detailed narrative is the prose version set forth in the ensuing chapters. Psalms 78:43–51 and 105:27–36 present highly condensed poetic paraphrases. The three sources vary in the sequence, number, and content of the plagues. Psalm 78 makes no mention of lice, boils, and darkness, whereas Psalm 105 ignores boils and pestilence. Due to the uncertain meaning of some of the Hebrew terms in those psalms, it is difficult to determine exactly how many and what kind of plagues the two compositions respectively present. Nor can one establish with certainty whether the differences represent variant traditions or poetic license.

The present narrative is a sophisticated and symmetric literary structure[18] with a pattern of three groups each comprising three plagues. The climactic tenth plague possesses a character all its own. The first two afflictions in each triad are forewarned; the last always strikes suddenly, unannounced. Furthermore, in the case of the first, fourth, and seventh plagues Pharaoh is informed in the morning and Moses is told to "station" himself before the king, whereas in the second of each series Moses is told to "come in before Pharaoh," that is, to confront him in the palace. Finally, in the first triad of plagues it is always Aaron who is the effective agent; in the third, it is always Moses.[19]

The controlling purpose behind this literary architecture is to emphasize the idea that the nine plagues are not random vicissitudes of nature; although they are natural disasters, they are the deliberate and purposeful acts of divine will—their intent being retributive, coercive, and educative. As God's judgments on Egypt for the enslavement of the Israelites, they are meant to crush Pharaoh's resistance to their liberation. They are to demonstrate to Egypt the impotence of its gods[20] and, by contrast, the incomparability of YHVH, God of Israel, as the one supreme sovereign God of Creation, who uses the phenomena of the natural order for His own purposes.[21]

In addition to this dominant motif of the plagues narrative, a secondary theme is also discernible: Israel as well as the Egyptians must "know" YHVH. This is made explicit in 10:2. The early Exodus narratives are very clear about the lack of the people's faith in its relationship with God.[22] In this regard, the mysterious silence of the Israelites throughout the course of the plagues may well be significant. True, the people is said to be shielded from the effects of the catastrophes, but only in the course of five of them;[23] nothing is said about this in connection with the others.[24] It is only after the culminating miracle at the sea that "the people feared the LORD; they had faith in the LORD and His servant Moses" (14:31).

THE FIRST PLAGUE: THE WATERS BECOME BLOODY (*dam*)　(7:14–25)[25]

This plague has been explained as the extreme intensification of a well-known phenomenon that occurs periodically in the Nile valley. The river is fed by melting snow and summer rains that pour down from the highlands of Ethiopia and carry with them sediment from the tropical red earth that

38

LORD, the God of the Hebrews, sent me to you to say, "Let My people go that they may worship Me in the wilderness." But you have paid no heed until now. ¹⁷Thus says the LORD, "By this you shall know that I am the LORD." See, I shall strike the water in the Nile with the rod that is in my hand, and it will be turned into blood; ¹⁸and the fish in the Nile will die. The Nile will stink so that the Egyptians will find it impossible to drink the water of the Nile.'"

¹⁹And the LORD said to Moses, "Say to Aaron: Take your rod and hold out your arm over the waters of Egypt—its rivers, its canals, its ponds, all its bodies of water—that they may turn to blood; there shall be blood throughout the land of Egypt, even in [vessels of] wood and stone."

16 וְאָמַרְתָּ֣ אֵלָ֗יו יְהֹוָ֞ה אֱלֹהֵ֤י הָעִבְרִים֙ שְׁלָחַ֣נִי
אֵלֶ֣יךָ לֵאמֹ֔ר שַׁלַּח֙ אֶת־עַמִּ֔י וְיַֽעַבְדֻ֖נִי
בַּמִּדְבָּ֑ר וְהִנֵּ֥ה לֹֽא־שָׁמַ֖עְתָּ עַד־כֹּֽה: 17 כֹּ֚ה אָמַ֣ר
יְהֹוָ֔ה בְּזֹ֣את תֵּדַ֔ע כִּ֖י אֲנִ֣י יְהֹוָ֑ה הִנֵּ֣ה אָֽנֹכִ֗י
מַכֶּ֣ה ׀ בַּמַּטֶּ֣ה אֲשֶׁר־בְּיָדִ֗י עַל־הַמַּ֛יִם אֲשֶׁ֥ר בַּיְאֹ֖ר
וְנֶהֶפְכ֥וּ לְדָֽם: 18 וְהַדָּגָ֧ה אֲשֶׁר־בַּיְאֹ֛ר תָּמ֖וּת וּבָאַ֣שׁ
הַיְאֹ֑ר וְנִלְא֣וּ מִצְרַ֔יִם לִשְׁתּ֥וֹת מַ֖יִם מִן־הַיְאֹֽר:
ס
19 וַיֹּ֨אמֶר יְהֹוָ֜ה אֶל־מֹשֶׁ֗ה אֱמֹ֣ר אֶֽל־אַהֲרֹ֡ן
קַ֣ח מַטְּךָ֣ וּנְטֵֽה־יָדְךָ֩ עַל־מֵימֵ֨י מִצְרַ֜יִם עַֽל־
נַהֲרֹתָ֣ם ׀ עַל־יְאֹרֵיהֶ֣ם וְעַל־אַגְמֵיהֶ֗ם וְעַ֤ל כָּל־מִקְוֵ֣ה
מֵֽימֵיהֶ֔ם וְיִֽהְיוּ־דָ֑ם וְהָ֤יָה דָם֙ בְּכָל־אֶ֣רֶץ מִצְרַ֔יִם
וּבָעֵצִ֖ים וּבָאֲבָנִֽים: 20 וַיַּֽעֲשׂוּ־כֵ֞ן מֹשֶׁ֤ה וְאַהֲרֹן֙

characterizes the region. Following from this explanation, the plague must have resulted from an abnormally heavy rainfall that led to an excessively high rise of the Nile and washed down inordinate amounts of the red sediment. The neutralization of this substance, which normally occurs in the course of the flow of the river, was now retarded, so that the entire river took on a bloody hue. As a result, flagellates and purple bacteria washed down from the high mountain lakes, together with the particles of red earth, disturbed the oxygen balance and killed off the fish, which produced a foul stench.²⁶

The Nile inundation, which reaches its height in September/October, has a bearing on the explanation for the next plague as well.

The Egyptians personified and deified the river Nile as the god Hapi, to whom offerings were made at the time of inundation. The flooding itself was regarded as a manifestation of the god Osiris. It is quite possible, then, that the contamination of the river served to discredit Egyptian polytheism.²⁷ Also, by commencing the series of plagues with the striking of the Nile waters, the text suggests an underlying notion of retribution, measure for measure, for Pharaoh's iniquitous decree that all newborn males be cast into the river.²⁸

This type of calamity is found elsewhere in the literature of the ancient Near East. A Sumerian text about the goddess Inanna tells of three plagues that she brought upon the world; in the first she turned all the waters of the land into blood.²⁹ An Egyptian literary work by a certain Ipuwer, which purports to be a description of contemporary chaotic conditions, mentions that "the river [Nile] is blood" and "people thirst for water."³⁰ In another Egyptian text, supposedly centering on the exploits of a magician who is one of the sons of Ramses II, the young man tells his mother that should he be defeated in a contest, the water she drinks would take on the color of blood.³¹

15. *as he is coming out to the water*   The significance of Pharaoh's act is unexplained. Perhaps it involves some ceremony associated with his morning rituals, or it may be for worship of the god of the Nile during the inundation period.³² It may also have been to measure the height of the river.³³

17. *Thus says the LORD*   See Comment to 4:22.

18.   The Nile and its pools teemed with fish, an important ingredient of the popular daily diet,³⁴ though taboo in certain pious Egyptian circles. The rotting of the fish was therefore a heavy blow.

impossible   The Hebrew stem *l-'-h* means "not to be able."³⁵

19. *in [vessels of] wood and stone*   "Vessels" is not in the Hebrew text, but is so understood by early exegesis.³⁶ However, the Hebrew phrase may be figurative, the opposites constituting a merism for nature in its entirety, that is, "everything."³⁷

²⁰Moses and Aaron did just as the Lᴏʀᴅ commanded: he lifted up the rod and struck the water in the Nile in the sight of Pharaoh and his courtiers, and all the water in the Nile was turned into blood ²¹and the fish in the Nile died. The Nile stank so that the Egyptians could not drink water from the Nile; and there was blood throughout the land of Egypt. ²²But when the Egyptian magicians did the same with their spells, Pharaoh's heart stiffened and he did not heed them—as the Lᴏʀᴅ had spoken. ²³Pharaoh turned and went into his palace, paying no regard even to this. ²⁴And all the Egyptians had to dig round about the Nile for drinking water, because they could not drink the water of the Nile.

²⁵When seven days had passed after the Lᴏʀᴅ struck the Nile, ²⁶the Lᴏʀᴅ said to Moses, "Go to Pharaoh and say to him, 'Thus says the Lᴏʀᴅ: Let My people go that they may worship Me. ²⁷If you refuse to let them go, then I will plague your whole country with frogs. ²⁸The Nile shall swarm with frogs, and they shall come up and enter your palace, your bedchamber and your bed, the houses of your courtiers and your people, and your ovens and your kneading bowls. ²⁹The frogs shall come up on you and on your people and on all your courtiers.'"

8 And the Lᴏʀᴅ said to Moses, "Say to Aaron: Hold out your arm with the rod over the rivers, the canals, and the

כַּאֲשֶׁר ׀ צִוָּה יְהֹוָה וַיָּרֶם בַּמַּטֶּה וַיַּךְ אֶת־
הַמַּיִם אֲשֶׁר בַּיְאֹר לְעֵינֵי פַרְעֹה וּלְעֵינֵי עֲבָדָיו
וַיֵּהָפְכ֥וּ כׇּל־הַמַּ֥יִם אֲשֶׁר־בַּיְאֹ֖ר לְדָ֑ם: 21 וְהַדָּגָ֣ה
אֲשֶׁר־בַּיְאֹ֥ר מֵ֙תָה֙ וַיִּבְאַ֣שׁ הַיְאֹ֔ר וְלֹא־יָכְל֣וּ
מִצְרַ֔יִם לִשְׁתּ֥וֹת מַ֖יִם מִן־הַיְאֹ֑ר וַיְהִ֥י הַדָּ֖ם בְּכׇל־
אֶ֥רֶץ מִצְרָֽיִם: 22 וַיַּֽעֲשׂוּ־כֵ֛ן חַרְטֻמֵּ֥י מִצְרַ֖יִם
בְּלָטֵיהֶ֑ם וַיֶּחֱזַ֤ק לֵב־פַּרְעֹה֙ וְלֹא־שָׁמַ֣ע אֲלֵהֶ֔ם
כַּאֲשֶׁ֖ר דִּבֶּ֥ר יְהֹוָֽה: 23 וַיִּ֣פֶן פַּרְעֹ֔ה וַיָּבֹ֖א אֶל־בֵּית֑וֹ
וְלֹא־שָׁ֥ת לִבּ֖וֹ גַּם־לָזֹֽאת: 24 וַיַּחְפְּר֧וּ כׇל־מִצְרַ֛יִם
סְבִיבֹ֥ת הַיְאֹ֖ר מַ֣יִם לִשְׁתּ֑וֹת כִּ֣י לֹ֤א יָֽכְלוּ֙ לִשְׁתֹּ֔ת
מִמֵּימֵ֖י הַיְאֹֽר:

25 וַיִּמָּלֵ֖א שִׁבְעַ֣ת יָמִ֑ים אַחֲרֵ֥י הַכּֽוֹת־יְהֹוָ֖ה אֶת־
הַיְאֹֽר: פ 26 וַיֹּ֤אמֶר יְהֹוָה֙ אֶל־מֹשֶׁ֔ה בֹּ֖א
אֶל־פַּרְעֹ֑ה וְאָמַרְתָּ֣ אֵלָ֗יו כֹּ֚ה אָמַ֣ר יְהֹוָ֔ה שַׁלַּ֥ח
אֶת־עַמִּ֖י וְיַֽעַבְדֻֽנִי: 27 וְאִם־מָאֵ֥ן אַתָּ֖ה לְשַׁלֵּ֑חַ הִנֵּ֣ה
אָנֹכִ֗י נֹגֵ֛ף אֶת־כׇּל־גְּבוּלְךָ֖ בַּֽצְפַרְדְּעִֽים: 28 וְשָׁרַ֣ץ
הַיְאֹר֮ צְפַרְדְּעִים֒ וְעָלוּ֙ וּבָ֣אוּ בְּבֵיתֶ֔ךָ וּבַחֲדַ֥ר
מִשְׁכָּבְךָ֖ וְעַל־מִטָּתֶ֑ךָ וּבְבֵ֤ית עֲבָדֶ֙יךָ֙ וּבְעַמֶּ֔ךָ
וּבְתַנּוּרֶ֖יךָ וּבְמִשְׁאֲרוֹתֶֽיךָ: 29 וּבְכָ֥ה* וּֽבְעַמְּךָ֖ וּבְכׇל־
עֲבָדֶ֑יךָ יַעֲל֖וּ הַֽצְפַרְדְּעִֽים:

ח וַיֹּ֤אמֶר יְהֹוָה֙ אֶל־מֹשֶׁ֔ה אֱמֹ֣ר אֶֽל־אַהֲרֹ֗ן נְטֵ֤ה
אֶת־יָֽדְךָ֙ בְּמַטֶּ֔ךָ עַל־הַ֙נְּהָרֹ֔ת עַל־הַיְאֹרִ֖ים וְעַל־

v. 29.• יתיר ה'

22.　　The magicians' success offsets the ominous effect of the plague.

25.　　The NJPS translation connects this verse with the next, implying that the second plague followed the first by a week.[38] The Hebrew could also signify that the first plague lasted seven days, a rendering favored by the Masoretic division of the Hebrew.

THE SECOND PLAGUE: FROGS (*tsefardea*ʿ)　(7:26–8:11)

During their reproductive period, frogs concentrate in particular areas such as ponds and lakes; as the Nile begins to recede in September/October, they usually mass on land. In the present circumstances their habitat had become polluted by the putrefying fish, so the amphibians would have been forced to invade the land much earlier than usual. But the dead fish would have been a source of infection carried by insects, so that the frogs died en masse.

It is possible that this plague, like the first one, was regarded as a judgment on Egyptian polytheism, for a frog-headed goddess named Heqt was the consort of the god Khnum, who was credited with having fashioned man out of clay. She was associated with fertility and was thought to assist women at childbirth. Hence, the plague may have been taken as retribution for the decree ordering the midwives to kill the newborn males at birth.[39]

26.　*Go to Pharaoh*　That is, to the palace.

28–29.　The victims are recorded in descending order of social status.

ponds, and bring up the frogs on the land of Egypt." ²Aaron held out his arm over the waters of Egypt, and the frogs came up and covered the land of Egypt. ³But the magicians did the same with their spells, and brought frogs upon the land of Egypt.

⁴Then Pharaoh summoned Moses and Aaron and said, "Plead with the Lord to remove the frogs from me and my people, and I will let the people go to sacrifice to the Lord." ⁵And Moses said to Pharaoh, "You may have this triumph over me: for what time shall I plead in behalf of you and your courtiers and your people, that the frogs be cut off from you and your houses, to remain only in the Nile?" ⁶"For tomorrow," he replied. And [Moses] said, "As you say—that you may know that there is none like the Lord our God; ⁷the frogs shall retreat from you and your courtiers and your people; they shall remain only in the Nile." ⁸Then Moses and Aaron left Pharaoh's presence, and Moses cried out to the Lord in the matter of the frogs which He had inflicted upon Pharaoh. ⁹And the Lord did as Moses asked; the frogs died out in the houses, the courtyards, and the fields. ¹⁰And they piled them up in heaps, till the land stank. ¹¹But when Pharaoh saw that there was relief, he became stubborn and would not heed them, as the Lord had spoken.

¹²Then the Lord said to Moses, "Say to Aaron: Hold out your rod and strike the dust of the earth, and it shall turn to lice throughout the land of Egypt." ¹³And they did so. Aaron held out his arm with the rod and struck the dust of the earth, and vermin came upon man and beast; all the dust of the earth turned to lice throughout the land of Egypt. ¹⁴The magicians did the like with their spells to

הָאֲגַמִּ֑ים וְהַ֥עַל אֶת־הַֽצְפַרְדְּעִ֖ים עַל־אֶ֥רֶץ מִצְרָֽיִם: ²וַיֵּ֤ט אַהֲרֹן֙ אֶת־יָד֔וֹ עַ֖ל מֵימֵ֣י מִצְרָ֑יִם וַתַּ֙עַל֙ הַצְּפַרְדֵּ֔עַ וַתְּכַ֖ס אֶת־אֶ֥רֶץ מִצְרָֽיִם: ³וַיַּֽעֲשׂוּ־כֵ֥ן הַֽחַרְטֻמִּ֖ים בְּלָֽטֵיהֶ֑ם וַיַּֽעֲל֥וּ אֶת־הַֽצְפַרְדְּעִ֖ים עַל־אֶ֥רֶץ מִצְרָֽיִם:

⁴וַיִּקְרָ֨א פַרְעֹ֜ה לְמֹשֶׁ֣ה וּֽלְאַהֲרֹ֗ן וַיֹּ֙אמֶר֙ הַעְתִּ֣ירוּ אֶל־יְהוָ֔ה וְיָסֵר֙ הַֽצְפַרְדְּעִ֔ים מִמֶּ֖נִּי וּמֵֽעַמִּ֑י וַֽאֲשַׁלְּחָה֙ אֶת־הָעָ֔ם וְיִזְבְּח֖וּ לַֽיהוָֽה: ⁵וַיֹּ֣אמֶר מֹשֶׁ֣ה לְפַרְעֹה֮ הִתְפָּאֵ֣ר עָלַי֒ לְמָתַ֣י | אַעְתִּ֣יר לְךָ֗ וְלַֽעֲבָדֶ֙יךָ֙ וּֽלְעַמְּךָ֔ לְהַכְרִ֤ית הַֽצְפַרְדְּעִים֙ מִמְּךָ֣ וּמִבָּתֶּ֔יךָ רַ֥ק בַּיְאֹ֖ר תִּשָּׁאַֽרְנָה: ⁶וַיֹּ֖אמֶר לְמָחָ֑ר וַיֹּ֙אמֶר֙ כִּדְבָ֣רְךָ֔ לְמַ֣עַן תֵּדַ֔ע כִּ֥י אֵ֖ין כַּֽיהוָ֥ה אֱלֹהֵֽינוּ: חמישי ⁷וְסָר֣וּ הַֽצְפַרְדְּעִ֗ים מִמְּךָ֙ וּמִבָּ֣תֶּ֔יךָ וּמֵֽעֲבָדֶ֖יךָ וּמֵֽעַמֶּ֑ךָ רַ֥ק בַּיְאֹ֖ר תִּשָּׁאַֽרְנָה: ⁸וַיֵּצֵ֥א מֹשֶׁ֛ה וְאַהֲרֹ֖ן מֵעִ֣ם פַּרְעֹ֑ה וַיִּצְעַ֤ק מֹשֶׁה֙ אֶל־יְהוָ֔ה עַל־דְּבַ֥ר הַֽצְפַרְדְּעִ֖ים אֲשֶׁר־שָׂ֥ם לְפַרְעֹֽה: ⁹וַיַּ֥עַשׂ יְהוָ֖ה כִּדְבַ֣ר מֹשֶׁ֑ה וַיָּמֻ֙תוּ֙ הַֽצְפַרְדְּעִ֔ים מִן־הַבָּתִּ֥ים מִן־הַֽחֲצֵרֹ֖ת וּמִן־הַשָּׂדֹֽת: ¹⁰וַיִּצְבְּר֥וּ אֹתָ֖ם חֳמָרִ֣ם חֳמָרִ֑ם וַתִּבְאַ֖שׁ הָאָֽרֶץ: ¹¹וַיַּ֣רְא פַּרְעֹ֗ה כִּ֤י הָֽיְתָה֙ הָֽרְוָחָ֔ה וְהַכְבֵּד֙ אֶת־לִבּ֔וֹ וְלֹ֥א שָׁמַ֖ע אֲלֵהֶ֑ם כַּֽאֲשֶׁ֖ר דִּבֶּ֥ר יְהוָֽה: ס

¹²וַיֹּ֣אמֶר יְהוָה֮ אֶל־מֹשֶׁה֒ אֱמֹר֙ אֶֽל־אַהֲרֹ֔ן נְטֵ֣ה אֶֽת־מַטְּךָ֔ וְהַ֖ךְ אֶת־עֲפַ֣ר הָאָ֑רֶץ וְהָיָ֥ה לְכִנִּ֖ם בְּכָל־אֶ֥רֶץ מִצְרָֽיִם: ¹³וַיַּֽעֲשׂוּ־כֵ֗ן וַיֵּט֩ אַהֲרֹ֨ן אֶת־יָד֤וֹ בְמַטֵּ֙הוּ֙ וַיַּךְ֙ אֶת־עֲפַ֣ר הָאָ֔רֶץ וַתְּהִי֙ הַכִּנָּ֔ם בָּֽאָדָ֖ם וּבַבְּהֵמָ֑ה כָּל־עֲפַ֥ר הָאָ֛רֶץ הָיָ֥ה כִנִּ֖ים בְּכָל־אֶ֥רֶץ מִצְרָֽיִם: ¹⁴וַיַּֽעֲשׂוּ־כֵ֨ן הַֽחַרְטֻמִּ֧ים

CHAPTER 8   **4.** The process of humbling Pharaoh now begins. His magicians can add to the number of frogs but cannot remove them.

plead with the Lord Pharaoh acknowledges the existence of YHVH for the first time. He makes a sweeping concession, only to rescind it soon after.

5. *triumph over me* The Hebrew phrase *hitpa'er 'al* usually means "to vaunt"[1] but here seems to connote "I defer to you" to select the time for removing the frogs.

THE THIRD PLAGUE: VERMIN (*kinnim*) (vv. 12–15)

In accordance with the pattern, the third in the series comes without warning. The land is suddenly hit by a devastating infestation of insects, identified by some as mosquitoes.[2] These carriers of deadly diseases, normally troublesome enough in Egypt during October/November, would have multiplied astronomically all over the land in the wake of the preceding plagues.

14–15. The magicians retire from the scene, their powers entirely exhausted.[3]

produce lice, but they could not. The vermin remained upon man and beast; [15]and the magicians said to Pharaoh, "This is the finger of God!" But Pharaoh's heart stiffened and he would not heed them, as the LORD had spoken.

[16]And the LORD said to Moses, "Early in the morning present yourself to Pharaoh, as he is coming out to the water, and say to him, 'Thus says the LORD: Let My people go that they may worship Me. [17]For if you do not let My people go, I will let loose swarms of insects against you and your courtiers and your people and your houses; the houses of the Egyptians, and the very ground they stand on, shall be filled with swarms of insects. [18]But on that day I will set apart the region of Goshen, where My people dwell, so that no swarms of insects shall be there, that you may know that I the LORD am in the midst of the land. [19]And I will make a

בְּלָטֵיהֶם לְהוֹצִיא אֶת־הַכִּנִּים וְלֹא יָכֹלוּ וַתְּהִי הַכִּנָּם בָּאָדָם וּבַבְּהֵמָה: 15 וַיֹּאמְרוּ הַחַרְטֻמִּם אֶל־פַּרְעֹה אֶצְבַּע אֱלֹהִים הִוא וַיֶּחֱזַק לֵב־פַּרְעֹה וְלֹא־שָׁמַע אֲלֵהֶם כַּאֲשֶׁר דִּבֶּר יְהוָה: ס 16 וַיֹּאמֶר יְהוָה אֶל־מֹשֶׁה הַשְׁכֵּם בַּבֹּקֶר וְהִתְיַצֵּב לִפְנֵי פַרְעֹה הִנֵּה יוֹצֵא הַמָּיְמָה וְאָמַרְתָּ אֵלָיו כֹּה אָמַר יְהוָה שַׁלַּח עַמִּי וְיַעַבְדֻנִי: 17 כִּי אִם־אֵינְךָ מְשַׁלֵּחַ אֶת־עַמִּי הִנְנִי מַשְׁלִיחַ בְּךָ וּבַעֲבָדֶיךָ וּבְעַמְּךָ וּבְבָתֶּיךָ אֶת־הֶעָרֹב וּמָלְאוּ בָּתֵּי מִצְרַיִם אֶת־הֶעָרֹב וְגַם הָאֲדָמָה אֲשֶׁר־הֵם עָלֶיהָ: 18 וְהִפְלֵיתִי בַיּוֹם הַהוּא אֶת־אֶרֶץ גֹּשֶׁן אֲשֶׁר עַמִּי עֹמֵד עָלֶיהָ לְבִלְתִּי הֱיוֹת־שָׁם עָרֹב לְמַעַן תֵּדַע כִּי אֲנִי יְהוָה

15. the finger of God A supernatural phenomenon beyond human control.[4]

THE FOURTH PLAGUE (ʿarov) (vv. 16–28)

The second triad of plagues now begins. Pharaoh is warned as he goes down to the river. The plague cannot be identified with certainty because Hebrew ʿarov occurs only in the present context. Indeed, diverse interpretive traditions already existed in ancient times. The word itself was taken to mean "mixture," and the most widely accepted understanding was "various kinds of wild animals."[5] An alternative tradition understands "swarms of insects,"[6] which the Septuagint and Philo specify as the dog fly. This would be the stable fly, or *Stomoxys calcitrans*, a vicious, bloodsucking insect that can multiply prodigiously in tropical and subtropical regions, given the proper environmental conditions. It is known to transmit anthrax and other animal diseases. If ʿarov indeed refers to this species, it would explain why Goshen, where the Israelites lived, was exempt, for its climate is Mediterranean. At any rate, for the first time a clear distinction is made between the Egyptians and the Israelites, and the time of the onset of the plague is fixed, both particulars leaving no doubt that the source of the plague is not just any god (v. 15) but YHVH, God of Israel.

18. the region Hebrew ʾerets is used here in the sense of a defined territory or district.[7]

Goshen In Genesis 45:10 this is the name given to the area of Israelite settlement in Egypt.[8] The name has not been identified as Egyptian and is most likely Semitic. It is probably connected with Hebrew *gush*, "a clod" (Job 7:5), referring to a type of soil. This element appears as a place-name in Gush-Ḥalav (Giscala) in Upper Galilee. Another "region of Goshen" is a strip of land south of Hebron in the Land of Israel; it is mentioned in Joshua 10:41 and 11:16. A hill city of the same name, situated in the southern extremity of Judah, southwest of Hebron, is listed in Joshua 15:51. The presence of such a name in Egypt accords with other Semitic place-names such as Succoth (Exod. 12:37), Migdol, and Baal-zephon (Exod. 14:1) in the same region, thus attesting to its early occupation by Semites.

Although no source defines the precise geographic location of Goshen, the cumulative effect of various items of evidence is to place it in the area of Wadi Tumeilat, which stretches from the eastern arm of the Nile to the Great Bitter Lake. Egyptian texts confirm the presence of Semites and other Asians in the northeastern part of the country, both at the end of the Sixth Dynasty (ca. 2250 B.C.E.) and about 1700 B.C.E., in the wake of the Hyksos invasion. Exodus 12:38 refers to a "mixed multitude," that is, foreign tribes, dwelling in the area of Israelite settlement.

distinction between My people and your people. Tomorrow this sign shall come to pass.'" [20]And the Lord did so. Heavy swarms of insects invaded Pharaoh's palace and the houses of his courtiers; throughout the country of Egypt the land was ruined because of the swarms of insects.

[21]Then Pharaoh summoned Moses and Aaron and said, "Go and sacrifice to your God within the land." [22]But Moses replied, "It would not be right to do this, for what we sacrifice to the Lord our God is untouchable to the Egyptians. If we sacrifice that which is untouchable to the Egyptians before their very eyes, will they not stone us! [23]So we must go a distance of three days into the wilderness and sacrifice to the Lord our God as He may command us." [24]Pharaoh said, "I will let you go to sacrifice to the Lord your God in the wilderness; but do not go very far. Plead, then, for me." [25]And Moses said, "When I leave your presence, I will plead with the Lord that the swarms of insects depart tomorrow from Pharaoh and his courtiers and his people; but let not Pharaoh again act deceitfully, not letting the people go to sacrifice to the Lord."

[26]So Moses left Pharaoh's presence and pleaded with the Lord. [27]And the Lord did as Moses asked: He removed the swarms of insects from Pharaoh, from his courtiers, and from his people; not one remained. [28]But Pharaoh became stubborn this time also, and would not let the people go.

בְּקֶרֶב הָאָרֶץ: שׁשׁי 19 וְשַׂמְתִּי פְדֻת בֵּין עַמִּי וּבֵין עַמֶּךָ לְמָחָר יִהְיֶה הָאֹת הַזֶּה: 20 וַיַּעַשׂ יְהוָה כֵּן וַיָּבֹא עָרֹב כָּבֵד בֵּיתָה פַרְעֹה וּבֵית עֲבָדָיו וּבְכָל־אֶרֶץ מִצְרַיִם תִּשָּׁחֵת הָאָרֶץ מִפְּנֵי הֶעָרֹב:

21 וַיִּקְרָא פַרְעֹה אֶל־מֹשֶׁה וּלְאַהֲרֹן וַיֹּאמֶר לְכוּ זִבְחוּ לֵאלֹהֵיכֶם בָּאָרֶץ: 22 וַיֹּאמֶר מֹשֶׁה לֹא נָכוֹן לַעֲשׂוֹת כֵּן כִּי תּוֹעֲבַת מִצְרַיִם נִזְבַּח לַיהוָה אֱלֹהֵינוּ הֵן נִזְבַּח אֶת־תּוֹעֲבַת מִצְרַיִם לְעֵינֵיהֶם וְלֹא יִסְקְלֻנוּ: 23 דֶּרֶךְ שְׁלֹשֶׁת יָמִים נֵלֵךְ בַּמִּדְבָּר וְזָבַחְנוּ לַיהוָה אֱלֹהֵינוּ כַּאֲשֶׁר יֹאמַר אֵלֵינוּ: 24 וַיֹּאמֶר פַרְעֹה אָנֹכִי אֲשַׁלַּח אֶתְכֶם וּזְבַחְתֶּם לַיהוָה אֱלֹהֵיכֶם בַּמִּדְבָּר רַק הַרְחֵק לֹא־תַרְחִיקוּ לָלֶכֶת הַעְתִּירוּ בַּעֲדִי: 25 וַיֹּאמֶר מֹשֶׁה הִנֵּה אָנֹכִי יוֹצֵא מֵעִמָּךְ וְהַעְתַּרְתִּי אֶל־יְהוָה וְסָר הֶעָרֹב מִפַּרְעֹה מֵעֲבָדָיו וּמֵעַמּוֹ מָחָר רַק אַל־יֹסֵף פַּרְעֹה הָתֵל לְבִלְתִּי שַׁלַּח אֶת־הָעָם לִזְבֹּחַ לַיהוָה:

26 וַיֵּצֵא מֹשֶׁה מֵעִם פַּרְעֹה וַיֶּעְתַּר אֶל־יְהוָה: 27 וַיַּעַשׂ יְהוָה כִּדְבַר מֹשֶׁה וַיָּסַר הֶעָרֹב מִפַּרְעֹה מֵעֲבָדָיו וּמֵעַמּוֹ לֹא נִשְׁאַר אֶחָד: 28 וַיַּכְבֵּד פַּרְעֹה אֶת־לִבּוֹ גַּם בַּפַּעַם הַזֹּאת וְלֹא שִׁלַּח אֶת־הָעָם: פ

---

19. *a distinction*   While the context requires such a meaning for Hebrew *pedut*,[9] it is unclear how it is obtained, for the other biblical usages of the noun mean "rescue, redemption," and the stem *p-d-h* invariably conveys "to ransom, redeem."[10]

21.   For the second time Pharaoh makes a concession, this time more limited.

within the land   Not in the wilderness.

22–23.   The Israelites do not yet know what animal sacrifice the Lord may demand of them. It may turn out to be one that Egyptians would regard as a sacrilegious provocation, given that their religion represents deities in animal form. Hence, the Israelites can only worship their God outside Egypt.

22. *untouchable*   Moses employs a deliberate ambiguity: Hebrew *to'evah* can mean "that which is taboo" to the Egyptians[11] and also "that which is an [Egyptian] abomination" in the sight of Israel,[12] namely, their animal divinities.

will they not stone us!   Would not such a sacrifice on our part evoke a violent reaction?

23. *three days*   See Comment to 3:18.

24.   Pharaoh seems to accept Moses' reasoning.

I will let you go   The Hebrew adds the personal pronoun before the verb to emphasize the subject. In this way Pharaoh asserts his superior authority while at the same time making a concession.

9 The Lord said to Moses, "Go to Pharaoh and say to him, 'Thus says the Lord, the God of the Hebrews: Let My people go to worship Me. ²For if you refuse to let them go, and continue to hold them, ³then the hand of the Lord will strike your livestock in the fields—the horses, the asses, the camels, the cattle, and the sheep—with a very severe pestilence. ⁴But the Lord will make a distinction between the livestock of Israel and the livestock of the Egyptians, so that nothing shall die of all that belongs to the Israelites. ⁵The Lord has fixed the time: tomorrow the Lord will do this thing in the land.'" ⁶And the Lord did so the next day: all the livestock of the Egyptians died, but of the livestock of the Israelites not a beast died. ⁷When Pharaoh inquired, he

ט וַיֹּאמֶר יְהוָה אֶל־מֹשֶׁה בֹּא אֶל־פַּרְעֹה וְדִבַּרְתָּ אֵלָיו כֹּה־אָמַר יְהוָה אֱלֹהֵי הָעִבְרִים שַׁלַּח אֶת־עַמִּי וְיַעַבְדֻנִי: 2 כִּי אִם־מָאֵן אַתָּה לְשַׁלֵּחַ וְעוֹדְךָ מַחֲזִיק בָּם: 3 הִנֵּה יַד־יְהוָה הוֹיָה בְּמִקְנְךָ אֲשֶׁר בַּשָּׂדֶה בַּסּוּסִים בַּחֲמֹרִים בַּגְּמַלִּים בַּבָּקָר וּבַצֹּאן דֶּבֶר כָּבֵד מְאֹד: 4 וְהִפְלָה יְהוָה בֵּין מִקְנֵה יִשְׂרָאֵל וּבֵין מִקְנֵה מִצְרָיִם וְלֹא יָמוּת מִכָּל־לִבְנֵי יִשְׂרָאֵל דָּבָר: 5 וַיָּשֶׂם יְהוָה מוֹעֵד לֵאמֹר מָחָר יַעֲשֶׂה יְהוָה הַדָּבָר הַזֶּה בָּאָרֶץ: 6 וַיַּעַשׂ יְהוָה אֶת־הַדָּבָר הַזֶּה מִמָּחֳרָת וַיָּמָת כֹּל מִקְנֵה מִצְרָיִם וּמִמִּקְנֵה בְנֵי־יִשְׂרָאֵל לֹא־מֵת אֶחָד: 7 וַיִּשְׁלַח פַּרְעֹה וְהִנֵּה לֹא־מֵת מִמִּקְנֵה

CHAPTER 9   THE FIFTH PLAGUE: PESTILENCE (*dever*)   (vv. 1–7)

Allusion to the importance of sacred animals in Egyptian religion is now followed by a visitation that exposes the inherent absurdity of such a notion. The God of Israel strikes the animals with pestilence. Most likely, the soil, contaminated by mounds of rotting frogs, became the breeding ground of disease, probably the highly infectious anthrax, which strikes the cattle in the fields. Once again, the livestock of the Israelites are unaffected, the time of the plague's onset is forecast, and Pharaoh is warned in his palace.

3. the hand of the Lord   As opposed to the "finger of God" in 8:15. The "hand" is the symbol of power, here exercised both punitively and coercively. In Akkadian, diseases are described as "the hand of Ishtar," "the hand of Nergal," or of other gods.[1]

will strike   Hebrew *hoyah* is undoubtedly a play on YHVH.[2]

camels   The presence of this animal here and in the patriarchal narratives is a problem because the camel does not figure in Egyptian texts and art until the Persian period. It is conspicuously absent from the published Mari texts from Mesopotamia, which are replete with information about pastoral nomadic groups and their way of life. Thousands of commercial and administrative texts from the Old Babylonian period (ca. 1950–1530 B.C.E.) maintain complete silence on the existence of this animal. All available evidence points to the conclusion that the effective domestication of the camel as a widely used beast of burden did not take place before the twelfth century B.C.E., which is long after the patriarchal and Exodus periods.

The key word in this formulation is "effective," for evidence of another kind does exist. Certain bilingual Sumerian-Akkadian lexical texts from Mesopotamia equate a domesticated animal called "donkey-of-the-sea-land" with a dromedary, thus proving a knowledge of the animal in southern Mesopotamia in Old Babylonian times (ca. 2000–1700 B.C.E.). Moreover, the scribes knew to differentiate between the dromedary and the Bactrian camel, and a Sumerian text from that period mentions the drinking of camel's milk. A braided cord made from camel hair (ca. 2000 B.C.E.) has been found in Egypt; a tiny bronze figurine of a camel from before 2100 B.C.E. turned up at Byblos; a frieze of a procession of typically Egyptian animals, including a camel, decorates a pot (1500–1400 B.C.E.) uncovered in Greece; a steatite seal from Minoan Crete (1800–1400 B.C.E.) features that animal; and a ration list from the North Syrian town of Alalakh from the 18th century B.C.E. in Old Babylonian includes fodder for the camel.

In light of all this, mention of the camel in Exodus and Genesis can be taken at face value. First domesticated in southern Arabia in the third millennium B.C.E., its presence spread very slowly and long remained a rarity. A wealthy man might acquire a few as a prestige symbol. Only much later did it become a beast of burden.[3]

found that not a head of the livestock of Israel had died; yet Pharaoh remained stubborn, and he would not let the people go.

⁸Then the LORD said to Moses and Aaron, "Each of you take handfuls of soot from the kiln, and let Moses throw it toward the sky in the sight of Pharaoh. ⁹It shall become a fine dust all over the land of Egypt, and cause an inflammation breaking out in boils on man and beast throughout the land of Egypt." ¹⁰So they took soot of the kiln and appeared before Pharaoh; Moses threw it toward the sky, and it caused an inflammation breaking out in boils on man and beast. ¹¹The magicians were unable to confront Moses because of the inflammation, for the inflammation afflicted the magicians as well as all the other Egyptians. ¹²But the LORD stiffened the heart of Pharaoh, and he would not heed them, just as the LORD had told Moses.

¹³The LORD said to Moses, "Early in the morning present yourself to Pharaoh and say to him, 'Thus says the LORD, the God of the Hebrews: Let My people go to worship Me.

יִשְׂרָאֵל עַד־אֶחָד וַיִּכְבַּד לֵב פַּרְעֹה וְלֹא שִׁלַּח אֶת־הָעָם: פ

⁸ וַיֹּאמֶר יְהֹוָה אֶל־מֹשֶׁה וְאֶל־אַהֲרֹן קְחוּ לָכֶם מְלֹא חָפְנֵיכֶם פִּיחַ כִּבְשָׁן וּזְרָקוֹ מֹשֶׁה הַשָּׁמַיְמָה לְעֵינֵי פַרְעֹה: ⁹ וְהָיָה לְאָבָק עַל כָּל־אֶרֶץ מִצְרָיִם וְהָיָה עַל־הָאָדָם וְעַל־הַבְּהֵמָה לִשְׁחִין פֹּרֵחַ אֲבַעְבֻּעֹת בְּכָל־אֶרֶץ מִצְרָיִם: ¹⁰ וַיִּקְחוּ אֶת־פִּיחַ הַכִּבְשָׁן וַיַּעַמְדוּ לִפְנֵי פַרְעֹה וַיִּזְרֹק אֹתוֹ מֹשֶׁה הַשָּׁמַיְמָה וַיְהִי שְׁחִין אֲבַעְבֻּעֹת פֹּרֵחַ בָּאָדָם וּבַבְּהֵמָה: ¹¹ וְלֹא־יָכְלוּ הַחַרְטֻמִּים לַעֲמֹד לִפְנֵי מֹשֶׁה מִפְּנֵי הַשְּׁחִין כִּי־הָיָה הַשְּׁחִין בַּחַרְטֻמִּם וּבְכָל־מִצְרָיִם: ¹² וַיְחַזֵּק יְהֹוָה אֶת־לֵב פַּרְעֹה וְלֹא שָׁמַע אֲלֵהֶם כַּאֲשֶׁר דִּבֶּר יְהֹוָה אֶל־מֹשֶׁה: ס

¹³ וַיֹּאמֶר יְהֹוָה אֶל־מֹשֶׁה הַשְׁכֵּם בַּבֹּקֶר וְהִתְיַצֵּב לִפְנֵי פַרְעֹה וְאָמַרְתָּ אֵלָיו כֹּה־אָמַר יְהֹוָה אֱלֹהֵי הָעִבְרִים שַׁלַּח אֶת־עַמִּי וְיַעַבְדֻנִי:

7.   Pharaoh's need to learn whether the prediction made in verse 4 was fulfilled betrays a weakened self-confidence. Yet the incontrovertible testimony of God's transcendent power only serves to reinforce his perversity.

THE SIXTH PLAGUE: BOILS (*sheḥin*)   (vv. 8–12)

As the third in the triad, this affliction arrives without prior warning. The plagues now become more intense. For the first time one of the plagues directly imperils human life. If the interpretation given to the preceding scourges is correct, then the disease referred to here would be anthrax, known to be transmitted by *Stomoxys calcitrans* to both human beings and animals; the latter are infected through grazing on contaminated pastures. There is much irony in the fact that Pharaoh's magicians were themselves afflicted by the disease to such an extent as to be totally immobilized. Incidentally, the disease called *sheḥin* must have been quite prevalent in Egypt and notorious for its exceptional virulence, for Deuteronomy 28:27 (cf. v. 35) singles out the Egyptian variety in a list of maledictions.

8. *soot*   The significance of this substance and of the accompanying action is unclear.

in the sight of Pharaoh   So that he knows that this particular outbreak is not the familiar, common type but one that has been sent by God for a particular time and purpose.

9. *inflammation*   Hebrew *sheḥin* derives from a stem meaning "to be hot."[4]

breaking out   Probably referring to the skin ulcerations and malignant pustules that characterize anthrax.[5]

12.   See Comment to 4:21.

THE SEVENTH PLAGUE: HAIL (*barad*)   (vv. 13–35)

The third and final triad of plagues now begins. The escalation in terror and ruin sets the stage for the climactic catastrophe. This accounts for the extraordinary length of the warning given to Pharaoh at

14For this time I will send all My plagues upon your person, and your courtiers, and your people, in order that you may know that there is none like Me in all the world. 15I could have stretched forth My hand and stricken you and your people with pestilence, and you would have been effaced from the earth. 16Nevertheless I have spared you for this purpose: in order to show you My power, and in order that My fame may resound throughout the world. 17Yet you continue to thwart My people, and do not let them go! 18This time tomorrow I will rain down a very heavy hail, such as has not been in Egypt from the day it was founded until now. 19Therefore, order your livestock and everything you have in the open brought under shelter; every man and beast that is found outside, not having been brought indoors, shall perish when the hail comes down upon them!'" 20Those among Pharaoh's courtiers who feared the Lord's word brought their slaves and livestock indoors to safety; 21but those who paid no regard to the word of the Lord left their slaves and livestock in the open.

22The Lord said to Moses, "Hold out your arm toward the sky that hail may fall on all the land of Egypt, upon man and beast and all the grasses of the field in the land of Egypt." 23So Moses held out his rod toward the sky, and the Lord sent thunder and hail, and fire streamed down to the ground, as the Lord rained down hail upon the land of Egypt. 24The hail was very heavy—fire flashing in the midst of the hail—such as had not fallen on the land of Egypt since it had become a nation. 25Throughout the land of Egypt the hail struck down all that were in the open, both man and beast; the hail also struck down all the grasses of the field and shattered all the trees of the field. 26Only in the

14 כִּי | בַּפַּעַם הַזֹּאת אֲנִי שֹׁלֵחַ אֶת־כָּל־מַגֵּפֹתַי אֶל־לִבְּךָ וּבַעֲבָדֶיךָ וּבְעַמֶּךָ בַּעֲבוּר תֵּדַע כִּי אֵין כָּמֹנִי בְּכָל־הָאָרֶץ: 15 כִּי עַתָּה שָׁלַחְתִּי אֶת־יָדִי וָאַךְ אוֹתְךָ וְאֶת־עַמְּךָ בַּדָּבֶר וַתִּכָּחֵד מִן־הָאָרֶץ: 16 וְאוּלָם בַּעֲבוּר זֹאת הֶעֱמַדְתִּיךָ בַּעֲבוּר הַרְאֹתְךָ אֶת־כֹּחִי וּלְמַעַן סַפֵּר שְׁמִי בְּכָל־הָאָרֶץ: שביעי 17 עוֹדְךָ מִסְתּוֹלֵל בְּעַמִּי לְבִלְתִּי שַׁלְּחָם: 18 הִנְנִי מַמְטִיר כָּעֵת מָחָר בָּרָד כָּבֵד מְאֹד אֲשֶׁר לֹא־הָיָה כָמֹהוּ בְּמִצְרַיִם לְמִן־הַיּוֹם הִוָּסְדָה וְעַד־עָתָּה: 19 וְעַתָּה שְׁלַח הָעֵז אֶת־מִקְנְךָ וְאֵת כָּל־אֲשֶׁר לְךָ בַּשָּׂדֶה כָּל־הָאָדָם וְהַבְּהֵמָה אֲשֶׁר־יִמָּצֵא בַשָּׂדֶה וְלֹא יֵאָסֵף הַבַּיְתָה וְיָרַד עֲלֵהֶם הַבָּרָד וָמֵתוּ: 20 הַיָּרֵא אֶת־דְּבַר יְהֹוָה מֵעַבְדֵי פַּרְעֹה הֵנִיס אֶת־עֲבָדָיו וְאֶת־מִקְנֵהוּ אֶל־הַבָּתִּים: 21 וַאֲשֶׁר לֹא־שָׂם לִבּוֹ אֶל־דְּבַר יְהֹוָה וַיַּעֲזֹב אֶת־עֲבָדָיו וְאֶת־מִקְנֵהוּ בַּשָּׂדֶה: פ 22 וַיֹּאמֶר יְהֹוָה אֶל־מֹשֶׁה נְטֵה אֶת־יָדְךָ עַל־הַשָּׁמַיִם וִיהִי בָרָד בְּכָל־אֶרֶץ מִצְרָיִם עַל־הָאָדָם וְעַל־הַבְּהֵמָה וְעַל כָּל־עֵשֶׂב הַשָּׂדֶה בְּאֶרֶץ מִצְרָיִם: 23 וַיֵּט מֹשֶׁה אֶת־מַטֵּהוּ עַל־הַשָּׁמַיִם וַיהֹוָה נָתַן קֹלֹת וּבָרָד וַתִּהֲלַךְ אֵשׁ אָרְצָה וַיַּמְטֵר יְהֹוָה בָּרָד עַל־אֶרֶץ מִצְרָיִם: 24 וַיְהִי בָרָד וְאֵשׁ מִתְלַקַּחַת בְּתוֹךְ הַבָּרָד כָּבֵד מְאֹד אֲשֶׁר לֹא־הָיָה כָמֹהוּ בְּכָל־אֶרֶץ מִצְרַיִם מֵאָז הָיְתָה לְגוֹי: 25 וַיַּךְ הַבָּרָד בְּכָל־אֶרֶץ מִצְרַיִם אֵת כָּל־אֲשֶׁר בַּשָּׂדֶה מֵאָדָם וְעַד־בְּהֵמָה וְאֵת כָּל־עֵשֶׂב הַשָּׂדֶה הִכָּה הַבָּרָד וְאֶת־כָּל־עֵץ הַשָּׂדֶה שִׁבֵּר: 26 רַק בְּאֶרֶץ גֹּשֶׁן אֲשֶׁר־שָׁם בְּנֵי יִשְׂרָאֵל לֹא הָיָה בָּרָד:

dawn. For the first time the Egyptians and their livestock are given the opportunity to take shelter, and some avail themselves of it. Also for the first time Pharaoh openly admits to being at fault.

The information given in verses 31–32 clearly dates the plague to early February.

14. all My plagues This phrase either introduces the last four plagues or alludes to their all-embracing consequences.

15–16. Pharaoh is instructed that he has thus far been spared, not because of any inherent merit or special power but solely by dint of God's forbearance, which serves a weightier, didactic purpose still to be accomplished.

17. thwart The meaning of this unique Hebrew phrase is uncertain.[6]

19. God shows concern for the needless loss of human and animal life. A rabbinic comment on this verse states: "Come and observe [the extent] of God's compassion. Even in a moment of anger He has compassion on the wicked and on their animals."[7]

23–25. The description is clearly of a long-lasting, savage hailstorm marked by repeated thunderclaps and continual flashes of lightning.[8]

region of Goshen, where the Israelites were, there was no hail.

27Thereupon Pharaoh sent for Moses and Aaron and said to them, "I stand guilty this time. The LORD is in the right, and I and my people are in the wrong. 28Plead with the LORD that there may be an end of God's thunder and of hail. I will let you go; you need stay no longer." 29Moses said to him, "As I go out of the city, I shall spread out my hands to the LORD; the thunder will cease and the hail will fall no more, so that you may know that the earth is the LORD's. 30But I know that you and your courtiers do not yet fear the LORD God."—31Now the flax and barley were ruined, for the barley was in the ear and the flax was in bud; 32but the wheat and the emmer were not hurt, for they ripen late.—33Leaving Pharaoh, Moses went outside the city and spread out his hands to the LORD: the thunder and the hail ceased, and no rain came pouring down upon the earth. 34But when Pharaoh saw that the rain and the hail

27 וַיִּשְׁלַח פַּרְעֹה וַיִּקְרָא לְמֹשֶׁה וּלְאַהֲרֹן וַיֹּאמֶר אֲלֵהֶם חָטָאתִי הַפָּעַם יְהֹוָה הַצַּדִּיק וַאֲנִי וְעַמִּי הָרְשָׁעִים: 28 הַעְתִּירוּ אֶל־יְהֹוָה וְרַב מִהְיֹת קֹלֹת אֱלֹהִים וּבָרָד וַאֲשַׁלְּחָה אֶתְכֶם וְלֹא תֹסִפוּן לַעֲמֹד: 29 וַיֹּאמֶר אֵלָיו מֹשֶׁה כְּצֵאתִי אֶת־הָעִיר אֶפְרֹשׂ אֶת־כַּפַּי אֶל־יְהֹוָה הַקֹּלוֹת יֶחְדָּלוּן וְהַבָּרָד לֹא יִהְיֶה־עוֹד לְמַעַן תֵּדַע כִּי לַיהֹוָה הָאָרֶץ: 30 וְאַתָּה וַעֲבָדֶיךָ יָדַעְתִּי כִּי טֶרֶם תִּירְאוּן מִפְּנֵי יְהֹוָה אֱלֹהִים: 31 וְהַפִּשְׁתָּה וְהַשְּׂעֹרָה נֻכָּתָה כִּי הַשְּׂעֹרָה אָבִיב וְהַפִּשְׁתָּה גִּבְעֹל: 32 וְהַחִטָּה וְהַכֻּסֶּמֶת לֹא נֻכּוּ כִּי אֲפִילֹת הֵנָּה: מפטיר 33 וַיֵּצֵא מֹשֶׁה מֵעִם פַּרְעֹה אֶת־הָעִיר וַיִּפְרֹשׂ כַּפָּיו אֶל־יְהֹוָה וַיַּחְדְּלוּ הַקֹּלוֹת וְהַבָּרָד וּמָטָר לֹא־נִתַּךְ אָרְצָה: 34 וַיַּרְא פַּרְעֹה כִּי־חָדַל

---

26.   Thunderstorms originating in Upper Egypt and moving northward may well be trapped within the narrow Nile valley, leaving unaffected the northeastern part of the Delta, where Goshen was located.

27.   Pharaoh's "this time" echoes the identical phrase used by God in His forewarning in verse 14.

28.   Pharaoh's concession now appears to be unqualified.

29.   *spread out my hands*   An attitude of prayer.[9]

that the earth is the LORD's   He, not the Egyptian gods, is sovereign over nature.

30.   Moses knows that Pharaoh's confession of guilt is just empty words.

31–32.   This note serves a double purpose. It creates suspense about Moses' response to Pharaoh's plea in light of verse 30, and it explains why, despite the devastation of crops caused by the hail, there still remained a residue for the locusts in the next plague (10:5). Ramban sees a didactic purpose in these verses, which he takes to be part of Moses' speech to Pharaoh—the king is told that if he sincerely repents, the wheat and emmer can still be saved.

In Egypt flax was normally sown at the beginning of January and was in bloom three weeks later; barley was sown in August and harvested in February. Flax was grown primarily for its linen fiber, which was made into yarn, woven into cloth, and then bleached. The linen-making industry was of considerable importance in the economy of Egypt because linen was the preferred fabric for clothing. Barley was cultivated extensively in Egypt; it was used for bread and brewed into beer. The destruction of these crops would be a severe blow.

31.   *in bud*   Hebrew *giv'ol* refers to the stage of development of the calyx.[10]

flax barley, barley flax   Note the chiastic design.[11]

32.   *emmer*   A species of wheat that along with barley and winter wheat made up the three chief cereals of Egypt. The identification of Hebrew *kussemet* as spelt, found in many translations, is erroneous for the reason that this cereal did not grow in the land of Egypt. *Kussemet* is mentioned several times in rabbinic texts as one of the principal products of the Land of Israel.[12]

ripen late   Wheat and emmer are planted in August and harvested in late spring or early summer. Hence, they were less vulnerable than the flax and barley.[13]

and the thunder had ceased, he became stubborn and reverted to his guilty ways, as did his courtiers. [35]So Pharaoh's heart stiffened and he would not let the Israelites go, just as the LORD had foretold through Moses.

הַמָּטָר וְהַבָּרָד וְהַקֹּלֹת וַיֹּסֶף לַחֲטֹא וַיַּכְבֵּד לִבּוֹ הוּא וַעֲבָדָיו: 35 וַיֶּחֱזַק לֵב פַּרְעֹה וְלֹא שִׁלַּח אֶת־בְּנֵי יִשְׂרָאֵל כַּאֲשֶׁר דִּבֶּר יְהוָה בְּיַד־מֹשֶׁה:
פ

10
BO'

Then the LORD said to Moses, "Go to Pharaoh. For I have hardened his heart and the hearts of his courtiers, in order that I may display these My signs among them, [2]and that you may recount in the hearing of your sons and of your sons' sons how I made a mockery of the Egyptians and how I displayed My signs among them—in order that you may know that I am the LORD." [3]So Moses and Aaron went

בא

י וַיֹּאמֶר יְהוָה אֶל־מֹשֶׁה בֹּא אֶל־פַּרְעֹה כִּי־אֲנִי הִכְבַּדְתִּי אֶת־לִבּוֹ וְאֶת־לֵב עֲבָדָיו לְמַעַן שִׁתִי אֹתֹתַי אֵלֶּה בְּקִרְבּוֹ: 2 וּלְמַעַן תְּסַפֵּר בְּאָזְנֵי בִנְךָ וּבֶן־בִּנְךָ אֵת אֲשֶׁר הִתְעַלַּלְתִּי בְּמִצְרַיִם וְאֶת־אֹתֹתַי אֲשֶׁר־שַׂמְתִּי בָם וִידַעְתֶּם כִּי־אֲנִי יְהוָה: 3 וַיָּבֹא מֹשֶׁה וְאַהֲרֹן אֶל־פַּרְעֹה וַיֹּאמְרוּ

---

34. Once again Pharaoh yields to his obstinate and perfidious impulses.

35. **through Moses** This implies that Moses had conveyed to the people God's foreknowledge of Pharaoh.

CHAPTER 10 THE EIGHTH PLAGUE: LOCUSTS (*'arbeh*) (vv. 1–20)

Bo'

The locust swarm has always been one of the worst scourges to afflict humanity. An area of one square kilometer can contain fifty million such insects, which in a single night can devour as much as one hundred thousand tons of vegetation. Their mass multiplication is fostered by heavy rains and unusually moist conditions.

The introduction to the onset of the plague is again unusually lengthy. It also contains several new features. The king's courtiers boldly challenge him; Pharaoh makes concessions in advance of the actual plague; the coercive function of the plague for the Egyptians is supplemented by an educative purpose for Israel.

1. **I have hardened his heart** See Comment to 4:21.

in order that . . . To the Egyptians, the multiplication of these "signs" enhances the evidence pointing to God's force and power.

2. **that you may recount** The singular form of the verb shows that Moses is addressed as the personification of the people of Israel, for whom the message is really intended. Hence, the last verb is in the plural form.

As the cycle of plagues inexorably draws to its inevitable conclusion, its larger historical and transcendent significance is brought into view. The events are to be indelibly marked upon the collective memory of the people of Israel and thus become a permanent part of the lore that is transmitted from generation to generation. The constant instruction of the young concerning God's mighty deeds is the medium of such transmission.[1] Psalms 78 and 105 provide biblical examples of this practice. The idea is that through the evocative power of narration, rather than by abstract theological discourse, the true knowledge of God is understood, is established in the mind of Israel, and is sustained. See also the Comment to 13:8.

I made a mockery[2] By humbling the mighty Egyptian state, by humiliating Pharaoh, its "divine king," and by exposing the impotence of its gods.

to Pharaoh and said to him, "Thus says the Lord, the God of the Hebrews, 'How long will you refuse to humble yourself before Me? Let My people go that they may worship Me. ⁴For if you refuse to let My people go, tomorrow I will bring locusts on your territory. ⁵They shall cover the surface of the land, so that no one will be able to see the land. They shall devour the surviving remnant that was left to you after the hail; and they shall eat away all your trees that grow in the field. ⁶Moreover, they shall fill your palaces and the houses of all your courtiers and of all the Egyptians —something that neither your fathers nor fathers' fathers have seen from the day they appeared on earth to this day.'" With that he turned and left Pharaoh's presence.

⁷Pharaoh's courtiers said to him, "How long shall this one be a snare to us? Let the men go to worship the Lord their God! Are you not yet aware that Egypt is lost?" ⁸So Moses and Aaron were brought back to Pharaoh and he said to them, "Go, worship the Lord your God! Who are the ones to go?" ⁹Moses replied, "We will all go, young and old: we will go with our sons and daughters, our flocks and herds; for we must observe the Lord's festival." ¹⁰But he said to them, "The Lord be with you the same as I mean to let your children go with you! Clearly, you are bent on mischief. ¹¹No! You menfolk go and worship the Lord, since that is what you want." And they were expelled from Pharaoh's presence.

אֵלָ֗יו כֹּֽה־אָמַ֤ר יְהוָה֙ אֱלֹהֵ֣י הָֽעִבְרִ֔ים עַד־מָתַ֗י מֵאַ֙נְתָּ֙ לֵעָנֹ֣ת מִפָּנָ֔י שַׁלַּ֥ח עַמִּ֖י וְיַֽעַבְדֻֽנִי׃ 4 כִּ֣י אִם־מָאֵ֤ן אַתָּה֙ לְשַׁלֵּ֣חַ אֶת־עַמִּ֔י הִנְנִ֨י מֵבִ֥יא מָחָ֛ר אַרְבֶּ֖ה בִּגְבֻלֶֽךָ׃ 5 וְכִסָּה֙ אֶת־עֵ֣ין הָאָ֔רֶץ וְלֹ֥א יוּכַ֖ל לִרְאֹ֣ת אֶת־הָאָ֑רֶץ וְאָכַ֣ל ׀ אֶת־יֶ֣תֶר הַפְּלֵטָ֗ה הַנִּשְׁאֶ֤רֶת לָכֶם֙ מִן־הַבָּרָ֔ד וְאָכַל֙ אֶת־כָּל־הָעֵ֔ץ הַצֹּמֵ֥חַ לָכֶ֖ם מִן־הַשָּׂדֶֽה׃ 6 וּמָלְא֨וּ בָתֶּ֜יךָ וּבָתֵּ֣י כָל־עֲבָדֶ֗יךָ וּבָתֵּ֣י כָל־מִצְרַ֔יִם אֲשֶׁ֙ר לֹֽא־רָא֤וּ אֲבֹתֶ֙יךָ֙ וַֽאֲב֣וֹת אֲבֹתֶ֔יךָ מִיּ֗וֹם הֱיוֹתָם֙ עַל־הָ֣אֲדָמָ֔ה עַ֖ד הַיּ֣וֹם הַזֶּ֑ה וַיִּ֥פֶן וַיֵּצֵ֖א מֵעִ֥ם פַּרְעֹֽה׃ 7 וַיֹּאמְרוּ֩ עַבְדֵ֨י פַרְעֹ֜ה אֵלָ֗יו עַד־מָתַי֙ יִהְיֶ֨ה זֶ֥ה לָ֙נוּ֙ לְמוֹקֵ֔שׁ שַׁלַּח֙ אֶת־הָ֣אֲנָשִׁ֔ים וְיַֽעַבְד֖וּ אֶת־יְהוָ֣ה אֱלֹהֵיהֶ֑ם הֲטֶ֣רֶם תֵּדַ֔ע כִּ֥י אָבְדָ֖ה מִצְרָֽיִם׃ 8 וַיּוּשַׁ֗ב אֶת־מֹשֶׁ֤ה וְאֶֽת־אַהֲרֹן֙ אֶל־פַּרְעֹ֔ה וַיֹּ֣אמֶר אֲלֵהֶ֔ם לְכ֥וּ עִבְד֖וּ אֶת־יְהוָ֣ה אֱלֹהֵיכֶ֑ם מִ֥י וָמִ֖י הַהֹלְכִֽים׃ 9 וַיֹּ֣אמֶר מֹשֶׁ֔ה בִּנְעָרֵ֥ינוּ וּבִזְקֵנֵ֖ינוּ נֵלֵ֑ךְ בְּבָנֵ֣ינוּ וּבִבְנוֹתֵ֗נוּ בְּצֹאנֵ֤נוּ וּבִבְקָרֵ֙נוּ֙ נֵלֵ֔ךְ כִּ֥י חַג־יְהוָ֖ה לָֽנוּ׃ 10 וַיֹּ֣אמֶר אֲלֵהֶ֗ם יְהִ֨י כֵ֤ן יְהוָה֙ עִמָּכֶ֔ם כַּאֲשֶׁ֛ר אֲשַׁלַּ֥ח אֶתְכֶ֖ם וְאֶֽת־טַפְּכֶ֑ם רְא֕וּ כִּ֥י רָעָ֖ה נֶ֥גֶד פְּנֵיכֶֽם׃ 11 לֹ֣א כֵ֗ן לְכֽוּ־נָ֤א הַגְּבָרִים֙ וְעִבְד֣וּ אֶת־יְהוָ֔ה כִּ֥י אֹתָ֖הּ אַתֶּ֣ם מְבַקְשִׁ֑ים וַיְגָ֣רֶשׁ אֹתָ֔ם מֵאֵ֖ת פְּנֵ֥י פַרְעֹֽה׃ פ
שני

---

6. your . . . fathers' fathers A neat counterpoint to "your sons' sons" in verse 2. For Israel, the future is invoked in a context of enduring inspiration and celebration. For Egypt, the past is recalled in order to paint a picture of impending catastrophe.

7. The threat of the plague of hail had fractured the ranks of Pharaoh's courtiers (9:20). The predicted invasion of locusts now leads to an open break with the king's policies.

this one A disrespectful allusion to Moses.

a snare We court disaster.

9. the Lord's festival See Comment to 5:1.

10. The Lord be Hebrew *yehi . . . YHVH*—another play on the divine name and the verb "to be," as in 3:14 and 9:3.

you are bent on mischief The literal meaning of the Hebrew—"evil is before your faces"— is ambiguous and has given rise to various interpretations: "You have evil intentions," that is, you do not intend returning after three days;[3] "you are foredoomed to disaster,"[4] an understanding that would seem to be supported by 32:12. Another explanation construes Hebrew *ra'ah,* here "mischief," as the name of a star; Pharaoh makes an astrological prediction that its configuration is an omen of disaster for the departing Israelites.[5] Finally, *ra'ah* has also been taken to be a Hebraized form of the name of the Egyptian god Re.[6]

11. The women and children are to be held hostage to ensure the return of the menfolk.

¹²Then the Lord said to Moses, "Hold out your arm over the land of Egypt for the locusts, that they may come upon the land of Egypt and eat up all the grasses in the land, whatever the hail has left." ¹³So Moses held out his rod over the land of Egypt, and the Lord drove an east wind over the land all that day and all night; and when morning came, the east wind had brought the locusts. ¹⁴Locusts invaded all the land of Egypt and settled within all the territory of Egypt in a thick mass; never before had there been so many, nor will there ever be so many again. ¹⁵They hid all the land from view, and the land was darkened; and they ate up all the grasses of the field and all the fruit of the trees which the hail had left, so that nothing green was left, of tree or grass of the field, in all the land of Egypt.

¹⁶Pharaoh hurriedly summoned Moses and Aaron and said, "I stand guilty before the Lord your God and before you. ¹⁷Forgive my offense just this once, and plead with the Lord your God that He but remove this death from me." ¹⁸So he left Pharaoh's presence and pleaded with the Lord. ¹⁹The Lord caused a shift to a very strong west wind, which lifted the locusts and hurled them into the Sea of Reeds; not a single locust remained in all the territory of Egypt. ²⁰But the Lord stiffened Pharaoh's heart, and he would not let the Israelites go.

²¹Then the Lord said to Moses, "Hold out your arm toward the sky that there may be darkness upon the land of Egypt, a darkness that can be touched." ²²Moses held out

יב וַיֹּאמֶר יְהֹוָה אֶל־מֹשֶׁה נְטֵה יָדְךָ עַל־אֶרֶץ מִצְרַיִם בָּאַרְבֶּה וְיַעַל עַל־אֶרֶץ מִצְרָיִם וְיֹאכַל אֶת־כָּל־עֵשֶׂב הָאָרֶץ אֵת כָּל־אֲשֶׁר הִשְׁאִיר הַבָּרָד: יג וַיֵּט מֹשֶׁה אֶת־מַטֵּהוּ עַל־אֶרֶץ מִצְרַיִם וַיהֹוָה נִהַג רוּחַ קָדִים בָּאָרֶץ כָּל־הַיּוֹם הַהוּא וְכָל־הַלָּיְלָה הַבֹּקֶר הָיָה וְרוּחַ הַקָּדִים נָשָׂא אֶת־הָאַרְבֶּה: יד וַיַּעַל הָאַרְבֶּה עַל כָּל־אֶרֶץ מִצְרַיִם וַיָּנַח בְּכֹל גְּבוּל מִצְרָיִם כָּבֵד מְאֹד לְפָנָיו לֹא־הָיָה כֵן אַרְבֶּה כָּמֹהוּ וְאַחֲרָיו לֹא יִהְיֶה־כֵּן: טו וַיְכַס אֶת־עֵין כָּל־הָאָרֶץ וַתֶּחְשַׁךְ הָאָרֶץ וַיֹּאכַל אֶת־כָּל־עֵשֶׂב הָאָרֶץ וְאֵת כָּל־פְּרִי הָעֵץ אֲשֶׁר הוֹתִיר הַבָּרָד וְלֹא־נוֹתַר כָּל־יֶרֶק בָּעֵץ וּבְעֵשֶׂב הַשָּׂדֶה בְּכָל־אֶרֶץ מִצְרָיִם: טז וַיְמַהֵר פַּרְעֹה לִקְרֹא לְמֹשֶׁה וּלְאַהֲרֹן וַיֹּאמֶר חָטָאתִי לַיהֹוָה אֱלֹהֵיכֶם וְלָכֶם: יז וְעַתָּה שָׂא נָא חַטָּאתִי אַךְ הַפַּעַם וְהַעְתִּירוּ לַיהֹוָה אֱלֹהֵיכֶם וְיָסֵר מֵעָלַי רַק אֶת־הַמָּוֶת הַזֶּה: יח וַיֵּצֵא מֵעִם פַּרְעֹה וַיֶּעְתַּר אֶל־יְהֹוָה: יט וַיַּהֲפֹךְ יְהֹוָה רוּחַ־יָם חָזָק מְאֹד וַיִּשָּׂא אֶת־הָאַרְבֶּה וַיִּתְקָעֵהוּ יָמָּה סּוּף לֹא נִשְׁאַר אַרְבֶּה אֶחָד בְּכֹל גְּבוּל מִצְרָיִם: כ וַיְחַזֵּק יְהֹוָה אֶת־לֵב פַּרְעֹה וְלֹא שִׁלַּח אֶת־בְּנֵי יִשְׂרָאֵל: פ כא וַיֹּאמֶר יְהֹוָה אֶל־מֹשֶׁה נְטֵה יָדְךָ עַל־הַשָּׁמַיִם וִיהִי חֹשֶׁךְ עַל־אֶרֶץ מִצְרָיִם וְיָמֵשׁ חֹשֶׁךְ:

13. an east wind Hebrew *kadim* is generally the hot, dry, withering wind known as the *khamsin*, or sirocco, such as in Genesis 41:6. Here, as in 14:21, it may signify the south wind that blows in from the Sahara, since Egypt was oriented southward to the source and headwaters of the Nile. The *kadim* is often used in the Bible as the instrument of God without any directional implication.[7]

all that day The locust migrates vast distances.

14-15. A bold overstatement to convey something of the magnitude of the plague.

18. Moses and Aaron, having been recalled by Pharaoh, make no response to his plea. Their cold silence must have been especially humiliating to Pharaoh, since he had summarily dismissed them only a short while before (v. 11).

19. west wind Literally, "sea wind."

THE NINTH PLAGUE: DARKNESS (*ḥoshekh*) (vv. 21–29)

Once again, the third in the series arrives without prior warning. For three days the land is engulfed in darkness, a spell corresponding to the three-day journey for worship that Pharaoh had repeatedly refused to grant the Israelites. This affliction can be explained in terms of the *khamsin* referred to above. This scorching sirocco wind blows in each spring from Saharan Africa or from Arabia, enveloping the land in thick sand and dust. It may often persist for several days and blacken the sky in its wake.

his arm toward the sky and thick darkness descended upon all the land of Egypt for three days. ²³People could not see one another, and for three days no one could get up from where he was; but all the Israelites enjoyed light in their dwellings.

²⁴Pharaoh then summoned Moses and said, "Go, worship the LORD! Only your flocks and your herds shall be left behind; even your children may go with you." ²⁵But Moses said, "You yourself must provide us with sacrifices and burnt offerings to offer up to the LORD our God; ²⁶our own livestock, too, shall go along with us—not a hoof shall remain behind: for we must select from it for the worship of the LORD our God; and we shall not know with what we are to worship the LORD until we arrive there." ²⁷But the LORD stiffened Pharaoh's heart and he would not agree to let them go. ²⁸Pharaoh said to him, "Be gone from me! Take care not to see me again, for the moment you look upon my face you shall die." ²⁹And Moses replied, "You have spoken rightly. I shall not see your face again!"

22 וַיֵּ֣ט מֹשֶׁ֗ה אֶת־יָד֖וֹ עַל־הַשָּׁמָ֑יִם וַיְהִ֧י חֹֽשֶׁךְ־אֲפֵלָ֛ה בְּכָל־אֶ֥רֶץ מִצְרַ֖יִם שְׁלֹ֥שֶׁת יָמִֽים: 23 לֹֽא־רָא֞וּ אִ֣ישׁ אֶת־אָחִ֗יו וְלֹא־קָ֛מוּ אִ֥ישׁ מִתַּחְתָּ֖יו שְׁלֹ֣שֶׁת יָמִ֑ים וּֽלְכָל־בְּנֵ֧י יִשְׂרָאֵ֛ל הָ֥יָה א֖וֹר בְּמוֹשְׁבֹתָֽם: שלישי

24 וַיִּקְרָ֨א פַרְעֹ֜ה אֶל־מֹשֶׁ֗ה וַיֹּ֙אמֶר֙ לְכ֣וּ עִבְד֣וּ אֶת־יְהוָ֔ה רַ֥ק צֹאנְכֶ֛ם וּבְקַרְכֶ֖ם יֻצָּ֑ג גַּֽם־טַפְּכֶ֖ם יֵלֵ֥ךְ עִמָּכֶֽם: 25 וַיֹּ֣אמֶר מֹשֶׁ֔ה גַּם־אַתָּ֛ה תִּתֵּ֥ן בְּיָדֵ֖נוּ זְבָחִ֣ים וְעֹלֹ֑ת וְעָשִׂ֖ינוּ לַֽיהוָ֥ה אֱלֹהֵֽינוּ: 26 וְגַם־מִקְנֵ֜נוּ יֵלֵ֣ךְ עִמָּ֗נוּ לֹ֤א תִשָּׁאֵר֙ פַּרְסָ֔ה כִּ֚י מִמֶּ֣נּוּ נִקַּ֔ח לַעֲבֹ֖ד אֶת־יְהוָ֣ה אֱלֹהֵ֑ינוּ וַאֲנַ֣חְנוּ לֹֽא־נֵדַ֗ע מַֽה־נַּעֲבֹד֙ אֶת־יְהוָ֔ה עַד־בֹּאֵ֖נוּ שָֽׁמָּה: 27 וַיְחַזֵּ֥ק יְהוָ֖ה אֶת־לֵ֣ב פַּרְעֹ֑ה וְלֹ֥א אָבָ֖ה לְשַׁלְּחָֽם: 28 וַיֹּֽאמֶר־ל֥וֹ פַרְעֹ֖ה לֵ֣ךְ מֵעָלָ֑י הִשָּׁ֣מֶר לְךָ֗ אַל־תֹּ֙סֶף֙ רְא֣וֹת פָּנַ֔י כִּ֗י בְּי֛וֹם רְאֹתְךָ֥ פָנַ֖י תָּמֽוּת: 29 וַיֹּ֥אמֶר מֹשֶׁ֖ה כֵּ֣ן דִּבַּ֑רְתָּ לֹֽא־אֹסִ֥ף ע֖וֹד רְא֥וֹת פָּנֶֽיךָ: פ

In the present case, the first *khamsin* to arrive in March would have been far more intense than usual. It would additionally have borne aloft the red soil deposited by the earlier torrential rains and now sunbaked and particulate following the destructive action of the locusts, which had already denuded the land of vegetation. Since the *khamsin* may travel northward in bands, rather than be diffused, the Israelite area of Goshen, situated at right angles to the Nile valley, could escape its effects.

The blotting out of the light of the sun for three days would have carried a powerful symbolic message for the Egyptians, for the sun was their supreme god, and its worship was pervasive in the official palace ritual.[8] The sun's diurnal rising was conceived to be a triumph over the demon Apophis, the embodiment of darkness, who struggled daily to vanquish him. The plague of darkness, therefore, would have had a devastating psychological impact. The impotence of the Egyptians' supreme god is exposed, thus foreboding imminent doom.

21. *that can be touched*   This probably refers to the vast quantities of sand, dust, and particles of soil that filled the air.[9]

25. *You yourself*   He who contemptuously denied all knowledge of YHVH will, in the end, provide sacrifices for Him in acknowledgment of His reality and power; compare 12:32.

CHAPTER 11   THE ANNOUNCEMENT OF THE TENTH PLAGUE   (vv. 1–10)

Pharaoh has closed the door on any further negotiations with Moses. Despite their concentrative force, their timing and intensity, the natural disasters have left the king even more uncompromising than before. Now one final, overwhelming blow is about to descend on the Egyptians, one that is wholly outside the range of nature or of previous human experience. This Moses announces to Pharaoh before he leaves the palace.

This chapter consists of three declarations. It connects with the past by registering the completion of the role of Moses and Aaron as the effective instruments of God's chastening and coercive measures against the Egyptians. At the same time, it foretells the impending, unmediated, and decisive intervention of God. By focusing on the initial preparations for the Exodus, it forges a transition to the Passover account in the next chapter.

י"א

11 And the Lord said to Moses, "I will bring but one more plague upon Pharaoh and upon Egypt; after that he shall let you go from here; indeed, when he lets you go, he will drive you out of here one and all. ²Tell the people to borrow, each man from his neighbor and each woman from hers, objects of silver and gold." ³The Lord disposed the Egyptians favorably toward the people. Moreover, Moses himself was much esteemed in the land of Egypt, among Pharaoh's courtiers and among the people.

⁴Moses said, "Thus says the Lord: Toward midnight I will go forth among the Egyptians, ⁵and every first-born in the land of Egypt shall die, from the first-born of Pharaoh who sits on his throne to the first-born of the slave girl who is behind the millstones; and all the first-born of the cattle.

א וַיֹּ֤אמֶר יְהֹוָה֙ אֶל־מֹשֶׁ֔ה ע֣וֹד נֶ֤גַע
אֶחָד֙ אָבִ֤יא עַל־פַּרְעֹה֙ וְעַל־מִצְרַ֔יִם אַחֲרֵי־כֵ֕ן
יְשַׁלַּ֥ח אֶתְכֶ֖ם מִזֶּ֑ה כְּשַׁלְּח֕וֹ כָּלָ֕ה גָּרֵ֛שׁ יְגָרֵ֥שׁ
אֶתְכֶ֖ם מִזֶּֽה: ב דַּבֶּר־נָ֣א בְּאָזְנֵ֣י הָעָ֑ם וְיִשְׁאֲל֞וּ אִ֣ישׁ ׀
מֵאֵ֣ת רֵעֵ֗הוּ וְאִשָּׁה֙ מֵאֵ֣ת רְעוּתָ֔הּ כְּלֵי־כֶ֖סֶף וּכְלֵ֥י
זָהָֽב: ג וַיִּתֵּ֧ן יְהֹוָ֛ה אֶת־חֵ֥ן הָעָ֖ם בְּעֵינֵ֣י מִצְרָ֑יִם גַּ֣ם ׀
הָאִ֣ישׁ מֹשֶׁ֗ה גָּד֤וֹל מְאֹד֙ בְּאֶ֣רֶץ מִצְרַ֔יִם בְּעֵינֵ֥י
עַבְדֵי־פַרְעֹ֖ה וּבְעֵינֵ֥י הָעָֽם: ס רביעי

ד וַיֹּ֣אמֶר מֹשֶׁ֔ה כֹּ֖ה אָמַ֣ר יְהֹוָ֑ה כַּחֲצֹ֣ת הַלַּ֔יְלָה
אֲנִ֥י יוֹצֵ֖א בְּת֥וֹךְ מִצְרָֽיִם: ה וּמֵ֣ת כָּל־בְּכוֹר֘ בְּאֶ֣רֶץ
מִצְרַיִם֒ מִבְּכ֤וֹר פַּרְעֹה֙ הַיֹּשֵׁ֣ב עַל־כִּסְא֔וֹ עַ֚ד
בְּכ֣וֹר הַשִּׁפְחָ֔ה אֲשֶׁ֖ר אַחַ֣ר הָרֵחָ֑יִם וְכֹ֖ל בְּכ֥וֹר
בְּהֵמָֽה: ו וְהָֽיְתָ֛ה צְעָקָ֥ה גְדֹלָ֖ה בְּכָל־אֶ֣רֶץ מִצְרָ֑יִם

1–3. These verses are a parenthetic aside. It must be assumed that Moses received this communication in the palace just as he was about to leave, for verse 8 shows that he conveyed its content to Pharaoh.

1. he will drive you out The Exodus will no longer be a concession on Pharaoh's part. He will earnestly desire your rapid departure.[1]

one and all Without restriction, exactly as Moses had demanded.[2]

2–3. See Comment to 3:22.

2. Tell the people Throughout the plagues episode, no communication of Moses with the Israelites has been reported. Now that his mission to Pharaoh is concluded, he once again turns his attention to internal affairs.

silver and gold The Septuagint and Samaritan texts add "and clothing," as in 3:22 and 12:35.

3. disposed . . . favorably The Egyptians willingly parted with their possessions.[3]

Moses himself An additional reason for the Egyptian people's response.

4–8. This section is a continuation of 10:29.

4. Toward midnight When everyone would be at home. For psychological effect, the specific night is not disclosed.

5. For the first time, Pharaoh personally will be afflicted.

from . . . Pharaoh . . . to . . . the slave girl A merism, in which totality is expressed by the extreme opposites of social status. None will be exempt.

the millstones Hebrew *reḥayim* is a dual form. The utensil with which the grain was ground into flour was the quern and muller type. The grain was placed between two pieces of stone. The smaller, upper one (Heb. *rekhev*, literally "rider" in Deut. 24:6) was moved by hand forward and backward over the larger, stationary stone. This tedious, menial labor was performed by slave girls and captives.[4] Sensitive to the problem as to why these unfortunates were to be victims of the tenth plague, the Mekhilta explains that they had gloated over the sufferings of the Israelites at the hands of the Egyptians.[5]

the first-born of the cattle These were included because they were objects of Egyptian veneration.[6] The Egyptians might have ascribed their misfortune to the work of their own animal-shaped gods instead of to YHVH.[7]

⁶And there shall be a loud cry in all the land of Egypt, such as has never been or will ever be again; ⁷but not a dog shall snarl at any of the Israelites, at man or beast—in order that you may know that the LORD makes a distinction between Egypt and Israel. ⁸Then all these courtiers of yours shall come down to me and bow low to me, saying, 'Depart, you and all the people who follow you!' After that I will depart." And he left Pharaoh's presence in hot anger.

⁹Now the LORD had said to Moses, "Pharaoh will not heed you, in order that My marvels may be multiplied in the land of Egypt." ¹⁰Moses and Aaron had performed all these marvels before Pharaoh, but the LORD had stiffened the heart of Pharaoh so that he would not let the Israelites go from his land.

12 The LORD said to Moses and Aaron in the land of Egypt: ²This month shall mark for you the beginning of the

אֲשֶׁר כָּמֹהוּ לֹא נִהְיָ֫תָה וְכָמֹ֫הוּ לֹא תֹסִֽף:
⁷ וּלְכֹ֣ל ׀ בְּנֵ֣י יִשְׂרָאֵ֗ל לֹ֤א יֶֽחֱרַץ־כֶּ֙לֶב֙ לְשֹׁנ֔וֹ לְמֵאִ֖ישׁ וְעַד־בְּהֵמָ֑ה לְמַ֙עַן֙ תֵּֽדְע֔וּן אֲשֶׁר֙ יַפְלֶ֣ה יְהֹוָ֔ה בֵּ֥ין מִצְרַ֖יִם וּבֵ֥ין יִשְׂרָאֵֽל: ⁸ וְיָרְד֣וּ כׇל־ עֲבָדֶ֩יךָ֩ אֵ֨לֶּה אֵלַ֜י וְהִשְׁתַּֽחֲווּ־לִ֣י לֵאמֹ֗ר צֵ֤א אַתָּה֙ וְכׇל־הָעָ֣ם אֲשֶׁר־בְּרַגְלֶ֔יךָ וְאַֽחֲרֵי־כֵ֖ן אֵצֵ֑א וַיֵּצֵ֥א מֵֽעִם־פַּרְעֹ֖ה בׇּֽחֳרִי־אָֽף: ס
⁹ וַיֹּ֤אמֶר יְהֹוָה֙ אֶל־מֹשֶׁ֔ה לֹא־יִשְׁמַ֥ע אֲלֵיכֶ֖ם פַּרְעֹ֑ה לְמַ֛עַן רְב֥וֹת מֽוֹפְתַ֖י בְּאֶ֥רֶץ מִצְרָֽיִם:
¹⁰ וּמֹשֶׁ֣ה וְאַֽהֲרֹ֗ן עָשׂ֛וּ אֶת־כׇּל־הַמֹּֽפְתִ֥ים הָאֵ֖לֶּה לִפְנֵ֣י פַרְעֹ֑ה וַיְחַזֵּ֤ק יְהֹוָה֙ אֶת־לֵ֣ב פַּרְעֹ֔ה וְלֹֽא־שִׁלַּ֥ח אֶת־בְּנֵֽי־יִשְׂרָאֵ֖ל מֵֽאַרְצֽוֹ: פ

י"ב וַיֹּ֤אמֶר יְהֹוָה֙ אֶל־מֹשֶׁ֣ה וְאֶֽל־אַֽהֲרֹ֔ן בְּאֶ֥רֶץ מִצְרַ֖יִם לֵאמֹֽר: ² הַחֹ֧דֶשׁ הַזֶּ֛ה לָכֶ֖ם רֹ֣אשׁ חֳדָשִׁ֑ים

6. *a loud cry*   Hebrew *tseʿakah* is the very term used to give expression to Israel's misery under Egyptian enslavement.⁸ The anguished cry of the oppressed yields to the cry of their oppressors and tormentors.

7.   By contrast, the departing, liberated Israelites will not encounter the slightest show of resistance.⁹

8. *in hot anger*   At Pharaoh's death threat (10:28).

9–10.   This summary is needed because Moses' negotiations with Pharaoh are over. He never speaks to him again. The verses conclude the saga that began in chapter 7, just as the summarizing verses of chapter 6 bring to completion the first section of the book.

CHAPTER 12

The Last Act   (vv. 1–51)

This chapter is a very complex composition. It divides into a number of clearly differentiated literary units, each centering on various aspects of the Exodus events. Some of these units deal with immediate concerns, such as the last-minute preparations for the departure from Egypt; others relate to the enduring impact of the events in shaping the future course of Israel's life as a people. Appropriately, the entire complex is framed by the phrase "the whole community of Israel" (vv. 3,47). Another salient feature of this composition is the sevenfold repetition of the Hebrew stem *sh-m-r*, "to observe, guard, preserve." There is considerable overlap among the various units but no exact duplication. The repetition amplifies the preceding data in various ways, either by the addition of explanatory material or by supplementary details or instructions. Without doubt, the chapter is a composite of several strands of tradition.

1. *in the land of Egypt*   The location is given because this chapter is an exception to the rule that all the laws were promulgated in the wilderness. The institution of the annual Passover celebration antedates the events it is to commemorate.

months; it shall be the first of the months of the year for you. ³Speak to the whole community of Israel and say that on the tenth of this month each of them shall take a lamb to a family, a lamb to a household. ⁴But if the household is too small for a lamb, let him share one with a neighbor who dwells nearby, in proportion to the number of persons; you shall contribute for the lamb according to what each household will eat. ⁵Your lamb shall be without blemish, a year-

רִאשׁ֥וֹן הוּא֙ לָכֶ֔ם לְחָדְשֵׁ֖י הַשָּׁנָֽה: 3 דַּבְּר֗וּ אֶל־
כָּל־עֲדַ֤ת יִשְׂרָאֵל֙ לֵאמֹ֔ר בֶּעָשֹׂ֖ר לַחֹ֣דֶשׁ הַזֶּ֑ה
וְיִקְח֣וּ לָהֶ֗ם אִ֛ישׁ שֶׂ֥ה לְבֵית־אָבֹ֖ת שֶׂ֥ה לַבָּֽיִת:
4 וְאִם־יִמְעַ֣ט הַבַּ֘יִת֮ מִהְי֣וֹת מִשֶּׂה֒ וְלָקַ֣ח ה֗וּא
וּשְׁכֵנ֛וֹ הַקָּרֹ֥ב אֶל־בֵּית֖וֹ בְּמִכְסַ֣ת נְפָשֹׁ֑ת אִ֚ישׁ לְפִ֣י
אָכְל֔וֹ תָּכֹ֖סּוּ עַל־הַשֶּֽׂה: 5 שֶׂ֧ה תָמִ֛ים זָכָ֥ר בֶּן־שָׁנָ֖ה

THE REFORM OF THE CALENDAR   (v. 2)

The impending Exodus is visualized as the start of a wholly new order of life that is to be dominated by the consciousness of God's active presence in history. The entire religious calendar of Israel is henceforth to reflect this reality by numbering the months of the year from the month of the Exodus.

This month   Elsewhere termed "the month of Abib,"[1] literally "when the ears of barley ripen," the spring (March/April), now known as Nisan. In other words, the calendar is lunisolar, the lunar reckoning being accommodated to the needs of agricultural life.

first of the months   The Hebrew months, like the days of the week, are given in ordinal numbers. The absence of names for either is probably due to a desire to avoid any confusion with the polytheistic calendars that associate days and months with astral bodies or pagan deities and rituals. There is evidence that at least some months once had names, for the biblical sources refer to the months of Ziv, Ethanim, and Bul.[2] The Hebrew month names now used by Jews were borrowed from the Babylonian calendar during the first exile.[3]

THE PASCHAL OFFERING   (vv. 3–13)

The laws relating to the sacrificial meal that is to occur immediately before the Exodus are now set forth in elaborate detail.

3.   community of Israel   Hebrew *'edah* is the premonarchic technical term for the people of Israel acting as a corporate political entity, a sort of people's assembly.[4]

the tenth of this month   The completion of the first decade of the lunar month apparently held some special significance. Yom Kippur, the most sacred day in the religious calendar, falls on the tenth of the seventh month, and in ancient times this same date ushered in the Jubilee year. Joshua chose the tenth of the first month to cross the Jordan.[5]

a lamb   As verse 5 and Deuteronomy 14:4 indicate, Hebrew *seh* covers both a lamb and a kid of the goats.[6] In light of the assertion in 8:22, this act broke the code of fear enforced by the Egyptian bondage and thereby removed the psychological barrier to liberation. According to a tradition in Shabbat 87b, that day was a Sabbath, which is one of the reasons adduced for entitling the Sabbath before Passover "the Great Sabbath" (Heb. *shabbat ha-gadol*).[7]

a family   Hebrew *bet 'avot*, literally "a house of fathers," is a subunit of a tribe.[8] It comprises a man, his wife or wives, unmarried daughters, and sons with their wives and unmarried children.

a household   The original festival was a domestic celebration. Later it became a pilgrimage festival held at the central sanctuary.[9]

4.   too small   According to Josephus, a minimum quorum of ten participants was required for this ritual in Second Temple times.[10] The actual slaughtering of the animal was performed in groups of no fewer than thirty.[11]

in proportion to the number[12]

54

ling male; you may take it from the sheep or from the goats. [6]You shall keep watch over it until the fourteenth day of this month; and all the assembled congregation of the Israelites shall slaughter it at twilight. [7]They shall take some of the blood and put it on the two doorposts and the lintel of the houses in which they are to eat it. [8]They shall eat the flesh that same night; they shall eat it roasted over the fire, with unleavened bread and with bitter herbs. [9]Do not eat

יִהְיֶה לָכֶם מִן־הַכְּבָשִׂים וּמִן־הָעִזִּים תִּקָּחוּ: 6 וְהָיָה לָכֶם לְמִשְׁמֶרֶת עַד אַרְבָּעָה עָשָׂר יוֹם לַחֹדֶשׁ הַזֶּה וְשָׁחֲטוּ אֹתוֹ כֹּל קְהַל עֲדַת־יִשְׂרָאֵל בֵּין הָעַרְבָּיִם: 7 וְלָקְחוּ מִן־הַדָּם וְנָתְנוּ עַל־שְׁתֵּי הַמְּזוּזֹת וְעַל־הַמַּשְׁקוֹף עַל הַבָּתִּים אֲשֶׁר־יֹאכְלוּ אֹתוֹ בָּהֶם: 8 וְאָכְלוּ אֶת־הַבָּשָׂר בַּלַּיְלָה הַזֶּה צְלִי־אֵשׁ וּמַצּוֹת עַל־מְרֹרִים יֹאכְלֻהוּ: 9 אַל־תֹּאכְלוּ

will eat   The consumption of the animal is an indispensable element of the ritual. By means of this sacrificial meal, kinship ties are strengthened, and family and neighborly solidarity is promoted, while communion with God is established.

5. without blemish   A defective gift is an insult to the recipient; hence, the harmony between the devotee and his God would be impaired by such a donation. The physical perfection of the sacrificial animal is therefore repeatedly demanded in the sacrificial regulations.[13] An extension of this principle is the rabbinic precept of *hiddur mitsvah*, the obligation to perform an act designated a *mitsvah* in the most elegant and choice manner.[14]

a yearling   Rather, "one within the first year" of life. An animal is acceptable as an offering once it is eight days old.[15]

6. keep watch   The animal, selected on the tenth of the month, is to be carefully protected from blemish for four days until it is slaughtered. No reason for the interval is given. It may be an act of defiance of the Egyptians—in light of 8:22—and a time of testing for Israel.

at twilight   Hebrew *bein ha-ʿarbayim*[16] literally means "between the two settings." Rabbinic sources take this to mean "from noon on."[17] According to Radak,[18] the first "setting" occurs when the sun passes its zenith just after noon and the shadows begin to lengthen, and the second "setting" is the actual sunset. Josephus testifies that the paschal lamb was slaughtered in the Temple between 3 and 5 P.M.[19]

7.   It is clear from verse 22 that the blood of the slaughtered lamb was first collected in a basin. According to verses 13 and 23, the daubing at the entrances served to identify the houses of the Israelites, for the blood is designated "a sign." Blood was a readily available coloring substance; it also possessed symbolic significance because it was looked upon as the life essence.[20] There is no warrant for the theory that it played a magic, apotropaic role, that is, as a means of averting or overcoming evil or danger. The deliverance of Israel is ascribed solely to divine decision.

The lintel and doorposts form the demarcation between the sacred Israelite interior and the profane world outside.

8–9.   The roasting is an indispensable requirement[21] either because it is the quickest means of preparation when time is short or because it is the most effective way of extracting the blood, the consumption of which is strictly forbidden.[22]

unleavened bread   Hebrew *matsot* (sing. *matsah*) is introduced without definition and without explanation. The implication, justified by biblical texts, is that *matsah* is already well known and, hence, a product independent of the Exodus events. The contexts suggest a kind of flat cake that can be speedily prepared for unexpected guests.[23] The present verse witnesses the integration of the originally distinct *matsot* festival with the Passover celebration, on which see Comment to verses 14–20.

bitter herbs   Hebrew *merorim* (sing. *maror*) is a generic term and probably referred originally to the kind of pungent condiment with which pastoral nomads habitually season their meals of roasted flesh. Mishnah Pesaḥim 2:6 specifies five kinds of herbs subsumed under the term *maror*. Traditionally, the preferred plant has been lettuce, in Hebrew *ḥassah*, a vegetable known to have been cultivated in ancient Egypt.[24] This choice allows for word play with Hebrew *ḥ-w-s*, "to have compassion," one of the meanings of the root of *pesaḥ* (Passover). According to Rabban Gamaliel, the

any of it raw, or cooked in any way with water, but roasted—head, legs, and entrails—over the fire. [10]You shall not leave any of it over until morning; if any of it is left until morning, you shall burn it.

[11]This is how you shall eat it: your loins girded, your sandals on your feet, and your staff in your hand; and you shall eat it hurriedly: it is a passover offering to the LORD. [12]For that night I will go through the land of Egypt and strike down every first-born in the land of Egypt, both man and beast; and I will mete out punishments to all the gods of Egypt, I the LORD. [13]And the blood on the houses where you are staying shall be a sign for you: when I see the blood I will pass over you, so that no plague will destroy you when I strike the land of Egypt.

מִמֶּ֣נּוּ נָ֔א וּבָשֵׁ֥ל מְבֻשָּׁ֖ל בַּמָּ֑יִם כִּ֣י אִם־צְלִי־אֵ֔שׁ רֹאשׁ֥וֹ עַל־כְּרָעָ֖יו וְעַל־קִרְבּֽוֹ׃ ¹⁰ וְלֹא־תוֹתִ֥ירוּ מִמֶּ֖נּוּ עַד־בֹּ֑קֶר וְהַנֹּתָ֥ר מִמֶּ֛נּוּ עַד־בֹּ֖קֶר בָּאֵ֥שׁ תִּשְׂרֹֽפוּ׃

¹¹ וְכָ֙כָה֙ תֹּאכְל֣וּ אֹת֔וֹ מָתְנֵיכֶ֣ם חֲגֻרִ֗ים נַֽעֲלֵיכֶם֙ בְּרַגְלֵיכֶ֔ם וּמַקֶּלְכֶ֖ם בְּיֶדְכֶ֑ם וַאֲכַלְתֶּ֤ם אֹתוֹ֙ בְּחִפָּז֔וֹן פֶּ֥סַח ה֖וּא לַֽיהוָֽה׃ ¹² וְעָֽבַרְתִּ֣י בְאֶֽרֶץ־מִצְרַ֘יִם֮ בַּלַּ֣יְלָה הַזֶּה֒ וְהִכֵּיתִ֤י כָל־בְּכוֹר֙ בְּאֶ֣רֶץ מִצְרַ֔יִם מֵֽאָדָ֖ם וְעַד־בְּהֵמָ֑ה וּבְכָל־אֱלֹהֵ֥י מִצְרַ֛יִם אֶֽעֱשֶׂ֥ה שְׁפָטִ֖ים אֲנִ֥י יְהוָֽה׃ ¹³ וְהָיָה֩ הַדָּ֨ם לָכֶ֜ם לְאֹ֗ת עַ֤ל הַבָּתִּים֙ אֲשֶׁ֣ר אַתֶּ֣ם שָׁ֔ם וְרָאִ֙יתִי֙ אֶת־הַדָּ֔ם וּפָֽסַחְתִּ֖י עֲלֵכֶ֑ם וְלֹֽא־יִֽהְיֶ֨ה בָכֶ֥ם נֶ֙גֶף֙ לְמַשְׁחִ֔ית בְּהַכֹּתִ֖י בְּאֶ֥רֶץ מִצְרָֽיִם׃

maror is a tangible symbol of the bitterness of the servitude endured by the Israelites, as related in Exodus 1:14 (Heb. *va-yemareru*).[25]

10. A sacrificial animal is devoted in its entirety to a sacred purpose. This is so even when the offering is of the kind that is eaten by the worshipers and not wholly burnt on the altar. The intentional act of eating at the designated time is an indispensable part of the ritual. Any leftovers (Heb. *notar*) retain their sacred status but can no longer be consumed and must therefore be burnt.[26] In rabbinic terminology sacrificial flesh that the officiant even intended to eat beyond the allotted time is called *piggul*,[27] "repugnant, offensive," that is, to God.

11. loins girded The standard dress consisted of a flowing shirtlike garment that was tightened by a sash wrapped around the waist when greater maneuverability was called for. Since the climactic moment of liberation is imminent, the Israelites must be ready for immediate departure.

hurriedly Hebrew *hippazon* expresses a sense of haste informed by anxiety. The noun is used only in connection with the Exodus.[28] The prophet Isaiah (52:12) implicitly contrasts the future unhurried and unagitated redemption of Israel from exile with the circumstances of the Exodus: "For you will not depart in haste [*hippazon*], / Nor will you leave in flight."

a passover offering Hebrew *pesah* has given birth to the English adjective "paschal," used to designate both the Passover lamb and Easter. Like *matsah*, *pesah* is assumed to be an immediately intelligible term, so it too must have a history antedating the Exodus. Three traditions about the meaning of the stem *p-s-h* have survived.[29] The oldest, and apparently the most reliable, is "to have compassion";[30] another is "to protect";[31] a third is "to skip over."[32] Although this last is the interpretation that has gained the widest currency, it is the least likely because the term was originally independent of the Exodus events. Strictly speaking, as noted below in the Comment to verses 14–20, only the fourteenth day of the month can be called *pesah*, but in the course of time this term was extended to cover the entire week of the festival.

to the LORD The frequency with which this modifier occurs with the paschal sacrifice[33] reinforces the conclusion that a pre-Israelite technical term has been adapted, transformed, and monotheized—and thus wholly disengaged from any previous association.

12. I will go through An anthropomorphism, or ascription to God of human activity, in order to make His active Presence in history more vividly and dramatically perceived.[34]

to all the gods of Egypt God's power to take Israel out of Egypt manifests His own exclusivity, mocks the professed divinity of the pharaoh, and exposes the deities of Egypt as nongods.[35]

13. This first section of the chapter is rounded out with an assurance that no harm will befall the Israelites. This is needed because fulfillment of the foregoing instructions is fraught with peril, and the ensuing period of inaction engenders anxiety.

¹⁴This day shall be to you one of remembrance: you shall celebrate it as a festival to the Lord throughout the ages; you shall celebrate it as an institution for all time. ¹⁵Seven

14 וְהָיָה֩ הַיֹּ֨ום הַזֶּ֤ה לָכֶם֙ לְזִכָּרֹ֔ון וְחַגֹּתֶ֥ם אֹתֹ֖ו חַ֣ג לַֽיהֹוָ֑ה לְדֹרֹ֣תֵיכֶ֔ם חֻקַּ֥ת עֹולָ֖ם תְּחָגֻּֽהוּ׃ 15 שִׁבְעַ֤ת יָמִים֙ מַצֹּ֣ות תֹּאכֵ֔לוּ אַ֚ךְ בַּיֹּ֣ום

when I see the blood See Comment to verse 7. Baḥya ben Asher explains this as follows: "The blood does not thwart the plague nor does its absence occasion it. Scripture teaches that the one who had perfect faith and confidence in God, and was not perturbed by Pharaoh's terror and evil decree but publicly sacrificed what to Egypt was an abomination, and who daubed the blood of the paschal offering on the doorposts and lintels—such a one was a righteous person, having confidence in God, and was worthy of divine protection from the plague and the destroyer."

destroy you See Comment to verse 23.

THE FESTIVAL OF *MATSOT* (vv. 14–20)

The foregoing rites relate solely to the specific situation at that time—the Passover of Egypt. In this section the events of the Exodus become an experience indelibly stamped for all time on Israel's memory and imagination, permanently shaping its religious consciousness and practice. Verse 14 establishes an annual commemorative festival; the succeeding verses explain how it is to be observed.

The focus is on the festival of *matsot*, unleavened bread. Without doubt, throughout the biblical period this remained a distinct celebration separate from the one-day paschal rite. Witness the fact that the next chapter (13:6–8) features the laws of *matsot* without so much as a mention of the paschal sacrifice. Leviticus 23:5–6 similarly differentiates the one from the other: "In the first month, on the fourteenth day of the month, at twilight, there shall be a passover offering to the Lord, and on the fifteenth day of that month the Lord's Feast of Unleavened Bread." During the Babylonian exile Ezekiel (45:21) likewise ordains: "On the fourteenth day of the first month you shall have the passover sacrifice; and during a festival of seven days unleavened bread shall be eaten." Finally, we are told in Ezra 6:19–22 that when the exiles returned from Babylon they "celebrated the Passover on the fourteenth day of the first month," and then "joyfully celebrated the Feast of Unleavened Bread for seven days."[36]

The paschal sacrifice is characteristically rooted in the life of the pastoral nomad who follows a lunar calendar; the *matsah* is grounded in the life of the soil and the farmer, which is governed by a solar calendar. Since the two festivals occurred in close propinquity to each other, and both coincided with the time of the Exodus, all three elements merged and were fused into a unified entity. The pre-Israelite ingredients were stripped of their former content and were invested with completely new associations and meanings connected with the events of the Exodus.

14. remembrance Hebrew *zikkaron* involves action. See Comment to 2:24.

throughout the ages Literally, "for your generations," that is, for future annual celebration. This is referred to in rabbinic parlance as *pesah dorot*. Mishnah Pesaḥim 9:5 notes that the initial requirements—to select the offering on the tenth day of the month, to daub the blood with hyssop on the lintel and doorposts, and to eat the meal in haste—do not apply. In addition, in the future the celebration, with the prohibition on leaven, is to last seven days instead of the original one day.[37]

15. The essential characteristics of the newly ordained festival are now set forth. These are specified as being one week's duration, the eating of *matsot*, and the removal of leaven.

Based on the emphasis "at evening" in the parallel description of verse 18, rabbinic interpretation understands that only on the first night is there a positive duty to eat *matsah*. For the rest of the week this is optional,[38] although the independent prohibition on leaven remains in effect.

unleavened bread Extraordinarily stringent regulations govern the manufacture of *matsot*. Their sole ingredients are flour and water. The flour may be made only from grains that are susceptible to fermentation. These are listed in Mishnah Pesaḥim 2:5[39] as wheat, barley, emmer, rye, and oats, although in practice only wheat is used. The water to be mixed with the flour is first left standing

days you shall eat unleavened bread; on the very first day you shall remove leaven from your houses, for whoever eats leavened bread from the first day to the seventh day, that person shall be cut off from Israel.

הָרִאשׁוֹן תַּשְׁבִּיתוּ שְּׂאֹר מִבָּתֵּיכֶם כִּי ׀ כָּל־אֹכֵל
חָמֵץ וְנִכְרְתָה הַנֶּפֶשׁ הַהִוא מִיִּשְׂרָאֵל מִיּוֹם
הָרִאשֹׁן עַד־יוֹם הַשְּׁבִעִי:

overnight. *Matsah shemurah*, "carefully guarded *matsah*," which many Jews use to fulfill the obligation to eat *matsah* on the first night of Passover, is made from flour milled from wheat that has been scrupulously supervised from the time of the harvesting on. Regular *matsah* is baked from wheat flour that has been specially milled for the purpose and has been carefully supervised from the time of milling through the baking. The entire manufacturing process from the kneading to completion must take no more than eighteen minutes, during which period the dough is continuously manipulated in order to retard fermentation. As a further precaution, perforation is applied to allow any bubbles of air to escape.

on the very first day   Since festivals commence in the evening,[40] this injunction has traditionally been taken to mean that the leaven must have been removed prior to the time for the paschal offering on the fourteenth of the month.[41]

remove leaven   The positive command to eat *matsah* is supplemented by the strict prohibition on retaining or eating leaven or leavened food throughout the entire festival. This rule is repeated in verses 19–20 and again in 13:7.[42] Leaven, Hebrew *se'or*, is the leavening agent known as sourdough; "leavened food," Hebrew *hamets*, is food to which sourdough has been added to accelerate the rising of the dough. The term traditionally also includes the above-mentioned five species of grain that are subject to fermentation as they decompose.[43]

No reason is given for the prohibition on leaven. Verses 34 and 39 intimate that it is in reenactment of the original circumstances at the time of the Exodus, when the Israelites left Egypt in haste before the dough they had prepared had time to rise. However, since leaven is also forbidden with certain types of sacrifices that are wholly unconnected with the Passover, it must be banned on other grounds, perhaps because of its use in some pagan rite. In postbiblical times fermentation was associated with decomposition and decay and taken figuratively to symbolize moral and spiritual corruption.[44]

No instructions are given as to the manner in which *hamets* is to be "removed." In Jewish law any food containing even a minute admixture of it must be disposed of at least two hours before noon on the eve of Passover. Thereafter, one may not own it, possess it, eat it, or derive any benefit from it. Immediately after dark on the night preceding the eve of the festival, a search for leaven, known in Hebrew as *bedikat hamets*, takes place—even though the dwelling has previously been thoroughly swept and cleaned. Then a declaration of nullification is made over the residual leaven, which is burnt the following morning and again annulled. Another mode of disposal is by sale to a non-Jew (Heb. *mekhirat hamets*).

shall be cut off   There are thirty-six instances of this formula in the Torah, all listed in Mishnah Keritot 1:1. This punishment, known as *[hik]karet* in rabbinic parlance, is peculiar to ritual texts and is largely confined to offenses of a cultic and sexual nature. The Torah gives no definition of *karet*, and no analogy exists in Near Eastern sources. In most texts the impersonal, passive form of the verb is used, as here, so that not only the type of punishment but also the executive authority is uncertain. In Leviticus 20:1–6 the active first person is used with God as the subject of the verb: "I will set My face against that man and will cut him off from among his people." This reasonably presupposes that *karet* is not a penalty enforced by the courts but a punishment left to divine execution. Such is the understanding of the term in rabbinic literature, where it specifically means premature death and, according to some, also childlessness.[45] Certainly the general idea is that one who deliberately excludes himself from the religious community of Israel cannot be a beneficiary of the covenantal blessings and thereby dooms himself and his line to extinction. See *The JPS Torah Commentary* to Leviticus, Excursus 1 and Numbers, Excursus 36.

16You shall celebrate a sacred occasion on the first day, and a sacred occasion on the seventh day; no work at all shall be done on them; only what every person is to eat, that alone may be prepared for you. 17You shall observe the [Feast of] Unleavened Bread, for on this very day I brought your ranks out of the land of Egypt; you shall observe this day throughout the ages as an institution for all time. 18In the first month, from the fourteenth day of the month at evening, you shall eat unleavened bread until the twenty-first day of the month at evening. 19No leaven shall be found in your houses for seven days. For whoever eats what is leavened, that person shall be cut off from the community of Israel, whether he is a stranger or a citizen of the country. 20You shall eat nothing leavened; in all your settlements you shall eat unleavened bread.

21Moses then summoned all the elders of Israel and said to them, "Go, pick out lambs for your families, and slaughter the passover offering. 22Take a bunch of hyssop, dip it in

‎16 וּבַיּוֹם הָרִאשׁוֹן מִקְרָא־קֹדֶשׁ וּבַיּוֹם
הַשְּׁבִיעִי מִקְרָא־קֹדֶשׁ יִהְיֶה לָכֶם כָּל־מְלָאכָה
לֹא־יֵעָשֶׂה בָהֶם אַךְ אֲשֶׁר יֵאָכֵל לְכָל־נֶפֶשׁ הוּא
לְבַדּוֹ יֵעָשֶׂה לָכֶם: ‎17 וּשְׁמַרְתֶּם אֶת־הַמַּצּוֹת כִּי
בְּעֶצֶם הַיּוֹם הַזֶּה הוֹצֵאתִי אֶת־צִבְאוֹתֵיכֶם
מֵאֶרֶץ מִצְרָיִם וּשְׁמַרְתֶּם אֶת־הַיּוֹם הַזֶּה
לְדֹרֹתֵיכֶם חֻקַּת עוֹלָם: ‎18 בָּרִאשֹׁן בְּאַרְבָּעָה
עָשָׂר יוֹם לַחֹדֶשׁ בָּעֶרֶב תֹּאכְלוּ מַצֹּת עַד
יוֹם הָאֶחָד וְעֶשְׂרִים לַחֹדֶשׁ בָּעָרֶב: ‎19 שִׁבְעַת
יָמִים שְׂאֹר לֹא יִמָּצֵא בְּבָתֵּיכֶם כִּי| כָּל־אֹכֵל
מַחְמֶצֶת וְנִכְרְתָה הַנֶּפֶשׁ הַהִוא מֵעֲדַת יִשְׂרָאֵל
בַּגֵּר וּבְאֶזְרַח הָאָרֶץ: ‎20 כָּל־מַחְמֶצֶת לֹא תֹאכֵלוּ
בְּכֹל מוֹשְׁבֹתֵיכֶם תֹּאכְלוּ מַצּוֹת: פ חמישי
‎21 וַיִּקְרָא מֹשֶׁה לְכָל־זִקְנֵי יִשְׂרָאֵל וַיֹּאמֶר
אֲלֵהֶם מִשְׁכוּ וּקְחוּ לָכֶם צֹאן לְמִשְׁפְּחֹתֵיכֶם
וְשַׁחֲטוּ הַפָּסַח: ‎22 וּלְקַחְתֶּם אֲגֻדַּת אֵזוֹב וּטְבַלְתֶּם

16.   The first and last days of the festival possess special sanctity but not quite to the same degree as the Sabbath and Day of Atonement. The preparation of food on those particular days is exempted from the prohibition on performing labor; other leniencies pertain as well.[46]

17.   The rationale for the festival is now given.

the [Feast of] Unleavened Bread   This understanding of the Hebrew phrase as ellipsis is based on the ensuing expression "on this very day" as well as on the parallel passage in 23:15.[47] However, traditional Jewish interpretation is literal: "guard the *matsot*," that is, supervise the process to ensure that no fermentation occurs.[48]

I brought   This is an example of the "prophetic perfect."[49] The future is described as having already occurred because God's will inherently and ineluctably possesses the power of realization so that the time factor is inconsequential.

your ranks   See Comment to 6:26.

18.   As specified in Leviticus 23:32, the duration of all festivals is from evening to evening.

19-20.   *a stranger*   Hebrew *ger* is a foreigner who has taken up permanent residence in Israel. Like his fellow Israelite, he is required to abstain from possessing leaven for this one week because its presence within the closely knit community interferes with the ability of others to fulfill their religious obligation. But only the Israelite has the duty to eat *matsah*. See further verses 48–49.

INSTRUCTIONS FOR THE *PESAH* ARE RELAYED (vv. 21–28)

Moses relays to the people the divinely given instructions and supplements them with some clarifications.

21.   *Go, pick out*   Lekaḥ Tov and Abravanel construe the two verbs as alternatives: "Select a lamb from your flock if you possess one; otherwise, purchase one."

the blood that is in the basin, and apply some of the blood that is in the basin to the lintel and to the two doorposts. None of you shall go outside the door of his house until morning. 23For when the LORD goes through to smite the Egyptians, He will see the blood on the lintel and the two doorposts, and the LORD will pass over the door and not let the Destroyer enter and smite your home.

24"You shall observe this as an institution for all time, for you and for your descendants. 25And when you enter the land that the LORD will give you, as He has promised, you shall observe this rite. 26And when your children ask you, 'What do you mean by this rite?' 27you shall say, 'It is the passover sacrifice to the LORD, because He passed over the houses of the Israelites in Egypt when He smote the Egyptians, but saved our houses.'"

The people then bowed low in homage. 28And the Israelites went and did so; just as the LORD had commanded Moses and Aaron, so they did.

בַּדָּם אֲשֶׁר־בַּסַּף וְהִגַּעְתֶּם אֶל־הַמַּשְׁקוֹף וְאֶל־שְׁתֵּי הַמְּזוּזֹת מִן־הַדָּם אֲשֶׁר בַּסָּף וְאַתֶּם לֹא תֵצְאוּ אִישׁ מִפֶּתַח־בֵּיתוֹ עַד־בֹּקֶר: 23 וְעָבַר יְהוָה לִנְגֹּף אֶת־מִצְרַיִם וְרָאָה אֶת־הַדָּם עַל־הַמַּשְׁקוֹף וְעַל שְׁתֵּי הַמְּזוּזֹת וּפָסַח יְהוָה עַל־הַפֶּתַח וְלֹא יִתֵּן הַמַּשְׁחִית לָבֹא אֶל־בָּתֵּיכֶם לִנְגֹּף: 24 וּשְׁמַרְתֶּם אֶת־הַדָּבָר הַזֶּה לְחָק־לְךָ וּלְבָנֶיךָ עַד־עוֹלָם: 25 וְהָיָה כִּי־תָבֹאוּ אֶל־הָאָרֶץ אֲשֶׁר יִתֵּן יְהוָה לָכֶם כַּאֲשֶׁר דִּבֵּר וּשְׁמַרְתֶּם אֶת־הָעֲבֹדָה הַזֹּאת: 26 וְהָיָה כִּי־יֹאמְרוּ אֲלֵיכֶם בְּנֵיכֶם מָה הָעֲבֹדָה הַזֹּאת לָכֶם: 27 וַאֲמַרְתֶּם זֶבַח־פֶּסַח הוּא לַיהוָה אֲשֶׁר פָּסַח עַל־בָּתֵּי בְנֵי־יִשְׂרָאֵל בְּמִצְרַיִם בְּנָגְפּוֹ אֶת־מִצְרַיִם וְאֶת־בָּתֵּינוּ הִצִּיל וַיִּקֹּד הָעָם וַיִּשְׁתַּחֲווּ: 28 וַיֵּלְכוּ וַיַּעֲשׂוּ בְּנֵי יִשְׂרָאֵל כַּאֲשֶׁר צִוָּה יְהוָה אֶת־מֹשֶׁה וְאַהֲרֹן כֵּן עָשׂוּ: ס ששי

---

22. a bunch of hyssop This explains how the directive of verse 7 is to be carried out. Three of the hyssop's thin, woody branches make an ideal applicator. It is often so used in purificatory rites.[50]

the basin This is how Rabbi Akiba understood Hebrew *saf*. It has much philological support.[51] The Septuagint, however, translates "threshold," which is also the rendering of Rabbi Ishmael. It too can be sustained,[52] but it implies that the paschal offering was actually slaughtered at the entrance to the house and that the entire doorframe was daubed with its blood. The absence of any mention of the threshold in verses 7 and 23 favors Rabbi Akiba's interpretation.

None . . . shall go outside On this night of danger and vigilance, the security of the Israelites lay in maintaining family solidarity within the portals of their hallowed homes.

23. the Destroyer The plague, although personified, is not an independent demonic being. It can only operate within the limits fixed by God.[53]

24. observe this As Ramban notes, the reference is to the slaughtering of the Passover offering, not to the daubing of the blood.

25. when you enter the land Apart from the celebration on the first anniversary of the Exodus, as described in Numbers 9:1–5, no further mention of the actual observance of Passover appears in the account of the wilderness wanderings until after the crossing of the river Jordan, as recorded in Joshua 5:1–12.

as He has promised To the patriarchs. See Comment to 6:8.

26–27. The ritual has a pedagogic function. Its peculiarities arouse the curiosity of children and so afford the opportunity to impart knowledge of the national traditions to the young.

27. our houses The passage of time never diminishes the contemporaneity of the events. The national culture is nurtured by the memory of them and by their continual reenactment, a theme stressed in the Passover Haggadah.

28. The reference is to the selection, guarding, and slaughtering of the lamb and to the application of its blood.

²⁹In the middle of the night the LORD struck down all the first-born in the land of Egypt, from the first-born of Pharaoh who sat on the throne to the first-born of the captive who was in the dungeon, and all the first-born of the cattle. ³⁰And Pharaoh arose in the night, with all his courtiers and all the Egyptians—because there was a loud cry in Egypt; for there was no house where there was not someone dead. ³¹He summoned Moses and Aaron in the night and said, "Up, depart from among my people, you and the Israelites with you! Go, worship the LORD as you said! ³²Take also your flocks and your herds, as you said, and begone! And may you bring a blessing upon me also!"

³³The Egyptians urged the people on, impatient to have them leave the country, for they said, "We shall all be dead." ³⁴So the people took their dough before it was leavened, their kneading bowls wrapped in their cloaks upon their shoulders. ³⁵The Israelites had done Moses' bidding and borrowed from the Egyptians objects of silver and gold, and clothing. ³⁶And the LORD had disposed the Egyptians favorably toward the people, and they let them have their request; thus they stripped the Egyptians.

³⁷The Israelites journeyed from Rameses to Succoth, about six hundred thousand men on foot, aside from children. ³⁸Moreover, a mixed multitude went up with them, and very much livestock, both flocks and herds.

29 וַיְהִי ׀ בַּחֲצִי הַלַּיְלָה וַיהוָה הִכָּה כָל־בְּכוֹר בְּאֶרֶץ מִצְרַיִם מִבְּכֹר פַּרְעֹה הַיֹּשֵׁב עַל־כִּסְאוֹ עַד בְּכוֹר הַשְּׁבִי אֲשֶׁר בְּבֵית הַבּוֹר וְכֹל בְּכוֹר בְּהֵמָה: 30 וַיָּקָם פַּרְעֹה לַיְלָה הוּא וְכָל־עֲבָדָיו וְכָל־מִצְרַיִם וַתְּהִי צְעָקָה גְדֹלָה בְּמִצְרָיִם כִּי־אֵין בַּיִת אֲשֶׁר אֵין־שָׁם מֵת: 31 וַיִּקְרָא לְמֹשֶׁה וּלְאַהֲרֹן לַיְלָה וַיֹּאמֶר קוּמוּ צְּאוּ מִתּוֹךְ עַמִּי גַּם־אַתֶּם גַּם־בְּנֵי יִשְׂרָאֵל וּלְכוּ עִבְדוּ אֶת־יְהוָה כְּדַבֶּרְכֶם: 32 גַּם־צֹאנְכֶם גַּם־בְּקַרְכֶם קְחוּ כַּאֲשֶׁר דִּבַּרְתֶּם וָלֵכוּ וּבֵרַכְתֶּם גַּם־אֹתִי:

33 וַתֶּחֱזַק מִצְרַיִם עַל־הָעָם לְמַהֵר לְשַׁלְּחָם מִן־הָאָרֶץ כִּי אָמְרוּ כֻּלָּנוּ מֵתִים: 34 וַיִּשָּׂא הָעָם אֶת־בְּצֵקוֹ טֶרֶם יֶחְמָץ מִשְׁאֲרֹתָם צְרֻרֹת בְּשִׂמְלֹתָם עַל־שִׁכְמָם: 35 וּבְנֵי־יִשְׂרָאֵל עָשׂוּ כִּדְבַר מֹשֶׁה וַיִּשְׁאֲלוּ מִמִּצְרַיִם כְּלֵי־כֶסֶף וּכְלֵי זָהָב וּשְׂמָלֹת: 36 וַיהוָה נָתַן אֶת־חֵן הָעָם בְּעֵינֵי מִצְרַיִם וַיַּשְׁאִלוּם וַיְנַצְּלוּ אֶת־מִצְרָיִם: פ

37 וַיִּסְעוּ בְנֵי־יִשְׂרָאֵל מֵרַעְמְסֵס סֻכֹּתָה כְּשֵׁשׁ־מֵאוֹת אֶלֶף רַגְלִי הַגְּבָרִים לְבַד מִטָּף: 38 וְגַם־עֵרֶב רַב עָלָה אִתָּם וְצֹאן וּבָקָר מִקְנֶה כָּבֵד מְאֹד:

THE TENTH PLAGUE   (vv. 29–36)

All preparations having been completed, the stage is set for the anticipated climactic plague that will finally secure the release of Israel from Egyptian bondage.[54] The Torah recognizes societal responsibility; thus, the entire Egyptian people is subject to judgment for having tolerated the inflexibly perverse will of the pharaoh.

29.   See Comment to 11:5.

30–32.   The king himself has to rise during the night, thereby compounding his humiliation at having to surrender unconditionally to Moses' demands. By summoning Moses and Aaron, he must retract the arrogant threat made at their last meeting (10:28). For him to seek their blessing is thus the ultimate humbling of the despot.

31.   *the Israelites*   Pharaoh uses this term for the first time, thereby granting recognition at last to Israel as a national entity. The story of the oppression, which opened with this term (1:1), now closes with it.

34.   *before it was leavened*   In verse 39 this note is amplified in such a way as to provide a clear, if implicit, explanation for the eating of *matsot* on Passover. A similar reason is given in Deuteronomy 16:3: "You shall eat unleavened bread, bread of distress—for you departed from the land of Egypt hurriedly." That statement is intelligible only in light of the two verses in the present chapter. Since the eating of the *matsot* was ordained and presumably carried out before the tenth plague struck (v. 8), the present rationale is a reinterpretation, transformation, and historicization of a preexisting practice.[55]

³⁹And they baked unleavened cakes of the dough that they had taken out of Egypt, for it was not leavened, since they had been driven out of Egypt and could not delay; nor had they prepared any provisions for themselves.

⁴⁰The length of time that the Israelites lived in Egypt was four hundred and thirty years; ⁴¹at the end of the four hundred and thirtieth year, to the very day, all the ranks of the LORD departed from the land of Egypt. ⁴²That was for

39 וַיֹּאפ֨וּ אֶת־הַבָּצֵ֜ק אֲשֶׁ֨ר הוֹצִ֧יאוּ מִמִּצְרַ֛יִם עֻגֹ֥ת מַצּ֖וֹת כִּ֣י לֹ֣א חָמֵ֑ץ כִּֽי־גֹרְשׁ֣וּ מִמִּצְרַ֗יִם וְלֹ֤א יָֽכְלוּ֙ לְהִתְמַהְמֵ֔הַּ וְגַם־צֵדָ֖ה לֹא־עָשׂ֥וּ לָהֶֽם׃
40 וּמוֹשַׁב֙ בְּנֵ֣י יִשְׂרָאֵ֔ל אֲשֶׁ֥ר יָשְׁב֖וּ בְּמִצְרָ֑יִם שְׁלֹשִׁ֣ים שָׁנָ֔ה וְאַרְבַּ֥ע מֵא֖וֹת שָׁנָֽה׃ 41 וַיְהִ֗י מִקֵּץ֙ שְׁלֹשִׁ֣ים שָׁנָ֔ה וְאַרְבַּ֥ע מֵא֖וֹת שָׁנָ֑ה וַיְהִ֗י בְּעֶ֙צֶם֙ הַיּ֣וֹם הַזֶּ֔ה יָ֥צְא֛וּ כָּל־צִבְא֥וֹת יְהוָ֖ה מֵאֶ֥רֶץ מִצְרָֽיִם׃

THE EXODUS (vv. 37–42)

37. *Rameses* This city served as the assembly point for the departing Israelites. For its location, see Comment to 1:11.

Succoth This is apparently Egyptian Tjeku, mentioned on several monuments and in a hieroglyphic papyrus. It is said to have been a day's journey from the royal palace at Rameses. Tjeku was the capital of the eighth nome of Lower Egypt in the eastern part of the Delta. The region is known to have served as pastureland for Semitic tribes and was the usual Egyptian gateway to and from Asia.

six hundred thousand This figure would yield a total Israelite population of over two million souls, a number that poses intractable problems. True, it reflects the phenomenal growth referred to in chapter 1, for over a sufficiently long period the original seventy adult male immigrants[56] could have increased to that number. Further, the demographic data given for the forty years of the wilderness wanderings are more or less internally consistent and accord with this figure.[57] Nevertheless, serious questions may be raised in relation to an estimated total Egyptian population of four to five million in the fourteenth century B.C.E., and in view of the inability of either the eastern part of the Nile Delta or the peninsula of Sinai to sustain such a vast population with water and food. There is, further, the logistics involved in moving two million people together with their cattle and herds across the Sea of Reeds with the Egyptian chariots in hot pursuit.

In response to these problems, it has been suggested that Hebrew *'elef*, usually rendered "thousand," here means a "clan"[58] or that it signifies a small military unit—the number of fighting men levied from each tribe.[59] Another theory construes the total number as envisaging the Israelite population at the close of the "Exodus era,"[60] which culminated with the completion of the Temple by King Solomon: 600,000 adult males would be a realistic statistic for this period.

38. *a mixed multitude* Varied groups of forced laborers seem to have taken advantage of the confused situation and fled the country with the Israelites. Ibn Ezra identified them with the people referred to as "riffraff" in Numbers 11:4.[61]

40–41. This historical summation does not exactly accord with the four hundred years of Egyptian oppression predicted in Genesis 15:13. The Mekhilta[62] resolves the discrepancy by attributing the thirty-year difference to the interval between God's covenant with Abraham and the birth of Isaac, although the text speaks clearly enough only of the Egyptian episode. The inclusion of the sojourn in Canaan in the computation is explicit in the texts of the Samaritan recension and Septuagint translation. The variant in this latter is noted in rabbinic sources.[63] Ibn Ezra begins the reckoning with the departure of Abraham from Haran for Canaan. And, in fact, exactly two hundred and fifteen years elapsed between that event and Jacob's migration to Egypt,[64] yielding the same time span for the stay of the Israelites in Egypt. This kind of symmetry follows a pattern well established in the patriarchal narratives and elsewhere in the Book of Genesis.[65] Thus, Abraham lived seventy-five years in the home of his father and seventy-five years in the lifetime of his son Isaac. He was one hundred years of age at the birth of Isaac, and he lived one hundred years in Canaan. Jacob lived seventeen years with Joseph in Canaan and a like period with him in Egypt. Ten generations separated Noah from Adam, and another ten generations, Abraham from Noah. In the light of these facts it

the LORD a night of vigil to bring them out of the land of Egypt; that same night is the LORD's, one of vigil for all the children of Israel throughout the ages.

⁴³The LORD said to Moses and Aaron: This is the law of the passover offering: No foreigner shall eat of it. ⁴⁴But any slave a man has bought may eat of it once he has been circumcised. ⁴⁵No bound or hired laborer shall eat of it. ⁴⁶It shall be eaten in one house: you shall not take any of the

42 לֵיל שִׁמֻּרִים הוּא לַיהוָה לְהוֹצִיאָם מֵאֶרֶץ מִצְרָיִם הוּא־הַלַּיְלָה הַזֶּה לַיהוָה שִׁמֻּרִים לְכָל־בְּנֵי יִשְׂרָאֵל לְדֹרֹתָם: פ

43 וַיֹּאמֶר יְהוָה אֶל־מֹשֶׁה וְאַהֲרֹן זֹאת חֻקַּת הַפָּסַח כָּל־בֶּן־נֵכָר לֹא־יֹאכַל בּוֹ: 44 וְכָל־עֶבֶד אִישׁ מִקְנַת־כָּסֶף וּמַלְתָּה אֹתוֹ אָז יֹאכַל בּוֹ: 45 תּוֹשָׁב וְשָׂכִיר לֹא־יֹאכַל־בּוֹ: 46 בְּבַיִת אֶחָד

may be that the neatly balanced periods of time are intended to be rhetorical rather than literal; that is, they underline the biblical ideal of history as the fulfillment of God's deliberate design. In the world view of the Bible, history cannot be merely a series of disconnected and haphazard incidents.

42. The final night in Egypt is described as one of vigil for both God and Israel. It was one that God, so to speak, watched over, having long designated it to be the night of redemption.[66] In turn, it was a night that Israel was enjoined to safeguard for all time. According to a talmudic interpretation, it was "a night ever under protection from malevolent beings."[67] Later Jewish history gave this particular exposition of the text an ironically tragic twist, for throughout Christian Europe in the Middle Ages, and in many lands even into the twentieth century, the night of Passover became a night of anguished vigil for Jews on account of the "blood accusation," the monstrous fabrication that Jews use Christian blood for the Passover rites. As a consequence of this calumny, the frenzied masses, incited by the clergy, would perpetrate bloody pogroms against Jews, and the night of vigil became a night of vigilance against malevolent human beings.

EXCLUSIONARY REGULATIONS (vv. 43–49)

This final section bears its own caption: "The Law of the Passover." It largely defines who is ineligible to celebrate the festival, with primary emphasis on the practice of circumcision. Being the physical token of God's covenant[68] and a symbol of consecration and commitment to a life lived in the consciousness of that covenant, it is the indispensable prerequisite for those who participate in the paschal offering.[69]

Thus the emphasis on the importance of that rite frames the story of Israel's redemption from Egyptian slavery. This emphasis was forcefully expressed in 4:24–26, when Moses set out to return to Egypt to commence his mission of liberation, and it is now stressed once again at the moment of the successful fulfillment of that mission.

43. *foreigner* Hebrew *ben nekhar* is a non-Israelite who resides in the land temporarily, usually for purposes of commerce.[70] He does not profess the religion of Israel and does not identify with the community's historical experiences. He is therefore exempted from the religious obligations and restrictions imposed on Israelites.[71] It is to be noted that an invocation for foreigners is included in King Solomon's prayer at the dedication of the Temple.[72] Rabbinic interpretation, based on the literal meaning of *nekhar*, "alienation," extended the exclusionary rule to a Jew who has apostatized[73] and thereby alienated himself from the community of Israel.

44. The privately owned slave, once circumcised in accordance with the law of Genesis 17:12–13, is treated as a member of the family and may participate in the Passover.[74]

45. *bound or hired laborer* Two categories of non-Israelite wage earners who do not have the status of members of a household.[75]

46. *in one house* This logically connects with the preceding verses, which stress that only those included within a household may participate. None may leave the house because every Israelite must be accounted for and accessible when the signal is given to depart.

flesh outside the house; nor shall you break a bone of it. [47]The whole community of Israel shall offer it. [48]If a stranger who dwells with you would offer the passover to the LORD, all his males must be circumcised; then he shall be admitted to offer it; he shall then be as a citizen of the country. But no uncircumcised person may eat of it. [49]There shall be one law for the citizen and for the stranger who dwells among you.

[50]And all the Israelites did so; as the LORD had commanded Moses and Aaron, so they did.

[51]That very day the LORD freed the Israelites from the land of Egypt, troop by troop.

יֹאכֵל לֹא־תוֹצִיא מִן־הַבַּיִת מִן־הַבָּשָׂר חוּצָה וְעֶצֶם לֹא תִשְׁבְּרוּ־בוֹ: 47 כָּל־עֲדַת יִשְׂרָאֵל יַעֲשׂוּ אֹתוֹ: 48 וְכִי־יָגוּר אִתְּךָ גֵּר וְעָשָׂה פֶסַח לַיהוָה הִמּוֹל לוֹ כָל־זָכָר וְאָז יִקְרַב לַעֲשֹׂתוֹ וְהָיָה כְּאֶזְרַח הָאָרֶץ וְכָל־עָרֵל לֹא־יֹאכַל בּוֹ: 49 תּוֹרָה אַחַת יִהְיֶה לָאֶזְרָח וְלַגֵּר הַגָּר בְּתוֹכְכֶם:

50 וַיַּעֲשׂוּ כָּל־בְּנֵי יִשְׂרָאֵל כַּאֲשֶׁר צִוָּה יְהוָה אֶת־מֹשֶׁה וְאֶת־אַהֲרֹן כֵּן עָשׂוּ: ס

51 וַיְהִי בְּעֶצֶם הַיּוֹם הַזֶּה הוֹצִיא יְהוָה אֶת־בְּנֵי יִשְׂרָאֵל מֵאֶרֶץ מִצְרַיִם עַל־צִבְאֹתָם: פ

שביעי

not break a bone Presumably, to suck out the marrow. Baal Ha-Turim suggests that such behavior would imply that they were still hungry, even though the Passover meal should have been completely satisfying.

48–49. These instructions relate unmistakably to the situation envisaged in verse 25. The stranger in Israel enjoyed numerous rights and privileges, such as the benefits of the Sabbath rest, the protection afforded by the cities of refuge, and access to a share of certain tithes and to the produce of the Sabbatical year.[76] He could offer sacrifices if he so pleased[77] and could even participate in religious festivals. He was also obligated to refrain from certain actions that undermined the social, moral, and spiritual well-being of the dominant society, such as immorality, idolatry, blasphemy, and the consumption of blood.[78] He was not required to celebrate the Passover; but if he desired to do so, and thus identify himself and his family with the national experience of Israel, he had first to submit to circumcision.[79] Having done so, no discrimination between him and the citizen was allowed.[80] Just like an uncircumcised non-Israelite, so an uncircumcised Israelite also was excluded.[81]

50. This refers to the eating of the paschal offering.

51. A resumptive repetition of verse 41. It picks up the narrative of verses 37–41 following the digression concerning ritual regulations. The Masoretic scribal division seems to reflect a tradition that connects the verse to the following chapter, indicating that the ensuing law of the first-born was promulgated on the very day of the Exodus. Rashbam, Ibn Ezra, and Ralbag all construe the verse in this manner.

CHAPTER 13

Commemorative Rituals   (vv. 1–16)

This section continues the process of historicizing existing institutions by reinterpreting them in terms of the Exodus experiences. The revitalized ancient rituals, now charged with new historical meaning, serve to perpetuate the memory of those events by making them living realities for succeeding generations.

In this section, the key to the association of topics—historical and natural events—is the coincidence of the liberation from Egypt with the spring (v. 4), the season of nature's rebirth. It is the time of the new barley harvest and the season when animals begin their reproductive cycle.

THE INSTALLATION OF THE FIRST-BORN   (vv. 1–2)

1. This simple formula always introduces some specific instruction given to Moses personally—a communication not relayed to the people. It usually requires that he initiate some action[1]—in this instance, the consecration of the first-born.

13 The LORD spoke further to Moses, saying, ²"Consecrate to Me every first-born; man and beast, the first issue of every womb among the Israelites is Mine."

³And Moses said to the people,

"Remember this day, on which you went free from Egypt, the house of bondage, how the LORD freed you from it with a mighty hand: no leavened bread shall be eaten. ⁴You go free on this day, in the month of Abib. ⁵So, when

יְ"ג וַיְדַבֵּר יְהֹוָה אֶל־מֹשֶׁה לֵּאמֹר: 2 קַדֶּשׁ־לִי
כָל־בְּכוֹר פֶּטֶר כָּל־רֶחֶם בִּבְנֵי יִשְׂרָאֵל
בָּאָדָם וּבַבְּהֵמָה לִי הוּא:
3 וַיֹּאמֶר מֹשֶׁה אֶל־הָעָם
זָכוֹר אֶת־הַיּוֹם הַזֶּה אֲשֶׁר יְצָאתֶם
מִמִּצְרַיִם מִבֵּית עֲבָדִים כִּי בְּחֹזֶק יָד הוֹצִיא
יְהֹוָה אֶתְכֶם מִזֶּה וְלֹא יֵאָכֵל חָמֵץ: 4 הַיּוֹם אַתֶּם
יֹצְאִים בְּחֹדֶשׁ הָאָבִיב: 5 וְהָיָה כִי־יְבִיאֲךָ יְהֹוָה

2. In many ancient cultures the miracle of new life was considered to be a divine gift. It was widely believed that the first fruits of the soil, of animal fecundity, and of human fertility were endowed by nature with intrinsic holiness. The present instruction to Moses to consecrate the first-born may therefore be a polemic against such pagan notions. The first-born belongs to God solely by reason of an act of divine will decreed at the time of the Exodus and not on account of any inherent sanctity. Their status is dissociated completely from the then contemporary ideas and practices.

It is explicitly related in Numbers 3:12 and 8:16,18 that in the course of the wilderness wanderings the Levites supplanted the first-born in assuming priestly and ritual functions. It may therefore be safely inferred that Moses is here instructed to install the first-born to fulfill priestly duties. Mishnah Zevaḥim 14:4 expresses the developments this way: "Before the creation of the Tabernacle, shrines (Heb. *bamot*) were permitted, and the worship was performed by the first-born; once the Tabernacle was erected, the shrines were prohibited, and the worship was performed by the priests [of the tribe of Levi]."

Consecrate to Me This instruction usually involves both a purificatory rite and an induction ceremony. The former requires bathing, laundering of clothes, and abstention from ritual defilement on the part of the initiate. The latter entails an investiture performed by a superior.[2]

beast Verse 12 restricts the requirement to the male animal, which would more likely be expendable, since animal breeding requires many females and few males.

Nothing is stated concerning the law of the first fruits of the soil because they cannot be connected with the events of the tenth plague and the Exodus itself, but only with the conquest and settlement of the land. They are treated in later texts.[3]

the first issue of every womb According to Baḥya ben Asher, the first-born of the mother rather than of the father is dedicated because paternity cannot be proved.

THE LAW OF *MATSOT* AND *TEFILLIN* (vv. 3–10)

Israel's liberation from Egypt is to be an event that is indelibly imprinted upon its memory, individually and collectively. A set of symbols is created to actualize the experiences.

3. Remember See Comment to 2:24.

this day The fifteenth of the first month.

the house of bondage Literally, "house of slaves."[4] This designation for Egypt, frequent in Deuteronomy, gives voice to the particular experience of Israel in that land. It may derive from the Egyptian practice of settling the labor gangs in workmen's villages in proximity to the site of the project for which they were conscripted. These villages were wholly enclosed by walls. One such has been uncovered at Deir el-Medinah, near Thebes. It served the laborers engaged in the construction of royal tombs in the Valley of the Kings. To the Israelite conscripts, such a village may have appeared to be a gigantic "slave house."

no leavened bread Denying oneself all benefit from anything containing leaven during Passover is one means by which the command to "remember" is fulfilled.

the LORD has brought you into the land of the Canaanites, the Hittites, the Amorites, the Hivites, and the Jebusites, which He swore to your fathers to give you, a land flowing with milk and honey, you shall observe in this month the following practice:

⁶"Seven days you shall eat unleavened bread, and on the seventh day there shall be a festival of the LORD. ⁷Throughout the seven days unleavened bread shall be eaten; no leavened bread shall be found with you, and no leaven shall be found in all your territory. ⁸And you shall explain to your son on that day, 'It is because of what the LORD did for me when I went free from Egypt.'

⁹"And this shall serve you as a sign on your hand and as a reminder on your forehead—in order that the Teaching of the LORD may be in your mouth—that with a mighty hand the LORD freed you from Egypt. ¹⁰You shall keep this institution at its set time from year to year.

אֶל־אֶרֶץ הַכְּנַעֲנִי וְהַחִתִּי וְהָאֱמֹרִי וְהַחִוִּי
וְהַיְבוּסִי אֲשֶׁר נִשְׁבַּע לַאֲבֹתֶיךָ לָתֶת לָךְ
אֶרֶץ זָבַת חָלָב וּדְבָשׁ וְעָבַדְתָּ אֶת־הָעֲבֹדָה הַזֹּאת
בַּחֹדֶשׁ הַזֶּה: ⁶ שִׁבְעַת יָמִים תֹּאכַל מַצֹּת וּבַיּוֹם הַשְּׁבִיעִי
חַג לַיהוָה: ⁷ מַצּוֹת יֵאָכֵל אֵת שִׁבְעַת הַיָּמִים
וְלֹא־יֵרָאֶה לְךָ חָמֵץ וְלֹא־יֵרָאֶה לְךָ שְׂאֹר
בְּכָל־גְּבֻלֶךָ: ⁸ וְהִגַּדְתָּ לְבִנְךָ בַּיּוֹם הַהוּא לֵאמֹר
בַּעֲבוּר זֶה עָשָׂה יְהוָה לִי בְּצֵאתִי מִמִּצְרָיִם:
⁹ וְהָיָה לְךָ לְאוֹת עַל־יָדְךָ וּלְזִכָּרוֹן בֵּין
עֵינֶיךָ לְמַעַן תִּהְיֶה תּוֹרַת יְהוָה בְּפִיךָ כִּי בְּיָד
חֲזָקָה הוֹצִאֲךָ יְהוָה מִמִּצְרָיִם: ¹⁰ וְשָׁמַרְתָּ אֶת־
הַחֻקָּה הַזֹּאת לְמוֹעֲדָהּ מִיָּמִים יָמִימָה: ס

5. See Comment to 3:8.

practice Hebrew 'avodah is word play on "bondage" in verse 3.[5] Service of God in freedom in Israel's own land is contrasted with the service to the pharaoh in Egyptian slavery.

6. Another commemorative stratagem, this one a positive action: the eating of *matsot*.

the seventh day By tradition it was on the seventh day of the Exodus that the pursuing Egyptians drowned in the Sea of Reeds. The emphasis here—before the Exodus—on the special character of the seventh day[6] disengages it from any celebration of Egypt's defeat.

7. See Comment to 12:15.

8. **you shall explain** Not necessarily in response to any question.[7] The parent must take the initiative in instructing the children. From Hebrew *ve-higgadta* comes Haggadah, the title of the book containing the rituals and readings for the Passover night ceremonials.

9. As Rashbam recognized, the idea is that observance of the foregoing precepts possesses the same commemorative function in relation to the Exodus as do physical memory-aiding devices placed on the hand and head.[8] Traditionally, the verse has been interpreted as instituting the *tefillin* (commonly rendered "phylacteries" in English), the wearing of which is incumbent upon adult Jewish males during the weekday morning prayers. See Excursus 5.

your hand Which one is not specified. Tradition takes it as referring to the left arm.[9]

forehead Literally, "between your eyes"; the Hebrew has always been interpreted to refer to the forehead. This is confirmed by Deuteronomy 14:1 and by the context of an Ugaritic passage in which the same phrase appears.[10]

Teaching of the LORD Hebrew *torat YHVH*. While this first appearance of this biblical phrase cannot yet refer to the canonized Torah, it does presuppose a fixed text that can be memorized and recited.[11]

THE REDEMPTION OF THE FIRST-BORN (vv. 11–16)

Verse 2 ordained the immediate consecration of the first-born. This section deals with the treatment of the first-born following settlement in the promised land. The animal firstling is to retain its status and so belong to God, but the priestly status of the human first-born is to be revoked and their

¹¹"And when the LORD has brought you into the land of the Canaanites, as He swore to you and to your fathers, and has given it to you, ¹²you shall set apart for the LORD every first issue of the womb: every male firstling that your cattle drop shall be the LORD's. ¹³But every firstling ass you shall redeem with a sheep; if you do not redeem it, you must break its neck. And you must redeem every first-born male among your children. ¹⁴And when, in time to come, your son asks you, saying, 'What does this mean?' you shall say to him, 'It was with a mighty hand that the LORD brought us out from Egypt, the house of bondage. ¹⁵When Pharaoh

יא וְהָיָ֞ה כִּֽי־יְבִֽאֲךָ֤ יְהוָה֙ אֶל־אֶ֣רֶץ הַֽכְּנַעֲנִ֔י
כַּאֲשֶׁ֛ר נִשְׁבַּ֥ע לְךָ֖ וְלַֽאֲבֹתֶ֑יךָ וּנְתָנָ֖הּ לָֽךְ׃
יב וְהַעֲבַרְתָּ֥ כָל־פֶּֽטֶר־רֶ֖חֶם לַֽיהוָ֑ה וְכָל־פֶּ֣טֶר ׀ שֶׁ֣גֶר
בְּהֵמָ֗ה אֲשֶׁ֨ר יִהְיֶ֥ה לְךָ֛ הַזְּכָרִ֖ים לַֽיהוָֽה׃ יג וְכָל־
פֶּ֤טֶר חֲמֹר֙ תִּפְדֶּ֣ה בְשֶׂ֔ה וְאִם־לֹ֥א תִפְדֶּ֖ה
וַֽעֲרַפְתּ֑וֹ וְכֹ֨ל בְּכ֥וֹר אָדָ֛ם בְּבָנֶ֖יךָ תִּפְדֶּֽה׃ מפטיר
יד וְהָיָ֞ה כִּֽי־יִשְׁאָלְךָ֥ בִנְךָ֛ מָחָ֖ר לֵאמֹ֣ר מַה־זֹּ֑את
וְאָמַרְתָּ֣ אֵלָ֔יו בְּחֹ֣זֶק יָ֗ד הֽוֹצִיאָ֧נוּ יְהוָ֛ה מִמִּצְרַ֖יִם
מִבֵּ֥ית עֲבָדִֽים׃ טו וַיְהִ֗י כִּֽי־הִקְשָׁ֣ה פַרְעֹה֘ לְשַׁלְּחֵנוּ֒

functions taken over by the tribe of Levi. Hence, first-born sons are to be desacralized by "redemption," which explains why this section does not immediately follow verse 2.

12. *set apart* Hebrew *le-haʿavir le-* denotes transference of property.¹²

issue of the womb A first-born by cesarean section is thus exempt from the redemption requirement.¹³

your cattle drop The Hebrew stem *sh-g-r* is used in biblical Hebrew only as a noun form *sheger* (construct *shegar*). In Aramaic the stem means "to cast, throw"; hence, the present translation. Elsewhere in the Torah the noun always appears in the phrase *shegar ʾalafeikha*, "the calving of your herd," and always in parallel with *ʿashterot tsoʾnekha*, "the lambing of your flock."¹⁴ *ʿAshterot* (construct pl.; sing. *ʿashtoret*) can be traced back to the name of the Canaanite goddess¹⁵ of generation and fecundity, identified with the Mesopotamian Ishtar and the Greek Astarte (the latter assimilated to the goddess Aphrodite). This makes it likely that the parallel *sheger*, too, is a term for fertility that is derived from the name of a fertility deity. Indeed, *shgr* as a divine name appears in a Punic personal name from Carthage, *ʾbdshgr*, "Servant of Shgr," and has turned up in a list of gods from Ugarit following *ʿttr* (Ishtar). Moreover, in the Balaam inscription from Deir ʿAlla in Jordan, a deity *shgr* occurs together with *ʿshtr*.¹⁶ There is no doubt that Hebrew *sheger* is a pagan divine name—the origin of which was lost in Israel—that was used as a metaphor for fecundity.

13. *firstling ass* This is the only ritually unclean animal that needs to be redeemed,¹⁷ in this case by giving a priest a sheep as a replacement. The ass was the standard means of transport and a beast of burden for nomadic peoples. As Ibn Ezra observes, it was most likely the only unclean domestic animal possessed by the Israelites in Egypt. The present instruction is repeated in 34:20.

break its neck Because the owner deprives the priest of a sheep by refusing to redeem the ass, he himself is denied the use of that animal.¹⁸ In rabbinic tradition the "breaking of the neck" was performed by a blow from behind with a hatchet.¹⁹ The reason for this exceptional form of slaughter is to avoid the appearance of performing a sacrifice of an unclean animal.

redeem every first-born male The mode of redemption is not given, presupposing some familiar and established practice. Numbers 18:16 makes clear that a payment of five silver shekels is to be made to the priest when the first-born is a month old.²⁰ The ceremony of *pidyon ha-ben*, "redemption of the [first-born] son," continues to this day. It is performed on the thirty-first day of life, unless it is a Sabbath or holy day, in which case it is postponed until the following day. It is the father's duty to have his son redeemed. Should he neglect to do so, the son is obligated to redeem himself on reaching the age of maturity. The son of a Kohen or Levite or of the daughter of a Kohen or Levite married to a Jew is exempt, as is one born by cesarean section.

The details of the ceremony are set forth in the traditional Jewish prayer book. It is customary nowadays to use special "redemption coins" minted for the purpose by the State of Israel.

14. See Comment to verse 8.

in time to come Hebrew *maḥar*, usually "tomorrow," sometimes refers to the indefinite future.²¹

stubbornly refused to let us go, the LORD slew every first-born in the land of Egypt, the first-born of both man and beast. Therefore I sacrifice to the LORD every first male issue of the womb, but redeem every first-born among my sons.'

16"And so it shall be as a sign upon your hand and as a symbol on your forehead that with a mighty hand the LORD freed us from Egypt."

וַיַּהֲרֹג יְהוָֹה כָּל־בְּכוֹר בְּאֶרֶץ מִצְרַיִם מִבְּכֹר אָדָם וְעַד־בְּכוֹר בְּהֵמָה עַל־כֵּן אֲנִי זֹבֵחַ לַיהוָֹה כָּל־פֶּטֶר רֶחֶם הַזְּכָרִים וְכָל־בְּכוֹר בָּנַי אֶפְדֶּה:

16 וְהָיָה לְאוֹת עַל־יָדְכָה וּלְטוֹטָפֹת בֵּין עֵינֶיךָ כִּי בְּחֹזֶק יָד הוֹצִיאָנוּ יְהוָֹה מִמִּצְרָיִם:
ס

BESHALLAH

17Now when Pharaoh let the people go, God did not lead them by way of the land of the Philistines, although it was nearer; for God said, "The people may have a change of heart when they see war, and return to Egypt." 18So God

בשלח

17 וַיְהִי בְּשַׁלַּח פַּרְעֹה אֶת־הָעָם וְלֹא־נָחָם אֱלֹהִים דֶּרֶךְ אֶרֶץ פְּלִשְׁתִּים כִּי קָרוֹב הוּא כִּי אָמַר אֱלֹהִים פֶּן־יִנָּחֵם הָעָם בִּרְאֹתָם מִלְחָמָה וְשָׁבוּ מִצְרָיְמָה:

this The ceremony of redemption.[22]

15. The "mighty hand" (v. 14) is explained as referring to the slaying of the Egyptian first-born.

16. See Comment to verse 9.

a symbol Hebrew *totefet* (pl. *totafot*) has not been satisfactorily explained. The term replaces *zikkaron*, "a reminder," of verse 9, and it appears again in the same context in Deuteronomy 6:8 and 11:18. In Mishnaic Hebrew it denotes a head ornament of some kind,[23] explained in the Gemara as encompassing a woman's head from ear to ear.[24] An alternative explanation cited there is "a charm containing balsam,"[25] apparently worn as an amulet to ward off the evil eye.[26] In Aramaic *totafta'* is the Targum's equivalent for Hebrew *pe'er*, "a turban," in Ezekiel 24:17,23,[27] and also for Hebrew *'ets'adah*, "an armlet," in 2 Samuel 1:10. The Arabic stem *ṭāfa*, "to go around, encircle," may underlie the term.

The Exodus (13:17–14:31)

INTO THE WILDERNESS (vv. 17–22)

Beshallaḥ The narrative, which was interrupted at 12:42, now continues.

17. *let ... go* The Hebrew verb *shillaḥ* is richly allusive. First, it reconnects with 12:33. Second, it carries the double juridical sense of divorce and of emancipation of a slave[28] and is highly evocative. Finally, because *shillaḥ* is the key term in each of the three divine promises of redemption given to Moses, its presence here intimates their fulfillment.[29]

God ... lead them Not Moses but God is the supreme actor.[30]

by way of the land of the Philistines The shortest land route from the Nile Delta to Canaan. It was the southern segment of the thousand-mile (1,600 km.) international artery of transportation that led up to Megiddo, into Asia Minor, and then on to Mesopotamia. Beginning at the Egyptian fortress city of Tjaru (Sile), the highway followed the shoreline fairly closely, except where the shifting sand dunes and the land formation dictated otherwise.[31] The army of Thutmose III took ten days to cover the 150-mile (240 km.) distance to Gaza. The Egyptian name for this part of the road was the "Ways of Horus"; it was the standard route followed by the pharaohs for incursions into Asia, and the pharaohs were considered to be the living embodiments on earth of the god Horus.

The "land of the Philistines" is the name given here to the stretch of territory in Canaan

led the people roundabout, by way of the wilderness at the Sea of Reeds.

Now the Israelites went up armed out of the land of Egypt. ¹⁹And Moses took with him the bones of Joseph, who had exacted an oath from the children of Israel, saying, "God will be sure to take notice of you: then you shall carry up my bones from here with you."

²⁰They set out from Succoth, and encamped at Etham, at the edge of the wilderness. ²¹The Lord went before them in

18 וַיַּסֵּב אֱלֹהִים ׀ אֶת־הָעָם דֶּרֶךְ הַמִּדְבָּר יַם־
סֽוּף
וַחֲמֻשִׁים עָלוּ בְנֵי־יִשְׂרָאֵל מֵאֶרֶץ מִצְרָֽיִם:
19 וַיִּקַּח מֹשֶׁה אֶת־עַצְמוֹת יוֹסֵף עִמּוֹ כִּי
הַשְׁבֵּעַ הִשְׁבִּיעַ אֶת־בְּנֵי יִשְׂרָאֵל לֵאמֹר
פָּקֹד יִפְקֹד אֱלֹהִים אֶתְכֶם וְהַעֲלִיתֶם אֶת־
עַצְמֹתַי מִזֶּה אִתְּכֶֽם:
20 וַיִּסְעוּ מִסֻּכֹּת וַיַּחֲנוּ בְאֵתָם בִּקְצֵה הַמִּדְבָּֽר:

alongside the highway—and the descriptive "Sea of Philistia" in 23:31 is used for the section of the Mediterranean adjacent to it. These terms testify to the dominant role later played by the Philistines in that part of the country. This people is first mentioned in historical records from the time of Ramses III (1183–1152 B.C.E.). They were one of a confederacy of "sea peoples" who invaded Egypt in the eighth year of that king's reign. They may have been among earlier waves of invaders who apparently came from the regions of Mycenae in Crete; their ultimate origin is unknown. Repulsed by Ramses III, the Philistines settled along the southern coastal plain of Canaan and, at first, became mercenaries of the Egyptian administration.[32]

a change of heart   Preferring Egyptian slavery to war.[33]

when they see war   Since the days of Pharaoh Seti I (ca. 1305–1290 B.C.E.), the coastal road to Canaan had been heavily fortified by the Egyptians. A chain of strongholds, way stations, reservoirs, and wells dotted the area as far as Gaza, the provincial capital. Many of these are pictured in great detail in the reliefs on the exterior of the walls of the temple of Amun at Karnak in the plain of Thebes, and they are also mentioned in Egyptian papyri.[34] Excavations at Deir el-Balaḥ, in the Gaza strip, unearthed an Egyptian garrison fortress, the components of which bear a striking correspondence to those on the Karnak reliefs.[35]

It is quite clear that it was the better part of wisdom for the Israelites to have avoided the "way of the land of the Philistines." They thereby avoided having to contend with the strongly entrenched Egyptian forces on what would have been hopelessly unequal terms.

18.   by way of the wilderness   This must refer to one of the ancient, natural tracks that traverse the Sinai peninsula. The vagueness of the designation and the inability to identify and locate most of the many wilderness stations recorded in the Torah[36] make it impossible to chart the route followed by the departing Israelites.

Sea of Reeds   The literal translation of Hebrew *yam suf*; not the Red Sea, which is more than 120 miles (192 km.) from the probable site of Goshen, too great a distance to cover even in a week in those days. Further, Hebrew *suf* is derived from the Egyptian for the papyrus reed,[37] which grows in fresh water; therefore, *yam suf* would not be an appropriate designation for the present Red Sea because the latter is saline and, as a consequence, does not favor the growth of that plant.[38] Since no lack of water is experienced until after the crossing of the *yam suf*, it may be surmised that this initial stage of the march took the Israelites to the far northeastern corner of Egypt, to one of the lagoons near the shore of the Mediterranean Sea.

armed   Hebrew *ḥamush(im)* is apparently a military term meaning "equipped for battle."[39] See Comment to 6:26.

19.   Joseph's dying request is implemented. The text reproduces almost verbatim his words as given in Genesis 50:25. The Mekhilta notes that while the other Israelites were busy plundering the Egyptians, Moses was preoccupied with disinterring Joseph and keeping faith with him. Joshua 24:32 records the reburial of Joseph in Shechem.

20.   Succoth   See Comment to 12:37.

Etham   The site, mentioned again in Numbers 33:6–8, has not been identified; nor is the distance between it and Succoth given.

a pillar of cloud by day, to guide them along the way, and in a pillar of fire by night, to give them light, that they might travel day and night. ²²The pillar of cloud by day and the pillar of fire by night did not depart from before the people.

כא וַיהוָה הֹלֵךְ לִפְנֵיהֶם יוֹמָם בְּעַמּוּד עָנָן לַנְחֹתָם הַדֶּרֶךְ וְלַיְלָה בְּעַמּוּד אֵשׁ לְהָאִיר לָהֶם לָלֶכֶת יוֹמָם וָלָיְלָה: כב לֹא־יָמִישׁ עַמּוּד הֶעָנָן יוֹמָם וְעַמּוּד הָאֵשׁ לָיְלָה לִפְנֵי הָעָם: פ

14 The LORD said to Moses: ²Tell the Israelites to turn back and encamp before Pi-hahiroth, between Migdol and the sea, before Baal-zephon; you shall encamp facing it, by the sea. ³Pharaoh will say of the Israelites, "They are astray

י״ד וַיְדַבֵּר יְהוָה אֶל־מֹשֶׁה לֵּאמֹר: ב דַּבֵּר אֶל־בְּנֵי יִשְׂרָאֵל וְיָשֻׁבוּ וְיַחֲנוּ לִפְנֵי פִּי הַחִירֹת בֵּין מִגְדֹּל וּבֵין הַיָּם לִפְנֵי בַּעַל צְפֹן נִכְחוֹ תַחֲנוּ עַל־הַיָּם: ג וְאָמַר פַּרְעֹה לִבְנֵי יִשְׂרָאֵל נְבֻכִים הֵם

21–22. A theme that recurs in the narratives of the wilderness wanderings is that God manifested his active, dynamic Presence throughout. This is conceptualized in accordance with the idea that the God of the Hebrew Bible is a Being who transcends the limits of time and space, and thus surpasses human imagining. Hence, God's indwelling Presence in the world is symbolized, however inadequately, by the mysterious, intangible, incorporeal elements of fire and cloud—actually a diaphanous, luminescent mist visible both by day and by night.[40] In these verses it functions to escort and guide the people through the untamed wilderness.[41] In other texts its movements signal the journeying and encamping of the people,[42] and it also provides a protective screen for the imperiled Israelites.[43] It should be noted that although God is portrayed as speaking "from the midst of the cloud," as in Exodus 24:16, this should always be understood as figurative language. There is never a question of His actually residing inside the cloud or being identified with it, as is clear from Exodus 19:20, when God "came down" upon Mount Sinai *after* it had been enveloped in cloud (v. 16).[44]

21. The LORD went Hebrew *holekh* is a participle, suggesting continuous occurrence. Verse 22 emphasizes the uninterrupted nature of the manifested Divine Presence.

CHAPTER 14   THE MIRACLE AT THE SEA   (vv. 1–31)

The liberated Israelites, having reached the edge of the wilderness, were suddenly ordered to change course. This new direction, fraught with great danger, was actually a stratagem to mislead the Egyptians and lure them to their doom. It was the culminating defeat of Pharaoh. Thereafter, Egypt does not again appear in Israelite history until the time of King Solomon.[1]

The miracle of the parting of the sea—known in Hebrew as *keriʿat yam suf*—left a deep impress on subsequent Hebrew literature and became the paradigm for the future redemption of Israel from exile. Remarkably, the overwhelming majority of the texts that celebrate the crossing of the sea relate solely to God's sovereign control over nature and history and do not mention the drowning of the Egyptians.[2]

INSTRUCTIONS TO CHANGE COURSE   (vv. 1–4)

2. None of the place-names mentioned here, and repeated in Numbers 33:7–8, can be identified with certainty.

Pi-hahiroth This may be a Hebraized form of Egyptian *Pr-Ḥthr,* "the house of [the deity] Hathḥor,"[3] or it may be connected with the Hebrew stem *ḥ-r-t,* "to dig," perhaps referring to one of the canals of the Nile and meaning "the mouth of the canal."[4] Jewish commentators associated the name with Hebrew *ḥerut,* "freedom."[5]

Migdol A pure Semitic word meaning "a watchtower" or "fortress." Several locations bearing this name are known. They testify to the heavy Semitic influence in the northeastern delta of the Nile.

in the land; the wilderness has closed in on them." [4]Then I will stiffen Pharaoh's heart and he will pursue them, that I may gain glory through Pharaoh and all his host; and the Egyptians shall know that I am the LORD.

And they did so.

[5]When the king of Egypt was told that the people had fled, Pharaoh and his courtiers had a change of heart about the people and said, "What is this we have done, releasing Israel from our service?" [6]He ordered his chariot and took his men with him; [7]he took six hundred of his picked chariots, and the rest of the chariots of Egypt, with officers in all of them. [8]The LORD stiffened the heart of Pharaoh

בְּאֶרֶץ סָגַר עֲלֵיהֶם הַמִּדְבָּר: 4 וְחִזַּקְתִּי אֶת־לֵב־
פַּרְעֹה וְרָדַף אַחֲרֵיהֶם וְאִכָּבְדָה בְּפַרְעֹה וּבְכָל־
חֵילוֹ וְיָדְעוּ מִצְרַיִם כִּי־אֲנִי יְהוָה
וַיַּעֲשׂוּ־כֵן:

5 וַיֻּגַּד לְמֶלֶךְ מִצְרַיִם כִּי בָרַח הָעָם וַיֵּהָפֵךְ
לְבַב פַּרְעֹה וַעֲבָדָיו אֶל־הָעָם וַיֹּאמְרוּ מַה־זֹּאת
עָשִׂינוּ כִּי־שִׁלַּחְנוּ אֶת־יִשְׂרָאֵל מֵעָבְדֵנוּ: 6 וַיֶּאְסֹר
אֶת־רִכְבּוֹ וְאֶת־עַמּוֹ לָקַח עִמּוֹ: 7 וַיִּקַּח שֵׁשׁ־
מֵאוֹת רֶכֶב בָּחוּר וְכֹל רֶכֶב מִצְרָיִם וְשָׁלִשִׁם
עַל־כֻּלּוֹ: 8 וַיְחַזֵּק יְהֹוָה אֶת־לֵב פַּרְעֹה מֶלֶךְ

Baal-zephon   In Ugaritic literature the second element of this name is a holy mountain[6] associated in particular with the Canaanite god Baal. The present combination also appears as a divine name.[7] Baal was the storm-god and also the patron of mariners. Several cult sites dedicated to him were built along the shores of the Mediterranean. A Phoenician letter from the sixth century B.C.E. seems to identify one Egyptian site named Baal-zephon with Tahpanhes,[8] modern Tell-Defneh, some 27 miles (48 km.) south-southwest of modern Port Said.

3. *astray*   Hebrew *nevukhim*[9] in the present context has the sense of "disoriented" or "hopelessly confused." The Israelites are hemmed in on all sides—by Egyptian border fortresses, by the wilderness, and by the sea.

4.   Pharaoh will be irresistibly drawn to chase after the Israelites. On the "stiffening, or hardening, of Pharaoh's heart," see Comment to 4:21.

that I may gain glory   Or "and I will . . ." The Hebrew leaves unclear whether this is the purpose of the tactic or its consequence. Either way, the idea is that the destruction of the wicked is a reaffirmation of the fundamental biblical principle that the world is governed by a divinely ordained moral order that must ultimately prevail. God is thereby glorified.[10] This point is further emphasized through the use of the stem *k-v-d*, which underlies the phrase "gain glory" and which is also frequently employed to express Pharaoh's obstinacy.[11] This character flaw of the monarch is self-destructive, and his downfall redounds to the glory of God.[12]

the Egyptians shall know   See Comments to 1:8 and 5:2.

THE EGYPTIANS RELENT AND GIVE CHASE (vv. 5–9)

5. *the people had fled*   It is clear that the Israelites are not coming back, for the "three-day journey" that Moses repeatedly requested[13] has come and gone, and they have not returned.

What is this . . .   "We have forfeited a most valuable source of cheap labor."

6. *He ordered his chariot*   Literally, "hitched."[14] A midrash utilizes this to suggest that in his perverse eagerness to pursue the Israelites, the king personally performed this menial task.[15]

took his men   Hebrew *'am*, "people," sometimes has the specific connotation of "armed force."[16]

7.   Pharaoh leads an elite chariot corps of six hundred, apparently the standard military unit.[17]

and the rest of the chariots   Literally, "every chariot/all the chariots/all the chariotry of Egypt," that is, in addition to the elite corps. The chariot was a revolutionary and powerful innovation in the art of warfare. It was introduced into Egypt from Canaan. Drawn by two horses, the weapon was used for massed charges; it required a crew with a high degree of skill and training. The charioteers enjoyed high social standing and became a military aristocracy.

king of Egypt, and he gave chase to the Israelites. As the Israelites were departing defiantly, [9]the Egyptians gave chase to them, and all the chariot horses of Pharaoh, his horsemen, and his warriors overtook them encamped by the sea, near Pi-hahiroth, before Baal-zephon.

[10]As Pharaoh drew near, the Israelites caught sight of the Egyptians advancing upon them. Greatly frightened, the Israelites cried out to the LORD. [11]And they said to Moses, "Was it for want of graves in Egypt that you brought us to die in the wilderness? What have you done to us, taking us out of Egypt? [12]Is this not the very thing we told you in Egypt, saying, 'Let us be, and we will serve the Egyptians, for it is better for us to serve the Egyptians than to die in the wilderness'?" [13]But Moses said to the people, "Have no fear! Stand by, and witness the deliverance which the LORD will work for you today; for the Egyptians whom you see today you will never see again. [14]The LORD will battle for you; you hold your peace!"

מִצְרַיִם וַיִּרְדֹּף אַחֲרֵי בְּנֵי יִשְׂרָאֵל וּבְנֵי יִשְׂרָאֵל יֹצְאִים בְּיָד רָמָה: שני 9 וַיִּרְדְּפוּ מִצְרַיִם אַחֲרֵיהֶם וַיַּשִּׂיגוּ אוֹתָם חֹנִים עַל־הַיָּם כָּל־סוּס רֶכֶב פַּרְעֹה וּפָרָשָׁיו וְחֵילוֹ עַל־פִּי הַחִירֹת לִפְנֵי בַּעַל צְפֹן:

10 וּפַרְעֹה הִקְרִיב וַיִּשְׂאוּ בְנֵי־יִשְׂרָאֵל אֶת־עֵינֵיהֶם וְהִנֵּה מִצְרַיִם ׀ נֹסֵעַ אַחֲרֵיהֶם וַיִּירְאוּ מְאֹד וַיִּצְעֲקוּ בְנֵי־יִשְׂרָאֵל אֶל־יְהוָה: 11 וַיֹּאמְרוּ אֶל־מֹשֶׁה הֲמִבְּלִי אֵין־קְבָרִים בְּמִצְרַיִם לְקַחְתָּנוּ לָמוּת בַּמִּדְבָּר מַה־זֹּאת עָשִׂיתָ לָּנוּ לְהוֹצִיאָנוּ מִמִּצְרָיִם: 12 הֲלֹא־זֶה הַדָּבָר אֲשֶׁר דִּבַּרְנוּ אֵלֶיךָ בְמִצְרַיִם לֵאמֹר חֲדַל מִמֶּנּוּ וְנַעַבְדָה אֶת־מִצְרָיִם כִּי טוֹב לָנוּ עֲבֹד אֶת־מִצְרַיִם מִמֻּתֵנוּ בַּמִּדְבָּר: 13 וַיֹּאמֶר מֹשֶׁה אֶל־הָעָם אַל־תִּירָאוּ הִתְיַצְּבוּ וּרְאוּ אֶת־יְשׁוּעַת יְהוָה אֲשֶׁר־יַעֲשֶׂה לָכֶם הַיּוֹם כִּי אֲשֶׁר רְאִיתֶם אֶת־מִצְרַיִם הַיּוֹם לֹא תֹסִפוּ לִרְאֹתָם עוֹד עַד־עוֹלָם: 14 יְהוָה יִלָּחֵם לָכֶם וְאַתֶּם תַּחֲרִישׁוּן: פ שלישי

---

officers Hebrew *shalish*, perhaps meaning "thirdling," may originally have been the third man in the chariot. Among the Hittites and Assyrians the chariot crew was comprised of a driver, a warrior, and a shieldbearer, but Egyptian chariots generally had only a two-man team. Hence, *shalish* may have assumed the extended meaning of "officer."[18]

8. departing defiantly Literally, "with upraised hand," a metaphor[19] drawn from the depiction of ancient Near Eastern gods menacingly brandishing a weapon in the upraised right hand. The self-confident Israelites are oblivious of the renewed Egyptian threat.

9. his horsemen Horseback riding was introduced into Egypt only in the fourteenth century B.C.E., and the use of mounted cavalry in warfare was unknown before the end of the second millennium. Hence, Hebrew *parash* must here have the meaning "steed," as in a few other biblical texts[20] and in Arabic *faras*; or it may be a term for "charioteer"—the one skilled at handling a horse.

overtook them Genesis 31:(23)25 shows that this refers not to direct contact but to being within sight of one another; that is, the Egyptians suddenly appeared on the horizon.

THE PEOPLE'S REACTION; MOSES' RESPONSE (vv. 10–14)

10. advancing The singular form of the Hebrew verb[21] suggested to the rabbis that the Egyptians were of one mind, acted in concert, and thus were deserving of their mass destruction.[22]

cried out to the LORD The self-assurance mentioned in verse 8 dissipated quickly. God alone can save them. The Hebrew here employs the same phrase as in 2:23, with a dialectic variant; thus, the entire narrative of Israel's oppression and liberation is framed by a record of Israel's heartfelt cry to God for help in dire distress.

11. This rebuke to Moses is a piece of bitter irony, for Egypt, with its death-obsessed religion, was the classic land of tombs.

12. Neither of the two previous repudiations of Moses, not that of 5:21 nor that of 6:9, contains this statement, which must reflect some incident not otherwise recorded in the Torah. Psalm 106:7 preserves a tradition of Israel's rebellion at the Sea of Reeds.

13–14. Moses ignores their censure and, instead, calms them and assuages their fear.

בשלח

15 וַיֹּאמֶר יְהֹוָה אֶל־מֹשֶׁה מַה־תִּצְעַק אֵלָי דַּבֵּר אֶל־בְּנֵי־יִשְׂרָאֵל וְיִסָּעוּ: 16 וְאַתָּה הָרֵם אֶת־מַטְּךָ וּנְטֵה אֶת־יָדְךָ עַל־הַיָּם וּבְקָעֵהוּ וְיָבֹאוּ בְנֵי־יִשְׂרָאֵל בְּתוֹךְ הַיָּם בַּיַּבָּשָׁה: 17 וַאֲנִי הִנְנִי מְחַזֵּק אֶת־לֵב מִצְרַיִם וְיָבֹאוּ אַחֲרֵיהֶם וְאִכָּבְדָה בְּפַרְעֹה וּבְכָל־חֵילוֹ בְּרִכְבּוֹ וּבְפָרָשָׁיו: 18 וְיָדְעוּ מִצְרַיִם כִּי־אֲנִי יְהֹוָה בְּהִכָּבְדִי בְּפַרְעֹה בְּרִכְבּוֹ וּבְפָרָשָׁיו:

19 וַיִּסַּע מַלְאַךְ הָאֱלֹהִים הַהֹלֵךְ לִפְנֵי מַחֲנֵה יִשְׂרָאֵל וַיֵּלֶךְ מֵאַחֲרֵיהֶם וַיִּסַּע עַמּוּד הֶעָנָן מִפְּנֵיהֶם וַיַּעֲמֹד מֵאַחֲרֵיהֶם: 20 וַיָּבֹא בֵּין | מַחֲנֵה מִצְרַיִם וּבֵין מַחֲנֵה יִשְׂרָאֵל וַיְהִי הֶעָנָן וְהַחֹשֶׁךְ וַיָּאֶר אֶת־הַלָּיְלָה וְלֹא־קָרַב זֶה אֶל־זֶה כָּל־הַלָּיְלָה: 21 וַיֵּט מֹשֶׁה אֶת־יָדוֹ עַל־הַיָּם וַיּוֹלֶךְ יְהֹוָה | אֶת־הַיָּם בְּרוּחַ קָדִים עַזָּה כָּל־הַלַּיְלָה וַיָּשֶׂם אֶת־הַיָּם לֶחָרָבָה וַיִּבָּקְעוּ הַמָּיִם: 22 וַיָּבֹאוּ בְנֵי־יִשְׂרָאֵל בְּתוֹךְ הַיָּם בַּיַּבָּשָׁה וְהַמַּיִם לָהֶם חֹמָה מִימִינָם וּמִשְּׂמֹאלָם: 23 וַיִּרְדְּפוּ מִצְרַיִם וַיָּבֹאוּ אַחֲרֵיהֶם כֹּל סוּס פַּרְעֹה רִכְבּוֹ וּפָרָשָׁיו אֶל־תּוֹךְ הַיָּם: 24 וַיְהִי בְּאַשְׁמֹרֶת הַבֹּקֶר וַיַּשְׁקֵף יְהֹוָה

15Then the LORD said to Moses, "Why do you cry out to Me? Tell the Israelites to go forward. 16And you lift up your rod and hold out your arm over the sea and split it, so that the Israelites may march into the sea on dry ground. 17And I will stiffen the hearts of the Egyptians so that they go in after them; and I will gain glory through Pharaoh and all his warriors, his chariots and his horsemen. 18Let the Egyptians know that I am LORD, when I gain glory through Pharaoh, his chariots, and his horsemen."

19The angel of God, who had been going ahead of the Israelite army, now moved and followed behind them; and the pillar of cloud shifted from in front of them and took up a place behind them, 20and it came between the army of the Egyptians and the army of Israel. Thus there was the cloud with the darkness, and it cast a spell upon the night, so that the one could not come near the other all through the night.

21Then Moses held out his arm over the sea and the LORD drove back the sea with a strong east wind all that night, and turned the sea into dry ground. The waters were split, 22and the Israelites went into the sea on dry ground, the waters forming a wall for them on their right and on their left. 23The Egyptians came in pursuit after them into the sea, all of Pharaoh's horses, chariots, and horsemen. 24At

GOD'S RESPONSE (vv. 15–20)

15. It is time for action, not for lengthy prayer. Moses is addressed as representative of the entire people.[23]

16. Moses is not instructed to strike the sea. In verse 21 the action of Moses with his rod is the signal for the strong wind to blow back the waters. Isaiah (63:12) makes clear that it is God who splits the sea.

17-18. See Comment to verse 4.

19. The symbol of God's indwelling Presence, the luminous pillar of cloud mentioned in 13:21 as leading and guiding the people, now serves as a protective screen separating the two camps.[24] This same tradition is recalled in Joshua 24:7: "They cried out to the LORD, and He put darkness between you and the Egyptians."

20. *cast a spell* This rendering derives the verb from the stem '-r-r, "to curse."[25] The usual meaning of Hebrew *va-ya'er*, "it lit up," would not seem to be consistent with the "cloud and the darkness." Traditional interpretation took it that the side of the cloud facing the Egyptians remained dark, while the other side illuminated the night for the Israelites.[26]

THE PARTING OF THE SEA (vv. 21–29)

21. Moses implements the instructions detailed in verse 16. It is not he but God who is the effective cause, the one who controls nature.

a strong east wind See Comment to 10:13.

23. Impelled by evil purposes, their judgment deranged by their brutal obstinacy, the Egyptian forces plunge headlong into the turbulent waters.

the morning watch, the Lord looked down upon the Egyptian army from a pillar of fire and cloud, and threw the Egyptian army into panic. ²⁵He locked the wheels of their chariots so that they moved forward with difficulty. And the Egyptians said, "Let us flee from the Israelites, for the Lord is fighting for them against Egypt."

²⁶Then the Lord said to Moses, "Hold out your arm over the sea, that the waters may come back upon the Egyptians and upon their chariots and upon their horsemen." ²⁷Moses held out his arm over the sea, and at daybreak the sea returned to its normal state, and the Egyptians fled at its approach. But the Lord hurled the Egyptians into the sea. ²⁸The waters turned back and covered the chariots and the horsemen—Pharaoh's entire army that followed them into the sea; not one of them remained. ²⁹But the Israelites had marched through the sea on dry ground, the waters forming a wall for them on their right and on their left.

³⁰Thus the Lord delivered Israel that day from the Egyptians. Israel saw the Egyptians dead on the shore of the sea.

אֶל־מַחֲנֵ֣ה מִצְרַ֔יִם בְּעַמּ֥וּד אֵ֖שׁ וְעָנָ֑ן וַיָּ֕הָם אֵ֖ת מַחֲנֵ֥ה מִצְרָֽיִם: 25 וַיָּ֗סַר אֵ֚ת אֹפַ֣ן מַרְכְּבֹתָ֔יו וַֽיְנַהֲגֵ֖הוּ בִּכְבֵדֻ֑ת וַיֹּ֣אמֶר מִצְרַ֗יִם אָנ֙וּסָה֙ מִפְּנֵ֣י יִשְׂרָאֵ֔ל כִּ֣י יְהֹוָ֔ה נִלְחָ֥ם לָהֶ֖ם בְּמִצְרָֽיִם: פ

רביעי [שלישי לספרדים]

26 וַיֹּ֤אמֶר יְהֹוָה֙ אֶל־מֹשֶׁ֔ה נְטֵ֥ה אֶת־יָדְךָ֖ עַל־הַיָּ֑ם וְיָשֻׁ֤בוּ הַמַּ֙יִם֙ עַל־מִצְרַ֔יִם עַל־רִכְבּ֖וֹ וְעַל־פָּרָשָֽׁיו: 27 וַיֵּט֩ מֹשֶׁ֨ה אֶת־יָד֜וֹ עַל־הַיָּ֗ם וַיָּ֨שָׁב הַיָּ֜ם לִפְנ֥וֹת בֹּ֙קֶר֙ לְאֵ֣יתָנ֔וֹ וּמִצְרַ֖יִם נָסִ֣ים לִקְרָאת֑וֹ וַיְנַעֵ֧ר יְהֹוָ֛ה אֶת־מִצְרַ֖יִם בְּת֥וֹךְ הַיָּֽם: 28 וַיָּשֻׁ֣בוּ הַמַּ֗יִם וַיְכַסּ֤וּ אֶת־הָרֶ֙כֶב֙ וְאֶת־הַפָּ֣רָשִׁ֔ים לְכֹל֙ חֵ֣יל פַּרְעֹ֔ה הַבָּאִ֥ים אַחֲרֵיהֶ֖ם בַּיָּ֑ם לֹֽא־נִשְׁאַ֥ר בָּהֶ֖ם עַד־אֶחָֽד: 29 וּבְנֵ֧י יִשְׂרָאֵ֛ל הָלְכ֥וּ בַיַּבָּשָׁ֖ה בְּת֣וֹךְ הַיָּ֑ם וְהַמַּ֤יִם לָהֶם֙ חֹמָ֔ה מִֽימִינָ֖ם וּמִשְּׂמֹאלָֽם: 30 וַיּ֨וֹשַׁע יְהֹוָ֜ה בַּיּ֥וֹם הַה֛וּא אֶת־יִשְׂרָאֵ֖ל מִיַּ֣ד מִצְרָ֑יִם וַיַּ֤רְא יִשְׂרָאֵל֙ אֶת־מִצְרַ֔יִם מֵ֖ת עַל־שְׂפַ֥ת הַיָּֽם: 31 וַיַּ֨רְא יִשְׂרָאֵ֜ל אֶת־הַיָּ֣ד הַגְּדֹלָ֗ה

24. ***the morning watch*** Between the hours of two and six A.M. In Israel the night was divided into three watches, the others covering the hours of six to ten P.M. and ten P.M. to two A.M.[27]

a pillar of fire and cloud The absence of the definite article may indicate that this is not identical with that mentioned in 13:21–22 and verse 19 above. Nevertheless, this pillar too is certainly a poetic objectification of God's immanence and providence.[28]

25. ***He locked*** The wheels got bogged down in the mud.[29]

with difficulty The same stem *k-v-d* that underlies "glorified" in verse 4. The verb is often used of the hardening of Pharaoh's heart—a subtle word play intimating causal connections.

Let us flee Literally, "Let me flee"; see Comment to verse 10.

the Lord is fighting for them The fulfillment of the prediction in verse 14.

27. ***its normal state*** Literally, "to its perennial flow."[30]

hurled . . . into the sea They were buffeted about in the sea.[31]

28. ***Pharaoh's entire army.***[32]

RECAPITULATION (vv. 30–31)

These two verses round out the preceding narrative and, at the same time, preface the following "Song at the Sea." Psalm 106:9–12 reflect this associative sequence: "He sent His blast against the Sea of Reeds; / it became dry; / He led them through the deep as through a wilderness. / He delivered them from the foe, / redeemed them from the enemy. / Water covered their adversaries; / not one of them was left. / Then they believed His promise, / and sang His praises."

30. ***from the Egyptians*** Literally, "from the hand of Egypt."

on the shore of the sea Rashbam and Ibn Ezra understand that the Israelites beheld the corpses of the Egyptians from the safety of the opposite shore. Bekhor Shor construes the verse to mean that the Israelites saw the Egyptian corpses that had been washed ashore by the waves.

³¹And when Israel saw the wondrous power which the LORD had wielded against the Egyptians, the people feared the LORD; they had faith in the LORD and His servant Moses.

אֲשֶׁ֨ר עָשָׂ֤ה יְהוָה֙ בְּמִצְרַ֔יִם וַיִּֽירְא֥וּ הָעָ֖ם אֶת־
יְהוָ֑ה וַיַּֽאֲמִ֙ינוּ֙ בַּֽיהוָ֔ה וּבְמֹשֶׁ֖ה עַבְדּֽוֹ׃ פ

31. the wondrous power Literally, "the great hand" of God that cut off the tyrannous "hand of Egypt." Hebrew *yad*, "hand," is a key word in this chapter, occurring seven times.³³

they had faith "Faith" in the Hebrew Bible is not belief in a doctrine or subscription to a creed. Rather, it refers to trust and loyalty that find expression in obedience and commitment.

His servant Moses As the faithful instrument of God's will, having successfully fulfilled his mission, it is fitting that the distinguishing title "servant of the Lord/of God" now be bestowed on Moses. He is so designated over thirty times in the Hebrew Bible, although he is never the object of a cult of personality. His faults are not obscured, and he is even punished for transgressing in anger the divine command. Yet he is Israel's leader par excellence. Of Moses, God says, "He is trusted throughout My household," and it is to him that God speaks "mouth to mouth" (Num. 12:7–8). The verdict of the Torah on his life is: "Never again did there arise in Israel a prophet like Moses—whom the LORD singled out, face to face" (Deut. 34:10).

CHAPTER 15

The Song at the Sea: Shirat ha-Yam   (vv. 1–19)

The Poetic and Prose Accounts After the narrative prose account of the extraordinary events at the Sea of Reeds, there follows what may be the oldest piece of sustained poetry in the Hebrew Bible: a paean of praise to God, the biblical way of expressing gratitude. It is not an epic narrative but a spontaneous, lyrical outpouring of emotion on the part of the people who experienced the great events of the Exodus. Because the topic is the glorification of God, a drastic shift of focus takes place. For this reason, it would be a misreading of the Song at the Sea—*shirat ha-yam*, as it is known in Hebrew—to expect from it a simple, poetic version of the prose report. The poem assumes that the audience is familiar with the course of events; there is no need, therefore, to repeat the pertinent facts, and there is considerable telescoping and condensation. The Song, little concerned with events on the human scene, is preoccupied with celebrating the mighty acts of God as He intervenes in human affairs. Thus, in place of the naturalistic "strong east wind" that blew through the night (14:21), there is the poetic "blast of [God's] nostrils" (15:8)—a sudden, brief, yet devastatingly effective breath that humbles human arrogance. Similarly, the change in perspective, together with the poetic diction, leads to a different description of the action of the waters and of the manner in which the advancing enemy is hurled to his destined fate. Moses, of course, plays no active role, for it is not he who holds out his arm over the sea, as in 14:16,21. Rather, it is the "right hand" of God that is extended (15:12). Nor is there any mention of the angel, the cloud, and the darkness, all so prominent in 14:19–20. These intermediaries signal the distance between God and Israel; by contrast, the "Song at the Sea" celebrates God's direct, unmediated, personal incursion into the world of humankind.

Analogues Chapters 14 and 15 in Exodus find a parallel in the Book of Judges, chapters 4 and 5. The latter tell of the battle against the Canaanite king Jabin of Hazor in the days of Deborah and Barak. There, too, a historic prose account is followed by a triumphal ode extolling the victory. Both compositions are Hebrew counterparts of an Egyptian literary genre, dating from the days of the New Kingdom, that features two accounts of the same event, the one prose, the other poetry. Examples are the narratives recounting the epic battle of Pharaoh Ramses II (1290–1224 B.C.E.) against the Hittites at Kadesh-on-the-Orontes,¹ and the battle of Pharaoh Merneptah (1224–1211 B.C.E.) against the Libyans.²

What distinguishes the *shirah*, as it is known in the tradition, from its analogues is its dominant God-centered theme. Whereas the Egyptian models are hyperbolic panegyrics to the superhuman heroic exploits of the pharaohs, in the Torah it is God alone who attracts the poet's interest.

Structure and Content There is little agreement among scholars as to how to demarcate the component units of the Song. Four main strophes seem to be discernible:

1. Verses 1–10 celebrate God's great triumph over the Egyptian foe;
2. Verses 11–13 tell of the incomparability of God;
3. Verses 14–16 describe the impact of these extraordinary events upon the surrounding peoples;
4. Verses 17–18 are forward-looking and anticipate future developments.

An inner logic binds together the four units, aside from the past, present, and future time sequences, respectively, of the first three. God's total and effortless destruction of the mighty Egyptian forces unqualifiedly demonstrates His total "otherness," which, in turn, provides infallible assurance of future victories. Israel responds with a glorious affirmation of God's eternal sovereignty.

The composition is encased within a historical prose framework that comprises an introductory statement identifying the singers[3] and a concluding recapitulation of the event that occasioned that triumphal ode (vv. 1a–b,19). The *shirah* itself opens and closes with an exaltation of God voiced in the third person.

The Language The language of the poem is thoroughly archaic, employing several features commonly found in Canaanite poetry: the heavy use of sentences structured in a variety of parallel forms, especially incremental repetition; the prefixed verbal *yqtl* (imperfect) construction is the standard narrative tense form; and the definite article never once appears with a noun. Another peculiarity is the frequent use of the pronominal suffix *-mo*. Other archaic features are noted in the Commentary.

The Antiphonal Arrangement The extensive use of parallel clauses, the opening prose statement that attributes the *shirah* to "Moses and the Israelites," and the notice about Miriam and the women also singing—all these suggest that it was sung antiphonally.[4] As early as the first century B.C.E. Philo of Alexandria imagined the Israelites forming two choruses, Moses leading the males and his sister, the females.[5] Rabbinic interpretation understood that the *shirah* was sung responsively by Moses and the people. Exactly how the antiphony was to have operated is left unclear and remains a matter of dispute. One view was that the people repeated or completed the phrase or verse that Moses initiated. Another held that the verses were recited by them in alternation. Still another view had the people reciting the entire song after Moses had finished it.[6]

Scribal Convention Recognition of the distinctive nature of the language and patterning of the *shirah* left its mark on scribal traditions. Along with one or two other highly poetic passages, the Song at the Sea enjoyed special treatment at the hands of the professional Torah scribes. Rabbinic laws[7] governing the particular mode of transcribing a Torah scroll stipulate that the *shirah* be copied so that the column imitates the bricklayer's art, with "a half brick over a whole brick and a whole brick over a half brick";[8] that is, the words must be spaced so that the writing on each line has a blank space below it, and the blank space will in turn have writing beneath it. The medieval biblical manuscript codices and later the printed editions largely adopted this aesthetic arrangement in a standardized manner.[9] The Hebrew of the present edition illustrates the convention.

The Shirah in the Liturgy The Song at the Sea assumed a special place in the Jewish liturgy quite early. In the days of the Second Temple it was customary for a Levitical choir to accompany the priestly *tamid* offering on Sabbath afternoons with a singing of the *shirah* in two parts, verses 1–10 being intoned one week and the rest on the next Sabbath.[10] After the destruction of the Temple, the Palestinian communities perpetuated the Levitical custom, although without the sacrifice. The Jews of Rome incorporated the entire *shirah* into the fixed, daily morning service, a practice that gradually became universal among Jews. This daily recitation assumed ever greater meaning as an affirmation of God's moral governance of the world, itself an assurance of the ultimate and inevitable downfall of tyrants. Such unassailable convictions took on increasing significance for Jews during the long dark

15 Then Moses and the Israelites sang this song to the Lord. They said:

טז

> I will sing to the Lord, for He has triumphed gloriously;
> Horse and driver He has hurled into the sea.
> [2]The Lord is my strength and might;
> He is become my deliverance.
> This is my God and I will enshrine Him;
> The God of my father, and I will exalt Him.
> [3]The Lord, the Warrior—
> Lord is His name!

אָ֣ז יָשִֽׁיר־מֹשֶׁה֩ וּבְנֵ֨י יִשְׂרָאֵ֜ל אֶת־הַשִּׁירָ֤ה הַזֹּאת֙ לַֽיהוָ֔ה וַיֹּאמְר֖וּ
לֵאמֹ֑ר   אָשִׁ֤ירָה לַֽיהוָה֙ כִּֽי־גָאֹ֣ה גָּאָ֔ה   ס֥וּס
וְרֹכְבֹ֖ו רָמָ֥ה בַיָּֽם׃   [2]עָזִּ֤י וְזִמְרָת֙ יָ֔הּ וַֽיְהִי־לִ֖י
לִֽישׁוּעָ֑ה   זֶ֤ה אֵלִי֙ וְאַנְוֵ֔הוּ   אֱלֹהֵ֥י
אָבִ֖י וַאֲרֹמְמֶֽנְהוּ׃   [3]יְהוָ֖ה אִ֣ישׁ מִלְחָמָ֑ה יְהוָ֖ה

---

nights of exile and persecution.[11] The Sabbath in the annual lectionary cycle on which the Torah reading is Exodus 13:17–17:16 (*Beshallaḥ*), receives the special designation *shabbat shirah*. The Song is also the scriptural reading for the seventh day of Passover, when the original event is believed to have occurred.

THE DEFEAT OF THE EGYPTIANS (vv. 1–10)

1. *Then* Hebrew *'az* inseparably connects the *shirah* to the situation summarized in 14:30–31.[12]

to the Lord As the Mekhilta observes, "to the Lord—and not to any mortal being."[13]

I will sing The first person formulation can refer only to Moses.[14]

for This gives the occasion of the Song.

triumphed Literally, "is most exalted," that is, He displayed His transcendence.

driver Hebrew *rokhev* here means the rider in the chariot, not one on horseback. See Comment to 14:9.[15]

2. *The Lord* Hebrew *yah* is an abbreviation of the divine name YHVH, which, in this form, is used exclusively in poetry.[16] Otherwise, it appears as an element in proper names such as Jeremiah (Heb. *yirmi-yahu*) and has survived in English in "hallelujah" (Heb. *hallelu-yah*).

my strength and might The source of my survival. Hebrew *zimrat* is a double entendre, for its stem can mean both "to sing, play music," and "to be strong," so that the phrase could also be rendered "my strength and [the theme of my] song."[17]

The Lord . . . my deliverance This passage appears in its entirety again in Isaiah 12:2 and Psalm 118:14: it must have had a liturgical function in ancient Israel as a personal confession of faith.[18]

This Baal Ha-Turim notes that the Hebrew demonstrative *zeh* may be used in reference to the unseen, as in Exodus 32:1.

I will enshrine Him Build Him a shrine or temple. This rendering is based on the Hebrew noun *naveh*, "a habitation."[19] See Comment to verse 13. Another interpretation takes the stem as a variant of Hebrew *na'eh*, "beautiful, lovely"; hence the alternative translation, "I will glorify Him"[20] in song. Rabbi Ishmael construed "glorifying God" to imply the performance of religious duties in the most elegant and attractive manner.[21] See Comment to 12:5.

The God of my father See Comment to 3:6.

3. *the Warrior* This divine epithet responds to 14:14, "The Lord will battle for you" and to verse 25, "the Egyptians said . . . the Lord is fighting for them against Egypt." Because the Egyptians came against Israel as an armed force, the Lord—to whom alone victory is attributed—is metaphorically described as a warrior. In the biblical view, the enemies of Israel are the enemies of

4Pharaoh's chariots and his army
He has cast into the sea;
And the pick of his officers
Are drowned in the Sea of Reeds.
5The deeps covered them;
They went down into the depths like a stone.
6Your right hand, O LORD, glorious in power,
Your right hand, O LORD, shatters the foe!
7In Your great triumph You break Your
　　opponents;
You send forth Your fury, it consumes them
　　like straw.
8At the blast of Your nostrils the waters piled up,
The floods stood straight like a wall;
The deeps froze in the heart of the sea.

שְׁמֽוֹ: 4 מַרְכְּבֹ֥ת פַּרְעֹ֛ה וְחֵיל֖וֹ יָרָ֣ה בַיָּ֑ם וּמִבְחַ֥ר

אָֽבֶן: שָֽׁלִשָׁ֖יו טֻבְּע֥וּ בְיַם־סֽוּף: 5 תְּהֹמֹ֖ת יְכַסְיֻ֑מוּ יָרְד֥וּ בִמְצוֹלֹ֖ת כְּמוֹ־

יְהֹוָ֖ה תִּרְעַ֥ץ אוֹיֵֽב: 6 יְמִֽינְךָ֣ יְהֹוָ֔ה נֶאְדָּרִ֖י בַּכֹּ֑חַ יְמִֽינְךָ֥

קָמֶ֑יךָ 7 וּבְרֹ֥ב גְּאֽוֹנְךָ֖ תַּהֲרֹ֣ס

אַפֶּ֖יךָ נֶ֣עֶרְמוּ מַ֔יִם תְּשַׁלַּח֙ חֲרֹ֣נְךָ֔ יֹאכְלֵ֖מוֹ כַּקַּֽשׁ: 8 וּבְר֤וּחַ

נֹֽזְלִ֑ים נִצְּב֥וּ כְמוֹ־נֵ֖ד קָֽפְא֥וּ תְהֹמֹ֖ת בְּלֶב־יָֽם: 9 אָמַ֥ר

God, so that Israel's wars for survival are portrayed as "the battles of the LORD."[22] Indeed, the Bible at times refers to a "Book of the Wars of the LORD," which is no longer extant.[23] A corollary of this concept is the humbling recognition that the decisive factor in war is ultimately not human prowess or the force of arms, but the free exercise of God's will. As David retorted to Goliath: "This whole assembly shall know that the LORD can give victory without sword or spear, for the battle is the LORD's. . . ."[24] The prophet Zechariah expresses the same idea this way: "Not by might, nor by power, but by My spirit, said the LORD of Hosts."[25] The poetic biblical notion of God as a warrior has nothing in common with the idea of "holy war" as it found expression in the crusades of medieval Christendom and in the Christian "wars of religion," or in the Islamic *jihad*, which regards the propagation of Islam by waging war against unbelievers as a religious duty.

LORD is His name! The divine name YHVH is invested with a dynamic quality. Thus, the statement evokes that essential power of God with which the Name is associated. See Comment to 6:3.[26]

4. *The pick of his officers* On Hebrew *shalish*, see Comment to 14:7.

5. *The deeps* Hebrew *tehomot* is the intensive plural form of *tehom*, the term for the cosmic, abyssal waters that lie beneath the earth, as mentioned in Genesis 1:2.[27]

6. An example of incremental parallelism. The first line, incomplete, receives its full expression in the second line.[28]

glorious The Hebrew stem '-d-r has the semantic range of "majestic, mighty, awe-inspiring."[29]

7. *fury* Hebrew *haron*, a term used exclusively of divine anger, here carries its primitive sense of "burning."

8. The waters are positioned in three stages.

the blast of Your nostrils Similar poetic imagery for the wind is found in 2 Samuel 22:16.[30]

piled up An ancient tradition, preserved in Targum Onkelos and the Mekhilta,[31] construes the unique Hebrew *ne'ermu* as though deriving not from *'aremah*, "a heap, pile,"[32] but from *'ormah*, "cunning, shrewdness."[33] This is taken as an allusion to retributive justice. The Egyptians "dealt shrewdly" with the Israelites, a policy that led to the decree to drown the Israelite males; now the waters deal with equal shrewdness in drowning the oppressors.[34]

like a wall Literally, "like a mound [of earth]."[35]

9The foe said,
"I will pursue, I will overtake,
I will divide the spoil;
My desire shall have its fill of them.
I will bare my sword—
My hand shall subdue them."
10You made Your wind blow, the sea covered them;
They sank like lead in the majestic waters.

11Who is like You, O Lord, among the celestials;
Who is like You, majestic in holiness,
Awesome in splendor, working wonders!

אוֹיֵב אֶרְדֹּף אַשִּׂיג אֲחַלֵּק שָׁלָל תִּמְלָאֵמוֹ
נַפְשִׁי 10 נָשַׁפְתָּ אָרִיק חַרְבִּי תּוֹרִישֵׁמוֹ יָדִי:
בְרוּחֲךָ כִּסָּמוֹ יָם צָלֲלוּ כַּעוֹפֶרֶת בְּמַיִם
אַדִּירִים: 11 מִי־כָמֹכָה בָּאֵלִם יְהֹוָה מִי
כָּמֹכָה נֶאְדָּר בַּקֹּדֶשׁ נוֹרָא תְהִלֹּת עֹשֵׂה־
פֶלֶא: 12 נָטִיתָ יְמִינְךָ תִּבְלָעֵמוֹ אָרֶץ: 13 נָחִיתָ

froze   They coagulated and formed a solid mass.[36]

9.   The poet reproduces what he imagines went on in the mind of the pharaoh. By means of a rapid, alliterative succession of words, he mimics the arrogant self-confidence and vainglorious boasting of the foe. The omission of the conjunctions[37] imparts to the series of verbs a staccato effect that bespeaks expectation of easy victory.

I will divide the spoil   This promise is an inducement to the reluctant soldiers to give chase.[38]

desire   Hebrew *nefesh*, like Ugaritic *npš* and Akkadian *napištu*, often has the sense of "throat, gullet, appetite."[39]

shall subdue   Literally, "my hand shall dispossess them," here meaning "I shall force them into slavery once again."[40]

10.   The first section of the Song at the Sea closes with a recital of God's effortless act that exposes the machinations of the enemy as mere empty rhetoric. It is to be noted that the waters do not act on their own accord but only when God energizes them.

wind blow   Most likely, the same blast as in verse 8. One brief, light puff, and the rampant sea engulfs the Egyptians.[41]

They sank   Hebrew *tsalelu* in this sense is unique. The verb may be formed from *metsulah*, "the depths," that is, "they plummeted."[42]

the majestic waters   The same phrase occurs in Psalm 93:4, where it parallels "the mighty waters," a phrase that alludes to the cosmic ocean.[43]

THE INCOMPARABILITY OF YHVH   (vv. 11–13)

11.   The foregoing recitation of God's sovereign control over nature logically culminates in an affirmation of His incomparability. This attribute is voiced through a rhetorical question that allows only an unqualifiedly negative response. The Book of Psalms several times echoes this phraseology.[44] Often the peerlessness of God is asserted categorically.[45]

It needs to be emphasized that the expression of God's uniqueness in comparative terms, and the mention of other celestial beings, cannot be interpreted literally to imply recognition of the existence of divinities other than the one God. Parallels in Mesopotamian religious poetry show that the poet is simply employing conventional, stereotypical language.[46] Moreover, many biblical texts utter similar statements along with an explicit denial of the reality of deities worshiped by other nations. Thus, the uncompromisingly monotheistic Narrator of Deuteronomy can state that "the Lord alone is God in

12You put out Your right hand,   בְּחַסְדְּךָ עַם־זוּ גָּאָלְתָּ   נֵהַלְתָּ בְעָזְּךָ אֶל־נְוֵה

The earth swallowed them.

13In Your love You lead the people You redeemed;   חָיִל   14 שָׁמְעוּ עַמִּים יִרְגָּזוּן   קָדְשֶׁךָ:

In Your strength You guide them to Your holy abode.

14The peoples hear, they tremble;   15 אָז נִבְהֲלוּ אַלּוּפֵי   אָחַז יֹשְׁבֵי פְּלָשֶׁת:

Agony grips the dwellers in Philistia.

heaven above and on earth below; there is no other" (4:39) and can refer to God's "powerful deeds that no god in heaven or on earth can equal" (3:24). The psalmist can declare, "There is none like You among the gods, O LORD," and can then add, "You alone are God" (Ps. 86:8,10). A psalmist can state that God "is held in awe by all divine beings. / All the gods of the peoples are mere idols" (Ps. 96:4–5), and can assert that "Our LORD is greater than all gods," and then deride the gods as being nothing but fetishes of silver and gold (Ps. 135:5,15–18).

the celestials   While Hebrew *'elim* (sing. *'el*) may certainly mean "gods," in some texts, as here, it refers to heavenly beings, the hosts of ministering angels that were imagined to surround the throne of God and to be at His service.[47]

majestic in holiness   Another possible translation is "majestic among the holy ones"—the members of the divine retinue. Some ancient versions so render it.[48]

Awesome in splendor   Or "awesome in regard to His laudable deeds"—recounted in the following verses.[49]

12.   The earth swallowed them   Figurative for "They met their death." Hebrew *'erets* here may well mean the underworld, as in some other biblical texts.[50]

13.   With the Egyptian menace finally eliminated, the movement of the poem shifts from the events that occurred at the sea and now focus on the march to the promised land. The use of *'erets* in verse 12 smooths the transition from the one to the other.[51]

In Your love   Hebrew *ḥesed* is a key term in the Bible. Depending on the context, it can express conduct conditioned by intimate relationship, covenantal obligation, or even undeserved magnanimity. The Decalogue and other texts specify *ḥesed* as one of God's supreme attributes.[52]

You redeemed   See Comment to 6:6.

You guide   The Hebrew stem *n-h-l* originates in the vocabulary of shepherding and denotes leading the sheep to a watering place.[53] Its use here thus evokes the idea of God's tender, loving care for His people—His "flock"—whom he leads from slavery to freedom and guides through the wilderness, while supplying all their needs. The image is reinforced by the following Hebrew *naveh*, which basically means "pastureland, abode of shepherds."[54] Psalm 78:52 gives a graphic depiction: "He set His people moving like sheep, / drove them like a flock in the wilderness."

Your holy abode   This phrase has been variously understood as referring to Mount Sinai,[55] the entire Land of Israel,[56] and the Temple on Mount Zion.[57] The account of the Exodus in Psalm 78:54 would seem to favor the first possibility because, following the notice of the drowning of the foe in the sea and preceding the conquest, the poet declares: "He brought them to His holy realm, / the mountain His right hand had acquired." This also accords with the theophany to Moses at the Burning Bush, which ordains that, following the Exodus, the people will worship God at the mount in the wilderness (3:12).

THE IMPACT ON THE NEIGHBORING PEOPLES   (vv. 14–16)

God's mighty deeds on Israel's behalf strike terror in the hearts of Israel's neighbors, their potential enemies.[58] These are listed in the order that Israel would have encountered them. The Philistines are mentioned first because they were closest to the northeastern border of Egypt and because they were

15Now are the clans of Edom dismayed;
The tribes of Moab—trembling grips them;
All the dwellers in Canaan are aghast.
16Terror and dread descend upon them;
Through the might of Your arm they are still as
stone—
Till Your people cross over, O LORD,
Till Your people cross whom You have ransomed.

אֱדֹום אֵילֵי מֹואָב יֹאחֲזֵמֹו רָעַד נָמֹגוּ
כֹּל יֹשְׁבֵי כְנָעַן: 16 תִּפֹּל עֲלֵיהֶם אֵימָתָה
וָפַחַד בִּגְדֹל זְרֹועֲךָ יִדְּמוּ כָּאָבֶן עַד־
יַעֲבֹר עַמְּךָ יְהוָה עַד־יַעֲבֹר עַם־זוּ

the most formidable. See Comment to 14:17. The other three appear in proper geographical and chronological order, according to the circuitous route followed: from south to north and then westward across the Jordan. The omission of the Ammonites from this list is puzzling; they are also omitted in Numbers 33:40–49.[59]

14. the dwellers Hebrew *yoshevei* here may well mean "rulers," literally "those who sit" [on thrones].[60]

15. the clans Hebrew *'alluf* might also mean "chieftain." Since it is used in combination only with the Edomites and with no other people, it may reflect local Edomite terminology.[61]

Edom The Edomites are descendants of Esau, also known as Edom, brother of Jacob. They occupied the southernmost part of Transjordan. They would later become inveterate enemies of Israel.[62]

The tribes An alternative is to take Hebrew *'eilei* literally as "rams" (sing. *'ayil*), a reference to the unusual wealth of sheep and rams found in Moab, as noted in 2 Kings 3:4. The term would then be a nickname for the inhabitants of the country. More likely "ram" is an honorific title for "chieftain." It is so used elsewhere in the Bible.[63]

Moab The plateau east of the Dead Sea between the wadis Arnon and Zered. It was occupied by the Moabites, who are traced back to Lot, nephew of Abraham. Numbers 22:1–7 recounts the alarm felt by the Moabites at the appearance of the Israelites close to their border.

dwellers in Canaan Or, as in verse 14, "rulers"—the thirty-one kings of the city-states listed in Joshua 12.

are aghast Literally, "melt away"; they are enervated, demoralized.[64]

16. The thought of the preceding verses is continued. The Israelites are perceived as a threat by the peoples who dwell in the vicinity of the wilderness route. This understanding requires that Hebrew *ya'avor* be rendered "pass by," unless it refers to the crossing of the Jordan into Canaan.

Till These last two clauses of the verse can hardly apply to the Canaanites, for they are to be dispossessed.

Your people The one You selected for a special relationship and destiny.

You have ransomed Hebrew *kanita* means literally "You acquired" (by purchase), "You own," as though God had purchased Israel from the Egyptians to be His own servants.[65] It is also possible that the Hebrew stem *k-n-h* is used here in its ancient meaning of "create." The idea that God "created" Israel is expressed explicitly in Deuteronomy 32:6.[66]

THE GRAND FINALE (vv. 17–18)

The Song at the Sea closes with an affirmation of confidence in the promise that God's redemption of Israel from Egypt will culminate in the building of a Temple. This idea is expressed in Deuteronomy 12:9–11[67] and echoed in King Solomon's dedicatory speech at the completion of the Temple in Jerusalem (1 Kings 8:56). That this event closes the Exodus era is well illustrated by the author of the

¹⁷You will bring them and plant them in
Your own mountain,
The place You made to dwell in, O L<small>ORD</small>,
The sanctuary, O Lord, which Your hands
established.
¹⁸The L<small>ORD</small> will reign for ever and ever!

¹⁹For the horses of Pharaoh, with his chariots and horse-
men, went into the sea; and the L<small>ORD</small> turned back on them
the waters of the sea; but the Israelites marched on dry
ground in the midst of the sea.

מָכ֑וֹן   בְּהַ֥ר נַחֲלָֽתְךָ֗   תְּבִאֵ֗מוֹ וְתִטָּעֵ֙מוֹ֙   ¹⁷   קָנִֽיתָ׃

מִקְּדָ֕שׁ אֲדֹנָ֖י כּוֹנְנ֥וּ   לְשִׁבְתְּךָ֙ פָּעַ֣לְתָּ יְהֹוָ֔ה   לְשִׁבְתְּךָ֙

כִּ֣י   ¹⁹   ¹⁸ יְהֹוָ֥ה ׀ יִמְלֹ֖ךְ לְעֹלָ֥ם וָעֶֽד׃   יָדֶֽיךָ׃

בַּיָּ֔ם   וּבְפָרָשָׁ֖יו   בְּרִכְבּ֥וֹ   פַּרְעֹ֜ה   ס֨וּס   בָ֣א

וַיָּ֨שֶׁב יְהֹוָ֤ה עֲלֵהֶם֙ אֶת־מֵ֣י הַיָּ֔ם וּבְנֵ֧י יִשְׂרָאֵ֛ל הָלְכ֥וּ

ב   בַיַּבָּשָׁ֖ה בְּת֥וֹךְ הַיָּֽם׃

Book of Kings, who dates the building of the Temple according to the Exodus, the only such
chronological reckoning in the Bible (1 Kings 6:1).

17. ***Your own mountain*** Hebrew *har naḥalatkha*, literally "the mountain of Your
possession," is a unique phrase in the Bible. It occurs in Ugaritic literature in relation to the sacred
mountain *Ṣapon*[68] on which stood the sanctuary of the Canaanite deity Baal. Here, this standard
religious phrase, prevalent in the ancient Near East, is employed by the poet in monotheized form,
totally emptied of its pagan content.

The place Hebrew *makhon* seems to mean the dais on which the divine throne rests.[69]

O Lord The Hebrew text has *'adonai* in place of the usual YHVH, possibly so that the
Tetragrammaton appears exactly ten times in the *shirah*.[70]

The sanctuary There is a widespread notion that the earthly sanctuary is but a replica of an
ideal celestial prototype. The two merge in the poet's mind.[71]

18. The *shirah* closes, as it opens, with the exaltation of God, now expressed in terms of
kingship—the earliest biblical use of this metaphor.[72] This climactic finale is the logical sequence of
the basic themes of the poem: God's absolute sovereignty over nature and history. The conception
and designation of the deity as king was pervasive throughout the ancient Near East long before Israel
appeared on the scene. It originated in the projection of the human institution onto the god. We do
not know when Israel first adopted the concept, but it must have preceded the founding of the
monarchy, for the prophet Samuel objected to the innovation on the grounds that it meant the
rejection of God's kingship over Israel (1 Sam. 8:7; 12:12).

The proclamation of the eternal kingship of God in the present context may suggest the contrast
between the ephemeral and illusory nature of Pharaoh's self-proclaimed royal divinity and the
permanent reality of God's sovereignty.

A CODA   (v. 19)

A brief prose summary of the occasion for the celebration closes the composition and reconnects it
with verse 1.[73]

THE SONG OF MIRIAM   (vv. 20–21)

This popular English title is somewhat misleading since the text states that Miriam recites only the
first line of the *shirah*. However, a midrash has it that Miriam and the women actually recite the entire
song. These verses affirm the custom, chronicled in Judges 11:34 and 1 Samuel 18:6, of women going
forth with music and dance[74] to hail the returning victorious hero, although in the present instance, it
is God and not man who is the victor.

²⁰Then Miriam the prophetess, Aaron's sister, took a timbrel in her hand, and all the women went out after her in dance with timbrels. ²¹And Miriam chanted for them:

Sing to the LORD, for He has triumphed gloriously;
Horse and driver He has hurled into the sea.

20 וַתִּקַּח מִרְיָם הַנְּבִיאָה אֲחֹות אַהֲרֹן אֶת־
הַתֹּף בְּיָדָהּ וַתֵּצֶאןָ כָל־הַנָּשִׁים אַחֲרֶיהָ בְּתֻפִּים
וּבִמְחֹלֹת: 21 וַתַּעַן לָהֶם מִרְיָם
שִׁירוּ לַיהֹוָה כִּי־גָאֹה גָּאָה
סוּס וְרֹכְבֹו רָמָה בַיָּם: ס

20. Miriam No longer anonymous as in Exodus 2:4,7–9, she is here given two titles.

the prophetess The other women with whom she shares this designation are Deborah, Huldah, and Noadiah.[75] Rabbinic tradition adds another three—Hannah, Abigail, and Esther—for a total of seven prophetesses active in Israel in biblical times.[76]

Aaron's sister Rashbam observes that the epithet reflects the practice of a younger daughter being known as the sister of the first-born male in the family; so Naamah, sister of Tubal-cain; Mahath, sister of Nebaioth; and Timna, sister of Lotan.[77] Behind this phenomenon may lie the well-documented Near Eastern social institution known as fratriarchy, in which, in certain circumstances, authority is invested in the eldest brother.[78]

timbrel Hebrew *tof* is most likely the portable frame drum, a percussion instrument constructed of two parallel membranes stretched over a loop or frame. It was apparently used exclusively by a special class of female musicians.[79]

Crises in the Wilderness   (15:22–17:16)

Freed from the Egyptian threat, the people begin the long trek through the wilderness toward the promised land. The rest of the Book of Exodus relates some major events of the first year of these wanderings, the central one, of course, being the experience at Sinai. But on the way to the mountain four crises occur: (1) a lack of drinking water (15:22–27), (2) a shortage of food (16:1–36), (3) a further lack of water (17:1–7), and (4) sudden, unprovoked aggression by a wild desert tribe (17:8–16).

These misfortunes reflect the harsh realities of life in the wilderness. The first three are imposed by the cruelties of nature; the last, by the cruelty of man. In each instance Israel's need is very real, and the popular discontent is quite understandable. These experiences illustrate both the precarious nature of Israel's survival and God's providential care of His people. Although in no case is divine anger displayed, the first three narratives nevertheless leave the unmistakable impression of being a negative judgment on Israel's behavior, an implicit critique of the people's ingratitude to God and their lack of faith in spite of their very recent experience of His wondrous protection and deliverance. And moreover, where one might expect popular resentment to diminish in the wake of the divine response to each successive deprivation, in fact just the opposite occurs. It appears that "faith in the LORD and His servant Moses," to which 14:31 bears witness, began to weaken under the strains of life in the wilderness.

These stories are part of a more extensive series of accounts about popular dissatisfaction and even rebellion in the course of the wanderings.

In serving its didactic purposes, the Torah focuses upon these particular incidents to draw a picture of a wayward generation. The same motif is taken up by both psalmist and prophet.[80] But the number of infractions is relatively few, after all, given the forty-year period in question and the difficult circumstances; and both Hosea and Jeremiah depict the wilderness period in a positive light. The former refers to Israel's future, loving response to God "as in the days of her youth, when she came up from the land of Egypt" (Hos. 2:16–17); the latter evokes memories of the halcyon days of the wilderness wanderings (Jer. 2:2): "I accounted to your favor / The devotion of your youth, / Your love as a bride— / How you followed Me in the wilderness, / In a land not sown."

22Then Moses caused Israel to set out from the Sea of Reeds. They went on into the wilderness of Shur; they traveled three days in the wilderness and found no water. 23They came to Marah, but they could not drink the water of Marah because it was bitter; that is why it was named Marah. 24And the people grumbled against Moses, saying, "What shall we drink?" 25So he cried out to the LORD, and the LORD showed him a piece of wood; he threw it into the water and the water became sweet.

There He made for them a fixed rule, and there He put them to the test. 26He said, "If you will heed the LORD your

22 וַיַּסַּע מֹשֶׁה אֶת־יִשְׂרָאֵל מִיַּם־סוּף וַיֵּצְאוּ אֶל־מִדְבַּר־שׁוּר וַיֵּלְכוּ שְׁלֹשֶׁת־יָמִים בַּמִּדְבָּר וְלֹא־מָצְאוּ מָיִם: 23 וַיָּבֹאוּ מָרָתָה וְלֹא יָכְלוּ לִשְׁתֹּת מַיִם מִמָּרָה כִּי מָרִים הֵם עַל־כֵּן קָרָא־שְׁמָהּ מָרָה: 24 וַיִּלֹּנוּ הָעָם עַל־מֹשֶׁה לֵּאמֹר מַה־נִּשְׁתֶּה: 25 וַיִּצְעַק אֶל־יְהוָה וַיּוֹרֵהוּ יְהוָה עֵץ וַיַּשְׁלֵךְ אֶל־הַמַּיִם וַיִּמְתְּקוּ הַמָּיִם

שָׁם שָׂם לוֹ חֹק וּמִשְׁפָּט וְשָׁם נִסָּהוּ: 26 וַיֹּאמֶר אִם־שָׁמוֹעַ תִּשְׁמַע לְקוֹל | יְהוָה אֱלֹהֶיךָ וְהַיָּשָׁר

THE BITTER WATERS AT MARAH (vv. 22–27)

This section, framed by notices designating the initial stations in the wilderness, resumes the narrative interrupted at 14:29. Numbers 33 sets forth the full itinerary in great detail. The present story is clearly abbreviated, for it presupposes knowledge of some legislation promulgated at Marah.

22. Moses caused Israel to set out This rather unusual formulation gave rise to a midrash that Moses had to compel the people to move on because they were preoccupied with collecting the spoils of the drowned Egyptians.[81]

the wilderness of Shur This region is designated "the wilderness of Etham" in Numbers 33:8. A location called Shur, along the route to Egypt, is mentioned several times in biblical texts.[82] The name means "a wall" and most probably refers to the wall of fortifications built by the pharaohs in the eastern Delta of the Nile along the line of the present-day Isthmus of Suez. It was meant to protect Egypt from Asian incursions. The Prophecy of Nefer-rohu (Neferti), purporting to derive from about 2650 B.C.E., already mentions the "Wall of the Ruler" to be built in order to keep Asiatics out of Egypt.[83] The Story of Sinuhe (20th cent. B.C.E.) similarly mentions the "Wall of the Ruler" made to oppose the Asiatics and to "crush the Sand-crossers."[84]

three days If intended literally, a distance of at most 45 miles (72.5 km.) would be involved. Three days is often used as a literary convention. See Comment to 3:18.

and found no water Since this would have been unlikely along the coastal region, it indicates an initial southerly march that had to be reversed for lack of water.

23. Marah Meaning "bitter" in Hebrew. The site has been plausibly identified with ʿAin Ḥawarah, a spring just south of Wadi ʿAmarah,[85] a name that probably gave rise to Marah as word play.

bitter Tormented by thirst, the people find only undrinkable water. Desert springs are frequently bitter.

24. It is only the opening phrase that shows the seemingly innocent and justifiable question to be accusatory and confrontational.[86]

25. Moses is not a wonder-worker; he can do nothing except by divine instruction.

a piece of wood Or "a log." Supposedly, the water passed through the porous wood, which filtered out enough of the impurities to make it potable.[87]

The Mekhilta turns the entire incident into a metaphor.[88] The living, life-sustaining water symbolizes the Torah; to be deprived of its spiritual sustenance for three days is life-threatening. (Hence, the Torah is read publicly each Sabbath, Monday, and Thursday.) The parable is reinforced by the Hebrew verb *va-yorehu*, "He showed him," which comes from the same stem as Torah, and by ʿ*ets*, "a tree log," which is a symbol of Torah described in Proverbs 3:18 (cf. 3:1) as "a tree of life to those who grasp her." The verse succeeding this Exodus passage further enhances the homily.

God diligently, doing what is upright in His sight, giving ear to His commandments and keeping all His laws, then I will not bring upon you any of the diseases that I brought upon the Egyptians, for I the LORD am your healer."

²⁷And they came to Elim, where there were twelve springs of water and seventy palm trees; and they encamped there beside the water.

בְּעֵינָיו תַּעֲשֶׂה וְהַאֲזַנְתָּ לְמִצְוֹתָיו וְשָׁמַרְתָּ כָּל־חֻקָּיו כָּל־הַמַּחֲלָה אֲשֶׁר־שַׂמְתִּי בְמִצְרַיִם לֹא־אָשִׂים עָלֶיךָ כִּי אֲנִי יְהוָה רֹפְאֶךָ: ס חמישי [רביעי לספרדים]

²⁷ וַיָּבֹאוּ אֵילִמָה וְשָׁם שְׁתֵּים עֶשְׂרֵה עֵינֹת מַיִם וְשִׁבְעִים תְּמָרִים וַיַּחֲנוּ־שָׁם עַל־הַמָּיִם:

16 Setting out from Elim, the whole Israelite community came to the wilderness of Sin, which is between Elim and Sinai, on the fifteenth day of the second month after their departure from the land of Egypt. ²In the wilderness, the whole Israelite community grumbled against Moses and Aaron. ³The Israelites said to them, "If only we had died by

ט״ז וַיִּסְעוּ מֵאֵילִם וַיָּבֹאוּ כָּל־עֲדַת בְּנֵי־יִשְׂרָאֵל אֶל־מִדְבַּר־סִין אֲשֶׁר בֵּין־אֵילִם וּבֵין סִינָי בַּחֲמִשָּׁה עָשָׂר יוֹם לַחֹדֶשׁ הַשֵּׁנִי לְצֵאתָם מֵאֶרֶץ מִצְרָיִם: ² וַיִּלּוֹנוּ כָּל־עֲדַת בְּנֵי־יִשְׂרָאֵל עַל־מֹשֶׁה וְעַל־אַהֲרֹן בַּמִּדְבָּר: 3 וַיֹּאמְרוּ אֲלֵהֶם בְּנֵי

וַיִּלּוֹנוּ ק' v. 2.

a fixed rule Apparently, the sentence is a parenthetic note that reflects a now lost tradition about some law(s) given to Israel at this site. The Mekhilta believes they were the Sabbath laws.[89] The next episode indeed presupposes knowledge of these laws prior to the Sinaitic revelation.[90]

He put them to the test Rashbam understands the lack of drinking water to have constituted a test of Israel's faith in God. The particular item of legislation might also have served the same purpose.

26. what is upright in His sight The Mekhilta understands this to refer to honesty in business dealings.[91]

the diseases Not necessarily the plagues, but those maladies that were endemic in Egypt, referred to elsewhere in the Torah as "the dreadful diseases of Egypt," "the Egyptian inflammation," and "the sicknesses of Egypt."[92]

your healer God is the ultimate source of all healing. Just as He cured the waters at Marah, so will He heal the ills of an obedient Israel.[93]

27. Elim So Numbers 33:9; a wooded, freshwater oasis, generally identified with Wadi Gharandel. Nearby is the plain of el-Marḥah, a convenient camp site.[94]

CHAPTER 16   THE SHORTAGE OF FOOD—MANNA AND QUAIL   (vv. 1–20)

It is now six weeks after the Exodus. With the oasis at Elim now behind them and the provisions brought from Egypt exhausted, the people face a severe shortage of food. The wilderness conditions offer little possibility of securing fresh supplies. Popular discontent flares, and harsh accusations are hurled against Moses and Aaron.

God responds to Israel's material and spiritual needs: He supplies manna and quail and institutes the weekly Sabbath rest day.

THE COMPLAINT (vv. 1–3)

1. The wilderness itinerary set forth in Numbers 33:10–11 refers to an intermediate encampment by the Sea of Reeds on the way to the region of Sinai, a clear indication that the present record is condensed.

2–3. The hardships of life in the wilderness arouse nostalgia for life in Egypt. Another

the hand of the LORD in the land of Egypt, when we sat by the fleshpots, when we ate our fill of bread! For you have brought us out into this wilderness to starve this whole congregation to death."

⁴And the LORD said to Moses, "I will rain down bread for you from the sky, and the people shall go out and gather each day that day's portion—that I may thus test them, to see whether they will follow My instructions or not. ⁵But

יִשְׂרָאֵ֔ל מִֽי־יִתֵּ֨ן מוּתֵ֤נוּ בְיַד־יְהֹוָה֙ בְּאֶ֣רֶץ מִצְרַ֔יִם בְּשִׁבְתֵּ֙נוּ֙ עַל־סִ֣יר הַבָּשָׂ֔ר בְּאׇכְלֵ֥נוּ לֶ֖חֶם לָשֹׂ֑בַע כִּֽי־הוֹצֵאתֶ֤ם אֹתָ֙נוּ֙ אֶל־הַמִּדְבָּ֣ר הַזֶּ֔ה לְהָמִ֛ית אֶת־ כׇּל־הַקָּהָ֥ל הַזֶּ֖ה בָּרָעָֽב׃ ס
4 וַיֹּ֤אמֶר יְהֹוָה֙ אֶל־מֹשֶׁ֔ה הִנְנִ֨י מַמְטִ֥יר לָכֶ֛ם לֶ֖חֶם מִן־הַשָּׁמָ֑יִם וְיָצָ֨א הָעָ֤ם וְלָֽקְטוּ֙ דְּבַר־יוֹם֙ בְּיוֹמ֔וֹ לְמַ֧עַן אֲנַסֶּ֛נּוּ הֲיֵלֵ֥ךְ בְּתוֹרָתִ֖י אִם־לֹֽא׃

popular idealizing of the past is chronicled in Numbers 11:5: "We remember the fish that we used to eat free in Egypt, the cucumbers, the melons, the leeks, the onions, and the garlic."

2. ***the whole Israelite community*** The suffering is more severe and more widespread than in the previous crisis, for in that instance the grumblers are described as simply "the people" (15:24).

3. ***died by the hand of the LORD*** That is, from natural causes.[1] Death in old age in slavery is deemed preferable to premature death by starvation in freedom.[2] These hypothetical options show a lack of faith in divine Providence.

fleshpots . . . bread[3] Since the people left Egypt with their flocks and herds,[4] they could hardly have been in danger of starvation. However, livestock is the most valuable possession of the pastoralist, who can seldom be induced to part with an animal. Besides, the people had probably already suffered losses for lack of adequate pasturage.

THE DIVINE RESPONSE (vv. 4–5)

Even before Moses can "cry out to the LORD," as in the preceding crisis (15:25), God responds to Israel's needs.[5] No anger is displayed at the people's complaint; nor is any recorded in the historical recapitulation of this episode in Deuteronomy 8:3,16. But in his sermon in Psalm 78:18–22, the psalmist portrays God as incensed at the disbelief and faithlessness inherent in the people's grumbling.[6]

It may well be that implicit in the Torah's narrative is the biblical teaching that human beings have an obligation to imitate divine qualities (***imitatio dei***). This Jewish doctrine is based on such passages as Leviticus 19:2—"You shall be holy, for I, the LORD your God, am holy"—and on the several texts in Deuteronomy that enjoin Israel "to walk" in God's way. The Sifrei phrases the teaching this way: "Just as He is compassionate, so be you; just as He is gracious, so be you."[7] It follows from the present narrative that Israel would be expected to emulate God's qualities of self-restraint in the face of base ingratitude and of solicitous concern for the hungry.

4. ***the LORD said to Moses*** Moses is privy to God's intentions, but he is not instructed to divulge the information to the people.

bread . . . from the sky This contrasts with the usual "bread from the earth." The substance is also poetically called "heavenly grain," "the bread of heroes," "heavenly bread," and "bread from heaven."[8]

each day Hebrew *devar yom be-yomo* is an administrative formula used in connection with work schedules, sacrifices, and rations.[9] The fixed daily allotment of manna to each individual ensured fair and equal distribution of this scarce commodity (v. 16). The insecurity of the people's day-to-day existence, wholly dependent on this unfamiliar substance, heightens their consciousness of absolute reliance upon God's beneficence.[10]

that I may thus test them Two interpretations of this phrase are possible: (1) the gift of manna is to be subject to restrictions that test Israel's obedience and trust;[11] and (2) God intentionally subjects Israel to hunger in order to demonstrate and inculcate the lesson of their absolute dependence upon Him for sustenance.[12] This follows the understanding of the manna episode in Deuteronomy 8:2–3.

on the sixth day, when they apportion what they have brought in, it shall prove to be double the amount they gather each day." ⁶So Moses and Aaron said to all the Israelites, "By evening you shall know it was the LORD who brought you out from the land of Egypt; ⁷and in the morning you shall behold the Presence of the LORD, because He has heard your grumblings against the LORD. For who are we that you should grumble against us? ⁸Since it is the LORD," Moses continued, "who will give you flesh to eat in the evening and bread in the morning to the full, because the LORD has heard the grumblings you utter against Him, what is our part? Your grumbling is not against us, but against the LORD!"

5 וְהָיָה֙ בַּיּ֣וֹם הַשִּׁשִּׁ֔י וְהֵכִ֖ינוּ אֵ֣ת אֲשֶׁר־יָבִ֑יאוּ וְהָיָ֣ה מִשְׁנֶ֔ה עַ֥ל אֲשֶֽׁר־יִלְקְט֖וּ י֥וֹם ׀ יֽוֹם׃ ס 6 וַיֹּ֤אמֶר מֹשֶׁה֙ וְאַהֲרֹ֔ן אֶֽל־כָּל־בְּנֵ֖י יִשְׂרָאֵ֑ל עֶ֕רֶב וִֽידַעְתֶּ֕ם כִּ֧י יְהֹוָ֛ה הוֹצִ֥יא אֶתְכֶ֖ם מֵאֶ֥רֶץ מִצְרָֽיִם׃ 7 וּבֹ֗קֶר וּרְאִיתֶם֙ אֶת־כְּב֣וֹד יְהֹוָ֔ה בְּשָׁמְע֥וֹ אֶת־תְּלֻנֹּתֵיכֶ֖ם עַל־יְהֹוָ֑ה וְנַ֣חְנוּ מָ֔ה כִּ֥י תלונו עָלֵֽינוּ׃ 8 וַיֹּ֣אמֶר מֹשֶׁ֗ה בְּתֵ֣ת יְהֹוָה֩ לָכֶ֨ם בָּעֶ֜רֶב בָּשָׂ֣ר לֶאֱכֹ֗ל וְלֶ֤חֶם בַּבֹּ֙קֶר֙ לִשְׂבֹּ֔עַ בִּשְׁמֹ֤עַ יְהֹוָה֙ אֶת־תְּלֻנֹּ֣תֵיכֶ֔ם אֲשֶׁר־אַתֶּ֥ם מַלִּינִ֖ם עָלָ֑יו וְנַ֣חְנוּ מָ֔ה לֹא־עָלֵ֥ינוּ תְלֻנֹּתֵיכֶ֖ם כִּ֥י עַל־יְהֹוָֽה׃

v. 7. תַּלִּינוּ ק׳

My instructions This may refer to laws specifically relating to the manna or to God's laws in general. Exodus 15:25 leads us to assume a tradition about laws given before the Sinaitic revelation.

5. *the sixth day* Of the week. The sentence is elliptical, meaning that "on Friday, twice the usual daily amount shall be collected and prepared."[13] Verses 22–23 show that this is precisely what the people did. The Mekhilta takes the sentence to mean that the regular day's allotment would miraculously double when brought home, but the Hebrew should then be *ve-hayah le-mishnah*.[14]

THE PEOPLE ARE INFORMED (vv. 6–10)

Even though Moses and Aaron are not commanded to relay God's message, they do so in order to pacify the populace. But they speak in generalities and say nothing about the sixth day. That is why the chieftains are later puzzled about the purpose of the double portion of manna (v. 22).

6. *Aaron* He is included because, along with Moses, he was the target of the people's complaint.

all the Israelites The comprehensive formulation echoes verse 2.

***it was the* LORD** And not we, as was charged in verse 2. The unexpected and timely satisfaction of the craving for meat will be incontestable proof that Israel's experiences are determined by God's sovereign will.

7. *The Presence of the* LORD This is the first biblical usage of the seminal Hebrew phrase *kevod YHVH*. Formerly rendered "the glory of God," it is now recognized to be multifaceted in meaning, its precise signification determined by the context.[15] The reference here, as Rashi and Rashbam note, is not to any visible symbol, as in verse 10, but to the manifestation of God's essential nature, as He caringly and beneficently provides for His people's needs.

***against the* LORD** The carping against Moses and Aaron is really a questioning of God, from whom their mission and authority derived.

For who are we . . .[16] A self-deprecating rhetorical question that is intensified by the use of Hebrew *mah*, literally "what," employed of things rather than persons.[17]

8. Moses reiterates the sentiment just voiced and expands it to emphasize that the people's complaint is really a challenge to God.

to eat . . . to the full The varying expressions indicate that the cravings for both flesh and bread are to be satisfied but that the former is an unreasonable need.[18]

⁹Then Moses said to Aaron, "Say to the whole Israelite community: Advance toward the LORD, for He has heard your grumbling." ¹⁰And as Aaron spoke to the whole Israelite community, they turned toward the wilderness, and there, in a cloud, appeared the Presence of the LORD.

¹¹The LORD spoke to Moses: ¹²"I have heard the grumbling of the Israelites. Speak to them and say: By evening you shall eat flesh, and in the morning you shall have your fill of bread; and you shall know that I the LORD am your God."

¹³In the evening quail appeared and covered the camp; in the morning there was a fall of dew about the camp.

9 וַיֹּאמֶר מֹשֶׁה אֶל־אַהֲרֹן אֱמֹר אֶל־כָּל־עֲדַת בְּנֵי יִשְׂרָאֵל קִרְבוּ לִפְנֵי יְהֹוָה כִּי שָׁמַע אֵת תְּלֻנֹּתֵיכֶם: 10 וַיְהִי כְּדַבֵּר אַהֲרֹן אֶל־כָּל־עֲדַת בְּנֵי־יִשְׂרָאֵל וַיִּפְנוּ אֶל־הַמִּדְבָּר וְהִנֵּה כְּבוֹד יְהֹוָה נִרְאָה בֶּעָנָן: פ ששי [חמישי לספרדים]

11 וַיְדַבֵּר יְהֹוָה אֶל־מֹשֶׁה לֵּאמֹר: 12 שָׁמַעְתִּי אֶת־תְּלוּנֹּת בְּנֵי יִשְׂרָאֵל דַּבֵּר אֲלֵהֶם לֵאמֹר בֵּין הָעַרְבַּיִם תֹּאכְלוּ בָשָׂר וּבַבֹּקֶר תִּשְׂבְּעוּ־לָחֶם וִידַעְתֶּם כִּי אֲנִי יְהֹוָה אֱלֹהֵיכֶם:

13 וַיְהִי בָעֶרֶב וַתַּעַל הַשְּׂלָו וַתְּכַס אֶת־הַמַּחֲנֶה וּבַבֹּקֶר הָיְתָה שִׁכְבַת הַטַּל סָבִיב לַמַּחֲנֶה:

---

9. Aaron acts as Moses' spokesman—now to Israel rather than to Pharaoh.

toward the LORD Literally, "before the Lord," a phrase that usually means in front of the altar, Ark, or Tabernacle.[19] Here, as Rashi notes, it must refer to the direction of the cloud.

10. *in a cloud* Rather, "in the cloud," that is, the luminous cloud that symbolizes God's active, dynamic, indwelling Presence in Israel during the wilderness period; see Comment to 13:22. The sudden appearance of the cloud is an affirmation of the declaration, announced by Aaron.

THE QUAIL AND MANNA ARRIVE (vv. 11–20)

The divine promise is fulfilled. The narrative is expansive on the manna but terse with respect to the quail, for several reasons: the cry for bread was reasonable, the craving for meat was not; the manna appeared with attendant supernatural features, but, except for its timing, the quail was a wholly natural phenomenon; and the manna was supplied continuously for forty years, whereas the quail was only occasional.

12. *I have heard* The repetition serves to introduce the account of the actual arrival of quail and manna. This is not fortuitous but determined by divine deliberation.

By evening On Hebrew *bein ha-ʿarbayim*, literally "at twilight"; see Comment to 12:6.

eat . . . have your fill See Comment to verse 8.

you shall know This echoes verse 6. Israel "knows" God through the experience of His actions on their behalf. On the meaning of the Hebrew verb *y-d-ʿ*, see Comments to 1:8 and 6:3.

13. *quail* These migratory birds of the pheasant family, scientifically known as *Coturnix coturnix*, are to this day caught in large numbers in northern Sinai and Egypt.[20] They migrate in vast flocks from central Europe to Africa in the autumn and return in the spring. They are small in size and make the long and tiring journey in stages. Flying low and landing exhausted, they are easily captured with nets or by hand. Numbers 11:31–32 gives a vivid description of this process. The tender meat of the baby quail is regarded as a great delicacy. It requires no oil for cooking and is speedily prepared over a hot flame. There is no suggestion in the narrative that the quail was other than a one-time provision. This is supported by the account in Numbers 11:4,6,13,21–22, which records that some people, bored with the manna beyond endurance, hankered after meat. Hence, the quail could not have been available regularly or even intermittently. That is why both Deuteronomy 8:3,16 and Nehemiah 9, which recount God's benefactions to Israel in the wilderness, ignore the gift of quail.[21]

13. *a fall of dew*[22] Numbers 11:9 reads: "When the dew fell on the camp at night, the manna would fall upon it." That text, read in combination with verses 13–14, here yields a description of the manna as enveloped in two layers of dew. It would thereby remain clean until collected in the

¹⁴When the fall of dew lifted, there, over the surface of the wilderness, lay a fine and flaky substance, as fine as frost on the ground. ¹⁵When the Israelites saw it, they said to one another, "What is it?"—for they did not know what it was. And Moses said to them, "That is the bread which the LORD has given you to eat. This is what the LORD has commanded: Gather as much of it as each of you requires to eat, an *omer* to a person for as many of you as there are; each of you shall fetch for those in his tent."

¹⁷The Israelites did so, some gathering much, some little. ¹⁸But when they measured it by the *omer,* he who had gathered much had no excess, and he who had gathered little had no deficiency: they had gathered as much as they needed to eat. ¹⁹And Moses said to them, "Let no one leave any of it over until morning." ²⁰But they paid no attention to Moses; some of them left of it until morning, and it became infested with maggots and stank. And Moses was angry with them.

²¹So they gathered it every morning, each as much as he needed to eat; for when the sun grew hot, it would melt.

14 וַתַּעַל שִׁכְבַת הַטָּל וְהִנֵּה עַל־פְּנֵי הַמִּדְבָּר דַּק מְחֻסְפָּס דַּק כַּכְּפֹר עַל־הָאָרֶץ: 15 וַיִּרְאוּ בְנֵי־ יִשְׂרָאֵל וַיֹּאמְרוּ אִישׁ אֶל־אָחִיו מָן הוּא כִּי לֹא יָדְעוּ מַה־הוּא וַיֹּאמֶר מֹשֶׁה אֲלֵהֶם הוּא הַלֶּחֶם אֲשֶׁר נָתַן יְהוָה לָכֶם לְאָכְלָה: 16 זֶה הַדָּבָר אֲשֶׁר צִוָּה יְהוָה לִקְטוּ מִמֶּנּוּ אִישׁ לְפִי אָכְלוֹ עֹמֶר לַגֻּלְגֹּלֶת מִסְפַּר נַפְשֹׁתֵיכֶם אִישׁ לַאֲשֶׁר בְּאָהֳלוֹ תִּקָּחוּ:

17 וַיַּעֲשׂוּ־כֵן בְּנֵי יִשְׂרָאֵל וַיִּלְקְטוּ הַמַּרְבֶּה וְהַמַּמְעִיט: 18 וַיָּמֹדּוּ בָעֹמֶר וְלֹא הֶעְדִּיף הַמַּרְבֶּה וְהַמַּמְעִיט לֹא הֶחְסִיר אִישׁ לְפִי־אָכְלוֹ לָקָטוּ: 19 וַיֹּאמֶר מֹשֶׁה אֲלֵהֶם אִישׁ אַל־יוֹתֵר מִמֶּנּוּ עַד־ בֹּקֶר: 20 וְלֹא־שָׁמְעוּ אֶל־מֹשֶׁה וַיּוֹתִרוּ אֲנָשִׁים מִמֶּנּוּ עַד־בֹּקֶר וַיָּרֻם תּוֹלָעִים וַיִּבְאַשׁ וַיִּקְצֹף עֲלֵהֶם מֹשֶׁה:

21 וַיִּלְקְטוּ אֹתוֹ בַּבֹּקֶר בַּבֹּקֶר אִישׁ כְּפִי אָכְלוֹ וְחַם הַשֶּׁמֶשׁ וְנָמָס: 22 וַיְהִי ׀ בַּיּוֹם הַשִּׁשִּׁי לָקְטוּ

early morning. Because of its association with dew, which in biblical times was thought to descend like rain from the sky,[23] the manna could be called "bread from heaven."

14. To the description "fine and flaky, as fine as frost" must be added the specification in Numbers 11:7 that the manna was like coriander seed, of the color of bdellium, and it tasted like rich cream when prepared. No natural phenomenon in the Sinai region entirely matches these details. Closest is a white honeylike substance excreted from the tamarisk bush and called manna to this day by the Bedouin who collect it and eat it. This sap, rich in carbohydrates, is sucked by insects, which excrete the surplus onto the twigs. These form tiny globules that crystallize and fall to the ground.[24] However, no naturalistic explanation can do justice to the manna tradition as it is presented in biblical literature. Here the substance possesses a numinous quality. Its bestowal is distinguished by certain wondrous features. However much one gathered, it amounted to only one omer; on Fridays the amount doubled; it did not fall on the Sabbath; any surplus beyond the allotted amount became rancid on weekdays but not on the Sabbath. What's more, although the manna collected by Bedouins in the Sinai is seasonal and of limited quantity, the biblical manna nourished the entire Israelite population throughout the forty years of the wilderness wanderings.

flaky[25]

15. **What is it?** Hebrew *man hu* is a folk explanation for the term by which the inhabitants of the wilderness knew the substance described above. The usual Hebrew would be *mah hu*, but the form *man* may be an ancient dialectic variant.[26]

16. **an omer** Hebrew *'omer* usually means a sheaf,[27] but in this chapter it appears as a measure of capacity. Quite likely, ours is a different word, perhaps connected with Arabic *ghumar*, "a small bowl" that was used for measuring. See Comment to verse 36.

19. Ibn Ezra understands the purpose behind this restriction to be a test of faith that the manna would appear again the next day.

20. **infested with maggots** Hebrew *va-yarum* may be a play on *rimmah*, "a worm" (cf. v. 24), as Ibn Janah suggests.

²²On the sixth day they gathered double the amount of food, two *omers* for each; and when all the chieftains of the community came and told Moses, ²³he said to them, "This is what the LORD meant: Tomorrow is a day of rest, a holy sabbath of the LORD. Bake what you would bake and boil what you would boil; and all that is left put aside to be kept until morning." ²⁴So they put it aside until morning, as Moses had ordered; and it did not turn foul, and there were no maggots in it. ²⁵Then Moses said, "Eat it today, for today is a sabbath of the LORD; you will not find it today on the plain. ²⁶Six days you shall gather it; on the seventh day, the sabbath, there will be none."

²⁷Yet some of the people went out on the seventh day to gather, but they found nothing. ²⁸And the LORD said to

לֶחֶם מִשְׁנֶה שְׁנֵי הָעֹמֶר לָאֶחָד וַיָּבֹאוּ כָּל־
נְשִׂיאֵי הָעֵדָה וַיַּגִּידוּ לְמֹשֶׁה: 23 וַיֹּאמֶר אֲלֵהֶם הוּא
אֲשֶׁר דִּבֶּר יְהֹוָה שַׁבָּתוֹן שַׁבַּת־קֹדֶשׁ לַיהֹוָה מָחָר
אֵת אֲשֶׁר־תֹּאפוּ אֵפוּ וְאֵת אֲשֶׁר־תְּבַשְּׁלוּ בַּשֵּׁלוּ
וְאֵת כָּל־הָעֹדֵף הַנִּיחוּ לָכֶם לְמִשְׁמֶרֶת עַד־הַבֹּקֶר:
24 וַיַּנִּיחוּ אֹתוֹ עַד־הַבֹּקֶר כַּאֲשֶׁר צִוָּה מֹשֶׁה וְלֹא
הִבְאִישׁ וְרִמָּה לֹא־הָיְתָה בּוֹ: 25 וַיֹּאמֶר מֹשֶׁה
אִכְלֻהוּ הַיּוֹם כִּי־שַׁבָּת הַיּוֹם לַיהֹוָה הַיּוֹם לֹא
תִמְצָאֻהוּ בַּשָּׂדֶה: 26 שֵׁשֶׁת יָמִים תִּלְקְטֻהוּ וּבַיּוֹם
הַשְּׁבִיעִי שַׁבָּת לֹא יִהְיֶה־בּוֹ:
27 וַיְהִי בַּיּוֹם הַשְּׁבִיעִי יָצְאוּ מִן־הָעָם לִלְקֹט וְלֹא
מָצָאוּ: 28 וַיֹּאמֶר יְהֹוָה אֶל־מֹשֶׁה עַד־   ס

THE LAW OF THE SABBATH   (vv. 21–30)

Divine abstention from creativity on the seventh day is the climax of the biblical cosmogony, as recounted in Genesis 2:1–3. For this, the Hebrew stem *sh-b-t* is used in its verbal form, with God as the subject. Now, for the first time, the noun *shabbat* occurs to designate the fixed institution that recurs with cyclic regularity.

21.   This verse introduces the entire section.

22.   Presumably, the people had been told to collect double the usual daily amount on Fridays, but had not been told why. The tribal chiefs report that the order was followed, and they await clarification.

double the amount of food   Hebrew *leḥem mishneh* occurs in the Bible only here. Verse 22 is the source of the Jewish custom of having two loaves of bread (referred to in later Hebrew as *leḥem mishneh*) on the table at the *kiddush*, the benedictory ceremony consecrating the Sabbath and festivals.[28]

23.   Rashbam takes this verse to mean that Moses deliberately withheld the information about the Sabbath from the people in order to use the element of mystery as a pedagogic device.

a day of rest   Hebrew *shabbaton* is an abstract form meaning "restfulness." It is also applied to the holy day later known as Rosh Hashanah, and to Tabernacles (*sukkot*).[29] However, the weekly Sabbath and the Day of Atonement are designated *shabbat shabbaton*,[30] a superlative signifying the highest degree of rest. Hence, "all manner of work (Heb. *mela'khah*) is proscribed on the *shabbat shabbaton* but only "laborious work" (Heb. *mele'khet 'avodah*) on the ordinary *shabbaton*.[31]

a holy sabbath   The holiness of the day flows from God's infusion of blessing and sanctity, as related in Genesis 2:3. Because it is an integral part of the divinely ordained cosmic order, its blessed and sacred character is a cosmic reality wholly independent of human initiative. Hence the frequent designation "a Sabbath of the LORD." See further the Comment to 20:8–12.

bake . . . boil   A fuller description of the way the manna was prepared is given in Numbers 11:8. "The people would go about and gather it, grind it between millstones or pound it in a mortar, boil it in a pot, and make it into cakes." The present passage is the biblical source for the prohibition against cooking on the Sabbath.

all that is left   That is, what was neither baked nor boiled on Friday but remained in its raw, though still edible, state.

26.   Six days . . . on the seventh   The law of the Sabbath is frequently styled this way.[32]

27.   Some people were skeptical of Moses' prediction that no manna would fall on the Sabbath (cf. v. 20), and they went out to test it. Ezekiel (20:10–13) most likely refers to this incident

Moses, "How long will you people refuse to obey My commandments and My teachings? 29Mark that the LORD has given you the sabbath; therefore He gives you two days' food on the sixth day. Let everyone remain where he is: let no one leave his place on the seventh day." 30So the people remained inactive on the seventh day.

31The house of Israel named it manna; it was like coriander seed, white, and it tasted like wafers in honey.

רְאוּ 29 וְתוֹרֹתָֽי׃ מִצְוֹתַ֖י לִשְׁמֹ֥ר מֵֽאַנְתֶּ֔ם אָ֚נָה
לָכֶ֑ם נֹתֵ֣ן ה֖וּא עַל־כֵּ֥ן הַשַּׁבָּ֔ת לָכֶ֣ם נָתַ֤ן כִּֽי־יְהֹוָ֨ה
אַל־ תַּחְתָּ֔יו אִ֣ישׁ שְׁב֣וּ׀ יוֹמָ֑יִם לֶ֣חֶם הַשִּׁשִּׁ֖י בַּיּ֥וֹם
הָעָ֖ם וַיִּשְׁבְּת֥וּ 30 הַשְּׁבִיעִֽי׃ בַּיּ֥וֹם מִמְּקֹמ֖וֹ אִ֥ישׁ יֵֽצֵא־
[ששי לספרדים] הַשְּׁבִיעִֽי׃ בַּיּ֥וֹם

וְה֕וּא מָ֑ן שְׁמ֖וֹ אֶת־ יִשְׂרָאֵ֛ל בֵּֽית־ וַיִּקְרְא֧וּ 31
וַיֹּ֣אמֶר 32 בִּדְבָֽשׁ׃ כְּצַפִּיחִ֥ת וְטַעְמ֖וֹ לָבָ֔ן גַּד֙ כְּזֶ֤רַע

when he recounts that Israel had already violated the Sabbath laws in the wilderness. If so, it suggests that the number involved was far greater than the text might indicate.[33]

28-29. There is an apparent disparity between the nature of the offense, which is lack of faith, and the content of the divine reproof,[34] which refers to a violation of some law. Hence, either the text is also referring to the incident reported in verse 20, or it tacitly assumes that not keeping God's "commandments and teachings" involves disbelief. At any rate, the verse—like verses 4 and 15:25—presupposes some prior lawgiving not otherwise detailed.

29. has given you the Sabbath The institution is God's gift to Israel. As the rabbis of the Talmud expressed it, "The Holy One Blessed Be He said to Moses, 'I have a precious gift in My treasure house, called the Sabbath, and I desire to give it to Israel.'"[35]

Let everyone remain where he is . . . his place And not go out to collect manna. Early on this verse was more broadly interpreted as a general restriction on mobility during the Sabbath. The definition of the synonymous terms "where he is" (Heb. *tahtav*) and "his place" (Heb. *mekomo*) was established to be two thousand cubits beyond the city wall. This distance was derived from Numbers 35:5, which fixes the boundaries of the Levitical cities. The same line of demarcation appears once again in Joshua 3:4 as a kind of *cordon sanitaire* separating the people from the Ark at the crossing of the river Jordan into the promised land.[36]

AN APPENDIX ON THE MANNA (vv. 31–36)

This section contains a note on the purported origin of the name *manna*, a description of the substance's appearance and taste, an instruction to preserve a sample, a historical retrospect, and a metrological note.

The appendix stems from a time later than the events just narrated. It presupposes the erection of the Tabernacle, the appointment of a priesthood, the termination of the fall of manna, the settlement in the land, and the obsolescence of the omer measure.

Medieval Jewish commentators recognized that verses 32–34 tell of events that took place later on. It was already well established in rabbinic times that the order of the pentateuchal narratives does not necessarily conform to chronological sequence. This observation was formulated in two ways: "There is no early and late in the Torah" (*'ein mukdam u-me'uhar ba-torah*); and "The pericopes of the Torah were not given in order" (*lo' nitnu parshiyoteiha shel torah 'al ha-seder*). This principle is the last of the "Thirty-two Rules" employed in the rabbinic interpretation of the Torah, a compilation ascribed to Rabbi Yose ben Eleazar of Galilee (second century C.E.).[37]

31. See Comment to verse 14. The information about the nature of the manna is provided for those who are no longer familiar with it. The comparison with coriander seed relates only to the shape and size, not to its color, which is dark. In Numbers 11:7 the manna is described as having the appearance of bdellium (Heb. *bedolah*). It is assumed that the reader is familiar with the term, whose precise meaning is now uncertain. In Genesis 2:12 it is associated with gold and lapis lazuli, and so should refer to some precious stone. The Septuagint understands the depiction of the manna in this way, as do Rashi and Saadia. Josephus, however, compares the manna with "the spicy herb called *bdellium*."[38] The Akkadian cognate *budulhu* is, in fact, an aromatic resin.[39] Genesis Rabba 16:2 cites both a "precious stone" and "the *bedolah* of perfumers." This was a fragrant semitransparent resin derived from trees of the genus *Commiphora*.

32Moses said, "This is what the Lord has commanded: Let one *omer* of it be kept throughout the ages, in order that they may see the bread that I fed you in the wilderness when I brought you out from the land of Egypt." 33And Moses said to Aaron, "Take a jar, put one *omer* of manna in it, and place it before the Lord, to be kept throughout the ages." 34As the Lord had commanded Moses, Aaron placed it before the Pact, to be kept. 35And the Israelites ate manna forty years, until they came to a settled land; they ate the manna until they came to the border of the land of Canaan. 36The *omer* is a tenth of an *ephah*.

מֹשֶׁה זֶה הַדָּבָר אֲשֶׁר צִוָּה יְהֹוָה מְלֹא הָעֹמֶר מִמֶּנּוּ לְמִשְׁמֶרֶת לְדֹרֹתֵיכֶם לְמַעַן ׀ יִרְאוּ אֶת־הַלֶּחֶם אֲשֶׁר הֶאֱכַלְתִּי אֶתְכֶם בַּמִּדְבָּר בְּהוֹצִיאִי אֶתְכֶם מֵאֶרֶץ מִצְרָיִם: 33 וַיֹּאמֶר מֹשֶׁה אֶל־אַהֲרֹן קַח צִנְצֶנֶת אַחַת וְתֶן־שָׁמָּה מְלֹא־הָעֹמֶר מָן וְהַנַּח אֹתוֹ לִפְנֵי יְהֹוָה לְמִשְׁמֶרֶת לְדֹרֹתֵיכֶם: 34 כַּאֲשֶׁר צִוָּה יְהֹוָה אֶל־מֹשֶׁה וַיַּנִּיחֵהוּ אַהֲרֹן לִפְנֵי הָעֵדֻת לְמִשְׁמָרֶת: 35 וּבְנֵי יִשְׂרָאֵל אָכְלוּ אֶת־הַמָּן אַרְבָּעִים שָׁנָה עַד־בֹּאָם אֶל־אֶרֶץ נוֹשָׁבֶת אֶת־הַמָּן אָכְלוּ עַד־בֹּאָם אֶל־קְצֵה אֶרֶץ כְּנָעַן: 36 וְהָעֹמֶר עֲשִׂרִית הָאֵיפָה הוּא: פ שביעי

like wafers Hebrew *tsapiḥit* is an unknown word.[40] In Numbers 11:8 the taste is compared to "cream of oil," that is, "rich cream." Either we are dealing with varying traditions, or, as Bekhor Shor and Ibn Ezra suggest, our verse describes the taste of the manna in its raw state, while the passage in Numbers characterizes its flavor when cooked.

32–34. For educational purposes, a sample of the manna—an amount equal to an individual's daily ration—is to be preserved as a kind of cultural relic. It is to serve future generations as a vivid reminder of God's providential care of Israel throughout the wilderness period.

33. Since the priesthood in Israel has not yet been established, this instruction cannot be contemporaneous with the events previously described.[41]

a jar Hebrew *tsintsenet* is a unique word. According to the context, it refers to a vessel of some kind. The Septuagint renders it *stamnos*, "a jar" (for storing wine). This is also the tradition of the Mekhilta.[42] Lekaḥ Tov cites Jeremiah 32:14: ". . . put them into an earthen jar, so that they may last a long time." Sealed with wax, jars of this type were the most common and effective receptacle for storing valuables. Some of the Dead Sea Scrolls found in the caves at Qumran had been preserved in earthenware jars.

before the Lord That is, in front of the Ark in the Holy of Holies of the Tabernacle, which was not erected until the first anniversary of the Exodus.[43]

34. ***the Pact*** Ellipsis for "the Ark of the Pact."[44] Hebrew *'edut* is synonymous with *berit*, "covenant." The Ark housed the two tablets of stone on which the Decalogue was inscribed. These are variously designated "the tablets of the Pact" (Heb. *luḥot ha-'edut*), as in 31:18 and elsewhere, and "the Tablets of the Covenant" (Heb. *luḥot ha-berit*), as in Deuteronomy 9:9,11. Following the revolt of Korah, Aaron's rod was similarly deposited "before the Lord," that is, "before the Pact," for safekeeping and for an educational purpose, as recounted in Numbers 17:19,22,25.

35. After the Israelites crossed the Jordan and celebrated the Passover in the Land of Israel for the first time, Joshua 5:11–12 reports that "on the day after the passover offering, on that very day, they ate of the produce of the country, unleavened bread and parched grain. On that same day, when they ate of the produce of the land, the manna ceased. The Israelites got no more manna; that year they ate of the yield of the land of Canaan."

to the border of the land of Canaan This note is obviously not consistent with the above-cited tradition, unless, with Ibn Ezra, the reference concerns Gilgal, the first encampment of Israel west of the Jordan. That locality is situated "on the eastern border [Heb. *ketseh*] of Jericho" (Josh. 4:19).

36. The omer as a measure never recurs in the Bible. The note is needed here because the omer became obsolete and unintelligible to later generations. A tenth of an ephah is otherwise termed *'issaron*.[45] The *ephah*, a word of Egyptian origin, was a dry measure frequently mentioned in the Bible.

17 From the wilderness of Sin the whole Israelite community continued by stages as the LORD would command. They encamped at Rephidim, and there was no water for the people to drink. ²The people quarreled with Moses.

י״ז וַיִּסְעוּ כָּל־עֲדַת בְּנֵי־יִשְׂרָאֵל מִמִּדְבַּר־סִין לְמַסְעֵיהֶם עַל־פִּי יְהוָה וַיַּחֲנוּ בִּרְפִידִים וְאֵין מַיִם לִשְׁתֹּת הָעָם: ² וַיָּרֶב הָעָם עִם־מֹשֶׁה וַיֹּאמְרוּ

It seems to have been the name of a vessel, a meaning it still has in Zechariah 5:6–10, where it is large enough to contain a person.

CHAPTER 17   MASSAH AND MERIBAH   (vv. 1–7)

For the third time the people grumble against Moses. Their rhetoric grows stronger and more threatening; they even question God's providence. The seriousness of the episode left an indelible impression on the national historical memory, and its locale was called by a derogatory, symbolic name: Massah-Meribah. The frequent mention of this narrative in the Bible indicates that it had become a favorite subject of homiletic and didactic interpretation in ancient Israel.

Biblical authors used the theme in various ways. Frequently the episode serves as the motif of Israel "trying" and "provoking" God. Numbers 14:22–23 makes a general statement of the many such occasions during the wilderness wanderings. Deuteronomy 6:16 and 9:22 specifically cite the grumbling at Massah as the prime example of such discontent. This theme is echoed and emphasized in Psalm 95:8. Furthermore, a few texts associate the testing of God with the keeping of His commandments; in Deuteronomy 6:16–17, 8:2 and Psalms 78:56, we find the idea that the people make obedience to God dependent upon His benefactions. Having already so richly experienced God's blessings and favors in the events connected with the liberation from Egypt, they must be judged guilty of lack of faith and gross ingratitude.

The Massah-and-Meribah theme also served as the paradigm of God's active presence in sustaining Israel during its moment of dire need. Deuteronomy 8:15 and particularly Psalms 78:15–16,20 relate to it in this way. And although Isaiah 48:21 and Psalm 114:7 do not specify the locale, it is almost certain that these texts have the present narrative in mind.

Most creative and original is the third usage of the Massah-and-Meribah theme in biblical literature. Here the situation is reversed; it is God who is seen as trying Israel. The trials and tribulations that the people experienced in the wilderness on their way to the promised land were intended to test their faith. It is one thing to be able to affirm that "when Israel saw the wondrous power which the LORD had wielded against the Egyptians, the people feared the LORD; they had faith in the LORD and His servant Moses" (Exod. 14:31). It is quite another matter to know whether that faith was powerful enough and disinterested enough to be sustained also in times of adversity and misfortune. Deuteronomy 8:2,16 explicitly declare that the experiences during the forty years of journeying in the wilderness took place in order "that He might test you by hardships to learn what was in your hearts: whether you would keep His commandments or not" and "in order to test you by hardships only to benefit you in the end." This interpretation is taken up in Psalm 81:8: "I tested you at the waters of Meribah."

Deuteronomy 33:8 seems to preserve an otherwise unrecorded tradition about the special role of the Levites in this incident. It is possible, however, that that text refers to quite a different narrative concerning "the waters of Meribah," an incident that occurred many years later and at another location, as recounted in Numbers 20:1–13 and cited often in biblical texts.[1]

*1. **Rephidim***   The last station on the journey from the Sea of Reeds to Sinai, according to Exodus 19:2 and Numbers 33:14–15. Its location is uncertain. Verse 6 in the present chapter shows that it must be very close to Horeb/Mount Sinai, but the identity of the latter is itself a matter of considerable scholarly controversy. Certainly, a wilderness station must be assumed to be an oasis. Why then was there no water at Rephidim? Unlike the situation at Marah (Exod. 15:23), potability is not mentioned as a problem here. Therefore, either drought conditions had caused severe depletion of the usually available local resources, or the people were forcibly denied access to them. The latter seems the more plausible explanation because it ties in with the next episode, verses 8–16. The hostile Amalekites were in control of this region and blocked the approaches to the sources of water.

"Give us water to drink," they said; and Moses replied to them, "Why do you quarrel with me? Why do you try the LORD?" ³But the people thirsted there for water; and the people grumbled against Moses and said, "Why did you bring us up from Egypt, to kill us and our children and livestock with thirst?" ⁴Moses cried out to the LORD, saying, "What shall I do with this people? Before long they will be stoning me!" ⁵Then the LORD said to Moses, "Pass before the people; take with you some of the elders of Israel, and take along the rod with which you struck the Nile, and set out. ⁶I will be standing there before you on the rock at Horeb. Strike the rock and water will issue from it, and the people will drink." And Moses did so in the sight of the elders of Israel. ⁷The place was named Massah and Meribah, because the Israelites quarreled and because they tried the LORD, saying, "Is the LORD present among us or not?"

תְּנוּ־לָ֤נוּ מַ֨יִם֙ וְנִשְׁתֶּ֔ה וַיֹּ֤אמֶר לָהֶם֙ מֹשֶׁ֔ה מַה־תְּרִיבוּן֙ עִמָּדִ֔י מַה־תְּנַסּ֖וּן אֶת־יְהוָֽה׃ 3 וַיִּצְמָ֨א שָׁ֤ם הָעָם֙ לַמַּ֔יִם וַיָּ֤לֶן הָעָם֙ עַל־מֹשֶׁ֔ה וַיֹּ֕אמֶר לָ֤מָּה זֶּה֙ הֶעֱלִיתָ֣נוּ מִמִּצְרַ֔יִם לְהָמִ֥ית אֹתִ֛י וְאֶת־בָּנַ֥י וְאֶת־מִקְנַ֖י בַּצָּמָֽא׃ 4 וַיִּצְעַ֤ק מֹשֶׁה֙ אֶל־יְהוָ֣ה לֵאמֹ֔ר מָ֥ה אֶעֱשֶׂ֖ה לָעָ֣ם הַזֶּ֑ה ע֥וֹד מְעַ֖ט וּסְקָלֻֽנִי׃ 5 וַיֹּ֤אמֶר יְהוָה֙ אֶל־מֹשֶׁ֔ה עֲבֹר֙ לִפְנֵ֣י הָעָ֔ם וְקַ֥ח אִתְּךָ֖ מִזִּקְנֵ֣י יִשְׂרָאֵ֑ל וּמַטְּךָ֗ אֲשֶׁ֨ר הִכִּ֤יתָ בּוֹ֙ אֶת־הַיְאֹ֔ר קַ֥ח בְּיָדְךָ֖ וְהָלָֽכְתָּ׃ 6 הִנְנִ֣י עֹמֵד֩ לְפָנֶ֨יךָ שָּׁ֥ם ׀ עַל־הַצּוּר֮ בְּחֹרֵב֒ וְהִכִּ֣יתָ בַצּ֗וּר וְיָצְא֤וּ מִמֶּ֨נּוּ֙ מַ֔יִם וְשָׁתָ֖ה הָעָ֑ם וַיַּ֤עַשׂ כֵּן֙ מֹשֶׁ֔ה לְעֵינֵ֖י זִקְנֵ֥י יִשְׂרָאֵֽל׃ 7 וַיִּקְרָא֙ שֵׁ֣ם הַמָּק֔וֹם מַסָּ֖ה וּמְרִיבָ֑ה עַל־רִ֣יב ׀ בְּנֵ֣י יִשְׂרָאֵ֗ל וְעַ֨ל נַסֹּתָ֤ם אֶת־יְהוָה֙ לֵאמֹ֔ר הֲיֵ֧שׁ יְהוָ֛ה בְּקִרְבֵּ֖נוּ אִם־אָֽיִן׃ פ

---

2. quarreled The two preceding stories about popular discontent employed the Hebrew verb *l-w-n/l-y-n*, "to grumble."² The present narrative uses *r-y-v* as its key word, a far stronger term that carries quasi-judicial overtones. It conjures up a picture of angry and hostile confrontation in which the people, professing to be an aggrieved party, levy charges against God and Moses.

Give us water The peremptory demand is, in effect, a denunciation and an accusation.

3–4. This situation has seriously deteriorated. The language of the mob is intemperate, the ugly mood is explosive, and a riot may break out any moment.

5. the rod This pointed allusion to the first plague, as described in 7:17–24, conveys a subtle lesson. Whereas, on the earlier occasion, striking with the rod had deprived the Egyptians of drinking water, the same action now serves to satisfy Israel's need for water.

6. I will be standing there This anthropomorphism, or use of human language for God, is a response to the people's skeptical questioning of God's continued support (v. 7). God's immediate and potent presence will indeed be manifest.

at Horeb This site is known as "the mountain of God,"³ apparently another name for Mount Sinai; see Comment to 3:1. Here Moses first received both the call to leadership and the promise of Israel's redemption. The name is probably evocative and heartening to the hard-pressed leader, for on that occasion God had given Moses the assurance, "I will be with you."

Strike the rock The phenomenon is most likely to be explained by the presence of water-bearing formations of soft porous limestone, which has high water-retaining capacity. A sharp blow to such rock may crack its crust and release a flow of groundwater. What is of importance is that the miracle is credited to God not Moses, something that is emphasized several times in the Bible.⁴ As often in times of crisis, Moses acts only by divine instruction as the agent of God's will; he does not act on his own initiative.

7. Massah Literally, "trial."

Meribah Literally, "quarrel." This double-barreled name arises out of the verbs used by Moses in verse 2 and repeated here. It is to be noted that Israel's grumbling and lack of faith here, as at Marah,⁵ goes unpunished, probably because it too occurred before the covenant between God and Israel at Sinai.

8Amalek came and fought with Israel at Rephidim. 9Moses said to Joshua, "Pick some men for us, and go out and do battle with Amalek. Tomorrow I will station myself on the top of the hill, with the rod of God in my hand." 10Joshua did as Moses told him and fought with Amalek, while Moses, Aaron, and Hur went up to the top of the hill. 11Then, whenever Moses held up his hand, Israel prevailed; but whenever he let down his hand, Amalek prevailed.

8 וַיָּבֹא עֲמָלֵק וַיִּלָּחֶם עִם־יִשְׂרָאֵל בִּרְפִידִם:
9 וַיֹּאמֶר מֹשֶׁה אֶל־יְהוֹשֻׁעַ בְּחַר־לָנוּ אֲנָשִׁים
וְצֵא הִלָּחֵם בַּעֲמָלֵק מָחָר אָנֹכִי נִצָּב עַל־רֹאשׁ
הַגִּבְעָה וּמַטֵּה הָאֱלֹהִים בְּיָדִי: 10 וַיַּעַשׂ יְהוֹשֻׁעַ
כַּאֲשֶׁר אָמַר־לוֹ מֹשֶׁה לְהִלָּחֵם בַּעֲמָלֵק וּמֹשֶׁה
אַהֲרֹן וְחוּר עָלוּ רֹאשׁ הַגִּבְעָה: 11 וְהָיָה כַּאֲשֶׁר
יָרִים מֹשֶׁה יָדוֹ וְגָבַר יִשְׂרָאֵל וְכַאֲשֶׁר יָנִיחַ יָדוֹ וְגָבַר
עֲמָלֵק: 12 וִידֵי מֹשֶׁה כְּבֵדִים וַיִּקְחוּ־אֶבֶן וַיָּשִׂימוּ

THE BATTLE WITH AMALEK   (vv. 8–16)

A somewhat more expansive account of this incident is given in Deuteronomy 25:17–19, which reports that the Amalekites made a surprise rear attack on the famished and exhausted Israelites not long after the escape from Egypt. They ruthlessly cut down the stragglers—the elderly, the weak, and the infirm. Israel was forced to fight its first defensive war for survival.

Who were the Amalekites? The name itself is non-Semitic; its origin is obscure. We first encounter Amalek as the thirteenth descendant of Esau-Edom in the lists in Genesis 36. He was born of Timna, a concubine of Esau's first-born son, Eliphaz.[6] She is said to have been a "Horite," which means that she belonged to the people who were indigenous to Mount Seir. The Edomites displaced them and largely wiped them out.[7]

Translating the genealogical shorthand of Genesis 36 into terms of historical reality, we may reconstruct the following situation: The tribe of Amalek had been a late and subordinate adherent to the twelve-tribe Edomite confederation. Forced out of its habitat, it pursued a nomadic existence in the Negeb and Sinai Peninsula.[8] The Amalekites interpreted the sudden appearance of the Israelites in this region as a menacing encroachment upon their territory and as a threat to their control of the oases and trading routes. The Amalekites thereupon savagely attacked the Israelites.

This episode, like the preceding one, occurred at Rephidim. Apart from the locale, the two narratives also share in common certain other features: the rod (vv. 5,9); the similar-sounding Hebrew stems *n-w-s, n-s-h,* and *n-s-s,* (vv. 2,7,15); and the demonstration of God's protective and supporting presence in times of adversity.

9. Joshua   Although not previously mentioned, he is not further identified, which suggests that he is already well known. Later he is revealed to be the son of Nun and grandson of Elishama, who was a chieftain of the tribe of Ephraim.[9] According to Joshua 24:30, Joshua was buried in the hill country of the tribal territory of Ephraim.

Joshua was Moses' faithful attendant and became his designated successor.[10] As commander-in-chief of the army, he led the conquest of Canaan, which is described in the biblical book that bears his name. The present incident is the only reference in the Torah to Joshua's military skill.

rod of God   See Comment to 4:20.

10. Hur   Like Joshua, he too must have been an important public figure at this time. Exodus 24:14 associates him with Aaron in judging the people during Moses' absence on Mount Sinai. A later tradition identifies him as the husband of Moses' sister, Miriam.[11] He may be identical with the Hur who was the grandfather of the master craftsman Bezalel.[12]

11. held up his hand   The significance of this gesture is unclear. The hand, often the symbol of action and power, is also the instrument of mediation. The expression "the laying on of the hands"[13] exemplifies this idea. Moses' action might therefore be interpreted as a sort of mysterious focusing of supernal power on Israel. If so, it is noteworthy that Moses is here presented as being subject to the ordinary human frailties, in possession of no superhuman or innate magical powers. Another interpretation, highly plausible, is that of Rashbam, according to which Moses held up a standard bearing some conspicuous symbol that signified the presence of God in the Israelite camp.

¹²But Moses' hands grew heavy; so they took a stone and put it under him and he sat on it, while Aaron and Hur, one on each side, supported his hands; thus his hands remained steady until the sun set. ¹³And Joshua overwhelmed the people of Amalek with the sword.

¹⁴Then the Lord said to Moses, "Inscribe this in a document as a reminder, and read it aloud to Joshua: I will utterly blot out the memory of Amalek from under heaven!" ¹⁵And Moses built an altar and named it Adonai-nissi. ¹⁶He said, "It means, 'Hand upon the throne of the Lord!' The Lord will be at war with Amalek throughout the ages."

תַּחְתָּיו וַיֵּשֶׁב עָלֶיהָ וְאַהֲרֹן וְחוּר תָּמְכוּ בְיָדָיו
מִזֶּה אֶחָד וּמִזֶּה אֶחָד וַיְהִי יָדָיו אֱמוּנָה עַד־בֹּא
הַשָּׁמֶשׁ: ¹³ וַיַּחֲלֹשׁ יְהוֹשֻׁעַ אֶת־עֲמָלֵק וְאֶת־עַמּוֹ
לְפִי־חָרֶב: פ מפטיר
¹⁴ וַיֹּאמֶר יְהֹוָה אֶל־מֹשֶׁה כְּתֹב זֹאת זִכָּרוֹן
בַּסֵּפֶר וְשִׂים בְּאָזְנֵי יְהוֹשֻׁעַ כִּי־מָחֹה אֶמְחֶה אֶת־
זֵכֶר עֲמָלֵק מִתַּחַת הַשָּׁמָיִם: ¹⁵ וַיִּבֶן מֹשֶׁה מִזְבֵּחַ
וַיִּקְרָא שְׁמוֹ יְהֹוָה | נִסִּי: ¹⁶ וַיֹּאמֶר כִּי־יָד עַל־כֵּס
יָהּ מִלְחָמָה לַיהֹוָה בַּעֲמָלֵק מִדֹּר דֹּר: פ

The name that Moses gave to the altar after the battle lends support to this explanation. Standards emblazoned with religious insignia are known to have been in military use in the ancient Near East.

A rabbinic comment on this verse reads as follows: "Did the hands of Moses control the course of war? [No! The text] teaches that as long as the Israelites set their sights on High and subjected themselves to their Father in Heaven, they prevailed; otherwise they failed."¹⁴

12. remained steady   Hebrew *'emunah*, "faithfulness," occurs in this physical sense only here. Generally, the word bespeaks a moral quality.

13. overwhelmed   This unique use of Hebrew *ḥ-l-sh*, "to be weak,"¹⁵ as a transitive verb seems to convey the notion of inflicting heavy casualties, rather than of victory. Therefore, the Amalekites were forced to break off the engagement and withdraw.

14. Inscribe   This is the first reference to writing in the Bible.

a reminder   On the Hebrew stem *z-k-r*, see Comment to 2:24. Deuteronomy 25:17–19 asserts an unconditional injunction to remember Amalek, which is reinforced by the negative admonition "Do not forget!"

I will   The parallel account in Deuteronomy 25 has "you shall blot out." The two versions are complementary. The present text is a theological statement, a divine assurance of ultimate victory over Amalek. The later one makes the fulfillment of that promise conditional upon Israelite initiative and action.

15. built an altar   As an expression of gratitude to God and as a memorial and witness to the battle and its portents. The practice of giving names to altars is attested in Genesis 33:20, 35:7, and Judges 6:24. In none of these examples is any sacrifice mentioned. In fact, Joshua 22:26–27 explicitly excludes sacrificial rites from such a commemorative altar. The practice of designating commemorative altars seems to have ceased with the founding of the monarchy.

Adonai-nissi   Literally, "The Lord is my standard." See Comment to verse 11.

16.   This enigmatic verse appears to be a fragmentary citation from some ancient poetic text, now lost—perhaps the Book of the Wars of the Lord, mentioned in Numbers 21:14, or the Book of Jashar, cited in Joshua 10:13 and 2 Samuel 1:18.¹⁶ These works seem to have contained collections of war songs and poetic accounts of battles. The present verse may well be excerpted from a poetic version of the battle against Amalek.

He said, "It means, . . ."   Although the passage purports to be an explanation of the altar's name,¹⁷ the relationship between the two is difficult to discern.

Hand upon the throne   Jewish exegesis, ancient and medieval, understood the unique *kes* as *kisse'*, "throne,"¹⁸ and interpreted the phrase to be an oath-formula uttered either by Moses or by God. It reinforces the promise of verse 14.

the Lord   Hebrew *yah*; see Comment to 15:2.

YITRO

18 Jethro priest of Midian, Moses' father-in-law, heard all that God had done for Moses and for Israel His people, how the LORD had brought Israel out from Egypt. ²So Jethro, Moses' father-in-law, took Zipporah, Moses' wife, after she had been sent home, ³and her two sons—of whom one was named Gershom, that is to say, "I have been a stranger in a foreign land"; ⁴and the other was named

יתרו

יח וַיִּשְׁמַע יִתְרוֹ כֹהֵן מִדְיָן חֹתֵן מֹשֶׁה אֶת־
כָּל־אֲשֶׁר עָשָׂה אֱלֹהִים לְמֹשֶׁה וּלְיִשְׂרָאֵל עַמּוֹ
כִּי־הוֹצִיא יְהוָה אֶת־יִשְׂרָאֵל מִמִּצְרָיִם: 2 וַיִּקַּח יִתְרוֹ
חֹתֵן מֹשֶׁה אֶת־צִפֹּרָה אֵשֶׁת מֹשֶׁה אַחַר שִׁלּוּחֶיהָ:
3 וְאֵת שְׁנֵי בָנֶיהָ אֲשֶׁר שֵׁם הָאֶחָד גֵּרְשֹׁם כִּי

throughout the ages Hebrew **mi-dor dor** is unparalleled and is probably a poetic form of the phrase "from generation to generation" found in Isaiah 34:10. In Ugaritic texts,[19] *dr dr* means "eternity" and is used in parallelism with *l'lm*, "forever." The Hebrew phrase envisages a protracted cycle of wars between Israel and Amalek. Several references to those wars are recorded in the biblical narratives. In the course of the wilderness wanderings, Amalekites and Canaanites jointly inflicted "a shattering blow" on an Israelite force, as told in Numbers 14:44–45. Amalekites, either as mercenaries of neighboring kingdoms or independently, made devastating incursions into Israelite settlements throughout the period of the judges.[20] It was King Saul who first dealt effectively with the recurring Amalekite menace,[21] and King David who finally confronted the implacable enemy on its home ground. He decisively neutralized its war-making capacities.[22] Still, it was not until the days of King Hezekiah (715–687/6 B.C.E.) that "the last surviving Amalekites" were destroyed, according to 1 Chronicles 4:43.

In later Jewish literature, Amalek became a synonym for the implacable enemies of Israel. Haman "the Agagite" was identified with Amalek;[23] Josephus made him a descendant of Amalek.[24] Rome, too, was given the code-name Amalek.

CHAPTER 18

Jethro's Visit and the Organization of the Judiciary (vv. 1–27)

Yitro

Two distinct but interrelated units make up this chapter: verses 1–12, describing the visit of Jethro to the camp of Israel; verses 13–26, dealing with his proposal for organizing the judicial system in Israel. The action of the two sections takes place over two days.

As early as the second century C.E., it was recognized that this chapter is not in its proper chronological sequence and that the episode took place after the revelation at Sinai. The internal evidence for this judgment is set forth in Zevahim 116a and in the Mekhilta (Yitro 1:1). It is summarized in the commentary of Abraham ibn Ezra as follows:

> The people are already encamped at "the mountain of God" (v. 5), that is, at Sinai, whereas the notice about their arrival there does not appear until 19:1–2; Jethro brings burnt offerings and sacrifices (v. 20), so that an altar must by this time exist; the only such mentioned so far was located at Rephidim, not Sinai, and was purely commemorative, not functional; therefore, the altar on which sacrifices are brought must be either that mentioned in 24:4 or the one in the Tabernacle, both belonging to the period following the theophany; Moses and his father-in-law refer to "the laws and the teachings of God" (vv. 16,20), a phrase that is far more appropriate following the giving of the Torah than before it; the account in Numbers 11:11,29–32 testifies to Jethro's presence in the camp of Israel in "the second month of the second year after the Exodus"; accordingly, the report of his departure given here in Exodus 18:27 must be dated to that time; finally, the story about the establishment of the judicial system is repeated in Deuteronomy 1:9–17 and is immediately followed by the notice that the people set out from Horeb. All this strongly suggests that the events took place toward the end of the sojourn at Sinai.

That the order of the narratives in the Torah need not necessarily be chronological was well

Eliezer, meaning, "The God of my father was my help, and He delivered me from the sword of Pharaoh." ⁵Jethro, Moses' father-in-law, brought Moses' sons and wife to him in the wilderness, where he was encamped at the mountain of God. ⁶He sent word to Moses, "I, your father-in-law Jethro, am coming to you, with your wife and her two sons." ⁷Moses went out to meet his father-in-law; he bowed

אָמַר גֵּר הָיִיתִי בְּאֶרֶץ נָכְרִיָּה: 4 וְשֵׁם הָאֶחָד
אֱלִיעֶזֶר כִּי־אֱלֹהֵי אָבִי בְּעֶזְרִי וַיַּצִּלֵנִי מֵחֶרֶב פַּרְעֹה:
5 וַיָּבֹא יִתְרוֹ חֹתֵן מֹשֶׁה וּבָנָיו וְאִשְׁתּוֹ אֶל־מֹשֶׁה
אֶל־הַמִּדְבָּר אֲשֶׁר־הוּא חֹנֶה שָׁם הַר הָאֱלֹהִים:
6 וַיֹּאמֶר אֶל־מֹשֶׁה אֲנִי חֹתֶנְךָ יִתְרוֹ בָּא אֵלֶיךָ
וְאִשְׁתְּךָ וּשְׁנֵי בָנֶיהָ עִמָּהּ: 7 וַיֵּצֵא מֹשֶׁה

recognized in rabbinic times. Radak, who subscribes to the view that this particular narrative is out of sequence, explains, in his comment to Judges 1:16, its intrusive position in the Torah as intending to contrast the treacherous behavior of the Amalekites with the friendliness of the Midianites/Kenites. It is to be noted that 1 Samuel 15:6 can be adduced in support of this explanation. Before King Saul punished the Amalekites for their treacherous attack on Israel at the Exodus, he first exhorted the Kenites to evacuate the war zone because they had shown "kindness to all the Israelites when they left Egypt." In fact, there is good reason to believe that the visit of Jethro to the Israelite camp belongs to a now lost record of a treaty of friendship between Israel and the Midianites/Kenites, probably contracted with a view to neutralizing the Amalekite menace. At any rate, 1 Samuel 15:6 provides the clue to the present literary arrangement, which places the Jethro episode immediately after the account of the war with the Amalekites. At the same time, the second part of this chapter, verses 13–26, focuses on God's "laws and teachings" and deals with the administrative arrangements for their implementation in the daily life of the people, thereby smoothing the transition to the theme of the succeeding chapters: the giving of the law.

THE ARRIVAL OF JETHRO (vv. 1–12)

1. Jethro   See Comments to 2:18 and 4:18.

2. after she had been sent home   We are treated to a fleeting glimpse into Moses' domestic life. The narrative in 4:20–26 affirms that Moses' wife and sons accompanied him as he set out to return to Egypt. Hence, this verse presumes a story, now lost, about how they separated and rejoined their family in Midian. A midrash has it that Aaron convinced Moses of the folly of bringing his family into Egypt at such a time, and so Zipporah and the children were sent back to Jethro. It is quite possible that the full story about the "bridegroom of blood," now abridged in 4:24–26, originally provided the details of Moses' separation from his wife.

The translation "sent home" for Hebrew *shilluhim* is by no means certain. The other biblical usages of this noun denote either "dowry," as in 1 Kings 9:16 and the cognate Ugaritic *tlḥ*, or "a farewell gift," as in Micah 1:14. Neither sense fits the context here. The verbal form *shillah* frequently means "to divorce";[1] but in light of Jethro's reference to his daughter as Moses' wife (v. 6), it cannot have this meaning here.

3. Gershom   See 2:22.

4. Eliezer   This fairly popular biblical name means literally "God is help."[2] Although the birth of this son is hinted at in 4:20, it has not been previously recorded.

The God of my father   See Comment to 3:6.

the sword of Pharaoh   This probably refers to the incident recorded in 2:10–15. The explanations given for the names of both Moses' sons are also symbolic of Israel's experience in Egypt.

5. the mountain of God   See Comment to 3:1.

6. He sent word   Literally, "He said." In view of verse 7, it can only imply that Jethro announced his arrival through a messenger. The Septuagint and Syriac versions translate, "It was told,"[3] presupposing a Hebrew reading *va-ye'amer* instead of *va-yo'mer*.

low and kissed him; each asked after the other's welfare, and they went into the tent.

[8]Moses then recounted to his father-in-law everything that the LORD had done to Pharaoh and to the Egyptians for Israel's sake, all the hardships that had befallen them on the way, and how the LORD had delivered them. [9]And Jethro rejoiced over all the kindness that the LORD had shown Israel when He delivered them from the Egyptians. [10]"Blessed be the LORD," Jethro said, "who delivered you from the Egyptians and from Pharaoh, and who delivered the people from under the hand of the Egyptians. [11]Now I know that the LORD is greater than all gods, yes, by the result of their very schemes against [the people]." [12]And Jethro, Moses' father-in-law, brought a burnt offering and sacrifices for God; and Aaron came with all the elders of Israel to partake of the meal before God with Moses' father-in-law.

לִקְרַאת חֹתְנוֹ וַיִּשְׁתַּחוּ וַיִּשַּׁק־לוֹ וַיִּשְׁאֲלוּ אִישׁ־
לְרֵעֵהוּ לְשָׁלוֹם וַיָּבֹאוּ הָאֹהֱלָה:
[8] וַיְסַפֵּר מֹשֶׁה לְחֹתְנוֹ אֵת כָּל־אֲשֶׁר עָשָׂה
יְהוָֹה לְפַרְעֹה וּלְמִצְרַיִם עַל אוֹדֹת יִשְׂרָאֵל אֵת
כָּל־הַתְּלָאָה אֲשֶׁר מְצָאָתַם בַּדֶּרֶךְ וַיַּצִּלֵם יְהוָה:
[9] וַיִּחַדְּ יִתְרוֹ עַל כָּל־הַטּוֹבָה אֲשֶׁר־עָשָׂה יְהוָה
לְיִשְׂרָאֵל אֲשֶׁר הִצִּילוֹ מִיַּד מִצְרָיִם: [10] וַיֹּאמֶר יִתְרוֹ
בָּרוּךְ יְהוָה אֲשֶׁר הִצִּיל אֶתְכֶם מִיַּד מִצְרַיִם וּמִיַּד
פַּרְעֹה אֲשֶׁר הִצִּיל אֶת־הָעָם מִתַּחַת יַד־מִצְרָיִם:
[11] עַתָּה יָדַעְתִּי כִּי־גָדוֹל יְהוָה מִכָּל־הָאֱלֹהִים כִּי
בַדָּבָר אֲשֶׁר זָדוּ עֲלֵיהֶם: [12] וַיִּקַּח יִתְרוֹ חֹתֵן מֹשֶׁה
עֹלָה וּזְבָחִים לֵאלֹהִים וַיָּבֹא אַהֲרֹן וְכֹל ׀ זִקְנֵי
יִשְׂרָאֵל לֶאֱכָל־לֶחֶם עִם־חֹתֵן מֹשֶׁה לִפְנֵי הָאֱלֹהִים:
שני

1 The Samaritan version reads "*hinneh*, "Lo," instead of our Hebrew '*ani*. This is also how the Septuagint and Syriac render it.[4]

7. Moses and Jethro engage in the formal civilities customary in the East.

10. Blessed be the LORD Jethro the Midianite invokes YHVH, the divine name of the God of Israel. It is not uncommon in the Bible for a non-Israelite to do so when dealing with Israelites.[5] In the present instance, the treaty background to the proceedings may well have influenced the usage.

who delivered you The Hebrew plural object probably refers to both Moses and Aaron, whose lives had been threatened by Pharaoh.[6]

11. Now I know This formula '*attah yada'ti* may either introduce something newly discovered or reaffirm what was hitherto accepted.[7] For Jethro, the divine superiority of YHVH has been demonstrated by the disaster suffered by the Egyptians in return for their machinations against Israel.[8] The sentiment may well echo the idea expressed in Exodus 12:12 that the Exodus constitutes a mockery of paganism.

yes... Most traditional Jewish commentators have understood this difficult clause to be an incomplete statement, its unexpressed complement being supplied by the imagination. It is taken to mean that the Egyptians were punished measure for measure. They perished by drowning—the very fate they had devised for the Israelites (Exod. 1:22).[9]

12. This ceremonial most likely possessed a juridical function. In the ancient Near East, treaties and pacts were often ratified by the involved parties participating in a solemn meal. This symbolic rite is mentioned in connection with the pact between Abimelech and Isaac, described in Genesis 26:30, and that between Laban and Jacob, as told in Genesis 31:54. Similarly, the covenant at Sinai is sealed with a sacrificial meal-sharing ceremony, detailed in Exodus 24:5,11.[10]

burnt offering and sacrifices These are the two main types of sacrifice offered in ancient Israel.[11] The first, the '*olah*, was wholly consumed by fire upon the altar as a tribute to the Lord; the second, the *zevaḥ*, was only partially offered up, the major portion being eaten at a festive meal.

THE ORGANIZATION OF THE JUDICIARY (vv. 13–27)

Jethro, observing the daily routine in the Israelite camp, is highly critical of the inefficient and tiresome procedure employed by Moses in judging the people. The narrative is remarkable in several

13Next day, Moses sat as magistrate among the people, while the people stood about Moses from morning until evening. 14But when Moses' father-in-law saw how much he had to do for the people, he said, "What is this thing that you are doing to the people? Why do you act alone, while all the people stand about you from morning until evening?" 15Moses replied to his father-in-law, "It is because the people come to me to inquire of God. 16When they have

יג וַיְהִי מִמָּחֳרָת וַיֵּשֶׁב מֹשֶׁה לִשְׁפֹּט אֶת־הָעָם
וַיַּעֲמֹד הָעָם עַל־מֹשֶׁה מִן־הַבֹּקֶר עַד־הָעָרֶב:
יד וַיַּרְא חֹתֵן מֹשֶׁה אֵת כָּל־אֲשֶׁר־הוּא עֹשֶׂה
לָעָם וַיֹּאמֶר מָה־הַדָּבָר הַזֶּה אֲשֶׁר אַתָּה עֹשֶׂה
לָעָם מַדּוּעַ אַתָּה יוֹשֵׁב לְבַדֶּךָ וְכָל־הָעָם נִצָּב
עָלֶיךָ מִן־בֹּקֶר עַד־עָרֶב: טו וַיֹּאמֶר מֹשֶׁה לְחֹתְנוֹ
כִּי־יָבֹא אֵלַי הָעָם לִדְרֹשׁ אֱלֹהִים: טז כִּי־יִהְיֶה

ways, not least because so important an Israelite institution as the judiciary is ascribed to the initiative and advice of a Midianite priest. This extraordinary fact testifies to the reliability of the tradition and to its antiquity. In light of the hostility that later characterized the relationships between the Midianites and the Israelites, it is hardly likely that anyone would invent such a story.

Also remarkable is the secular nature of the judicial agency. Its organizational structure is humanly devised, and its personnel are drawn "from among all the people" (v. 21), from "all Israel" (v. 25)—from the civil and not the ecclesiastical sphere. Elsewhere in the Torah—for instance, in Deuteronomy 17:9 and 19:17—priests and Levites are also involved in the judicial process. Furthermore, it seems that Moses bypasses the existing power structure. The "elders," who usually exercise judicial functions in a tribal-patriarchal society, are, surprisingly, not mentioned. In fact, the tribal divisions are wholly ignored in the appointments to this new judiciary. The restructuring creates a centralized, supratribal system.

The judicial machinery itself is decentralized to a certain extent by an internal hierarchy of authorities. Moses, who acts as the supreme judicial authority, functions as the mediator of divine will, but not as lawmaker or as one who dispenses justice by virtue of superior wisdom.

The origin of the judiciary in Israel is also recounted in Moses' farewell address. There too it is not attributed to divine command, although no mention is made of Jethro's role. Deuteronomy 1:9–18 tells that Moses found the people too numerous and too litigious for him to bear the judicial burden alone. He therefore suggested that the people select representatives from each of the tribes to share it with him, men who are "wise, discerning, and experienced." The proposal met with popular approval and was promptly put into effect. It involved the same multilevel system as is set forth in Exodus 18:21,25. An added feature is Moses' charge to the judges: "Hear out your fellow men, and decide justly between any man and a fellow Israelite or a stranger. You shall not be partial in judgment: hear out low and high alike. Fear no man, for judgment is God's" (Deut. 1:16–17).

Two interesting parallels to these narratives in Exodus and Deuteronomy may be cited. The first comes from Egypt, from the days of Pharaoh Haremhab (ca. 1333–1306 B.C.E.). This pharaoh, who lived not too long before the Exodus, issued a decree for the reformation of the Egyptian judiciary. He writes that he sought out "persons of integrity, good in character," and placed them in the towns of Egypt. He charged them as follows: "Do not enter into close relations with other people, do not accept a gift from another."

The other parallel comes from 2 Chronicles 19:5–8, where we are told that King Jehoshaphat (873–849 B.C.E.) appointed judges "in all the fortified towns of Judah, in each and every town," and charged them as follows: "Consider what you are doing, for you judge not on behalf of man, but on behalf of the LORD, and He is with you when you pass judgment. Now let the dread of the LORD be upon you; act with care, for there is no injustice or favoritism or bribe-taking with the LORD our God."

14. act Literally, "sit," as in verse 13.[12]

15. to inquire of God This biblical phrase originally meant to seek divine guidance in a situation in which human wisdom has unavailingly exhausted itself.[13] Here it has acquired a legal nuance with the sense of "seeking a judgment or decision," "making judicial inquiry."[14] This usage reflects the conception of true justice as being ultimately the expression of the will of God communicated through the human judge.[15]

a dispute, it comes before me, and I decide between one person and another, and I make known the laws and teachings of God."

¹⁷But Moses' father-in-law said to him, "The thing you are doing is not right; ¹⁸you will surely wear yourself out, and these people as well. For the task is too heavy for you; you cannot do it alone. ¹⁹Now listen to me. I will give you counsel, and God be with you! You represent the people before God: you bring the disputes before God, ²⁰and enjoin upon them the laws and the teachings, and make known to them the way they are to go and the practices they are to follow. ²¹You shall also seek out from among all the people capable men who fear God, trustworthy men who spurn ill-gotten gain. Set these over them as chiefs of thousands, hundreds, fifties, and tens, and ²²let them judge the people at all times. Have them bring every major dispute to you, but let them decide every minor dispute themselves. Make it easier for yourself by letting them share the burden with you. ²³If you do this—and God so commands you—you will be able to bear up; and all these people too will go home unwearied."

לָהֶם דָּבָר בָּא אֵלַי וְשָׁפַטְתִּי בֵּין אִישׁ וּבֵין רֵעֵהוּ וְהוֹדַעְתִּי אֶת־חֻקֵּי הָאֱלֹהִים וְאֶת־תּוֹרֹתָיו: ¹⁷ וַיֹּאמֶר חֹתֵן מֹשֶׁה אֵלָיו לֹא־טוֹב הַדָּבָר אֲשֶׁר אַתָּה עֹשֶׂה: ¹⁸ נָבֹל תִּבֹּל גַּם־אַתָּה גַּם־הָעָם הַזֶּה אֲשֶׁר עִמָּךְ כִּי־כָבֵד מִמְּךָ הַדָּבָר לֹא־תוּכַל עֲשֹׂהוּ לְבַדֶּךָ: ¹⁹ עַתָּה שְׁמַע בְּקֹלִי אִיעָצְךָ וִיהִי אֱלֹהִים עִמָּךְ הֱיֵה אַתָּה לָעָם מוּל הָאֱלֹהִים וְהֵבֵאתָ אַתָּה אֶת־הַדְּבָרִים אֶל־הָאֱלֹהִים: ²⁰ וְהִזְהַרְתָּה אֶתְהֶם אֶת־הַחֻקִּים וְאֶת־הַתּוֹרֹת וְהוֹדַעְתָּ לָהֶם אֶת־הַדֶּרֶךְ יֵלְכוּ בָהּ וְאֶת־הַמַּעֲשֶׂה אֲשֶׁר יַעֲשׂוּן: ²¹ וְאַתָּה תֶחֱזֶה מִכָּל־הָעָם אַנְשֵׁי־חַיִל יִרְאֵי אֱלֹהִים אַנְשֵׁי אֱמֶת שֹׂנְאֵי בָצַע וְשַׂמְתָּ עֲלֵהֶם שָׂרֵי אֲלָפִים שָׂרֵי מֵאוֹת שָׂרֵי חֲמִשִּׁים וְשָׂרֵי עֲשָׂרֹת: ²² וְשָׁפְטוּ אֶת־הָעָם בְּכָל־עֵת וְהָיָה כָּל־הַדָּבָר הַגָּדֹל יָבִיאוּ אֵלֶיךָ וְכָל־הַדָּבָר הַקָּטֹן יִשְׁפְּטוּ־הֵם וְהָקֵל מֵעָלֶיךָ וְנָשְׂאוּ אִתָּךְ: ²³ אִם אֶת־הַדָּבָר הַזֶּה תַּעֲשֶׂה וְצִוְּךָ אֱלֹהִים וְיָכָלְתָּ עֲמֹד וְגַם כָּל־הָעָם הַזֶּה עַל־מְקֹמוֹ יָבֹא בְשָׁלוֹם:
שלישי

16.   Moses does not function as lawgiver but as adjudicator. He operates by known rules— the laws and teachings of God. Doubtless, in practice, the interpretation of the law in a specific situation creates a precedent that then becomes the basis of future adjudication.

17–18.   The inefficiency of the system is bound to have a debilitating effect on Moses and to impose hardship on the public.[16]

19.   Jethro volunteers his services as a management consultant. He fills for Moses the role that Joseph had filled for Pharaoh.

21.   Jethro now defines the ideal social, spiritual, and moral qualifications for judges— those necessary to create and maintain a healthy and just legal order. In the corresponding account in Deuteronomy 1:13 the requirements for judges are given as "wisdom, discernment and experience."

chiefs of thousands   Israel is frequently depicted in the Torah as an army marching out of Egypt and proceeding in military formation through the wilderness to the promised land.[17] The administrative structure recommended here corresponds to the organization of the army in the days of the united monarchy.[18] The setup seems also to have been in wide use beyond the Israelite sphere.[19] The analogy between the military and the judiciary may have its origin in the practice of assigning judicial functions to military officers. This would explain why the judge is here termed "chief" (Heb. *sar*), a military title. This situation is well illustrated by an inscription discovered at an Israelite fortress at Yavneh-yam (ca. 630 B.C.E.). It is an appeal for justice addressed to the commander (*sar*) by one of the company.[20]

22. at all times   So verse 26. This new judiciary is to be a permanent, professional institution, not one that is convened on an ad hoc basis.

every major dispute   In verse 26 this is defined as "the difficult matters." To act as supreme judge was traditionally the prerogative of the leader and king.[21]

23. will go home unwearied   In contrast to what is described in verse 18. The phrase translates literally as "will go to its place in peace." It may well mean that the new court system will fulfill its assigned function to keep domestic peace and preserve the social order.

²⁴Moses heeded his father-in-law and did just as he had said. ²⁵Moses chose capable men out of all Israel, and appointed them heads over the people—chiefs of thousands, hundreds, fifties, and tens; ²⁶and they judged the people at all times: the difficult matters they would bring to Moses, and all the minor matters they would decide themselves. ²⁷Then Moses bade his father-in-law farewell, and he went his way to his own land.

24 וַיִּשְׁמַע מֹשֶׁה לְקוֹל חֹתְנוֹ וַיַּעַשׂ כֹּל אֲשֶׁר אָמָר: 25 וַיִּבְחַר מֹשֶׁה אַנְשֵׁי־חַיִל מִכָּל־יִשְׂרָאֵל וַיִּתֵּן אֹתָם רָאשִׁים עַל־הָעָם שָׂרֵי אֲלָפִים שָׂרֵי מֵאוֹת שָׂרֵי חֲמִשִּׁים וְשָׂרֵי עֲשָׂרֹת: 26 וְשָׁפְטוּ אֶת־הָעָם בְּכָל־עֵת אֶת־הַדָּבָר הַקָּשֶׁה יְבִיאוּן אֶל־מֹשֶׁה וְכָל־הַדָּבָר הַקָּטֹן יִשְׁפּוּטוּ הֵם: 27 וַיְשַׁלַּח מֹשֶׁה אֶת־חֹתְנוֹ וַיֵּלֶךְ לוֹ אֶל־אַרְצוֹ: פ רביעי

27. Numbers 10:29–32 relate that Moses tried to persuade his father-in-law to act as guide for the Israelites through the wilderness.

CHAPTER 19

The Covenant at Sinai (19:1–20:21)

The arrival at Sinai inaugurates the culminating stage in the process of forging Israel's national identity and spiritual destiny. The shared experiences of bondage and liberation are to be supplemented and given ultimate meaning by a great communal encounter with God. Henceforth, Israel is to be a people inextricably bound to God by a covenantal relationship.

The Hebrew term for a covenant is the seminal biblical word *berit*. The Christian designation of sacred Scripture as "testament" reflects this understanding of the covenant concept as the controlling idea of biblical faith; "testament" is a now largely obsolete word for the written record of a compact.

In the ancient world, relationships between individuals as well as between states were ordered and regulated by means of covenants, or treaties. Numerous examples of such instruments of international diplomacy have survived, deriving from various parts of the ancient Near East. These divide into two basic categories: (1) a parity treaty, where the contracting parties negotiate as equals; (2) a suzerain-vassal treaty, where one party transparently imposes its will on the other.

A study of these documents, particularly those of the latter type, leaves no doubt as to the influence of the ancient Near Eastern treaty patterns on the external, formal, literary aspects of the biblical *berit*. The affinities are to be expected. In order for the *berit* to be intelligible to the Israelites, it made sense to structure it according to the accepted patterns of the then universally recognized legal instruments.

The Decalogue and its contents are, however, in a class by themselves. The idea of a covenantal relationship between God and an entire people is unparalleled. Similarly unique is the setting of the covenant in a narrative context. It is the latter that imparts to the covenant its meaning and significance; the covenant would be devalued were the link between them to be severed. Another major and original feature is the manner in which the content of the *berit* embraces the internal life of the "vassal" by regulating individual behavior and human relationships. Such a preoccupation with social affairs is beyond the scope and intent of all other ancient treaties, whose sole concern is with the external affairs of the vassal.

The uniqueness of the Decalogue notwithstanding, it is undeniable that many of its provisions are closely paralleled in the wisdom and ethical literature of the ancient world. Several other ancient law collections rest upon foundations of ethical and moral principles of justice and morality. Sins of a moral and ethical nature, such as bearing false witness, disrespect of parents, theft, adultery, and murder, are all listed in the magic texts from Mesopotamia known as the *Shurpu* series. The "Declaration of Innocence," located in chapter 125 of the Egyptian "Book of the Dead," is formulated in negative terms and clearly testifies to the reality of positive moral ideals. It is obvious that the great civilizations of the Nile and Mesopotamian valleys could not have functioned without a commitment to a set of ethical ideals and principles of morality.

What is revolutionary about the Decalogue in Israel is not so much its content as the way in which these norms of conduct are regarded as being expressions of divine will, eternally binding on

19 On the third new moon after the Israelites had gone forth from the land of Egypt, on that very day, they entered the wilderness of Sinai. [2]Having journeyed from Rephidim, they entered the wilderness of Sinai and encamped in the wilderness. Israel encamped there in front of the mountain, [3]and Moses went up to God. The LORD called to him from the mountain, saying, "Thus shall you say to the house of Jacob and declare to the children of Israel: [4]'You have seen what I did to the Egyptians, how I bore you on eagles' wings and brought you to Me. [5]Now then, if you will obey Me faithfully and keep My covenant, you shall be My treasured possession among all the peoples. Indeed, all the earth is Mine, [6]but you shall be to Me a kingdom of priests

יְ"ט בַּחֹדֶשׁ הַשְּׁלִישִׁי לְצֵאת בְּנֵי־יִשְׂרָאֵל מֵאֶרֶץ מִצְרָיִם בַּיּוֹם הַזֶּה בָּאוּ מִדְבַּר סִינָי: 2 וַיִּסְעוּ מֵרְפִידִים וַיָּבֹאוּ מִדְבַּר סִינַי וַיַּחֲנוּ בַּמִּדְבָּר וַיִּחַן־ שָׁם יִשְׂרָאֵל נֶגֶד הָהָר: 3 וּמֹשֶׁה עָלָה אֶל־הָאֱלֹהִים וַיִּקְרָא אֵלָיו יְהֹוָה מִן־הָהָר לֵאמֹר כֹּה תֹאמַר לְבֵית יַעֲקֹב וְתַגֵּיד לִבְנֵי יִשְׂרָאֵל: 4 אַתֶּם רְאִיתֶם אֲשֶׁר עָשִׂיתִי לְמִצְרָיִם וָאֶשָּׂא אֶתְכֶם עַל־כַּנְפֵי נְשָׁרִים וָאָבִא אֶתְכֶם אֵלָי: 5 וְעַתָּה אִם־שָׁמוֹעַ תִּשְׁמְעוּ בְּקֹלִי וּשְׁמַרְתֶּם אֶת־בְּרִיתִי וִהְיִיתֶם לִי סְגֻלָּה מִכָּל־הָעַמִּים כִּי־לִי כָּל־הָאָרֶץ: 6 וְאַתֶּם

the individual and on society as a whole. Both are equally answerable to the deity, which was not the case in pagan cultures.

Another extraordinary Israelite innovation is the amalgamation of what in modern times would be classified separately as "religious" and "secular," or social, obligations. This distinction is meaningless in a biblical context, where both categories alike are accepted as emanating from God. Social concern, therefore, is rooted in the religious conscience.

Still another outstanding feature of the Decalogue is the apodictic nature of its stipulations—the simple, absolute, positive and negative imperatives are devoid of qualification and mostly presented without accompanying penalties or threats of punishment. The idea is that the covenant is a self-enforcing document. The motivation for fulfilling its stipulations is not to be fear of retribution but the desire to conform to divine will, reinforced by the spiritual discipline and moral fiber of the individual.

NARRATIVE INTRODUCTION   (vv. 1–3)

1. On the third new moon   The closer definition "on that very day" shows that Hebrew *ḥodesh*, usually "month," is here used in its original sense of "new moon."[1]

on that very day   Midrash Tanḥuma comments that the Hebrew has "this" instead of "that" in order to teach that the revelation at Sinai—the words of the Torah—should be newly experienced each day.

2. Rephidim   See Comment to 17:1.

the mountain   The one selected to be the site of the revelation.

ISRAEL'S DESTINY DEFINED   (vv. 3c–6)

These verses express the essence of the covenant idea. Israel is chosen to enter into a special and unique relationship with God. This bond imposes obligations and responsibilities. The prophet Amos (3:2) formulated it this way: "You alone have I singled out / Of all the families of the earth— / That is why I will call you to account / For all your iniquities."

4. on eagles' wings   The king of the birds, the eagle, impressed the biblical writers for the prodigious expanse of its outstretched wings,[2] its solicitous and protective carrying of its young on its back,[3] and its ability to soar to great heights[4] at considerable speed[5] and to fly over long distances.[6]

5. My covenant   The stipulations soon to be set forth. This is the first mention of the covenant in the Exodus narrative. A new dimension is now introduced into the relationship between God and Israel.

and a holy nation.' These are the words that you shall speak to the children of Israel."

⁷Moses came and summoned the elders of the people and put before them all that the LORD had commanded him. ⁸All the people answered as one, saying, "All that the LORD has spoken we will do!" And Moses brought back the people's words to the LORD. ⁹And the LORD said to Moses, "I will come to you in a thick cloud, in order that the people may hear when I speak with you and so trust you ever after." Then Moses reported the people's words to the LORD, ¹⁰and the LORD said to Moses, "Go to the people and

תִּהְיוּ־לִי מַמְלֶכֶת כֹּהֲנִים וְגוֹי קָדוֹשׁ אֵלֶּה הַדְּבָרִים
אֲשֶׁר תְּדַבֵּר אֶל־בְּנֵי יִשְׂרָאֵל: חמישי
7 וַיָּבֹא מֹשֶׁה וַיִּקְרָא לְזִקְנֵי הָעָם וַיָּשֶׂם לִפְנֵיהֶם
אֵת כָּל־הַדְּבָרִים הָאֵלֶּה אֲשֶׁר צִוָּהוּ יְהוָה: 8 וַיַּעֲנוּ
כָל־הָעָם יַחְדָּו וַיֹּאמְרוּ כֹּל אֲשֶׁר־דִּבֶּר יְהוָה נַעֲשֶׂה
וַיָּשֶׁב מֹשֶׁה אֶת־דִּבְרֵי הָעָם אֶל־יְהוָה: 9 וַיֹּאמֶר
יְהוָה אֶל־מֹשֶׁה הִנֵּה אָנֹכִי בָּא אֵלֶיךָ בְּעַב
הֶעָנָן בַּעֲבוּר יִשְׁמַע הָעָם בְּדַבְּרִי עִמָּךְ וְגַם־בְּךָ
יַאֲמִינוּ לְעוֹלָם וַיַּגֵּד מֹשֶׁה אֶת־דִּבְרֵי הָעָם אֶל־יְהוָה:

My treasured possession Hebrew *segullah*, like its Akkadian cognate *sikiltum*, originally denoted valued property to which one has an exclusive right of possession. It has this literal meaning in Ecclesiastes 2:8 and 1 Chronicles 29:3,[7] and it is also so used in rabbinic texts.[8] It then came to be employed in a figurative sense in theological and political contexts in the ancient Near East. A royal seal of Abban of Alalakh designates its owner as the *sikiltum* of the god, his "servant" and "beloved." A letter from the Hittite sovereign to the king of Ugarit characterizes his vassal as his "servant" and *sglt*, "treasured possession." The biblical description of Israel as God's *segullah* or as his *'am segullah*, "treasured people," as in Deuteronomy (7:6; 14:2; 26:18–19), thus expresses God's special covenantal relationship with Israel and His love for His people. At the same time, those biblical texts, as well as Exodus 19:6, all uniquely emphasize the inextricable association between being God's *segullah* and the pursuit of holiness.[9]

6. This statement further defines the implications of being God's "treasured people." National sovereignty, here expressed by "kingdom," is indispensable for the proper fulfillment of Israel's mission. Without it, the nation becomes the passive tool of historical forces beyond its control. At the same time, the priest's place and function within society must serve as the ideal model for Israel's self-understanding of its role among the nations. The priest is set apart by a distinctive way of life consecrated to the service of God and dedicated to ministering to the needs of the people.

The present verse finds an echo in Psalm 114:1–2. The striving for holiness in the life of the people is to be the hallmark of Israel's existence. Time and again the Book of Leviticus repeats this exhortation. Holiness is to be achieved by human imitation of God's attributes (Lev. 19:1).

THE POPULAR RESPONSE (vv. 7–8)

Moses conveys the divine message through the agency of the elders. On this institution, see Comment to 3:16. The unanimous and unhesitating response is to accept, readily and freely, God's charge—even before hearing the terms of the covenant (cf. 24:3,7). Moses, in turn, reports this to God.

PREPARATIONS FOR THE THEOPHANY (vv. 9–25)

The mood has now been set for the solemn, formal enactment of the covenant between God and Israel. Preparations are begun at once. They comprise the following elements: authentication of the role of Moses; purification, which involves sexual abstinence and, most likely, bathing, and laundering of clothes; and repeated warnings against encroachment upon the holy domain of the mountain.

9. This passage may well allude to the declaration in 3:12 that the climactic Sinai experience would be the ultimate validation of Moses' leadership. Here, in addition, the point is made that the

warn them to stay pure today and tomorrow. Let them wash their clothes. ¹¹Let them be ready for the third day; for on the third day the LORD will come down, in the sight of all the people, on Mount Sinai. ¹²You shall set bounds for the people round about, saying, 'Beware of going up the mountain or touching the border of it. Whoever touches the mountain shall be put to death: ¹³no hand shall touch

¹⁰ וַיֹּ֤אמֶר יְהוָה֙ אֶל־מֹשֶׁ֔ה לֵ֥ךְ אֶל־הָעָ֖ם וְקִדַּשְׁתָּ֥ם הַיּ֖וֹם וּמָחָ֑ר וְכִבְּס֖וּ שִׂמְלֹתָֽם: ¹¹ וְהָי֥וּ נְכֹנִ֖ים לַיּ֣וֹם הַשְּׁלִישִׁ֑י כִּ֣י ׀ בַּיּ֣וֹם הַשְּׁלִשִׁ֗י יֵרֵ֧ד יְהוָ֛ה לְעֵינֵ֥י כָל־הָעָ֖ם עַל־הַ֥ר סִינָֽי: ¹² וְהִגְבַּלְתָּ֤ אֶת־הָעָם֙ סָבִ֣יב לֵאמֹ֔ר הִשָּׁמְר֥וּ לָכֶ֛ם עֲל֥וֹת בָּהָ֖ר וּנְגֹ֣עַ בְּקָצֵ֑הוּ כָּל־הַנֹּגֵ֥עַ בָּהָ֖ר מ֥וֹת יוּמָֽת: ¹³ לֹא־תִגַּ֨ע

public nature of the forthcoming revelation would further verify his authenticity. Finally, the statement anticipates the awestruck and fearful reaction of the people to the revelation as described in verses 16 and 20:18–19. As a result, according to Deuteronomy 5:5,20–24, the people requested that the divine pronouncements be conveyed through the intermediacy of Moses rather than directly to them. For this reason, it is of vital importance that Moses' credibility as the true bearer of God's message be unchallengeable. This is achieved by a sign visible to all: the sudden appearance of a thick cloud, understood to symbolize God's corroborative presence.

a thick cloud   Compare 13:21. Anthropomorphism is carefully avoided.

Then Moses reported   This phrase refers not to the immediate antecedent but to the quote in verse 8. It is an instance of resumptive repetition, a literary device in which the text, following a digression, reconnects with an earlier text. Classic examples are to be found in Genesis 37:36, 39:1, 43:17, and 43:24.

10. to stay pure   This is defined in verse 15. It most likely includes bathing, which is taken for granted.[10]

11. the third day   In biblical consciousness, three days constitute a significant segment of time. As with Abraham at the Akedah (Gen. 22:4), so here the longish interval is crucial to the trial of faith. The people's immediate assent to God's declaration may otherwise have been given impulsively, without proper consideration. The three days of preparation and self-restraint allow time for sober reflection, so that acceptance of the covenant can be considered an undoubted act of free will.

According to Jewish tradition, the third day fell on the sixth of Sivan and is identified with the harvest festival of Shavuot, which consequently came to commemorate the giving of the Torah.[11]

will come down   This fairly frequent figurative depiction of God's action in terms of human motion expresses at one and the same time God's infinite transcendence and His personal and intimate involvement with humanity.[12]

in the sight of   The people will become intensely conscious of the Divine Presence.

12–25.   As Ramban noted,[13] Mount Sinai assumes the character of a sanctuary for the duration of the theophany. A close similarity to the wilderness Tabernacle is suggested by several shared characteristics. Both Sinai and the Tabernacle evidence a tripartite division. The summit corresponds to the inner sanctum, or Holy of Holies.[14] The second zone, partway up the mountain, is the equivalent of the Tabernacle's outer sanctum, or Holy Place.[15] The third zone, at the foot of the mountain, is analogous to the outer court.[16] As with the Tabernacle, the three distinct zones of Sinai feature three gradations of holiness in descending order. Just as Moses alone may ascend to the peak of the mountain, so all but one are barred from the Holy of Holies in the Tabernacle.[17] Just as the Holy Place is the exclusive preserve of the priesthood, so only the priests and elders are allowed to ascend to a specific point on the mountain.[18] The confinement of the laity to the outer court of the Tabernacle, where the altar of burnt offering was located, evokes the parallel with Sinai in the restriction of the laity to the foot of the mountain, where the altar was built.[19] The graduated restrictions on access, touch, and sight are the counterparts of the repeated regulations about the unlawful invasion of sacred domain in the same three ways.[20] God is said to "descend" upon the mountain as upon the Tabernacle,[21] and He communicates with Moses on the summit as He does in the Holy of Holies.[22] Finally, the vivid descriptions of smoke, dense cloud, and fire that issued from and enveloped Sinai are paralleled by the cloud and fire that become associated with the Tabernacle.[23]

him, but he shall be either stoned or shot; beast or man, he shall not live.' When the ram's horn sounds a long blast, they may go up on the mountain."

בֹּ֣ו יָ֗ד כִּֽי־סָק֤וֹל יִסָּקֵל֙ אֽוֹ־יָרֹ֣ה יִיָּרֶ֔ה אִם־בְּהֵמָ֖ה אִם־אִ֣ישׁ לֹ֣א יִחְיֶ֑ה בִּמְשֹׁךְ֙ הַיֹּבֵ֔ל הֵ֖מָּה יַעֲל֥וּ בָהָֽר׃

[שׁשׁי לספרדים]

¹⁴Moses came down from the mountain to the people and warned the people to stay pure, and they washed their clothes. ¹⁵And he said to the people, "Be ready for the third day; do not go near a woman."

¹⁴ וַיֵּ֧רֶד מֹשֶׁ֛ה מִן־הָהָ֖ר אֶל־הָעָ֑ם וַיְקַדֵּשׁ֙ אֶת־הָעָ֔ם וַֽיְכַבְּס֖וּ שִׂמְלֹתָֽם׃ ¹⁵ וַיֹּ֙אמֶר֙ אֶל־הָעָ֔ם הֱי֥וּ נְכֹנִ֖ים לִשְׁלֹ֣שֶׁת יָמִ֑ים אַֽל־תִּגְּשׁ֖וּ אֶל־אִשָּֽׁה׃

¹⁶On the third day, as morning dawned, there was thunder, and lightning, and a dense cloud upon the mountain, and a very loud blast of the horn; and all the people who were in the camp trembled. ¹⁷Moses led the people out of the camp toward God, and they took their places at the foot of the mountain.

¹⁶ וַיְהִי֩ בַיּ֨וֹם הַשְּׁלִישִׁ֜י בִּֽהְיֹ֣ת הַבֹּ֗קֶר וַיְהִי֩ קֹלֹ֨ת וּבְרָקִ֜ים וְעָנָ֤ן כָּבֵד֙ עַל־הָהָ֔ר וְקֹ֥ל שֹׁפָ֖ר חָזָ֣ק מְאֹ֑ד וַיֶּחֱרַ֥ד כָּל־הָעָ֖ם אֲשֶׁ֥ר בַּֽמַּחֲנֶֽה׃ ¹⁷ וַיּוֹצֵ֨א מֹשֶׁ֧ה אֶת־הָעָ֛ם לִקְרַ֥את הָֽאֱלֹהִ֖ים מִן־הַֽמַּחֲנֶ֑ה וַיִּֽתְיַצְּב֖וּ בְּתַחְתִּ֥ית הָהָֽר׃

¹⁸Now Mount Sinai was all in smoke, for the LORD had come down upon it in fire; the smoke rose like the smoke of a kiln, and the whole mountain trembled violently. ¹⁹The

¹⁸ וְהַ֤ר סִינַי֙ עָשַׁ֣ן כֻּלּ֔וֹ מִ֠פְּנֵ֠י אֲשֶׁ֨ר יָרַ֥ד עָלָ֛יו יְהוָ֖ה בָּאֵ֑שׁ וַיַּ֤עַל עֲשָׁנוֹ֙ כְּעֶ֣שֶׁן הַכִּבְשָׁ֔ן וַיֶּחֱרַ֥ד כָּל־הָהָ֖ר מְאֹֽד׃ ¹⁹ וַיְהִי֙ ק֣וֹל הַשּׁוֹפָ֔ר הוֹלֵ֖ךְ וְחָזֵ֣ק מְאֹ֑ד

12. **shall be put to death** By human agency, as verse 13 makes clear.

13. **no hand shall touch him** The trespasser shall not be seized since this would itself bring another person to violate the restriction. He shall be executed when he is beyond the limits of the mountain.

ram's horn Hebrew *yovel* seems originally to have meant a sheep or a ram, as in Joshua 6:4,5. It is also so used in the Punic Marseilles Tariff (line 7) of the fourth century B.C.E. However, it came to be restricted to the horn. *Yovel* lies behind the word "Jubilee," which was inaugurated by the sounding of the ram's horn (Lev. 25:9).

they may go up Sinai possesses no inherent or "natural" holiness, nor does it acquire such by virtue of the theophany. Its sanctity and hence untouchability do not outlast the limited duration of the event. See Comment to 3:5.

15. **for the third day** Literally, "for three days," but verse 16 determines the precise meaning.

16-19. Violent atmospheric disturbances are said to precede and accompany the theophany. The Bible frequently portrays upheavals of nature in association with God's self-manifestation. Apart from the present context, such mention is always confined to poetic texts.[24] The conventional and stereotypical nature of the language employed here, and the numerous parallels found in ancient Near Eastern religious compositions, prove that a widespread and well-entrenched literary tradition lies behind it. However, the gods in the pagan religions inevitably inhere in nature, for they are actually personifications of natural phenomena. The upheavals and disturbances are taken literally as aspects of the lives of the gods. In Israelite monotheism, by contrast, God the Creator is wholly independent of His creation and is sovereign over it. The picturesque imagery constitutes, so to speak, the overture that sets the emotional tone for the grand drama that is to follow. The vivid, majestic, and terrifying depictions, which draw their ultimate inspiration from the storm and the earthquake, are meant to convey in human terms something of the awe-inspiring impact of the event upon those who experienced it. The narrative of 1 Kings 19:11–12 is intended to dispel any possibility of mistaking the atmospherics for the substance of the theophany.

17. **toward God** Toward the site of the theophany.

the foot of the mountain The lowest part, on the level ground.

blare of the horn grew louder and louder. As Moses spoke, God answered him in thunder. ²⁰The Lᴏʀᴅ came down upon Mount Sinai, on the top of the mountain, and the Lᴏʀᴅ called Moses to the top of the mountain and Moses went up. ²¹The Lᴏʀᴅ said to Moses, "Go down, warn the people not to break through to the Lᴏʀᴅ to gaze, lest many of them perish. ²²The priests also, who come near the Lᴏʀᴅ, must stay pure, lest the Lᴏʀᴅ break out against them." ²³But Moses said to the Lᴏʀᴅ, "The people cannot come up to Mount Sinai, for You warned us saying, 'Set bounds about the mountain and sanctify it.'" ²⁴So the Lᴏʀᴅ said to him, "Go down, and come back together with Aaron; but let not the priests or the people break through to come up to the Lᴏʀᴅ, lest He break out against them." ²⁵And Moses went down to the people and spoke to them.

מֹשֶׁה יְדַבֵּר וְהָאֱלֹהִים יַעֲנֶנּוּ בְקוֹל: [שביעי
לספרדים] 20 וַיֵּרֶד יְהֹוָה עַל־הַר סִינַי אֶל־רֹאשׁ הָהָר
וַיִּקְרָא יְהֹוָה לְמֹשֶׁה אֶל־רֹאשׁ הָהָר וַיַּעַל מֹשֶׁה:
21 וַיֹּאמֶר יְהֹוָה אֶל־מֹשֶׁה רֵד הָעֵד בָּעָם פֶּן־
יֶהֶרְסוּ אֶל־יְהֹוָה לִרְאוֹת וְנָפַל מִמֶּנּוּ רָב: 22 וְגַם
הַכֹּהֲנִים הַנִּגָּשִׁים אֶל־יְהֹוָה יִתְקַדָּשׁוּ פֶּן־יִפְרֹץ בָּהֶם
יְהֹוָה: 23 וַיֹּאמֶר מֹשֶׁה אֶל־יְהֹוָה לֹא־יוּכַל הָעָם
לַעֲלֹת אֶל־הַר סִינָי כִּי־אַתָּה הַעֵדֹתָה בָּנוּ לֵאמֹר
הַגְבֵּל אֶת־הָהָר וְקִדַּשְׁתּוֹ: 24 וַיֹּאמֶר אֵלָיו יְהֹוָה
לֶךְ־רֵד וְעָלִיתָ אַתָּה וְאַהֲרֹן עִמָּךְ וְהַכֹּהֲנִים וְהָעָם
אַל־יֶהֶרְסוּ לַעֲלֹת אֶל־יְהֹוָה פֶּן־יִפְרָץ־בָּם: 25 וַיֵּרֶד
מֹשֶׁה אֶל־הָעָם וַיֹּאמֶר אֲלֵהֶם: ס

18. mountain Some Hebrew manuscripts, as well as the Septuagint, read here "people" as in verse 16. Bekhor Shor observes: "The terror of God was over the mountain so that all who observed it were terror-struck."

19. the horn Hebrew *shofar*, not the same term as in verse 13. A celestial flourish heralding the arrival of the King is imagined; compare 20:15. In Zechariah 9:14 the Lord Himself is poetically said to "sound the ram's horn" and advance in a stormy tempest as He manifests His presence. The shofar in these texts is figurative for the blasts of thunder.

20. Moses alone is privileged to ascend to the top.

21. to gaze One to whom God's majesty and holiness are not unapproachable, and who is indifferent to the divine potency with which the mountain is charged, is no longer a participant but a mere spectator, a detached observer disengaged from the covenantal experience.

22. the priests According to Exodus 28 and 29, the priesthood was not established in Israel until after the Sinaitic revelation, which would make the present reference to priests, like that in verse 24, an anachronism. Many modern scholars regard these verses as reflecting a different strand of tradition about the origins of the priestly institution. Jewish commentators understood "priests" here as referring to first-born males, in that the latter functioned as priests until they were replaced by the Aaronides, as recounted in Numbers 3:11–13 and 8:16–18.[25]

break out So in verse 24. The effect of such action is given in verse 21. The verb, with God as the subject, connotes a visitation that is sudden, violent, and destructive, as in the case of Uzzah, described in 2 Samuel 6:7–8.[26]

CHAPTER 20   THE DECALOGUE   (vv. 1–14[17])

The Title The present chapter carries no designation for this document. The popular English title "The Ten Commandments" is derived from the traditional, although inaccurate, English rendering of the Hebrew phrase *ʿaseret ha-devarim* that appears in Exodus 34:28 and in Deuteronomy 4:13 and 10:4. In fact, the term "commandment" (Heb. *mitsvah*, pl. *mitsvot*) is not employed in the present context. The Hebrew means, rather, "The Ten Words," which the Jews of ancient Alexandria in Egypt translated literally into Greek as *deka logoi*. This gave rise to the more accurate English alternative "Decalogue." In fact, traditional exegesis derived thirteen, not ten, commandments from the Decalogue as, for instance, in the *Sefer ha-Ḥinnukh* (13th cent.).

Hebrew *devarim* does appear in the introductory verse as well as in the epilogue to the repetition of the Decalogue found in Deuteronomy 5. In rabbinic texts, and generally in Hebrew down to modern times, the common designation is *'aseret ha-dibrot*. This latter word is the plural of *diber*, which in Jeremiah 5:13 denotes the revealed word of God, a meaning that is singularly appropriate in the present context.[1]

The Tablets of Stone

The Tablets of Stone Several biblical texts testify to the inscribing of the Decalogue on two stone tablets.[2] The practice of recording covenants on tablets was well rooted in the biblical world, as was also the custom, mentioned in Exodus 25:16, of depositing the document in the sanctuary.[3] A treaty between the Hittite King Shuppiluliumas (ca. 1375–1335 B.C.E.) and King Mattiwaza of Mittani in Upper Mesopotamia noted that each of the contracting parties deposited a copy in his respective temple before the shrine of the deity.[4] Similarly, when Ramses II of Egypt and the Hittite King Hattusilis concluded a treaty around the year 1269 B.C.E., the clauses were inscribed on a tablet of silver, which was placed "at the feet of the god."[5] In Rome, too, treaties (Latin *foedera*) were written on tablets—bronze—and stored in the Capitol.

In Israel a special container was fashioned to house the stone tablets. When the portable Tabernacle was erected in the wilderness, the container was placed in the Holy of Holies. In fact, the Ark, as the container was called, was designated the "Ark of the Covenant" (*'aron ha-berit*) or the "Ark of the Pact" (*'aron ha-'edut*). It was the only item of furniture in the most sacred part of the Tabernacle.

Why two tablets were needed for the Decalogue is unclear; nor do we know the spatial distribution of the text. The Mekhilta[6] assumes that five declarations were incised on each tablet, which is the tradition reflected in Jewish art since the thirteenth-century Spanish illuminated Bible manuscripts. However, such an arrangement would have resulted in a grave imbalance; one tablet would have contained 146 Hebrew words and the other only 26. The Palestinian Talmud[7] has preserved a different tradition, there given as the majority view, that each tablet contained the entire Decalogue. Saadia maintained that the two tablets featured respectively the variant versions as found in Exodus 20 and Deuteronomy 5.

The Internal Division

The Internal Division As noted, the Decalogue has come down to us in two distinct versions. The differences between them are minute and generally insignificant, except with regard to the Sabbath commandment, which is discussed in the Commentary below. Of greater importance is the matter of the internal division and numbering.

Context, style, and language suggest a basic division of the Decalogue into two distinct groups. The first governs the relations between God and the individual Israelite; the second regulates human relationships. The first group is characterized by the fivefold use of the phrase "the LORD your God," while the second contains no reference to Him. In addition, there is the striking fact that the document opens with "the LORD your God" and closes with "your neighbor." Further, the first group features obligations unique to the religion of Israel, while the second series, which consists entirely of prohibitions, is of universal application and has numerous parallels in other literature of the ancient world. Only in Israel, however, are these injunctions presented as divine imperatives rather than as the fruit of human wisdom.

While these broad, basic divisions are clear and convincing, less obvious is the manner in which the number ten is attained. Here, there are varying traditions that center on (1) whether verse 2 is an independent declaration on a par with the others or simply an introduction to the entire document; and (2) whether verses 3 and 4 are treated as a single item or as two distinct commandments. On each of these issues, rabbinic tradition favors the first alternative. This is reasonable, given the understanding of *'aseret ha-devarim* as "Ten (divine) Pronouncements." Another approach is taken by Philo of Alexandria (d. 50 C.E.), in his work on the Decalogue, and by Josephus[8] (d. after 100 C.E.); both reflect early Jewish traditions that make verse 3 the first commandment and verses 4–6 the second. Roman Catholic and Lutheran traditions interpret verses 3–6 as the first commandment and divide verse 14(17) into two commandments.

It should be noted that from verses 13 on there are differences in the numbering in many editions of the Bible. These are here given in parentheses.

The Decalogue in Liturgy and Ritual

The Decalogue in Liturgy and Ritual From Mishnah Tamid 4:3 and 5:1 we learn that in the days of the Second Jewish Commonwealth, the Decalogue enjoyed a special status, next to the

20 God spoke all these words, saying:

²I the LORD am your God who brought you out of the land of Egypt, the house of bondage: ³You shall have no other gods besides Me.

כ וַיְדַבֵּ֣ר אֱלֹהִ֔ים אֵ֛ת כָּל־הַדְּבָרִ֥ים הָאֵ֖לֶּה לֵאמֹֽר׃
ס
² אָֽנֹכִי֙ יְהֹוָ֣ה אֱלֹהֶ֔יךָ אֲשֶׁ֣ר הוֹצֵאתִ֩יךָ֩ מֵאֶ֨רֶץ
מִצְרַ֖יִם מִבֵּ֣ית עֲבָדִ֑ים׃ 3 לֹֽא־יִהְיֶ֥ה־לְךָ֛ אֱלֹהִ֥ים
אֲחֵרִ֖ים עַל־פָּנָֽי׃

Shemaʿ, in the daily morning service held in the Chamber of Hewn Stones within the Temple precincts. A Hebrew papyrus from Egypt, known as the Nash Papyrus and dating from about 150 B.C.E., contains the Decalogue followed immediately by the *Shemaʿ*. This must be either a liturgical text or part of a ritual object such as a *mezuzah* or *tefillin*. There is indeed evidence that the Decalogue once constituted one of the biblical passages contained in the *tefillin*, at least among certain segments of Jewry. *Tefillin* of this type have been found at Qumran, near the Dead Sea.

Rabbinic sources[9] inform us that at some unspecified time the liturgical use of the Decalogue was discontinued so as not to give credence to sectarian claims that the Decalogue alone, and not the rest of the law, was given at Sinai.

1. This introductory statement is unique in the Torah in that it does not indicate to whom the divine declaration is addressed. The lack of specification satisfies an inherent complexity. On the one hand, it is "all the people" as a corporate entity, a psychic unity, that enters into the covenantal relationship with God. On the other hand, each member of the community is addressed individually, as is shown by the consistent use of the second person singular. Moreover, from verses 15–18(18–21), and from the recapitulation of events found in Deuteronomy 5:4–5, it is clear that at some point in the course of the revelation the people, out of fear, demanded that Moses act as mediator between them and God. According to rabbinic tradition,[10] the people heard the divine voice utter only the first two pronouncements; the rest of the Decalogue was mediated by Moses. This understanding receives support from the use of the first person by God through verse 6, followed by the third person in reference to God in the subsequent verses. The omission of an indirect object allows the opening statement to encompass all aspects of the situation as it unfolded.

In rabbinic legend,[11] the Decalogue was offered by God to all the other peoples of the earth only to be rejected by them. That it was proclaimed in the wilderness, and not within any national boundaries, highlights its universality. It is also said to have been simultaneously translated into all the languages of humankind.[12] Again, because the audience in verse 1 is left undefined, the text permits of various readings.

2. For the origin of this royal, self-identifying formula, see Comment to 3:6. In the present case its use not only underlines the unimpeachable sovereign authority behind the ensuing pronouncements but it also emphasizes that the demands of the Decalogue have their source and sanction in divine will, not in human wisdom. Hence they remain eternally valid and unaffected by temporal considerations.

As noted above, Jewish tradition came to regard this verse as the first of the ten divine pronouncements and understood it as enjoining the belief in the existence of God who is the ultimate controller of the processes of history.

who brought you out In this historical review God bases His claim to Israel's allegiance on His role as the Liberator of Israel, not as Creator.

house of bondage See Comment to 13:3.

3-6. Rabbinic tradition treats these verses as a single unit.[13]

3. You shall have no Hebrew does not feature a verb "to have" but expresses possession by *h-y-h le-*, literally "to be to." Since the idea of possession necessarily involves relationship, the same term is used for entering into the marriage bond[14] and for establishing the covenant between God and Israel.[15] This command, therefore, warns against violating the covenant by recognizing in any manner or form what other peoples accept as deities. Israel's God demands uncompromising and exclusive loyalty.

⁴You shall not make for yourself a sculptured image, or any likeness of what is in the heavens above, or on the earth below, or in the waters under the earth. ⁵You shall not bow down to them or serve them. For I the LORD your God am an impassioned God, visiting the guilt of the parents upon the children, upon the third and upon the fourth generations of those who reject Me, ⁶but showing kindness to the

4 לֹא תַעֲשֶׂה־לְךָ פֶסֶל ׀ וְכָל־תְּמוּנָה אֲשֶׁר בַּשָּׁמַיִם ׀ מִמַּעַל וַאֲשֶׁר בָּאָרֶץ מִתַּחַת וַאֲשֶׁר בַּמַּיִם ׀ מִתַּחַת לָאָרֶץ: 5 לֹא־תִשְׁתַּחֲוֶה לָהֶם וְלֹא תָעָבְדֵם כִּי אָנֹכִי יְהוָה אֱלֹהֶיךָ אֵל קַנָּא פֹּקֵד עֲוֹן אָבֹת עַל־בָּנִים עַל־שִׁלֵּשִׁים וְעַל־רִבֵּעִים

4. The forms of worship are now regulated. The revolutionary Israelite concept of God entails His being wholly separate from the world of His creation and wholly other than what the human mind can conceive or the human imagination depict. Therefore, any material representation of divinity is prohibited, a proscription elaborated in Deuteronomy 4:12,15–19, where it is explained that the people heard "the sound of words" at Sinai "but perceived no shape—nothing but a voice." In the Israelite view any symbolic representation of God must necessarily be both inadequate and a distortion, for an image becomes identified with what it represents and is soon looked upon as the place and presence of the Deity. In the end the image itself will become the locus of reverence and an object of worship, all of which constitutes the complete nullification of the singular essence of Israelite monotheism.

5. *an impassioned God* The Hebrew stem *k-n-'*, in its primitive meaning, seems to have denoted "to become intensely red." Because extreme and intense emotions affect facial coloration, the term came, by extension, to express ardor,[16] zeal,[17] rage,[18] and jealousy.[19] It is used in a variety of contexts, even with God as the referent. The limitations of language necessitate the application to God of phraseology that typically belongs in the human sphere. The present epithet *'el kanna'* is most frequently translated "a jealous God," a rendering that understands the marriage bond to be the implied metaphor for the covenant between God and His people. God demands exclusive loyalty from Israel, and, according to this interpretation, His reaction to their infidelity is expressed in terms of human jealousy. It should be noted, however, that the form *kanna'* is used in the Bible solely of God,[20] never of a human being, a distinction that testifies to a consciousness that the emotion referred to differs qualitatively from the human variety. Whether one renders *kanna'* as "jealous" or "impassioned," the term emphasizes that God cannot be indifferent to His creatures and that He is deeply involved in human affairs. It underscores the vigorous, intensive, and punitive[21] nature of the divine response to apostasy and to modes of worship unacceptable to Himself.

visiting the guilt . . . The Israelite conception of itself as a community bound to God by a covenant has dual implications. Society is collectively responsible for its actions, and the individual too is accountable for behavior that affects the life of the community. There is thus forged a mutuality of responsibility and consequences. It is further recognized that contemporary conduct inevitably has an impact upon succeeding generations. These historical effects are perceived in terms of God "visiting the sins" of one faithless generation upon the next or of His "showing kindness," that is, rewarding fidelity, far into the future. This understanding of God's governance of the world recurs many times in the Bible,[22] and it has an educational function. Over time, however, intensification of the problem of evil led to a revision of this view, for it was perceived as engendering or deepening a pervasive feeling of hopelessness and apathy in an era of acute national crisis. The popular mood is well illustrated in Lamentations 5:7: "Our fathers sinned and are no more; / And we must bear their guilt." Jeremiah and Ezekiel felt compelled to deny cross-generational punishment: "People shall no longer say, 'Parents have eaten sour grapes and children's teeth are blunted,' but everyone shall die for his own sins; whosoever eats sour grapes, his teeth shall be blunted." Such is the teaching of Jeremiah.[23] Similarly, his contemporary Ezekiel denounced the popular belief:

> What do you mean by quoting this proverb upon the soil of Israel, "Parents eat sour grapes and their children's teeth are blunted"? As I live—declares the Lord God—this proverb shall no longer be current among you in Israel. Consider, all lives are Mine; the life of the parent and the life of the child are both Mine. The person who sins, only he shall die. . . . A child shall not share the burden of a parent's guilt, nor shall a parent share the burden of a child's

thousandth generation of those who love Me and keep My commandments.

⁷You shall not swear falsely by the name of the LORD your God; for the LORD will not clear one who swears falsely by His name.

⁸Remember the sabbath day and keep it holy. ⁹Six days

לִשְׂנְאָ֑י: ⁶ וְעֹ֥שֶׂה חֶ֖סֶד לַאֲלָפִ֑ים לְאֹהֲבַ֖י וּלְשֹׁמְרֵ֥י מִצְוֺתָֽי: ס

⁷ לֹ֥א תִשָּׂ֛א אֶת־שֵֽׁם־יְהוָ֥ה אֱלֹהֶ֖יךָ לַשָּׁ֑וְא כִּ֣י לֹ֤א יְנַקֶּה֙ יְהוָ֔ה אֵ֛ת אֲשֶׁר־יִשָּׂ֥א אֶת־שְׁמ֖וֹ לַשָּֽׁוְא: פ

⁸ זָכ֛וֹר אֶת־י֥וֹם הַשַּׁבָּ֖ת לְקַדְּשֽׁוֹ:

guilt; the righteousness of the righteous shall be accounted to him alone, and the wickedness of the wicked shall be accounted to him alone.[24]

And the Talmud in Makkot 24a asserts: "Moses pronounced an adverse sentence on Israel—the visiting of the iniquities of the fathers on the children—and it was revoked by Ezekiel."

It is important to note that the statement in the Decalogue concerning the generational extension of punishment has nothing whatsoever to do with the administration of justice in Israel's legal system. There, vicarious punishment is never mandated; indeed, it is explicitly outlawed in Deuteronomy 24:16.[25]

the third and . . . fourth generations   This conventional phrase is otherwise always found in a context of longevity as a divine reward for righteousness, not only in the Bible[26] but also in Aramaic inscriptions.[27] Here, it is used to describe the enduring, baneful effects of evil.

who reject Me   This phrase may modify "parents" or "children" or both. Rabbinic exegesis seized on the ambiguity to soften the apparent harshness of the statement: The verdict applies only when subsequent generations perpetuate the evils of their parents.[28]

6. *showing kindness*   On Hebrew ḥesed, see Comment to 15:13.

thousandth generation   The corresponding text in Deuteronomy 7:9 shows that this is the correct rendering of Hebrew la-'alafim. The rabbis were quick to point out the contrast between God's boundless beneficence and the limited extent of His punishment.[29]

7.   This command deals with the abuse of the divine name.

swear   Hebrew n-s-', literally "to take up," is here an ellipsis for "to take upon the lips," that is, "to utter" the divine name.[30]

falsely   Hebrew la-shav' can mean this[31] as well as "for nothing, in vain."[32] The ambiguities allow for the proscription of perjury by the principals in a lawsuit, swearing falsely,[33] and the unnecessary or frivolous use of the divine Name. In Berakhot 33a the view is expressed that even the recitation of an unnecessary blessing is a transgression of this command. It should be noted that several biblical passages favor the use of God's name in oath-taking when done in sincerity and truthfulness.[34]

will not clear   That is, God will not allow the deed to go unpunished even though it may go undetected or not be actionable in a human court of law.[35]

8.   The Sabbath, as a noun, is not found in Genesis 2:1–3. Only the verbal form, with God as the subject, is used. Already implied in 16:23–30, the Sabbath (Heb. shabbat) is now established by the Decalogue as a fixed, weekly institution. With the Creation as its rationale (as also reiterated in Exodus 31:13–17), the seventh day of each week is invested with blessing and holiness. It is an integral part of the divinely ordained cosmic order and exists independent of human effort. For this reason it is described here as "a sabbath of the LORD Your God."

The Sabbath is wholly an Israelite innovation. There is nothing analogous to it in the entire ancient Near Eastern world. This is surprising since seven-day units of time are well known throughout the region. Yet the Sabbath is the sole exception to the otherwise universal practice of basing all the major units of time—months and seasons, as well as years—on the phases of the moon and solar cycle. The Sabbath, in other words, is completely dissociated from the movement of celestial bodies. This singularity, together with Creation as the basis for the institution, expresses the quintessential idea of Israel's monotheism: God is entirely outside of and sovereign over nature.

you shall labor and do all your work, [10]but the seventh day is a sabbath of the LORD your God: you shall not do any work—you, your son or daughter, your male or female slave, or your cattle, or the stranger who is within your settlements. [11]For in six days the LORD made heaven and

9 שֵׁ֣שֶׁת יָמִ֣ים תַּֽעֲבֹד֮ וְעָשִׂ֣יתָ כָּל־מְלַאכְתֶּֽךָ׃ 10 וְי֙וֹם֙ הַשְּׁבִיעִ֔י שַׁבָּ֖ת ׀ לַיהֹוָ֣ה אֱלֹהֶ֑יךָ לֹֽא־תַעֲשֶׂ֣ה כָל־מְלָאכָ֡ה אַתָּ֣ה ׀ וּבִנְךָֽ־וּבִתֶּ֣ךָ עַבְדְּךָ֣ וַאֲמָֽתְךָ�(֙) וּבְהֶמְתֶּ֔ךָ וְגֵרְךָ֖ אֲשֶׁ֥ר בִּשְׁעָרֶֽיךָ׃ 11 כִּ֣י שֵֽׁשֶׁת־יָמִים֩ עָשָׂ֨ה יְהֹוָ֜ה אֶת־

The etymology of Hebrew *shabbat* has been debated. It is uncertain whether the noun is derived from the verbal stem meaning "to desist from labor," or vice versa. Semitists have long drawn attention to the similarity of sound to the Akkadian *shabattum* (or *shapattum*) which designated the fifteenth day of the lunar month, that is, the full moon. This is described in cuneiform texts as "the day of the quieting of the heart (of the god)," the meaning of which is uncertain. It has also been noted that in the Mesopotamian lunar calendar the seventh, fourteenth, twenty-first, and twenty-eighth days of certain months, corresponding to the four phases of the moon, were all regarded as days of baneful character, controlled by evil spirits. Special magical rites had to be performed, and the king, in particular, had to refrain from all sorts of activities. These days, however, were not called *shab/pattu*. Whatever the true etymology of the Hebrew term may be, the institution itself has no connection with any known Mesopotamian observance.

Remember   See Comment to 2:24. It is fitting that the law of the seventh day commences with the seventh letter of the Hebrew alphabet. The narrative about the manna in Exodus 16:5,22–30 presupposes the institution of the Sabbath prior to the Sinaitic revelation.

keep it holy   Its intrinsic sacred character derives from God. By following a pattern of living and observance in conformity with that intrinsic holiness, Israel transforms its mundane existence into a spiritual experience one day a week. Texts like Hosea 2:13 and Isaiah 58:13–14 show that already in biblical times the Sabbath was a day of "rejoicing" and "delight." It was these aspects of the day that rabbinic authorities sought to intensify in making the Sabbath "the cornerstone of Judaism."

10.   work   The definition of prohibited labor (*mela'khah*) is not given here. Elsewhere in the Bible certain types of work are specified: "leaving one's place,"[36] that is, walking beyond certain limits, agricultural activities,[37] kindling fire,[38] gathering wood,[39] conducting business,[40] carrying burdens,[41] treading the winepress, and loading asses.[42]

The rabbis of the talmudic period formulated the rules governing the Sabbath in systematic fashion. They were guided by the close proximity in the Torah of the prohibition of work on the Sabbath and the instructions for building the Tabernacle.[43] Acts that were essential in the construction of the Tabernacle are termed "principal" categories (*'avot*); thirty-nine such acts are listed in Mishnah Shabbat 7:2. Other subcategories, analogous but not essential in the construction of the Tabernacle, are called "derivatives" (*toladot*).[44] Of course, all Sabbath prohibitions are suspended when human life is deemed to be in danger (*pikkuaḥ nefesh*)—in such a situation it is a religious duty to violate them if that is what is required to save a life.[45] This principle is grounded in Leviticus 18:5: "You shall keep My laws and My rules, by the pursuit of which man shall live; I am the LORD."

you . . . the stranger   The order of Creation is translated into a social pattern and woven into the fabric of society. By proscribing work and creativity on that day, and by enjoining the inviolability of nature one day a week, the Torah delimits human autonomy and restores nature to its original state of pristine freedom. Human liberty is immeasurably enhanced, human equality is strengthened, and the cause of social justice is promoted by legislating the inalienable right of every human being, irrespective of social class, and of draft animals as well, to twenty-four hours of complete rest every seven days. Exodus 23:12 emphasizes the social function of the Sabbath—"in order that your ox and your ass may rest, and that your bondman and the stranger may be refreshed." This humanitarian approach is the only one given in the Deuteronomic version of the Decalogue: "Remember that you were a slave in the land of Egypt and the LORD your God freed you from there with a mighty hand and an outstretched arm; therefore the LORD your God has commanded you to observe the sabbath day." Appropriately, the list in the present verse comprises seven categories of God's creatures who benefit from the rest on the seventh day.

earth and sea, and all that is in them, and He rested on the
seventh day; therefore the LORD blessed the sabbath day and
hallowed it.

¹²Honor your father and your mother, that you may long
endure on the land that the LORD your God is assigning to
you.

¹³You shall not murder.

You shall not commit adultery.

You shall not steal.

You shall not bear false witness against your neighbor.

הַשָּׁמַ֣יִם וְאֶת־הָאָ֗רֶץ אֶת־הַיָּם֙ וְאֶת־כָּל־אֲשֶׁר־בָּ֔ם
וַיָּ֖נַח בַּיּ֣וֹם הַשְּׁבִיעִ֑י עַל־כֵּ֗ן בֵּרַ֧ךְ יְהוָ֛ה אֶת־י֥וֹם
הַשַּׁבָּ֖ת וַֽיְקַדְּשֵֽׁהוּ׃ ס

¹² כַּבֵּ֣ד אֶת־אָבִ֖יךָ וְאֶת־אִמֶּ֑ךָ לְמַ֙עַן֙ יַאֲרִכ֣וּן
יָמֶ֔יךָ עַ֚ל הָֽאֲדָמָ֔ה אֲשֶׁר־יְהוָ֥ה אֱלֹהֶ֖יךָ נֹתֵ֥ן לָֽךְ׃

ס ¹³ לֹ֥א תִּרְצָֽח׃ ס לֹ֖א תִּנְאָֽף׃

ס לֹ֣א תִּגְנֹֽב׃ ס לֹֽא־תַעֲנֶ֥ה בְרֵעֲךָ֖ עֵ֥ד
שָֽׁקֶר׃ ס

the stranger   In the ancient world strangers were often without rights and were outside the protection of the law. The Torah is particularly sensitive to their feelings and solicitous of their needs and welfare. Numerous injunctions and obligations are set forth to ensure their humane treatment.[46]

12.   This command forms the transition from the first to the second group of divine declarations, in that it simultaneously possesses both religious and social dimensions. It shares with the preceding command the formula "the LORD your God." Also, the relationship of Israel to God is often expressed metaphorically in filial terms,[47] and the same verbs of "honoring" and "revering" are used in expressing proper human attitudes to both God and parents.[48] In fact, the obligation to respect is enjoined only for God and parents, and the offender in either instance is liable to the extreme penalty. The parallels point up the supreme importance that the Torah assigns to the integrity of the family for the sake of the stability of society and generational continuity. Family life is the bedrock on which Jewish society stands. No other item in the Decalogue is similarly formulated wholly in positive terms, and for none other is there a promise of reward. The prophet Ezekiel includes the dishonoring of parents among the grievous sins that characterized the generation of the destruction of the First Temple.[49]

father . . . mother   The command applies equally to son and daughter irrespective of their age, and it holds for both parents.[50]

long endure   Respect for parents is deemed to be vital for the preservation of the social fabric; dishonoring parents imperils the well-being of society.

13. murder   The Hebrew stem r-ts-ḥ, as noted by Rashbam and Bekhor Shor, applies only to illegal killing and, unlike other verbs for the taking of life, is never used in the administration of justice or for killing in war. Also, it is never employed when the subject of the action is God or an angel. This command, therefore, cannot be used to justify either pacifism or the abolition of the death penalty, both of which would have to be argued on other grounds. Genesis 9:6 provides the rationale for the prohibition on murder: "Whoever sheds the blood of man, / By man shall his blood be shed; / For in His image / Did God make man." This means that society must exact satisfaction for the crime of murder because life, being derived from God, is infinitely precious and is His alone to give and to take. By his unspeakable act, the murderer usurps the divine prerogative and infringes upon God's sovereignty; and, because human beings are created in the divine image, he also affronts God's majesty. For this reason, it is not in the power of human beings to forgive a murderer or to commute the death penalty into ransom, as Numbers 35:31 makes clear. In practice, however, at least in Second Temple times, imposition of the death penalty was a rare occurrence. Mishnah Makkot 1:10 states:

> A Sanhedrin that carries out the death penalty once in seven years is designated destructive. Rabbi Eliezar ben Azariah says: Once in seventy years. Rabbi Tarfon and Rabbi Akiba say: Had we been members of the Sanhedrin, no one would ever have received the death penalty. Rabbi Simeon ben Gamaliel says: They would also have multiplied those who shed blood in Israel.

Significantly, the narrative about the first murder notes the obvious fraternal relationship of Cain to Abel seven times, a way of indicating that all homicide is fratricide. Commenting on God's censure

¹⁴You shall not covet your neighbor's house: you shall not covet your neighbor's wife, or his male or female slave, or his ox or his ass, or anything that is your neighbor's.

לֹא תַחְמֹד בֵּית רֵעֶךָ לֹא־תַחְמֹד אֵשֶׁת רֵעֶךָ ¹⁴
וְעַבְדּוֹ וַאֲמָתוֹ וְשׁוֹרוֹ וַחֲמֹרוֹ וְכֹל אֲשֶׁר לְרֵעֶךָ:
פ   שביעי

of Cain in that text—"Hark, your brother's blood cries out to Me from the ground" (Gen. 4:10)—the rabbis in Mishnah Sanhedrin 4:5 interpreted the use of the plural form (*demei*) in the Hebrew to encompass not only the blood of the victim but also that of all his potential offspring, now doomed never to be born. They further commented: "Why was only one man created by God?—to teach that whoever takes a single life destroys thereby a whole world [of human beings]."

adultery   In a society in which polygamy but not polyandry is socially acceptable, the definition of adultery is sexual intercourse by mutual consent between a married woman and a man who is not her lawful husband. Such was the case throughout the ancient Near East. Adultery was a private wrong committed against the husband, an infringement of his exclusive rights of possession. Hence, the punishment or pardon of the violators was left to his discretion. True, adultery is termed "the great sin" in both Egypt and Ugarit, but the gods were not involved in its interdiction or in its legal consequences. In Israel, by contrast, the marriage bond has a sacral dimension,[51] and the prohibition of adultery is divinely ordained. Since adultery is treated as both a public wrong and an offense against God, the husband has no legal power to pardon his faithless wife or her paramour. The gravity of adultery in Israelite law may be gauged both by its place in the Decalogue—between murder and theft—and by the extreme severity of the penalty.[52]

steal   The precise application of this prohibition is complicated by the lack of specifics. The Hebrew verb *g-n-v* may cover theft of chattels and kidnapping. Rabbinic tradition interpreted the command according to the latter meaning.[53] Many modern scholars do likewise, arguing that otherwise there would be an overlapping with the last commandment; that, in the context of the foregoing items, a capital offense rather than a tort is more likely;[54] and that, in the kind of pastoral society that is presupposed in the Decalogue, the protection of individual property rights would not have played sufficiently significant a role to have warranted inclusion. These considerations are not entirely persuasive. The summaries of the Decalogue's provisions found in Leviticus 19:11, Jeremiah 7:9, and Hosea 4:2 also fail to specify the category of theft that is intended. It would seem best, then, not to define this command so narrowly as to exclude from its scope the protection of property rights.

false witness   Each individual is here directly addressed as a potential witness in a juridical forum. This is not the same as "swearing falsely," discussed above, for witnesses did not testify under oath in ancient Israel. The purpose of court procedure was to establish the truth, on which decisions could be based. The witnesses, whose testimony about the facts with which they were acquainted was always given orally, constituted the key factor in the judicial process. False evidence not only hindered the administration of justice in any particular case, but also undermined public confidence in the integrity of the judicial system—and thereby jeopardized the very stability of society. As a consequence, various measures were taken to discourage false testimony. Two witnesses were necessary in order for the evidence to be valid,[55] and false witnesses were punished according to the principle of talion. That is, for their mendacious, damaging testimony, they would receive the same punishment that would have been meted out to the accused. Also, the witnesses themselves had to initiate the execution in cases involving capital punishment.[56]

14. *covet*   A study of the biblical contexts in which the Hebrew stem *ḥ-m-d* occurs discloses that it does not signify the general human proclivity for acquisitiveness and cupidity; rather it always focuses upon a specific object of desire, the sight of which stimulates the craving to possess it. However, because of an inherent ambiguity in the biblical usages of that Hebrew stem, the meaning of the present command has been a matter of dispute. Action, not just a hidden mental state, is certainly implied in Exodus 34:24: "No one will covet your land when you go up to appear before the LORD." Yet a decidedly inward feeling is understood in Proverbs 6:25, literally, "Do not desire her beauty in your heart." Further, passages like Deuteronomy 7:25, Joshua 7:21, and Micah 2:2 indicate that *ḥ-m-d*, itself having a passive nuance, is of sufficient intensity to stimulate active measures to gratify the desire. The issue is further complicated by such questions as whether desire or

15All the people witnessed the thunder and lightning, the blare of the horn and the mountain smoking; and when the people saw it, they fell back and stood at a distance. 16"You speak to us," they said to Moses, "and we will obey; but let not God speak to us, lest we die." 17Moses answered the people, "Be not afraid; for God has come only in order to test you, and in order that the fear of Him may be ever with you, so that you do not go astray." 18So the people remained at a distance, while Moses approached the thick cloud where God was.

19The Lord said to Moses:

Thus shall you say to the Israelites: You yourselves saw that I spoke to you from the very heavens: 20With Me,

טו וְכָל־הָעָם רֹאִים אֶת־הַקּוֹלֹת וְאֶת־
הַלַּפִּידִם וְאֵת קוֹל הַשֹּׁפָר וְאֶת־הָהָר עָשֵׁן וַיַּרְא
הָעָם וַיָּנֻעוּ וַיַּעַמְדוּ מֵרָחֹק: 16 וַיֹּאמְרוּ אֶל־מֹשֶׁה
דַּבֵּר־אַתָּה עִמָּנוּ וְנִשְׁמָעָה וְאַל־יְדַבֵּר עִמָּנוּ אֱלֹהִים
פֶּן־נָמוּת: 17 וַיֹּאמֶר מֹשֶׁה אֶל־הָעָם אַל־תִּירָאוּ
כִּי לְבַעֲבוּר נַסּוֹת אֶתְכֶם בָּא הָאֱלֹהִים וּבַעֲבוּר
תִּהְיֶה יִרְאָתוֹ עַל־פְּנֵיכֶם לְבִלְתִּי תֶחֱטָאוּ:
18 וַיַּעֲמֹד הָעָם מֵרָחֹק וּמֹשֶׁה נִגַּשׁ אֶל־הָעֲרָפֶל
אֲשֶׁר־שָׁם הָאֱלֹהִים: מפטיר   פ   19 וַיֹּאמֶר
יְהוָה אֶל־מֹשֶׁה כֹּה תֹאמַר אֶל־בְּנֵי יִשְׂרָאֵל אַתֶּם
רְאִיתֶם כִּי מִן־הַשָּׁמַיִם דִּבַּרְתִּי עִמָּכֶם: 20 לֹא

its avoidance can be commanded or legislated, and whether there can be liability for mere intention or feeling. But this poses no greater difficulty than does the oft repeated command to love God, one's neighbor, and the stranger, and not to abhor an Edomite or an Egyptian, or not to hate one's brother in one's heart.[57] The Mekhilta, citing Deuteronomy 7:25, decides that one is culpable only when actions accompany the covetous feelings. Ibn Ezra, on the other hand, understands the thrust of the commandment to be an obligation to discipline and condition the mind so that its automatic response to covetousness is a sense of repulsion.

It must be remembered that the Decalogue deals with the ideal. It does not concern itself with penalties, if any, to be imposed by a court of law.

house   Hebrew *bayit* here, as frequently elsewhere, means "household."[58] The following six items, listed in decreasing order of importance or worth, constitute the components of the household. They reflect a seminomadic society. In contrast to Deuteronomy 5:18, land is not included here.

THE PEOPLE'S REACTION   (vv. 15–16)

15–16. (18–19.)   *witnessed*   Hebrew *r-'-h*, "to see," is extended to encompass sound, thus creating a "sense paradox." The figurative language indicates the profound awareness among the assembled throng of the overpowering majesty and mystery of God's self-manifestation. It is an experience that cannot be adequately described by the ordinary language of the senses. The encounter with the Holy universally inspires fascination; inevitably and characteristically it also arouses feelings of awe, even terror (see Comment to 3:1–6). Fear of death is a frequent reaction.[59] The unique, transcendent, supernal holiness of the Divine Presence is felt to be beyond human endurance.

17. (20.)   Moses allays their fears. The purpose of the personal, direct, unmediated nature of the mass experience was to prove the quality of their faith. The enduring, living memory of the encounter should instill the fear of God and so be a deterrent to sin.

18. (21.)   *the thick cloud*   Hebrew *'arafel*. The dense, dark cloud poetically expresses God's mysteriously perceptible yet invisible presence.[60]

THE REGULATION OF WORSHIP   (vv. 19–23 [22–26])

These verses bridge the foregoing and following sections. They continue the preceding narrative by featuring the instructions that Moses received as he "approached the thick cloud"; they also serve as a crucial introduction to the following laws because without verse 19 (22) there would be no antecedents to 21:1. At the same time, these verses, together with 23:19, encase the regulations controlling

therefore, you shall not make any gods of silver, nor shall you make for yourselves any gods of gold. ²¹Make for Me an altar of earth and sacrifice on it your burnt offerings and your sacrifices of well-being, your sheep and your oxen; in every place where I cause My name to be mentioned I will come to you and bless you. ²²And if you make for Me an

תַּעֲשׂוּן אִתִּי אֱלֹהֵי כֶסֶף וֵאלֹהֵי זָהָב לֹא תַעֲשׂוּ לָכֶם: [מפטיר לספרדים] ²¹ מִזְבַּח אֲדָמָה תַּעֲשֶׂה־לִּי וְזָבַחְתָּ עָלָיו אֶת־עֹלֹתֶיךָ וְאֶת־שְׁלָמֶיךָ אֶת־ צֹאנְךָ וְאֶת־בְּקָרֶךָ בְּכָל־הַמָּקוֹם אֲשֶׁר אַזְכִּיר אֶת־ שְׁמִי אָבוֹא אֵלֶיךָ וּבֵרַכְתִּיךָ: ²² וְאִם־מִזְבַּח

interpersonal and societal behavior within a framework of prescriptions that govern the relationship of the individual to God.

It is to be noted that verses 19–20 (22–23) are of general concern, being addressed to all Israel and couched in the plural. Verses 21–23 (24–26) are formulated in the singular and pertain to the individual in a specific circumstance. The delineation of the authentic modes of divine worship is the unifying theme of the entire section.

19–20. (22–23.) The theophany was direct, public, and communal. All Israel was witness to the phenomenon of God speaking from heaven; that is, His abode is neither on nor of the earth. He is wholly removed from the natural confines of this material world. The noncorporeal nature of God's unmediated self-manifestation was apparent to all. As Deuteronomy 4:12,15–18,36 emphasize, the experience was entirely auditory. Those present "perceived no shape—nothing but a voice." Therefore, God may never be represented by any shape or form; nor may God be associated with any idol such as other peoples accept as gods.

21–23. (24–26.) These laws, addressed to the individual, reflect and regulate the altars and worship that characterized the popular lay religion before the implementation of Deuteronomic law concentrated all sacrificial worship exclusively in one official national-religious center.⁶¹ The altars referred to are the kind erected ad hoc by Noah,⁶² the patriarchs,⁶³ Gideon,⁶⁴ Manoah,⁶⁵ and the people of Beth Shemesh.⁶⁶ See Comment to 27:1–8.

21. (24.) altar of earth One made by heaping up a mound of earth in an open field. It was just such an altar that the Syrian commander probably had in mind, as told in 2 Kings 5:17, when he requested two mule-loads of the earth of the land of Israel to take back home with him. There, in Damascus, he could offer sacrifices on the earthen altar.

in every place Hebrew *makom*, like Arabic *maqam*, most likely means here "sacred site," that is, a site rendered sacred by the location there of an altar to God, as in Genesis 12:6 and other texts.⁶⁷ If the verse is to be integrated into its surrounding context, it must convey the teaching that God is content with a simple earthen altar and requires no elaborate structure.

I cause . . . mentioned This construction, with both subject and object referring to God, is unparalleled. God would not be expected to call on Himself or evoke His own name in worship. Hence, the medieval Jewish commentators, followed by the present translation, understood the verb '*azkir* to be causative.⁶⁸ In this way, the sentence is harmonized with the Deuteronomic demands for the centralization of the sacrificial worship at one site chosen by God, be it Shiloh, Nob, or Jerusalem.

In order to make the same point, Rabbi Yoshiah, in Sotah 38a, transposes the order of the clauses to read: "In whichever place I will come to you and bless you I will cause My name to be uttered." He, of course, identifies the "place" with the Temple in Jerusalem, where the full divine name YHVH was uttered in worship in the days of the Second Jewish Commonwealth.⁶⁹

22. (25.) This prohibition is reiterated in Deuteronomy 27:5–6 in regard to the instructions for the altar to be erected on Mount Ebal, and Joshua strictly enforced it.⁷⁰ We are told that in the construction of Solomon's Temple "only finished stones cut at the quarry were used, so that no hammer or ax or any iron tool was heard in the House while it was being built."⁷¹ Many centuries later, when Judah Maccabee built a new altar following the liberation of Jerusalem, he was careful to use only uncut stones.⁷² Josephus, describing Herod's Temple, reports that no iron was used in the construction of the altar.⁷³

tool This is undefined, but Deuteronomy 27:5 and 1 Kings 6:7 specify iron. Mishnah Middot 3:4 explains the prohibition as follows: "Iron was created to shorten man's days [it being used

altar of stones, do not build it of hewn stones; for by wielding your tool upon them you have profaned them. 23Do not ascend My altar by steps, that your nakedness may not be exposed upon it.

אֲבָנִים֙ תַּעֲשֶׂה־לִּ֔י לֹא־תִבְנֶ֥ה אֶתְהֶ֖ן גָּזִ֑ית כִּ֧י חַרְבְּךָ֛ הֵנַ֥פְתָּ עָלֶ֖יהָ וַתְּחַֽלְלֶֽהָ׃ 23 וְלֹא־תַעֲלֶ֥ה בְמַעֲלֹ֖ת עַל־מִזְבְּחִ֑י אֲשֶׁ֛ר לֹֽא־תִגָּלֶ֥ה עֶרְוָתְךָ֖ עָלָֽיו׃
פ

to fashion weapons of destruction], while the altar was created to prolong man's days [by effecting reconciliation with God]. It is unseemly that that which shortens [life] should be wielded against that which prolongs [it]." Put another way, it means that it is illegitimate to promote spiritual ends by violent means.

Rashbam suggests that the ban on the use of a tool blunted the temptation to decorate the altar stones with images.

23. (26.) The altar must be so designed as to permit access to it with suitable propriety. This contrasts with many scenes in ancient Near Eastern art that feature priests officiating in the nude.[74] Ritual nudity is a phenomenon known to many religions. It is symbolically associated with both death and rebirth, and it also has a variety of magical uses.

The instruction is clearly intended for the layman at a private altar since the uniform of the priests included "linen breeches to cover their nakedness."[75] The priests who removed the ashes from the altar each morning had to wear such a garment.[76] It would seem, then, that the official altar was approached by steps. This inference is supported by Ezekiel's vision of the renewed altar; explicit mention is made of steps (*ma'alot*), and the priests wear "linen breeches on their loins."[77] Breeches are otherwise unknown in the Bible and Near East in preexilic times. The dress of the ordinary person included a shirtlike garb but not breeches. The Israelite altar excavated at Tell Dan, dating from the first half of the eighth century B.C.E., has a wide, monumental stairway built against the southern face of the platform on which it stands. In the Second Temple, however, the altar was approached by a ramp.[78]

CHAPTER 21

The Book of the Covenant: The Laws (21:1–24:18)

These chapters, containing the first body of Torah legislation, have become known in English as the "Book of the Covenant," Hebrew *sefer ha-berit*. This name is based on 24:4,7, which recount that Moses put the divine commands into writing and then read aloud the covenant document to the people, who gave it their assent. The title is of major importance, for it underscores the outstanding characteristic of the collection: its divine source. Social rules, moral imperatives, ethical injunctions, civil and criminal laws, and cultic prescriptions are all equally conceived to be expressions of divine will; all form the stipulations of the covenant between God and Israel enacted at Sinai. Unlike the ancient Near Eastern corpora of laws, the document here is not a self-contained, independent entity; rather, it is an inseparable part of the Exodus narratives. The narrative context is essential to the meaning and significance of the document.

The Book of the Covenant falls into four distinct parts. The first, 21:2–22:16, treats a variety of legal topics that relate to civil and criminal matters. They are mostly couched in the casuistic style that is typical of all ancient Near Eastern collections of laws. The individual topics are presented in the form of specific rulings about hypothetical, concrete contingencies, not as abstract legal principles. The implementation of the rulings is left to the jurisdiction of the courts.

It should also be noted that this body of legislation cannot strictly be called a law code. It is not comprehensive in scope and is silent on important areas of legal practice, such as inheritance, the transfer of property, commerce, and marriage. The gaps must have been filled by orally transmitted customary law that regulated vast areas of human relationships. The items dealt with in the Torah must be regarded as innovations and amendments to existing practice. For the connections with the cuneiform collections, see Excursus 6.

The second part of the legal corpus, 22:17–23:19, is quite different. The style is mainly that of the Decalogue, categorical and apodictic. It encompasses a wide variety of discrete topics, with special

MISHPATIM

21 These are the rules that you shall set before them:

²When you acquire a Hebrew slave, he shall serve six years; in the seventh year he shall go free, without payment. ³If he came single, he shall leave single; if he had a wife, his

כ"א וְאֵ֗לֶּה הַמִּשְׁפָּטִ֔ים אֲשֶׁ֥ר תָּשִׂ֖ים לִפְנֵיהֶֽם: ² כִּ֤י תִקְנֶה֙ עֶ֣בֶד עִבְרִ֔י שֵׁ֥שׁ שָׁנִ֖ים יַעֲבֹ֑ד וּבַ֨שְּׁבִעִ֔ת יֵצֵ֥א לַֽחָפְשִׁ֖י חִנָּֽם: ³ אִם־בְּגַפּ֥וֹ יָבֹ֖א בְּגַפּ֣וֹ יֵצֵ֑א אִם־בַּ֤עַל אִשָּׁה֙ ה֔וּא וְיָצְאָ֥ה אִשְׁתּ֖וֹ עִמּֽוֹ:

emphasis on humanitarian considerations. In the main, these laws are not enforced through juridical forms; enforcement is left to the promptings of conscience informed by the conviction that the source and authority of the laws is divine.

The third section, 23:20–33, is an appendix that affirms the divine promises to Israel and warns against the dangers of assimilation to paganism.

The fourth section, chapter 24, rounds out the entire pericope of the Book of the Covenant with a ritual of ratification of the document and with Moses receiving the Decalogue incised in stone.

JUDICIAL RULINGS   (21:2–22:16)

Mishpatim   *1.*   This verse serves as a heading for the entire section.

These are   Hebrew *ve-'elleh*, literally "And these are," the conjunction indicating continuity. It connects the following laws with the preceding Decalogue, all of which emanated from the same Source at Sinai. This interpretation of Rabbi Ishmael in the Mekhilta[1] is supported by the recapitulation of events found in Deuteronomy 4:13–14 and 5:28–6:17, where it is explicitly stated that in addition to the Decalogue many other laws were promulgated at Sinai. Nehemiah 9:13 similarly features this same tradition: "You came down on Mount Sinai and spoke to them from heaven; You gave them right rules [*mishpatim*] and true teachings, good laws and commandments."

the rules   Hebrew *mishpatim* originally meant "judicial rulings," and then came to be used for legal enactments in general, that is, authoritative standards of conduct. Here they are specifically formulated in the casuistic style.

you shall set before them   Knowledge of the law is to be the privilege and obligation of the entire people, not the prerogative of specialists.

LAWS CONCERNING SLAVES (vv. 2–11)

The list of *mishpatim* (enactments) begins with ten laws regulating the institution of slavery. None of the other law collections from the ancient Near East opens with this topic. Hammurabi's, for example, deals with slavery last (pars. 278–282). The priority given to this subject by the Torah doubtless has a historical explanation: Having recently experienced liberation from bondage, the Israelite is enjoined to be especially sensitive to the condition of the slave.

This association of the Exodus with the regulation of slavery already appeared in the opening words of the Decalogue, where God is identified as the One who freed Israel from the thralldom of Egypt. The Decalogue then mandates the right of the slave to enjoy the weekly Sabbath rest.[2] The same correlation of the themes of Exodus and slavery is present in the laws of Deuteronomy 15:13–15 and in the narrative of Jeremiah 34:13–14.

All the law collections of the ancient Near East deal with the topic of slavery. However, there is no evidence that this evil institution, although widespread, persistent, and socially sanctioned, was of major economic importance in the region. Everywhere the attitude to the slave was marked by ambivalence: He was a human being in close daily contact with the master and other members of his family; but he was also an item of property to be assessed in terms of monetary value. Biblical legislation is directed toward enhancing the social and legal status of this human chattel. This humanitarian approach expresses itself in a variety of ways: The slave is termed "your brother";[3] he possesses an inalienable right to rest on the Sabbath day and on festivals;[4] when circumcised, and thus

wife shall leave with him. ⁴If his master gave him a wife, and she has borne him children, the wife and her children shall belong to the master, and he shall leave alone. ⁵But if the slave declares, "I love my master, and my wife and children: I do not wish to go free," ⁶his master shall take him before

4 אִם־אֲדֹנָיו֙ יִתֶּן־ל֣וֹ אִשָּׁ֔ה וְיָלְדָה־ל֥וֹ בָנִ֖ים א֣וֹ בָנ֑וֹת הָאִשָּׁ֣ה וִֽילָדֶ֗יהָ תִּהְיֶה֙ לַֽאדֹנֶ֔יהָ וְה֖וּא יֵצֵ֥א בְגַפּֽוֹ: 5 וְאִם־אָמֹ֤ר יֹאמַר֙ הָעֶ֔בֶד אָהַ֙בְתִּי֙ אֶת־אֲדֹנִ֔י אֶת־אִשְׁתִּ֖י וְאֶת־בָּנָ֑י לֹ֥א אֵצֵ֖א חָפְשִֽׁי: 6 וְהִגִּישׁ֤וֹ

identified with the covenant between God and Israel, he participates in the Passover offering;[5] he is to be "avenged" if he dies from a beating by his master;[6] and the loss of a limb, even a tooth, at the hands of his master automatically gains him his freedom.[7] A fugitive slave may not be extradited and is accorded protection from maltreatment and the right to live wherever he chooses.[8] Finally, a six-year limit is set on his term of service. No wonder the rabbis observed in Kiddushin 20a that he who buys a Hebrew slave is like one buying himself a master.

The Male Slave (vv. 2–6)

2. When you acquire The reduction of an Israelite to slave status could result from poverty or insolvency. By self-sale, the desperately poor could gain a measure of security. The labors of a debtor or a thief could discharge the debt or compensate for the stolen property.

There are scriptural indications that, in practice, defaulting debtors or members of their family would be subject to seizure by a creditor and forced into service.[9] Whereas the prophets denounce this practice, Mesopotamian laws actually provide for the seizure of debtors.[10] Rabbinic tradition interpreted the present text as referring specifically to an Israelite thief who is legally sentenced to work off the value of stolen goods.[11]

a Hebrew slave A fellow Israelite, called a "brother" in Deuteronomy 15:12 and Jeremiah 34:9,14.

six years The slave laws of Leviticus 25:40 rule that this maximum limit on his term of service is shortened should the Jubilee year occur in the meantime. Hammurabi (par. 117) limited a debtor's service to three years.[12]

in the seventh year Rabbinic tradition understood this to mean the seventh year from the commencement of his indentureship. However, Targum Jonathan, representing an earlier stratum of halakhic interpretation, interpreted it as referring to the Sabbatical year. So did Bekhor Shor.[13]

free, without payment Emancipation is his by right, and no compensation is due to the master. The parallel law in Deuteronomy 15:12–15 requires the master to make generous provision for the slave on leaving his service.

free Hebrew ḥofshi, on the basis of its Akkadian cognate ḥupshu and Ugaritic ḫpt, originally seems to have been a technical term for one who belongs to the low social class composed of emancipated slaves. By a shift of meaning in the Bible, it came to mean simply "free."

3. if he had a wife The master would have been responsible for the maintenance of the slave's wife and children throughout the period of his service.

4. In the ancient Near East it was common practice for a master to mate a slave with a foreign bondwoman solely for the purpose of siring "house born" slaves.[14] In such instances, no matrimonial or emotional bond was necessarily involved, and the woman and her offspring remained the property of the master.

5. It must have been a fairly frequent occurrence that the slave felt comfortable and at home in his master's household and also formed an emotional attachment to the bondwoman and to the children he had begotten through her. In addition, he did not relish the prospect of freedom in poverty. These considerations might lead him voluntarily to surrender his right to personal freedom. In such a case, he had to make a solemn declaration to that effect.[15]

God. He shall be brought to the door or the doorpost, and his master shall pierce his ear with an awl; and he shall then remain his slave for life.

אֲדֹנָיו֙ אֶל־הָ֣אֱלֹהִ֔ים וְהִגִּישׁוֹ֙ אֶל־הַדֶּ֔לֶת א֖וֹ אֶל־הַמְּזוּזָ֑ה וְרָצַ֨ע אֲדֹנָ֤יו אֶת־אָזְנוֹ֙ בַּמַּרְצֵ֔עַ וַעֲבָד֖וֹ לְעֹלָֽם: ס

7When a man sells his daughter as a slave, she shall not be freed as male slaves are. 8If she proves to be displeasing to

7 וְכִֽי־יִמְכֹּ֥ר אִ֛ישׁ אֶת־בִּתּ֖וֹ לְאָמָ֑ה לֹ֥א תֵצֵ֖א כְּצֵ֥את הָעֲבָדִֽים: 8 אִם־רָעָ֗ה בְּעֵינֵ֤י אֲדֹנֶ֙יהָ֙ אֲשֶׁר־

6. A change from temporary to permanent slavery is a step of transcendental human importance. In order to avoid abuse on the part of a master and to safeguard the rights of the slave, it must be carried out according to a procedure fixed by law.

before God This term appears again in 22:7–8, also in a legal context. There, the accompanying verb is in the plural so that ʾelohim is not likely to have the literal meaning of "God." The court records from Nuzi frequently mention the administering of an "oath of the gods" taken by a litigant in the presence of, or perhaps by actually holding, the figurines of the gods. The phrase "before ʾelohim," an echo of pre-Israelite legal terminology, is in the Torah divested of its original association with gods and most likely simply means "in the sanctuary." Probably the slave had to repeat, in the presence of witnesses or the local authorities, the formal declaration of his intention, uncompelled, to forgo his freedom. Rabbinic tradition understood the phrase in question to mean "in the presence of the judges."[16]

the door or the doorpost Of the sanctuary. This interpretation is supported by an analogy with the laws of Eshnunna, which mandate, in a certain case, "an oath in the gate of Tishpak," the chief god of the city.[17]

pierce his ear Rashbam took this as a sign of permanent slave status. Rabbinic tradition specified the right ear.[18] It saw in this act a symbolic punishment: "Because the ear heard on Mount Sinai: 'For they are My servants, whom I freed from the land of Egypt; they may not give themselves over into servitude [Lev. 25:42],' and it divested itself of the yoke of Heaven and accepted the hegemony of a human yoke—let it be pierced!"[19]

for life Rashbam took this literally; the rest of his life. But according to rabbinic interpretation, the new term of service ends at the next Jubilee year or at the death of the master, whichever comes first.[20]

The Female Slave (vv. 7–11)

The Hebrew term ʾamah, used here, does not mean a slave girl in the usual sense, since her status is quite different from that of the male slave. The following laws safeguard her rights and protect her from sexual exploitation.

In the ancient world, a father, driven by poverty, might sell his daughter into a well-to-do family in order to ensure her future security. The sale presupposes marriage to the master or his son. Documents recording legal arrangements of this kind have survived from Nuzi. The Torah stipulates that the girl must be treated as a free woman; should the designated husband take an additional wife, he is still obligated to support her. A breach of faith gains her her freedom, and the master receives no compensation for the purchase price.

Rabbinic interpretation restricted the power of the father to dispose of his daughter in this way. He could do so only so long as she was a minor, that is, below the age of twelve years and a day, and then only if he was utterly destitute. She could not sell herself into slavery nor could she be sold by a court as an insolvent thief, as could a male, in order to make restitution for the stolen articles. Further, she could not be designated to be the wife of the master or his son without her knowledge.[21]

The status of the ʾamah in biblical times is demonstrated in practice through the discovery of a preexilic epitaph of a royal steward from the village of Siloam outside Jerusalem. The inscription mentions his ʾamah, and it is clear that he arranged to be buried next to her. Another discovery is the seal of "Alyah the ʾamah of Hananel," who obviously enjoyed superior social rank. In like vein, an extant Babylonian document mentions a slave girl of a married couple who is described as both the aššat, "wife," of the husband and the ʾamat of the wife.

her master, who designated her for himself, he must let her be redeemed; he shall not have the right to sell her to outsiders, since he broke faith with her. 9And if he designated her for his son, he shall deal with her as is the practice with free maidens. 10If he marries another, he must not withhold from this one her food, her clothing, or her conjugal rights. 11If he fails her in these three ways, she shall go free, without payment.

לֹא יְעָדָהּ וְהֶפְדָּהּ לְעַם נָכְרִי לֹא־יִמְשֹׁל לְמָכְרָהּ בְּבִגְדוֹ־בָהּ: 9 וְאִם־לִבְנוֹ יִיעָדֶנָּה כְּמִשְׁפַּט הַבָּנוֹת יַעֲשֶׂה־לָּהּ: 10 אִם־אַחֶרֶת יִקַּח־לוֹ שְׁאֵרָהּ כְּסוּתָהּ וְעֹנָתָהּ לֹא יִגְרָע: 11 וְאִם־שְׁלָשׁ־אֵלֶּה לֹא יַעֲשֶׂה לָהּ וְיָצְאָה חִנָּם אֵין כָּסֶף: ס

לוֹ ק' v. 8.

8. outsiders Hebrew 'am nokhri means one outside the nuclear family.[22] This ancient technical term preserves the original meaning of 'am, "kin"; it has survived vestigially in the expression "to be gathered into one's kin."[23]

broke faith That is, the master has repudiated the presumption that accompanied his acquisition of the girl.[24]

9. the practice with free maidens The girl is to be raised within the family and given the status of a daughter. As such, she would normally be protected from sexual abuse.

10. The laws of Lipit-Ishtar similarly stipulate that if a man takes a second wife, now his favorite, he must continue to support his first wife.[25] The Torah extends this protection to the slave girl and here specifies three basic necessities of life to which she is entitled. The formulation once again gives every appearance of being ancient technical legal language. It is generally agreed (1) that Hebrew she'er, literally "flesh," is an ancient word for "meat,"[26] perhaps, like lehem, extended to cover food in general, and (2) that kesut is certainly "clothing."[27] It is the unique word 'onah that has generated debate. The Septuagint, Peshitta, and Targums all understood it to refer to the woman's conjugal rights. This interpretation, which has no philological support, is also found in rabbinic sources.[28] If correct, it would reflect a singular recognition in the laws of the ancient Near East that a wife is legally entitled to sexual gratification.

Rashbam and Bekhor Shor favor another rendering of 'onah as "dwelling," "shelter," which is supported etymologically by the Hebrew noun ma'on, me'onah, "dwelling, habitation."[29]

A persuasive, although as yet philologically unsustained, argument has been made for understanding the term to mean "oil, ointment." In many ancient Near Eastern texts there are clauses that make provision for "food, clothing, and ointment." This same triad of commodities is found in Hosea 2:7 and Ecclesiastes 9:7–9. Likewise, the Egyptian wisdom text known as "The Instruction of the Vizier Ptah-hotep" advises "a man of standing" to fill his wife's belly, clothe her back, and provide ointment for her body.[30]

11. in these three ways Any of the aforementioned possibilities: marriage to the master, or to his son, or allowing her to be redeemed.

THREE CAPITAL OFFENSES (vv. 12–17)

This section elaborates on three of the topics of the Decalogue: murder, dishonoring parents, and kidnapping. Violation of each law, under specific conditions, incurs the death penalty.

Murder (vv. 12–14)

The reference here is to criminal homicide where malice aforethought has been established beyond question. The same law appears again in Leviticus 24:17,21. Deuteronomy 17:6 and 19:15 stipulate that capital punishment is to be carried out only on the evidence of two witnesses. Numbers 35:30–31 add that monetary compensation cannot substitute for the murderer's execution. This last provision has no parallel in other ancient Near Eastern law collections, which view murder only in terms of economic loss to the family or clan. For the rationale behind the biblical approach, see Comment to 20:13. Although the text does not prescribe the mode of execution, rabbinic sources specify decapitation.[31]

[12]He who fatally strikes a man shall be put to death. [13]If he did not do it by design, but it came about by an act of God, I will assign you a place to which he can flee.

[14]When a man schemes against another and kills him treacherously, you shall take him from My very altar to be put to death.

[15]He who strikes his father or his mother shall be put to death.

יב מַכֵּה אִישׁ וָמֵת מוֹת יוּמָת: יג וַאֲשֶׁר לֹא צָדָה וְהָאֱלֹהִים אִנָּה לְיָדוֹ וְשַׂמְתִּי לְךָ מָקוֹם אֲשֶׁר יָנוּס שָׁמָּה: ס

יד וְכִי־יָזִד אִישׁ עַל־רֵעֵהוּ לְהָרְגוֹ בְעָרְמָה מֵעִם מִזְבְּחִי תִּקָּחֶנּוּ לָמוּת: ס

טו וּמַכֵּה אָבִיו וְאִמּוֹ מוֹת יוּמָת:

ASYLUM (vv. 13–14)   Unintentional homicide is treated differently from murder. Here the implicit issue is the ancient and widespread phenomenon of the blood feud. In the absence of centralized authority, family and clan solidarity led people to administer private justice. The "avenger of blood," Hebrew *go'el ha-dam*—generally the nearest relative of the victim of homicide—would be duty-bound to seek revenge. With the development of the concept that crime should be punished by the state, and not by means of private vengeance, it became imperative to eliminate the blood feud. The present measures are designed to protect the innocent manslayer and allow established legal procedure to take its course. The law of asylum, which also covers the prevention of its abuse, is therefore set forth. The considerable attention given to the blood feud in the legal texts of the Torah and the attempts to exert social control over it are indicative of the tenacity of the institution.[32]

13. *by design*   With premeditation.[33]

by an act of God   The theological assumption is that the death of the victim occurred by the intervention of Providence; thus, the manslayer was the unwitting agent.

I will assign you   The manslayer is to be guaranteed temporary asylum pending judicial disposition of the case. This is the only instance in the enactments (*mishpatim*) of God that addresses Israel directly. The anomaly emphasizes the high degree of concern for the protection of life.

a place   Hebrew *makom*, like its Arabic cognate *maqam*, probably means here "sacred site," a sanctuary.[34] Its precincts are inviolable. The other biblical sources dealing with this topic specifically provide for "cities of refuge."

14. Even the sacred area of the altar loses its inviolable, extraterritorial status if abused by the willful murderer. Rabbinic exegesis derives from this text the rule that a priest who is a convicted murderer is to be summarily interrupted and removed from the Temple even if he is engaged in the act of performing his sacred duties.[35]

altar   The narratives about Adonijah in 1 Kings 1:50–53 and Joab in 1 Kings 2:28–34 illustrate in practice the custom of claiming asylum by seizing "the horns of the altar," that is, the four corner projections. In these two cases, however, the particular circumstances rendered the claim ineffective.

Abuse of Parents (vv. 15,17)

Although separated by the law of the kidnapper, these two verses belong together and, in fact, are so placed in the Septuagint. Verse 15 concerns violent assault on a parent by a son or daughter; verse 17 deals with verbal abuse. The extreme severity with which both offenses are treated clearly indicates the importance that biblical religion attached to the integrity of the family as the indispensable prerequisite for a wholesome society. There is also here the unassailable conviction that the dissolution of the family unit must inevitably rend to shreds the entire social fabric. See Comment to 20:12.

The corresponding law in Hammurabi's collection (par. 195) prescribes the amputation of the hand of a son who strikes his father. The mother as the victim is not mentioned there.[36]

15. *strikes*   According to rabbinic exegesis, only the actual infliction of physical injury by an adult son or daughter entails the death penalty.[37]

16He who kidnaps a man—whether he has sold him or is still holding him—shall be put to death.

17He who insults his father or his mother shall be put to death.

16 וְגֹנֵב אִישׁ וּמְכָרוֹ וְנִמְצָא בְיָדוֹ מוֹת יוּמָת׃
ס

17 וּמְקַלֵּל אָבִיו וְאִמּוֹ מוֹת יוּמָת׃ ס

17. insults This law is repeated even more forcefully in Leviticus 20:9.[38] For several reasons, "insult" is too weak a rendering for the Hebrew stem *k-l-l*. First, its frequent antonym is *b-r-k*, "to bless,"[39] and second, it is used with God as the object, as in Leviticus 24:11,15. The kind of behavior understood here includes uttering a curse. The horrendous nature of this offense is intensified in a culture that believed the malediction to possess potent force and to take on a devastating life of its own, especially if uttered in the name of God.[40] The stem *k-l-l* is also used in both Hebrew[41] and Akkadian[42] as an antonym of *k-b-d*, "to honor." It denotes "treating with contempt and humiliating"; in other words, the flagrant violation of the Decalogue's imperative in Exodus 20:12. It also encompasses the kind of misdeeds described in Deuteronomy 21:18–19 in the case of the "wayward and defiant son" who is disobedient, incorrigible, disloyal, a glutton, and a drunkard.

Kidnapping (v. 16)

The prevalence of the slave trade clearly spurred this item of legislation. The principal motive for kidnapping was to coerce the victim into servitude, either to the kidnapper himself or to another master who is willing to pay for the human merchandise. The sale of Joseph, as reported in Genesis 37:25–28,36 and 39:1, vividly illustrates this type of traffic in human misery.

Hammurabi's laws (par. 14) also prescribe the death penalty for kidnapping but define the victim as "the young son of a [free] man." The context in which the law appears shows that it was considered an economic crime. The Hittite laws (pars. 19–24) also treat kidnapping as an economic offense, the penalty for which is restitution not execution.

The law in Exodus is formulated comprehensively; it applies whoever is the victim. The parallel in Deuteronomy 24:7 is more restrictive. According to Mishnah Sanhedrin 11:1 the mode of execution for assaulting parents and for kidnapping is strangulation. Ramban explains the close association of two such different laws in the Hebrew text as a function of their common penalty. For the offense of verse 17, the punishment is death by stoning, according to the rabbis.

BODILY INJURY INFLICTED BY PERSONS (vv. 18–27)

These laws deal with the redress of personal injuries caused by the physical attack of one human being upon another. The basic principle here centers on intention—whether or not the assailant intended to inflict the injury. The section is famous for its formulation of the *lex talionis*, or "eye for an eye," system of justice.

Injury Resulting from a Quarrel (vv. 18–19)

quarrel The Hebrew stem *r-y-v* essentially denotes an exchange of words. What starts out as a verbal quarrel degenerates into a brawl, as one strikes a blow that temporarily incapacitates the other. The aggressor must indemnify the victim for loss of income, here called "idleness," and for medical expenses as well. This text is curiously silent on the law governing the infliction of permanent injury.

unpunished Presumably, if a fatality ensues, then the laws set forth in verses 12–14 are operative. Rabbinic tradition required the assailant to be held in custody pending the victim's full and certain recovery.[43] The extenuating circumstances in the present case are the clear absence of unlawful or prior intention to cause bodily injury. The corresponding laws in Hammurabi's collection (pars. 206–208) deal not with a verbal dispute but with a brawl; the assailant must swear that he did not "strike wittingly," and he then pays only the medical expenses. Should the victim die

[18]When men quarrel and one strikes the other with stone or fist, and he does not die but has to take to his bed—[19]if he then gets up and walks outdoors upon his staff, the assailant shall go unpunished, except that he must pay for his idleness and his cure.

[20]When a man strikes his slave, male or female, with a rod, and he dies there and then, he must be avenged. [21]But if he survives a day or two, he is not to be avenged, since he is the other's property.

18 וְכִי־יְרִיבֻן אֲנָשִׁים וְהִכָּה־אִישׁ אֶת־רֵעֵהוּ בְּאֶבֶן אוֹ בְאֶגְרֹף וְלֹא יָמוּת וְנָפַל לְמִשְׁכָּב: 19 אִם־יָקוּם וְהִתְהַלֵּךְ בַּחוּץ עַל־מִשְׁעַנְתּוֹ וְנִקָּה הַמַּכֶּה רַק שִׁבְתּוֹ יִתֵּן וְרַפֹּא יְרַפֵּא: ס שני

20 וְכִי־יַכֶּה אִישׁ אֶת־עַבְדּוֹ אוֹ אֶת־אֲמָתוֹ בַּשֵּׁבֶט וּמֵת תַּחַת יָדוֹ נָקֹם יִנָּקֵם: 21 אַךְ אִם־יוֹם אוֹ יוֹמַיִם יַעֲמֹד לֹא יֻקַּם כִּי כַסְפּוֹ הוּא: ס

from the blow, monetary compensation must be paid, the amount determined in accordance with the social status of the victim.

Injury to a Slave (vv. 20–21)

This law—the protection of slaves from maltreatment by their masters—is found nowhere else in the entire existing corpus of ancient Near Eastern legislation. It represents a qualitative transformation in social and human values and expresses itself once again in the provisions of verses 26–27. The underlying issue, as before, is the determination of intent on the part of the assailant at the time the act was committed.

his slave   The final clause of verse 21 seems to indicate that the slave in question is a foreigner. Otherwise the terminology would be inappropriate, given the conditions under which an Israelite might become enslaved.[44]

a rod   Hebrew *shevet*, the customary instrument of discipline.[45] The right of a master to discipline his slave within reason is recognized. But according to rabbinic exegesis, it is restricted to the use of an implement that does not normally have lethal potentiality, and it may not be applied to a part of the body considered to be particularly vulnerable.[46]

there and then   Literally, "under his hand," in contrast to "a day or two" in verse 21. The direct, immediate, causal relationship between the master's act and the death of the slave is undisputed. The master has unlawfully used deadly force, and homicidal intent is assumed.

he must be avenged   The master is criminally liable and faces execution, in keeping with the law of verse 12.

Rabbinic tradition prescribes decapitation.[47] This interpretation—that the Hebrew stem *n-k-m* means the death penalty—is supported by the early tradition behind the Samaritan version, which, in place of our received Hebrew text, actually reads here, "He must be put to death" (*mot yumat*). Ibn Ezra notes that the verb *n-k-m*, as used in the Bible, principally involves meting out the death penalty. In the absence of the office of public executioner, it would generally be the victim's next of kin who would administer the supreme penalty, as provided for in Numbers 35:19 and Deuteronomy 19:12. This would hardly be the situation in the case of a slave, who would be unlikely to have local relatives. Hence, the obligation to exact the penalty falls on the community, which is probably why *n-k-m* is used here and not the usual *yumat*.

The verb *n-k-m* is popularly taken to signify "revenge." Actually, it means "to avenge," that is, to vindicate, or redress, the imbalance of justice. Its use in the Bible is overwhelmingly with God as the subject, and in such cases it always serves the ends of justice. It is employed in particular in situations in which normal judicial procedures are not effective or cannot be implemented. It does not focus on the desire to get even or to retaliate; indeed, Leviticus 19:18 forbids private vengeance.

21.   Should the beaten slave linger more than a day before succumbing, certain new and mitigating circumstances arise. The direct, causal relationship between the master's conduct and the slave's death is now in doubt, for there may have been some unknown intermediate cause. The intent of the master appears less likely to have been homicidal and more likely to have been disciplinary. He is given the benefit of the doubt, especially since he is losing his financial investment, the price of the slave.

124

משפטים

22When men fight, and one of them pushes a pregnant woman and a miscarriage results, but no other damage ensues, the one responsible shall be fined according as the woman's husband may exact from him, the payment to be based on reckoning. 23But if other damage ensues, the penalty shall be life for life, 24eye for eye, tooth for tooth,

22 וְכִי־יִנָּצוּ אֲנָשִׁים וְנָגְפוּ אִשָּׁה הָרָה
וְיָצְאוּ יְלָדֶיהָ וְלֹא יִהְיֶה אָסוֹן עָנוֹשׁ יֵעָנֵשׁ כַּאֲשֶׁר
יָשִׁית עָלָיו בַּעַל הָאִשָּׁה וְנָתַן בִּפְלִלִים: 23 וְאִם־
אָסוֹן יִהְיֶה וְנָתַתָּה נֶפֶשׁ תַּחַת נָפֶשׁ: 24 עַיִן תַּחַת
עַיִן שֵׁן תַּחַת שֵׁן יָד תַּחַת יָד רֶגֶל תַּחַת רָגֶל:

Unintended Harm to a Pregnant Woman (vv. 22–25)

The legal issues in this case are complicated by several additional factors. Unlike the earlier instance of a verbal quarrel that was initially not unlawful (vv. 18–19), the present one involves physical violence from the beginning. There was prior intent on the part of each antagonist to cause bodily harm to the other, and thus their activity was intrinsically unlawful and hazardous. Since the possibility of indirect damage was foreseeable, the antagonists are liable for injury caused to an innocent bystander, in this case, a pregnant woman. Restitution is to be made, but there is no retaliation if death does not ensue.

Unfortunately, the Hebrew text is replete with difficulties, which are further compounded by the attachment of the law of talion (vv. 23–25). For example, it is not clear why the phrase expressing expulsion of the fetus should speak of "children" in the plural; nor do we know whether stillbirth, premature birth, or term delivery is intended. Nor is it certain to what and to whom the Hebrew 'ason, here rendered "other damage," refers.

The legal consequences of causing a woman to miscarry are treated also in the Sumerian law fragments,[48] in Hammurabi's collection,[49] in the Middle Assyrian Laws,[50] and in the Hittite laws.[51] All call for monetary compensation for the loss of the fetus. Only the Sumerian laws distinguish between accidental and intentional assault. Hammurabi's provide for vicarious punishment: Should the parties involved belong to the upper class, the assailant's daughter is put to death if the victim dies. The Middle Assyrian laws are particularly harsh. They too mandate vicarious punishment and vary the penalty according to social status, but, in addition, they inflict multiple torments on the aggressor. The Hittite laws, alone, take into account the age of the fetus in estimating the fine imposed on the assailant. In none of the cuneiform parallels do the particulars correspond exactly to the details of the case presented here in the Torah, so they shed little light on the complexities of our text.

fight The Hebrew stem *n-ts-h* implies the use of physical force.[52]

a miscarriage results Literally, "her children emerge." The common Hebrew stem *y-ts-'*, "to go out, emerge," is used of parturition.[53]

damage Hebrew 'ason elsewhere always signifies a major calamity;[54] therefore, the most likely issue here is whether or not death ensues. Rabbinic tradition construes the phrase in this way and understands it as referring to the mother.[55]

based on reckoning Hebrew *pelilim* means "estimation," "assessment,"[56] the idea being that the husband makes a claim based on some recognized system. Rabbinic interpretation takes *pelilim* to mean "the judges," that is, those who are to approve the sum demanded by the husband.[57]

23. other damage Presumably, the death of the mother, in which case the principle of life for life is invoked, as opposed to monetary fine. This accords with the rule that the killing of a human being cannot be compensated for by the payment of money (Num. 35:31).

Lex Talionis (vv. 23–25)

These verses formulate the law of talion, or exact equivalence for injury, usually understood to mean identical physical injury inflicted in retaliation for physical injury suffered. This legal principle was first introduced by Hammurabi and finds expression in such laws as these:

hand for hand, foot for foot, ²⁵burn for burn, wound for
wound, bruise for bruise.

²⁶When a man strikes the eye of his slave, male or female,

כ״ה כְּוִיָּה תַּחַת כְּוִיָּה פֶּצַע תַּחַת פָּצַע פֶּצַע חַבּוּרָה
תַּחַת חַבּוּרָה: ס

כ״ו וְכִי־יַכֶּה אִישׁ אֶת־עֵין עַבְדּוֹ אוֹ־אֶת־עֵין

> If a seignior has destroyed the eye of a member of the aristocracy, they shall destroy his eye.
> If he has broken a(nother) seignior's bone, they shall break his bone.
> If a seignior has knocked out a tooth of a seignior of his own rank, they shall knock out his tooth.⁵⁸

Another law of this type decrees that if a house collapsed and killed its owner as a result of faulty construction, then the builder is put to death. If the casualty was the owner's son, then the builder's son is put to death.⁵⁹

Prior to Hammurabi, monetary compensation, not physical retaliation, was the rule for inflicting bodily injury. This principle is operative in the laws of Ur-nammu,⁶⁰ Eshnunna,⁶¹ and the Hittites,⁶² as well as in the Middle Assyrian laws.⁶³

It is now recognized by legal anthropologists that before the time of Hammurabi, assault and battery was considered a private wrong to be settled between the families of the assailant and the victim. As a result of the socially disruptive effects of the cycle of violence and counterviolence, it became acceptable to take monetary compensation for the wrong committed. With the growth of urbanization and centralized government as well as the increased importance of maintaining domestic tranquillity, the state more and more tended to encroach upon the private domain. Physical violence became an issue of public welfare, and the state began to regulate the payments for various types of injuries. In a revolutionary development, Hammurabi categorized assault and battery as criminal conduct to be prosecuted by the state. The central government took on the responsibility of protecting the public and preserving the security of its citizens. The lex talionis strove to achieve exact justice: only one life for one life, only one eye for one eye, and so forth. In pursuit of this goal, however, the laws allowed physical retaliation and vicarious punishment and did not accept the principle of equal justice for all but, rather, adjusted penalties according to social class.

The same legal principles that underlie the lex talionis of Hammurabi are present in biblical law. The formulation appears three times in the legal texts of the Torah: here, in Leviticus 24:17–22, and in Deuteronomy 19:18–19,21. The list found here, the most comprehensive of the three, begins with the maximum penalty, loss of life, and then cites four instances of loss of limb, arranged in anatomical order from head to foot. These are followed by three types of painful surface wounds.

Rabbinic tradition understood the biblical formulation to mean monetary payment and not physical retaliation.⁶⁴ The present Exodus passage exhibits several strange features indicating that such was indeed the original intent. The section is introduced in the Hebrew text by a verb in the second person—"you shall pay." That this stylistic formulation is unique in these otherwise impersonally and casuistically formulated laws indicates that the passage in question is not an organic part of the wider text. Another peculiarity lies in the fact that the list of damages is singularly inappropriate to the circumstances described. Other than "life for life," none of the injuries listed can be included under the rubric of the term 'ason used in verses 22 and 23. Nor can loss of limb be relevant to the case in hand. If the mother who carries the fetus is killed, any other injuries would be irrelevant. If she only suffers loss of limb but survives, then the fact of her pregnancy is immaterial.

Remarkably, the two other citations of the talion formula in the Torah are also inapplicable to the legal context in which they are embedded. The Leviticus passage deals with blasphemy, and talion is extraneous to it. The passage in Deuteronomy concerns false witnesses, and the law states that they are subject to the very penalty that would have been inflicted on the accused had their falsehood not been exposed. Since, with the singular exception of Deuteronomy 25:12, mutilation is not a penalty in biblical law, the entire list, other than "life for life," is again irrelevant.

The most reasonable conclusion to be drawn from the foregoing is that the talion list is a citation from some extrabiblical compendium of laws and has been incorporated intact into the Torah. That is why the stylistic variant "you shall pay," noted above, appears in our Exodus text. The list is actually a general statement of legal policy that formulates the abstract principle of equivalence and restitution in concrete terms.

and destroys it, he shall let him go free on account of his eye. ²⁷If he knocks out the tooth of his slave, male or female, he shall let him go free on account of his tooth.

²⁸When an ox gores a man or a woman to death, the ox shall be stoned and its flesh shall not be eaten, but the owner of the ox is not to be punished. ²⁹If, however, that ox

אֲמָתוֹ וְשִׁחֲתָהּ לַחָפְשִׁי יְשַׁלְּחֶנּוּ תַּחַת עֵינוֹ: ס 27 וְאִם־שֵׁן עַבְדּוֹ אוֹ־שֵׁן אֲמָתוֹ יַפִּיל לַחָפְשִׁי יְשַׁלְּחֶנּוּ תַּחַת שִׁנּוֹ: פ 28 וְכִי־יִגַּח שׁוֹר אֶת־אִישׁ אוֹ אֶת־אִשָּׁה וָמֵת סָקוֹל יִסָּקֵל הַשּׁוֹר וְלֹא יֵאָכֵל אֶת־בְּשָׂרוֹ וּבַעַל הַשּׁוֹר נָקִי: 29 וְאִם שׁוֹר נַגָּח הוּא מִתְּמֹל

Of all the equivalency items in the list, it is obvious that only "life for life" can be implemented literally because all human beings are created equal. But exact equivalency in respect of bodily injury is inherently unattainable. Therefore, the only available avenue of redress is monetary compensation.

Additional evidence in support of the nonliteral interpretation of the biblical "eye for eye" phraseology lies in Leviticus 24:18: "One who kills a beast shall make restitution for it [lit. "shall pay for it"]: life for life." Here the legal prose can be sensibly construed only in terms of monetary compensation. Further, in Judges 15:11, when Samson butchered the Philistines because they had burnt alive his wife and her father, he justified his act by saying, "As they did to me, so I did to them," even though the punishment he inflicted did not correspond exactly to the crime they had committed. Finally, there is the law in Numbers 35:31 forbidding ransom for the life of a murderer and insisting on his death. The clear implication is that monetary compensation was the usual practice in respect of other, nonfatal physical assaults.

To sum up: Biblical law accepted the principle that assault and battery are public crimes and not simply private wrongs. However, it instituted monetary compensation not retaliation for bodily injury. It also insisted on equal justice for all citizens (for the slave, see vv. 20,26–27). And it outlawed vicarious punishment.

How was the amount of restitution calculated? The Torah information itself provides no answer. According to rabbinic tradition, however, it was to be based on the diminution in value of a slave who sustained a similar injury.⁶⁵

Injury by a Master to his Slave (vv. 26–27)

Verse 20 established the culpability of one who kills his own slave. These clauses deal with the case of a master who causes his slave irreparable bodily injury. The biblical law does not give the master the benefit of the doubt that only disciplinary chastisement was intended; were that the case, it would indeed have been cruel and unusual punishment. Intent to cause injury is assumed, and the master is guilty of aggravated assault. He has robbed his slave of his humanity and dignity, and for this the slave, male or female, gains freedom. As Ibn Ezra points out, the prospect of losing his financial investment [not to mention the services performed] must inevitably in such circumstances act as a deterrent to cruel treatment on the part of the master.

This biblical law, like that of verses 20–21, is without parallel in other ancient Near Eastern legislation; the latter simply does not concern itself with the well-being of the slave.

his slave According to rabbinic tradition,⁶⁶ a non-Israelite.

eye ... tooth Or any other of the chief external organs of the body. Rabbinic law lists twenty-four such, including the fingers, toes, tips of the ears, and the tip of the nose.⁶⁷ Should the master injure any of these, the slave is given his freedom.

THE HOMICIDAL BEAST (vv. 28–32)

This section contains three cases involving the attack of a homicidal beast—here exemplified by an ox⁶⁸—upon human beings. They are the cases of (1) the beast that has no previous record of viciousness; (2) the beast that has such a previous history and whose owner has been so warned; and (3) the beast that gores a slave.

The legal topic of the goring ox is treated in the laws of both Eshnunna⁶⁹ and Hammurabi.⁷⁰ The former deal only with cases 2 and 3, but the latter include all three and in the same sequence as the

has been in the habit of goring, and its owner, although warned, has failed to guard it, and it kills a man or a woman—the ox shall be stoned and its owner, too, shall be put to death. [30]If ransom is laid upon him, he must pay whatever is laid upon him to redeem his life. [31]So, too, if it gores a minor, male or female, [the owner] shall be dealt

שְׁלְשֹׁם וְהוּעַד בִּבְעָלָיו וְלֹא יִשְׁמְרֶנּוּ וְהֵמִית אִישׁ אוֹ
אִשָּׁה הַשּׁוֹר יִסָּקֵל וְגַם־בְּעָלָיו יוּמָת: 30 אִם־כֹּפֶר
יוּשַׁת עָלָיו וְנָתַן פִּדְיֹן נַפְשׁוֹ כְּכֹל אֲשֶׁר־יוּשַׁת עָלָיו:
31 אוֹ־בֵן יִגָּח אוֹ־בַת יִגָּח כַּמִּשְׁפָּט הַזֶּה יֵעָשֶׂה לּוֹ:

Torah. All three collections share in common the general principle that the owner who has been duly warned about his vicious ox is responsible for guarding it. Beyond this, there are considerable differences between the Mesopotamian and biblical approaches. Eshnunna and Hammurabi interest themselves exclusively in the economic aspects of the case. The incident itself is treated as a relatively minor affair. Eshnunna, for instance, imposes the same penalty on the forewarned owner of the ox that kills a man as it does for the offense of cutting off someone's finger. Neither law collection recommends any action against the ox, and Hammurabi explicitly disavows as an actionable offense the first-time killing of a man by an ox.

By contrast, the entire treatment of the case in the Torah is grounded in religious and moral considerations. Thus, legislation here demands the destruction of an ox that has fatally gored a human being, whatever the past history of the beast, and it proscribes the eating of its flesh. If the owner had been forewarned, it regards him as being worthy of the death penalty. The gender of the victim is immaterial. The two Mesopotamian law collections mention only the goring of a male.

28. *the ox shall be stoned*   The killer ox is not destroyed solely because it is dangerous. This is clear from the fact that it is not destroyed when the victim is another ox and from the prescribed mode of destruction—not ordinary slaughter but stoning. The execution of the ox was carried out in the presence, and with the participation, of the entire community—implying that the killing of a human being is a source of mass pollution and that the proceedings had an expiatory function.[71] The killing of a homicidal beast is ordained in Genesis 9:5–6: "For your own life-blood I will require a reckoning: I will require it of every beast. . . . Whoever sheds the blood of man, by man shall his blood be shed; for in His image did God make man." The sanctity of human life is such as to make bloodshed the consummate offense, one viewed with unspeakable horror. Both man and beast that destroy human life are thereafter tainted by bloodguilt.

its flesh   This hardly needs mention since the stoning would in any case render the flesh of the animal inedible. The proscription rests on the notion that a beast tainted by the taking of human life cannot be fit for human consumption.

not to be punished   In contrast to the next case. Here there is no implicit negligence.

29.   This is a case of unmistakable criminal negligence. The owner is guilty of reckless disregard of the safety and rights of others. His liability is therefore great.

has failed to guard it   Hebrew *ve-lo' yishmerennu*; the Septuagint reads, "he did not destroy it," apparently based on a Hebrew text: *ve-lo' yashmidennu*. This accords with the interpretation of Rabbi Eliezer, who understood the term "guarding" to mean putting the knife to the ox.[72]

30. *ransom*   Numbers 35:31 forbids the acceptance of ransom for the life of one found guilty of murder. This man is not, strictly speaking, a murderer since he did not directly cause the homicide and did not have such intent; the sentence is therefore mitigated. Rabbinic exegesis interprets the death penalty mentioned in verse 29 to mean "death by the hand of Heaven," not by a human court.[73]

whatever is laid upon him   Presumably by the family of the victim (cf. v. 22). Targum Jonathan preserves a tradition that it is the court that fixes the amount of the ransom.

31.   Such an amplification of a law is unparalleled in the Torah legislation. It is thought to emend or polemicize against some earlier Semitic law that stipulated vicarious punishment. Although such practice is indeed attested in Hammurabi (pars. 116,210,230), it is not applied there in the present case, which enjoins a fine for the owner only in the case of an ox that kills a man.

with according to the same rule. ³²But if the ox gores a slave, male or female, he shall pay thirty shekels of silver to the master, and the ox shall be stoned.

³³When a man opens a pit, or digs a pit and does not cover it, and an ox or an ass falls into it, ³⁴the one responsible for the pit must make restitution; he shall pay the price to the owner, but shall keep the dead animal.

³⁵When a man's ox injures his neighbor's ox and it dies, they shall sell the live ox and divide its price; they shall also divide the dead animal. ³⁶If, however, it is known that the ox was in the habit of goring, and its owner has failed to guard it, he must restore ox for ox, but shall keep the dead animal. ³⁷When a man steals an ox or a sheep, and slaugh-

32 אִם־עֶ֣בֶד יִגַּ֥ח הַשּׁ֖וֹר א֣וֹ אָמָ֑ה כֶּ֣סֶף ׀ שְׁלֹשִׁ֣ים
שְׁקָלִים֙ יִתֵּ֣ן לַֽאדֹנָ֔יו וְהַשּׁ֖וֹר יִסָּקֵֽל׃ ס
33 וְכִֽי־יִפְתַּ֨ח אִ֜ישׁ בּ֗וֹר א֠וֹ כִּֽי־יִכְרֶ֥ה אִ֛ישׁ
בֹּ֖ר וְלֹ֣א יְכַסֶּ֑נּוּ וְנָֽפַל־שָׁ֥מָּה שּׁ֖וֹר א֥וֹ חֲמֽוֹר׃ 34 בַּ֤עַל
הַבּוֹר֙ יְשַׁלֵּ֔ם כֶּ֖סֶף יָשִׁ֣יב לִבְעָלָ֑יו וְהַמֵּ֖ת יִֽהְיֶה־לּֽוֹ׃
ס
35 וְכִֽי־יִגֹּ֧ף שֽׁוֹר־אִ֛ישׁ אֶת־שׁ֥וֹר רֵעֵ֖הוּ וָמֵ֑ת
וּמָ֣כְר֗וּ אֶת־הַשּׁ֤וֹר הַחַי֙ וְחָצ֣וּ אֶת־כַּסְפּ֔וֹ וְגַ֥ם אֶת־
הַמֵּ֖ת יֶֽחֱצֽוּן׃ 36 א֣וֹ נוֹדַ֗ע כִּ֠י שׁ֣וֹר נַגָּ֥ח הוּא֙
מִתְּמ֣וֹל שִׁלְשֹׁ֔ם וְלֹ֥א יִשְׁמְרֶ֖נּוּ בְּעָלָ֑יו שַׁלֵּ֨ם יְשַׁלֵּ֤ם
שׁוֹר֙ תַּ֣חַת הַשּׁ֔וֹר וְהַמֵּ֖ת יִֽהְיֶה־לּֽוֹ׃ ס
37 כִּ֤י יִגְנֹֽב־אִישׁ֙ שׁ֣וֹר אוֹ־שֶׂ֔ה וּטְבָח֖וֹ א֣וֹ מְכָר֑וֹ
חֲמִשָּׁ֣ה בָקָ֗ר יְשַׁלֵּם֙ תַּ֣חַת הַשּׁ֔וֹר וְאַרְבַּע־צֹ֖אן
תַּ֥חַת הַשֶּֽׂה׃

32. ***thirty shekels*** This is the evaluation, for purposes of vows, of a woman between the ages of twenty and sixty, as given in Leviticus 27:4. It is also the fine imposed by Hammurabi's laws (par. 251) on the owner of an ox that gored to death a member of the aristocracy. The same laws (par. 252) impose only twenty shekels if the victim was the aristocrat's slave. The laws of Eshnunna (par. 55) exact fifteen shekels. In the law of the Torah, the stoning of the ox means that it was regarded as having incurred bloodguilt, just as it had for killing a free person.

DAMAGE TO LIVESTOCK (vv. 33–36)

33–34. The presumption is that the pit or cistern was located on public property or that there was unobstructed access to it from public property.[74] Behavioral norms would expect the individual to exercise reasonable prudence and not leave such hazards exposed. For this act of omission, which constitutes negligence, the offender must make restitution for the value of the animal.

The last phrase of the Hebrew text, which literally translates "and the carcass shall be his," is ambiguous. As noted by Rashbam, the straightforward meaning favors the present translation. Rabbinic exegesis awards the carcass to the claimant, but its value is deducted from the compensation paid for the loss of the animal.[75] The carcass would be valued for its hide.

35–36. Here, one ox kills another of presumed equal worth.[76] The amount of compensation will depend on whether or not the attacking ox had a history of viciousness. If it had none, then, because neither party was at fault, they share the loss. If it had such a history, then its owner was negligent and must make full restitution for the dead ox.

Paragraph 53 of the laws of Eshnunna is almost identical with verse 35 here but lacks the circumstance of verse 36.

THE LAW OF THEFT (21:37–22:3)

37. This verse, in some editions of the Bible numbered 22:1, must be taken together with 22:2b(3b) and 3(4). The operative principle here is that the slaughter or sale of the stolen animal constitutes unmistakable evidence of *mens rea*, that is, evil intent on the part of the thief. The theft cannot be interpreted as merely an impulsive act. The thief must pay back in kind fivefold for the ox and fourfold for the sheep. Rabbinic tradition understood this to mean replacing the animal plus four more or three more animals respectively.[77]

The reason for the difference in compensation for the two animals has been a matter of conjecture. Targum Jonathan and Rabbi Meir maintain that since the ox, unlike the sheep, is a draft

ters it or sells it, he shall pay five oxen for the ox,
22 and four sheep for the sheep.—[1]the thief is seized
while tunneling, and he is beaten to death, there is no

כ"ב אִם־בַּמַּחְתֶּרֶת יִמָּצֵא הַגַּנָּב וְהֻכָּה וָמֵת
אֵין לוֹ דָּמִים: ² אִם־זָרְחָה הַשֶּׁמֶשׁ עָלָיו דָּמִים לוֹ
שַׁלֵּם יְשַׁלֵּם אִם־אֵין לוֹ וְנִמְכַּר בִּגְנֵבָתוֹ: 3 אִם־

animal, its comparative worth, and hence the loss, is greater. Rabbi Johanan ben Zakkai argues that
the Torah is sensitive to human dignity, even in the case of a thief. Since the miscreant had to carry the
sheep—a very humiliating experience—a lesser penalty is imposed.[78] Bekhor Shor explains that the
owner is compensated for his considerable investment of effort and toil in training the ox, as well as
for the loss of its labors. In the case of the stolen sheep, it may be added that the owner has been
deprived of the potential value of its fleece, milk, flesh, and hide. Doubtless, the multiple restitution
also takes into account the benefit derived by the thief from slaughtering or selling the animal. It also
functions punitively as a deterrent to crime. Mishnah Ketubbot 3:9 rules that a thief who voluntarily
confesses his crime before the court makes restitution only for the stolen item and is exempt from the
penalties.

Verse 2b(3b) stipulates that the aforementioned restitution must be made and that an insolvent
thief is to be indentured by the court to work off the value of his debt. Hammurabi[79] sentences an
insolvent thief to death.

Verse 3(4) specifies that should the animals be discovered unharmed and still in the possession of
the rustler, then only double restitution is to be made. In this instance, the loss to the owner has been
minimal and temporary. From 22:6,8 it is clear that, apart from the case of 21:37, the standard penalty
was double restitution. Mishnah Bava Kamma 7:1 applies this penalty uniformly to all goods and
effects.

Violations of property rights occupy much attention in the laws of Hammurabi, Assyria, and the
Hittites. Hammurabi's laws show that in the earlier period the penalty for theft was death; later, the
penalty became multiple restitution, which might be ten times the value of the stolen article and, in
the case of theft from a temple or the royal palace, as high as thirty times.[80] The Middle Assyrian laws
deal with women thieves and inflict mutilation as a punishment.[81] The Hittite laws are dispropor-
tionately preoccupied with issues of property violations. In all cases, multiple restitution is enforced.
In the Torah, by contrast, theft, while a serious offence and a sin, is not particularly emphasized. As
the following verses show, the humanity even of the thief is of concern.

CHAPTER 22   **22:1–2a.**   The particular case of a thief who is surprised in the act of breaking and entering is
parenthetically injected into the law dealing with theft. The contrast between the phrases, "If the sun
has risen" and "while tunneling" shows the latter to presuppose a nighttime setting. This is confirmed
by Job 24:16, as well as by the fact that the presence of bystanders outside would discourage such a
laborious mode of entry by day. Because the burglar is likely to encounter the occupants and must
anticipate that they will use force, his nocturnal timing creates a presumption of homicidal intent.
The condition of imminent threat, necessary to satisfy lawful self-defense by the householder, is thus
fulfilled. Hence, no bloodguilt is incurred should the intruder be killed. The operative moral principle, as formulated in Bava Metsia 62a, is that "your life takes precedence" over his. For this reason,
as Sanhedrin 72a puts it, "If one comes to slay you, you forestall by slaying him."

If the break-in occurred in broad daylight, however, it is not presumed to present imminent
danger to life; the use of deadly force is therefore deemed to be unwarranted, and bloodguilt would
ensue. Here the issue is the hierarchy of values. The biblical scale gives priority to the protection of
life—even the life of the burglar—over the protection of property.

According to the Mekhilta,[1] Rabbi Ishmael understood the phrase "If the sun has risen" to be
figurative for absolute certainty. In other words, he eliminates the distinction between the nighttime
and daytime slaying of the burglar and restricts the privileged killing to the circumstance in which the
murderous intent of the intruder is absolutely beyond doubt.

The laws of Eshnunna[2] also deal with the topic of theft and likewise distinguish between daytime
and nighttime offenses, but they are concerned solely with the protection of property and ignore the
humanitarian issue. Hammurabi[3] simply prescribes the death penalty for the thief who made a breach
in a house or committed robbery.

bloodguilt in his case. [2]If the sun has risen on him, there is bloodguilt in that case.—He must make restitution; if he lacks the means, he shall be sold for his theft. [3]But if what he stole—whether ox or ass or sheep—is found alive in his possession, he shall pay double.

[4]When a man lets his livestock loose to graze in another's land, and so allows a field or a vineyard to be grazed bare, he must make restitution for the impairment of that field or vineyard.

[5]When a fire is started and spreads to thorns, so that stacked, standing, or growing grain is consumed, he who started the fire must make restitution.

הַמְצֵא תִמָּצֵא בְיָדוֹ הַגְּנֵבָה מִשּׁוֹר עַד־חֲמוֹר
עַד־שֶׂה חַיִּים שְׁנַיִם יְשַׁלֵּם: ס   שלישי
4 כִּי יַבְעֶר־אִישׁ שָׂדֶה אוֹ־כֶרֶם וְשִׁלַּח אֶת־
בְּעִירֹה וּבִעֵר בִּשְׂדֵה אַחֵר מֵיטַב שָׂדֵהוּ וּמֵיטַב
כַּרְמוֹ יְשַׁלֵּם: ס
5 כִּי־תֵצֵא אֵשׁ וּמָצְאָה קֹצִים וְנֶאֱכַל
גָּדִישׁ אוֹ הַקָּמָה אוֹ הַשָּׂדֶה שַׁלֵּם יְשַׁלֵּם הַמַּבְעִר
אֶת־הַבְּעֵרָה: ס

v. 4   בְּעִירוֹ ק'

DAMAGE TO CROPS (vv. 4–5)

Two cases are under consideration: the destruction of crops (1) by livestock or (2) by fire. The first is treated more severely—the cattle owner must compensate for the choice crops of the yield—because he carelessly, although without malicious intent, allowed his beast to stray into another's field. In the second case restitution of choice produce is not required because the damage was wholly accidental. These two cases are wedged between laws relating to theft because all are viewed under the broad heading of damage to property.

The Hittite laws similarly feature and juxtapose the same two legal topics although in reverse order, and they likewise insert them among laws of theft.

The Hebrew text contains several obscurities, discussed below.

4. lets . . . loose to graze The two Hebrew clauses are complementary, the second (*ve-shillaḥ*) accounting for the action of the first, with the connecting *vav* being explanatory.[4] The Hebrew stem *b-ʿ-r* most frequently means "to set fire, burn," as in verse 5. But it can also mean "to ravage,"[5] which is the action of a beast (Heb. *beʿir*). Isaiah 5:5 illustrates the present case: "Now I am going to tell you / What I will do to My vineyard: / I will remove its hedge, / That it may be ravaged [*le-vaʿer*]; / I will break down its wall, / That it may be trampled." The Septuagint similarly understood the verb *b-ʿ-r* in the Hebrew text in the sense of "graze over."

for the impairment Hebrew *meitav*, literally "the best." In tannaitic sources there is a difference of opinion as to the intent of this law. It is unclear whether the compensation imposed on the owner of the beast is calculated according to the best property of the defendant or of the plaintiff.[6] Both the Septuagint and the Samaritan texts interpolate a clause making the normal crop the criterion of compensation when the crop was only partly destroyed, and the top of the crop the standard when the entire field was grazed over.

5. When a fire is started For legitimate purposes, but the flames spread by the wind to someone else's property.

thorns These would be collected and used as fuel by the poor and for building hedges.

growing grain Literally, "the field."

THE LAW OF BAILMENT (vv. 6–14)

With the exception of verse 8, this section deals with the stipulations governing various types of guardianship of another's movables or livestock, and the degree of each bailee's responsibility. The general principle is that liability increases with the benefit that the bailee receives or expects for his services or that he gains from the entrusted property.

Mishnah Bava Metsia 7:8 (= Shevu. 8:1) distinguishes the following four categories: (1) a gratuitous bailee (Heb. *shomer ḥinnam*), (2) a borrower (*shoʾel*), (3) one who takes a fee (*noseʾ sakhar*),

⁶When a man gives money or goods to another for safekeeping, and they are stolen from the man's house—if the thief is caught, he shall pay double; ⁷if the thief is not caught, the owner of the house shall depose before God that he has not laid hands on the other's property. ⁸In all

6 כִּי־יִתֵּן אִישׁ אֶל־רֵעֵהוּ כֶּסֶף אוֹ־כֵלִים לִשְׁמֹר וְגֻנַּב מִבֵּית הָאִישׁ אִם־יִמָּצֵא הַגַּנָּב יְשַׁלֵּם שְׁנָיִם: 7 אִם־לֹא יִמָּצֵא הַגַּנָּב וְנִקְרַב בַּעַל־הַבַּיִת אֶל־הָאֱלֹהִים אִם־לֹא שָׁלַח יָדוֹ בִּמְלֶאכֶת רֵעֵהוּ:

and (4) a hirer (sokher). "The gratuitous bailee must swear [to innocence of negligence] in all cases [of loss of the deposit, and is then freed from liability]; the borrower must make restitution in all cases; both the paid bailee and the hirer take the oath [in a case] pertaining to an animal that was injured, carried off, or died, but must make restitution if it was lost or stolen."

Movable Goods (vv. 6–7)

A bailee claims that movable goods entrusted to him for safekeeping have been stolen. If the thief is not caught, the bailee must clear himself of suspicion of misappropriation by taking an oath before the proper authorities.

Since "money or goods" are kept in the house together with the bailee's own possessions, they require no special attention or effort, and there is no expectation of benefit or consideration. As a gratuitous bailee (shomer ḥinnam), he is not liable for loss or theft that does not result from his own negligence.[7]

Similar cases are dealt with in the other law collections of the ancient Near East. The laws of Eshnunna[8] rule that where a deposit disappears, and there is no evidence of a break-in, the bailee must replace the property. However, if the house collapses or is burglarized and the bailee's own property is also lost, he takes an exculpatory oath to that effect before the chief god of the city and is then free of all liability.

Hammurabi's laws contain several clauses relating to issues of this kind;[9] they reflect a highly developed commercial society in which witnesses and written contracts govern such transactions. They are not, however, strictly analogous to those detailed in the Torah.

6. **they are stolen**   So the bailee claims.

pay double   In accordance with the rule of verse 3.

7. **shall depose**   Literally, "shall draw near." The Hebrew stem k-r-v often has legal force in the sense of applying for a judicial determination.[10] In the present instance the term means to make a statement under oath, which becomes determinative.

before God   See Comment to 21:6.

laid hands on   That is, misappropriated. If he made use of the deposit for his own benefit, he has become a paid bailee and thus liable for theft or loss.

property   Hebrew mela'khah, "labor, the product or fruit of labor," covers both money and goods.[11]

A Claim of Tortious Conversion (v. 8)

This is a general, comprehensive formulation that deals with an allegation that another has wrongfully taken possession of the claimant's chattel and has contested his right of ownership.

As was recognized by Rabbi Ḥiyya bar Joseph, recorded in Bava Kamma 107a, "an interweaving of sections" ('eruv parashiyyot) has occurred here. This observation is explained by Rashi to mean that the verse is an interpolation and is extraneous to its immediate context. We may conjecture that it has been wedged in between the two types of bailment because, like them, the dispute involves a claim of illegal assumption of ownership, and because it shares legal phraseology in common with them both: "before God," "shall pay double," "ox, an ass, and a sheep."

charges of misappropriation   Hebrew devar pesha'. Davar frequently carries the legal denotation of "case, suit, action, controversy at law."[12] Pesha' basically connotes the denial or

charges of misappropriation—pertaining to an ox, an ass, a sheep, a garment, or any other loss, whereof one party alleges, "This is it"—the case of both parties shall come before God: he whom God declares guilty shall pay double to the other.

⁹When a man gives to another an ass, an ox, a sheep or any other animal to guard, and it dies or is injured or is carried off, with no witness about, ¹⁰an oath before the LORD shall decide between the two of them that the one has not laid hands on the property of the other; the owner must acquiesce, and no restitution shall be made. ¹¹But if [the animal] was stolen from him, he shall make restitution to its owner. ¹²If it was torn by beasts, he shall bring it as evidence; he need not replace what has been torn by beasts.

עַל־כָּל־דְּבַר־פֶּ֫שַׁע עַל־שׁ֡וֹר עַל־חֲמוֹר עַל־
שֶׂה עַל־שַׂלְמָה עַל־כָּל־אֲבֵדָה אֲשֶׁר יֹאמַר
כִּי־ה֣וּא זֶה עַד הָאֱלֹהִים יָבֹא דְּבַר־שְׁנֵיהֶם אֲשֶׁר
יַרְשִׁיעֻן אֱלֹהִים יְשַׁלֵּם שְׁנַיִם לְרֵעֵהוּ׃ ס
⁹ כִּי־יִתֵּן אִישׁ אֶל־רֵעֵהוּ חֲמוֹר אוֹ־שׁוֹר
אוֹ־שֶׂה וְכָל־בְּהֵמָה לִשְׁמֹר וּמֵת אוֹ־נִשְׁבַּר אוֹ־
נִשְׁבָּה אֵין רֹאֶה׃ ¹⁰ שְׁבֻעַת יְהוָה תִּהְיֶה בֵּין
שְׁנֵיהֶם אִם־לֹא שָׁלַח יָדוֹ בִּמְלֶאכֶת רֵעֵהוּ וְלָקַח
בְּעָלָיו וְלֹא יְשַׁלֵּם׃ ¹¹ וְאִם־גָּנֹב יִגָּנֵב מֵעִמּוֹ יְשַׁלֵּם
לִבְעָלָיו׃ ¹² אִם־טָרֹף יִטָּרֵף יְבִאֵהוּ עֵד הַטְּרֵפָה
לֹא יְשַׁלֵּם׃ פ

repudiation of the right of another to exercise dominion and control. Hence, it is used in the political context of renunciation of the status of vassalage, an act of treachery in the ancient world; and it is used in a religious sense of violating God's covenant,[13] transgressing His law.[14] Here *pesha'* bears a legal nuance: a breach of trust, a case of lawbreaking.

"This is it" The plaintiff claims to identify his property. Alternatively, the phrase might be rendered "This is he," referring to the alleged offender.

shall pay double The livestock or movable property has remained intact in the possession of the guilty party, so the rule of 22:3 applies.

Livestock (vv. 9–12)

Unlike the case of "money or goods," the safeguarding of animals is complicated by their being out in the fields and requiring much attention and labor. It may be assumed, therefore, that the bailee is paid for his services (*nose'/shomer sakhar*), and this fact alone affects the degree of responsibility that is expected of him. Three contingencies are presented: (1) The bailee claims that the loss to the owner was caused by an "act of God," an unforeseeable and unpreventable natural phenomenon. In the absence of corroborating witnesses, an oath of innocence is required to free him from liability (vv. 9–10). (2) The loss is blamed on theft. A measure of negligence is presumed, and the bailee must make restitution (v. 11). (3) The entrusted animal was savaged by a wild beast. The burden of proof is on the bailee; if he can prove his claim, he is exempt from liability.

Hammurabi's laws similarly discuss the case of the entrusted animal. They stipulate that the shepherd is free of liability if the beast was killed in the sheepfold by an "act of god" or by a lion—provided that he prove himself innocent "in the presence of the god." In that case, the owner receives the dead animal. If, however, the animal be lamed in the fold due to negligence, the shepherd must make good the loss.[15]

carried off A case of cattle rustling, as in Job 1:15,17, not the same as ordinary theft mentioned in verse 11.[16]

10. an oath before the LORD Rather, "an oath by the Lord." The use of YHVH here in place of "God" (*'elohim*) reflects the actual wording of the Israelite oath, just as in the regular oath-formula *hai YHVH*, "as the Lord lives."[17]

between the two of them It is uncertain whether both parties have to swear.[18]

must acquiesce Literally, "accept"—the oath as incontestable.[19]

12. he shall bring it as evidence He would be expected to attempt to save at least some part of the animal, as David notes in 1 Samuel 17:34–35.[20] Amos 3:12 illustrates this custom: "As a

[13]When a man borrows [an animal] from another and it dies or is injured, its owner not being with it, he must make restitution. [14]If its owner was with it, no restitution need be made; but if it was hired, he is entitled to the hire.

13 וְכִי־יִשְׁאַל אִישׁ מֵעִם רֵעֵהוּ וְנִשְׁבַּר אוֹ־מֵת בְּעָלָיו אֵין־עִמּוֹ שַׁלֵּם יְשַׁלֵּם: 14 אִם־בְּעָלָיו עִמּוֹ לֹא יְשַׁלֵּם אִם־שָׂכִיר הוּא בָּא בִּשְׂכָרוֹ: ס

shepherd rescues from the lion's jaws / Two shank bones or the tip of an ear . . . " The material circumstantial evidence suffices to exempt him from responsibility.

In place of *'ed*, "witness, evidence," some ancient versions read the preposition *'ad*, "up to": "He shall bring him [i.e., the owner] to the savaged animal."[21]

Borrowing (and Hiring?) (vv. 13–14)

The act of borrowing falls within the category of bailment. Since the use of the object is obtained gratis, entirely for the borrower's benefit, his degree of responsibility and liability exceeds that in the previous cases, unless certain conditions are fulfilled.

As will be shown below, it is not entirely clear whether the contingency of hiring actually appears in the Torah's legislation. The preserved fragments of the laws of Lipit-Ishtar[22] deal with the various payments to be made for different kinds of injuries caused by the hirer. Hammurabi[23] absolves the hirer if a rented ox or ass is killed by a lion in the open, but he requires full restitution if the death of the animal was caused by negligence or maltreatment; a tariff of payments for various types of injuries is also included.

13. borrows The verb has no object.[24] The theme of verses 9–12 and the phrase "it dies or is injured" make it certain that an animal, most likely a work animal, is meant.

14. If its owner was with it This provision may presuppose the borrowing of the services of the owner together with his animal.[25] At any rate, the presence of the owner at the time of the mishap absolves the borrower from liability. The reason may be that the owner has the responsibility of supervision and is expected to save his own animal.

if it was hired This rendering presupposes that Hebrew *sakhir* has adjectival force and refers back to the unmentioned but posited animal, thus creating a fourth category of bailment. However, other than the poetic phrase in Isaiah 7:20, "the razor that is hired," *sakhir* is always a noun meaning "a hired man, a day laborer,"[26] so that the translation could well be, "If he [the borrower] was a hired laborer," implying that the latter borrowed the animal from his employer.

he is entitled to the hire Hebrew *ba' bi-skharo* is puzzling. The present rendering means that the owner who hired out his animal—which then suffered misfortune—is not compensated for it but is entitled to receive only the hiring fee. Another possible rendering is "It came with his hiring fee"; that is, the owner is assumed to have taken the risk into account when he rented out the animal and therefore receives no restitution. Still a third translation could be "It comes out of his pay";[27] that is, the restitution is deducted from the wages of the hired laborer, who is fully responsible.

In the times of the Mishnah the responsibility of the hirer was a matter of dispute. Rabbi Meir classed him with the gratuitous bailee; Rabbi Judah, with the paid bailee.[28]

THE LAW OF SEDUCTION (vv. 15–16)

The Book of the Covenant does not regulate the laws of marriage. Long established by custom in Israel, they were transmitted orally over the generations. The present law must be an amendment to existing practice. The extant corpora of laws from the ancient Near East devote much attention to the case of rape but none to the specific issue dealt with here.

Ibn Ezra points out that the sequence of legal topics is "from the case of stolen property to that of a stolen heart." Both are offenses that occasion economic loss and entail payment of compensation.

A man has seduced an unattached virgin. Ordinarily, her father would receive the *mohar*, or bride-price, customarily paid him by the husband-to-be. This is in compensation for the loss of the daughter's services and potential value to the family. But the *mohar* was predicated on the woman's

¹⁵If a man seduces a virgin for whom the bride-price has not been paid, and lies with her, he must make her his wife by payment of a bride-price. ¹⁶If her father refuses to give her to him, he must still weigh out silver in accordance with the bride-price for virgins.

15 וְכִי־יְפַתֶּה אִישׁ בְּתוּלָה אֲשֶׁר לֹא־אֹרָשָׂה וְשָׁכַב עִמָּהּ מָהֹר יִמְהָרֶנָּה לּוֹ לְאִשָּׁה: 16 אִם־מָאֵן יְמָאֵן אָבִיהָ לְתִתָּהּ לּוֹ כֶּסֶף יִשְׁקֹל כְּמֹהַר הַבְּתוּלֹת: ס

premarital virginity, which was expected on moral and social grounds and was essential to the marriage contract.²⁹ Thus, the deflowering of the girl caused her a loss of social status and resulted in her father's forfeiture of the *mohar*. Consequently, the seducer had to make good the lost sum, regardless of whether the father permitted him to marry his daughter.

The origin of the technical term *mohar* is uncertain. Since it is common to Hebrew, Ugaritic, Aramaic, and Arabic, the practice must have been widespread. A similar institution, known as *tirḥatum* in Akkadian, is regulated in the cuneiform law collections. From the story of Dinah and Shechem, as told in Genesis 34, it is clear that the *mohar* was in force in pre-Israelite Canaan (v. 12).

The *mohar* was occasionally paid in services or heroic deeds instead of in money, as was the case with David's marriage to Saul's daughter,³⁰ Othniel's betrothal to Achsah, daughter of Caleb,³¹ and Jacob's many years of service in return for Laban's two daughters.³²

The *mohar* was paid to the bride's father, who in most cases would only enjoy the usufruct, that is, the profit and utility it produced. The original sum would eventually be turned over to the daughter. This practice seems to underlie the complaint of Laban's two daughters in Genesis 31:15 that their father "had used up [the] purchase price," that is, the original capital. In the Aramaic legal documents of the Jewish colony in Elephantine, in Egypt, deriving from the second half of the fifth century B.C.E., the *mohar* was paid to the father but counted among the wife's possessions.³³

seduces   By persuasion³⁴ or deception³⁵ but not by coercion. There is a presumption of consent on the part of the girl. For the law of rape, see Deuteronomy 22:22–29.

the bride-price has not been paid   Hebrew *'asher lo' 'orasah* means that she had never been betrothed; that is, she has not previously had a fiancé, one who paid the *mohar* for her but had not yet consummated the marriage.

Biblical marriage comprised two separate stages. The first is expressed through the stem *'-r-s* used here. The origin of the term is uncertain, but it may mean "to ask"³⁶—for the girl's hand in marriage. Once the *mohar* was paid, the girl was considered betrothed (Heb. *me'orasah*) and had the legal status of a married woman even though she was still entirely under the care and authority of her father.³⁷ This status explains Hosea's (2:21–22) figurative use of this verb to describe the binding love relationship between God and Israel.

15.   He must make her his wife   Hebrew *mahor yimharennah* are verbs formed from the noun *mohar*.

16.   the bride-price   The amount is not specified, it being assumed that the existing practice was well known. Based upon Deuteronomy 22:29, rabbinic tradition understood fifty shekels to be the average amount.³⁸

CATEGORICAL COMMANDS   (22:17–23:19)

The second section of the Book of the Covenant now opens. It comprises a miscellany of social, ethical, moral and religious stipulations that fall under the rubric of *devarim*, divine commands. These are overwhelmingly formulated in the categorical, apodictic style characteristic of the Decalogue, rather than in the casuistic, hypothetical style of the preceding laws. Most of the proscriptions and prescriptions are of the sort that do not come within the scope of the judicial powers of the court. Their enforcement is left to the human conscience, conditioned and quickened by the knowledge and conviction that they are standards of behavior imposed by a transcendent divine will, not salutary maxims born of human experience and wisdom.

¹⁷You shall not tolerate a sorceress.
¹⁸Whoever lies with a beast shall be put to death.

מְכַשֵּׁפָה לֹא תְחַיֶּה: ס   ¹⁷

כָּל־שֹׁכֵב עִם־בְּהֵמָה מוֹת יוּמָת: ס   ¹⁸

17–19. Three offenses are grouped together for several reasons: Each is a foreign importation alien to and subversive of the religion of Israel; each incurs the death penalty; each is regarded as an abomination and so designated elsewhere in the Bible—described by the Hebrew term *to'evah*, something utterly abhorrent.[39]

THE PROHIBITION OF SORCERY (v. 17)

The belief in and practice of magic was universal in the ancient world. It was an inevitable by-product of polytheism. The multiplicity of divine forces limited the power of any one of them; and since gods were but the divinization of nature's powers and phenomena, gods and humans were thought to share the same world. Like humans, gods were thought to be born, grow old, and die. Hence, within the intellectual system of polytheism, the reality of a realm of existence independent of the gods and ultimately in control of them was a logical inference. The attempt to activate and manipulate to one's advantage the mysterious supernatural forces inherent in this realm constituted the essence of magic. Elaborate techniques were developed to this end, and magic became an indispensable ingredient of religion. Apart from the practical and verbal procedures, and the personnel who specialized in them, there were also individuals who were thought to possess inherent mystical powers capable of exploiting the occult properties of the extramundane realm. Like all productions of the human mind, magic could be put to benevolent or malevolent use. The latter was outlawed in all societies.

Biblical monotheism, with its uncompromising insistence on the absolute omnipotence of one universal, sovereign, creator God, was totally irreconcilable with the underlying postulates of magic. The religion of Israel ruthlessly and relentlessly fought to extirpate such beliefs and practices. The classic statement on the subject appears in Deuteronomy 18:9–14:

> When you enter the land that the LORD your God is giving you, you shall not learn to imitate the abhorrent practices of those nations. Let no one be found among you who consigns his son or daughter to the fire, or who is an augur, a soothsayer, a diviner, a sorcerer, one who casts spells, or one who consults ghosts or familiar spirits, or one who inquires of the dead. For anyone who does such things is abhorrent to the LORD, and it is because of these abhorrent things that the LORD your God is dispossessing them before you. You must be wholehearted with the LORD your God. Those nations that you are about to dispossess do indeed resort to soothsayers and augurs; to you, however, the LORD your God has not assigned the like.

The non-Israelite seer Balaam noted this distinctiveness of Israel: "Lo, there is no augury in Jacob, / No divining in Israel" (Num. 23:23). Yet the frequency with which magical practices are mentioned in the Bible is sure testimony to their hold on the popular imagination and to the difficulty encountered in combating them.[40]

not tolerate Literally, "not let live," a unique legal expression in place of the usual "shall be put to death." Ramban regards the phrasing as indicative of the exceptional severity with which this antisocial offense is viewed.[41]

a sorceress The same penalty certainly applies to the male practitioner. The feminine specification here probably reflects a historical reality that the clandestine operators of this officially outlawed cult were mostly women.[42] This phenomenon, together with the fact that sorcery and witchcraft are forms of deception, most likely accounts for the association of this law with the preceding rule about the seducer.

THE PROHIBITION OF BESTIALITY (v. 18)

This particular perversion is again prohibited in Leviticus 18:23 and 20:15–16, where it is presented as one of the abominations of the pre-Israelite inhabitants of Canaan. Deuteronomy 27:21 also includes its perpetrators in its list of the accursed. It is not known to what extent the biblical allusions are representational of Syro-Palestinian culture. Quite possibly, they are aimed at idolatrous practices,

¹⁹Whoever sacrifices to a god other than the LORD alone shall be proscribed.

²⁰You shall not wrong a stranger or oppress him, for you were strangers in the land of Egypt.

יט זֹבֵחַ לָאֱלֹהִים יָחֳרָם בִּלְתִּי לַיהוָה לְבַדּוֹ:

כ וְגֵר לֹא־תוֹנֶה וְלֹא תִלְחָצֶנּוּ כִּי־גֵרִים הֱיִיתֶם בְּאֶרֶץ מִצְרָיִם:

otherwise unrecorded, of the official pagan religious or popular cults. Of the law collections of the ancient Near East, only the Hittite legislates against bestiality, imposing the death penalty—except for copulation between a human and a horse or mule, which, inexplicably, is not an offense![43] Hittite ritual texts dating back to the second half of the thirteenth century B.C.E. describe the purificatory rites for the removal of the impurity of bestiality (and incest) from a man. Otherwise, references to this abomination are restricted to mythological literature and to records of dream experience. Mishnah Avodah Zarah 2:1 mentions that contemporary heathens in the Greco-Roman world were suspected of copulating with animals.

THE PROHIBITION OF APOSTASY (v. 19)

The generalized prohibition of idolatry in the Decalogue (Exod. 20:3) is now specifically directed against sacrifice, here designated by the verb *z-v-ḥ*, which means "to slaughter." The sacrifice called *zevaḥ* was essentially a sacrificial feast shared by the worshiper and the deity. It was widespread throughout the religions of the ancient Near East.

to a god Rather, "to the gods"—of other nations. This understanding is indicated by the vocalization of the Hebrew: *la-'elohim*, as distinct from *le'lohim*, which refers to the one God.[44] The last Hebrew clause of the verse acts as an explanatory gloss to clarify the possible ambiguity in the consonantal text; to the same end, the Samaritan recension adds *'aḥerim*, "other" gods, while omitting that clause.

proscribed The Hebrew verb, formed from the noun *ḥerem*, implies a greater stringency than does the simple death penalty formula. It implies total annihilation and includes the destruction of the criminal's property, as Targum Jonathan was careful to note.[45]

CONCERN FOR THE DISADVANTAGED OF SOCIETY (vv. 20–26)

Four social groups especially vulnerable to exploitation are now singled out as being the object of God's special concern. These are the stranger, the widow, the orphan, and the poor. The Torah here enjoins sensitivity to their condition not simply out of humanitarian considerations but as a divine imperative. Insensitivity is consequently sinful, a violation of a commandment that expresses God's will. A striking feature of the Hebrew legal formulation is the manner in which the audience is addressed in the singular and the plural, following the pattern of the Decalogue. It recognizes both the individual and society as equally responsible and accountable for the terms of the covenantal relationship between God and Israel. Social evil is thus a sin against humanity and God.

The seminal importance of these laws in the religion of Israel is apparent from their frequent reiteration in the biblical literature,[46] as well as by the twin motives that actuate them: Israel's empathetic regard for the disadvantaged of society should be stimulated by her own historical experience (v. 20); God's concern arises out of His essential nature, His intolerance of injustice, and His compassionate qualities (vv. 22–23,26).[47]

These humanitarian stipulations may have been set down after the preceding cultic laws in order to establish a contrast between the moral corruption of paganism (vv. 17–19) and the moral nature of the God of Israel. In addition, they serve to inculcate the idea that the rejection of the non-Israelite religious practices (v. 19) has no bearing on the inalienable right of the alien to civilized treatment free of victimization (v. 20).

The Stranger (v. 20)

The Hebrew term *ger*, "stranger," denotes a foreign-born permanent resident whose status was intermediate between the native-born citizen (*'ezraḥ*) and the foreigner temporarily residing outside his community (*nokhri*). Because he could not fall back upon local family and clan ties, he lacked the

²¹You shall not ill-treat any widow or orphan. ²²If you do mistreat them, I will heed their outcry as soon as they cry out to Me, ²³and My anger shall blaze forth and I will put you to the sword, and your own wives shall become widows and your children orphans.

21 כָּל־אַלְמָנָה וְיָתוֹם לֹא תְעַנּוּן: 22 אִם־
עַנֵּה תְעַנֶּה אֹתוֹ כִּי אִם־צָעֹק יִצְעַק אֵלַי שָׁמֹעַ
אֶשְׁמַע צַעֲקָתוֹ: 23 וְחָרָה אַפִּי וְהָרַגְתִּי אֶתְכֶם
בֶּחָרֶב וְהָיוּ נְשֵׁיכֶם אַלְמָנוֹת וּבְנֵיכֶם יְתֹמִים:
פ

social and legal protection that these ordinarily afforded. Being dependent on the goodwill of others, he could easily fall victim to discrimination and exploitation.

The numerous biblical prohibitions against the maltreatment of strangers are supplemented in the legislation by positive injunctions to love them,⁴⁸ even as God does,⁴⁹ which entails supplying their basic needs and extending to them the same social services and amenities to which disadvantaged Israelites were entitled.⁵⁰ It was inevitable that over time strangers would be absorbed into the body politic of Israel and take upon themselves the obligations and duties that devolved upon a member of the covenantal society. Hence, in postbiblical Hebrew the term *ger* (fem. *giyyoret*) eventually came to be synonymous with "proselyte." See *The JPS Torah Commentary,* Numbers, Excursus 34, p. 398.

wrong . . . oppress   The two verbs heighten the stringency of the prohibition. Rabbinic exegesis interprets the first, *honah*, to mean verbal and emotional abuse, and the second, *l-ḥ-ts*, to connote defrauding.⁵¹ However, as Mishnah Bava Metsia 4:10 makes clear, *honah* can also encompass victimizing and defrauding.⁵²

The Widow and the Orphan (vv. 21–23)

The exploitation of these unfortunates was so tempting, and apparently so widespread and seemingly beyond the reach of the law, that the Torah amplifies the ordinary apodictic formulation with a passionate emphasis on the gravity of the sin in the eyes of God. The absence of a human protector of the widow and the orphan should not delude the unscrupulous or the society that tolerates them. God Himself champions the cause of the downtrodden. The same conviction is expressed in Proverbs 22:22–23: "Do not rob the wretched because he is wretched; / Do not crush the poor in the gate; / For the Lord will take up their cause / And despoil those who despoil them of life." Proverbs 23:10–11 puts it this way: "Do not encroach upon the field of the orphans, / For they have a mighty Kinsman, / And He will surely take up their cause with you."

21.   *widow or orphan*   Rabbi Ishmael,⁵³ followed by Rashi, adds, "or any other human being."

22.   *mistreat . . . heed . . . cry out*⁵⁴

23.   *the sword*   That is, in warfare. Social injustice leads to social disaster.

The Poor and Loans (vv. 24–26)

These laws are aimed at protecting the desperate poor from exploitation by the more fortunate. They are the first of several such examples in the Torah that regulate loans and forbid the taking of interest. The others are Leviticus 25:35–38, Deuteronomy 23:20–21, and 24:10–13. The association of loan giving with the poor provides the social background to the prohibition. Prior to Solomon's time, Israelite society was composed overwhelmingly of peasants in villages operating in an agrarian economy. Tribal affiliation carried with it the obligation of mutual cooperation and support. In these circumstances, the need for a loan would be occasioned not by business and commerce but by dire poverty. Those who habitually lived at little more than subsistence level would need to borrow either money or grain if disaster struck. The taking of interest was therefore a moral not an economic issue—to do so was to shirk responsibility to one's fellow Israelite and to profit from another's misery. It also opened the door to the eventual enslavement of the borrower and his family, since in most instances the payment of the interest, let alone repayment of the loan, was unfeasible. The story in 2 Kings 4:1 illustrates the case.

²⁴If you lend money to My people, to the poor among you, do not act toward them as a creditor: exact no interest from them. ²⁵If you take your neighbor's garment in pledge, you must return it to him before the sun sets; ²⁶it is

²⁴ אִם־כֶּסֶף ׀ תַּלְוֶה אֶת־עַמִּי אֶת־הֶעָנִי עִמָּךְ
לֹא־תִהְיֶה לוֹ כְּנֹשֶׁה לֹא־תְשִׂימוּן עָלָיו נֶשֶׁךְ:
²⁵ אִם־חָבֹל תַּחְבֹּל שַׂלְמַת רֵעֶךָ עַד־בֹּא הַשֶּׁמֶשׁ
תְּשִׁיבֶנּוּ לוֹ: ²⁶ כִּי הִוא כְסוּתֹה לְבַדָּהּ הִוא

v. 26. כְּסוּתוֹ ק'

The present laws, like similar ones found elsewhere in the Torah, are designed to safeguard the dignity and protect the means of subsistence of the impoverished debtor. True, several biblical texts indicate that there were times when the ideal was ignored in practice.[55] Nevertheless, biblical law is unique in the ancient Near East in imposing an absolute ban on lending and borrowing with interest.

In the urbanized and commercialized society of Mesopotamia, loans on interest were commonplace and regulated by both law and custom. Loan contracts from Nuzi show that rates of interest at times reached 50 percent per annum. The laws of Eshnunna and Hammurabi pay much attention to loans. Generally, interest rates specify 33⅓ percent per annum on loans of grain and 20–25 percent on loans of silver. The system resulted in the granting of legal sanction to the practice of seizing the nonpaying debtor or members of his family and depriving them of their freedom.

24. *if you lend* The hypothetical, or casuistic, formulation is only apparent. No penalties are specified, the direct address in the second person is employed, and there is a concluding apodictic prohibition—none of which is characteristic of the true type of casuistic law. Hence, Rabbi Ishmael could construe the opening Hebrew *'im* not as a voluntary act but as implying an obligation.[56]

to My people Deuteronomy 23:20–21 expressly permits the exaction of interest on loans made to a foreigner (Heb. *nokhri*), that is, to one who resides in an Israelite locality only temporarily. Likewise, debts incurred by a foreigner are not canceled in the Sabbatical year (Deut. 15:3). These distinctions are drawn because the foreigner referred to would most likely be a traveling trader who takes a loan for commercial and business reasons. Because of his mobility, such an individual would constitute a high risk. This situation is well documented in the ramified and far-flung trading operations carried on in the Assyrian Empire, which were financed through private enterprise. A further consideration is reciprocity; an Israelite abroad would certainly be subject to local business practices and be required to pay the exorbitant interest rates.

act . . . as a creditor That is, do not harass the borrower.[57]

interest Hebrew *neshekh* derives from the stem *n-sh-k*, "to bite." Here, it is a general term for interest on a loan.[58] In other texts[59] it is used in association with *tarbit/marbit*, literally "increase." Mishnah Bava Metsia 5:1 understands *neshekh* to be advance interest that is initially "bitten off" or deducted from the amount of the loan. Some understand *marbit* to mean accrued interest. Bava Metsia 60a takes them all to be synonymous.

25. *garment* Hebrew *salmah* (also *simlah*) was a large piece of cloth wrapped around the body. For the poor it also served as a blanket at night and might have been their only possession. Texts such as Amos 2:8, Proverbs 20:16, 27:13, and Job 22:6 testify to the practice of taking the garment as a pledge. An interesting light is shed on this custom by a seventh century B.C.E. Hebrew inscription from an Israelite fortress uncovered near Yavneh-yam. It registers the complaint of an agricultural laborer that the officer in charge was holding his garment pending satisfaction of a disputed claim that the worker had not fulfilled his obligations.[60]

in pledge While the exaction of interest is prohibited, the taking of a pledge to secure repayment of the loan is permitted. In the case set forth here the pledge would largely serve a symbolic purpose. Elsewhere in the Torah the creditor is forbidden to take in pledge the garment of a widow or, more generally, anything that would deprive a person of the basic necessities of life. Furthermore, he may not invade the privacy of the debtor in order to obtain the pledge, for the dignity and freedom of the poor may not be violated.[61]

before the sun sets Deuteronomy 24:12–13 repeats this obligation and adds: "that he may sleep in his cloth and bless you; and it will be to your merit before the LORD your God."

139

his only clothing, the sole covering for his skin. In what else shall he sleep? Therefore, if he cries out to Me, I will pay heed, for I am compassionate.

²⁷You shall not revile God, nor put a curse upon a chieftain among your people.

²⁸You shall not put off the skimming of the first yield of your vats. You shall give Me the first-born among your sons. ²⁹You shall do the same with your cattle and your

שִׂמְלָתוֹ לְעֹרוֹ בַּמֶּה יִשְׁכָּב וְהָיָה כִּי־יִצְעַק אֵלַי
וְשָׁמַעְתִּי כִּי־חַנּוּן אָנִי: ס רביעי
27 * אֱלֹהִים לֹא תְקַלֵּל וְנָשִׂיא בְעַמְּךָ לֹא
תָאֹר:
28 מְלֵאָתְךָ וְדִמְעֲךָ לֹא תְאַחֵר בְּכוֹר בָּנֶיךָ
תִּתֶּן־לִי: 29 כֵּן־תַּעֲשֶׂה לְשֹׁרְךָ לְצֹאנֶךָ שִׁבְעַת

חצי הספר בפסוקים v. 27.

26. for I am compassionate Hebrew ḥannun is one of God's essential traits. It is invariably included in the numerous formulaic listings of the qualities that characterize God's actions in relation to humankind.[62]

The extraordinary omission of the term ra(ḥ)ḥum, "merciful," which always accompanies God's attribute ḥannun, perhaps underscores the point that the poor man is entitled to the return of his garment by right, not as an act of mercy. The outcry of the poor at their deprivation is a plea for justice to which God responds because the poor are His special concern.

Duties to God (vv. 27–30)

The characterization of God in verse 26 is followed by laws that regulate the proper attitude toward Him.

27. revile God Bekhor Shor and Ibn Ezra explain the sequence of topics in verses 20–26 and in this verse on the basis of Isaiah 8:21, which tells of the wretched and the hungry who, in desperation, rage and utter curses against God. Implicit in the juxtaposition may also be the idea that to ignore the misery of the disadvantaged of society is to revile God.

Reviling God as a judicial issue is mentioned in Leviticus 24:10–23, where the penalty is death by stoning. That was the fate of Naboth, who was falsely convicted of the same offense through perjured testimony, as told in 1 Kings 21:1–16.

Rabbi Ishmael,[63] as well as the Targums, interpreted 'elohim here as meaning "judges" (see Comment to 21:6). This rendering is most likely conditioned by the parallel Hebrew term for "chieftain" and by the fact that, although God is the speaker, the first person is not used, in contrast to verses 28–30.

chieftain Hebrew nasi' is the title given to the chief of a clan or tribe in the period before the monarchy.[64]

28–29. These verses deal in a general way with the requirement to donate to God the firstling of the produce of the soil, of the human womb, and of domesticated animals. The laws are formulated in a terse, absolute manner without further definition or specification. This style presupposes a background on the part of the reader as to the proper procedures. Several other texts supply such details.[65]

28. You shall not put off Tardiness in presenting God with what is rightfully His is an act of disrespect; it deprives the offering of its value as an expression of religious inwardness. Rabbinic exegesis understands the phrase to mean that the various offerings must be made in their proper sequence.[66]

the skimming of the first yield of your vats The meaning of the two Hebrew agricultural terms mele'ah and dema' is uncertain. The first noun, literally "fullness," appears again in Numbers 18:27 in connection with the vat and in association with "the new grain from the threshing floor." It is also mentioned in Deuteronomy 22:9 in relation to the sowing of seed and "the yield of the vineyard." The term is ambiguous and does not yield a precise definition; nor do we know if it is specific to grain and cereals or to wine and oil, or whether it can include both categories. Moreover, dema' is a unique word; it may contrast with mele'ah or form a compound with it (a hendiadys) to

flocks: seven days it shall remain with its mother; on the
eighth day you shall give it to Me.

³⁰You shall be holy people to Me: you must not eat flesh
torn by beasts in the field; you shall cast it to the dogs.

יָמִים יִהְיֶה עִם־אִמּוֹ בַּיּוֹם הַשְּׁמִינִי תִּתְּנוֹ־לִי:
30 וְאַנְשֵׁי־קֹדֶשׁ תִּהְיוּן לִי וּבָשָׂר בַּשָּׂדֶה טְרֵפָה
לֹא תֹאכֵלוּ לַכֶּלֶב תַּשְׁלִכוּן אֹתוֹ: ס

express a single idea: "your abundant harvest." Many scholars, ancient and modern, connect *demaʿ*
with *dimʿah*, "tear" and take it as a figurative use for liquid products, wine and oil.[67] Indeed, Arabic
dammāʿ means liquor oozing from the vine, and Ibn Janaḥ points to the Arabic phrase "tear of the
vineyard" as a poetic epithet for wine. In the mishnaic period *demaʿ* was still in use in the spoken
language with the general meaning of *terumah*, or gifts, to the Temple priesthood.[68] It even had a
verbal form and could refer to both cereals and liquids.[69] Still, a good case has been made for
separating *demaʿ* in the present verse from *dimʿah*, "tear." The Samaritan Targum renders *ḥelev*, "fat,
best portion of" in Genesis 45:18 and Deuteronomy 32:14 by *dmʿ*, which has a cognate in Arabic
dimāḡ and is applied to cereals. On this basis, our Hebrew phrase would be rendered, "your crop in
full bloom, namely, the best part of it."[70]

You shall give Me   This phrase is not explained. The following clause would appear to
indicate that, as with animals, the human first-born was to be sacrificed to God. But such an
interpretation is impossible in Israel. Hence, the unqualified, categorical prescription must be an
archaic, fossilized, legal formulary from pre-Israelite times. In Israel it was understood to mean that
the first-born had sacral status and performed sacral duties as is proved by 1 Samuel 1:11. Once the
hereditary priesthood was established, his sacerdotal functions ceased. See Comment to 13:2,11–15.

29.   You shall do the same   That is, dedicate the first-born animals for sacral purposes (cf.
Deut. 15:19).

seven days   The dedication of the first fruits of the soil is not to be delayed, but for the first-
born of animals there is a minimum waiting period of seven days. Leviticus 22:27 prescribes that no
animal is fit to be offered to the Lord until it is eight days old. Like the rite of human circumcision on
the eighth day,[71] the present ruling may reflect the notion that the newborn has completed a seven-
day unit of time corresponding to the process of Creation. This law may also reflect the desire to avoid
cruelty to animals and, more broadly, to foster humane feelings in human beings. These ideas are
suggested by mention of the mother and by the extension of the Levitical law to include a prohibition
on slaughtering both the young and its mother on the same day. Similar notions are expressed by the
proscriptions against taking a fledgling or eggs from a nest in which the mother bird is present (Deut.
22:6–7), yoking together an ox and an ass (Deut. 22:10)—two animals of unequal strength; and
muzzling an ox while it is threshing (Deut. 25:4).

30.   The preceding law enjoined the dedication of certain animals to God. The present law
forbids the human consumption of animals that are in a loathsome state.

holy people   This is the ideal for Israel set forth at Sinai (19:6). In the pursuit of this end, one
must, among other things, avoid polluting substances and defiling actions, for these disturb the
relationship with God. Strict adherence to the dietary laws (*kashrut*) as an essential ingredient of holy
living is reiterated in both Leviticus 11:44–45 and Deuteronomy 14:21; they serve to elevate, spiri-
tualize, and hallow the animalistic act of eating.

flesh torn by beasts   Hebrew *terefah* in rabbinic texts refers to a clean animal inflicted with
an organic defect, a mortal injury, or a fatal disease. In modern Jewish parlance, the term is popularly
used for food that does not meet the requirements of the laws of *kashrut*.[72] According to Leviticus
17:15 the eating of *terefah* renders the eater ritually impure.

CHAPTER 23   In the Mekhilta verse 30 of chapter 22 opens the following section instead of closing the preceding
one, as it does in the traditional Hebrew text. This variant may be intended to teach that the
definition of holiness encompasses not only the culinary and the cultic but also the ethical and the
moral—as in the classic presentation of holy living set forth in Leviticus 19.

23 You must not carry false rumors; you shall not join hands with the guilty to act as a malicious witness: ²You shall neither side with the mighty to do wrong—you shall not give perverse testimony in a dispute so as to pervert it in favor of the mighty—³nor shall you show deference to a poor man in his dispute.

⁴When you encounter your enemy's ox or ass wandering, you must take it back to him.

⁵When you see the ass of your enemy lying under its burden and would refrain from raising it, you must nevertheless raise it with him.

⁶You shall not subvert the rights of your needy in their

כ"ג לֹא תִשָּׂא שֵׁמַע שָׁוְא אַל־תָּשֶׁת יָדְךָ
עִם־רָשָׁע לִהְיֹת עֵד חָמָס: ס 2 לֹא־תִהְיֶה
אַחֲרֵי־רַבִּים לְרָעֹת וְלֹא־תַעֲנֶה עַל־רִב לִנְטֹת
אַחֲרֵי רַבִּים לְהַטֹּת: 3 וְדָל לֹא תֶהְדַּר בְּרִיבוֹ:
ס
4 כִּי תִפְגַּע שׁוֹר אֹיִבְךָ אוֹ חֲמֹרוֹ תֹּעֶה הָשֵׁב
תְּשִׁיבֶנּוּ לוֹ: ס
5 כִּי־תִרְאֶה חֲמוֹר שֹׂנַאֲךָ רֹבֵץ תַּחַת מַשָּׂאוֹ
וְחָדַלְתָּ מֵעֲזֹב לוֹ עָזֹב תַּעֲזֹב עִמּוֹ: ס חמישי
6 לֹא תַטֶּה מִשְׁפַּט אֶבְיֹנְךָ בְּרִיבוֹ: 7 מִדְּבַר־

JUDICIAL INTEGRITY (vv. 1–3)

1–3. Five prohibitions outlaw behavior in courts of law that would jeopardize the integrity and impartiality of the judicial process.

1. The first clause addresses the litigants, the witnesses, and, by implication, also the judge.[1] Giving unfounded hearsay testimony in judicial proceedings is prohibited and inadmissible. The second clause outlaws collusion on the part of a witness with one of the parties for a fraudulent or deceitful purpose.

2. In the interest of impartial justice, no consideration is to be given to the social standing of the litigants.[2] The verse has also been taken to express a warning not to pervert justice by deferring to the majority view if one is convinced that it is erroneous. Tannaitic exegesis utilized this text to support the rule that two different judicial procedures are to be adopted for acquittal and conviction, the former requiring only a simple majority, the latter a majority of two.[3]

3. The frequency with which the Torah enjoins compassion for the poor dictates the need for caution against allowing one's emotions, however desirable and noble, to color one's judgment.[4] The same warning appears in Leviticus 19:15 and Deuteronomy 1:17.

HUMANE TREATMENT OF THE ENEMY (vv. 4–5)

4–5. A prohibition against permitting one's hostile and vindictive emotions to overcome one's humanity. The moral duty to show concern for the plight of one's enemy is stressed in Proverbs 25:21: "If your enemy is hungry, give him bread to eat; / If he is thirsty, give him water to drink." These injunctions intuit the psychological truth that such civilized conduct must inevitably disarm mutual animosity. It is taken for granted that one would naturally help a friend or acquaintance in difficulty; therefore, only the imperative of assisting one's enemy needs to be stressed here. The more general obligation of returning lost property—known in Hebrew as *hashavat 'avedah*—is explicated in Deuteronomy 22:1–3.

4. **enemy's** Four different definitions of the "enemy" in this context are suggested in the Mekhilta:[5] a gentile idolater, a relapsed convert to Judaism, a Jewish apostate, and a Jew who exhibits enmity toward another.

5. This case involves humanitarian considerations and the prevention of cruelty to animals. The latter, an important biblical and rabbinic principle, is known in Hebrew as *tsaʿar baʿalei ḥayyim*, literally "[prevention of] pain to living things."[6]

raising . . . raise The Hebrew stem *ʿ-z-v* here, as in Nehemiah 3:8,34, corresponds to Ugaritic *ʿdb*, "to make, prepare, set."[7]

A SERIES OF MISCELLANEOUS LAWS (vv. 6–9)

6. **your needy** Those who depend on you for justice.

142

disputes. ⁷Keep far from a false charge; do not bring death on those who are innocent and in the right, for I will not acquit the wrongdoer. ⁸Do not take bribes, for bribes blind the clear-sighted and upset the pleas of those who are in the right.

⁹You shall not oppress a stranger, for you know the feelings of the stranger, having yourselves been strangers in the land of Egypt.

¹⁰Six years you shall sow your land and gather in its yield; ¹¹but in the seventh you shall let it rest and lie fallow. Let the needy among your people eat of it, and what they leave let the wild beasts eat. You shall do the same with your vineyards and your olive groves.

שֶׁקֶר תִּרְחָק וְנָקִי וְצַדִּיק אַל־תַּהֲרֹג כִּי לֹא־
אַצְדִּיק רָשָׁע: ⁸ וְשֹׁחַד לֹא תִקָּח כִּי הַשֹּׁחַד
יְעַוֵּר פִּקְחִים וִיסַלֵּף דִּבְרֵי צַדִּיקִים:
⁹ וְגֵר לֹא תִלְחָץ וְאַתֶּם יְדַעְתֶּם אֶת־נֶפֶשׁ
הַגֵּר כִּי־גֵרִים הֱיִיתֶם בְּאֶרֶץ מִצְרָיִם:
¹⁰ וְשֵׁשׁ שָׁנִים תִּזְרַע אֶת־אַרְצֶךָ וְאָסַפְתָּ אֶת־
תְּבוּאָתָהּ: ¹¹ וְהַשְּׁבִיעִת תִּשְׁמְטֶנָּה וּנְטַשְׁתָּהּ
וְאָכְלוּ אֶבְיֹנֵי עַמֶּךָ וְיִתְרָם תֹּאכַל חַיַּת הַשָּׂדֶה
כֵּן־תַּעֲשֶׂה לְכַרְמְךָ לְזֵיתֶךָ:

7. *a false charge*　Hebrew *davar* here, as in 18:16–22, means a cause or case for judicial investigation. A judge should have nothing to do with a claim he knows to be fraudulent.

do not bring death　The final clause, which affirms that God brings the guilty to account, suggests that the legal topic here is the fear that excessive concern on the part of judges that a criminal not go unpunished might lead to a miscarriage of justice and the wrongful execution of an innocent person.

Rabbinic exegesis utilized this admonition to outlaw double jeopardy by taking "innocent and in the right" to mean that a defendant who has already been so judged is not to be given a second trial for the same offense.[8]

8.　The Hebrew syntax highlights the severity of the offense by placing "bribe" in the emphatic initial position. The text apparently cites some well-known proverb—repeated almost verbatim in Deuteronomy 16:19.

The corruption of the judicial process by bribery is frequently mentioned in the Bible.[9] It is emphasized that God "shows no favor and takes no bribe,"[10] and the one who takes bribes is included in the list of those who are under a divine curse.[11] Rabbinic bribery legislation extended the crime to include "verbal bribery"; even a perfunctory courtesy proffered by a litigant to a judge immediately disqualifies the latter.[12] A judge who accepts a bribe in violation of the biblical prohibition is subject to the penalty of flogging.

9.　This is a repetition of the substance of 22:20 with an expansion of the motive clause. Whereas the earlier injunction was aimed at each individual Israelite, the present one is directed at the judge.[13] As Shadal points out, in verse 8 the perversion of justice resulted from familiarity between litigant and judge; here it issues from estrangement.

THE AGRICULTURAL PRESCRIPTIONS　(vv. 10–13)

10–19.　These are seasonal and calendrical observances that relate to the rhythms of nature. Unlike the preceding laws, they apply to the entire community.

10–11.　The concern for the underprivileged and unfortunates of society determines immediate association with the topics of verses 6–9 and 12–13.[14]

Verses 10–11 deal solely with the prohibition on sowing the land in the seventh year of the Sabbatical cycle. This same law is repeated with greater emphasis on its humanitarian purpose in Leviticus 25:1–7,18–22, while Deuteronomy 15:1–1 extends the provisions of the Sabbatical year to include remission of debts.

Continuous cultivation of arable land leads to serious depletion of its nutrients and consequent loss of productivity. Hence, the effect of the Torah's seventh-year fallow system is conservationist. It

¹²Six days you shall do your work, but on the seventh day you shall cease from labor, in order that your ox and your ass may rest, and that your bondman and the stranger may be refreshed.

¹³Be on guard concerning all that I have told you. Make no mention of the names of other gods; they shall not be heard on your lips.

¹⁴Three times a year you shall hold a festival for Me:

יב שֵׁ֣שֶׁת יָמִים֮ תַּעֲשֶׂ֣ה מַעֲשֶׂיךָ֒ וּבַיּ֣וֹם הַשְּׁבִיעִ֖י תִּשְׁבֹּ֑ת לְמַ֣עַן יָנ֗וּחַ שֽׁוֹרְךָ֙ וַחֲמֹרֶ֔ךָ וְיִנָּפֵ֥שׁ בֶּן־אֲמָתְךָ֖ וְהַגֵּֽר׃

יג וּבְכֹ֛ל אֲשֶׁר־אָמַ֥רְתִּי אֲלֵיכֶ֖ם תִּשָּׁמֵ֑רוּ וְשֵׁ֨ם אֱלֹהִ֤ים אֲחֵרִים֙ לֹ֣א תַזְכִּ֔ירוּ לֹ֥א יִשָּׁמַ֖ע עַל־פִּֽיךָ׃

יד שָׁלֹ֣שׁ רְגָלִ֔ים תָּחֹ֥ג לִ֖י בַּשָּׁנָֽה׃ 15 אֶת־חַ֣ג

preserves the fertility of the soil and enhances future productivity. The economic benefit is fully recognized in Leviticus 25:18–22, Here, however, the motivation of the Sabbatical institution, like that for the Sabbath day itself, is expressed in purely social and humanitarian terms.

11. **let it rest** That is, lie unworked. The Hebrew verbal stem used here, *sh-m-t*, is at the base of the noun *shemittah*, "Sabbatical year."

12. On the weekly Sabbath, see Comment to 20:8–12. The obvious thematic connection with the seven-year cycle is enhanced by the parallel formulaic style,[15] as well as by the chiasmic arrangement:

Radak notes that two different verbs are employed to describe the benefit of the Sabbath for man and beast. The beast "rests" physically; man is "refreshed" spiritually.

13. The first clause closes the preceding legislation,[16] which concentrates on human relationships; the second clause opens the final section of the Book of the Covenant, which focuses on obligations to God.

The prohibition on mentioning the names of pagan gods, although seemingly intrusive, is actually quite relevant since the rest of the section deals with the celebrations of the seasonal cycle, which in the pagan world were invariably accompanied by magical rites aimed at propitiating divine powers and enlisting their aid in the regeneration of the soil, the ripening of the crops, and the fecundity of the herds and flocks. Such cults must have been very attractive to the Israelites. Hence the need to commence the section by outlawing the invocation of pagan gods. Note the emphatic "festival for Me" in the next verse, meaning "for Me exclusively." This is further explicated in verse 17, "the Sovereign, the Lord [YHVH]."

THE RELIGIOUS CALENDAR (vv. 14–17)

14–17. These verses present the triad of agricultural festivals that form the core of Israel's sacral calendar. Rosh Hashanah, Yom Kippur, and the Passover day are omitted because they are not rooted in the life of the soil, which is the encompassing topic of the larger section of verses 10–19. The smaller unit is framed by parallel introductory and concluding statements. A shorter version appears in Exodus 34:18–24. The three agricultural festivals are again listed in Deuteronomy 16:1–17; the complete annual cycle of the sacred days is given in Leviticus 23; and the calendrical sacrificial rituals that accompany those occasions are featured in Numbers 28–29.[17]

The absence of fixed dates in the present verses for any of the festivals is striking, although in the case of the Feast of Unleavened Bread, the phrase "at the set time" undoubtedly refers back to Exodus 12:6,14–20. The name of each festival bears the definite article and suggests that these institutions are well known; indeed, they are by their very essence universal in character, reflecting as they do the rhythms of nature. The distinctive quality of Israel's festivals lies both in their being grateful acknowledgments of God's bounty, wholly divested of mythological accretions and magical fertility rites, and in their becoming historicized, so that the theme of commemoration of the Exodus is interwoven with the agrarian strands.[18] Each of the three festivals is called a *ḥag*. This term indicates that the festival entails an obligatory pilgrimage to a sanctuary, a meaning that endures in the Muslim institution of the *haj*, the religious duty to undertake a pilgrimage to Mecca. See Comment to 5:1.

15You shall observe the Feast of Unleavened Bread—eating unleavened bread for seven days as I have commanded you—at the set time in the month of Abib, for in it you went forth from Egypt; and none shall appear before Me empty-handed; 16and the Feast of the Harvest, of the first fruits of your work, of what you sow in the field; and the Feast of Ingathering at the end of the year, when you gather

הַמַּצּוֹת תִּשְׁמֹר שִׁבְעַת יָמִים תֹּאכַל מַצּוֹת כַּאֲשֶׁר צִוִּיתִךָ לְמוֹעֵד חֹדֶשׁ הָאָבִיב כִּי־בוֹ יָצָאתָ מִמִּצְרָיִם וְלֹא־יֵרָאוּ פָנַי רֵיקָם: 16 וְחַג הַקָּצִיר בִּכּוּרֵי מַעֲשֶׂיךָ אֲשֶׁר תִּזְרַע בַּשָּׂדֶה וְחַג הָאָסִף בְּצֵאת הַשָּׁנָה בְּאָסְפְּךָ אֶת־מַעֲשֶׂיךָ מִן

The sequence of festivals listed here conforms to the rule of 12:2 that the religious year is to commence with the spring.

14. Three times Hebrew *shalosh regalim*, synonymous with *shalosh pe'amim* in verse 17, still has this original meaning in Numbers 22:28,32,33. In postbiblical Hebrew the phrase came to signify the three pilgrimage festivals; the singular *regel* became interchangeable with *ḥag* and was used for a pilgrimage in general, for which the rabbinic term is *'aliyah le-regel*.

for Me Exclusively.

15. the Feast of Unleavened Bread That is, the beginning of the barley harvest. As noted above, Passover day, strictly speaking the holiday of the paschal lamb, is not mentioned here because it was not originally established as a farmers' festival.

as I have commanded you In Exodus 12:14–20.

Abib Renamed Nisan in postexilic times. See Comment to 13:4.

you went forth The agricultural festival is invested with new historical significance.[19]

shall appear before Me Hebrew *yera'u panai*, literally "My face shall be seen," is a technical term for making a pilgrimage to a sanctuary.[20]

empty-handed Without bringing the appropriate offerings.[21] In the period of the Second Temple these were the pilgrim's burnt offering (Heb. *'olat re'iyyah*), the festal offering (*shalmei ḥagigah*), and the offering of rejoicing (*shalmei simḥah*).

16. the Feast of the Harvest This, the second of the three great festivals, is better known as "the Feast of Weeks"—Shavuot.[22] It is also called "the day of the first fruits."[23] The Greek-speaking Jews knew it as "Pentecoste" (fiftieth), whence the English name "Pentecost," because the festival falls, as Leviticus 23:15–16 prescribes, on "the day after the seventh week—fifty days" from "the day after the Sabbath" of Passover. This has traditionally been interpreted to mean counting from the second day of Passover; thus, Shavuot is celebrated on the sixth of Sivan.

In rabbinic literature the festival is known as *'atseret*, which seems to mean "concluding feast"—of Passover.[24] This close connection between the two festivals functions on two levels. Shavuot marks the completion of the wheat harvest even as Passover registers the beginning of barley harvesting. Shavuot also traditionally celebrates the revelation on Mount Sinai, "the time of the giving of our Torah" (*zeman mattan toratenu*), thereby expressing some of the fundamental ideas of Judaism: that liberation and freedom must be grounded in and controlled by law and that "man does not live by bread alone"—that there is also a spiritual dimension to life.

The association of Shavuot with the establishment of the covenant between God and Israel, although not explicit in the Bible, is exceedingly ancient. Exodus 19:1 has the Israelites arriving at Sinai on the New Moon of the third month after the Exodus, that is, in the month of Sivan. A report in 2 Chronicles 15:10–13 tells that King Asa of Judah (913–873 B.C.E.) called a great assembly of the people "in the third month" for a national ceremony of covenant renewal. The pilgrimage festival of Shavuot, falling in that month, would have been the most likely occasion for that ceremony. The Jewish sectarian community at Qumran by the Dead Sea (destroyed by the Romans ca. 70 C.E.) annually held a "covenant feast" on Shavuot, doubtless following an ancient and widespread tradition. The Book of Jubilees 6:17 (2nd cent. B.C.E.) explicitly identifies Shavuot with the giving of the Torah, although on a different date from the one accepted by normative Judaism.

As long as the Temple in Jerusalem existed, Shavuot was observed by bringing to the priest on

in the results of your work from the field. ¹⁷Three times a year all your males shall appear before the Sovereign, the LORD.

¹⁸You shall not offer the blood of My sacrifice with anything leavened; and the fat of My festal offering shall not be left lying until morning.

הַשָּׂדֶה: 17 שָׁלֹשׁ פְּעָמִים בַּשָּׁנָה יֵרָאֶה כָּל־זְכוּרְךָ אֶל־פְּנֵי הָאָדֹן ׀ יְהוָה: 18 לֹא־תִזְבַּח עַל־חָמֵץ דַּם־זִבְחִי וְלֹא־יָלִין חֵלֶב־חַגִּי עַד־בֹּקֶר:

duty there "a wave offering" consisting of two loaves of bread baked from flour made of the finest wheat grown that year in the Land of Israel, as well as a basket of the first ripe fruits of the seven species mentioned in Deuteronomy 8:8. The ceremonies and rituals are described in Leviticus 23:15–22 and Deuteronomy 26:1–2 and are elaborated in Mishnah Bikkurim.

the Feast of Ingathering   The third in the series of pilgrimage festivals also has this name, in Hebrew *'asif*, in Exodus 34:22 and in a tenth-century B.C.E. agricultural calendar from Gezer, in Israel. The designation derives from the harvest and thanksgiving character of the festival—the celebration of the final ingathering of the yield of the fields and orchards and of its storage in the barns before the onset of the rainy season.²⁵ Sukkot, known in English as "Tabernacles,"²⁶ has its origin in the practice of constructing booths from branches and vines for protection from the weather and for guarding the orchards during the harvesting period.²⁷ As with the other two agricultural festivals, this too was historicized in Israel and interpreted as commemorating the wilderness wanderings following the Exodus.²⁸ The date of the festival is the fifteenth to the twenty-first of the seventh month, Tishrei.²⁹ Sukkot assumed such great importance in the course of time that it came to be known as "the Festival" (*he-ḥag*) par excellence.³⁰

at the end of the year   At the close of the agricultural year. In 34:22 the synonymous phrase "at the turn of the year" is used, thereby signifying the transition from one agricultural season to the other.

17.   An expansive restatement of verse 14 elucidating the meaning of "festival" (*ḥag*) used there.

times   Hebrew *pe'amin*, a synonym of *regalim* (v. 14), both meaning "feet, times."³¹

males   The story of Hannah in 1 Samuel 1 shows that it must not have been uncommon for women, too, to make the pilgrimage.³² Deuteronomy 16:11,14 include women and children among those who are to appear "before the LORD" on these festivals.

the Sovereign   Hebrew *'adon*, literally "master,"³³ is often used as a royal title and is applied to God as Sovereign of the universe to whom all creation is subordinate and to whom all owe homage.³⁴ In the parallel passage in 34:23, the title of God is given as "the Sovereign LORD, the God of Israel."

18–19.   This appendix to verses 14–17 contains four laws regulating ritual and ceremonial aspects of the three foregoing celebrations. The same, also following the religious calendar, appears in the parallel version of 34:25–26, although with some variations:

(1) The first rule forbids the slaughtering of the paschal lamb on the fourteenth of Nisan while leaven is still in possession of the participants in the sacrifice. The same prohibition is repeated in Deuteronomy 16:2–4. The rabbis inferred that the obligation to remove all *ḥamets* (leaven) commences from the time that the offering was made in the Temple, that is, at midday. But due to the severity of the prohibition on leaven, the deadline was moved back two hours as a precaution.³⁵ For the idea of leaven as symbolic of corruption, see Comment to 12:15.

(2) The second rule requires that the fatty portions of the paschal sacrifice, those that attach to the stomach and intestines, be burnt before dawn. The parallel passage in 34:25 reads: "The sacrifice of the Feast of Passover shall not be left lying until the morning." The same restriction governed the original paschal offering,³⁶ which had to be eaten during the night hours, and all the leftovers had to be burnt.

(3) The third rule relates to the Festival of Shavuot.³⁷ The choicest³⁸ of the first fruits must be brought to the sanctuary, as described more fully in Deuteronomy 26:2–11; compare Numbers 18:12–13.

¹⁹The choice first fruits of your soil you shall bring to the house of the LORD your God.

19 רֵאשִׁ֗ית בִּכּוּרֵי֙ אַדְמָ֣תְךָ֔ תָּבִ֕יא בֵּ֖ית יְהֹוָ֣ה אֱלֹהֶ֑יךָ

You shall not boil a kid in its mother's milk.

לֹֽא־תְבַשֵּׁ֥ל גְּדִ֖י בַּחֲלֵ֥ב אִמּֽוֹ׃ ס   ששי

²⁰I am sending an angel before you to guard you on the way and to bring you to the place that I have made ready. ²¹Pay heed to him and obey him. Do not defy him, for he

20 הִנֵּ֨ה אָנֹכִ֜י שֹׁלֵ֤חַ מַלְאָךְ֙ לְפָנֶ֔יךָ לִשְׁמׇרְךָ֖ בַּדָּ֑רֶךְ וְלַהֲבִ֣יאֲךָ֔ אֶל־הַמָּק֖וֹם אֲשֶׁ֥ר הֲכִנֹֽתִי׃ 21 הִשָּׁ֧מֶר מִפָּנָ֛יו וּשְׁמַ֥ע בְּקֹל֖וֹ אַל־תַּמֵּ֣ר

(4) The fourth rule largely remains an enigma. Its importance may be measured by its being repeated twice more in the Torah, in Exodus 34:26 and Deuteronomy 14:21. In this latter source the prohibition appears in the context of the dietary laws, but the other two sources indicate that its origin lies in the overall context of the festivals. The juxtaposition of this rule with the law of the first fruits led Menahem ibn Saruq[39] (10th cent.) to interpret *gedi* not as a kid of the goats but as "berries." This eccentric explanation was taken up by Menahem ben Solomon[40] (first half 12th cent.), who took "mother's milk" to be figurative for the juice of the bud that contains the berry. The entire passage conveyed to him a proscription on bringing the first fruits before they are ripe.[41] Many scholars, medieval and modern, follow the suggestion of Maimonides that this law prohibits some pagan rite[42]—although no such rite is presently known.

Rashbam, Bekhor Shor, Ibn Ezra, and Abravanel all, in various ways, adduce a humanitarian motivation akin to that cited in the Comment to 22:29. Rashbam further suggests that because festivals were celebrated with feasts of meat, and because goats are generally multiparous and have a high yield of milk, it was customary to slaughter one of the kids of a fresh litter and to cook it in its mother's milk. The Torah looks upon such a practice as exhibiting insensitivity to the animal's feelings. The explanation of Rashbam has been buttressed by the modern observation that in biblical times goats were far more plentiful than sheep in the Land of Israel and were the main source of milk. The flesh of the young kid is more tender and more delicate in flavor than lamb. Also, since the estrous cycle of goats occurs during the summer months and parturition takes place in the rainy season, the earliest litter would be produced just around the time of Sukkot. This injunction, therefore, regulates the festivities at the Festival of the Ingathering of the Harvest.

The interdiction of boiling a kid in its mother's milk was generalized to outlaw the mixing of all meat and milk (meaning all dairy products). Its threefold repetition in the Torah was explained by Rabbi Simeon bar Yoḥai as indicative of three aspects of the prohibition: cooking such a mixture, eating it, and deriving any benefit from it.[43]

RENEWAL OF THE DIVINE PROMISES   (vv. 20–33)

The complex of laws closes with a peroration that contains divine promises and admonitions. The laws in the preceding section, verses 10–19, all presume settled life in the promised land following the anticipated conquest. The closing oration emphasizes that the ability to enjoy the happy cycle of harvest festivals is conditional upon Israel's fidelity to its covenant with God. The exhortation is appropriate because the narrative at this point considers the experience at Sinai to be nearing its conclusion, with the people soon to be on their way to Canaan to engage in a series of battles with the native population.

The hortatory style of the epilogue, with its conditional blessings and misfortunes, is reminiscent of ancient Near Eastern law codes and covenants, which often close with a series of blessings and curses, much like those in Deuteronomy 27–30 and Leviticus 26. Here, however, this feature has been supplemented by several didactic elements of a theological, historical, and geographical nature. The characteristic themes are divine help for Israel in conquering the land, divine blessings on Israel after the settlement, and prohibitions on making peace with the native population or accepting their cult. The entire section has close parallels in Deuteronomy 6:10–25 and 7.

20. *an angel*   On angels in the Bible, see Comment to 3:2. Classical Jewish commentators are divided on whether a heavenly[44] or human[45] messenger is here intended by Hebrew *mal'akh*.[46]

will not pardon your offenses, since My Name is in him; ²²but if you obey him and do all that I say, I will be an enemy to your enemies and a foe to your foes.

²³When My angel goes before you and brings you to the Amorites, the Hittites, the Perizzites, the Canaanites, the Hivites, and the Jebusites, and I annihilate them, ²⁴you shall not bow down to their gods in worship or follow their practices, but shall tear them down and smash their pillars to bits. ²⁵You shall serve the Lord your God, and He will bless your bread and your water. And I will remove sickness from your midst. ²⁶No woman in your land shall miscarry or be barren. I will let you enjoy the full count of your days.

²⁷I will send forth My terror before you, and I will throw into panic all the people among whom you come, and I will make all your enemies turn tail before you. ²⁸I will send a

בֹּו כִּי לֹא יִשָּׂא לְפִשְׁעֲכֶם כִּי שְׁמִי בְּקִרְבֹּו:
22 כִּי אִם־שָׁמֹעַ תִּשְׁמַע בְּקֹלֹו וְעָשִׂיתָ כֹּל אֲשֶׁר אֲדַבֵּר וְאָיַבְתִּי אֶת־אֹיְבֶיךָ וְצַרְתִּי אֶת־צֹרְרֶיךָ:
23 כִּי־יֵלֵךְ מַלְאָכִי לְפָנֶיךָ וֶהֱבִיאֲךָ אֶל־הָאֱמֹרִי וְהַחִתִּי וְהַפְּרִזִּי וְהַכְּנַעֲנִי הַחִוִּי וְהַיְבוּסִי וְהִכְחַדְתִּיו:
24 לֹא־תִשְׁתַּחֲוֶה לֵאלֹהֵיהֶם וְלֹא תָעָבְדֵם וְלֹא תַעֲשֶׂה כְּמַעֲשֵׂיהֶם כִּי הָרֵס תְּהָרְסֵם וְשַׁבֵּר תְּשַׁבֵּר מַצֵּבֹתֵיהֶם: 25 וַעֲבַדְתֶּם אֵת יְהוָה אֱלֹהֵיכֶם וּבֵרַךְ אֶת־לַחְמְךָ וְאֶת־מֵימֶיךָ וַהֲסִרֹתִי מַחֲלָה מִקִּרְבֶּךָ: שביעי 26 לֹא תִהְיֶה מְשַׁכֵּלָה וַעֲקָרָה בְּאַרְצֶךָ אֶת־מִסְפַּר יָמֶיךָ אֲמַלֵּא:
27 אֶת־אֵימָתִי אֲשַׁלַּח לְפָנֶיךָ וְהַמֹּתִי אֶת־כָּל־הָעָם אֲשֶׁר תָּבֹא בָּהֶם וְנָתַתִּי אֶת־כָּל־אֹיְבֶיךָ אֵלֶיךָ עֹרֶף: 28 וְשָׁלַחְתִּי אֶת־הַצִּרְעָה לְפָנֶיךָ

The phrase may simply be an idiom expressing the activity of Divine Providence, as in Genesis 24:7.[47]

the place that I have made ready   Apparently, a reference to the land of Canaan, in which the Israelites will take possession of "great and flourishing cities . . . houses full of all good things . . . hewn cisterns . . . vineyards and olive groves," in the words of Deuteronomy 6:10–11. Since Hebrew *makom,* "place," frequently means "sacred space," it is possible that this unusual designation of the land carries with it the idea of the Holy Land.

21. Do not defy him   The verbal stem *m-r-h* is overwhelmingly used of rebellion against God.[48]

your offenses   Hebrew *pesha',* originally a term for the violation of vassal treaty obligations,[49] was transferred from the political to the religious sphere to express an infringement of God's covenant with Israel. See Comment to 22:8.

My name is in him   The Divine Will and Power manifests itself through this heaven-sent messenger.

22.   This statement seems to belong to the language of treaties. Similar sentiments are found in the peace treaty made between the Hittite Hattusilis and the Egyptian Ramses II, as well as in a Northwest Semitic treaty.[50]

24.   Worship of the gods of the native peoples is prohibited as is also the adoption of their cultic practices—even in the service of the God of Israel. Their cultic appurtenances are to be destroyed.

pillars   Hebrew *matsevah* derives from the stem *n-ts-v,* "to stand." It denotes a single, upright slab of stone. Believed to be the repository of a divinity or spirit, it was often used as a cultic object and was therefore considered by Israelite religion to be idolatrous.[51]

25–26.   For a fuller description of the blessings that flow from fidelity to the covenant, see Deuteronomy 7:13–15.

26. the full count of your days   Long life.[52]

27. My terror   That is, He will cause the enemy to be struck with terror.[53]

throw into panic   Such will be the impact of the "terror."[54]

plague ahead of you, and it shall drive out before you the Hivites, the Canaanites, and the Hittites. ²⁹I will not drive them out before you in a single year, lest the land become desolate and the wild beasts multiply to your hurt. ³⁰I will drive them out before you little by little, until you have increased and possess the land. ³¹I will set your borders from the Sea of Reeds to the Sea of Philistia, and from the wilderness to the Euphrates; for I will deliver the inhabitants of the land into your hands, and you will drive them out before you. ³²You shall make no covenant with them and their gods. ³³They shall not remain in your land, lest

וְגֵרַשְׁתָּ֛ אֶת־הַחִוִּ֥י אֶת־הַֽכְּנַעֲנִ֖י וְאֶת־הַחִתִּ֑י מִלְּפָנֶֽיךָ: 29 לֹ֧א אֲגָרְשֶׁ֛נּוּ מִפָּנֶ֖יךָ בְּשָׁנָ֣ה אֶחָ֑ת פֶּן־תִּהְיֶ֤ה הָאָ֙רֶץ֙ שְׁמָמָ֔ה וְרַבָּ֥ה עָלֶ֖יךָ חַיַּ֥ת הַשָּׂדֶֽה: 30 מְעַ֥ט מְעַ֛ט אֲגָרְשֶׁ֖נּוּ מִפָּנֶ֑יךָ עַ֚ד אֲשֶׁ֣ר תִּפְרֶ֔ה וְנָחַלְתָּ֖ אֶת־הָאָֽרֶץ: 31 וְשַׁתִּ֣י אֶת־גְּבֻֽלְךָ֮ מִיַּם־ס֜וּף וְעַד־יָ֣ם פְּלִשְׁתִּ֗ים וּמִמִּדְבָּר֮ עַד־הַנָּהָר֒ כִּ֣י ׀ אֶתֵּ֣ן בְּיֶדְכֶ֗ם אֵ֚ת יֹשְׁבֵ֣י הָאָ֔רֶץ וְגֵרַשְׁתָּ֖מוֹ מִפָּנֶֽיךָ: 32 לֹא־תִכְרֹ֥ת לָהֶ֛ם וְלֵאלֹֽהֵיהֶ֖ם בְּרִֽית: 33 לֹ֣א

28. *a plague* Hebrew *tsirʿah* occurs again in the Bible only in Deuteronomy 7:20 and in Joshua 24:12, also in reference to the conquest of Canaan. One rendering is "hornet,"[55] which, if taken literally, must reflect some tradition of a plague of hornets sent against the Canaanites on the pattern of the Egyptian plagues. If taken figuratively, the divinely sent agency may have been none other than the pharaohs whose successive and devastating campaigns in Canaan drained the country of its resources, ruined its economy, and destroyed its fortifications, thereby facilitating its collapse under the Israelite onslaught. If such be the case, it is not just that *tsirʿah* may evoke word play with *mitsrayim*, "Egypt," but that the *tsirʿah* may be the word for the insect that was the symbol of kingship of Lower Egypt. Another understanding of the term is some epidemic or perhaps leprosy, *tsaraʿat*.[56]

29-30. This passage qualifies the foregoing promises, which imply the speedy conquest of the entire land. That would leave large areas of the country uninhabited because the people of Israel was insufficiently numerous to fill the void that would be created following the expulsion of the native population. Deuteronomy 7:22 gives the same explanation. That the initial campaigns were unable to complete the conquest is explicitly stated in the books of Joshua and Judges.[57] This historic reality generated varied responses. Judges 2:20–21 explains it as divine punishment for infidelity to the covenant; Judges 2:22–23 and 3:1,4 see it as a means of trying Israel's faith; and Judges 3:2 understands the protracted nature of the conquest as a prudent strategy for training successive generations in the art of warfare.

31. The ideal boundaries of the land are now set forth. As in Genesis 15:18–21, the ethnographic description of verses 23,28 is supplemented by a closer geographic definition. At no time in Israelite history, even at the height of the Davidic-Solomonic empire, were these boundaries a reality.[58] They are believed to have their origin in the pre-Israelite Egyptian province of Canaan, which included Palestine and Syria as a single political and geographical entity. It was Thutmose III and IV who, in the course of the fifteenth century B.C.E., carried out numerous military expeditions to Palestine and Syria and the pharaohs of the thirteenth and twelfth centuries who established Egyptian imperial rule over these lands.[59]

Sea of Reeds Here, undoubtedly, the Gulf of Akaba.

Sea of Philistia The Mediterranean Sea. See Comment to 13:17.

the wilderness Probably a general term for the desert and steppeland.

the Euphrates Literally, "the river."

32-33. The covenant demands exclusive recognition of YHVH as the Sovereign King to whom is owed undivided and uncompromising loyalty. Hence, a warning against making covenants with the native peoples is appropriate. Such compacts would imperil the integrity of Israel's religion and pose a dire threat to its national existence. Other biblical texts emphasize the dangers of intermarriage and resulting apostasy that flow from intermingling with the pagans.[60]

they cause you to sin against Me; for you will serve their gods—and it will prove a snare to you.

יֵשְׁבוּ בְּאַרְצְךָ פֶּן־יַחֲטִיאוּ אֹתְךָ לִי כִּי תַעֲבֹד אֶת־אֱלֹהֵיהֶם כִּי־יִהְיֶה לְךָ לְמוֹקֵשׁ: פ

24 Then He said to Moses, "Come up to the Lord, with Aaron, Nadab and Abihu, and seventy elders of Israel, and bow low from afar. ²Moses alone shall come near the Lord;

כ"ד וְאֶל־מֹשֶׁה אָמַר עֲלֵה אֶל־יְהֹוָה אַתָּה וְאַהֲרֹן נָדָב וַאֲבִיהוּא וְשִׁבְעִים מִזִּקְנֵי יִשְׂרָאֵל וְהִשְׁתַּחֲוִיתֶם מֵרָחֹק: 2 וְנִגַּשׁ מֹשֶׁה

CHAPTER 24   RATIFICATION OF THE COVENANT   (vv. 1–18)

The stipulations of the covenant between God and Israel—the rules and principles that are henceforth to govern Israelite society—have been promulgated. The climactic scene in the historic covenant drama is about to be enacted. An elaborate rite of ratification takes place, after which Moses is called upon to ascend Mount Sinai in order to receive the tangible, permanent symbol of the covenant: the two stone tablets into which the Decalogue is incised.

The present chapter rounds out the literary complex that began with chapter 19. It frames the unit by the sevenfold use of the key stem d-b-r, "to speak, word," in both the opening and closing chapters,[1] and by the sevenfold employment of the stem y-r-d, "to go down," in chapter 19[2] and of its antonym ʿ-l-h, "to go up," in this chapter.[3]

POPULAR ASSENT (vv. 1–11)

1–11. This section actually constitutes the earliest stage in the process of canonizing the Torah literature. It registers the beginning of the long history of the development of the authoritative corpus of sacred literature that came to be known as *Tanakh* in Hebrew and Bible in English.[4]

The initial step was the unanimous popular assent to the divine initiative for a covenant, as recorded in 19:8: "All that the Lord has spoken we will do!" Then Moses mediated the commandments orally to the entire people assembled at the foot of Sinai. Having heard the stipulations, they now orally bind themselves to obedience, using the same formula of affirmation as before (24:3). The stipulations are then put into writing, and a sacrificial ritual and a blood rite take place (vv. 4–6). The written document is read to the people who again make a collective pledge of affirmation and loyalty, whereupon the blood rite is completed (vv. 7–8). The representatives of the people ascend partway up the mountain and there experience a manifestation of the divine majesty. A solemn covenantal meal concludes the entire episode (vv. 9–11).

*1. **Then He said to Moses*** The Hebrew inverts the usual syntactical order and literally reads, "And to Moses He said," thus emphasizing that this particular instruction pertains specifically to Moses and not to the assembled Israelites, as in previous instances.[5] The point is reiterated in verse 2.

Come up According to 20:18(21), Moses had already "approached the thick cloud where God was," that is, the summit of the mountain; it must therefore be presumed that he had since descended. In chapter 19 there is repeated ascent and descent.[6]

Nadab and Abihu Their introduction without any descriptive identity presupposes knowledge of Aaron's genealogy given in 6:23. The two later perished while performing some sinful ritual act.[7] Their inclusion in the present delegation and the exclusion of their two younger brothers, who succeeded them in the priesthood,[8] attest to the antiquity of this tradition.

elders of Israel See Comment to 3:16. Seventy elders are mentioned again only in Numbers 11:16,24–25 and Ezekiel 8:11. As in Exodus 1:5, the number seventy has symbolic force expressing totality, comprehensiveness. It represents the entire community of Israel.

bow low Throughout the ancient Near East full-length prostration of the body was a conventional gesture expressing unconditional submission and homage to a superior authority.[9] The

but the others shall not come near, nor shall the people come up with him."

³Moses went and repeated to the people all the commands of the LORD and all the rules; and all the people answered with one voice, saying, "All the things that the LORD has commanded we will do!" ⁴Moses then wrote down all the commands of the LORD.

Early in the morning, he set up an altar at the foot of the mountain, with twelve pillars for the twelve tribes of Israel. ⁵He designated some young men among the Israelites, and they offered burnt offerings and sacrificed bulls as offerings of well-being to the LORD. ⁶Moses took one part of the

לְבַדּוֹ אֶל־יְהֹוָה וְהֵם לֹא יִגָּשׁוּ וְהָעָם לֹא יַעֲלוּ
עִמּוֹ:
3 וַיָּבֹא מֹשֶׁה וַיְסַפֵּר לָעָם אֵת כָּל־דִּבְרֵי
יְהֹוָה וְאֵת כָּל־הַמִּשְׁפָּטִים וַיַּעַן כָּל־הָעָם קוֹל
אֶחָד וַיֹּאמְרוּ כָּל־הַדְּבָרִים אֲשֶׁר־דִּבֶּר יְהֹוָה
נַעֲשֶׂה: 4 וַיִּכְתֹּב מֹשֶׁה אֵת כָּל־דִּבְרֵי יְהֹוָה
וַיַּשְׁכֵּם בַּבֹּקֶר וַיִּבֶן מִזְבֵּחַ תַּחַת הָהָר וּשְׁתֵּים
עֶשְׂרֵה מַצֵּבָה לִשְׁנֵים עָשָׂר שִׁבְטֵי יִשְׂרָאֵל:
5 וַיִּשְׁלַח אֶת־נַעֲרֵי בְּנֵי יִשְׂרָאֵל וַיַּעֲלוּ עֹלֹת
וַיִּזְבְּחוּ זְבָחִים שְׁלָמִים לַיהֹוָה פָּרִים: 6 וַיִּקַּח

present instruction is to be understood as part of the formal ceremonial attending the ratification of the covenant; it was not simply an act of worshipful reverence.

from afar   This phrase might be construed to mean that they are to keep their distance from the mountain summit. However, the figurative use of the idiom "to prostrate from afar" is found in letters to royalty from Ugarit in both the native language[10] and in Akkadian,[11] suggesting a recognized diplomatic courtesy on the part of a vassal, who makes repeated prostrations starting at a distance from the suzerain's presence. Jacob's performance in meeting Esau, as told in Genesis 33:3, illustrates this practice: "He himself went on ahead and bowed low to the ground seven times until he was near his brother."

2. Moses alone   Mount Sinai is divided into three zones, each of which has restricted access. Moses alone reaches the summit; a site partway up is reserved for Aaron and his delegation; the people are confined to the foot of the mountain. See Comment to 19:12–25.

3. went and repeated   In response to the instructions given to Moses in 20:19(22) and 21:1.

commands . . . rules   The Hebrew terms *devarim* and *mishpatim*, respectively, distinguish the two types of laws in the foregoing legal corpus. The "commands" are those formulated in concise apodictic style—the Decalogue and the bulk of 22:17–23:19. Their enforcement is left to the individual conscience. The "rules," contained in 21:1–22:16, fall within the scope of the coercive power of the state and the jurisdiction of the law courts.

4. wrote down   This document is termed *sefer ha-berit*, "book of the covenant," in verse 7. (See introduction to chap. 21 and Comment to v. 7 below.) The commitment to writing was an essential part of the ratification process of treaties in the ancient Near East. It made the treaty a legal reality.

set up an altar   Doubtless, in accord with the provisions of 20:21(24). This altar not only had a practical use for sacrifices (v. 5), but it also symbolized the Divine Presence, just as the twelve pillars represented the other contracting party,[12] the twelve tribes.

twelve pillars   It is likely that the dashing of the blood "on the people" described in verse 8 was effectuated by sprinkling it over the pillars. In Genesis 31:45–54 an upright pillar (*matsevah*) served as a mute witness to a treaty between Jacob and Laban. A large stone was similarly used to commemorate the covenant between God and Israel made at Shechem. The note in Joshua 24:27 is instructive:[13] "See, this very stone shall be a witness against us, for it heard all the words that the LORD spoke to us."

5. young men   The strenuous task of slaughtering bulls and preparing them for the altar could only be performed by young men. It is likely, in light of the designation of Samuel the Ephraimite and of Eli's sons in 1 Samuel 2:13–17 and 3:1, that the *neʿarim* constituted a class of subordinate cultic assistants. A guild of temple servitors named *nʿrm* existed at Ugarit.[14] Rabbinic

blood and put it in basins, and the other part of the blood he dashed against the altar. ⁷Then he took the record of the covenant and read it aloud to the people. And they said, "All that the LORD has spoken we will faithfully do!" ⁸Moses took the blood and dashed it on the people and said, "This is the blood of the covenant that the LORD now makes with you concerning all these commands."

⁹Then Moses and Aaron, Nadab and Abihu, and seventy elders of Israel ascended; ¹⁰and they saw the God of Israel:

מֹשֶׁה חֲצִי הַדָּם וַיָּשֶׂם בָּאַגָּנֹת וַחֲצִי הַדָּם זָרַק עַל־הַמִּזְבֵּחַ: 7 וַיִּקַּח סֵפֶר הַבְּרִית וַיִּקְרָא בְּאָזְנֵי הָעָם וַיֹּאמְרוּ כֹּל אֲשֶׁר־דִּבֶּר יְהוָה נַעֲשֶׂה וְנִשְׁמָע: 8 וַיִּקַּח מֹשֶׁה אֶת־הַדָּם וַיִּזְרֹק עַל־הָעָם וַיֹּאמֶר הִנֵּה דַם־הַבְּרִית אֲשֶׁר כָּרַת יְהוָה עִמָּכֶם עַל כָּל־הַדְּבָרִים הָאֵלֶּה: 9 וַיַּעַל מֹשֶׁה וְאַהֲרֹן נָדָב וַאֲבִיהוּא וְשִׁבְעִים מִזִּקְנֵי יִשְׂרָאֵל: 10 וַיִּרְאוּ אֵת אֱלֹהֵי יִשְׂרָאֵל

tradition identified the "young men" as the first-born males upon whom devolved cultic duties prior to the establishment of the priesthood in Israel.¹⁵

they offered The two types of sacrifice are the *ʿolah* and the *shelamim*; the latter term, often rendered "peace offerings," is more accurately "an offering of well-being" or "a sacrifice of greeting." The first was wholly consumed by fire upon the altar; the second was shared, certain parts being burnt and the rest consumed by the worshiper. The sacrifice of *shelamim* was a kind of shared sacred meal. See Comment to verse 11.

6. The blood of the *ʿolah* and the *shelamim* was always collected and dashed against the sides of the altar. In the present ceremony Moses performs this standard ritual with only half of the blood; he stored the other half in basins for later sprinkling on the people (v. 8). The two parts were for the two parties to the covenant, God and Israel, respectively.¹⁶

The significance of the sprinkling of the blood is never explained. However, the prevailing notion in Israel was that the blood, the vital bodily fluid, constituted the life-force. As such, like life itself, it belonged to God alone. For that reason, its consumption by humans is strictly forbidden,¹⁷ and the blood of sacrifices is dashed on the altar. The use of blood in a covenant is found nowhere else in the Bible. The ordination of Aaron as High Priest, as related in Leviticus 8, involved daubing the blood of the sacrificial lamb of ordination on parts of his body and on the altar.¹⁸ It is likely that in both these ceremonies—covenant and ordination—the blood functions mysteriously to cement the bond between the involved parties. Through God's sharing, as it were, of the vital fluid with Israel or with Aaron, the life of the recipient is thought to take on a new dimension and to be elevated to a higher level of intimate relationship with the Deity.

basins Hebrew *ʾaggan*, mentioned again only in Isaiah 22:24 and Song 7:3, has turned up in the Hebrew inscriptions found at Arad,¹⁹ as well as in several other Semitic languages.²⁰ The *ʾaggan* has been established archaeologically to be a large and deep two-handled bowl.

7. ***the record of the covenant*** Hebrew *sefer ha-berit*, usually rendered "the Book of the Covenant," occurs only once again in the Bible, in a context very similar to the present one. It is the designation given to the "scroll of the Torah" that was found in the Temple by the High Priest Hilkiah in the days of King Josiah. On the basis of that scroll, the king convened a national assembly and publicly read its entire text, after which the people entered into "a covenant before the LORD" to be bound by the laws inscribed in the scroll of the Torah.²¹ This ceremony of covenant-renewal indicates that the public reading and popular assent were necessary elements of the ratification process. Interestingly, some Hittite treaty texts require periodic public recital of the terms of the pact before the vassal and his people.²²

we will faithfully do Literally, "we will do and obey." Since this is the last act of public participation, the formula of consent is expanded to give it finality.

8. With the conclusion of the formalities of popular consent, Moses completes the blood-sprinkling rite.

concerning all these commands The essence of the covenant is obedience to the laws of the Torah.

under His feet there was the likeness of a pavement of
sapphire, like the very sky for purity. [11]Yet He did not raise
His hand against the leaders of the Israelites; they beheld
God, and they ate and drank.

וְתַחַת רַגְלָיו כְּמַעֲשֵׂה לִבְנַת הַסַּפִּיר וּכְעֶצֶם
הַשָּׁמַיִם לָטֹהַר: [11] וְאֶל־אֲצִילֵי בְּנֵי יִשְׂרָאֵל לֹא
שָׁלַח יָדוֹ וַיֶּחֱזוּ אֶת־הָאֱלֹהִים וַיֹּאכְלוּ וַיִּשְׁתּוּ:
ס

9. The authorized, select representatives of the people now advance partway up the
mountain where they experience a vision of the divine majesty. Rashbam draws an analogy with the
covenant between God and Abraham: There too God projects a visual manifestation of His Presence
by appearing as "a flaming torch which passed between those pieces" (Gen. 15:17).

10. Maimonides maintains that "seeing" God refers not to perception by the senses but to
perception by the intellect.[23] Ibn Ezra understands the experience to be a prophetic vision similar to
those described in 1 Kings 22:19, Isaiah 6:1, Ezekiel 1, and Amos 9:1.

the God of Israel This name befits the context of the special relationship now being forged
between God and Israel.

under His feet The language is circumspect. There is no description of God Himself, only
of the celestial setting beneath the visionary heavenly throne. Even so, the Hebrew particle *k-* is used
in order to indicate mere similarity and approximation.

a pavement of sapphire Hebrew *livnat*, from *levenah*, "brick," suggests a decorative floor
area of covered bricks or tiles. Hebrew *sappir*, rendered "sapphire," is not the modern blue gemstone
(corundum), which was unknown in the ancient Near East, but the widely used deep blue lapis lazuli.
In the vision of Ezekiel (1:26; 10:1) God's throne is made of this material. The decorative use of lapis
lazuli in a palace is mentioned in Ugaritic literature.[24]

the very sky for purity The same word, *ṭhr*, is used in Ugaritic to describe lapis lazuli and
can mean both purity and brightness.[25]

11. *did not raise His hand* Exceptionally, they survived the experience. See Comment
to 3:6 and 33:20.

the leaders Those listed in verse 9. The unusual term *'atsilim* seems to be connected with
Arabic *'aṣula*, "to be distinguished."

they beheld God The repetition points up the extraordinary nature of the experience. The
general verb *r-'-h*, "to see," is replaced by the stronger *ḥ-z-h*, "to behold," which connotes far greater
intensity, belongs to the vocabulary of prophetic vision, and qualifies the earlier statement by taking
the encounter outside the range of natural ocular experience.

and they ate and drank Possibly another figurative way of saying they survived.[26] More
likely, it describes a formal element in the conclusion of the covenant. See the Comment to 18:12 for
evidence of such solemn covenant meals as an integral part of treaty-making. The meal would have
consisted of the sacrifices mentioned in verse 5.

MOSES RECEIVES THE TABLETS (vv. 12–18)

These verses contain subtle intimations of the two themes that occupy the last section of Exodus
(chaps. 25–40). They prepare us for, and make the transition to, the account of the building of the
Tabernacle and the episode of the golden calf.

Mention of the "stone tablets" (v. 12) is indispensable both for explaining the purpose of
constructing the Ark (25:10–22) and for understanding Moses' reaction to the apostasy (32:15–16,19).
It was Moses' prolonged stay on the mountain (v. 18) that precipitated the crisis (32:1). The stem
sh-k-n used of God's Presence on Sinai (v. 16) is also employed in connection with the Tabernacle
(25:8,19; 40:34–38). The Divine Presence (*kevod YHVH*) rests on Sinai (vv. 16,17) and in the completed Tabernacle (40:34–35), and the cloud covers the mountain (v. 15) and the Tent of Meeting
(40:34). Finally, Joshua's partial ascent of Sinai (vv. 13–14) explains his puzzled reaction to the
worshipers' noisy revelry around the calf (32:17–18).

12The Lord said to Moses, "Come up to Me on the mountain and wait there, and I will give you the stone tablets with the teachings and commandments which I have inscribed to instruct them." 13So Moses and his attendant Joshua arose, and Moses ascended the mountain of God. 14To the elders he had said, "Wait here for us until we return to you. You have Aaron and Hur with you; let anyone who has a legal matter approach them."

15When Moses had ascended the mountain, the cloud covered the mountain. 16The Presence of the Lord abode on Mount Sinai, and the cloud hid it for six days. On the seventh day He called to Moses from the midst of the cloud. 17Now the Presence of the Lord appeared in the sight of the Israelites as a consuming fire on the top of the mountain. 18Moses went inside the cloud and ascended the

יב וַיֹּאמֶר יְהֹוָה אֶל־מֹשֶׁה עֲלֵה אֵלַי הָהָרָה
וֶהְיֵה־שָׁם וְאֶתְּנָה לְךָ אֶת־לֻחֹת הָאֶבֶן
וְהַתּוֹרָה וְהַמִּצְוָה אֲשֶׁר כָּתַבְתִּי לְהוֹרֹתָם:
יג וַיָּקׇם מֹשֶׁה וִיהוֹשֻׁעַ מְשָׁרְתוֹ וַיַּעַל מֹשֶׁה אֶל־
הַר הָאֱלֹהִים: יד וְאֶל־הַזְּקֵנִים אָמַר שְׁבוּ־לָנוּ
בָזֶה עַד אֲשֶׁר־נָשׁוּב אֲלֵיכֶם וְהִנֵּה אַהֲרֹן וְחוּר
עִמָּכֶם מִי־בַעַל דְּבָרִים יִגַּשׁ אֲלֵהֶם: [מפטיר
לספרדים]

טו וַיַּעַל מֹשֶׁה אֶל־הָהָר וַיְכַס הֶעָנָן אֶת־הָהָר:
מפטיר טז וַיִּשְׁכֹּן כְּבוֹד־יְהֹוָה עַל־הַר סִינַי וַיְכַסֵּהוּ
הֶעָנָן שֵׁשֶׁת יָמִים וַיִּקְרָא אֶל־מֹשֶׁה בַּיּוֹם הַשְּׁבִיעִי
מִתּוֹךְ הֶעָנָן: יז וּמַרְאֵה כְּבוֹד יְהֹוָה כְּאֵשׁ
אֹכֶלֶת בְּרֹאשׁ הָהָר לְעֵינֵי בְּנֵי יִשְׂרָאֵל: יח וַיָּבֹא

---

12. Come up to Me Either Moses had descended with the entire delegation and is now instructed to ascend once again or he is still on the mountain and is directed to ascend to its highest level. The former is favored by verses 13–14, which imply that he has been down among the people. The latter is supported by the parallel account in Deuteronomy 5:28 in which Moses is told, "But you remain here with Me." Two strands of tradition appear to have been interwoven here.

the stone tablets This follows the widespread Near Eastern practice of recording important public documents, particularly treaty stipulations, on imperishable materials. See the introductory Comment to chapter 20.[27]

13. his attendant Joshua See Comment to 17:9.[28]

mountain of God See Comment to 3:1. The site is identified as Sinai in verse 16.

14. Moses is concerned about the welfare of Israel during his absence. Aaron and Hur are to substitute for Moses—either as sole magistrates or as the court of final appeal, depending on whether the establishment of the judiciary took place before or after the Sinai episode. This issue is discussed in the introductory Comment to chapter 18.

for us Even though only Moses is mentioned in verses 13 and 15, the plural indicates that Joshua too ascended up to a certain level. As Bekhor Shor notes, Joshua was not able to observe the scene of the golden calf from his position on the mountain (32:17).

Hur See Comment to 17:10.

15. the cloud The symbol of the Divine Presence in the wilderness wanderings. See Comment to 13:21.

16. Presence Hebrew *kavod*, the glory or majesty of God, is used for His manifested presence. See Comment to 16:7.

abode Hebrew stem *sh-k-n*, "to tent, abide,"[29] is the base of the postbiblical term *Shekhinah*, the presence, or indwelling of God in the life of the world.

six days. On the seventh day This is an example of a well-known literary phenomenon—the climactic use of numbers. It appears in Akkadian and Ugaritic literature and often in the Bible.[30] An action continues for six consecutive days, and then a new event occurs on the seventh. Here the six days are probably intended for spiritual preparation.

17. appeared Hebrew *mar'eh* is literally "the appearance of." The term serves to translate the supernatural reality into terms approximating human experience.[31]

mountain; and Moses remained on the mountain forty
days and forty nights.

מֹשֶׁה בְּתוֹךְ הֶעָנָן וַיַּעַל אֶל־הָהָר וַיְהִי מֹשֶׁה
בָּהָר אַרְבָּעִים יוֹם וְאַרְבָּעִים לָיְלָה: פ

a consuming fire For the imagery, see Comment to 3:2.[32] This instance manifests the twin aspects of the visible emblem of God's invisible presence at the Exodus: the "pillar of cloud" and the "pillar of fire." See Comment to 13:21–22.

18. *forty days and forty nights* A tradition repeated several times.[33] Forty is frequently used as a symbolic number, and forty days expresses a significant period of time,[34] often connected with purification and purging of sin.

THE TABERNACLE (25:1–31:17; 35:1–40:38)

With the conclusion of the revelation at Sinai, preparations are made for the spiritual welfare of the people during their trek through the wilderness on their way to the promised land. This requires the construction of a central, mobile sanctuary to serve as the symbol of God's continued Presence in the midst of Israel, to accommodate the organized practice of religion. Additionally, it became the focus of national unity. It is not designed, as are modern places of worship, for communal use.

The detailed narrative that recounts the building and functioning of this sanctuary, known in English as the Tabernacle, is divided into two parts: the series of instructions (25:1–31:17) and the account of its construction (35:1–40:38). Interposed between these two is the episode of the violation of the covenant through the making and worship of the golden calf.

The Ground Plan The Tabernacle is an oblong structure comprising three zones. These are, in descending order of holiness: the Holy of Holies, the Holy Place, and the Court. The structure is oriented longitudinally, on an east-west axis, with the most sacred zone in the west. An outer perimeter demarcates the sacred area. This is divided into two equal squares. The first two zones lie in

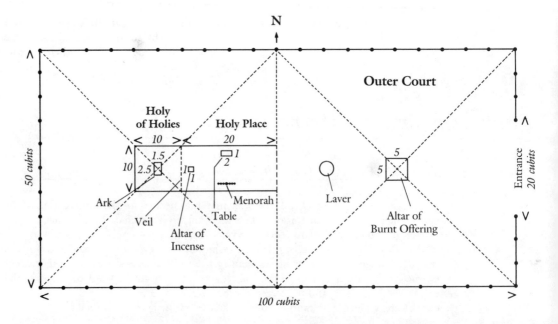

THE WILDERNESS TABERNACLE. *All numbers within the rectangle refer to cubits. The Ark was 1.5 cubits high; the Altar of Incense was 2 cubits high; the Table was 1.5 cubits high; the Altar of Burnt Offering was 3 cubits high.*

TERUMAH

25 The LORD spoke to Moses, saying: ²Tell the Israelite people to bring Me gifts; you shall accept gifts for Me from every person whose heart so moves him. ³And these are the

one square and the Court constitutes the other square. From the Ark in the Holy of Holies, God reaches out to Israel; from the altar of sacrifice, the Israelites reach out to God. Each seems to be located exactly at the point of intersection of the diagonals of the squares. See diagram, page 155.

Ancient Parallels Mobile sanctuaries are known to us from Arab Bedouin practices, pre-Islamic and Islamic, and even from pre-Christian times. They are also documented in Phoenician and Egyptian sources, the latter from the period of Rameses II (ca. 1290–1224 B.C.E.). Furthermore, the method of construction described here in our chapters is now known to be based on well-established Egyptian techniques.[1]

The Celestial Blueprint A prominent characteristic of the narrative in both its parts is the repeated reference to divinely given instructions and celestial patterns for the terrestrial edifice and for its contents.[2] Such a conception of a sanctuary is not unknown elsewhere in the ancient world. It is attested as early as about 2200 B.C.E. in the narration of a building project by the Sumerian King Gudea of Lagash. It also occurs in Egyptian texts that treat of similar enterprises. This idea of divine inspiration, initiation, and specification of a religious institution generally communicates the deity's sanction and acceptance of the sacred structure, which is thereby endowed with legitimacy.[3]

The Tabernacle and Creation The series of instructions for the components of the Tabernacle is made up of seven subsections, each of which is introduced by the formula "The Lord spoke/said to Moses."[4] Six of them deal with creativity, and the seventh features the Sabbath law. This latter is explicitly grounded in creation. The association of the Tabernacle with the Sabbath is given prominence in Leviticus 19:30 and 26:2: "You shall keep my Sabbaths and venerate My sanctuary: I am the Lord." Further, the completed Tabernacle is erected on New Year's day, as Exodus 40:17 records. This underscores the idea that a new era in the life of the people has begun and the cosmogonic association of the Tabernacle is thereby strengthened. Finally, other thematic and verbal echoes of the Genesis Creation narrative in our account[5] confirm their interdependence.

CHAPTER 25

Instructions for the Tabernacle (25:1–31:18)

Terumah   THE MATERIALS (vv. 1–9)

The account opens with a list of the basic materials needed for the construction of the Tabernacle, its appurtenances, and its operation. These are grouped in seven categories: metals, dyed yarns, fabrics, timber, oil, spices, and gems. All are to be acquired through public donations. A singular peculiarity of the fabrics is that some of them are fashioned of a mixture of wool and linen. Such a mixture, termed *kil'ayim* or *sha'atnez* in Leviticus 19:19 and Deuteronomy 22:11, is otherwise forbidden.[6] This is true of the lower covers of the Tabernacle, the curtain in front of the Ark, the screen for the entrance of the Tent, and the screen for the gate of the Enclosure. It also applies to the High Priest's ephod, breastpiece, sash, and the pomegranates on the hem of his robe.

     1. The LORD spoke to Moses During the forty days he spent in seclusion on Mount Sinai.[7]

     2. the Israelite people The sanctuary is to serve the entire community, and its construction is therefore to be accomplished through the generosity of all.

gifts that you shall accept from them: gold, silver, and copper; [4]blue, purple, and crimson yarns, fine linen, goats' hair; [5]tanned ram skins, dolphin skins, and acacia wood;

3 וְזֹאת הַתְּרוּמָה אֲשֶׁר תִּקְחוּ מֵאִתָּם זָהָב וָכֶסֶף וּנְחֹשֶׁת: 4 וּתְכֵלֶת וְאַרְגָּמָן וְתוֹלַעַת שָׁנִי וְשֵׁשׁ וְעִזִּים: 5 וְעֹרֹת אֵילִם מְאָדָּמִים וְעֹרֹת תְּחָשִׁים

to bring Me . . . for Me   The phrasing indicates a religious function, but the full purpose of the donations is withheld until the end of the unit (vv. 8–9).

gifts   Hebrew *terumah* is a technical term referring specifically to that which is set aside by its owner and dedicated for sacred use.[8]

3.   The metals are listed in descending order of value. This, in turn, determines their use for various objects; the closer the object is to the Holy of Holies, the more valuable the metal of which it is made. Iron is notably absent, either on account of its great rarity at this time or because its utilization for more efficient weapons of death made it incompatible with the spiritual ends that the sanctuary was intended to serve. See Comment to 20:22.[9]

copper   Hebrew *nehoshet* most likely designates bronze, an alloy of copper and tin. This metal was used extensively in the Near East as early as the third millennium B.C.E.

4. blue, purple, and crimson yarns   These are the most expensive dyed yarns of antiquity.[10] The sequence, once again, reflects their relative value and thus the degree of sanctity that attaches to the objects in which they are used, starting with the Holy of Holies. The dyes were all obtained from animal sources, and the yarns were to be used for the Tabernacle hangings and coverings and for the priestly vestments.

blue   In the Bible, Hebrew *tekhelet* is frequently paired with Hebrew *'argaman*, purple, both being dyes produced from the murex, a marine snail termed *hillazon* in rabbinic tradition.[11] This creature exudes a yellow fluid that becomes a dye in the red-purple range when exposed to sunlight. The desired shade was obtained by varying the species of murex and by adding other ingredients. *Tekhelet* was probably closer to a violet tint, while *'argaman* had a more reddish hue.

The Phoenician coast was famous for its dyeing industry. Immense quantities of marine-snail shells dating to the fifteenth century B.C.E. have been found at Ugarit. Modern attempts to reconstruct the process have shown that it required thousands of snails to produce sufficient dye for one robe. This, together with the intensity of the labor and the superiority of the dye's richness and stability, made the products very costly. Hence, possession of *tekhelet*-dyed or *'argaman*-dyed fabrics were marks of wealth, nobility, and royalty.[12]

crimson   Hebrew *tola'at shani*. The first word means "a worm"; the second signifies the color. The combination designates the brilliant red dye produced from the eggs of scale insects of the Coccidae family that feed on oak trees.[13]

fine linen   Hebrew *shesh* is a very early term, borrowed from Egyptian *šš*, used for cloth of exceptional quality.[14] In late biblical Hebrew *shesh* was replaced by *buts*, from which Greek *byssos*, Latin *byssus*, and English "byssus" are all derived.

goats' hair   The Hebrew is elliptical, omitting the word "hair," which is left to the imagination.[15] Goats' hair grows in long locks and was left undyed. As Exodus 35:26 shows, the spinning of goat's hair was a specialized skill of women.

5. skins   The use of animal hides and skins for human needs is very ancient and is widely attested in the Bible,[16] although the technique of leather production is never described. Hence, it is unclear whether Hebrew *me'oddamim*, literally "made red," refers to the tanning or dyeing process.

Dolphin   Hebrew *tehashim* (sing. *tahash*), with one exception,[17] always refers to the coverings of the Tabernacle. Its exact meaning is uncertain.[18] In rabbinic times the *tahash* was invested with mythical association and identified with the unicorn. Because of the similarity with Arabic *tuhas*, *duhs*, which denote both the dolphin and the dugong found in the Red Sea, modern scholars have variously identified the biblical creature with one or the other. A suggestion to equate the term with Akkadian *dušu* (= *tahšia*), the name of a precious stone of either yellow or orange color, seems more

⁶oil for lighting, spices for the anointing oil and for the aromatic incense; ⁷lapis lazuli and other stones for setting, for the ephod and for the breastpiece. ⁸And let them make Me a sanctuary that I may dwell among them. ⁹Exactly as I

וְעֲצֵי שִׁטִּים: 6 שֶׁמֶן לַמָּאֹר בְּשָׂמִים לְשֶׁמֶן הַמִּשְׁחָה וְלִקְטֹרֶת הַסַּמִּים: 7 אַבְנֵי־שֹׁהַם וְאַבְנֵי מִלֻּאִים לָאֵפֹד וְלַחֹשֶׁן: 8 וְעָשׂוּ לִי מִקְדָּשׁ וְשָׁכַנְתִּי בְּתוֹכָם: 9 כְּכֹל אֲשֶׁר אֲנִי מַרְאֶה אוֹתְךָ אֵת

plausible since that word is also used to describe leather that is dyed and tanned the color of the stone.[19] Significantly, only the hides of goats (and sheep) were so treated.

acacia wood   Other than in Isaiah 41:19, Hebrew *shittim* always refers to the timbers used in the construction of the Tabernacle and its appurtenances. A few biblical place-names testify to the presence of acacia groves in the region of the Land of Israel.[20] There are about eight hundred different species of acacias, but only a few have an upright trunk suitable for cutting timbers for construction. These yield very hard, durable, but lightweight planks. The Hebrew *shittah* may well be an Egyptian loan word.[21]

6. oil   This is later specified as olive oil.[22]

for lighting   As distinct from oil for food preparation and for anointing. See Comment to 27:20.

spices   The ingredients of this aromatic oil are listed in 30:23–25. The oil will be used to desecularize the Tabernacle, its appurtenances, and its personnel, and to consecrate them for the service of God. The Hebrew stem *m-sh-ḥ*, "anoint," is the base of the term *mashiaḥ*, "messiah," which means "anointed one," and which in the Hebrew Bible is never used of anyone to whom supernatural power is ascribed.

aromatic incense   See Comment to 30:7. The set of aromatics is listed in 30:34.

7.   These precious stones are to adorn the vestments of the priests.

lapis lazuli   Hebrew *shoham* is an oft-mentioned gem of uncertain identity. The ancient versions and rabbinic sources preserve no consistent traditions about it. In Genesis 2:12 it is mentioned as one of the gems native to the mysterious "land of Havilah" near the Garden of Eden, and Ezekiel 28:13 places it in the garden itself.

for setting   Their identity and function are detailed in chapter 28.

the ephod and . . . breast-piece   These, too, are described in chapter 28.

8.   The purpose of assembling all these materials is to construct a sanctuary, in Hebrew, *mikdash*. This term defines that which is clearly enclosed and recognized as sacred space. In later Hebrew, *mikdash*—or more fully *beit ha-mikdash*—became the common designation for the Temple in Jerusalem.

dwell   Careful analysis of the language used here is essential for a proper understanding of the underlying concept and role of the sanctuary. First, the text speaks of God dwelling not "in it," that is in the sanctuary, but "among them," that is, among the people of Israel (v. 2). Then, the verb "to dwell" is not the common Hebrew stem *y-sh-v* but the rarer *sh-k-n*, which has a different connotation. This verb conveys the idea of temporary lodging in a tent and characterizes the nomadic style of life. That is why the structure is called a *mishkan* (e.g., v. 9) and why the verbal form is frequently used together with *'ohel*,[23] the common word for "a tent," and in connection with nomads.[24] The noun *mishkan* is often employed in synonymous parallelism with *'ohel*,[25] and the other designations of the wilderness Tabernacle are the "Tent of the Pact"[26] and the "Tent of Meeting."[27]

Thus, the sanctuary is not meant to be understood literally as God's abode, as are other such institutions in the pagan world. Rather, it functions to make perceptible and tangible the conception of God's immanence, that is, of the indwelling of the Divine Presence in the camp of Israel, to which the people may orient their hearts and minds. A postbiblical extension of this usage of the verb *sh-k-n* is the Hebrew term *shekhinah* for the Divine Presence.

show you—the pattern of the Tabernacle and the pattern of all its furnishings—so shall you make it.

תַּבְנִית הַמִּשְׁכָּן וְאֵת תַּבְנִית כָּל־כֵּלָיו וְכֵן תַּעֲשׂוּ:
ס

¹⁰They shall make an ark of acacia wood, two and a half cubits long, a cubit and a half wide, and a cubit and a half high. ¹¹Overlay it with pure gold—overlay it inside and out—and make upon it a gold molding round about.

¹⁰ וְעָשׂוּ אֲרוֹן עֲצֵי שִׁטִּים אַמָּתַיִם וָחֵצִי אָרְכּוֹ וְאַמָּה וָחֵצִי רָחְבּוֹ וְאַמָּה וָחֵצִי קֹמָתוֹ: ¹¹ וְצִפִּיתָ אֹתוֹ זָהָב טָהוֹר מִבַּיִת וּמִחוּץ תְּצַפֶּנּוּ וְעָשִׂיתָ עָלָיו זֵר זָהָב סָבִיב: ¹² וְיָצַקְתָּ לּוֹ אַרְבַּע

9. The Tabernacle and its furnishings are conceived either as earthly replicas of celestial archetypes or as constructions based upon divinely given blueprints and pictorial representations.²⁸ Both notions are found elsewhere in the Bible. According to the Chronicler's account of the building of Solomon's Temple (1 Chron. 28:11–19), David had received the specifications from God. Ezekiel's detailed vision of the reconstructed Temple in Jerusalem is likewise said to have been received by the prophet while standing on "a very high mountain," as is told in Ezekiel 40–2. The notion of a celestial temple, a sort of cosmic sanctuary, is clearly conveyed in the vision of Isaiah 6:1–8. It is explicit in Micah 1:2–3, which foresees the Lord coming down from "His holy abode," from "His dwelling-place" to "stride upon the heights of the earth." The psalmist, too, declares that "the LORD is in His holy palace; the LORD—His throne is in heaven" (Ps. 11:4).

Exactly as I show you A general admonition, later specified in relation to the menorah, the Tabernacle structure, and the outer altar, apparently all items that were difficult to conceptualize.²⁹

THE ARK (vv. 10–16)

The directions for constructing the Tabernacle commence with the order to fashion an Ark. This takes up the point made in 24:12, that Moses is to ascend the mountain in order to receive the two stone tablets on which the Decalogue is incised. The Ark will permanently house them, and it is therefore the focus of the entire enterprise. That is why the Tabernacle as a whole, including the Ark, features the instruction formula in the third person: "They shall make," the people being the subject. This is distinct from the otherwise uniform wording for the other components: "You shall make," addressed to Moses. It is the Ark and its contents, the symbol of the covenant between God and Israel, that give meaning to the Tabernacle, for the religio-moral imperatives of the Decalogue constitute the foundation of Israelite society. The maintenance of the community's spiritual and moral environment is the responsibility of the entire people. Hence the directive "They shall make."

10. an ark This has the shape of a wooden chest open at the top. In later times, Hebrew *'aron*, in full *'aron kodesh*, "sacred Ark," was transferred to the receptacle for the scrolls of the Torah in the synagogue.

cubits Hebrew *'ammah* means literally "forearm," that is, the distance between the elbow and the tip of the middle finger of an average-sized person.³⁰ The standard biblical cubit is about 18 inches (45 cm.). This would give external dimensions of approximately 3¾ feet in length and 2¼ feet in both width and height (1.12 cm. × .67 cm.)

11. Overlay it According to some rabbinic authorities, a nest of three separate chests of slightly varying dimensions was constructed; one was of wood and two were of gold. The main wooden chest, referred to in verse 10, was inserted inside one gold one, which became its jacket; the other gold chest was fitted inside the wooden chest as a lining.³¹ Another tradition has the wooden chest simply overlaid with gold inside and out.³² Either design would have been familiar to contemporary Egyptian artisans. King Tutankhamen's body was discovered reposing within a nest of three coffins, the innermost having been made of solid gold and the two outer ones of hammered gold over wooden frames.

pure gold Of the highest grade, having undergone extra steps in the refining process to free it from impurities. See Comment to verse 31.

12Cast four gold rings for it, to be attached to its four feet, two rings on one of its side walls and two on the other. 13Make poles of acacia wood and overlay them with gold; 14then insert the poles into the rings on the side walls of the ark, for carrying the ark. 15The poles shall remain in the rings of the ark: they shall not be removed from it. 16And deposit in the Ark [the tablets of] the Pact which I will give you.

טַבְּעֹת זָהָב וְנָתַתָּה עַל אַרְבַּע פַּעֲמֹתָיו וּשְׁתֵּי
טַבָּעֹת עַל־צַלְעוֹ הָאֶחָת וּשְׁתֵּי טַבָּעֹת עַל־צַלְעוֹ
הַשֵּׁנִית: 13 וְעָשִׂיתָ בַדֵּי עֲצֵי שִׁטִּים וְצִפִּיתָ אֹתָם
זָהָב: 14 וְהֵבֵאתָ אֶת־הַבַּדִּים בַּטַּבָּעֹת עַל צַלְעֹת
הָאָרֹן לָשֵׂאת אֶת־הָאָרֹן בָּהֶם: 15 בְּטַבְּעֹת
הָאָרֹן יִהְיוּ הַבַּדִּים לֹא יָסֻרוּ מִמֶּנּוּ: 16 וְנָתַתָּ אֶל־
הָאָרֹן אֵת הָעֵדֻת אֲשֶׁר אֶתֵּן אֵלֶיךָ:   שני

molding   The top of the chest is to be rimmed by a gold band that slightly overlaps its perimeter.[33]

12–15.   The Ark is to be transported from station to station in the wilderness by means of gold-plated wooden poles inserted through gold rings attached to its sides. The poles remained in place even when the Ark was stationary. This injunction was observed even after the Ark found its permanent resting-place in Solomon's Temple, as noted in 1 Kings 8:8. This arrangement probably originated as a precautionary measure to protect the Ark from contact with profane hands. It was the one item of furniture considered to possess supreme holiness and was regarded as endowed with a numinous quality. The tragic fate of a certain Uzzah son of Abinadab, who inadvertently touched the Ark as it was being transported to Jerusalem in the days of King David, well illustrates the point. The parallel text to 2 Samuel 6:3–7, which recounts the story, explicitly mentions that Uzzah's death came about "because he laid a hand on the Ark" (1 Chron. 13:9–10).

The use of poles for transportation is mentioned again in connection with the spies whom Moses sent from the wilderness to reconnoiter the land of Canaan, as reported in Numbers 13:23. It is of interest that underneath the decorated cedar chest found in Tutankhamen's tomb were four poles that had been inserted into bronze rings attached to its base. The Torah is almost silent as to the precise placement of the rings on the sides of the Ark, specifying only that they are affixed to its "four feet."[34] But we are not otherwise told about the Ark having feet, and this meaning of the Hebrew feminine plural *paʿamot*[35] is not certain. The Targums rendered this term as "corners," which Rashi understood to mean the upper ones, and Rashbam took as referring to the lower ones. Ibn Ezra speculates that the Ark stood on legs and not directly on the ground.

16.   *[the tablets of] the Pact*   Hebrew *ha-ʿedut* is elliptical, standing for *lukhot ha-ʿedut*,[36] itself a variant of *lukhot ha-berit*,[37] "the tablets of the Covenant." The Hebrew terms *ʿedut* and *berit* are synonymous; *ʿedut* is a very ancient Semitic term[38] that fell into disuse in Hebrew and was displaced by *berit*. This latter word is exclusive to Hebrew.

The sole function of the Ark is to house the tablets of stone. According to the testimony of 1 Kings 8:9, in the Solomonic Temple "there was nothing inside the Ark but the two tablets of stone that Moses placed there at Horeb, when the LORD made [a covenant] with the Israelites after their departure from the land of Egypt." The practice of depositing legal documents in a sacred place was quite widespread in the ancient Near East. It symbolically underscored the importance of the document and projected the idea that the presiding deity witnessed and guarded it and oversaw its implementation. The disposition of such legal instruments in this manner is exemplified by, among others, the treaty of nonaggression and mutual assistance contracted between King Mattiwaza of Mitanni in Upper Mesopotamia and the Hittite monarch Suppiluliumas (ca. 1375–1335 B.C.E.). One copy was deposited "before the Sun-goddess of Arinna" and another "before the deity Tessub."[39] The phrasing means in front of the image of the god. In Egypt, Ramses II, who made a treaty with the Hittite king Hattusilis, confirms that duplicates of the document lie "beneath the feet" of the respective gods of the contracting parties.[40] Another Egyptian text, a copy of the Book of the Dead, carries a note that it was discovered in Hermopolis "beneath the feet of the god."[41]

Thus, when Moses deposits in the Ark the tablets of stone that contained the fundamentals of the covenant between God and Israel, he is following an ancient and widespread Near Eastern legal tradition. His action also carries implications for the symbolic meaning of the Ark. God is never said to reside in it or to speak from it, only to communicate with Moses from above it (v. 22). It is therefore likely that the Ark represented the footstool of God's throne, which was imagined to be

¹⁷You shall make a cover of pure gold, two and a half cubits long and a cubit and a half wide. ¹⁸Make two cherubim of gold—make them of hammered work—at the two ends of the cover. ¹⁹Make one cherub at one end and the other cherub at the other end; of one piece with the cover shall you make the cherubim at its two ends. ²⁰The

17 וְעָשִׂיתָ כַפֹּרֶת זָהָב טָהוֹר אַמָּתַיִם וָחֵצִי
אָרְכָּהּ וְאַמָּה וָחֵצִי רָחְבָּהּ: 18 וְעָשִׂיתָ שְׁנַיִם
כְּרֻבִים זָהָב מִקְשָׁה תַּעֲשֶׂה אֹתָם מִשְּׁנֵי קְצוֹת
הַכַּפֹּרֶת: 19 וַעֲשֵׂה כְּרוּב אֶחָד מִקָּצָה מִזֶּה
וּכְרוּב־אֶחָד מִקָּצָה מִזֶּה מִן־הַכַּפֹּרֶת תַּעֲשׂוּ אֶת־
הַכְּרֻבִים עַל־שְׁנֵי קְצוֹתָיו: 20 וְהָיוּ הַכְּרֻבִים

situated above it. In fact, it is metaphorically so described in 1 Chronicles 28:2.[42] The footstool, like the throne, was an important prerogative of royalty, a token of dignity and power in the Near East. It was a distinctive and unique piece of furniture often symbolically ornamented and placed in the royal tomb together with the throne. A richly decorated one was recovered from the tomb of Tutankhamen.

THE "KAPPORET" AND THE CHERUBIM   (vv. 17–22)

A solid slab of pure gold is to be placed above the Ark, which was open at the top. The dimensions of the slab correspond exactly to those of the Ark.[43] This object is called in Hebrew *kapporet*, a word that has traditionally been rendered "mercy-seat" in the English versions. This is based on the Septuagint and Vulgate translations, which mean "an instrument of propitiation," and follow the usual sense of the Hebrew stem *k-p-r*, "to atone, make expiation." This understanding would appear to be strengthened by the instruction in Leviticus 16:15–16 that at this spot in the Holy of Holies the High Priest is to perform expiatory rites on the Day of Atonement. Nevertheless, "mercy-seat" is not a satisfactory translation of *kapporet*, since the aspect of "mercy" is an interpretation and is not inherent in the word. The present translation, "a cover," rests on a supposed primary meaning "to cover" for the Hebrew verb *k-p-r*, as in Arabic *kafara*.[44]

Whatever its precise meaning, the *kapporet* was far more than a mere lid for the Ark. It was a distinct entity with its own identity and symbolism. The Ark and *kapporet* are listed several times as two items in the various inventories of the contents of the Tabernacle.[45] The fact that the *kapporet* has its own instruction formula and that its dimensions are separately measured reinforce this conclusion.

At either end of the *kapporet* a cherub was hammered out. The two cherubim faced each other, with their heads bent slightly downward. Their fully outstretched wings were turned upward, sheltering the main body of the lid and the Ark below it. Verse 22 as well as Numbers 7:89 make clear that the divine voice was thought to issue from the space above the lid and between the two cherubim. Therefore, just as the Ark may poetically be the footstool, the *kapporet* with its cherubim would support the invisible throne of God. This explains a frequently employed epithet of God as the One who is "Enthroned on the Cherubim."[46] It is also said that "He mounted a cherub and flew."[47] The outstretched wings of the cherubim also signify flight and mobility.

As noted above, the biblical references, in assuming prior familiarity with the cherubim, suggest a connection with an existing tradition. Closest is the Akkadian term *kuribu*,[48] a protective genius fashioned for the entrances of temples and palaces in Mesopotamia. These creatures are composites of human, animal, and avian features. Hybrids of this kind have turned up over a wide area of the ancient Near East and the Mediterranean lands, including Canaan.[49] Such representations are highly reminiscent of the description of the cherubim in Ezekiel 1:6–11 and 10:14–22. However, a comparison of the non-Israelite creatures with the cherubim of the Tabernacle and with Ezekiel 41:18–19 shows considerable variation in the artistic theme.

Whatever the original inspiration, the cherubim of the Tabernacle certainly communicate some concepts of God that are fundamental to the religion of Israel. As bearers of the celestial throne, they evoke belief in divine, transcendent sovereignty. Their permanent place above the Ark expresses God's immanence—His enduring presence in the covenanted community of Israel. Their outstretched wings represent the idea of consummate mobility, that is, of God's omnipresence.

cherubim shall have their wings spread out above, shielding the cover with their wings. They shall confront each other, the faces of the cherubim being turned toward the cover. [21]Place the cover on top of the Ark, after depositing inside the Ark the Pact that I will give you. [22]There I will meet with you, and I will impart to you—from above the cover, from between the two cherubim that are on top of the Ark of the Pact—all that I will command you concerning the Israelite people.

[23]You shall make a table of acacia wood, two cubits long, one cubit wide, and a cubit and a half high. [24]Overlay it with pure gold, and make a gold molding around it. [25]Make a rim of a hand's breadth around it, and make a gold molding for its rim round about. [26]Make four gold

פֹּרְשֵׂי כְנָפַ֙יִם לְמַ֔עְלָה סֹכְכִ֤ים בְּכַנְפֵיהֶם֙ עַל־
הַכַּפֹּ֔רֶת וּפְנֵיהֶ֖ם אִ֣ישׁ אֶל־אָחִ֑יו אֶל־הַכַּפֹּ֔רֶת יִהְי֖וּ
פְּנֵ֥י הַכְּרֻבִֽים׃ [21] וְנָתַתָּ֧ אֶת־הַכַּפֹּ֛רֶת עַל־הָאָרֹ֖ן
מִלְמָ֑עְלָה וְאֶל־הָ֣אָרֹ֔ן תִּתֵּן֙ אֶת־הָ֣עֵדֻ֔ת אֲשֶׁ֥ר אֶתֵּ֖ן
אֵלֶֽיךָ׃ [22] וְנוֹעַדְתִּ֣י לְךָ֮ שָׁם֒ וְדִבַּרְתִּ֨י אִתְּךָ֜
מֵעַ֣ל הַכַּפֹּ֗רֶת מִבֵּין֙ שְׁנֵ֣י הַכְּרֻבִ֔ים אֲשֶׁ֖ר עַל־אֲרֹ֣ן
הָעֵדֻ֑ת אֵ֣ת כָּל־אֲשֶׁ֧ר אֲצַוֶּ֛ה אוֹתְךָ֖ אֶל־בְּנֵ֥י
יִשְׂרָאֵֽל׃ פ

[23] וְעָשִׂ֥יתָ שֻׁלְחָ֖ן עֲצֵ֣י שִׁטִּ֑ים אַמָּתַ֤יִם אָרְכּוֹ֙
וְאַמָּ֣ה רָחְבּ֔וֹ וְאַמָּ֥ה וָחֵ֖צִי קֹמָתֽוֹ׃ [24] וְצִפִּיתָ֤ אֹתוֹ֙
זָהָ֣ב טָה֔וֹר וְעָשִׂ֥יתָ לּ֛וֹ זֵ֥ר זָהָ֖ב סָבִֽיב׃ [25] וְעָשִׂ֤יתָ
לּוֹ֙ מִסְגֶּ֤רֶת טֹ֨פַח֙ סָבִ֔יב וְעָשִׂ֧יתָ זֵר־זָהָ֛ב לְמִסְגַּרְתּ֖וֹ
סָבִֽיב׃ [26] וְעָשִׂ֣יתָ לּ֔וֹ אַרְבַּ֖ע טַבְּעֹ֣ת זָהָ֑ב וְנָתַתָּ֙

22. The imagery of the footstool and throne evoke the conception of God as King. In this capacity, He issues His royal decrees to Israel through the instrumentality of Moses. Hence, God may be said to "meet" with Moses by the Ark and *kapporet*, a function of the latter object that is repeated several times.[50] This gave rise to the term *'ohel mo'ed*, "Tent of Meeting," as an alternative designation for the Tabernacle.[51] We also find the combination *mishkan 'ohel mo'ed*, "the Tabernacle of the Tent of Meeting."[52]

I will meet with you Hebrew *no'adeti* derives from the stem *y-'-d*, "to appoint, to come at the appointed time, to meet by appointment." By popular etymology, the similar sounding, although distinct, stem *'-w-d*, which is at the base of *'edut*, "pact," was connected with it so that the two words often appear together in these texts.

THE TABLE AND ITS APPURTENANCES   (vv. 23–30)

Having dealt with the contents of the most sacred space, the text now presents instructions relating to the furniture and utensils that are to be housed in the second sacred zone of the Tabernacle. Of these, the table comes first because it is next in holiness, after the Ark. Made of acacia wood and overlaid with pure gold, the table top measures 2 cubits by 1 cubit (approximately 3 ft. × 1½ ft., or 0.9 m. × .45 m.) and stands 1½ cubits from the ground (approximately 2½ ft. or 0.67 m.). It is supported by four wooden legs to which golden rings are attached. Poles are inserted into these rings when the Table is to be transported. Its proper location in the Tabernacle is on the north side of the Holy Place, the second zone.[53]

Some of the constructional details are unclear. It appears that gilded molding embellished the top, and the legs were fastened to an underframe equipped with molding to afford greater stability.[54] The Torah is silent about the shape and decoration of the legs. Josephus claims that they "were exquisitely finished" in the lower half.[55]

The main function of the table was to accommodate the bread of display. Hence, it is called "the table of display" in Numbers 4:7. Another name, found in 2 Chronicles 29:18, is "the table of the row [of breads]." Still a third designation, "the pure table," is used in Leviticus 24:6. This last refers either to the plating of pure gold,[56] or it means that the rows of bread be placed "on the table proper" and not on the side attachments.[57]

24. **molding** See Comment to verse 11.

25. **a rim** Hebrew *misgeret* is exclusive to this artifact, but it appears again as a technical term in connection with the laver in Solomon's Temple.[58] The stem *s-g-r* denotes "to close"; hence *misgeret* might mean "an enclosure," "a frame."[59]

rings for it, and attach the rings to the four corners at its four legs. ²⁷The rings shall be next to the rim, as holders for poles to carry the table. ²⁸Make the poles of acacia wood, and overlay them with gold; by these the table shall be carried. ²⁹Make its bowls, ladles, jars and jugs with which to offer libations; make them of pure gold. ³⁰And on the table you shall set the bread of display, to be before Me always.

אֶת־הַטַּבָּעֹת עַל אַרְבַּע הַפֵּאֹת אֲשֶׁר לְאַרְבַּע רַגְלָיו: 27 לְעֻמַּת הַמִּסְגֶּרֶת תִּהְיֶיןָ הַטַּבָּעֹת לְבָתִּים לְבַדִּים לָשֵׂאת אֶת־הַשֻּׁלְחָן: 28 וְעָשִׂיתָ אֶת־הַבַּדִּים עֲצֵי שִׁטִּים וְצִפִּיתָ אֹתָם זָהָב וְנִשָּׂא־בָם אֶת־הַשֻּׁלְחָן: 29 וְעָשִׂיתָ קְּעָרֹתָיו וְכַפֹּתָיו וּקְשׂוֹתָיו וּמְנַקִּיֹּתָיו אֲשֶׁר יֻסַּךְ בָּהֵן זָהָב טָהוֹר תַּעֲשֶׂה אֹתָם: 30 וְנָתַתָּ עַל־הַשֻּׁלְחָן לֶחֶם פָּנִים לְפָנַי תָּמִיד: פ　　[שלישי לספרדים]

29. Four utensils were displayed on the table. These are referred to in other texts as "service vessels" (Heb. *kelei sharet*) and also as "sacred utensils."[60] Their functions are uncertain.

bowls Hebrew *ke'arot* (sing. *ke'arah*) are understood in the Talmud to be the molds in which the loaves of bread were placed after baking so that they would retain their shape.[61] Bekhor Shor understands them to be the pans in which the dough is baked.

ladles Hebrew *kappot* (sing. *kaf*), literally "palm [of the hand]," hence a palm-shaped vessel.[62] These most likely contained the frankincense mentioned in Leviticus 24:7 that was placed on the table of the bread of display and that was burnt when the loaves were removed each Sabbath. In later Hebrew these two incense containers were known as *bazikhin*.[63]

jars Hebrew *kesavot*. In Numbers 4:7 they are called *kesot ha-nesekh*, "libation jugs," so that the following clause of the present verse—"with which to offer libations"—also applies to these "jars." This presents a difficulty, however, in that Exodus 30:9 expressly prohibits libations on the altar in this Holy Place. Either some ritual not otherwise recorded took place in connection with the bread of display, or these jars were simply symbolic. According to Bekhor Shor, they were water containers for use in kneading the dough. However, in Menaḥot 97a the *kesavot* are defined as "props" (Heb. *senifin*) for the loaves of bread on display.[64]

jugs Hebrew *menakiyyot* (sing. *menakit*) appears only in lists of ritual accessories.[65] Their identity and function are uncertain. The literal meaning of the word should be "cleansers"; indeed, Bekhor Shor takes them to be utensils for clearing ashes from the oven and for cleaning the table. Menaḥot 97a takes them to be rods in the shape of hollow reeds broken in two that were placed on the table to permit free circulation of air between the cakes to keep them clean and fresh.

30. *the bread of display* Hebrew *leḥem panim* has been variously translated, depending on the understanding of *panim*, which usually means "face, presence, interior." Ibn Ezra's explanation that they are perpetually set out before the Lord—hence "the bread of the presence"—is supported by the end of this verse and by 1 Samuel 21:7. Rashi took the phrase figuratively: "bread fit for dignitaries."[66] Mishnah Menaḥot 11:4 interprets "that all its surfaces [Heb. *panim*] should be visible." According to Menaḥot 94b, the loaves were flat and oblong-shaped, "like a broken box" that has neither front nor back but only a base with two upright sides.

As prescribed in Leviticus 24:5–9, there were twelve loaves in all, each prepared from two-tenths of an ephah measure of choice flour. This is twice the daily per capita ration of manna in the wilderness. According to Josephus, the loaves were unleavened.[67] The significance of the number twelve is not explained, but it may symbolize the twelve tribes of Israel.[68] The loaves were set out on the table in two equal rows,[69] and they remained undisturbed for the entire week until the Sabbath, when they were replaced by freshly baked loaves. The old ones were eaten by the priests in the sacred precincts. From the manner in which they were displayed, the bread also became known as "the bread [arranged in] rows" (Heb. *leḥem ha-ma'arekhet*)[70] and "the regular bread" (Heb. *leḥem ha-tamid*).[71] The story of David and the priest Ahimelech of the sanctuary at Nob, as told in 1 Samuel 21:2–7, gives an insight into the actual use of the bread, although the story contains features that do not conform to the Torah's legislation.

The Levitical clan of Kohathites was charged with the weekly task of baking the bread and arranging the loaves on the table. This was apparently a specialized skill, and in the days of the Second

³¹You shall make a lampstand of pure gold; the lampstand shall be made of hammered work; its base and its
shaft, its cups, calyxes, and petals shall be of one piece. ³²Six

לא וְעָשִׂ֥יתָ מְנֹרַ֖ת זָהָ֣ב טָה֑וֹר מִקְשָׁה֩ תֵּעָשֶׂ֨ה
הַמְּנוֹרָ֜ה יְרֵכָ֣הּ וְקָנָ֗הּ גְּבִיעֶ֛יהָ כַּפְתֹּרֶ֥יהָ וּפְרָחֶ֖יהָ
מִמֶּ֣נָּה יִהְי֑וּ: לב וְשִׁשָּׁ֣ה קָנִ֔ים יֹצְאִ֖ים מִצִּדֶּ֑יהָ

Temple it seems to have been the preserve of "the house of Garmu," which kept the process a closely
guarded trade secret.

THE MENORAH[72]   (vv. 31–40)

The second sacred item of furniture that stood in the outer sanctum was the seven-branched
menorah, the lampstand. It was positioned on the south side of the Tabernacle opposite the table.[73] A
talmudic statement has it that Moses himself found it difficult to conceptualize the object.[74] The
statement in Numbers 8:4 that God showed Moses a heavenly prototype no doubt reinforced that
idea. Although the instructions about the menorah are very detailed, the text is obscure on many
points and is characterized by a paucity of verbs of action, which complicates our understanding.
Further, we are not told whether the lamps on the six side branches were level with that of the central
shaft; and no information is forthcoming as to the material, clay or metal, from which the lamps were
to be made. Also, for reasons unknown, the dimensions of the lampstand are not given.[75] Equally exceptional is the specification of the weight of the gold from which it was to be manufactured (v. 39).
Another unique feature is the requirement that the entire object be fashioned out of one solid block
of gold (v. 36); the other articles of furniture were made of wood overlaid with gold. Finally, some of
the technical vocabulary is still imperfectly understood.

No lampstand that incorporates all or even most of the features of the Tabernacle menorah has
yet been uncovered in the Near East. The famous menorah relief on the Arch of Titus cannot be used
to reconstruct that of the Tabernacle. It deviates in important details from the prescriptions given
here in Exodus, from the rabbinic sources, and from the account of Josephus, who was himself a
priest and very likely actually saw the menorah in Herod's Temple. The Roman artist may have
changed some details for his own aesthetic purposes, or he may have used a model other than that of
the Temple. Moreover, it is likely that Herod's menorah, dating from at least one thousand years after
the one in the Tabernacle, was itself the product of change and development.

The menorah prescribed here is not an idealized retrojection from the furniture in Solomon's
Temple. The narrative in Kings[76] that depicts the construction of the Temple does not mention such
a cultic object; rather, it tells of ten lampstands fashioned for that edifice. They are not clearly
described, and there is no evidence that they were of the branched type. Also, they were manufactured
of "solid gold" (Heb. *zahav sagur*), whereas the Tabernacle one was made of "pure gold" (Heb. *zahav
tahor*). The difference in technical terminology is significant. The former term is of Akkadian origin[77]
and indicates a northern source for the gold. The latter term is much closer to Egyptian metallurgic
nomenclature,[78] suggesting a more local, southern provenance.

Other affinities with Egypt are also discernible. The term for the shaft (Heb. *kaneh*) (v. 31) really
means "a reed" or "cane plant." It usually appears in the Bible in Egyptian contexts, for the reed
flourishes in the Egyptian marshlands.[79] The word here translated "cups" (Heb. *gaviʿa*) is probably of
Egyptian origin,[80] and other Pentateuchal usages also have an Egyptian context.[81] Above all, it is the
extraordinary cluster of botanical terms and motifs that provides the strongest evidence of the world
of ancient Egypt, where art and architecture are distinguished by renditions of plant life. Typical are
the treelike columns with their floral decorations on the capitals.

The contrasts between the Tabernacle menorah and the lamps of Solomon's Temple, together
with the Egyptian affinities, are particularly significant in light of the fact that the designs and
architectonics are distinctive of the Late Bronze Age—the period of the Exodus. The structure points
in the same direction. A central shaft with six branches, the floral ring molding, the bowl element,
and the form of the so-called base have all been shown to belong to that period.[82]

As verse 37 and other biblical sources make clear, the primary function of the menorah was
utilitarian: to illuminate the area around it at nighttime.[83] The responsibility for lighting and tending
the lamps was the exclusive prerogative of Aaron and his sons.[84] Still, since the elaborate design

branches shall issue from its sides; three branches from one side of the lampstand and three branches from the other side of the lampstand. [33]On one branch there shall be three cups shaped like almond-blossoms, each with calyx and petals, and on the next branch there shall be three cups shaped like almond-blossoms, each with calyx and petals; so for all six branches issuing from the lampstand. [34]And

שְׁלֹשָׁה ׀ קְנֵי מְנֹרָה מִצִּדָּהּ הָאֶחָד וּשְׁלֹשָׁה קְנֵי מְנֹרָה מִצִּדָּהּ הַשֵּׁנִי: 33 שְׁלֹשָׁה גְבִעִים מְשֻׁקָּדִים בַּקָּנֶה הָאֶחָד כַּפְתֹּר וָפֶרַח וּשְׁלֹשָׁה גְבִעִים מְשֻׁקָּדִים בַּקָּנֶה הָאֶחָד כַּפְתֹּר וָפָרַח כֵּן לְשֵׁשֶׁת הַקָּנִים הַיֹּצְאִים מִן־הַמְּנֹרָה: 34 וּבַמְּנֹרָה אַרְבָּעָה

motifs in no way pertain to the practical use, it may be assumed that an additional, symbolic significance attaches to the sacred menorah, which, of all the furnishings in the sanctuary, is the only one repeatedly accorded the epithet "pure."[85] The shape of the lampstand—the trunk with its branches extending on either side—unmistakably evokes the image of a tree. Quite possibly, it represents the tree of life. The inflorescence of the almond tree most certainly bears symbolic value, for that tree (Heb. *shaked*) is the earliest spring-flowering plant in the Land of Israel, often even before the end of February. The stem *sh-k-d* means "to be watchful, wakeful, vigilant"; thus, the almond flower is a symbol of life renewed and sustained.[86] The number seven, the totality of the lamps, is the outstanding symbolic number in the Bible, an expression of completeness and perfection. Finally, the lights constitute the most powerful symbol of all, for light intimates both life itself[87] and the presence of the Giver of all life.[88] This is the interpretation given in Shabbat 22b: The light of the menorah is testimony that the Divine Presence resides in the midst of Israel. Hence, in the prophet Zechariah's vision of the menorah, its light represents the invincible power of the spirit over brute force: "Not by might, nor by power, but by My spirit—said the LORD of Hosts" (Zech. 4:6).

Following the destruction of the Temple, rabbinic law proscribed the production of a facsimile of the seven-branch menorah,[89] but it has remained a pervasive symbol of Judaism and has been found as a frequent pictorial motif in early synagogues, catacombs, tombs, manuscripts, and on artifacts.[90] Because the menorah has always been imbued with emotive and conceptual significance for Jews, it was adopted as the emblem of the State of Israel.

31. a lampstand "Candlestick" or "candelabrum" are anachronistic translations for biblical Hebrew *menorah*, since candles did not appear before the Roman period.

pure gold See Comment to verse 11.

hammered work See Comment to verse 18.

its base Hebrew *yarekh*, literally "loins, thigh." The regular pattern of ancient Near Eastern lampstands featured a gradual increase in the width toward the bottom. This type of flared base is probably what is meant here by *yarekh*, rather than the boxlike form featured on the menorah of the Arch of Titus.[91]

shaft Hebrew *kaneh*, literally "cane, reed," here refers to the branches.

cups Hebrew *gaviaʿ* is a goblet, hence a bulbous-shaped receptacle.

calyxes Hebrew *kaftor* appears as an architectural term in Amos 9:1 and Zephaniah 2:14, where it designates the capital of a column. Since such were ornamented with a florid design, *kaftor* most likely refers to the calyx motif. Elsewhere in the Bible, Caphtor denotes the isle of Crete,[92] where this type of ornamentation may have originated. Interestingly, Menahot 28b compares the shape of the *kaftor* to "Cretan apples."

petals Hebrew *peraḥ*, usually meaning "flower," is here rendered "lily" by the ancient versions.[93] In Egypt the lotus blossom, that is, the water lily, was for long highly popular as a floral decoration of columns. It symbolized nascent life. Solomon's Temple, too, had a lily design on the capitals of the columns.[94] Menahot 28b compares the menorah's floral decoration to "the blossoms around the [capitals of] columns."

of one piece Literally, "they shall be of it." All the above-mentioned elements, together with the central shaft, are to be made of a single block of gold and not assembled from individual parts.

on the lampstand itself there shall be four cups shaped like almond-blossoms, each with calyx and petals: 35a calyx, of one piece with it, under a pair of branches; and a calyx, of one piece with it, under the second pair of branches, and a calyx, of one piece with it, under the last pair of branches; so for all six branches issuing from the lampstand. 36Their calyxes and their stems shall be of one piece with it, the whole of it a single hammered piece of pure gold. 37Make its seven lamps—the lamps shall be so mounted as to give the light on its front side—38and its tongs and fire pans of pure gold. 39It shall be made, with all these furnishings, out of a talent of pure gold. 40Note well, and follow the patterns for them that are being shown you on the mountain.

גְּבִעִים מְשֻׁקָּדִים כַּפְתֹּרֶיהָ וּפְרָחֶיהָ: 35 וְכַפְתֹּר
תַּחַת שְׁנֵי הַקָּנִים מִמֶּנָּה וְכַפְתֹּר תַּחַת שְׁנֵי
הַקָּנִים מִמֶּנָּה וְכַפְתֹּר תַּחַת־שְׁנֵי הַקָּנִים מִמֶּנָּה
לְשֵׁשֶׁת הַקָּנִים הַיֹּצְאִים מִן־הַמְּנֹרָה:
36 כַּפְתֹּרֵיהֶם וּקְנֹתָם מִמֶּנָּה יִהְיוּ כֻּלָּהּ מִקְשָׁה
אַחַת זָהָב טָהוֹר: 37 וְעָשִׂיתָ אֶת־נֵרֹתֶיהָ שִׁבְעָה
וְהֶעֱלָה אֶת־נֵרֹתֶיהָ וְהֵאִיר עַל־עֵבֶר פָּנֶיהָ:
38 וּמַלְקָחֶיהָ וּמַחְתֹּתֶיהָ זָהָב טָהוֹר: 39 כִּכַּר זָהָב
טָהוֹר יַעֲשֶׂה אֹתָהּ אֵת כָּל־הַכֵּלִים הָאֵלֶּה:
40 וּרְאֵה וַעֲשֵׂה בְּתַבְנִיתָם אֲשֶׁר־אַתָּה מָרְאֶה
בָּהָר: ס   שלישי

35.   The "lampstand" refers to the central shaft; its ornamentation is to be located just beneath the points from which the side branches extend.

37.   *the lamps*   The containers for the wick and oil. The text leaves unclear whether they were all of a piece with the rest of the menorah or were separate and removable.[95] If the latter, they were most likely ceramic. Genesis Rabba 20:18 refers to a gold menorah with ceramic lamps (Heb. *ner*) on top.

shall be so mounted   The meaning of Hebrew *ve-he'elah* depends on the resolution of the issue discussed in the preceding note as to whether the lamps were removable. The term could either mean "causing the flame to rise" or "placing the removable lamps on top of the extremities of the branches." The statement is parenthetical. The verbs are phrased in the third person singular instead of the second person like the others, and they deal with the daily utilization of the menorah, not with its construction.

on its front side   The lamps are to be arranged in such a way that the light is thrown forward toward the table facing it.[96] Less likely is the interpretation that the lights are to focus upon the central shaft.[97]

38.   *tongs . . . fire pans*   These nouns are objects of the verb "make" in verse 37. The "tongs" (Heb. *melkaḥayim*) were used[98] to remove the burned wicks; the fire pans (Heb. *maḥtah*), to receive them.[99]

39.   *a talent*   The value of Hebrew *kikkar* cannot be accurately determined, since there was no uniform weight system. See Comment to 38:24–30.

CHAPTER 26   THE TABERNACLE COVERINGS   (vv. 1–14)

Now that the instructions regarding the furnishing of the Holy of Holies and the Holy Place have been given, the text turns to the coverings that serve as the roof. These comprise four separate layers: linen, goats' hair, ram skins, and, uppermost, *taḥash* leather.

THE LOWEST LAYER (vv. 1–6)

The lowest layer is to comprise ten multicolored sheets of fine linen decorated with the cherubim motif, each sheet measuring 28 cubits × 4 cubits (42 ft. × 6 ft. = 12.8 × 8 m.). They are sewn together in paired sets of five, yielding two long sheets, each 28 cubits × 20 cubits (42 ft. × 30 ft. = 12.8 m.

26 As for the Tabernacle, make it of ten strips of cloth; make these of fine twisted linen, of blue, purple, and crimson yarns, with a design of cherubim worked into them. ²The length of each cloth shall be twenty-eight cubits, and the width of each cloth shall be four cubits, all the cloths to have the same measurements. ³Five of the cloths shall be joined to one another, and the other five cloths shall be joined to one another. ⁴Make loops of blue wool on the edge of the outermost cloth of the one set; and do likewise on the edge of the outermost cloth of the other set: ⁵make fifty loops on the one cloth, and fifty loops on the edge of the end cloth of the other set, the loops to be opposite one another. ⁶And make fifty gold clasps, and couple the cloths to one another with the clasps, so that the Tabernacle becomes one whole.

כ"ו וְאֶת־הַמִּשְׁכָּן תַּעֲשֶׂה עֶשֶׂר יְרִיעֹת שֵׁשׁ
מָשְׁזָר וּתְכֵלֶת וְאַרְגָּמָן וְתֹלַעַת שָׁנִי כְּרֻבִים
מַעֲשֵׂה חֹשֵׁב תַּעֲשֶׂה אֹתָם: 2 אֹרֶךְ ׀ הַיְרִיעָה
הָאַחַת שְׁמֹנֶה וְעֶשְׂרִים בָּאַמָּה וְרֹחַב אַרְבַּע
בָּאַמָּה הַיְרִיעָה הָאֶחָת מִדָּה אַחַת לְכָל־הַיְרִיעֹת:
3 חֲמֵשׁ הַיְרִיעֹת תִּהְיֶיןָ חֹבְרֹת אִשָּׁה אֶל־אֲחֹתָהּ
וְחָמֵשׁ יְרִיעֹת חֹבְרֹת אִשָּׁה אֶל־אֲחֹתָהּ:
4 וְעָשִׂיתָ לֻלְאֹת תְּכֵלֶת עַל שְׂפַת הַיְרִיעָה
הָאֶחָת מִקָּצָה בַּחֹבָרֶת וְכֵן תַּעֲשֶׂה בִּשְׂפַת
הַיְרִיעָה הַקִּיצוֹנָה בַּמַּחְבֶּרֶת הַשֵּׁנִית: 5 חֲמִשִּׁים
לֻלָאֹת תַּעֲשֶׂה בַּיְרִיעָה הָאֶחָת וַחֲמִשִּׁים לֻלָאֹת
תַּעֲשֶׂה בִּקְצֵה הַיְרִיעָה אֲשֶׁר בַּמַּחְבֶּרֶת הַשֵּׁנִית
מַקְבִּילֹת הַלֻּלָאֹת אִשָּׁה אֶל־אֲחֹתָהּ: 6 וְעָשִׂיתָ
חֲמִשִּׁים קַרְסֵי זָהָב וְחִבַּרְתָּ אֶת־הַיְרִיעֹת אִשָּׁה
אֶל־אֲחֹתָהּ בַּקְּרָסִים וְהָיָה הַמִּשְׁכָּן אֶחָד:
פ

× 9.1 m.). Fifty blue loops are fixed along one of the edges of each section. The two sets are fastened together by gold clasps inserted into the loops, resulting in a total measurement of 40 cubits × 28 cubits (60 ft. × 42 ft. = 18.2 m. × 12.8 m.). The linen drapes are then to be placed lengthwise over the Tabernacle, which measures 30 cubits × 10 cubits (35 ft. × 15 ft. = 10.7 m. × 4.6 m.), so that on the north and south walls they hang down 1 cubit (1½ ft. = 0.45 m.) short of the full height and, on the west side, they touch the ground. There is no overlap on the east side. These calculations disregard the thickness of the walls, on which see the introductory Comment to verses 15–30 below.

1. *the Tabernacle*   Already mentioned above in 25:8–9. Here, Hebrew *mishkan* has the restricted sense of the two sacred zones.

strips of cloth   Hebrew *yeriʿah* (sing.) invariably refers to the fabrics of which tents are made.[1]

twisted   Hebrew *moshzar*, a technical term found only in connection with the linen of the Tabernacle. It is most likely related to the Arabic stem *shazara* meaning "to twist cord." Twisting is the all-important operation in spinning. Hence, the lowest layer is to be made of a fine grade of linen that is woven of ply yarns. According to talmudic sources, the yarns of linen were to consist of six strands of multicolored threads.[2]

a design of cherubim   Hebrew *keruvim maʿaseh ḥoshev*, literally "cherubs, the work of a thinker/designer," that is, of a creative and imaginative artist.[3] This phrase apparently refers to some highly specialized technique of weaving, different from that mentioned in verses 36 and 28:32. Yoma 72b records a difference of opinion on the meaning of the technical terms. One view holds that double-faced weaving is intended; that is, the design is so woven into the fabric as to appear the same on both sides. The other view has different designs on the obverse and reverse.[4] Ibn Ezra suggests that the linen fabric was decorated with ink or pigment. Examples of such are, in fact, well known from ancient Egypt.[5]

3. *joined*   Apparently stitched together with needle and thread.

4. *loops*   Hebrew *lulaʾot* is used only in the context of the Tabernacle.[6]

6. *clasps*   Hebrew *keres* is another technical term exclusive to this context.[7] The clasps, probably S-shaped, are to be inserted through the two parallel sets of loops.

one whole   The ten separate fabrics that cover the area that constitutes the Tabernacle in its restricted sense become a unified entity.

7You shall then make cloths of goats' hair for a tent over the Tabernacle; make the cloths eleven in number. 8The length of each cloth shall be thirty cubits, and the width of each cloth shall be four cubits, the eleven cloths to have the same measurements. 9Join five of the cloths by themselves, and the other six cloths by themselves; and fold over the sixth cloth at the front of the tent. 10Make fifty loops on the edge of the outermost cloth of the one set, and fifty loops on the edge of the cloth of the other set. 11Make fifty copper clasps, and fit the clasps into the loops, and couple the tent together so that it becomes one whole. 12As for the overlapping excess of the cloths of the tent, the extra half-cloth shall overlap the back of the Tabernacle, 13while the extra cubit at either end of each length of tent cloth shall hang down to the bottom of the two sides of the Tabernacle and cover it. 14And make for the tent a covering of tanned ram skins, and a covering of dolphin skins above.

7 וְעָשִׂיתָ יְרִיעֹת עִזִּים לְאֹהֶל עַל־הַמִּשְׁכָּן עַשְׁתֵּי־עֶשְׂרֵה יְרִיעֹת תַּעֲשֶׂה אֹתָם: 8 אֹרֶךְ ׀ הַיְרִיעָה הָאַחַת שְׁלֹשִׁים בָּאַמָּה וְרֹחַב אַרְבַּע בָּאַמָּה הַיְרִיעָה הָאֶחָת מִדָּה אַחַת לְעַשְׁתֵּי עֶשְׂרֵה יְרִיעֹת: 9 וְחִבַּרְתָּ אֶת־חֲמֵשׁ הַיְרִיעֹת לְבָד וְאֶת־שֵׁשׁ הַיְרִיעֹת לְבָד וְכָפַלְתָּ אֶת־הַיְרִיעָה הַשִּׁשִּׁית אֶל־מוּל פְּנֵי הָאֹהֶל: 10 וְעָשִׂיתָ חֲמִשִּׁים לֻלָאֹת עַל שְׂפַת הַיְרִיעָה הָאֶחָת הַקִּיצֹנָה בַּחֹבָרֶת וַחֲמִשִּׁים לֻלָאֹת עַל שְׂפַת הַיְרִיעָה הַחֹבֶרֶת הַשֵּׁנִית: 11 וְעָשִׂיתָ קַרְסֵי נְחֹשֶׁת חֲמִשִּׁים וְהֵבֵאתָ אֶת־הַקְּרָסִים בַּלֻּלָאֹת וְחִבַּרְתָּ אֶת־הָאֹהֶל וְהָיָה אֶחָד: 12 וְסֶרַח הָעֹדֵף בִּירִיעֹת הָאֹהֶל חֲצִי הַיְרִיעָה הָעֹדֶפֶת תִּסְרַח עַל אֲחֹרֵי הַמִּשְׁכָּן: 13 וְהָאַמָּה מִזֶּה וְהָאַמָּה מִזֶּה בָּעֹדֵף בְּאֹרֶךְ יְרִיעֹת הָאֹהֶל יִהְיֶה סָרוּחַ עַל־צִדֵּי הַמִּשְׁכָּן מִזֶּה וּמִזֶּה לְכַסֹּתוֹ: 14 וְעָשִׂיתָ מִכְסֶה לָאֹהֶל עֹרֹת אֵילִם מְאָדָּמִים וּמִכְסֵה עֹרֹת תְּחָשִׁים מִלְמָעְלָה: פ רביעי

THE SECOND LAYER (vv. 7–13)

A coarser covering made of goats' hair was to be laid above the linen fabric. It comprised eleven strips, each measuring 30 cubits × 4 cubits (45 ft. × 6 ft. = 13.7 m. × 1.8 m.). Five strips and six strips were to be stitched together, yielding an area of 44 cubits × 30 cubits (66 ft. × 45 ft. = 20.1 m. × 13.7 m.) when secured by loops and clasps. The text does not specify the color of the loops, which suggests that they were not dyed. The clasps were made of bronze. The long fabric was to be spread lengthwise over the entire area of the Tabernacle starting from the eastern entrance and extending toward the rear. The outermost strip, called "the sixth," which began at the entrance, was to be doubled over, thus leaving an overhang of 10 cubits on the north and south sides so that the coverings of goats' hair just touched the ground. On the west side, the fabric, which was 12 cubits (18 ft. = 5.5 m.) long, would trail 2 cubits (3 ft. = 0.9 m.) along the ground.

7. *goats' hair* See Comment to 25:4.

for a tent As a protective shield over the ornamented linen cover.

eleven One strip more than the number of linen cloths.

12. *overlap* The Hebrew stem *s-r-ḥ* means "to overrun limits."[8]

the tent The covering.

THE THIRD AND FOURTH LAYERS (v. 14)

The measurements of the two uppermost leather coverings are not given. A difference of opinion about them is recorded in Shabbat 28a. Rabbi Judah understands that there were to be two layers, one of dyed ram skins and one of *taḥash* skins, while Rabbi Nehemiah holds that there was only one more layer, consisting half of ram skins and half of *taḥash* skins.

dolphin See Comment to 25:5.

15You shall make the planks for the Tabernacle of acacia wood, upright. 16The length of each plank shall be ten cubits and the width of each plank a cubit and a half. 17Each plank shall have two tenons, parallel to each other; do the same with all the planks of the Tabernacle. 18Of the planks of the Tabernacle, make twenty planks on the south side:

15 וְעָשִׂיתָ אֶת־הַקְּרָשִׁים לַמִּשְׁכָּן עֲצֵי שִׁטִּים
עֹמְדִים: 16 עֶשֶׂר אַמּוֹת אֹרֶךְ הַקָּרֶשׁ וְאַמָּה
וַחֲצִי הָאַמָּה רֹחַב הַקֶּרֶשׁ הָאֶחָד: 17 שְׁתֵּי יָדוֹת
לַקֶּרֶשׁ הָאֶחָד מְשֻׁלָּבֹת אִשָּׁה אֶל־אֲחֹתָהּ כֵּן
תַּעֲשֶׂה לְכֹל קַרְשֵׁי הַמִּשְׁכָּן: 18 וְעָשִׂיתָ אֶת־
הַקְּרָשִׁים לַמִּשְׁכָּן עֶשְׂרִים קֶרֶשׁ לִפְאַת נֶגְבָּה

THE WOODEN STRUCTURE (vv. 15–30)

The instructions now proceed to outline the structure that is to hold the drapes. Three walls are to be constructed of gilded timber planks (or frames) cut from acacia trees. Twenty such planks (or frames) make up the northern and southern walls; the western wall requires eight; the eastern side has none. The northwestern and southwestern corners are each reinforced by an additional wooden support.

Each plank (or frame) measured 10 cubits (15 ft. = 4.6 m.) in height and 1½ cubits (2 ft. 3 in. = 0.3 m.) in width. The thickness is not given; Josephus claims that each was "four fingers."[9] In Shabbat 98b Rabbi Nehemiah asserts that the thickness of the wood was uniformly 1 cubit (1½ ft. = 0.45 m.), whereas Rabbi Judah maintains that each plank tapered from 1 cubit at the bottom to a fingerbreadth at the top. The entire structure would have measured 30 cubits (45 ft. = 13.7 m.) in length and 10 cubits (15 ft. = 4.6 m.) in both width and height. As such, the Tabernacle was exactly half the size of Solomon's Temple in length and width and one-third its height, according to the dimensions given in 1 Kings 6:2.

It is not entirely clear how all the wooden pieces were held in place. Several devices seem to have been adopted. Two grooves were hollowed out at the top of each upright, and gold ringlike fasteners were inserted into each groove. These were just large enough to fit into the adjacent groove of the plank alongside it as well. In addition, two tenons were cut into the bottom of each upright and were mortised into silver sockets. There were ninety-six tenons in all. To provide still greater stability, five gilded crossbars made from acacia wood were inserted into gold ringlike holders affixed to the uprights on each of the three walls.

15. the planks Hebrew *kerashim* (sing. *keresh*). Abravanel notes that the word appears with the definite article because the use of planks is taken for granted in the construction of a sanctuary. In Ugaritic texts the singular form of the same noun is the regular designation of the shrine of the Canaanite god Il.[10] According to a widely held scholarly view, *keresh* indicates a wooden frame rather than a plank; this is based on the fact that the massive weight of the forty-eight (or fifty) planks of wood required for the Tabernacle would have imposed an intolerable burden on those charged with transporting them in the wilderness.[11] In response, it has been pointed out that the Levitical clan of Merarites were provided with four wagons drawn by eight oxen for the purpose, as stated in Numbers 7:8.[12] While the latter argument is persuasive, it is not decisive, since frames of the number and size given would also have required wagons.[13] Moreover, the clan of Gershonites was also given ox-drawn wagons even though their porterage duties involved a relatively light load, as specified in Numbers 4:22–27 and 7:6–7.

acacia See Comment to 25:5.

upright Literally, "standing," which may specify straight-trunked trees; or it may refer to the placement of the planks vertically, and not horizontally as is usual in log construction.[14]

17. tenons The traditional rendering of Hebrew *yadot*, from *yad*, "hand."[15]

parallel Hebrew *meshullavot* is of uncertain meaning. In 1 Kings 7:28–29, *shelabbim* (sing. *shalav*) seems to mean "crossbars."[16]

18. on the south side Hebrew *negbah teimanah*. Both terms mean "to the south." The first derives from the name Negeb, "dry, arid," given to the southern part of Israel; the second stems from *yamin*, "right hand, south," the direction to the right when one faces the rising sun.[17]

¹⁹making forty silver sockets under the twenty planks, two sockets under the one plank for its two tenons and two sockets under each following plank for its two tenons; ²⁰and for the other side wall of the Tabernacle, on the north side, twenty planks, ²¹with their forty silver sockets, two sockets under the one plank and two sockets under each following plank. ²²And for the rear of the Tabernacle, to the west, make six planks; ²³and make two planks for the corners of the Tabernacle at the rear. ²⁴They shall match at the bottom, and terminate alike at the top inside one ring; thus shall it be with both of them: they shall form the two corners. ²⁵Thus there shall be eight planks with their sockets of silver: sixteen sockets, two sockets under the first plank, and two sockets under each of the other planks.

²⁶You shall make bars of acacia wood: five for the planks of the one side wall of the Tabernacle, ²⁷five bars for the planks of the other side wall of the Tabernacle, and five bars for the planks of the wall of the Tabernacle at the rear to the west. ²⁸The center bar halfway up the planks shall run from end to end. ²⁹Overlay the planks with gold, and make their rings of gold, as holders for the bars; and overlay the bars with gold. ³⁰Then set up the Tabernacle according to the manner of it that you were shown on the mountain.

תֵימָנָה: 19 וְאַרְבָּעִים אַדְנֵי־כֶסֶף תַּעֲשֶׂה תַּחַת עֶשְׂרִים הַקָּרֶשׁ שְׁנֵי אֲדָנִים תַּחַת־הַקֶּרֶשׁ הָאֶחָד לִשְׁתֵּי יְדֹתָיו וּשְׁנֵי אֲדָנִים תַּחַת־הַקֶּרֶשׁ הָאֶחָד לִשְׁתֵּי יְדֹתָיו: 20 וּלְצֶלַע הַמִּשְׁכָּן הַשֵּׁנִית לִפְאַת צָפוֹן עֶשְׂרִים קָרֶשׁ: 21 וְאַרְבָּעִים אַדְנֵיהֶם כָּסֶף שְׁנֵי אֲדָנִים תַּחַת הַקֶּרֶשׁ הָאֶחָד וּשְׁנֵי אֲדָנִים תַּחַת הַקֶּרֶשׁ הָאֶחָד: 22 וּלְיַרְכְּתֵי הַמִּשְׁכָּן יָמָּה תַּעֲשֶׂה שִׁשָּׁה קְרָשִׁים: 23 וּשְׁנֵי קְרָשִׁים תַּעֲשֶׂה לִמְקֻצְעֹת הַמִּשְׁכָּן בַּיַּרְכָתָיִם: 24 וְיִהְיוּ תֹאֲמִים מִלְּמַטָּה וְיַחְדָּו יִהְיוּ תַמִּים עַל־רֹאשׁוֹ אֶל־הַטַּבַּעַת הָאֶחָת כֵּן יִהְיֶה לִשְׁנֵיהֶם לִשְׁנֵי הַמִּקְצֹעֹת יִהְיוּ: 25 וְהָיוּ שְׁמֹנָה קְרָשִׁים וְאַדְנֵיהֶם כֶּסֶף שִׁשָּׁה עָשָׂר אֲדָנִים שְׁנֵי אֲדָנִים תַּחַת הַקֶּרֶשׁ הָאֶחָד וּשְׁנֵי אֲדָנִים תַּחַת הַקֶּרֶשׁ הָאֶחָד: 26 וְעָשִׂיתָ בְרִיחִם עֲצֵי שִׁטִּים חֲמִשָּׁה לְקַרְשֵׁי צֶלַע־הַמִּשְׁכָּן הָאֶחָד: 27 וַחֲמִשָּׁה בְרִיחִם לְקַרְשֵׁי צֶלַע־הַמִּשְׁכָּן הַשֵּׁנִית וַחֲמִשָּׁה בְרִיחִם לְקַרְשֵׁי צֶלַע הַמִּשְׁכָּן לַיַּרְכָתַיִם יָמָּה: 28 וְהַבְּרִיחַ הַתִּיכֹן בְּתוֹךְ הַקְּרָשִׁים מַבְרִחַ מִן־הַקָּצֶה אֶל־הַקָּצֶה: 29 וְאֶת־הַקְּרָשִׁים תְּצַפֶּה זָהָב וְאֶת־טַבְּעֹתֵיהֶם תַּעֲשֶׂה זָהָב בָּתִּים לַבְּרִיחִם וְצִפִּיתָ אֶת־הַבְּרִיחִם זָהָב: 30 וַהֲקֵמֹתָ אֶת־הַמִּשְׁכָּן כְּמִשְׁפָּטוֹ אֲשֶׁר הָרְאֵיתָ בָּהָר: ס חמישי

19. sockets Hebrew 'eden can also mean "base, pedestal."[18]

22. the rear Hebrew yarkatayim, literally "two thighs," is often used figuratively to connote the extremities, remotest parts, in this case, the west.[19]

to the west Hebrew yammah, literally "seaward," that is, in the direction of the Mediterranean.

23. corners Hebrew mekutsa'ot (miktso'ot in v. 24 and elsewhere) is an architectural term for some kind of special corner structure. Here it seems to involve two extra supports, one at each corner of the western wall.[20]

24. This verse has not been satisfactorily interpreted. It apparently means that the corner buttresses are to be perfectly aligned and secured at both top and bottom.

match ... terminate The Hebrew features the word play to'amim = tammim. The first verb means "to twin."

26. bars Hebrew beriah denotes a crossbar, usually one that secures doors and gates.[21] The location and arrangement of the bars here are uncertain.

30. This refers back to 25:9.

THE INNER CURTAIN (*parokhet*) (vv. 31–35)

The Tabernacle is to be partitioned into two unequal sections by means of a dividing curtain, or veil, called in Hebrew *parokhet*. Its function is stated in verse 33. The inner section will form a perfect cube

³¹You shall make a curtain of blue, purple, and crimson yarns, and fine twisted linen; it shall have a design of cherubim worked into it. ³²Hang it upon four posts of acacia wood overlaid with gold and having hooks of gold, [set] in four sockets of silver. ³³Hang the curtain under the clasps, and carry the Ark of the Pact there, behind the curtain, so that the curtain shall serve you as a partition between the Holy and the Holy of Holies. ³⁴Place the cover upon the Ark of the Pact in the Holy of Holies. ³⁵Place the table outside the curtain, and the lampstand by the south wall of the Tabernacle opposite the table, which is to be placed by the north wall.

³⁶You shall make a screen for the entrance of the Tent, of blue, purple, and crimson yarns, and fine twisted linen, done in embroidery. ³⁷Make five posts of acacia wood for

31 וְעָשִׂיתָ פָרֹכֶת תְּכֵלֶת וְאַרְגָּמָן וְתוֹלַעַת שָׁנִי וְשֵׁשׁ מָשְׁזָר מַעֲשֵׂה חֹשֵׁב יַעֲשֶׂה אֹתָהּ כְּרֻבִים:
32 וְנָתַתָּה אֹתָהּ עַל־אַרְבָּעָה עַמּוּדֵי שִׁטִּים מְצֻפִּים זָהָב וָוֵיהֶם זָהָב עַל־אַרְבָּעָה אַדְנֵי־כָסֶף:
33 וְנָתַתָּה אֶת־הַפָּרֹכֶת תַּחַת הַקְּרָסִים וְהֵבֵאתָ שָׁמָּה מִבֵּית לַפָּרֹכֶת אֵת אֲרוֹן הָעֵדוּת וְהִבְדִּילָה הַפָּרֹכֶת לָכֶם בֵּין הַקֹּדֶשׁ וּבֵין קֹדֶשׁ הַקֳּדָשִׁים: 34 וְנָתַתָּ אֶת־הַכַּפֹּרֶת עַל אֲרוֹן הָעֵדֻת בְּקֹדֶשׁ הַקֳּדָשִׁים: 35 וְשַׂמְתָּ אֶת־הַשֻּׁלְחָן מִחוּץ לַפָּרֹכֶת וְאֶת־הַמְּנֹרָה נֹכַח הַשֻּׁלְחָן עַל צֶלַע הַמִּשְׁכָּן תֵּימָנָה וְהַשֻּׁלְחָן תִּתֵּן עַל־צֶלַע צָפוֹן:
36 וְעָשִׂיתָ מָסָךְ לְפֶתַח הָאֹהֶל תְּכֵלֶת וְאַרְגָּמָן וְתוֹלַעַת שָׁנִי וְשֵׁשׁ מָשְׁזָר מַעֲשֵׂה רֹקֵם:

measuring 10 cubits (15 ft. = 4.6 m.) on each side. This is the Holy of Holies, which will contain the Ark and the *kapporet*, as prescribed in 25:17. The outer section will measure 10 cubits in width, 20 cubits in length, and 10 cubits in height (15 ft. × 30 ft. × 15 ft.). It is called the "Holy Place" and will receive the table, the menorah, and the altar of incense.

The *parokhet*, a term used in the Bible solely in the present context, is also variously known as "the curtain for screening" (Heb. *parokhet ha-masakh*)²² because of its function in screening off the most sacred area; "the curtain of the Pact" (Heb. *parokhet ha'edut*),²³ an ellipsis for "the curtain of the Ark of the Pact," because the latter was veiled by it; and "the curtain of the Shrine" (Heb. *parokhet ha-kodesh*),²⁴ referring to the Holy Place in front of it. The term *parokhet* probably derives from a stem meaning "to bar the way, to mark off an area."²⁵

The *parokhet* is made from the same fabric and designed with the same colors as the lowest coverings. It, too, is adorned with figures of cherubim. Its size is not given, but both reason and tradition require 10 × 10 cubits (15 ft. square = 4.6 m. sq.).²⁶

In later Hebrew the term *parokhet* was transferred to the ornamented curtain covering the Ark that contains the Torah scrolls in the synagogue. Ashkenazim hang it in front of the doors, while Sephardim place it behind them. Jewish religious law requires that a *parokhet* no longer in use not be destroyed; it must be stored away.²⁷

32. hooks Hebrew *vav*, the name of the sixth letter of the Hebrew alphabet. In the ancient script it was shaped like a two-pronged fork.²⁸

sockets of silver In 38:27, the same are called "the sockets of the sanctuary."

33. Ramban notes that the sequence here does not reflect the reality of the construction and assembly. As 40:3 shows, the Ark was to be put in place first and the curtain thereafter.

THE OUTER CURTAIN (vv. 36–37)

A second screen (Heb. *masakh*)²⁹ separated the entrance of the Holy Place on the eastern side from the outer court. It was made of the same multicolored fabric as the *parokhet* but was not decorated with cherubs. It also differed from it in that it was embroidered (v. 36) and rested on five pillars instead of four, and its pillars fitted into bronze rather than silver sockets.

36. done in embroidery Hebrew *ma'aseh rokem*, another specialized type of weaving, required less skill than that required for the coverings of the Tabernacle and the *parokhet*.

the screen and overlay them with gold—their hooks being of gold—and cast for them five sockets of copper.

27 You shall make the altar of acacia wood, five cubits long and five cubits wide—the altar is to be square—and three cubits high. ²Make its horns on the four corners, the horns to be of one piece with it; and overlay it with copper. ³Make the pails for removing its ashes, as well as its scrapers, basins, flesh hooks, and fire pans—make all its utensils of copper. ⁴Make for it a grating of meshwork in

³⁷ וְעָשִׂ֤יתָ לַמָּסָךְ֙ חֲמִשָּׁ֣ה עַמּוּדֵ֣י שִׁטִּ֔ים וְצִפִּיתָ֤ אֹתָם֙ זָהָ֔ב וָוֵיהֶ֖ם זָהָ֑ב וְיָצַקְתָּ֣ לָהֶ֔ם חֲמִשָּׁ֖ה אַדְנֵ֥י נְחֹֽשֶׁת׃ ס ששי

כ״ז וְעָשִׂ֤יתָ אֶת־הַמִּזְבֵּ֨חַ֙ עֲצֵ֣י שִׁטִּ֔ים חָמֵשׁ֩ אַמּ֨וֹת אֹ֜רֶךְ וְחָמֵ֧שׁ אַמּ֣וֹת רֹ֗חַב רָב֤וּעַ יִהְיֶה֙ הַמִּזְבֵּ֔חַ וְשָׁלֹ֥שׁ אַמּ֖וֹת קֹמָתֽוֹ׃ ² וְעָשִׂ֣יתָ קַרְנֹתָ֗יו עַ֚ל אַרְבַּ֣ע פִּנֹּתָ֔יו מִמֶּ֖נּוּ תִּהְיֶ֣יןָ קַרְנֹתָ֑יו וְצִפִּיתָ֥ אֹת֖וֹ נְחֹֽשֶׁת׃ ³ וְעָשִׂ֤יתָ סִּֽירֹתָיו֙ לְדַשְּׁנ֔וֹ וְיָעָ֗יו וּמִזְרְקֹתָיו֙ וּמִזְלְגֹתָ֣יו וּמַחְתֹּתָ֔יו לְכָל־כֵּלָ֖יו תַּעֲשֶׂ֥ה נְחֹֽשֶׁת׃ ⁴ וְעָשִׂ֤יתָ לּוֹ֙ מִכְבָּ֔ר מַעֲשֵׂ֖ה רֶ֣שֶׁת נְחֹ֑שֶׁת

CHAPTER 27   THE OUTER ALTAR OF SACRIFICES AND ITS ACCESSORIES (vv. 1–8)

The prescriptions now move from the Holy Place to the enclosure of the Tabernacle. Once again, they begin with the most important item in it, the "altar of burnt offering" (Heb. *mizbaḥ ha-ʿolah*),[1] so-called because that specific sacrifice, performed twice daily,[2] was the mainstay of the cult. This altar was also known as "the altar of bronze,"[3] on account of its metal overlay and also to distinguish it from the altar of gold, which was used for incense. A third name, found in rabbinic literature, is "the outer altar." This name derives from its location and is to be contrasted with the "inner altar," the golden incense altar that stood in the Holy Place.[4]

The precise position of the altar of burnt offering is not specified, but its approximate location is given in 30:18 and 40:6–7,29–30. The details of its construction are quite complicated and imperfectly understood. It formed a square of 5 cubits (7½ ft. = 2.3 m.) and stood 3 cubits high (4½ ft. = 1.35 m.). It also had four bronzed, horn-shaped projections on top of each corner. The inside was hollow. No mention is made of the "top" of the altar, in contrast to the incense altar (30:3). It is assumed that it was filled with fieldstones and earth in the wilderness encampments. This would have satisfied the requirement of 20:24 that there be "an altar of earth." It would also have protected the wooden structure below from the fire on the altar. Porterage was facilitated by means of bronzed poles inserted, when necessary, into rings affixed to its sides.

1. *the altar*   The patriarchs frequently built altars, and Moses himself did so twice.[5] Since an altar was an indispensable implement of worship and ritual, its presence in the Tabernacle is taken for granted—hence, the use of the definite article. The altar for burnt offerings uncovered in the Judean temple at Arad in the Negeb corresponds exactly to the dimensions of the altar in the Tabernacle.[6]

2.   The horn-shaped projections at the upper corners were to be carved out of the wooden structure and then bronzed, so as to become integral parts of the altar. They were not to be made separately and then attached to it. According to the tradition cited in Zevaḥim 54b, they were hollow. The golden altar of incense also had horns, and Ezekiel envisages a horned altar for the rebuilt Temple.[7] A Canaanite horned altar was found at Megiddo, and Israelite examples have been excavated at both Dan and Beer-sheba.[8]

All this shows that great importance was attached to the horns, a conclusion reinforced by the ritual connected with them. They were daubed with blood from the slaughtered animal sacrifices in rites of consecration and expiation.[9] It also seems to have been an ancient custom for fugitives to seek asylum by clutching the horns of the altar, as demonstrated by the stories in 1 Kings 1:5–53 and 2:28–34. See Comment to Exodus 21:14.

The Megiddo altar and others prove that the horned altar was not exclusively Israelite. Its origin and significance are shrouded in mystery. The horn may have been widely regarded as a symbol of strength, power, and fertility.[10] The altar horns also appear to have served a practical function; as Psalm 118:27 indicates: "Bind the festal offering to the horns of the altar with cords."

copper; and on the mesh make four copper rings at its four corners. ⁵Set the mesh below, under the ledge of the altar, so that it extends to the middle of the altar. ⁶And make poles for the altar, poles of acacia wood, and overlay them with copper. ⁷The poles shall be inserted into the rings, so that the poles remain on the two sides of the altar when it is carried. ⁸Make it hollow, of boards. As you were shown on the mountain, so shall they be made.

וְעָשִׂיתָ עַל־הָרֶשֶׁת אַרְבַּע טַבְּעֹת נְחֹשֶׁת עַל אַרְבַּע קְצוֹתָיו: 5 וְנָתַתָּה אֹתָהּ תַּחַת כַּרְכֹּב הַמִּזְבֵּחַ מִלְּמָטָּה וְהָיְתָה הָרֶשֶׁת עַד חֲצִי הַמִּזְבֵּחַ: 6 וְעָשִׂיתָ בַדִּים לַמִּזְבֵּחַ בַּדֵּי עֲצֵי שִׁטִּים וְצִפִּיתָ אֹתָם נְחֹשֶׁת: 7 וְהוּבָא אֶת־בַּדָּיו בַּטַּבָּעֹת וְהָיוּ הַבַּדִּים עַל־שְׁתֵּי צַלְעֹת הַמִּזְבֵּחַ בִּשְׂאֵת אֹתוֹ: 8 נְבוּב לֻחֹת תַּעֲשֶׂה אֹתוֹ כַּאֲשֶׁר הֶרְאָה אֹתְךָ בָּהָר כֵּן יַעֲשׂוּ: ס   שביעי

3. Five accessories needed for the performance of the sacrificial rites are now listed. The number of each is not given.

pails Hebrew *sir* is usually a large vessel with a wide mouth.[11]

scrapers Hebrew *ya'eh* is a kind of shovel with which the refuse on the altar is gathered up and placed in the pails for removal.[12]

basins Hebrew *mizrak*, from the stem *z-r-k*, "to sprinkle," is a vessel in which the blood of the sacrificial animal is collected for sprinkling on the altar.[13] This exercise was an integral and important part of the ritual. The biblical idea is that blood constitutes the life essence and therefore belongs exclusively to God, the Giver of all life.[14] That is why the Torah strictly and repeatedly forbids its consumption.[15] The act of sprinkling the blood on the altar symbolizes its return to God. See Comment to 24:6.

flesh hooks Hebrew *mizlagah* is an implement that is dug into the flesh to turn it over while it is being burnt on the altar.[16] In 1 Samuel 2:13 a *mazleg*, used on the meat by the priest, is clearly a three-pronged large fork.

fire pans Hebrew *maḥtah*. See Comment to 25:38. The verbal stem means "to scoop up coals, to rake embers." Thus, the noun would be an instrument with which to perform this task.[17]

4–5. More detailed instructions for the design of the altar are now given.

4. ***a grating*** Hebrew *mikhbar* is presumed to be connected with *kevarah*, which means "a sieve" in Amos 9:9 and later Hebrew. It is here further defined by "a meshwork." As Rashi notes, the order of the Hebrew words is inverted and should be understood to mean, "Make for it a bronze grating, a meshwork." The function of this item is not defined. It is to be placed beneath a ledge that runs all the way around the altar. It may perhaps be intended to catch falling embers.

5. ***the ledge*** Hebrew *karkov*. It may have been purely decorative. The Megiddo and Arad altars both have ledges near the top, although the two items are not identical. According to some rabbinic authorities, the ledge was a projection that served as a walkway for the priests officiating on the altar.[18]

the middle Depending on the category of sacrifice, the blood had to be sprinkled either above or below this line.[19]

6–7. ***poles*** For porterage.

8. Assyrian altars were also often hollow.

THE ENCLOSURE (vv. 9–19)

As in all temples and sanctuaries, the sacred area must be well demarcated to separate it from the profane space outside. The prescriptions now deal with the enclosure of the entire Tabernacle compound, termed *ḥatser* in Hebrew. This area constitutes an oblong measuring 100 cubits (150 ft. = 45.7 m.) on the north and south sides, and 50 cubits (75 ft. = 22.9 m.) on the east and west sides, thus giving a total of 5,000 square cubits (approximately 11,250 square feet). The perimeter measures 300

⁹You shall make the enclosure of the Tabernacle:

On the south side, a hundred cubits of hangings of fine twisted linen for the length of the enclosure on that side—¹⁰with its twenty posts and their twenty sockets of copper, the hooks and bands of the posts to be of silver.

¹¹Again a hundred cubits of hangings for its length along the north side—with its twenty posts and their twenty sockets of copper, the hooks and bands of the posts to be of silver.

¹²For the width of the enclosure, on the west side, fifty cubits of hangings, with their ten posts and their ten sockets.

¹³For the width of the enclosure on the front, or east side, fifty cubits: ¹⁴fifteen cubits of hangings on the one flank, with their three posts and their three sockets; ¹⁵fifteen cubits of hangings on the other flank, with their three posts and their three sockets; ¹⁶and for the gate of the enclosure,

9 וְעָשִׂ֗יתָ אֵ֚ת חֲצַ֣ר הַמִּשְׁכָּ֔ן
לִפְאַ֣ת נֶֽגֶב־תֵּימָ֗נָה קְלָעִ֤ים לֶֽחָצֵר֙ שֵׁ֣שׁ
מָשְׁזָ֔ר מֵאָ֤ה בָֽאַמָּה֙ אֹ֔רֶךְ לַפֵּאָ֖ה הָֽאֶחָֽת: 10 וְעַמֻּדָ֣יו עֶשְׂרִ֔ים וְאַדְנֵיהֶ֥ם עֶשְׂרִ֖ים נְחֹ֑שֶׁת וָוֵ֧י
הָֽעַמֻּדִ֛ים וַֽחֲשֻׁקֵיהֶ֖ם כָּֽסֶף: 11 וְכֵ֨ן לִפְאַ֤ת צָפוֹן֙ בָּאֹ֔רֶךְ קְלָעִ֖ים מֵ֣אָה אֹ֑רֶךְ וְעַמֻּדָ֣יו עֶשְׂרִ֔ים וְאַדְנֵיהֶ֥ם עֶשְׂרִ֖ים נְחֹ֑שֶׁת וָוֵ֧י
הָֽעַמֻּדִ֛ים וַֽחֲשֻׁקֵיהֶ֖ם כָּֽסֶף: 12 וְרֹ֤חַב הֶֽחָצֵר֙ לִפְאַת־יָ֔ם קְלָעִ֖ים חֲמִשִּׁ֣ים
אַמָּ֑ה עַמֻּֽדֵיהֶ֥ם עֲשָׂרָ֖ה וְאַדְנֵיהֶ֥ם עֲשָׂרָֽה: 13 וְרֹ֣חַב הֶֽחָצֵ֗ר לִפְאַ֛ת קֵ֥דְמָה מִזְרָ֖חָה חֲמִשִּׁ֣ים
אַמָּֽה: 14 וַֽחֲמֵ֨שׁ עֶשְׂרֵ֥ה אַמָּ֛ה קְלָעִ֖ים לַכָּתֵ֑ף
עַמֻּֽדֵיהֶ֥ם שְׁלֹשָׁ֖ה וְאַדְנֵיהֶ֥ם שְׁלֹשָֽׁה: 15 וְלַכָּתֵף֙
הַשֵּׁנִ֔ית חֲמֵ֥שׁ עֶשְׂרֵ֖ה קְלָעִ֑ים עַמֻּֽדֵיהֶ֥ם שְׁלֹשָׁ֖ה
וְאַדְנֵיהֶ֖ם שְׁלֹשָֽׁה: 16 וּלְשַׁ֨עַר֙ הֶֽחָצֵ֔ר מָסָ֣ךְ ׀

וְעַמֻּדָיו ק׳ v. 11.

cubits (450 ft. = 137.2 m.) and is surrounded on three sides by hangings of fine white twisted linen fabric. On the east side, the entrance, an area of 15 cubits from each end toward the center, was covered by hangings; the 20 remaining cubits in the middle were enclosed by a screen. The hangings were to be suspended from sixty pillars, each 5 cubits (7½ ft. = 2.3 m.) high and spaced at intervals of 5 cubits. These are distributed as follows: twenty pillars on both north and south sides, and ten on the west side. Three pillars are to uphold the fabrics on each of the extremities of the east side, and four to support the entrance screen. The pillars rest in sockets of bronze. The hangings are held down by pegs and guy-ropes (v. 19).

The instructions do not fix the location of the Tabernacle proper within the larger area of the enclosure. It is widely assumed that the entrance to the Holy Place on the eastern side was positioned along a north-south line that divided the enclosure into two equal squares of 50 by 50 cubits. Since the length of the Tabernacle on the east-west axis was 30 cubits, it follows that 20 cubits separated its western wall from the western boundary of the enclosure. It is also likely that the Tabernacle was equidistant from the enclosure on the northern and southern sides. Because the Tabernacle was 10 cubits wide, there would have been a space of 20 cubits on either side.

Such positioning would have placed the point of intersection of the diagonals of the western square precisely in the center of the Holy of Holies. It is likely that the Ark was at exactly this location. Similarly, for the sake of symmetry, the altar of sacrifice would most likely have been placed at the point of intersection of the diagonals of the other square, the outer court, east of the Holy Place. Between it and the altar stood a bronze laver (30:18; 38:8).

9. *south side* See Comment to 26:18.

hangings Hebrew kelaʿim (sing. kelaʿ), literally "plaited, basket work," probably refers to the type of textile manufactured by basketry technique. Linen of this type has been found in Egypt dating to around 2500 B.C.E..[20]

10. *posts* According to 38:17, the bronze posts had silver tops.

bands The stem of Hebrew ḥashuk means "to be attached to." Some kind of fillet or connecting rod seems intended.

12. *west* See Comment to 26:22.

13. *on the front, or east side* Hebrew kedmah mizraḥah, literally "on the front toward the rising sun."

a screen of twenty cubits, of blue, purple, and crimson yarns, and fine twisted linen, done in embroidery, with their four posts and their four sockets.

¹⁷All the posts round the enclosure shall be banded with silver and their hooks shall be of silver; their sockets shall be of copper.

¹⁸The length of the enclosure shall be a hundred cubits, and the width fifty throughout; and the height five cubits—[with hangings] of fine twisted linen. The sockets shall be of copper: ¹⁹all the utensils of the Tabernacle, for all its service, as well as all its pegs and all the pegs of the court, shall be of copper.

עֶשְׂרִ֣ים אַמָּ֗ה תְּכֵ֧לֶת וְאַרְגָּמָ֛ן וְתוֹלַ֥עַת שָׁנִ֖י
וְשֵׁ֣שׁ מָשְׁזָ֑ר מַעֲשֵׂ֣ה רֹקֵ֔ם עַמֻּדֵיהֶ֣ם אַרְבָּעָ֔ה
וְאַדְנֵיהֶ֖ם אַרְבָּעָֽה: מפטיר

¹⁷ כָּל־עַמּוּדֵ֨י הֶֽחָצֵ֤ר סָבִיב֙ מְחֻשָּׁקִ֣ים כֶּ֔סֶף
וָוֵיהֶ֖ם כָּ֑סֶף וְאַדְנֵיהֶ֖ם נְחֹֽשֶׁת:

¹⁸ אֹ֣רֶךְ הֶֽחָצֵר֩ מֵאָ֨ה בָֽאַמָּ֜ה וְרֹ֣חַב ׀
חֲמִשִּׁ֣ים בַּחֲמִשִּׁ֗ים וְקֹמָ֛ה חָמֵ֥שׁ אַמּ֖וֹת שֵׁ֣שׁ מָשְׁזָ֑ר
וְאַדְנֵיהֶ֖ם נְחֹֽשֶׁת: ¹⁹ לְכֹל֙ כְּלֵ֣י הַמִּשְׁכָּ֔ן בְּכֹ֖ל
עֲבֹֽדָת֑וֹ וְכָל־יְתֵֽדֹתָ֛יו וְכָל־יִתְדֹ֥ת הֶחָצֵ֖ר נְחֹֽשֶׁת:
ס

TETSAVVEH

²⁰You shall further instruct the Israelites to bring you clear oil of beaten olives for lighting, for kindling lamps regularly. ²¹Aaron and his sons shall set them up in the

תצוה

²⁰ וְאַתָּ֞ה תְּצַוֶּ֣ה ׀ אֶת־בְּנֵ֣י יִשְׂרָאֵ֗ל וְיִקְח֨וּ
אֵלֶ֜יךָ שֶׁ֣מֶן זַ֥יִת זָ֛ךְ כָּתִ֖ית לַמָּא֑וֹר לְהַעֲלֹ֥ת נֵ֖ר
תָּמִֽיד: ²¹ בְּאֹ֣הֶל מוֹעֵד֩ מִח֨וּץ לַפָּרֹ֜כֶת אֲשֶׁ֣ר

---

16. *done in embroidery*   See Comment to 26:36.

A SUMMATION   (vv. 18–19)

19. *the Tabernacle*   Here, Hebrew *mishkan* means the entire Tabernacle compound and not the Tabernacle proper, in which the accessories were of gold, not bronze.

pegs   Pegs and guy-ropes are mentioned several times in connection with the enclosure.[21]

THE OIL FOR LIGHTING (vv. 20–21)

Tetsavveh   The instructions for constructing the menorah have been given above. Here the text deals with the fuel that is to be used to provide the illumination. "Oil for lighting" was originally listed in 25:6 but without any specification.

20. *You shall further instruct*   Placing the personal pronoun before the verb at the beginning of the sentence is a way of introducing a new topic.[22]

to bring you   The same Hebrew verb *l-k-ḥ*, literally "to take," as is used in 25:2. Ramban points out that the frequently used formula "they shall make" would be inappropriate here because they had no facilities in the wilderness for acquiring olives and extracting the oil. Oil had to be brought in its prepared state. Hence, it was to be brought to Moses for inspection as to its quality. The oil was either included among the supplies carried out of Egypt or was acquired in the wilderness from caravaneers.

clear oil of beaten olives   The oil listed in 25:6, like the other items mentioned there, refers to a one-time donation for the making of the Tabernacle. The present prescription mandates an ongoing obligation.[23] Oil extracted from olives is specified because several other sources of oil, including sesame seed, flax, and animal fats, were utilized in the ancient Near East. The oil used for the Tabernacle lamps had to be "clear" (Heb. *zakh*), that is, refined so as to be free of lees. This condition was obtained by pounding the olives in a mortar with a pestle rather than by grinding them in a mill—hence Hebrew *katit*, "beaten."[24] The oil was then passed through a strainer, resulting in a

Tent of Meeting, outside the curtain which is over [the Ark of] the Pact, [to burn] from evening to morning before the LORD. It shall be a due from the Israelites for all time, throughout the ages.

עַל־הָעֵדָת יַעֲרֹךְ אֹתוֹ אַהֲרֹן וּבָנָיו מֵעֶרֶב עַד־
בֹּקֶר לִפְנֵי יְהֹוָה חֻקַּת עוֹלָם לְדֹרֹתָם מֵאֵת בְּנֵי
יִשְׂרָאֵל: ס

clear, refined grade that yields a far brighter light and produces a minimum of smoke. The category of *zakh* oil is used in the Bible exclusively for the Tabernacle lamps. Baḥya points out that this is contrary to everyday practice in which the clear olive oil of this grade was reserved for culinary purposes, while the cruder type was used as fuel for lamps, that is, "lampante oil."

for kindling lamps Hebrew *ner* is here a collective, as shown by the parallel passage in Leviticus 24:2–4, in which *ner* and the plural *nerot* are used interchangeably.

regularly Hebrew *tamid* may mean "with unfailing regularity" or "uninterruptedly." Thus, the *'olat tamid* refers to the burnt offering brought twice daily, while *'esh tamed* is the fire that burns perpetually on the altar and is never extinguished. Regarding the present case, verse 21 and Leviticus 24:3 explicitly state that the lamps are to burn from evening until morning.[25] Further, 1 Samuel 3:3 mentions that "the lamp of God had not yet gone out" in the sanctuary at Shiloh. Accordingly, as Rashi and Ibn Ezra recognize, *ner tamid* means a lamp kindled on a regular basis each evening. However, Josephus, referring to the Second Temple, records that on the lampstand "there is a light which is never extinguished by day or night."[26] Ramban is of the opinion that the *ner tamid* is indeed a perpetually lit lamp from which light was taken at dusk each day to kindle the menorah.

In later Judaism the *ner tamid* was understood to mean "eternal light" and to refer to the perpetually lit lamp usually suspended from the ceiling above the Torah Ark in the synagogue. This lamp serves as a symbolic reminder of the original menorah, although the assigned place of that lampstand was on the western side of the Tabernacle, not on the eastern side where the "eternal light" is now placed in synagogues. The *ner tamid* also symbolizes the Divine Presence, the Shekhinah that accompanies the community of Israel through its dispersal.[27]

21. Aaron and his sons Rather, "Aaron or his sons," as Ḥizkuni observes. This tradition that the ritual of lighting the lamps may be performed by any priest is reflected in 2 Chronicles 13:10–11. It is also taken for granted in the description of the Temple service given in Mishnah Tamid 3:9. In other biblical passages, however, the duty to attend to the lamps seems to be the exclusive prerogative of Aaron, that is, of the High Priest. This apparently variant tradition is found in Exodus 30:7–8, Leviticus 24:3, and Numbers 8:1–3.[28] Mention of Aaron anticipates the next section, for he has not yet been appointed to the priesthood.

Tent of Meeting Hebrew *'ohel mo'ed* is a variant term for the Tabernacle. See Comment to 25:8. For the understanding of *mo'ed*, see Comment to 25:22. The designation "Tent of Meeting" stresses the oracular function of the Tabernacle: that is, the place where God communicates His word to Moses.

outside the curtain That is, in the Holy Place.

a due Provision of the oil is henceforth to be a permanent public obligation.

CHAPTER 28 <u>THE PRIESTHOOD AND THE PRIESTLY VESTMENTS   (vv. 1–43)</u>

A sanctuary requires officiants, and Moses is ordered to appoint Aaron and his sons to fill this role. Clearly, the office is to be hereditary.

Just as sacred space must be differentiated from profane space, so the occupants of the sacred office must be distinguishable from the laity. Hence, special attire, the insignia of office, is ordained for Aaron, the archetypal High Priest, and for his sons, the priests of lower rank.

The main concern of this chapter is with the vestments of the High Priest, the chief cultic officiant. The vestments of the ordinary priests are detailed only in verses 40 and 42. However, there

28 You shall bring forward your brother Aaron, with his sons, from among the Israelites, to serve Me as priests: Aaron, Nadab and Abihu, Eleazar and Ithamar, the sons of Aaron. ²Make sacral vestments for your brother Aaron, for dignity and adornment. ³Next you shall instruct all who are

כ"ח וְאַתָּה הַקְרֵב אֵלֶיךָ אֶת־אַהֲרֹן אָחִיךָ
וְאֶת־בָּנָיו אִתּוֹ מִתּוֹךְ בְּנֵי יִשְׂרָאֵל לְכַהֲנוֹ־לִי
אַהֲרֹן נָדָב וַאֲבִיהוּא אֶלְעָזָר וְאִיתָמָר בְּנֵי אַהֲרֹן:
2 וְעָשִׂיתָ בִגְדֵי־קֹדֶשׁ לְאַהֲרֹן אָחִיךָ לְכָבוֹד
וּלְתִפְאָרֶת: 3 וְאַתָּה תְּדַבֵּר אֶל־כָּל־חַכְמֵי־לֵב

is an overlap in the two sets of ceremonial robes. The High Priest dresses in eight articles of clothing, the ordinary priest, in four of these (with some slight differences); the description of the latter is really encompassed by the detailed account of the former. No mention is made of footwear, for the priests officiated barefoot. See Comment to 3:5.[1]

THE HIGH PRIEST (vv. 1–39)

The attire of the High Priest is colorful, distinguished by the prominent use of gold. Hence, in rabbinic Hebrew parlance it is referred to as *bigdei zahav*, "golden attire." On Yom Kippur, however, the officiant performed his duties clothed in white linen garments, as prescribed in Leviticus 16:4. These are called *bigdei lavan*, "white attire."[2]

Some idea of the impression made upon the worshipers by the appearance of the High Priest attired in his full regalia may be gained from this description in Ben Sira (ca. 190 B.C.E.) 50:5ff: "How glorious was he when / he looked forth from the Tent / and emerged from behind the / Temple veil! / He was like the morning star / appearing between the clouds, / Like the full moon on a festival day. . . ."

Although the various items of dress are given in detail, not all the specialized technical terms have been fully clarified. Our understanding is enhanced by the living traditions from Second Temple times, which are found in Ben Sira,[3] Josephus,[4] and rabbinic literature.[5] But allowances must be made for adjustments and changes that may have occurred over the centuries.

1. You shall bring forward To the Tent of Meeting, once it is erected.[6] Until now Moses has acted in the capacity of chief cultic officiant; he is the one who is to "bring forward," that is, induct into office, the newly appointed chief priest.[7]

from among the Israelites 1 Chronicles 23:13 explains this phrase: "Aaron was set apart, he and his sons, forever, to be consecrated as most holy, to make burnt offerings to the LORD and serve Him and pronounce blessings in His name forever."[8]

Nadab and Abihu Aaron's four sons are first listed in the genealogy of 6:23. The two mentioned here accompanied their father and the elders of Israel partway up Mount Sinai, to the point from which Moses ascended alone to perform the covenantal ceremony, as described in 24:1–11. They later perished while discharging their priestly duties.[9]

Eleazar and Ithamar These two sons continued to exercise the priestly functions after the death of their brothers.[10] Eleazar succeeded to the high priesthood on the death of his father.[11] Ithamar directed the building of the Tabernacle.[12] The priestly house of Eli seems to have been descended from him.[13]

2. Make That is, you are responsible for having them made.

sacral vestments Hebrew *bigdei kodesh*,[14] so-called either because the High Priest wore them while officiating in the Holy Place[15] or because the vestments themselves were regarded as endowed with sanctity since they were anointed with the sacred oil, as 29:21 prescribes.[16] They are also called "service vestments" (Heb. *bigdei serad*)[17] and "officiating vestments" (*bigdei sharet*)[18] in rabbinic sources.

for dignity and adornment As befits the exalted office. Maimonides points out that this attire was worn not for the self-glorification of the High Priest but solely because it was divinely commanded.[19]

skillful, whom I have endowed with the gift of skill, to make Aaron's vestments, for consecrating him to serve Me as priest. ⁴These are the vestments they are to make: a breastpiece, an ephod, a robe, a fringed tunic, a headdress, and a sash. They shall make those sacral vestments for your brother Aaron and his sons, for priestly service to Me; ⁵they, therefore, shall receive the gold, the blue, purple, and crimson yarns, and the fine linen.

אֲשֶׁר מִלֵּאתִיו רוּחַ חָכְמָה וְעָשׂוּ אֶת־בִּגְדֵי אַהֲרֹן לְקַדְּשׁוֹ לְכַהֲנוֹ־לִי: 4 וְאֵלֶּה הַבְּגָדִים אֲשֶׁר יַעֲשׂוּ חֹשֶׁן וְאֵפוֹד וּמְעִיל וּכְתֹנֶת תַּשְׁבֵּץ מִצְנֶפֶת וְאַבְנֵט וְעָשׂוּ בִגְדֵי־קֹדֶשׁ לְאַהֲרֹן אָחִיךָ וּלְבָנָיו לְכַהֲנוֹ־לִי: 5 וְהֵם יִקְחוּ אֶת־הַזָּהָב וְאֶת־הַתְּכֵלֶת וְאֶת־הָאַרְגָּמָן וְאֶת־תּוֹלַעַת הַשָּׁנִי וְאֶת־הַשֵּׁשׁ: פ

3. **skillful** Literally, "wise of heart." The heart is regarded as the seat of intelligence. Wisdom in the biblical view, is as much concerned with the practical realities of life as with considerations of moral conduct. The term is therefore frequently applied to the possession of exceptional skill and talent in a specialized field. The "gift of skill" is literally "the spirit of wisdom," which is considered to be divinely bestowed.[20]

4. Only six of the eight articles of clothing are listed. The other two—the frontlet and the breeches—are prescribed in verses 36–38 and 42–43. Each item is separately described below.

5. These elements are made of the same materials as the Tabernacle fabrics.

they . . . shall receive That is, the skilled craftsmen are to receive these contributions directly from the people.[21]

The Ephod (vv. 6–12)

Following the pattern of the prescriptions for building the Tabernacle, the instructions for the priestly vestments commence with the most important item, the ephod. Its preeminence is indicated by its utilization of all five colors. And here again the definite article implies an object already well known. This is borne out by the use of the word in the cognate form *ipd* in Ugaritic,[22] where it refers to some kind of expensive robe, and in the form *epattu* in Assyrian and Akkadian,[23] where it also signifies some costly garment.

An ephod is mentioned several times in the Bible, but the name seems to apply to different kinds of cultic objects, some of them idolatrous. It is connected with *teraphim* in many passages, and also with sculptured and molten images, all of which are illegitimate in the religion of Israel.[24] Gideon is said to have made a golden ephod after which "all Israel went astray" and which "became a snare to Gideon and his household."[25] In 1 Samuel 21:10 it is related that an ephod had a fixed place in the sanctuary at Nob and that Goliath's sword was kept behind it. Elsewhere the ephod was an object that could be "carried" in the hand[26] and that was "girded on" the body.[27] It is explicitly stated that it was used to ascertain divine will.[28] This is particularly pertinent to the understanding of the function of the ephod as a vestment of the High Priest because the "breastpiece" (Heb. *ḥoshen*) in verse 29 was attached to it and served a similar purpose.

It is not easy to reconcile all these varied references to the ephod. It may quite possibly have been an item of apparel that was once widespread among the upper classes in the Near East and that eventually became outmoded. The innate conservatism of religious institutions made for its retention in ecclesiastical circles alone, where it developed into a sacral vestment. A modern analogy to this process would be the distinctive dress of Hasidim, which evolved from the one-time attire of the Polish gentry. The association of the ephod with idols may derive from the pagan practice of robing the god.

The biblical description of the priest's ephod includes four elements: the main body of the garment, two shoulder straps, and a richly decorated band. Left unclear is whether the ephod covered the lower and/or upper parts of the body and whether the back and/or front. Josephus, himself a priest in the last days of the Second Temple, likens the ephod to the upper part of a woman's tunic that had shoulder straps and sleeves and was fastened by brooches—a sort of waistcoat.[29] Rashi

⁶They shall make the ephod, of gold, of blue, purple, and crimson yarns, and of fine twisted linen, worked into designs. ⁷It shall have two shoulder-pieces attached; they shall be attached at its two ends. ⁸And the decorated band that is upon it shall be made like it, of one piece with it: of gold, of blue, purple, and crimson yarns, and of fine twisted linen. ⁹Then take two lazuli stones and engrave on them the names of the sons of Israel: ¹⁰six of their names on the one stone, and the names of the remaining six on the other stone, in the order of their birth. ¹¹On the two stones you shall make seal engravings—the work of a lapidary—of the names of the sons of Israel. Having bordered them with frames of gold, ¹²attach the two stones to the shoulder-pieces of the ephod, as stones for remembrance of the Israelite people, whose names Aaron shall carry upon his two shoulder-pieces for remembrance before the LORD.

6 וְעָשׂוּ אֶת־הָאֵפֹד זָהָב תְּכֵלֶת וְאַרְגָּמָן תּוֹלַעַת שָׁנִי וְשֵׁשׁ מָשְׁזָר מַעֲשֵׂה חֹשֵׁב: 7 שְׁתֵּי כְתֵפֹת חֹבְרֹת יִהְיֶה־לּוֹ אֶל־שְׁנֵי קְצוֹתָיו וְחֻבָּר: 8 וְחֵשֶׁב אֲפֻדָּתוֹ אֲשֶׁר עָלָיו כְּמַעֲשֵׂהוּ מִמֶּנּוּ יִהְיֶה זָהָב תְּכֵלֶת וְאַרְגָּמָן וְתוֹלַעַת שָׁנִי וְשֵׁשׁ מָשְׁזָר: 9 וְלָקַחְתָּ אֶת־שְׁתֵּי אַבְנֵי־שֹׁהַם וּפִתַּחְתָּ עֲלֵיהֶם שְׁמוֹת בְּנֵי יִשְׂרָאֵל: 10 שִׁשָּׁה מִשְּׁמֹתָם עַל הָאֶבֶן הָאֶחָת וְאֶת־שְׁמוֹת הַשִּׁשָּׁה הַנּוֹתָרִים עַל־הָאֶבֶן הַשֵּׁנִית כְּתוֹלְדֹתָם: 11 מַעֲשֵׂה חָרַשׁ אֶבֶן פִּתּוּחֵי חֹתָם תְּפַתַּח אֶת־שְׁתֵּי הָאֲבָנִים עַל־שְׁמֹת בְּנֵי יִשְׂרָאֵל מֻסַבֹּת מִשְׁבְּצוֹת זָהָב תַּעֲשֶׂה אֹתָם: 12 וְשַׂמְתָּ אֶת־שְׁתֵּי הָאֲבָנִים עַל כִּתְפֹת הָאֵפֹד אַבְנֵי זִכָּרֹן לִבְנֵי יִשְׂרָאֵל וְנָשָׂא אַהֲרֹן אֶת־שְׁמוֹתָם לִפְנֵי יְהוָה עַל־שְׁתֵּי כְתֵפָיו לְזִכָּרֹן: ס שני

compares the ephod to a pinafore worn by upper-class Frenchwomen when they went horseback riding; that garment fully covers the upper part of the back. Rashbam describes it as being wrapped around the body from the loins down.

8. band Hebrew ḥeshev appears only in connection with the ephod. It probably derives from the stem ḥ-v-sh, "to bind," with the order of the second and third consonants reversed.[30]

9–12. The names of all the tribes engraved on the gems and affixed to his vestments serve as a perpetual and humbling reminder of the High Priest's role as the representative of the entire community of Israel before God.

9. engrave on them The technique of miniature engraving on precious stones was highly developed in the Near East. A gem-engraving industry existed in Egypt in the period of the Eighteenth Dynasty (16th–14th cent. B.C.E.).

10. in the order of their birth As recounted in Genesis 30 and 35:16–18. According to Josephus, the names of the six elder sons were listed on the stone of the right shoulder and the six others, on the left. Rabbi Hanina ben Gamaliel, in Sotah 36b, understood the arrangement to be that of the tribal listing in Exodus 1:1–5, which is matrilineal (see Comment to 1:1–5). According to Maimonides,[31] the order on the right side was Reuben, Levi, Issachar, Naphtali, Gad, and Joseph,[32] and on the left, Simeon, Judah, Zebulun, Dan, Asher, and Benjamin. This totaled twenty-five Hebrew consonants on each side.

11. seal Hebrew ḥotam is of Egyptian origin.[33]

12. for remembrance This twice-repeated word points to the dual function of the engraved stones: as a reminder to the High Priest, as noted above; and as an invocation to God to be mindful of His people Israel, with whom He enacted a covenant.

The Breastpiece and the Urim and Thummim (vv. 13–30)

Fastened to the ephod, and made of the same fine multicolored fabric, was a pouch about nine inches square worn over the breast. Twelve different gemstones were affixed to it, and each was engraved with the name of one of the tribes of Israel. These stones were arranged in four rows of three. The pouch, called in Hebrew ḥoshen, contained the Urim and Thummim, on which, see verse 30 below.

¹³Then make frames of gold ¹⁴and two chains of pure gold; braid these like corded work, and fasten the corded chains to the frames.

¹⁵You shall make a breastpiece of decision, worked into a design; make it in the style of the ephod: make it of gold, of blue, purple, and crimson yarns, and of fine twisted linen. ¹⁶It shall be square and doubled, a span in length and a span in width. ¹⁷Set in it mounted stones, in four rows of stones. The first row shall be a row of carnelian, chrysolite, and emerald; ¹⁸the second row: a turquoise, a sapphire, and an amethyst; ¹⁹the third row: a jacinth, an agate, and a crystal; ²⁰and the fourth row: a beryl, a lapis lazuli, and a jasper. They shall be framed with gold in their mountings. ²¹The stones shall correspond [in number] to the names of the sons of Israel: twelve, corresponding to their names. They shall be engraved like seals, each with its name, for the twelve tribes.

²²On the breastpiece make braided chains of corded work in pure gold. ²³Make two rings of gold on the breastpiece,

יג וְעָשִׂיתָ מִשְׁבְּצֹת זָהָב: יד וּשְׁתֵּי שַׁרְשְׁרֹת זָהָב טָהוֹר מִגְבָּלֹת תַּעֲשֶׂה אֹתָם מַעֲשֵׂה עֲבֹת וְנָתַתָּה אֶת־שַׁרְשְׁרֹת הָעֲבֹתֹת עַל־הַמִּשְׁבְּצֹת: ס

טו וְעָשִׂיתָ חֹשֶׁן מִשְׁפָּט מַעֲשֵׂה חֹשֵׁב כְּמַעֲשֵׂה אֵפֹד תַּעֲשֶׂנּוּ זָהָב תְּכֵלֶת וְאַרְגָּמָן וְתוֹלַעַת שָׁנִי וְשֵׁשׁ מָשְׁזָר תַּעֲשֶׂה אֹתוֹ: טז רָבוּעַ יִהְיֶה כָּפוּל זֶרֶת אָרְכּוֹ וְזֶרֶת רָחְבּוֹ: יז וּמִלֵּאתָ בוֹ מִלֻּאַת אֶבֶן אַרְבָּעָה טוּרִים אָבֶן טוּר אֹדֶם פִּטְדָה וּבָרֶקֶת הַטּוּר הָאֶחָד: יח וְהַטּוּר הַשֵּׁנִי נֹפֶךְ סַפִּיר וְיָהֲלֹם: יט וְהַטּוּר הַשְּׁלִישִׁי לֶשֶׁם שְׁבוֹ וְאַחְלָמָה: כ וְהַטּוּר הָרְבִיעִי תַּרְשִׁישׁ וְשֹׁהַם וְיָשְׁפֵה מְשֻׁבָּצִים זָהָב יִהְיוּ בְּמִלּוּאֹתָם: כא וְהָאֲבָנִים תִּהְיֶיןָ עַל־שְׁמֹת בְּנֵי־יִשְׂרָאֵל שְׁתֵּים עֶשְׂרֵה עַל־שְׁמֹתָם פִּתּוּחֵי חוֹתָם אִישׁ עַל־שְׁמוֹ תִּהְיֶיןָ לִשְׁנֵי עָשָׂר שָׁבֶט: כב וְעָשִׂיתָ עַל־הַחֹשֶׁן שַׁרְשֹׁת גַּבְלֻת מַעֲשֵׂה עֲבֹת זָהָב טָהוֹר: כג וְעָשִׂיתָ עַל־הַחֹשֶׁן שְׁתֵּי

13–14. These two verses prescribe the means by which the ḥoshen is to be attached to the ephod. The braiding is to provide greater strength. Further details are given in verses 22–28.

15. _a breastpiece of decision_ Hebrew ḥoshen mishpat was usually rendered "breastplate of judgment" in earlier translations. But it was not a plate, and all available sources indicate that it was a device for determining divine will;[34] see Comment to verse 30. The origin of the term ḥoshen is uncertain. It may be related to an Arabic word ḥasuna, "to be excellent, beautiful," and designate the most splendid article of the High Priest's attire. Another possibility is to connect the word with Hebrew ḥosen, "store, treasure,"[35] and with postbiblical maḥsan, "storage place," hence, "a receptacle."[36]

16. _square and doubled_ By doubling over the piece of cloth, it became a square, taking the form of a pouch.

a span Hebrew zeret is the maximum distance between the top of the little finger and the thumb, approximately 9 inches, or half a cubit.[37] The word seems to be of Egyptian origin.[38]

17–20. The identity of the twelve stones cannot be established with certainty. Three are unique to this passage and to its parallel text in 39:10–13, namely, _leshem, shevo, 'aḥlamah_; three appear several times in the Bible and were clearly the most easily obtainable by the Israelites, namely, _sappir,_[39] _tarshish,_[40] _shoham_;[41] nine of the twelve are listed in Ezekiel 28:13 as gems found in the Garden of Eden. Whether this is coincidence or whether it has any intentional bearing on the selection of stones for the High Priest's vestment is uncertain.[42]

21. According to Maimonides[43] and Rashi, the tribal names were engraved in order of their birth; see Comment to verse 10. A tradition recorded in Yoma 73b adds that the names of the three patriarchs, Abraham, Isaac, and Jacob, were also inscribed on the gems, as was the Hebrew phrase _shivtei yeshurun,_ "the tribes of Jeshurun."[44] Once again, the insignia of office symbolize the role of the High Priest as the representative of the entire community and the personification of its historic ideals.

22–28. Instructions for fastening the breastpiece to the ephod and keeping it in position utilize the items mentioned in verses 13–14.

and fasten the two rings at the two ends of the breastpiece, ²⁴attaching the two golden cords to the two rings at the ends of the breastpiece. ²⁵Then fasten the two ends of the cords to the two frames, which you shall attach to the shoulder-pieces of the ephod, at the front. ²⁶Make two rings of gold and attach them to the two ends of the breastpiece, at its inner edge, which faces the ephod. ²⁷And make two other rings of gold and fasten them on the front of the ephod, low on the two shoulder-pieces, close to its seam above the decorated band. ²⁸The breastpiece shall be held in place by a cord of blue from its rings to the rings of the ephod, so that the breastpiece rests on the decorated band and does not come loose from the ephod. ²⁹Aaron shall carry the names of the sons of Israel on the breastpiece of decision over his heart, when he enters the sanctuary, for remembrance before the LORD at all times. ³⁰Inside the breastpiece of decision you shall place the Urim and Thummim, so that they are over Aaron's heart when he comes before the LORD. Thus Aaron shall carry the instrument of decision for the Israelites over his heart before the LORD at all times.

טַבְּעֹות זָהָב וְנָתַתָּ אֶת־שְׁתֵּי הַטַּבָּעֹות עַל־שְׁנֵי קְצֹות הַחֹשֶׁן: 24 וְנָתַתָּה אֶת־שְׁתֵּי עֲבֹתֹת הַזָּהָב עַל־שְׁתֵּי הַטַּבָּעֹת אֶל־קְצֹות הַחֹשֶׁן: 25 וְאֵת שְׁתֵּי קְצֹות שְׁתֵּי הָעֲבֹתֹת תִּתֵּן עַל־שְׁתֵּי הַמִּשְׁבְּצֹות וְנָתַתָּה עַל־כִּתְפֹות הָאֵפֹד אֶל־מוּל פָּנָיו: 26 וְעָשִׂיתָ שְׁתֵּי טַבְּעֹות זָהָב וְשַׂמְתָּ אֹתָם עַל־שְׁנֵי קְצֹות הַחֹשֶׁן עַל־שְׂפָתֹו אֲשֶׁר אֶל־עֵבֶר הָאֵפֹד בָּיְתָה: 27 וְעָשִׂיתָ שְׁתֵּי טַבְּעֹות זָהָב וְנָתַתָּה אֹתָם עַל־שְׁתֵּי כִתְפֹות הָאֵפֹוד מִלְּמַטָּה מִמּוּל פָּנָיו לְעֻמַּת מֶחְבַּרְתֹּו מִמַּעַל לְחֵשֶׁב הָאֵפֹוד: 28 וְיִרְכְּסוּ אֶת־הַחֹשֶׁן מטבעתו אֶל־טַבְּעֹת הָאֵפֹד בִּפְתִיל תְּכֵלֶת לִהְיֹות עַל־חֵשֶׁב הָאֵפֹוד וְלֹא־יִזַּח הַחֹשֶׁן מֵעַל הָאֵפֹוד: 29 וְנָשָׂא אַהֲרֹן אֶת־שְׁמֹות בְּנֵי־יִשְׂרָאֵל בְּחֹשֶׁן הַמִּשְׁפָּט עַל־לִבֹּו בְּבֹאֹו אֶל־הַקֹּדֶשׁ לְזִכָּרֹן לִפְנֵי־יְהוָה תָּמִיד: 30 וְנָתַתָּ אֶל־חֹשֶׁן הַמִּשְׁפָּט אֶת־הָאוּרִים וְאֶת־הַתֻּמִּים וְהָיוּ עַל־לֵב אַהֲרֹן בְּבֹאֹו לִפְנֵי יְהוָה וְנָשָׂא אַהֲרֹן אֶת־מִשְׁפַּט בְּנֵי־יִשְׂרָאֵל עַל־לִבֹּו לִפְנֵי יְהוָה תָּמִיד: ס   שלישי

מִטַּבְּעֹתָיו ק'   v. 28.

28. held in place   Hebrew *ve-yirkesu*; the stem *r-k-s* appears in both Akkadian and Ugaritic with the meaning "to bind."[45]

a cord of blue   Hebrew *petil tekhelet* is the same phrase used in Numbers 15:38 in connection with the *tsitsit*; see Comment to 25:4.

29.   See Comment to verse 10.

30. Urim and Thummim   It is quite clear from the association with "the breastpiece of decision" and "the instrument of decision" that these two items constituted a device for determining the will of God in specific matters that were beyond human ability to decide. The reference in Numbers 27:21 spells this out: "He shall present himself to Eleazar the priest, who shall on his behalf seek the decision of the Urim before the LORD. By such instruction they shall go out and by such instruction they shall come in, he and all the Israelites, the whole community." In 1 Samuel 28:6, it is told that "Saul inquired of the LORD, but the LORD did not answer him, either by dreams or by Urim or by prophets." And Ezra 2:63 (= Neh. 7:65) reports that among those Jews who returned from the Babylonian exile following the Cyrus Declaration were some who could not substantiate their claim to priestly genealogy. They were therefore forbidden to eat of the most holy offerings "until a priest with Urim and Thummim should appear," through whose instrumentality a divine decision would be obtained.

The use of the definite article with the Hebrew terms in this passage indicates that the Urim and Thummim are not an innovation here but are already well known. This conclusion is reinforced by the instruction "you shall place" instead of the usual formula, "you shall make."[46] While the function of this device is clear, neither the above-cited texts nor the only other references to it in the Torah— Leviticus 8:8 and Deuteronomy 33:8—carry a description of it or of the technique employed in its use. A revealing text is 1 Samuel 14:37–41, which tell that King Saul had "inquired of the Lord" without success, and he then begged the Lord to "show Thammim [*sic*]." The Greek version of this text reads as follows: "Why have You not responded to Your servant today? If this iniquity was due to my son Jonathan or to me, O Lord God of Israel, show Urim; and if You say it was due to Your people Israel,

³¹You shall make the robe of the ephod of pure blue. ³²The opening for the head shall be in the middle of it; the opening shall have a binding of woven work round about —it shall be like the opening of a coat of mail—so that it does not tear. ³³On its hem make pomegranates of blue, purple, and crimson yarns, all around the hem, with bells of gold between them all around: ³⁴a golden bell and a pome-

לא וְעָשִׂיתָ אֶת־מְעִיל הָאֵפוֹד כְּלִיל תְּכֵלֶת: 31 וְהָיָה פִי־רֹאשׁוֹ בְּתוֹכוֹ שָׂפָה יִהְיֶה לְפִיו סָבִיב מַעֲשֵׂה אֹרֵג כְּפִי תַחְרָא יִהְיֶה־לּוֹ לֹא יִקָּרֵעַ: 33 וְעָשִׂיתָ עַל־שׁוּלָיו רִמֹּנֵי תְּכֵלֶת וְאַרְגָּמָן וְתוֹלַעַת שָׁנִי עַל־שׁוּלָיו סָבִיב וּפַעֲמֹנֵי זָהָב בְּתוֹכָם סָבִיב: 34 פַּעֲמֹן זָהָב וְרִמּוֹן פַּעֲמֹן זָהָב

show Thummim." This reading is apparently based on a tradition that each object was a kind of counter and that the required decision depended on which one the priest drew out of the ḥoshen, or breastpiece, in which the two were kept. This procedure is similar to the casting of lots, which is mentioned several times in the Bible.⁴⁷ Although numerous pagan divinatory devices are condemned, the Urim and Thummim, like lots, are permitted. There is no mention of them ever being used in an idolatrous context. They are in the exclusive possession of the priest and are always administered on behalf of the leader of the people in matters of national import.

This mode of discovering the divine will never appears beyond the Davidic age. Ezra 2:63, cited above, implies that it was not available in early Second Temple times. Josephus reports that it had ceased to operate two hundred years before his time, in the days of the Hasmonean High Priest John Hyrcanus (135–104 B.C.E.).⁴⁸ Mishnah Sotah 9:12 relates that "with the death of the first prophets, the Urim and Thummim ceased"; but it is unclear precisely to which period this refers.⁴⁹ Yoma 21b claims that they were present in the Second Temple but did not function as before.⁵⁰

The meaning of the two terms remains obscure. Yoma 73b connects Urim with Hebrew 'or, "light," that is, "they made their words enlightening," and Thummim with tam, "complete," that is, "they fulfilled their words." The Septuagint understands "instruction and truth," that is, "true instruction." The Vulgate similarly renders doctrina et veritas.

The Robe (vv. 31–35)

Beneath the ephod and the ḥoshen the High Priest is to wear a long robe (Heb. me'il) woven entirely of woolen thread dyed the aristocratic color tekhelet, on which, see Comment to 25:4. In 39:22 this garment is described as "woven work." It seems to have been ankle-length,⁵¹ with armholes but no sleeves, and rather free flowing.⁵² The neck opening is reinforced to prevent fraying. The hem of the robe is fringed with tassels of three colors representing pomegranates, and with gold bells. Other biblical references to the robe suggest a garment distinctive of persons of high social rank.⁵³

31. of pure blue With no admixture of the other two characteristic colors listed in 25:4.⁵⁴

32. a binding Hebrew safah, literally "lip, edge," here "edging," implying something like a turnover collar.

a coat of mail The unique Hebrew taḥra' (so 39:23) has traditionally been so understood. The reference is probably to the leather collar that protected the neck, a feature of the kind of armor worn by Canaanite charioteers and depicted in a chariot relief of Thutmose IV.⁵⁵

so that . . . tear Hebrew lo' yikkarea' either explains the reason for reinforcing the collar, or it is a prohibition: "It may not be torn." Both interpretations are given in Yoma 72a.

33. hem Hebrew shulayim otherwise refers to the skirt of a garment.⁵⁶

pomegranates This is one of the seven characteristic fruits of the Land of Israel as listed in Deuteronomy 8:8.⁵⁷ The columns of Solomon's Temple were adorned with hundreds of pomegranate figures.⁵⁸ In Second Temple times the fruit appears as a motif on the coins struck by the Hasmonean kings from Alexander Yannai (103–76 B.C.E.) to Mattathias Antigonus (40–37 B.C.E.), as well as by Herod (37–4 B.C.E.). It also appears on coins struck during the first two years of the Jewish revolt against Rome (66–68 C.E.). The significance of this use of the pomegranate is not clear.⁵⁹ In the Song of Songs, however, it is mentioned several times as a symbol of beauty and fertility.⁶⁰

granate, a golden bell and a pomegranate, all around the hem of the robe. [35]Aaron shall wear it while officiating, so that the sound of it is heard when he comes into the sanctuary before the LORD and when he goes out—that he may not die.

וְרִמֹּן עַל־שׁוּלֵי הַמְּעִיל סָבִיב: [35] וְהָיָה עַל־אַהֲרֹן לְשָׁרֵת וְנִשְׁמַע קוֹלוֹ בְּבֹאוֹ אֶל־הַקֹּדֶשׁ לִפְנֵי יְהוָה וּבְצֵאתוֹ וְלֹא יָמוּת: ס

between them   Hebrew *betokham* may also mean "inside them." Hence the difference of opinion among the commentators as to whether verse 34 prescribes an alternation of bells and pomegranates, as held by Rashi, Rashbam, and Maimonides, or whether the bells were to be fixed inside the pomegranate-shaped figures, as maintained by Ramban.

34. all around   In Zevaḥim 88b the sages are divided as to whether there were seventy-two or thirty-six bells in all.

35. while officiating   Hebrew *le-sharet*, literally "to officiate," implying that anything short of scrupulous and undeviating adherence to the detailed prescriptions disqualifies the officiant and renders his priestly service null and void.[61]

the sound of it is heard   The unexplained role of the bells has given rise to various conjectures. Rashbam refers to the requirement of Leviticus 16:16–17 that only the High Priest—and nobody else—shall be present in the Tent of Meeting when he enters it to make expiation. Thus the tinkling of the bells alerts the other priests to vacate the premises. The cited text speaks only of Yom Kippur, however.

Bekhor Shor and Ramban draw an analogy from the convention governing the entry of a subject to a royal palace. Just as one should not appear abruptly and unceremoniously before royalty, so the delicate sounds of the bells signal one's presence and intention. Still other suggestions are that the tinkling attracts the attention of the worshipers outside the Tent to the fact that the High Priest is performing the ritual; or the bells sent out a message that no mishap had occurred in the course of the priestly duties such as had happened to Aaron's two sons (see Leviticus 10). Another possibility is that the High Priest is himself reminded by the sound of the bells on his robe that he is to attune his heart and mind to his solemn duties and that he must be fully conscious of the fact that he is in the presence of God.

that he may not die   This conventional formula[62] probably refers to the entire section and not just to the matter of the bells. Any deviation from the prescribed rules places the priest in the category of an unauthorized person and invalidates his service. He is thus an encroacher—Hebrew *zar*—in the sacred precincts. The formula expresses the severity with which such an offense is viewed.

The Frontlet (vv. 36–38)

The prescriptions now turn to the High Priest's headwear. Once again, they follow the pattern of commencing with the most important and most sacred element; in this instance it is the gold plate worn on the forehead over the head-dress and bearing the inscription *kodesh l-YHWH*, "Holy to the Lord." According to one tradition, cited in Shabbat 63b, the gold plate extended from ear to ear and was two fingerbreadths wide. The plate is termed *tsits* in Hebrew, a word that usually means "a blossom, flower."[63]

In biblical texts, the *tsits* is used in parallelism with *'atarah*, "a crown,"[64] and is either identical with or associated with the *nezer*, "a diadem," or the ornamental headband,[65] which was emblematic of royalty and aristocracy.[66] The diadem is well known from Egyptian paintings. Its outstanding feature is the lotus flower, a symbol of nascent life.[67]

The Hebrew inscription most likely signified the sacred nature of the office and person of the High Priest, the one who is consecrated and committed to the service of God all his life. Several biblical texts testify to this understanding.[68] Additionally, "Holy to the Lord" may also refer to Israel, who is explicitly so referred to by this term in Jeremiah 2:3, as Rashbam notes. The role of the High Priest as Israel's representative before God is visibly projected by his vestments, as vv. 9–12, 21, and 29–30 demonstrate.

36You shall make a frontlet of pure gold and engrave on it the seal inscription: "Holy to the Lord." 37Suspend it on a cord of blue, so that it may remain on the headdress; it shall remain on the front of the headdress. 38It shall be on Aaron's forehead, that Aaron may take away any sin arising from the holy things that the Israelites consecrate, from any of their sacred donations; it shall be on his forehead at all times, to win acceptance for them before the Lord.

לו וְעָשִׂיתָ צִּיץ זָהָב טָהוֹר וּפִתַּחְתָּ עָלָיו
פִּתּוּחֵי חֹתָם קֹדֶשׁ לַיהוָה: 37 וְשַׂמְתָּ אֹתוֹ עַל־
פְּתִיל תְּכֵלֶת וְהָיָה עַל־הַמִּצְנָפֶת אֶל־מוּל פְּנֵי־
הַמִּצְנֶפֶת יִהְיֶה: 38 וְהָיָה עַל־מֵצַח אַהֲרֹן וְנָשָׂא
אַהֲרֹן אֶת־עֲוֹן הַקֳּדָשִׁים אֲשֶׁר יַקְדִּישׁוּ בְּנֵי
יִשְׂרָאֵל לְכָל־מַתְּנֹת קָדְשֵׁיהֶם וְהָיָה עַל־מִצְחוֹ
תָּמִיד לְרָצוֹן לָהֶם לִפְנֵי יְהוָה:

36. "Holy to the Lord" The ancient sources differ as to how the two Hebrew words were inscribed on the *tsits*. One talmudic view is that the divine name alone appeared on the left side of the upper line, and KDShL ("Holy to") was placed on the right side of the lower line. Eliezer ben Rabbi Yose, who claimed to have seen the object in Rome, said that the entire two words were inscribed on one line.[69] Both the Letter of Aristeas (2nd cent. b.c.e.) and Josephus record that only the tetragrammaton, YHVH, the most sacred name of God, was written on the *tsits*, and in the ancient Hebrew script.[70]

37. a cord of blue This was apparently threaded through holes punched in the *tsits* and served to hold it in place.

the headdress Hebrew *mitsnefet* is not actually prescribed until v. 39. Its mention here, with the definite article, implies an item of apparel that is taken for granted. Elsewhere in the Bible it is a symbol of royalty. It clearly means "a turban."[71]

38. It shall be on Aaron's forehead This instruction is repeated with the addition of Hebrew *tamid*, "at all times," meaning, "whenever the High Priest performs the service." (See Comment to 27:20.) Rashi and Bekhor Shor, contrary to the traditional accentuation, connect *tamid* with the following clause.

to take away any sin Because the Hebrew expression *nasa' 'avon* may mean both "to remove sin"[72] and "to bear sin,"[73] that is, incur responsibility, the present verse is ambiguous. Analogous texts like Leviticus 22:15–16 and Numbers 18:1 indicate that the reference is to the High Priest's assumption of responsibility for any infraction of the rules governing the sacred offerings. The wearing of the *tsits* inscribed with the legend "Holy to the Lord" helps to concentrate his thoughts on his duties and on his accountability. At the same time, this consciousness effectively secures atonement for such offenses.

The Tunic (v. 39)

Once again, the definite article indicates a well-known garment, and Hebrew *kuttonet* is mentioned many times in the Bible. It was fashionable in the Near East in the Late Bronze Age, and became standard dress in the Iron Age.[74] Both men and women wore it, mainly as an ankle-length undergarment, usually next to the skin.[75] Some types were clearly marks of prestige, such as the garment that Jacob gave to Joseph as well as those worn by princesses in the days of David (see Gen. 37:3 and 2 Sam. 13:18–19).

The High Priest's tunic is defined as the *tashbets* type, and the same verbal stem, *sh-b-ts*, is used here.[76] Usually understood as "chequered work," it is here translated "fringed," but neither rendering is certain. Josephus reports that the tunic of the High Priest was "of a double texture," of ankle-length, and had long sleeves tightly laced around the arms.[77]

The Headdress (v. 39)

This item has been discussed in the Comment to verse 37. According to one account of Josephus,[78] the headdress was a tiara wreathed with blue and encircled by a crown of gold. However, in a second report,[79] he describes it as a nonconical cap over which was stitched another cap embroidered in blue, encircled by a three-tiered golden crown, and topped by a golden calyx. The origin of these descriptions is not known.

39You shall make the fringed tunic of fine linen. You shall make the headdress of fine linen. You shall make the sash of embroidered work.

40And for Aaron's sons also you shall make tunics, and make sashes for them, and make turbans for them, for dignity and adornment. 41Put these on your brother Aaron and on his sons as well; anoint them, and ordain them and consecrate them to serve Me as priests.

42You shall also make for them linen breeches to cover their nakedness; they shall extend from the hips to the thighs. 43They shall be worn by Aaron and his sons when

39 וְשִׁבַּצְתָּ הַכְּתֹנֶת שֵׁשׁ וְעָשִׂיתָ מִצְנֶפֶת
שֵׁשׁ וְאַבְנֵט תַּעֲשֶׂה מַעֲשֵׂה רֹקֵם: 40 וְלִבְנֵי אַהֲרֹן
תַּעֲשֶׂה כֻתֳּנֹת וְעָשִׂיתָ לָהֶם אַבְנֵטִים וּמִגְבָּעוֹת
תַּעֲשֶׂה לָהֶם לְכָבוֹד וּלְתִפְאָרֶת: 41 וְהִלְבַּשְׁתָּ
אֹתָם אֶת־אַהֲרֹן אָחִיךָ וְאֶת־בָּנָיו אִתּוֹ
וּמָשַׁחְתָּ אֹתָם וּמִלֵּאתָ אֶת־יָדָם וְקִדַּשְׁתָּ אֹתָם
וְכִהֲנוּ לִי:
42 וַעֲשֵׂה לָהֶם מִכְנְסֵי־בָד לְכַסּוֹת בְּשַׂר
עֶרְוָה מִמָּתְנַיִם וְעַד־יְרֵכַיִם יִהְיוּ: 43 וְהָיוּ עַל־

The Sash (v. 39)

Hebrew 'avnet[80] is specified in 39:29 as being made of "fine twisted linen, blue, purple, and crimson yarns, done in embroidery." It was girded over the tunic. Beyond the priestly context, the 'avnet is mentioned only in Isaiah 22:21, where it belongs to the regalia of a high official. According to Maimonides,[81] the cloth of the 'avnet was three finger-breadths wide[82] and thirty-two cubits (48 ft. = 14.6 m.) in length, and it was wound around the body. He maintains that its function was to demarcate the upper from the lower part of the body.

THE VESTMENTS OF ORDINARY PRIESTS (vv. 40–43)

Four in number, the last of which is mentioned in verse 42.

40. turbans These probably differ from the High Priest's headdress because a different Hebrew word, *migba'ot* (pl.), is used, although no description is given.[83] Josephus[84] describes the item as a nonconical—that is, flattish—cap that only partially covered the head. It consisted of a band of woven linen wound round and round, and repeatedly stitched with a muslin veil enveloping it from the top down to the forehead in order to hide the unsightly stitches.

41. This verse and the following chapter prescribe the manner in which the priesthood, anticipated in verse 1, is to be officially installed into office once the Tabernacle is erected. The ritual involves laving the body, robing, anointing, ordination, animal sacrifices, and offerings of unleavened bread. The actual consecration of the priests is described in Leviticus 8.

put these That is, the vestments, as they apply respectively to Aaron and his sons.

anoint them The formula for compounding the special aromatic oil for this rite is specified in 30:22–25. The oil was forbidden to be duplicated for any other purpose. The vestments for both Aaron and his sons were sprinkled with the oil;[85] in addition, the High Priest had oil poured over his head.[86] The Tabernacle vessels too were anointed.[87] This symbolic ceremony effectuates the transition from the profane to the sacred.

ordain them The Hebrew idiom *mille' yad* literally means "to fill the hand." It is most frequently used in the sense of installing persons into priestly office.[88] The phrase must have originated in some concrete situation wherein some object was ceremoniously placed in the hand of the novitiate.[89] It then became a mere figure of speech meaning "commissioning, issuing a mandate." This last English word itself derives from Latin *manus + dare*, "to give into the hand."[90]

consecrate them This probably does not signify another distinct ceremony but sums up the consequence of performing the entire complement of rituals. Ibn Ezra understands the verb to be declarative: "and so declare them to be consecrated."

42. Hebrew *mikhnasayim*, "breeches," occurs in the Bible solely in connection with the priestly attire.[91] They are here listed separately because they cannot be subsumed under the rubric of vestments that are "for dignity and adornment" (v. 40), and also because, to avoid unseemliness, the priest put these on by himself, unlike the vestments, into which he is helped by others (v. 41).

they enter the Tent of Meeting or when they approach the altar to officiate in the sanctuary, so that they do not incur punishment and die. It shall be a law for all time for him and for his offspring to come.

אַהֲרֹ֨ן וְעַל־בָּנָ֜יו בְּבֹאָ֣ם ׀ אֶל־אֹ֣הֶל מוֹעֵ֗ד א֣וֹ בְגִשְׁתָּ֤ם אֶל־הַמִּזְבֵּ֨חַ֙ לְשָׁרֵ֣ת בַּקֹּ֔דֶשׁ וְלֹא־ יִשְׂא֥וּ עָוֺ֖ן וָמֵ֑תוּ חֻקַּ֥ת עוֹלָ֛ם ל֖וֹ וּלְזַרְע֥וֹ אַחֲרָֽיו׃ ס רביעי

29 This is what you shall do to them in consecrating them to serve Me as priests: Take a young bull of the herd and two rams without blemish; ²also unleavened bread, unleavened cakes with oil mixed in, and unleavened wafers spread with oil—make these of choice wheat flour. ³Place these in one basket and present them in the basket, along with the bull and the two rams. ⁴Lead Aaron and his sons up to the entrance of the Tent of Meeting, and wash them with water. ⁵Then take the vestments, and clothe Aaron

כ״ט וְזֶ֨ה הַדָּבָ֜ר אֲשֶֽׁר־תַּעֲשֶׂ֥ה לָהֶ֛ם לְקַדֵּ֥שׁ אֹתָ֖ם לְכַהֵ֣ן לִ֑י לְ֠קַ֠ח פַּ֣ר אֶחָ֧ד בֶּן־בָּקָ֛ר וְאֵילִ֥ם שְׁנַ֖יִם תְּמִימִֽם׃ ² וְלֶ֣חֶם מַצּ֗וֹת וְחַלֹּ֤ת מַצֹּת֙ בְּלוּלֹ֣ת בַּשֶּׁ֔מֶן וּרְקִיקֵ֥י מַצּ֖וֹת מְשֻׁחִ֣ים בַּשָּׁ֑מֶן סֹ֥לֶת חִטִּ֖ים תַּעֲשֶׂ֥ה אֹתָֽם׃ ³ וְנָתַתָּ֤ אוֹתָם֙ עַל־סַ֣ל אֶחָ֔ד וְהִקְרַבְתָּ֥ אֹתָ֖ם בַּסָּ֑ל וְאֶ֨ת־הַפָּ֔ר וְאֵ֖ת שְׁנֵ֥י הָאֵילִֽם׃ ⁴ וְאֶת־אַהֲרֹ֤ן וְאֶת־בָּנָיו֙ תַּקְרִ֔יב אֶל־פֶּ֖תַח אֹ֣הֶל מוֹעֵ֑ד וְרָחַצְתָּ֥ אֹתָ֖ם בַּמָּֽיִם׃ ⁵ וְלָקַחְתָּ֣ אֶת־

---

to cover their nakedness   See Comment to 20:26.

43.   This instruction most likely refers to the aggregate of vestments and not just to the last item.

CHAPTER 29

The Installation of the Priests   (29:1–46)

All the details regarding the priestly vestments having been set forth, the instructions to Moses now concentrate on the rituals for the installation of the priests themselves. Moses is to preside over the ceremonies, during which he will act as the sole priest. This role underlies Psalm 99:6, which speaks of "Moses and Aaron among His priests."

The installation rituals, which are to last seven days, comprise animal sacrifices, cereal offerings, the washing of the body, robing, and anointing. The performance of the installation is reported and described in Leviticus chapters 8–9.[1]

THE MATERIALS   (vv. 1–3)

These are listed first, just as in 25:1–7, and their functions are specified subsequently.

1.   In the narrative of Leviticus 8 the three animals are termed "the bull of sin offering," "the ram of burnt offering," and "the ram of ordination," respectively.

to them   To Aaron and his sons.[2]

Take[3]

without blemish   This requirement applies to all three animals.

2.   The cereal offerings are to consist of three varieties of unleavened bread, *matsah*, made of choice wheat flour: (1) plain, oven-baked; (2) with the dough mixed and kneaded with oil; (3) with oil smeared on top after the baking.[4] The significance of the variations is unknown. These unleavened breads are only for the ram of ordination.

3.   ***present***   Literally, "bring forward," that is, to the Tent of Meeting.[5]

with the tunic, the robe of the ephod, the ephod, and the breastpiece, and gird him with the decorated band of the ephod. ⁶Put the headdress on his head, and place the holy diadem upon the headdress. ⁷Take the anointing oil and pour it on his head and anoint him. ⁸Then bring his sons forward; clothe them with tunics ⁹and wind turbans upon them. And gird both Aaron and his sons with sashes. And so they shall have priesthood as their right for all time.

You shall then ordain Aaron and his sons. ¹⁰Lead the bull up to the front of the Tent of Meeting, and let Aaron and his sons lay their hands upon the head of the bull. ¹¹Slaugh-

הַבְּגָדִים וְהִלְבַּשְׁתָּ אֶת־אַהֲרֹן אֶת־הַכֻּתֹּנֶת וְאֵת מְעִיל הָאֵפֹד וְאֶת־הָאֵפֹד וְאֶת־הַחֹשֶׁן וְאָפַדְתָּ לוֹ בְּחֵשֶׁב הָאֵפֹד: 6 וְשַׂמְתָּ הַמִּצְנֶפֶת עַל־רֹאשׁוֹ וְנָתַתָּ אֶת־נֵזֶר הַקֹּדֶשׁ עַל־הַמִּצְנָפֶת: 7 וְלָקַחְתָּ אֶת־שֶׁמֶן הַמִּשְׁחָה וְיָצַקְתָּ עַל־רֹאשׁוֹ וּמָשַׁחְתָּ אֹתוֹ: 8 וְאֶת־בָּנָיו תַּקְרִיב וְהִלְבַּשְׁתָּם כֻּתֳּנֹת: 9 וְחָגַרְתָּ אֹתָם אַבְנֵט אַהֲרֹן וּבָנָיו וְחָבַשְׁתָּ לָהֶם מִגְבָּעֹת וְהָיְתָה לָהֶם כְּהֻנָּה לְחֻקַּת עוֹלָם וּמִלֵּאתָ יַד־אַהֲרֹן וְיַד־בָּנָיו: 10 וְהִקְרַבְתָּ אֶת־הַפָּר לִפְנֵי אֹהֶל מוֹעֵד וְסָמַךְ אַהֲרֹן וּבָנָיו אֶת־יְדֵיהֶם עַל־רֹאשׁ הַפָּר: 11 וְשָׁחַטְתָּ אֶת־הַפָּר לִפְנֵי

THE WASHING (v. 4)

Before being dressed in the sacred garments of office for the first time, Aaron and his sons must undergo ritual purification by immersion of the entire body in water.⁶ For the regular daily services, only the hands and feet need to be washed, as prescribed in 30:17–21.

THE ROBING AND ANOINTING OF AARON ALONE (vv. 5–7)

For reasons of delicacy, the linen breeches are not mentioned. Aaron puts on this undergarment himself.⁷ The order of robing prescribed here inexplicably differs from that described in the narrative of Leviticus 8:7–9.

6. diadem Hebrew *nezer*, on which see the introductory Comment to 28:36–38.

7. See Comment to 28:41. The present verse implies that Aaron alone is to be anointed. The narrative of Leviticus 8:12 also makes no mention of the anointing of Aaron's sons. In fact, the biblical title "the anointed priest" (Heb. *ha-kohen ha-mashiah*), refers exclusively to the High Priest.⁸ Other passages, however, make clear that the ordinary priests were indeed anointed.⁹ Either the texts reflect two strands of tradition,¹⁰ or the citations pertaining to the sons refer to the ceremony of sprinkling the oil on their vestments, as prescribed in verse 21 and as described in Leviticus 8:30.

THE ROBING OF AARON AND HIS SONS (vv. 8–9)

In the Hebrew text these instructions deal in turn with the vestments of the ordinary priests and with the items common to them and Aaron. For the sake of clarity, the present English rendering rearranges the order of the clauses.¹¹

8. turbans Hebrew *migba'ot* applies only to the headdress of the ordinary priests. That of the High Priest, called *mitsnefet*, was mentioned in verse 6.

sashes The sash of the High Priest was described in 28:4,39, but was not mentioned in the instructions of verses 5–6 above.

9. their right for all time According to Sanhedrin 83b, the instructions for the investiture close with this pronouncement in order to signify that the priestly prerogative is effective only so long as the priest is fully and properly attired in his sacerdotal vestments.

You shall ordain See Comment to 28:4.

ter the bull before the LORD, at the entrance of the Tent of Meeting, 12and take some of the bull's blood and put it on the horns of the altar with your finger; then pour out the rest of the blood at the base of the altar. 13Take all the fat that covers the entrails, the protuberance on the liver, and the two kidneys with the fat on them, and turn them into smoke upon the altar. 14The rest of the flesh of the bull, its hide, and its dung shall be put to the fire outside the camp; it is a sin offering.

15Next take the one ram, and let Aaron and his sons lay their hands upon the ram's head. 16Slaughter the ram, and take its blood and dash it against all sides of the altar. 17Cut up the ram into sections, wash its entrails and legs, and put

יְהוָה פֶּתַח אֹהֶל מוֹעֵד: 12 וְלָקַחְתָּ מִדַּם הַפָּר
וְנָתַתָּה עַל־קַרְנֹת הַמִּזְבֵּחַ בְּאֶצְבָּעֶךָ וְאֶת־כָּל־
הַדָּם תִּשְׁפֹּךְ אֶל־יְסוֹד הַמִּזְבֵּחַ: 13 וְלָקַחְתָּ אֶת־
כָּל־הַחֵלֶב הַמְכַסֶּה אֶת־הַקֶּרֶב וְאֵת הַיֹּתֶרֶת
עַל־הַכָּבֵד וְאֵת שְׁתֵּי הַכְּלָיֹת וְאֶת־הַחֵלֶב אֲשֶׁר
עֲלֵיהֶן וְהִקְטַרְתָּ הַמִּזְבֵּחָה: 14 וְאֶת־בְּשַׂר הַפָּר
וְאֶת־עֹרוֹ וְאֶת־פִּרְשׁוֹ תִּשְׂרֹף בָּאֵשׁ מִחוּץ לַמַּחֲנֶה
חַטָּאת הוּא:
15 וְאֵת־הָאַיִל הָאֶחָד תִּקָּח וְסָמְכוּ אַהֲרֹן
וּבָנָיו אֶת־יְדֵיהֶם עַל־רֹאשׁ הָאָיִל: 16 וְשָׁחַטְתָּ
אֶת־הָאָיִל וְלָקַחְתָּ אֶת־דָּמוֹ וְזָרַקְתָּ עַל־הַמִּזְבֵּחַ
סָבִיב: 17 וְאֶת־הָאַיִל תְּנַתֵּחַ לִנְתָחָיו וְרָחַצְתָּ

THE ANIMAL SACRIFICES (vv. 10–22, 31–42)

Immediately before the slaughtering of each of the three animals listed in verse 1, the priests are to perform "the laying on of the hands" (Heb. *semikhah*).[12] The text clarifies neither the manner in which this is to be done nor the meaning of the ceremony. According to rabbinic tradition, it applies, with only rare exceptions, to the sacrifices brought by individuals and not to communal sacrifices, and it is always done by the owner of the animal, who presses down on the head with bare hands.[13]

In certain circumstances the rite is also performed on persons,[14] and no single explanation accounts for all the occasions that require it. It sometimes seems to designate the animal or person for a specific role or fate; at other times it serves to identify and affirm ownership of the sacrificial animals. And in the case of the installation of the Levites prescribed in Numbers 8:10 and of the appointment of Joshua as Moses' successor recorded in Numbers 27:18,23 and Deuteronomy 34:9, the action appears to signify the transfer of authority. It is this last interpretation that gave rise to the use of the Hebrew term *semikhah* for rabbinical ordination.

THE BULL OF SIN OFFERING (vv. 10–14)

This is essentially a purificatory and expiatory sacrifice.

10. hands The plural is always employed when the object of the rite is a person;[15] the singular is mostly used in connection with an animal.[16] However, on the basis of the cardinal number "two" defining the singular form of the Hebrew consonantal spelling of the noun (*shetei ydw* not *ydyv*) in Leviticus 16:21, rabbinic exegesis inferred that two hands are required in all cases.[17]

12. See Comments to 24:6–8 and 27:2. The precise significance of daubing specifically the horns of the altar with blood is not known.

13. the protuberance on the liver Hebrew *yoteret ha-kaved* literally means "the redundance of/upon the liver." In Mishnah Tamid 4:3 the same is called "the finger of the liver," and without doubt the reference is to the *lobus caudatus*. The requirement to remove and burn this part is quite likely a reaction against the great importance attached to the liver in ancient Near Eastern divination, a reference to which appears in Ezekiel 21:26. Numerous clay models of the liver have been uncovered in Mesopotamia, some divided into fifty sections and inscribed with omens and magical formulas for the use of diviners.[18]

THE RAM OF BURNT OFFERING (vv. 15–18)

The first of the rams is to be an *ʿolah* offering, one that is completely consumed by fire on the altar.

16. against all sides The blood was collected in a vessel and dashed against the altar from diagonally opposite corners in such a way that each of the two sprinklings spattered two of the sides.[19]

them with its quarters and its head. [18]Turn all of the ram into smoke upon the altar. It is a burnt offering to the LORD, a pleasing odor, an offering by fire to the LORD.

[19]Then take the other ram, and let Aaron and his sons lay their hands upon the ram's head. [20]Slaughter the ram, and take some of its blood and put it on the ridge of Aaron's right ear and on the ridges of his sons' right ears, and on the thumbs of their right hands, and on the big toes of their right feet; and dash the rest of the blood against every side of the altar round about. [21]Take some of the blood that is on the altar and some of the anointing oil and sprinkle upon Aaron and his vestments, and also upon his sons and his sons' vestments. Thus shall he and his vestments be holy, as well as his sons and his sons' vestments.

[22]You shall take from the ram the fat parts—the broad tail, the fat that covers the entrails, the protuberance on the liver, the two kidneys with the fat on them—and the right thigh; for this is a ram of ordination. [23]Add one flat loaf of bread, one cake of oil bread, and one wafer, from the basket of unleavened bread that is before the LORD. [24]Place all these on the palms of Aaron and his sons, and offer them as an elevation offering before the LORD. [25]Take them from

קִרְבּוֹ וּכְרָעָיו וְנָתַתָּ עַל־נְתָחָיו וְעַל־רֹאשׁוֹ:
18 וְהִקְטַרְתָּ אֶת־כָּל־הָאַיִל הַמִּזְבֵּחָה עֹלָה
הוּא לַיהוָה רֵיחַ נִיחוֹחַ אִשֶּׁה לַיהוָה הוּא: חמישי
19 וְלָקַחְתָּ אֵת הָאַיִל הַשֵּׁנִי וְסָמַךְ אַהֲרֹן
וּבָנָיו אֶת־יְדֵיהֶם עַל־רֹאשׁ הָאָיִל: 20 וְשָׁחַטְתָּ
אֶת־הָאַיִל וְלָקַחְתָּ מִדָּמוֹ וְנָתַתָּה עַל־תְּנוּךְ אֹזֶן
אַהֲרֹן וְעַל־תְּנוּךְ אֹזֶן בָּנָיו הַיְמָנִית וְעַל־בֹּהֶן
יָדָם הַיְמָנִית וְעַל־בֹּהֶן רַגְלָם הַיְמָנִית וְזָרַקְתָּ
אֶת־הַדָּם עַל־הַמִּזְבֵּחַ סָבִיב: 21 וְלָקַחְתָּ מִן־הַדָּם
אֲשֶׁר עַל־הַמִּזְבֵּחַ וּמִשֶּׁמֶן הַמִּשְׁחָה וְהִזֵּיתָ עַל־
אַהֲרֹן וְעַל־בְּגָדָיו וְעַל־בָּנָיו וְעַל־בִּגְדֵי בָנָיו אִתּוֹ
וְקָדַשׁ הוּא וּבְגָדָיו וּבָנָיו וּבִגְדֵי בָנָיו אִתּוֹ:
22 וְלָקַחְתָּ מִן־הָאַיִל הַחֵלֶב וְהָאַלְיָה וְאֶת־
הַחֵלֶב | הַמְכַסֶּה אֶת־הַקֶּרֶב וְאֵת יֹתֶרֶת הַכָּבֵד
וְאֵת | שְׁתֵּי הַכְּלָיֹת וְאֶת־הַחֵלֶב אֲשֶׁר עֲלֵהֶן
וְאֵת שׁוֹק הַיָּמִין כִּי אֵיל מִלֻּאִים הוּא: 23 וְכִכַּר
לֶחֶם אַחַת וַחַלַּת לֶחֶם שֶׁמֶן אַחַת וְרָקִיק
אֶחָד מִסַּל הַמַּצּוֹת אֲשֶׁר לִפְנֵי יְהוָה: 24 וְשַׂמְתָּ
הַכֹּל עַל כַּפֵּי אַהֲרֹן וְעַל כַּפֵּי בָנָיו וְהֵנַפְתָּ אֹתָם
תְּנוּפָה לִפְנֵי יְהוָה: 25 וְלָקַחְתָּ אֹתָם מִיָּדָם

18. a pleasing odor This phrase is a technical term in ritual texts connoting divine acceptance of the sacrifice.[20]

an offering by fire This rendering of Hebrew *'ishsheh* assumes a derivation from *'esh*, "fire." Another possibility connects it with Ugaritic *'uśn*, "a gift."[21]

THE RAM OF ORDINATION (vv. 19–34)

This comes under the category of Hebrew *zevaḥ shelamim*, "an offering of well-being" or "a sacred gift of greeting."[22] It is only partly burnt on the altar. The rest belongs to the priests. This offering consummates the entire ceremony of installation and is accompanied by elaborate rites.

20. The daubing of the blood of the sacrifice on the priest's extremities has its counterpart only in the law of Leviticus 14:14ff., governing one who has recovered from the severe dermatological affliction called *tsaraʿat* in Hebrew. There the ceremony has a purificatory function, and it most likely serves the same purpose here. The singling out of the ear, hand, and foot may well symbolize the idea that the priest is to attune himself to the divine word and be responsive to it in deed and direction in life.

the ridge It is uncertain whether the part of the ear denoted by Hebrew *tenukh* refers to the cartilage or the lobe.

21. As the text explains, and as the description of Leviticus 8:30 repeats, this ritual effectuated the consecration of the priests.

22. for this is a ram of ordination This explanatory note is needed because normally the right thigh of the animal is assigned to the priest and not, as here, offered up in smoke on the altar.[23]

24. an elevation offering Hebrew *tenufah* is the technical term for an offering that undergoes the special ritual of being "raised up." Mishnah Menaḥot 5:6 describes the procedure as follows: The priest places his hands beneath the pile of offerings and waves it forward and backward,

their hands and turn them into smoke upon the altar with the burnt offering, as a pleasing odor before the LORD; it is an offering by fire to the LORD.

²⁶Then take the breast of Aaron's ram of ordination and offer it as an elevation offering before the LORD; it shall be your portion. ²⁷You shall consecrate the breast that was offered as an elevation offering and the thigh that was offered as a gift offering from the ram of ordination—from that which was Aaron's and from that which was his sons' —²⁸and those parts shall be a due for all time from the Israelites to Aaron and his descendants. For they are a gift; and so shall they be a gift from the Israelites, their gift to the LORD out of their sacrifices of well-being.

²⁹The sacral vestments of Aaron shall pass on to his sons after him, for them to be anointed and ordained in. ³⁰He among his sons who becomes priest in his stead, who enters the Tent of Meeting to officiate within the sanctuary, shall wear them seven days.

³¹You shall take the ram of ordination and boil its flesh in the sacred precinct; ³²and Aaron and his sons shall eat the

וְהִקְטַרְתָּ הַמִּזְבֵּחָה עַל־הָעֹלָה לְרֵיחַ נִיחוֹחַ לִפְנֵי יְהֹוָה אִשֶּׁה הוּא לַיהֹוָה: ²⁶ וְלָקַחְתָּ אֶת־הֶחָזֶה מֵאֵיל הַמִּלֻּאִים אֲשֶׁר לְאַהֲרֹן וְהֵנַפְתָּ אֹתוֹ תְּנוּפָה לִפְנֵי יְהֹוָה וְהָיָה לְךָ לְמָנָה: ²⁷ וְקִדַּשְׁתָּ אֵת ׀ חֲזֵה הַתְּנוּפָה וְאֵת שׁוֹק הַתְּרוּמָה אֲשֶׁר הוּנַף וַאֲשֶׁר הוּרָם מֵאֵיל הַמִּלֻּאִים מֵאֲשֶׁר לְאַהֲרֹן וּמֵאֲשֶׁר לְבָנָיו: ²⁸ וְהָיָה לְאַהֲרֹן וּלְבָנָיו לְחָק־עוֹלָם מֵאֵת בְּנֵי יִשְׂרָאֵל כִּי תְרוּמָה הוּא וּתְרוּמָה יִהְיֶה מֵאֵת בְּנֵי־יִשְׂרָאֵל מִזִּבְחֵי שַׁלְמֵיהֶם תְּרוּמָתָם לַיהֹוָה: ²⁹ וּבִגְדֵי הַקֹּדֶשׁ אֲשֶׁר לְאַהֲרֹן יִהְיוּ לְבָנָיו אַחֲרָיו לְמָשְׁחָה בָהֶם וּלְמַלֵּא־בָם אֶת־יָדָם: ³⁰ שִׁבְעַת יָמִים יִלְבָּשָׁם הַכֹּהֵן תַּחְתָּיו מִבָּנָיו אֲשֶׁר יָבֹא אֶל־אֹהֶל מוֹעֵד לְשָׁרֵת בַּקֹּדֶשׁ: ³¹ וְאֵת אֵיל הַמִּלֻּאִים תִּקָּח וּבִשַּׁלְתָּ אֶת־בְּשָׂרוֹ בְּמָקֹם קָדֹשׁ: ³² וְאָכַל אַהֲרֹן וּבָנָיו אֶת־

upward and downward. Based on this source, the *tenufah* has traditionally been rendered "wave-offering" in English. A different tradition has been preserved by the Aramaic Targums, which employ the stem *r-w-m*, "to raise up," in both nominal and verbal forms. This understanding is supported by the inherent difficulty in performing a waving motion: it would tend to unbalance the pile of offerings. Further, several biblical passages support a meaning of "elevate" for the stem *n-w-f*.²⁴

Shadal suggests that the function of this ritual was to signify that the object elevated has passed from the domain of the owner to the domain of God.

26. Here, because the installation ceremonies are not quite completed and because Moses acts in a priestly capacity, he is entitled to that which would routinely be the priest's portion in the future.²⁵

THE INSTALLATION OF FUTURE PRIESTS (vv. 27–30)

These verses interrupt the theme. They explain that the foregoing applies only to the present inaugural and that different rules will govern the installation of priestly successors.

28. *their gift to the LORD* Who assigns these parts to the priests.

29–30. The eight garments that are the uniform of the High Priest, as described in 28:3–4, 42, are to be handed down from father to son to be worn for the successor's installation ceremony, which is also to last for seven days. Numbers 20:22–29 narrates the death of Aaron and the investiture of his son as the successor High Priest: "Moses stripped Aaron of his vestments and put them on his son Eleazar."

THE SACRIFICIAL MEAL (vv. 31–34)

The instructions for the present installation of Aaron and his sons now resume.

31. *in the sacred precinct* In the enclosed court of the Tabernacle.²⁶

flesh of the ram, and the bread that is in the basket, at the entrance of the Tent of Meeting. ³³These things shall be eaten only by those for whom expiation was made with them when they were ordained and consecrated; they may not be eaten by a layman, for they are holy. ³⁴And if any of the flesh of ordination, or any of the bread, is left until morning, you shall put what is left to the fire; it shall not be eaten, for it is holy.

³⁵Thus you shall do to Aaron and his sons, just as I have commanded you. You shall ordain them through seven days, ³⁶and each day you shall prepare a bull as a sin offering for expiation; you shall purge the altar by performing purification upon it, and you shall anoint it to consecrate it. ³⁷Seven days you shall perform purification for the altar to consecrate it, and the altar shall become most holy; whatever touches the altar shall become consecrated.

³⁸Now this is what you shall offer upon the altar: two yearling lambs each day, regularly. ³⁹You shall offer the one

בְּשַׂר הָאַיִל וְאֶת־הַלֶּחֶם אֲשֶׁר בַּסָּל פֶּתַח אֹהֶל מוֹעֵד: 33 וְאָכְלוּ אֹתָם אֲשֶׁר כֻּפַּר בָּהֶם לְמַלֵּא אֶת־יָדָם לְקַדֵּשׁ אֹתָם וְזָר לֹא־יֹאכַל כִּי־קֹדֶשׁ הֵם: 34 וְאִם־יִוָּתֵר מִבְּשַׂר הַמִּלֻּאִים וּמִן־הַלֶּחֶם עַד־הַבֹּקֶר וְשָׂרַפְתָּ אֶת־הַנּוֹתָר בָּאֵשׁ לֹא יֵאָכֵל כִּי־קֹדֶשׁ הוּא: 35 וְעָשִׂיתָ לְאַהֲרֹן וּלְבָנָיו כָּכָה כְּכֹל אֲשֶׁר־צִוִּיתִי אֹתָכָה שִׁבְעַת יָמִים תְּמַלֵּא יָדָם: 36 וּפַר חַטָּאת תַּעֲשֶׂה לַיּוֹם עַל־הַכִּפֻּרִים וְחִטֵּאתָ עַל־הַמִּזְבֵּחַ בְּכַפֶּרְךָ עָלָיו וּמָשַׁחְתָּ אֹתוֹ לְקַדְּשׁוֹ: 37 שִׁבְעַת יָמִים תְּכַפֵּר עַל־הַמִּזְבֵּחַ וְקִדַּשְׁתָּ אֹתוֹ וְהָיָה הַמִּזְבֵּחַ קֹדֶשׁ קָדָשִׁים כָּל־הַנֹּגֵעַ בַּמִּזְבֵּחַ יִקְדָּשׁ: ס ששי
38 וְזֶה אֲשֶׁר תַּעֲשֶׂה עַל־הַמִּזְבֵּחַ כְּבָשִׂים בְּנֵי־שָׁנָה שְׁנַיִם לַיּוֹם תָּמִיד: 39 אֶת־הַכֶּבֶשׂ הָאֶחָד

32–33. The ritual of the *shelamim* offering involves a sacrificial meal, as prescribed in Leviticus 7:15. See Comments to 18:12 and 24:6,11.

33. *a layman* Hebrew *zar*, literally "strange, alien, removed," is used in cultic contexts to refer to an outsider or an unauthorized person or thing in relation to specific roles or functions.

34. On the law of *notar* in connection with sacrifices, see Comment to 12:10.

A WEEK-LONG OBSERVANCE (vv. 35–37)

These verses appear to mean that the entire installation ceremony is to be repeated each day for seven days. Leviticus 8:33–36 is less explicit on this point, but there the priests are forbidden, in addition, to leave the Tabernacle precincts throughout the seven-day period.

36. As a piece of furniture fashioned by human beings, the altar is assumed to possess a natural impurity. Hence, it must be anointed, purged of defilement and consecrated before being used for its sacred function. Ezekiel, in his vision of the Temple rebuilt, similarly provides for a seven-day period of purification for the altar (43:18–27).

37. *most holy* Hebrew *kodesh kodashim*, literally "holy of holies," is usually a technical term for the inner sanctum of the Tabernacle. However, it is also used, as here, in the sense of superior, rather than superlative, holiness.

shall become holy That is, its holiness is contagious.[27] In Mishnah Zevahim 9:1 some sages restrict the application of this principle to those items for which the altar is the proper place. Libations, for instance, would not contract holiness by coming into contact with the altar, according to this view.

THE REGULAR BURNT OFFERING (vv. 38–42)

The fourfold mention of the altar in the previous two verses affords appropriate occasion for introducing its primary, permanent function: to accommodate the daily burnt offering. This was the

lamb in the morning, and you shall offer the other lamb at twilight. [40]There shall be a tenth of a measure of choice flour with a quarter of a *hin* of beaten oil mixed in, and a libation of a quarter *hin* of wine for one lamb; [41]and you shall offer the other lamb at twilight, repeating with it the meal offering of the morning with its libation—an offering by fire for a pleasing odor to the LORD, [42]a regular burnt offering throughout the generations, at the entrance of the Tent of Meeting before the LORD.

For there I will meet with you, and there I will speak with you, [43]and there I will meet with the Israelites, and it shall be sanctified by My Presence. [44]I will sanctify the Tent of Meeting and the altar, and I will consecrate Aaron and his sons to serve Me as priests. [45]I will abide among the Israelites, and I will be their God. [46]And they shall know

תַּעֲשֶׂה בַבֹּקֶר וְאֵת הַכֶּבֶשׂ הַשֵּׁנִי תַּעֲשֶׂה בֵּין
הָעַרְבָּיִם: 40 וְעִשָּׂרֹן סֹלֶת בָּלוּל בְּשֶׁמֶן
כָּתִית רֶבַע הַהִין וְנֵסֶךְ רְבִיעִת הַהִין יַיִן לַכֶּבֶשׂ
הָאֶחָד: 41 וְאֵת הַכֶּבֶשׂ הַשֵּׁנִי תַּעֲשֶׂה בֵּין
הָעַרְבָּיִם כְּמִנְחַת הַבֹּקֶר וּכְנִסְכָּהּ תַּעֲשֶׂה־לָּהּ
לְרֵיחַ נִיחֹחַ אִשֶּׁה לַיהוָה: 42 עֹלַת תָּמִיד
לְדֹרֹתֵיכֶם פֶּתַח אֹהֶל־מוֹעֵד לִפְנֵי יְהוָה
אֲשֶׁר אִוָּעֵד לָכֶם שָׁמָּה לְדַבֵּר אֵלֶיךָ שָׁם:
43 וְנֹעַדְתִּי שָׁמָּה לִבְנֵי יִשְׂרָאֵל וְנִקְדַּשׁ בִּכְבֹדִי:
44 וְקִדַּשְׁתִּי אֶת־אֹהֶל מוֹעֵד וְאֶת־הַמִּזְבֵּחַ וְאֶת־
אַהֲרֹן וְאֶת־בָּנָיו אֲקַדֵּשׁ לְכַהֵן לִי: 45 וְשָׁכַנְתִּי
בְּתוֹךְ בְּנֵי יִשְׂרָאֵל וְהָיִיתִי לָהֶם לֵאלֹהִים:

core of the whole sacrificial system. Twice daily, a lamb was wholly burnt on the altar. Called in Hebrew *ʿolat ha-tamid*, "the regular burnt offering," the sacrifice came to be known simply as the *tamid* in postexilic times. First instituted with the installation of the priesthood, it was thereafter to be continued on a regular basis. The prescription is repeated in the comprehensive register of public offerings given in Numbers 28–29, where it heads the list.

The great importance that attached to the *tamid* in Temple times may be gauged by the fact that its suspension by the Seleucid king Antiochus IV Epiphanes in the year 167 B.C.E. was regarded by Jews as a disaster. The Book of Daniel (8:11–12; 11:31; 12:11) and 1 Maccabees 1:41–45 record the calamitous event. Mishnah Taʿanit 4:6 includes the abolition of the *tamid* among the disasters to be commemorated by the Fast of the Seventeenth of Tammuz.[28]

38. *regularly*   On the meaning of Hebrew *tamid*, see Comment to 25:30 and 27:20.

39. *at twilight*   On Hebrew *bein ha-ʿarbayim*, see Comment to 12:6.

40. *a tenth of a measure*   Specifically of the *ephah*, on which see Comment to 16:36.

hin   This term for a liquid measure is of Egyptian origin, as Ibn Ezra observed. It appears originally to have designated a type of vessel.[29]

42. *there*   This refers back to the Tent of Meeting, not to the entrance. See Comment to 33:9.

A SUMMATION   (vv. 43–46)

The wealth of technical detail relating to the physical structure of the Tabernacle, its constitutive elements, and its ritual and practitioners may tend to obscure its original higher purpose. Therefore, the chapter closes with an emphatic reaffirmation of its religious and spiritual content, values, and meanings.

43. *I will meet*   See Comment to 25:22.

it shall be sanctified   That is, the Tent of Meeting.

My Presence   See Comment to 16:10.

44.   The Tabernacle as such possesses no innate sanctity, nor does the regimen of ritual produce it. No efficacious magic derives from them. The sacred status of the priests and of the edifice, with its furniture and utensils, flows solely from Divine will.

45. *I will abide*   See Comment to 25:8.

that I the LORD am their God, who brought them out from the land of Egypt that I might abide among them, I the LORD their God.

46 וְיָדְע֗וּ כִּ֣י אֲנִ֤י יְהוָֹה֙ אֱלֹ֣הֵיהֶ֔ם אֲשֶׁ֨ר הוֹצֵ֧אתִי אֹתָ֛ם מֵאֶ֥רֶץ מִצְרַ֖יִם לְשָׁכְנִ֣י בְתוֹכָ֑ם אֲנִ֖י יְהוָ֥ה אֱלֹהֵיהֶֽם: פ   שביעי

I will be their God   See Comment to 6:7.[30]

46.   they shall know   A key phrase in the Exodus narratives. See Comment to 1:8. God's Presence is manifest and meaningful to Israel through His intervention in the events of history.

CHAPTER 30

An Appendix to the Instructions   (30:1–38)

This chapter comprises supplementary instructions relating to the construction of the Tabernacle and to its rituals. It contains five sections in all: (1) the incense altar (vv. 1–10); (2) the expiation money (vv. 11–16); (3) the bronze laver (vv. 17–21); (4) the aromatic anointing oil (vv. 22–23); and (5) the ingredients of the incense (vv. 34–38). All the materials needed for these final items were anticipated in the list of invited donations in 25:3–6. There may be a specific reason why each of these items is relegated to an appendix and not included in the preceding instructions.

THE INCENSE ALTAR   (vv. 1–10)

The use of incense in rites of worship was widespread and had a long history in the ancient world. It is surprising, therefore, that the instruction to build an altar for the ritual burning of incense in the Tabernacle is not included in the main pericope. A possible answer is that although incense is foretokened in 25:6, it plays no role in the installation ceremonies of the priesthood. Hence, notice of its use is deferred until those directives are completed. As to the reason for omitting the incense offering from those rituals, the symbolism that attached to it made it inappropriate to the occasion. There are grounds for believing that the cloud of aromatic incense in the Tabernacle and later in the Temple was perceived to be emblematic or a reminder of God's invisible, active Presence, just as was the cloud that accompanied the Israelites at the Exodus from Egypt and in the course of the wanderings in the wilderness, as noted in the Comment to 13:21. The ritual for the Day of Atonement requires that the High Priest "shall put the incense on the fire before the LORD so that the cloud from the incense screens the cover that is over" the Ark (Lev. 16:13). It is explained that God appears "in the cloud over the cover" (Lev. 16:2). Thus, the cloud of incense screens the High Priest from the Divine Presence even as it serves as a constant reminder of It. The cloud of glory is said to descend on the Tabernacle and to suffuse it only after the structure is entirely completed and only at the end of the seven days of ceremony.[1] That phenomenon expresses divine satisfaction and acceptance of the shrine and signifies its divine legitimation as the house of worship.[2] Hence, it would have been premature to produce the cloud of incense at the installation of the priesthood.

The present sequence of topics also allows for certain verbal and thematic connectives with both the previous chapter and the following section: Mention of God's "meeting" with Moses appears in 29:42–43 and 30:6; the performance of purification occurs in 29:36–37 and 30:10; the phrase "throughout the ages/generations"[3] is featured in 29:42 and 30:8,10; and the description "most holy" is applied in 29:37 and 30:10. Moreover, both the incense of verses 1–10 and the half-shekel of verses 11–16 fulfill an expiatory function.

The importance attached to the altar for incense is shown by its placement in the Holy Place just outside the curtain that veils the Holy of Holies. This contrasts with the siting of the altar of burnt offerings in the outer court.

The altar is known by several names: "the altar of gold"[4] (Heb. *mizbaḥ ha-zahav*), to distinguish it from the "altar of bronze" used for animal sacrifices; "the altar of incense"[5] (Heb. *mizbaḥ ha-*

30 You shall make an altar for burning incense; make it of acacia wood. ²It shall be a cubit long and a cubit wide—it shall be square—and two cubits high, its horns of one piece with it. ³Overlay it with pure gold: its top, its sides round about, and its horns; and make a gold molding for it round about. ⁴And make two gold rings for it under its molding; make them on its two side walls, on opposite sides. They shall serve as holders for poles with which to carry it. ⁵Make the poles of acacia wood, and overlay them with gold.

⁶Place it in front of the curtain that is over the Ark of the Pact—in front of the cover that is over the Pact—where I will meet with you. ⁷On it Aaron shall burn aromatic incense: he shall burn it every morning when he tends the lamps, ⁸and Aaron shall burn it at twilight when he lights the lamps—a regular incense offering before the LORD throughout the ages. ⁹You shall not offer alien incense on it, or a burnt offering or a meal offering; neither shall you pour a libation on it. ¹⁰Once a year Aaron shall perform

לְ וְעָשִׂ֨יתָ מִזְבֵּ֖חַ מִקְטַ֣ר קְטֹ֑רֶת עֲצֵ֥י שִׁטִּ֖ים
תַּעֲשֶׂ֥ה אֹתֽוֹ: 2 אַמָּ֨ה אָרְכּ֜וֹ וְאַמָּ֤ה רָחְבּוֹ֙ רָב֣וּעַ
יִהְיֶ֔ה וְאַמָּתַ֖יִם קֹֽמָת֑וֹ מִמֶּ֖נּוּ קַרְנֹתָֽיו: 3 וְצִפִּיתָ֨
אֹת֜וֹ זָהָ֣ב טָה֗וֹר אֶת־גַּגּ֤וֹ וְאֶת־קִֽירֹתָיו֙ סָבִ֔יב
וְאֶת־קַרְנֹתָ֑יו וְעָשִׂ֥יתָ לּ֛וֹ זֵ֥ר זָהָ֖ב סָבִֽיב: 4 וּשְׁתֵּי֩
טַבְּעֹ֨ת זָהָ֜ב תַּעֲשֶׂה־לּ֣וֹ ׀ מִתַּ֣חַת לְזֵר֗וֹ עַ֚ל
שְׁתֵּ֣י צַלְעֹתָ֔יו תַּעֲשֶׂ֖ה עַל־שְׁנֵ֣י צִדָּ֑יו וְהָיָה֙
לְבָתִּ֣ים לְבַדִּ֔ים לָשֵׂ֥את אֹת֖וֹ בָּהֵֽמָּה: 5 וְעָשִׂ֥יתָ
אֶת־הַבַּדִּ֖ים עֲצֵ֣י שִׁטִּ֑ים וְצִפִּיתָ֥ אֹתָ֖ם זָהָֽב:

6 וְנָתַתָּ֣ה אֹת֗וֹ לִפְנֵ֤י הַפָּרֹ֙כֶת֙ אֲשֶׁ֣ר עַל־אֲרֹ֣ן
הָֽעֵדֻ֔ת לִפְנֵ֣י הַכַּפֹּ֔רֶת אֲשֶׁ֖ר עַל־הָֽעֵדֻ֑ת אֲשֶׁ֛ר
אִוָּעֵ֥ד לְךָ֖ שָֽׁמָּה: 7 וְהִקְטִ֥יר עָלָ֛יו אַהֲרֹ֖ן קְטֹ֣רֶת
סַמִּ֑ים בַּבֹּ֣קֶר בַּבֹּ֗קֶר בְּהֵיטִיב֛וֹ אֶת־הַנֵּרֹ֖ת יַקְטִירֶֽנָּה:
8 וּבְהַעֲלֹ֨ת אַהֲרֹ֧ן אֶת־הַנֵּרֹ֛ת בֵּ֥ין הָֽעַרְבַּ֖יִם
יַקְטִירֶ֑נָּה קְטֹ֧רֶת תָּמִ֛יד לִפְנֵ֥י יְהֹוָ֖ה לְדֹרֹֽתֵיכֶֽם:
9 לֹא־תַעֲל֥וּ עָלָ֛יו קְטֹ֥רֶת זָרָ֖ה וְעֹלָ֣ה וּמִנְחָ֑ה וְנֵ֕סֶךְ
לֹ֥א תִסְּכ֖וּ עָלָֽיו: 10 וְכִפֶּ֤ר אַהֲרֹן֙ עַל־קַרְנֹתָ֔יו אַחַ֖ת

מפטיר

---

ketoret), to designate its exclusive function; and, in rabbinic literature, "the inner altar"[6] (Heb. *mizbeah ha-penimi*), to differentiate it from the other altar of the outer court.

The object in question was quite small, measuring a mere 1.5 feet (0.45 m.) square at the top and standing 3 feet (0.9 m.) high. This is 9 inches higher than the table. It had a flat top, unlike the other altar, which was hollow and had none.[7] Like the Ark and the table, it was embellished with a molding,[8] and also like them, it was transported through the wilderness by means of poles inserted through rings affixed to its sides.[9]

1. an altar   Hebrew *mizbeah*, literally "place of slaughter," is strictly applicable only to an altar for animal sacrifice but is used for this object because of its similar shape.[10]

for burning incense   Maimonides maintains that the use of incense was originally instituted to ameliorate and sweeten the stench of the burning flesh of the sacrifices.[11] While this may be so, there is no doubt that it became an independent ritual in its own right, with its own significance and mystique. The ingredients of which the incense is to be compounded are listed in verses 34–38.

3. pure gold   See Comment to 25:11,31.

7–8.   Although it would appear from these verses that both the incense offering and the tending and lighting of the lamps are to be the prerogatives of the High Priest, we know that the daily performance of these rituals was carried out by the ordinary priests as well. Not only does 27:21 make this clear in respect of the lamp lighting, but 2 Chronicles 26:8, Mishnah Yoma 4:4, and Mishnah Tamid 6:3 all attest to it in regard to the incense offering.

7. aromatic incense   Hebrew *ketoret sammim*. The noun *ketoret* derives from a stem meaning "to burn, smoke"; it eventually became the generic term for the substance that produces the aroma. The identical semantic development is seen in the English words "incense," from Latin *incendere*, "to burn," and "perfume" from a combination of Latin *per*, "through," and *fumum*, "smoke." The second Hebrew word, *sammim*, is of uncertain origin. It points to a specific type of incense. In later Hebrew *sam* denotes a drug, medicine, or poison.

tends   Literally, "makes good," that is, cleans the lamps of refuse and replaces the wicks and the oil.[12]

9. alien incense   Hebrew *ketoret zarah*. On the latter word, see Comment to 29:33. Any

purification upon its horns with blood of the sin offering of
purification; purification shall be performed upon it once a
year throughout the ages. It is most holy to the LORD.

בְּשָׁנָ֡ה מִדַּם֩ חַטַּ֨את הַכִּפֻּרִ֜ים אַחַ֣ת בַּשָּׁנָ֗ה יְכַפֵּ֨ר
עָלָ֜יו לְדֹרֹ֣תֵיכֶ֗ם קֹֽדֶשׁ־קָֽדָשִׁ֥ים ה֖וּא לַיהוָֽה:
פ

KI TISSA'

11The LORD spoke to Moses, saying: 12When you take a
census of the Israelite people according to their enroll-
ment, each shall pay the LORD a ransom for himself on

כי תשא

11 וַיְדַבֵּ֥ר יְהוָ֖ה אֶל־מֹשֶׁ֥ה לֵּאמֹֽר: 12 כִּ֣י תִשָּׂ֞א
אֶת־רֹ֥אשׁ בְּנֵֽי־יִשְׂרָאֵל֮ לִפְקֻֽדֵיהֶם֒ וְנָֽתְנ֗וּ אִ֛ישׁ
כֹּ֧פֶר נַפְשׁ֛וֹ לַֽיהוָ֖ה בִּפְקֹ֣ד אֹתָ֑ם וְלֹא־יִֽהְיֶ֥ה בָהֶ֛ם

incense not precisely compounded according to the formula of verses 34–36 is invalid. Compare the
narrative about the infraction of the cultic rules by Aaron's two sons, as told in Leviticus 10:1–7.

or a burnt offering . . .   It is to be used exclusively for the prescribed incense offering.

10.   The sole exception to the last-mentioned rule is when the High Priest has to perform
the purificatory rites for reconsecrating the altar each Yom Kippur, as prescribed in Leviticus 16:16–19.

most holy   See Comment to 29:37.

THE CENSUS AND THE POLL TAX[13]   (vv. 11–16)

Ki Tissa'   A census of males above the age of twenty is to be accompanied by the imposition of a poll tax of one
half-shekel on each. This payment is considered to be a ransom for the life of the individual; it serves
to avert a plague. In other words, it has an expiatory function, which connects this topic with the one
immediately preceding it. Both feature a threefold emphasis of the Hebrew stem *k-p-r*, variously
translated "purification, ransom, expiation."

This passage recognizes that census taking is a necessary administrative measure but regards it as
fraught with danger to the public. The several such head counts recorded in the Bible are usually
related to army service and warfare.[14] In only one other instance is there any mention of the payment
of ransom money or of ill consequences—the remarkable exception of the census ordered by David,
which resulted in a visitation of pestilence, as told in 2 Samuel 24. Joab's reluctance to undertake the
assignment, and David's subsequent uneasy conscience about it, reflect the same underlying notion
as stated here: a peacetime census is a perilous enterprise that engenders popular anxiety. There may
have been sound historical reasons for Joab's reaction, for a census almost invariably portended
preparation for war or the imposition of some new tax. It is of interest that the postbiblical term
kenas, a Hebraized form of Latin *census*, means "a penalty," and the verbal form denotes "to sentence,
impose a fine, confiscate property."

The head count envisaged in the present section is separate from that commanded in Numbers 1.
This one precedes the construction of the Tabernacle, as 38:24–28 shows; the collected half-shekels
are used for casting the sockets of the sanctuary. The census of Numbers 1 must postdate the
completion of the Tent of Meeting, since it was ordained to Moses from inside it.

The present poll tax is a one-time imposition for the building of the Tabernacle, and not an
annual obligation. In later times, however, the injunction was treated as a precedent, and the text
came to be interpreted as such.[15] In Second Temple times Jews contributed the half-shekel annually
from all the lands of their dispersal.[16] The money was used to maintain the communal offerings and
for other public projects.[17] Following the destruction of the Temple in about 70 C.E., the emperor
Vespasian forced the Jews to contribute the annual tax to the imperial treasury for the god Jupiter
Capitolinus in Rome.[18] This levy, known as the *Fiscus Judaicus*, was still in force in the third century.

In Temple times the payment of the half-shekel was due during the month of Adar. On the first
thereof, messengers departed to all the Jewish communities to collect the tax.[19] Hence, on the
Sabbath before that date, or on the New Moon of that month should it fall on a Sabbath, Exodus
30:11–16 is added to the weekly Torah reading, and the day is known as *shabbat shekalim*.

being enrolled, that no plague may come upon them through their being enrolled. ¹³This is what everyone who is entered in the records shall pay: a half-shekel by the sanctuary weight—twenty *gerahs* to the shekel—a half-shekel as an offering to the LORD. ¹⁴Everyone who is entered in the records, from the age of twenty years up, shall give the LORD's offering: ¹⁵the rich shall not pay more and the poor shall not pay less than half a shekel when giving the LORD's offering as expiation for your persons. ¹⁶You shall take the expiation money from the Israelites and assign it to the service of the Tent of Meeting; it shall serve the Israelites as a reminder before the LORD, as expiation for your persons.

נֶגֶף בִּפְקֹד אֹתָם: ¹³ זֶה ׀ יִתְּנוּ כָּל־הָעֹבֵר עַל־הַפְּקֻדִים מַחֲצִית הַשֶּׁקֶל בְּשֶׁקֶל הַקֹּדֶשׁ עֶשְׂרִים גֵּרָה הַשֶּׁקֶל מַחֲצִית הַשֶּׁקֶל תְּרוּמָה לַיהוָה: ¹⁴ כֹּל הָעֹבֵר עַל־הַפְּקֻדִים מִבֶּן עֶשְׂרִים שָׁנָה וָמָעְלָה יִתֵּן תְּרוּמַת יְהוָה: ¹⁵ הֶעָשִׁיר לֹא־יַרְבֶּה וְהַדַּל לֹא יַמְעִיט מִמַּחֲצִית הַשָּׁקֶל לָתֵת אֶת־תְּרוּמַת יְהוָה לְכַפֵּר עַל־נַפְשֹׁתֵיכֶם: ¹⁶ וְלָקַחְתָּ אֶת־כֶּסֶף הַכִּפֻּרִים מֵאֵת בְּנֵי יִשְׂרָאֵל וְנָתַתָּ אֹתוֹ עַל־עֲבֹדַת אֹהֶל מוֹעֵד וְהָיָה לִבְנֵי יִשְׂרָאֵל לְזִכָּרוֹן לִפְנֵי יְהוָה לְכַפֵּר עַל־נַפְשֹׁתֵיכֶם: פ

12. take a census The Hebrew phrase literally means "to raise the head," that is, to take a head count. The idiom in this sense is peculiar to priestly texts.[20]

a ransom for himself Hebrew *kofer* is a monetary payment made in lieu of a physical penalty incurred.[21] See Comment to 21:30. Numbers 35:31–32 proscribes taking such redemption money for the life of a murderer. In the present case, the idea seems to be that a census places the lives of those counted in jeopardy.

13. who is entered in the records An idiomatic rendering of the Hebrew, which literally means "who passes by the numbered ones."[22] The stem ʿ-v-r, "to pass," used here is found a few times in connection with the method of counting sheep.[23] Mishnah Bekhorot 9:7 describes the system of tithing sheep as follows: The animals are taken into an enclosed area that has an opening large enough to permit only one sheep at a time to go through. The officer counts them as they emerge and places a mark on every tenth one. A similar system may have been in vogue for taking a census. Those mustered passed single file before the officer in charge. It is also possible that the tally was made indirectly by counting the number of half-shekels.

a half-shekel Not a coin but a unit of weight for gold and silver.[24] The present such is defined as "the sanctuary weight."[25] This would have been heavier than the shekel "at the going merchants' rate."[26] There was also a standard known as "the royal weight."[27] Many marked shekel weights have been found in Israel. Although they are not uniform, they indicate an average weight of 11.4 grams.[28]

twenty gerahs The *gerah* was the smallest subdivision of the shekel. The term, which probably means "a grain," is derived from Akkadian *giru*, which was one twenty-fourth of a shekel in the Mesopotamian system. Weights marked *gerah* that have been found in Israel have an average weight of 0.5658 grams.[29]

14. twenty years This is the age at which an Israelite became subject to military service.[30]

15. The contribution of the half-shekel has two purposes: to support the work of the Tabernacle and to effect expiation for each individual. The Tabernacle belongs equally to every Israelite, irrespective of one's social status or wealth. As all human beings are equal before God, there is to be one standard contribution from all, to be neither exceeded nor reduced.

16. expiation money Hebrew *kesef ha-kippurim*, a designation based on the use of the stem k-p-r in verses 12,15.

the service of the Tent Hebrew ʿavodah may refer both to the maintenance of the worship and to the work of construction. It has this latter meaning in 39:32. And since the silver was used for casting the sockets of the sanctuary and for the manufacture of other items (38:25–28), it should be so understood here.

196

¹⁷The LORD spoke to Moses, saying: ¹⁸Make a laver of copper and a stand of copper for it, for washing; and place it between the Tent of Meeting and the altar. Put water in it, ¹⁹and let Aaron and his sons wash their hands and feet [in water drawn] from it. ²⁰When they enter the Tent of Meeting they shall wash with water, that they may not die; or when they approach the altar to serve, to turn into smoke an offering by fire to the LORD, ²¹they shall wash their hands and feet, that they may not die. It shall be a law for all time for them—for him and his offspring—throughout the ages.

יז וַיְדַבֵּר יְהוָה אֶל־מֹשֶׁה לֵּאמֹר: 18 וְעָשִׂיתָ
כִּיּוֹר נְחֹשֶׁת וְכַנּוֹ נְחֹשֶׁת לְרָחְצָה וְנָתַתָּ אֹתוֹ בֵּין־
אֹהֶל מוֹעֵד וּבֵין הַמִּזְבֵּחַ וְנָתַתָּ שָׁמָּה מָיִם:
19 וְרָחֲצוּ אַהֲרֹן וּבָנָיו מִמֶּנּוּ אֶת־יְדֵיהֶם וְאֶת־
רַגְלֵיהֶם: 20 בְּבֹאָם אֶל־אֹהֶל מוֹעֵד יִרְחֲצוּ־מַיִם
וְלֹא יָמֻתוּ אוֹ בְגִשְׁתָּם אֶל־הַמִּזְבֵּחַ לְשָׁרֵת
לְהַקְטִיר אִשֶּׁה לַיהוָה: 21 וְרָחֲצוּ יְדֵיהֶם וְרַגְלֵיהֶם
וְלֹא יָמֻתוּ וְהָיְתָה לָהֶם חָק־עוֹלָם לוֹ וּלְזַרְעוֹ
לְדֹרֹתָם: פ

THE BRONZE LAVER   (vv. 17–21)

This vessel was not included in the earlier instructions for several reasons: (1) The use to which it was put was not an act of divine worship but was preparatory to it. (2) It was not needed for the installation ceremony because that required immersion of the entire body, whereas the laver was solely for washing the hands and feet. (3) It was not fashioned with materials provided by the public donations but from the bronze mirrors of the women who served at the entrance of the Tabernacle. See Comment to 38:8.

For practical reasons, the laver was placed between the entrance of the Tabernacle and the altar of sacrifice, so that the priest entered the sanctuary in a state of ritual purity and bodily cleanliness. Its importance may be weighed by its inclusion among the vessels that were consecrated by being anointed with oil (v. 28).

The dimensions of the laver are not given. According to Zevaḥim 19b, it had to be large enough to contain sufficient water for the washing of four priests. The same source reports that the priests washed in a standing position, but with each hand on the corresponding foot so that each pair was washed simultaneously.

20. *that they may not die*   On this formula, see Comment to 28:35. The washing is an indispensable requirement; its neglect renders the priest's service invalid.

THE AROMATIC ANOINTING OIL   (vv. 22–33)

The anointing oil and the spices needed for it were mentioned in 25:6. Ibn Ezra points out[31] that because the ingredients were supplied by the tribal chieftains and were not acquired by donations from the public,[32] the instructions for compounding the oil were deferred to this appendix. The association of washing and anointing the body may have determined the sequence of topics.[33]

Spices and perfumes were rare, highly prized commodities in the ancient world. As 1 Kings 10:2, 10 relate, the queen of Sheba arrived in Jerusalem bearing gifts of spices, gold, and precious stones for King Solomon. Like silver and gold, fragrant oils and spices were stored in the Judean royal treasury (2 Kings 20:13). These products were costly due to the huge amounts of raw materials needed to manufacture the desired quantity and to the great distances they had to be transported by land caravan or by sea from distant locations in Arabia, Somaliland, India, and even China.[34] It will be remembered that the caravan of Ishmaelites to whom Joseph was sold by his brothers was on its way to Egypt from Gilead with a load of precious spices (Gen. 37:25). Finally, the highly specialized art of perfumery demanded a high level of skill and experience.

The formula for blending the anointing oil given here specifies four "choice spices"[35] mixed with olive oil.

²²The LORD spoke to Moses, saying: ²³Next take choice spices: five hundred weight of solidified myrrh, half as much—two hundred and fifty—of fragrant cinnamon, two hundred and fifty of aromatic cane, ²⁴five hundred—by the sanctuary weight—of cassia, and a *hin* of olive oil. ²⁵Make of this a sacred anointing oil, a compound of ingredients expertly blended, to serve as sacred anointing oil. ²⁶With it anoint the Tent of Meeting, the Ark of the Pact, ²⁷the table and all its utensils, the lampstand and all its fittings, the altar of incense, ²⁸the altar of burnt offering and all its utensils, and the laver and its stand. ²⁹Thus you shall consecrate them so that they may be most holy; whatever touches them shall be consecrated. ³⁰You shall also anoint Aaron and his sons, consecrating them to serve Me as priests.

³¹And speak to the Israelite people, as follows: This shall be an anointing oil sacred to Me throughout the ages. ³²It must not be rubbed on any person's body, and you must not make anything like it in the same proportions; it is sacred, to be held sacred by you. ³³Whoever compounds its like, or puts any of it on a layman, shall be cut off from his kin.

²² וַיְדַבֵּ֥ר יְהוָ֖ה אֶל־מֹשֶׁ֥ה לֵּאמֹֽר: ²³ וְאַתָּ֣ה קַח־לְךָ֮ בְּשָׂמִ֣ים רֹאשׁ֒ מָר־דְּרוֹר֙ חֲמֵ֣שׁ מֵא֔וֹת וְקִנְּמָן־בֶּ֥שֶׂם מַחֲצִית֖וֹ חֲמִשִּׁ֣ים וּמָאתָ֑יִם וּקְנֵה־בֹ֖שֶׂם חֲמִשִּׁ֥ים וּמָאתָֽיִם: ²⁴ וְקִדָּ֕ה חֲמֵ֥שׁ מֵא֖וֹת בְּשֶׁ֣קֶל הַקֹּ֑דֶשׁ וְשֶׁ֥מֶן זַ֖יִת הִֽין: ²⁵ וְעָשִׂ֣יתָ אֹת֗וֹ שֶׁ֚מֶן מִשְׁחַת־קֹ֔דֶשׁ רֹ֥קַח מִרְקַ֖חַת מַעֲשֵׂ֣ה רֹקֵ֑חַ שֶׁ֥מֶן מִשְׁחַת־קֹ֖דֶשׁ יִהְיֶֽה: ²⁶ וּמָשַׁחְתָּ֥ ב֖וֹ אֶת־אֹ֣הֶל מוֹעֵ֑ד וְאֵ֖ת אֲר֥וֹן הָעֵדֻֽת: ²⁷ וְאֶת־הַשֻּׁלְחָן֙ וְאֶת־כָּל־כֵּלָ֔יו וְאֶת־הַמְּנֹרָ֖ה וְאֶת־כֵּלֶ֑יהָ וְאֵ֖ת מִזְבַּ֥ח הַקְּטֹֽרֶת: ²⁸ וְאֶת־מִזְבַּ֥ח הָעֹלָ֖ה וְאֶת־כָּל־כֵּלָ֑יו וְאֶת־הַכִּיֹּ֖ר וְאֶת־כַּנּֽוֹ: ²⁹ וְקִדַּשְׁתָּ֣ אֹתָ֔ם וְהָי֖וּ קֹ֣דֶשׁ קָֽדָשִׁ֑ים כָּל־הַנֹּגֵ֥עַ בָּהֶ֖ם יִקְדָּֽשׁ: ³⁰ וְאֶת־אַהֲרֹ֥ן וְאֶת־בָּנָ֖יו תִּמְשָׁ֑ח וְקִדַּשְׁתָּ֥ אֹתָ֖ם לְכַהֵ֥ן לִֽי:

³¹ וְאֶל־בְּנֵ֥י יִשְׂרָאֵ֖ל תְּדַבֵּ֣ר לֵאמֹ֑ר שֶׁ֣מֶן מִשְׁחַת־קֹ֜דֶשׁ יִהְיֶ֥ה זֶ֛ה לִ֖י לְדֹרֹתֵיכֶֽם: ³² עַל־בְּשַׂ֤ר אָדָם֙ לֹ֣א יִיסָ֔ךְ וּבְמַ֨תְכֻּנְתּ֔וֹ לֹ֥א תַעֲשׂ֖וּ כָּמֹ֑הוּ קֹ֣דֶשׁ ה֔וּא קֹ֖דֶשׁ יִהְיֶ֥ה לָכֶֽם: ³³ אִ֚ישׁ אֲשֶׁ֣ר יִרְקַ֣ח כָּמֹ֔הוּ וַאֲשֶׁ֛ר יִתֵּ֥ן מִמֶּ֖נּוּ עַל־זָ֑ר וְנִכְרַ֖ת מֵעַמָּֽיו: ס

---

23. The list is set out in decreasing order of value.

solidified myrrh Southern Arabia and Somaliland were the sources of this aromatic gum resin.³⁶ The substance exudes naturally as globules from the ducts of the trunk and branches of the trees, but it flows freely if one makes a cut in the bark. It hardens slowly when exposed to air.

fragrant cinnamon As Rashi notes, the adjective is needed because there are nonaromatic species of cinnamon.³⁷ The tree is indigenous to Ceylon (modern Sri Lanka) but was also cultivated elsewhere in Asia.

aromatic cane Although Hebrew *kaneh* is mentioned several times in the Bible,³⁸ its identity is uncertain. Here again there appear to be nonaromatic species of the plant. Jeremiah 6:20 refers to the "fragrant" (literally "good") cane from a distant land.

24. cassia Hebrew *kiddah*,³⁹ so rendered by the Targums (*ketsi'ata*),⁴⁰ has not been identified with certainty. The Greek translation understood it to be calamus.

25. expertly blended Literally, "the work of a perfumer." The skill was practiced by both men and women.⁴¹

26–28. The sacred aromatic oil is to be applied both to the priests and to the articles of furniture and their utensils.⁴² The act of anointing consecrates them to divine service. Henceforth, their holiness is contagious. See Comment to 29:37.

31–33. This sacred aromatic anointing oil, with its specific ingredients blended in the appropriate proportions, must never be duplicated or used for any purpose other than that here stipulated.

a layman See Comment to 29:33.

34And the LORD said to Moses: Take the herbs stacte, onycha, and galbanum—these herbs together with pure frankincense; let there be an equal part of each. 35Make them into incense, a compound expertly blended, refined, pure, sacred. 36Beat some of it into powder, and put some before the Pact in the Tent of Meeting, where I will meet with you; it shall be most holy to you. 37But when you make this incense, you must not make any in the same proportions for yourselves; it shall be held by you sacred to the LORD. Whoever makes any like it, to smell of it, shall be cut off from his kin.

לד וַיֹּאמֶר יְהוָה אֶל־מֹשֶׁה קַח־לְךָ סַמִּים נָטָף ׀ וּשְׁחֵלֶת וְחֶלְבְּנָה סַמִּים וּלְבֹנָה זַכָּה בַּד בְּבַד יִהְיֶה: לה וְעָשִׂיתָ אֹתָהּ קְטֹרֶת רֹקַח מַעֲשֵׂה רוֹקֵחַ מְמֻלָּח טָהוֹר קֹדֶשׁ: לו וְשָׁחַקְתָּ מִמֶּנָּה הָדֵק וְנָתַתָּה מִמֶּנָּה לִפְנֵי הָעֵדֻת בְּאֹהֶל מוֹעֵד אֲשֶׁר אִוָּעֵד לְךָ שָׁמָּה קֹדֶשׁ קָדָשִׁים תִּהְיֶה לָכֶם: לז וְהַקְּטֹרֶת אֲשֶׁר תַּעֲשֶׂה בְּמַתְכֻּנְתָּהּ לֹא תַעֲשׂוּ לָכֶם קֹדֶשׁ תִּהְיֶה לְךָ לַיהוָה: לח אִישׁ אֲשֶׁר־יַעֲשֶׂה כָמוֹהָ לְהָרִיחַ בָּהּ וְנִכְרַת מֵעַמָּיו: ס

THE INGREDIENTS OF THE INCENSE   (vv. 34–38)

The original list of materials to be assembled for the construction of the Tabernacle and the order of divine service included "spices . . . for the aromatic incense" (25:6) but without specification. Instructions for the fabrication of the golden altar of incense were given above, in verses 1–10. Now the four ingredients of the incense to be offered on it are listed.

An ancient rabbinic text in Keritot 6a and TJ Yoma 4:5 (41a) enumerates eleven kinds of spices used for the incense offerings in the days of the Second Temple and treats the precise implementation of the prescription as a matter of the utmost seriousness. Several sources report that the priestly family of Abtinas retained a monopoly on the compounding of the incense and jealously guarded the secret formula.[43]

34. stacte   Hebrew *nataf*, derived from a stem meaning "to drip, drop," refers to a resin of a certain tree, apparently balsam or persimmon.[44]

onycha   The identity of Hebrew *sheḥelet* is uncertain. The Greek and Latin translations have *onyx*, literally "a nail," apparently referring to a nail-shaped mollusk from which an aromatic substance was produced. A similar tradition seems to be behind the corresponding rabbinic term *tsipporen*, literally "a fingernail."

galbanum   Hebrew *ḥelbenah*, a gum resin extracted from a plant of the ferula class that grows in Turkistan, Persia, and Crete. It emits a disagreeable odor when burned; but this is diffused when the substance is blended with the other aromatics, and it has the effect of making the latter more pungent.[45]

This phenomenon gave rise to a rabbinic homily about tolerance. Just as the galbanum with its unpleasant odor is an indispensable ingredient of the incense offering, so the sinners of Israel must be included in the prayer services on a fast day, otherwise it is no fast.[46]

frankincense   Also called "olibanum"; cf. Hebrew *levonah*, literally "whiteness," so called because of the white smoke it emits when burned. It is a gum resin extracted from trees of the genus Boswellia that is native to southern Arabia and northern Somaliland.[47]

35. refined   Hebrew *memullaḥ* literally means "salted" and refers to the addition of salt to the incense, for the practical purpose of enhancing the rate of burning and smoking. This was commonly done in the ancient world in regard to sacred as well as profane incense. There is no warrant for the rendering "refined."[48]

36.   Each day, morning and evening, some of the blended and pulverized incense is to be placed on the golden altar for the incense offerings.

37-38.   Like the aromatic oil (vv. 31–33), the incense, in composition and function, must not be produced for use in any but its prescribed ritual.

31 The LORD spoke to Moses: ²See, I have singled out by name Bezalel son of Uri son of Hur, of the tribe of Judah. ³I have endowed him with a divine spirit of skill, ability, and knowledge in every kind of craft; ⁴to make designs for work in gold, silver, and copper, ⁵to cut stones for setting and to carve wood—to work in every kind of craft. ⁶Moreover, I have assigned to him Oholiab son of Ahisamach, of the tribe of Dan; and I have also granted skill to all who are skillful, that they may make everything that I have commanded you: ⁷the Tent of Meeting, the Ark for the Pact and the cover upon it, and all the furnishings of the Tent; ⁸the table and its utensils, the pure lampstand and all its fittings, and the altar of incense; ⁹the altar of burnt offering and all its utensils, and the laver and its stand; ¹⁰the service vestments, the sacral vestments of Aaron the priest and the vestments of his sons, for their service as priests; ¹¹as well as

לֹ״א וַיְדַבֵּר יְהוָה אֶל־מֹשֶׁה לֵּאמֹר: 2 רְאֵה קָרָאתִי בְשֵׁם בְּצַלְאֵל בֶּן־אוּרִי בֶן־חוּר לְמַטֵּה יְהוּדָה: 3 וָאֲמַלֵּא אֹתוֹ רוּחַ אֱלֹהִים בְּחָכְמָה וּבִתְבוּנָה וּבְדַעַת וּבְכָל־מְלָאכָה: 4 לַחְשֹׁב מַחֲשָׁבֹת לַעֲשׂוֹת בַּזָּהָב וּבַכֶּסֶף וּבַנְּחֹשֶׁת: 5 וּבַחֲרֹשֶׁת אֶבֶן לְמַלֹּאת וּבַחֲרֹשֶׁת עֵץ לַעֲשׂוֹת בְּכָל־מְלָאכָה: 6 וַאֲנִי הִנֵּה נָתַתִּי אִתּוֹ אֵת אָהֳלִיאָב בֶּן־אֲחִיסָמָךְ לְמַטֵּה־דָן וּבְלֵב כָּל־חֲכַם־לֵב נָתַתִּי חָכְמָה וְעָשׂוּ אֵת כָּל־אֲשֶׁר צִוִּיתִךָ: 7 אֵת אֹהֶל מוֹעֵד וְאֶת־הָאָרֹן לָעֵדֻת וְאֶת־הַכַּפֹּרֶת אֲשֶׁר עָלָיו וְאֵת כָּל־כְּלֵי הָאֹהֶל: 8 וְאֶת־הַשֻּׁלְחָן וְאֶת־כֵּלָיו וְאֶת־הַמְּנֹרָה הַטְּהֹרָה וְאֶת־כָּל־כֵּלֶיהָ וְאֵת מִזְבַּח הַקְּטֹרֶת: 9 וְאֶת־מִזְבַּח הָעֹלָה וְאֶת־כָּל־כֵּלָיו וְאֶת־הַכִּיּוֹר וְאֶת־כַּנּוֹ: 10 וְאֵת בִּגְדֵי הַשְּׂרָד וְאֶת־בִּגְדֵי הַקֹּדֶשׁ לְאַהֲרֹן הַכֹּהֵן וְאֶת־בִּגְדֵי בָנָיו לְכַהֵן: 11 וְאֵת

CHAPTER 31   APPOINTMENT OF CONSTRUCTION PERSONNEL   (vv. 1–11)

The final instruction to Moses that directly relates to the work of the Tabernacle concerns the appointment of a supervisory master craftsman named Bezalel, a Judahite, and his associate Oholiab, a Danite. Presumably, Moses, Bezalel, and Oholiab are to recruit the subordinate workers, here described as those "who are skillful." In 38:21 special mention is made of Levites who work under the direction of Ithamar son of Aaron.

2. *singled out by name*   Commissioned for the task.[1]

Bezalel   The name means "in the shadow [that is, protection] of God."[2]

Uri   Probably a short form of Uriel or Uriah, meaning "God/Yah is my light."[3]

Hur   Six different persons bear this name in the Bible. Its origin is obscure, and it is uncertain if the one mentioned here is the same Hur who is frequently associated with Aaron.[4] See Comment to 17:10.

3. *a divine spirit*   See Comment to 28:3.

6. *Oholiab*   The name may mean either "the tent of the father" or "the father is my tent" (that is, my protection). It may contain a word play since it is the person with this name who is to construct the Tent of Meeting (v. 7).[5]

granted skill to all who are skillful   Citing Daniel 2:21, Rabbi Johanan states: "The Holy One Blessed Be He imparts wisdom only to one who already possesses it."[6]

7–11.   These verses summarize the components of the Tabernacle, its furnishings, and appurtenances in an order that differs slightly from that of the foregoing instructions.

7. *the Ark for the Pact*   The Ark that is intended to house the two tablets that symbolize the pact between God and Israel. See Comment to 25:22.[7]

8. *the pure lampstand*   See Comment to 25:31.

10. *the service vestments*   Hebrew *bigdei serad*. *Serad* is an obscure term for which there is no satisfactory Hebrew etymology.[8] Rashi, Rashbam, and Ibn Ezra connect it with Aramaic *s-r-d*, meaning "to plait" and so understand the phrase to mean "plaited cloths." They connect it with the coverings spread over the Tabernacle and its furnishings during the wilderness journeyings, as

שֶׁמֶן הַמִּשְׁחָה וְאֶת־קְטֹרֶת הַסַּמִּים לַקֹּדֶשׁ כְּכֹל
אֲשֶׁר־צִוִּיתִךָ יַעֲשׂוּ: פ
12 וַיֹּאמֶר יְהֹוָה אֶל־מֹשֶׁה לֵּאמֹר: 13 וְאַתָּה
דַּבֵּר אֶל־בְּנֵי יִשְׂרָאֵל לֵאמֹר אַךְ אֶת־שַׁבְּתֹתַי
תִּשְׁמֹרוּ כִּי אוֹת הִוא בֵּינִי וּבֵינֵיכֶם
לְדֹרֹתֵיכֶם לָדַעַת כִּי אֲנִי יְהֹוָה מְקַדִּשְׁכֶם:
14 וּשְׁמַרְתֶּם אֶת־הַשַּׁבָּת כִּי קֹדֶשׁ הִוא לָכֶם
מְחַלְלֶיהָ מוֹת יוּמָת כִּי כָּל־הָעֹשֶׂה בָהּ
מְלָאכָה וְנִכְרְתָה הַנֶּפֶשׁ הַהִוא מִקֶּרֶב עַמֶּיהָ:
15 שֵׁשֶׁת יָמִים יֵעָשֶׂה מְלָאכָה וּבַיּוֹם הַשְּׁבִיעִי
שַׁבַּת שַׁבָּתוֹן קֹדֶשׁ לַיהֹוָה כָּל־הָעֹשֶׂה מְלָאכָה
בְּיוֹם הַשַּׁבָּת מוֹת יוּמָת: 16 וְשָׁמְרוּ בְנֵי־יִשְׂרָאֵל
אֶת־הַשַּׁבָּת לַעֲשׂוֹת אֶת־הַשַּׁבָּת לְדֹרֹתָם בְּרִית
עוֹלָם: 17 בֵּינִי וּבֵין בְּנֵי יִשְׂרָאֵל אוֹת הִוא לְעֹלָם

prescribed in Numbers 4:7–14. In Yoma 72b the term *serad* is associated with the priestly vestments. The Targums and the Peshitta, as well as the Septuagint and the Vulgate, all take it to mean "service vestments." This rendering is supported both by the explanatory phrase "for officiating in the sanctuary" and by the appositional "sacral vestments," which follows all other usages of the term.[9]

THE OBSERVANCE OF THE SABBATH (vv. 12–17)

The concluding—and, appropriately, the seventh—literary unit within the pericope of the instructions for the Tabernacle is devoted to the observance of the law of the Sabbath. Correspondingly, the resumption of the Tabernacle narrative in chapter 35 commences with the Sabbath law. This structural pattern is intended to make an emphatic statement about the hierarchy of values that informs the Torah: The Tabernacle enshrines the concept of the holiness of space; the Sabbath embodies the concept of the holiness of time. The latter takes precedence over the former, and the work of the Tabernacle must yield each week to the Sabbath rest.

Quite deliberately the present unit features Creation as the rationale for the Sabbath (v. 17), as is found in the Decalogue (20:8–11), rather than the Exodus, as in the version in Deuteronomy (5:12–15). It is in the Creation narrative of Genesis that the first occurrence of the idea of the holy is encountered, and it relates to time—the Sabbath. This is in striking contrast to the Babylonian cosmology, which culminates in the erection of a temple to Marduk, thereby asserting the antithetical primacy of the holiness of space. See Comments to 3:5 and 20:8–11.

13. Nevertheless Hebrew *'akh* has restrictive force.[10] Even though building the Tabernacle is a divine command, it does not supersede the observance of the Sabbath.

My sabbaths This phrase is defined in verses 15 and 17. The Sabbath, that is, the sanctity of the seventh day of the week, is an integral part of the cosmic order ordained by God.

a sign The idea of the Sabbath as a sign is reiterated in verse 17.[11] Its observance is a declaration of faith, an affirmation that Israel is a holy nation not inherently but by an act of divine will; that the relationship between God and Israel is regulated by a covenant; and that the universe is wholly the purposeful product of divine intelligence, the work of a transcendent Being outside of nature and sovereign over space and time.

15. a sabbath of complete rest See Comment to 16:23.[12]

16. The obligation to observe the Sabbath is eternally encumbent upon those who participate in the covenant with God.

shall be a sign for all time between Me and the people of Israel. For in six days the LORD made heaven and earth, and on the seventh day He ceased from work and was refreshed.

18When He finished speaking with him on Mount Sinai, He gave Moses the two tablets of the Pact, stone tablets inscribed with the finger of God.

32 When the people saw that Moses was so long in coming down from the mountain, the people gathered against Aaron and said to him, "Come, make us a god who shall go before us, for that man Moses, who brought us

כִּי־שֵׁשֶׁת יָמִים עָשָׂה יְהוָה אֶת־הַשָּׁמַיִם וְאֶת־הָאָרֶץ וּבַיּוֹם הַשְּׁבִיעִי שָׁבַת וַיִּנָּפַשׁ: ס

שני

18 וַיִּתֵּן אֶל־מֹשֶׁה כְּכַלֹּתוֹ לְדַבֵּר אִתּוֹ בְּהַר סִינַי שְׁנֵי לֻחֹת הָעֵדֻת לֻחֹת אֶבֶן כְּתֻבִים בְּאֶצְבַּע אֱלֹהִים:

ל"ב וַיַּרְא הָעָם כִּי־בֹשֵׁשׁ מֹשֶׁה לָרֶדֶת מִן־הָהָר וַיִּקָּהֵל הָעָם עַל־אַהֲרֹן וַיֹּאמְרוּ אֵלָיו קוּם ׀ עֲשֵׂה־לָנוּ אֱלֹהִים אֲשֶׁר יֵלְכוּ לְפָנֵינוּ כִּי־זֶה ׀

17. **and was refreshed** Hebrew *va-yinnafash* is derived from the noun *nefesh*, a multivalent term that can refer to a person's life essence, vitality, psychic energy, or essential character.[13] The verbal form used here conveys the notion of a fresh infusion of spiritual and physical vigor, the reinvigoration of the totality of one's being. Of course, as applied to God, it is an anthropomorphism, the ascription to the Deity of human characteristics. But such language has a didactic purpose: to impress upon the Israelite an awareness of the transcendent value of Sabbath observance. Thus, the same verb is used in 23:12 to describe the invigorating consequences of the Sabbath rest: "that your bondman and the stranger may be refreshed [*ve-yinnafesh*]."

A CODA (v. 18)

This concluding verse, recording the receipt of the tablets of stone, picks up where the last narrative left off—Moses' ascent of Mount Sinai to receive those tokens of the covenant (24:12–18). It also serves as the transition to the next episode, which involves the smashing of those very tablets.

stone tablets Bekhor Shor notes that stone, as an enduring substance, is emblematic of the eternity of the content.

inscribed with the finger of God On this figurative language, see Comment to 32:16.[14]

The Violation of the Covenant: The Golden Calf (32:1–33:23)

The account of the Tabernacle is interrupted by the story of the making and worship of a golden calf. This episode separates the detailed set of instructions from the report of their implementation. The literary arrangement conveys the impression that the apostasy of the people—that is, their alienation from God—interfered with the building of the intended sanctuary that was to be the "Tent of Meeting" between God and Israel. The work could begin only after their reconciliation through the mediation of Moses.

CHAPTER 32   THE MAKING OF A GOLDEN CALF (vv. 1–6)

1. This verse is intelligible only in reference to 24:18, which told of Moses' ascent of the cloud-enveloped mountain and of his seclusion there for forty days and nights. Because Moses has until now fulfilled the role of exclusive mediator between God and Israel—at the urgent request of

from the land of Egypt—we do not know what has happened to him." ²Aaron said to them, "Take off the gold rings that are on the ears of your wives, your sons, and your daughters, and bring them to me." ³And all the people took off the gold rings that were in their ears and brought them to Aaron. ⁴This he took from them and cast in a mold, and made it into a molten calf. And they exclaimed, "This is your god, O Israel, who brought you out of the land of Egypt!" ⁵When Aaron saw this, he built an altar before it;

מֹשֶׁה הָאִישׁ אֲשֶׁר הֶעֱלָנוּ מֵאֶרֶץ מִצְרַיִם לֹא יָדַעְנוּ מֶה־הָיָה לוֹ: 2 וַיֹּאמֶר אֲלֵהֶם אַהֲרֹן פָּרְקוּ נִזְמֵי הַזָּהָב אֲשֶׁר בְּאָזְנֵי נְשֵׁיכֶם בְּנֵיכֶם וּבְנֹתֵיכֶם וְהָבִיאוּ אֵלָי: 3 וַיִּתְפָּרְקוּ כָּל־הָעָם אֶת־נִזְמֵי הַזָּהָב אֲשֶׁר בְּאָזְנֵיהֶם וַיָּבִיאוּ אֶל־אַהֲרֹן: 4 וַיִּקַּח מִיָּדָם וַיָּצַר אֹתוֹ בַּחֶרֶט וַיַּעֲשֵׂהוּ עֵגֶל מַסֵּכָה וַיֹּאמְרוּ אֵלֶּה אֱלֹהֶיךָ יִשְׂרָאֵל אֲשֶׁר הֶעֱלוּךָ מֵאֶרֶץ מִצְרָיִם: 5 וַיַּרְא אַהֲרֹן וַיִּבֶן מִזְבֵּחַ לְפָנָיו וַיִּקְרָא

the people, as told in 20:15–18[1]—his protracted absence generates deep anxiety, a mood exacerbated by the awareness of the impending departure from Sinai.

gathered against   Hebrew *nikhal ʿal* always carries a menacing nuance.[2]

make us a god   Something that is emblematic of immanent divinity. Rashbam suggests that they had in mind some instrument for determining the divine will as a replacement for Moses, the absent human medium of divine revelation.[3]

that man Moses   A disrespectful manner of speaking.[4]

who brought us from   And has now abandoned us.

3. *gold rings*   These may have been among the items the Israelites received from neighbors when they left Egypt, as related in 11:2–3 and 12:35–36. From the story in Genesis 35:4, where earrings are coupled with "alien gods" and are ritually buried with them, it is clear that they were not mere adornments but also had some cultic significance. This conclusion is reinforced by the narrative about Gideon in Judges 8:24–27. He too specifically requested gold earrings and manufactured from them an ephod, after which "all Israel went astray" and which "became a snare to Gideon and his household."

4. *cast in a mold*   The meaning of the Hebrew phrase is uncertain. The verb *va-yatsar* can denote "he fashioned"[5] or "he tied up";[6] the noun *ḥeret* can signify "a stylus" or "an engraving tool."[7] The phrase may therefore mean that Aaron fashioned the gold with a tool. This, however, would be inconsistent with the description of the image as being "molten,"[8] and one does not use an engraving tool on gold. It is possible that *ḥeret* is a variant form of *ḥarit*, "a bag,[9] which appears with the same verb as here in a similar context in 2 Kings 5:23: "He wrapped [*va-yatsar*] the two talents of silver in two bags [*haritim*]." In Exodus, then, Aaron tied up the gold earrings in a bag.[10] It is noteworthy that when Gideon made his image, he "spread out a cloth, and everyone threw onto it the earring."[11] Finally, the Hebrew phrase may well have originated in the technical vocabulary of ancient metallurgy and then become a metaphor simply expressing the imparting of shape to metal, regardless of the technique employed.[12]

molten   Most likely a wooden model was overlaid with gold.[13]

calf   Hebrew *ʿegel* is a young ox or bull. Thus, Psalm 106:19–20, in reference to this episode, alternates *ʿegel* with *shor*, "ox." Throughout the Near East the bull was a symbol of lordship, leadership, strength, vital energy, and fertility. As such, it was either deified and worshiped or employed in representation of divinity. Often the bull or some other animal served as the pedestal on which the god stood, elevated above human level.[14] The particular animal might be suggestive of the attributes ascribed to the god who was mounted upon it. Aaron seems to have followed contemporary artistic convention. The young bull would have been the pedestal upon which the invisible God of Israel was popularly believed to be standing. His presence would be left to human imagination.

This last interpretation is supported by the people's association of the manufactured image with the God who operates in history, not with some deity possessing mythological associations. It is strengthened by Aaron's proclamation (v. 5) that the following day would be "a festival of the LORD [*YHVH*]." In other words, the people, in demanding "a god" because of Moses' disappearance,

and Aaron announced: "Tomorrow shall be a festival of the LORD!" ⁶Early next day, the people offered up burnt offerings and brought sacrifices of well-being; they sat down to eat and drink, and then rose to dance.

⁷The LORD spoke to Moses, "Hurry down, for your people, whom you brought out of the land of Egypt, have acted basely. ⁸They have been quick to turn aside from the way that I enjoined upon them. They have made themselves a molten calf and bowed low to it and sacrificed to it, saying: 'This is your god, O Israel, who brought you out of the land of Egypt!'"

⁹The LORD further said to Moses, "I see that this is a stiffnecked people. ¹⁰Now, let Me be, that My anger may

אַהֲרֹן וַיֹּאמַר חַג לַיהֹוָה מָחָר: 6 וַיַּשְׁכִּימוּ מִמָּחֳרָת וַיַּעֲלוּ עֹלֹת וַיַּגִּשׁוּ שְׁלָמִים וַיֵּשֶׁב הָעָם לֶאֱכֹל וְשָׁתוֹ וַיָּקֻמוּ לְצַחֵק: פ

7 וַיְדַבֵּר יְהֹוָה אֶל־מֹשֶׁה לֶךְ־רֵד כִּי שִׁחֵת עַמְּךָ אֲשֶׁר הֶעֱלֵיתָ מֵאֶרֶץ מִצְרָיִם: 8 סָרוּ מַהֵר מִן־ הַדֶּרֶךְ אֲשֶׁר צִוִּיתִם עָשׂוּ לָהֶם עֵגֶל מַסֵּכָה וַיִּשְׁתַּחֲווּ־לוֹ וַיִּזְבְּחוּ־לוֹ וַיֹּאמְרוּ אֵלֶּה אֱלֹהֶיךָ יִשְׂרָאֵל אֲשֶׁר הֶעֱלוּךָ מֵאֶרֶץ מִצְרָיִם: 9 וַיֹּאמֶר יְהֹוָה אֶל־מֹשֶׁה רָאִיתִי אֶת־הָעָם הַזֶּה וְהִנֵּה עַם־קְשֵׁה־עֹרֶף הוּא: 10 וְעַתָּה הַנִּיחָה

wanted an appropriate visible object that would recall the Divine Presence in their midst. It should be noted that in verse 8 the focus of the indictment is on the making of a molten calf, not on worshiping "other gods."

they exclaimed   The ringleaders of the people, not Aaron.

This is your god   Rashbam and other medieval Jewish commentators have pointed out that the people "could not have been so stupid" as to believe that this freshly manufactured image was itself a deity responsible for the Exodus from Egypt. Rather, they felt that the object was a potent symbol that acquired a numinous quality, and that they could invoke the Deity through it.

It is to be noted that the demonstrative pronoun ('elleh) and the verb governed by 'elohim, "God," are in the plural form, and that a plural verb is also used in verses 1 and 23. Plural forms with 'elohim are found in a monotheistic context several times in the Bible,[15] and there is as yet no satisfactory explanation for this anomaly. In the present chapter the plural usage may be a scribal device to emphasize the unacceptable nature of the object. Aaron made only one image, and, significantly, Nehemiah 9:18, in recalling this episode, has the cry of the people in the singular, "This [zeh] is your God who brought you out [he'elkha] of Egypt."

6.   Aaron plays no further role. The rabble has taken over and has plunged into pagan orgiastic rites. Five verbs of action are employed to describe popular behavior. See Comment to verses 19–20.

to dance   This appears to be the meaning of tsaḥek in Judges 16:25. Verse 19 below explicitly refers to dancing. However, the same verb in Genesis 26:8 and 39:14,17 connotes sexual activity.

GOD'S ANGER AND MOSES' INTERCESSION   (vv. 7–14)

7–8.   When the boisterous revelry has reached its height, God informs Moses of what is happening in the camp below.

7.   *your people*   A strong intimation of their alienation from God[16] in contrast to "My people," repeatedly employed hitherto in divine speech.[17]

have acted basely   The calf, even if only intended as the pedestal of the invisible God of Israel, was very much an image of a living entity. It would inevitably divert human attention to itself and away from the invisible One that it was meant to invoke. The popular mind would regard the image-pedestal as an object endowed with divinity. By putting God back into nature, the people violated and nullified the fundamental distinctive idea of the religion of Israel.

8.   *to turn aside from the way*   Significantly, the text does not say "from Me"; they have adopted pagan modes of worship, but in worship of the God of Israel.[18]

9.   *I see*   Divine "seeing" as opposed to Aaron's "seeing" in verse 5.

blaze forth against them and that I may destroy them, and make of you a great nation." [11]But Moses implored the LORD his God, saying, "Let not Your anger, O LORD, blaze forth against Your people, whom You delivered from the land of Egypt with great power and with a mighty hand. [12]Let not the Egyptians say, 'It was with evil intent that He delivered them, only to kill them off in the mountains and annihilate them from the face of the earth.' Turn from Your blazing anger, and renounce the plan to punish Your

לִ֠י וְיִֽחַר־אַפִּ֤י בָהֶם֙ וַאֲכַלֵּ֔ם וְאֶֽעֱשֶׂ֥ה אוֹתְךָ֖ לְג֥וֹי גָּד֑וֹל: 11 וַיְחַ֣ל מֹשֶׁ֔ה אֶת־פְּנֵ֖י יְהוָ֣ה אֱלֹהָ֑יו וַיֹּ֗אמֶר לָמָ֤ה יְהוָה֙ יֶחֱרֶ֤ה אַפְּךָ֙ בְּעַמֶּ֔ךָ אֲשֶׁ֤ר הוֹצֵ֙אתָ֙ מֵאֶ֣רֶץ מִצְרַ֔יִם בְּכֹ֥חַ גָּד֖וֹל וּבְיָ֥ד חֲזָקָֽה: 12 לָ֣מָּה יֹאמְר֣וּ מִצְרַ֗יִם לֵאמֹ֞ר בְּרָעָ֣ה הֽוֹצִיאָ��,ם לַהֲרֹ֤ג אֹתָם֙ בֶּֽהָרִ֔ים וּלְכַלֹּתָ֔ם מֵעַ֖ל פְּנֵ֣י הָֽאֲדָמָ֑ה שׁ֚וּב מֵחֲר֣וֹן אַפֶּ֔ךָ וְהִנָּחֵ֥ם עַל־הָרָעָ֖ה

this . . . people　　God sardonically turns on the people their disrespectful reference to Moses (v. 1).

stiffnecked　　A frequent image of willful obstinacy, derived from the farmer's experience with work animals.

10. _let Me be_　　This phrase both intimates and anticipates intercession for Israel on the part of Moses.[19] As such, it is a tacit comment on Moses' extraordinary character. At the same time it implies that such intercession can be effective. Thus, it is also a statement about the nature of God: He is responsive to human entreaty. Intercession before God on behalf of man is an indispensable aspect of the prophetic role. In fact, the first scriptural usage of the term _navi'_, "prophet," appears in such a context. In Genesis 20:7 Abimelech is told, "Since he [Abraham] is a prophet, he will intercede for you." Moses frequently acts as intercessor,[20] as do Samuel,[21] Amos,[22] and especially Jeremiah.[23]

a great nation　　The phrase evokes the divine promises to the patriarch.[24] This is seized on at once by Moses.

11-14.　　These verses together with 34:1-10 comprise the Torah reading at the afternoon (_minḥah_) service on fast days other than Yom Kippur. Ibn Ezra takes note of an inconsistency. The present section concludes with a declaration of divine forbearance (v. 14); nevertheless, verses 30-34 record Moses' entreaty of God and conclude with his hope, "perhaps I may win forgiveness for your sin." To this complication may be added the fact that the parallel account in Deuteronomy 9:15-21 has Moses descending the mountain immediately after being apprised of the situation below and making intercession only after breaking the tablets.

Many modern scholars explain the anomalies as resulting from the amalgamation of varying traditions. Ibn Ezra concludes that verses 11-14 are out of chronological sequence and belong after verse 31. They have been placed here because they are Moses' response to God's intimation (v. 10) that intercession would be effective. Understanding the text differently, Ramban believes that verses 11-14 are in the correct place and that Moses made two separate intercessions. The first (vv. 11-14) was intended to gain rescission of the threat to destroy Israel, whereas the second (vv. 30-34) was to obtain forgiveness after the pulverization of the golden calf and the punishment of the transgressors. Ramban notes that in the version in Deuteronomy, events are telescoped because the story appears in a different context and is narrated for a different purpose.

Moses' petition rests on the following considerations: Israel is God's chosen people; God manifested His power in delivering Israel from Egypt; the destruction of Israel would diminish God's honor in the eyes of the Egyptians; further, God made promises to the patriarchs.

11.　　Moses' love of Israel is such that he nobly and selflessly rejects God's offer to make his own descendants the sole heirs to the promises made to the patriarchs. This same characteristic is once again displayed in verse 32.

The language of Moses' prayer echoes that of God's censure. God stated (v. 10), "My anger may blaze forth," and Moses prays, "Let not Your anger, O LORD, blaze forth," "Turn from Your blazing anger." God spoke of "your people, whom you brought out" (v. 7), and Moses counters with "Your people, whom You delivered."

12.　　The thrust of the events in Egypt was that the Egyptians might "know" the Lord,[25] that

205

people. ¹³Remember Your servants, Abraham, Isaac, and
Israel, how You swore to them by Your Self and said to
them: I will make your offspring as numerous as the stars of
heaven, and I will give to your offspring this whole land of
which I spoke, to possess forever." ¹⁴And the LORD renounced the punishment He had planned to bring upon
His people.

¹⁵Thereupon Moses turned and went down from the
mountain bearing the two tablets of the Pact, tablets inscribed on both their surfaces: they were inscribed on the
one side and on the other. ¹⁶The tablets were God's work,

לְעַמֶּֽךָ׃ 13 זְכֹר לְאַבְרָהָם לְיִצְחָק וּלְיִשְׂרָאֵל
עֲבָדֶיךָ אֲשֶׁר נִשְׁבַּעְתָּ לָהֶם בָּךְ וַתְּדַבֵּר אֲלֵהֶם
אַרְבֶּה אֶֽת־זַרְעֲכֶם כְּכוֹכְבֵי הַשָּׁמָיִם וְכָל־
הָאָרֶץ הַזֹּאת אֲשֶׁר אָמַרְתִּי אֶתֵּן לְזַרְעֲכֶם
וְנָחֲלוּ לְעֹלָֽם׃ 14 וַיִּנָּחֶם יְהוָה עַל־הָרָעָה אֲשֶׁר
דִּבֶּר לַעֲשׂוֹת לְעַמּֽוֹ׃ פ
15 וַיִּפֶן וַיֵּרֶד מֹשֶׁה מִן־הָהָר וּשְׁנֵי לֻחֹת
הָעֵדֻת בְּיָדוֹ לֻחֹת כְּתֻבִים מִשְּׁנֵי עֶבְרֵיהֶם מִזֶּה
וּמִזֶּה הֵם כְּתֻבִים׃ 16 וְהַלֻּחֹת מַעֲשֵׂה אֱלֹהִים
הֵמָּה וְהַמִּכְתָּב מִכְתַּב אֱלֹהִים הוּא חָרוּת עַל־

is, recognize His incomparability. The theological impact of the events of the Exodus would now be
undone. This sensitivity concerning God's reputation is a recurrent motif in the Bible.²⁶

13. Remember See Comment to 2:24.

14. the LORD renounced Moses' intercession succeeded in averting the threatened punishment. As the psalmist has it, "He would have destroyed them had not Moses, His chosen one,
confronted Him in the breach to avert His destructive wrath."²⁷

MOSES SMASHES THE TABLETS AND DESTROYS THE CALF (vv. 15–20)

15–16. The description of the tablets is not germane to the present context; it more
appropriately belongs in 31:18. Ramban suggests that it functions here to point up the strikingly
audacious nature of Moses' action in smashing the precious objects.

15. bearing the two tablets Their size is not recorded here, but their maximum dimensions are determined by the size of the Ark in which they were to repose. This was given in 25:10 as
being 2.5 cubits in length and 1.5 cubits in width and height (approximately 3.75 ft. × 2.25 ft. = 1.12 cm.
× 0.67 cm.). A rabbinic tradition recorded in Bava Batra 14a has the size of the tablets as 1 cubit by 1.5
cubits. At any rate, they could certainly have been carried without difficulty.

tablets of the Pact See Comment to 31:18.

inscribed The description here and in the next verse is obscure, but it is clearly intended to
express its singular nature.

16. God's work . . . God's writing This verse amplifies the statement in 24:12. Rashi
observes that these descriptions may be taken either literally or figuratively. If the latter, they convey
the idea that the Torah is God's preoccupation. Maimonides²⁸ rejects the literal interpretation that a
physical action on the part of God occurred. He cites Mishnah Avot 5:6, which places the inscribed
tablets of stone among the extraordinary phenomena that were created just before the onset of the
Sabbath at Creation. He explains this verse to imply that the tablets came into being at Creation by
divine will as part of the cosmic order. He notes that references to God's "work" and God's "finger"
appear also in Psalm 8:4 in reference to the creation of the heavens, which were brought into existence
by divine will (Ps. 33:6). Put a different way, our text expresses the fundamental biblical teaching that
the Ten Commandments are divine imperatives that are as much constitutive of the cosmic order as
are the laws of nature.

incised Hebrew ḥarut is unique in the Bible.²⁹ Mishnah Avot 6:2 utilizes it for word play
on ḥerut, "freedom": "No person is free except the one who labors in the Torah"; that is, the spiritual
and moral discipline instilled by the Torah is the essence of true freedom because it liberates human
beings from servitude to animal appetites and depraved instincts.

and the writing was God's writing, incised upon the tablets.
¹⁷When Joshua heard the sound of the people in its boister-
ousness, he said to Moses, "There is a cry of war in the
camp." ¹⁸But he answered,

"It is not the sound of the tune of triumph,
Or the sound of the tune of defeat;
It is the sound of song that I hear!"

¹⁹As soon as Moses came near the camp and saw the calf
and the dancing, he became enraged; and he hurled the
tablets from his hands and shattered them at the foot of the
mountain. ²⁰He took the calf that they had made and
burned it; he ground it to powder and strewed it upon the
water and so made the Israelites drink it.

²¹Moses said to Aaron, "What did this people do to you
that you have brought such great sin upon them?" ²²Aaron

הַלֻּחֹת: 17 וַיִּשְׁמַע יְהוֹשֻׁעַ אֶת־קוֹל הָעָם בְּרֵעֹה
וַיֹּאמֶר אֶל־מֹשֶׁה קוֹל מִלְחָמָה בַּמַּחֲנֶה: 18 וַיֹּאמֶר
אֵין קוֹל עֲנוֹת גְּבוּרָה
וְאֵין קוֹל עֲנוֹת חֲלוּשָׁה
קוֹל עַנּוֹת אָנֹכִי שֹׁמֵעַ:
19 וַיְהִי כַּאֲשֶׁר קָרַב אֶל־הַמַּחֲנֶה וַיַּרְא אֶת־
הָעֵגֶל וּמְחֹלֹת וַיִּחַר־אַף מֹשֶׁה וַיַּשְׁלֵךְ מִידוֹ אֶת־
הַלֻּחֹת וַיְשַׁבֵּר אֹתָם תַּחַת הָהָר: 20 וַיִּקַּח אֶת־
הָעֵגֶל אֲשֶׁר עָשׂוּ וַיִּשְׂרֹף בָּאֵשׁ וַיִּטְחַן עַד
אֲשֶׁר־דָּק וַיִּזֶר עַל־פְּנֵי הַמַּיִם וַיַּשְׁקְ אֶת־בְּנֵי
יִשְׂרָאֵל:
21 וַיֹּאמֶר מֹשֶׁה אֶל־אַהֲרֹן מֶה־עָשָׂה לְךָ
הָעָם הַזֶּה כִּי־הֵבֵאתָ עָלָיו חֲטָאָה גְדֹלָה:

v. 17. מִידָיו ק׳   v. 19. בְּרֵעוֹ ק׳

17. *Joshua* He was stationed partway up the mountain awaiting Moses' return, as told in 24:13; thus, he could hear the rising din but could not view the scene.

18. *But he answered* Moses has already been informed (vv. 7–8).

song Hebrew ʿannot is an intensive (Piel) form of the preceding ʿanot. It may designate a specific type of cultic singing.[30]

19–20. As he approaches the camp and personally witnesses the scene, Moses realizes the full extent of the degradation and recognizes the enormity of the people's sin.

enraged The same Hebrew term is used of God's reaction in verse 10.

he hurled the tablets This was not an impetuous act; rather, it quite deliberately signified the abrogation of the covenant. In Akkadian legal terminology to "break the tablet" (tuppam ḥepû) means to invalidate or repudiate a document or agreement. Moses is no longer the intercessor but the decisive, energetic leader. His actions are recorded in a series of ten verbs, delivered in quick succession (vv. 19–21).

at the foot of the mountain Where the people were assembled.[31]

20. The same series of destructive acts is found in Ugaritic literature.[32] It conveys a picture of the total annihilation of the obnoxious object.[33] This parallel suggests that our narrative has been crafted in conformity with conventional literary patterns. For this reason, it is hypercritical to question the burning and pulverizing of the golden calf on the grounds that the metal is neither combustible nor friable.[34]

the water Unidentified here, the water is characterized in the duplicate account of Deuter-onomy 9:21 as "the brook that comes down from the mountain." This implies a single source of water for the entire camp, the idea being, apparently, that no individual could escape drinking the mixture.

made the Israelites drink it In Avodah Zarah 44a this move is seen as a trial by ordeal modeled upon that administered to the sotah, or suspected adulteress, whose treatment is described in Numbers 5:12–31.[35] She was forced to drink the bitter water mingled with dust taken from the floor of the sanctuary. Supporting this interpretation is a phrase in the next verse and also the frequent use of the unfaithful wife motif in biblical literature as a metaphor for Israel's infidelity to the covenant with God.[36] The purpose of the ordeal was to identify the transgressors.

said, "Let not my lord be enraged. You know that this people is bent on evil. ²³They said to me, 'Make us a god to lead us; for that man Moses, who brought us from the land of Egypt—we do not know what has happened to him.' ²⁴So I said to them, 'Whoever has gold, take it off!' They gave it to me and I hurled it into the fire and out came this calf!"

²⁵Moses saw that the people were out of control—since Aaron had let them get out of control—so that they were a menace to any who might oppose them. ²⁶Moses stood up in the gate of the camp and said, "Whoever is for the Lᴏʀᴅ, come here!" And all the Levites rallied to him. ²⁷He said to

כב וַיֹּאמֶר אַהֲרֹן אַל־יִחַר אַף אֲדֹנִי אַתָּה יָדַעְתָּ אֶת־הָעָם כִּי בְרָע הוּא: כג וַיֹּאמְרוּ לִי עֲשֵׂה־לָנוּ אֱלֹהִים אֲשֶׁר יֵלְכוּ לְפָנֵינוּ כִּי־זֶה ׀ מֹשֶׁה הָאִישׁ אֲשֶׁר הֶעֱלָנוּ מֵאֶרֶץ מִצְרַיִם לֹא יָדַעְנוּ מֶה־הָיָה לוֹ: כד וָאֹמַר לָהֶם לְמִי זָהָב הִתְפָּרָקוּ וַיִּתְּנוּ־לִי וָאַשְׁלִכֵהוּ בָאֵשׁ וַיֵּצֵא הָעֵגֶל הַזֶּה: כה וַיַּרְא מֹשֶׁה אֶת־הָעָם כִּי פָרֻעַ הוּא כִּי־פְרָעֹה אַהֲרֹן לְשִׁמְצָה בְּקָמֵיהֶם: כו וַיַּעֲמֹד מֹשֶׁה בְּשַׁעַר הַמַּחֲנֶה וַיֹּאמֶר מִי לַיהוָה אֵלָי וַיֵּאָסְפוּ אֵלָיו כָּל־בְּנֵי לֵוִי: כז וַיֹּאמֶר לָהֶם כֹּה־אָמַר

AARON'S APOLOGIA   (vv. 21–24)

Moses now breaks his silence. His questioning of Aaron is really a harsh rebuke.

21. *this people* See Comment to verse 9.

great sin This is a legal term found in documents from Ugarit and in Egyptian marriage contracts, always referring to adultery. This same usage appears in Abimelech's reproof of Abraham in Genesis 20:9, which is couched in language almost identical to that used here. A reflex of it shows itself in Joseph's rebuff of Potiphar's wife in Genesis 39:9. There are four other biblical occurrences of "the great sin," all in reference to idolatry.[37]

22–24. Aaron excuses himself by vilifying the people. He repeats their words but abbreviates his own response to their demand and glosses over his own involvement in the fashioning of the calf image.

24. *out came this calf* As though it fabricated itself![38] Moses does not respond. In recounting the episode in Deuteronomy 9:12–22, he ignores Aaron's excuse as though unworthy of consideration, and he clearly states that "the Lᴏʀᴅ was angry enough with Aaron to have destroyed him." Only by Moses' intercession was he saved.

SELECTION OF THE LEVITES   (vv. 25–29)

The destruction of the golden calf seems to have triggered a riot among its worshipers. The Levites are called in to suppress it and to punish the guilty ones.

25. *out of control* The consonants of the Hebrew verb *p-r-ʿ* are the same as those used in connection with the *sotah*, the alleged adulteress, in Numbers 5:18—which provides another point of association between the two themes.[39]

Aaron . . . out of control An unequivocal rejection of Aaron's lame excuse and a condemnation of his action.

menace The unique Hebrew *shimtsah* has usually been understood as "an object of derision" or of "malignant joy." In Job 4:12 and 26:14 the masculine form *shemets* means "a whisper"; it offers no clue to the meaning here.

26. *Whoever is for the Lᴏʀᴅ* The question implies that regardless of the intention of the worshipers at the calf, the use of an image is irreconcilable with true monotheism.

all the Levites Moses' own tribe. They remained faithful to the covenant and loyally maintained the purity of Israel's worship. This note, as verse 29 and Deuteronomy 10:8 imply, is intended to provide a background for the election of the tribe of Levi to be in charge of the Taber-

them, "Thus says the LORD, the God of Israel: Each of you put sword on thigh, go back and forth from gate to gate throughout the camp, and slay brother, neighbor, and kin." 28The Levites did as Moses had bidden; and some three thousand of the people fell that day. 29And Moses said, "Dedicate yourselves to the LORD this day—for each of you has been against son and brother—that He may bestow a blessing upon you today."

30The next day Moses said to the people, "You have been guilty of a great sin. Yet I will now go up to the LORD; perhaps I may win forgiveness for your sin." 31Moses went back to the LORD and said, "Alas, this people is guilty of a great sin in making for themselves a god of gold. 32Now, if You will forgive their sin [well and good]; but if not, erase me from the record which You have written!" 33But the

יְהוָֹה אֱלֹהֵי יִשְׂרָאֵל שִׂימוּ אִישׁ־חַרְבּוֹ עַל־יְרֵכוֹ עִבְרוּ וָשׁוּבוּ מִשַּׁעַר לָשַׁעַר בַּמַּחֲנֶה וְהִרְגוּ אִישׁ־אֶת־אָחִיו וְאִישׁ אֶת־רֵעֵהוּ וְאִישׁ אֶת־קְרֹבוֹ: 28 וַיַּעֲשׂוּ בְנֵי־לֵוִי כִּדְבַר מֹשֶׁה וַיִּפֹּל מִן־הָעָם בַּיּוֹם הַהוּא כִּשְׁלֹשֶׁת אַלְפֵי אִישׁ: 29 וַיֹּאמֶר מֹשֶׁה מִלְאוּ יֶדְכֶם הַיּוֹם לַיהוָה כִּי אִישׁ בִּבְנוֹ וּבְאָחִיו וְלָתֵת עֲלֵיכֶם הַיּוֹם בְּרָכָה: 30 וַיְהִי מִמָּחֳרָת וַיֹּאמֶר מֹשֶׁה אֶל־הָעָם אַתֶּם חֲטָאתֶם חֲטָאָה גְדֹלָה וְעַתָּה אֶעֱלֶה אֶל־יְהוָה אוּלַי אֲכַפְּרָה בְּעַד חַטַּאתְכֶם: 31 וַיָּשָׁב מֹשֶׁה אֶל־יְהוָה וַיֹּאמַר אָנָּא חָטָא הָעָם הַזֶּה חֲטָאָה גְדֹלָה וַיַּעֲשׂוּ לָהֶם אֱלֹהֵי זָהָב: 32 וְעַתָּה אִם־תִּשָּׂא חַטָּאתָם וְאִם־אַיִן מְחֵנִי נָא מִסִּפְרְךָ אֲשֶׁר כָּתָבְתָּ: 33 וַיֹּאמֶר יְהוָה אֶל־מֹשֶׁה מִי אֲשֶׁר

nacle[40] and to be surrogates for the first-born.[41] It is quite likely that the first-born played a leading role in the worship of the golden calf and for that reason were displaced as cultic officiants.

27. *Thus says the LORD* See Comment to 5:1. This solemn formula is employed here to signify that the assignment to the Levites is extraordinary, that is, beyond the purview of any human authority to impose. It cannot be taken as a precedent for the disposition of future cases. The presumption is, as explained above, that the water ordeal exposed the guilty ones. See Comment to verse 35.

slay brother They must be absolutely impartial and evenhanded in carrying out their grim task. It is likely that Moses' farewell blessing of Levi in Deuteronomy 33:9 refers to this episode: "Who said of his father and mother, / 'I consider them not.' / His brothers he disregarded, / Ignored his own children. / Your precepts alone they observed, / And kept Your covenant."

29. *dedicate yourselves* On this idiom, see Comment to 28:41.

MOSES' SECOND INTERCESSION (vv. 30–34)

Having secured annulment of the decree to destroy Israel by his first intercession, Moses now attempts to gain complete forgiveness for the people.

30. *The next day* After the carnage.

go up To the summit of Sinai.

31-32. As would be expected, the prayer blends confession with a plea for pardon; but another element is introduced. Moses nobly ties his personal destiny to his people's fate. There can hardly be a more impressive example of selfless "love of Israel" (in Hebrew 'ahavat yisra'el).

31. *Alas* Hebrew 'anna' often introduces an entreaty.[42]

32. *[well and good]* This phrase is to be supplied by the context—a literary device known as aposiopesis.[43]

erase me from the record This request seems to reflect a well-rooted and widespread Near Eastern popular belief in the existence of heavenly "books." The Hebrew Bible differentiates three types. There is the book of life, mentioned in Psalm 69:28, in which God is thought to inscribe the names of all living.[44] This notion undoubtedly drew its inspiration from the civil census lists that were kept by municipal or state authorities.[45] Then there is the book of divine decrees,[46] in which the destinies of men and women and of peoples are recorded. Lastly, there is the book of remembrance in

LORD said to Moses, "He who has sinned against Me, him only will I erase from My record. ³⁴Go now, lead the people where I told you. See, My angel shall go before you. But when I make an accounting, I will bring them to account for their sins."

³⁵Then the LORD sent a plague upon the people, for what they did with the calf that Aaron made.

חָטָא־לִ֔י אֶמְחֶ֖נּוּ מִסִּפְרִֽי׃ 34 וְעַתָּ֞ה לֵ֣ךְ ׀ נְחֵ֣ה אֶת־הָעָ֗ם אֶ֤ל אֲשֶׁר־דִּבַּ֙רְתִּי֙ לָ֔ךְ הִנֵּ֥ה מַלְאָכִ֖י יֵלֵ֣ךְ לְפָנֶ֑יךָ וּבְי֣וֹם פׇּקְדִ֔י וּפָקַדְתִּ֥י עֲלֵיהֶ֖ם חַטָּאתָֽם׃ 35 וַיִּגֹּ֥ף יְהֹוָ֖ה אֶת־הָעָ֑ם עַ֚ל אֲשֶׁ֣ר עָשׂ֣וּ אֶת־הָעֵ֔גֶל אֲשֶׁ֥ר עָשָׂ֖ה אַהֲרֹֽן׃ ס

33 Then the LORD said to Moses, "Set out from here, you and the people that you have brought up from the land of Egypt, to the land of which I swore to Abraham, Isaac, and Jacob, saying, 'To your offspring will I give it'—²I will send

ל״ג וַיְדַבֵּ֨ר יְהֹוָ֤ה אֶל־מֹשֶׁה֙ לֵ֣ךְ עֲלֵ֣ה מִזֶּ֔ה אַתָּ֣ה וְהָעָ֔ם אֲשֶׁ֥ר הֶעֱלִ֖יתָ מֵאֶ֣רֶץ מִצְרָ֑יִם אֶל־הָאָ֗רֶץ אֲשֶׁ֣ר נִ֠שְׁבַּ֠עְתִּי לְאַבְרָהָ֨ם לְיִצְחָ֤ק וּֽלְיַעֲקֹב֙ לֵאמֹ֔ר לְזַרְעֲךָ֖ אֶתְּנֶֽנָּה׃ 2 וְשָׁלַחְתִּ֥י

Malachi 3:16 in which the deeds of human beings, both good and evil, are written up.[47] This last must have its origin in ancient court procedure. It is hard to decide whether or not the notion of heavenly books was taken literally in ancient Israel. Maimonides[48] unambiguously emphasizes the figurative, nonliteral nature of the biblical phraseology. The perennial Jewish greeting on the High Holy Days—"May you be inscribed . . ." —echoes the ancient idea.

In the present instance, Moses' request is framed in the figurative language of the book of life, so that he is really asking to die if Israel is not forgiven.[49]

33–34. God responds to Moses' entreaty: There must be individual accountability (see Comment to 20:5). But the people also bears collective responsibility. Divine promises of national territory to the people of Israel are immutable, but total absolution for the sin of the golden calf cannot be given. Israel receives a suspended sentence; the people is on probation.

34. *my angel* See Comment to 23:20–23.

35. This verse more appropriately belongs after verse 20, where it would indicate that the water-ordeal caused the guilty ones to be stricken—as the similar procedure was designed to do in the case of the suspected adulteress. The calf worshipers would thus have been readily identifiable to the Levites.

for what they did This difficult sentence seems to mean that Aaron and the people shared the blame equally; they, for demanding a visible "god"; he, for yielding to them.

CHAPTER 33   There was a tragic irony in the episode of the golden calf. The people wanted to provide themselves with a reassuring symbol of God's continued presence in their midst; yet that very symbol became the instrument of their alienation from God. Although Moses' intercession saves the people from annihilation, Israel has not yet secured full pardon and reconciliation with God.

The unifying theme of this chapter is Moses' concern for the continued presence of God in the midst of His people, as symbolized by the mobile sanctuary.

WITHDRAWAL OF THE DIVINE PRESENCE   (vv. 1–6)

The chapter opens with a reiteration of the command to lead the people to Canaan, but it is clearly implied that the punitive decree of 32:10 was canceled because of the oaths to the patriarchs (32:13), not because of the people's merit.

1. set out Hebrew *lekh ʿaleh*, literally "go, ascend," in contrast to 32:7, *lekh red*, "go, descend," signifies that a reversal of fate has taken place.[1]

You Moses' request in 32:32 is emphatically denied.

an angel before you, and I will drive out the Canaanites, the Amorites, the Hittites, the Perizzites, the Hivites, and the Jebusites—³a land flowing with milk and honey. But I will not go in your midst, since you are a stiffnecked people, lest I destroy you on the way."

⁴When the people heard this harsh word, they went into mourning, and none put on his finery.

⁵The Lord said to Moses, "Say to the Israelite people, 'You are a stiffnecked people. If I were to go in your midst for one moment, I would destroy you. Now, then, leave off your finery, and I will consider what to do to you.'" ⁶So the Israelites remained stripped of the finery from Mount Horeb on.

⁷Now Moses would take the Tent and pitch it outside the camp, at some distance from the camp. It was called the Tent of Meeting, and whoever sought the Lord would go

לְפָנֶיךָ מַלְאָךְ וְגֵרַשְׁתִּי אֶת־הַכְּנַעֲנִי הָאֱמֹרִי וְהַחִתִּי וְהַפְּרִזִּי הַחִוִּי וְהַיְבוּסִי: 3 אֶל־אֶרֶץ זָבַת חָלָב וּדְבָשׁ כִּי לֹא אֶעֱלֶה בְּקִרְבְּךָ כִּי עַם־קְשֵׁה־עֹרֶף אַתָּה פֶּן־אֲכֶלְךָ בַּדָּרֶךְ:

4 וַיִּשְׁמַע הָעָם אֶת־הַדָּבָר הָרָע הַזֶּה וַיִּתְאַבָּלוּ וְלֹא־שָׁתוּ אִישׁ עֶדְיוֹ עָלָיו:

5 וַיֹּאמֶר יְהוָה אֶל־מֹשֶׁה אֱמֹר אֶל־בְּנֵי־יִשְׂרָאֵל אַתֶּם עַם־קְשֵׁה־עֹרֶף רֶגַע אֶחָד אֶעֱלֶה בְקִרְבְּךָ וְכִלִּיתִיךָ וְעַתָּה הוֹרֵד עֶדְיְךָ מֵעָלֶיךָ וְאֵדְעָה מָה אֶעֱשֶׂה־לָּךְ: 6 וַיִּתְנַצְּלוּ בְנֵי־יִשְׂרָאֵל אֶת־עֶדְיָם מֵהַר חוֹרֵב:

7 וּמֹשֶׁה יִקַּח אֶת־הָאֹהֶל וְנָטָה־לוֹ מִחוּץ לַמַּחֲנֶה הַרְחֵק מִן־הַמַּחֲנֶה וְקָרָא לוֹ אֹהֶל מוֹעֵד וְהָיָה כָּל־מְבַקֵּשׁ יְהוָה יֵצֵא אֶל־אֹהֶל מוֹעֵד

the people   It is no longer "your people" as God said to Moses in 32:7. The shift connotes some mitigation of the impact of Israel's alienation from God.

2. an angel   The promise of 23:20–33 and 32:34 is repeated, but the emissary is not here designated "My" angel.[2] The change is ominous.

Canaanites . . .   On the list, see Comment to 3:8.

3. a land . . .   For this standard description, see Comment to 3:8.

I will not go   This statement contradicts the promise of verses 2 and 32:34. Even assuming that the "angel" is to be understood as an entity apart from God, God has nevertheless just pledged to drive out the native peoples. Accordingly, God's absence from the midst of Israel should be understood, with Ibn Ezra, to mean the cancellation of the order to construct the Tabernacle.[3]

lest I destroy you   Paradoxically, God's withdrawal of His presence is a mercifully preventive measure; it is intended to avert what would inevitably be the very destructive consequences of another episode such as that of the golden calf.

4.   This decision has a shattering effect, for it was the want of a mediating representation of God's immanence that generated the demand for a material image in the first place.

5. leave off   Hebrew imperative *hored* can only mean "remove!" But the people have already done this. Hence, it is best to invert the order of verses 4–5 and to take verse 4 as the response to the divine command.

6. from Mount Horeb on   From that time on, throughout the wilderness wanderings. It is a sign of remorse by the people over their transgression. On Horeb, see Comment to 3:1.

MOSES' EXCEPTIONAL STATUS (vv. 7–11)

This section continues the theme of the presence of God and connects directly with verse 3. Because God withholds His indwelling in the camp of Israel, Moses employs an extraordinary stratagem. He pitches "the Tent" outside the camp. This is not the Tabernacle—which is not yet constructed—but a private tent where he might commune with God. There is no priesthood, cult, or ritual of any sort. The Tent was also accessible to the individual Israelite worshiper.

This highlighting of the special status of Moses serves as preparation for the succeeding episodes.

out to the Tent of Meeting that was outside the camp. [8]Whenever Moses went out to the Tent, all the people would rise and stand, each at the entrance of his tent, and gaze after Moses until he had entered the Tent. [9]And when Moses entered the Tent, the pillar of cloud would descend and stand at the entrance of the Tent, while He spoke with Moses. [10]When all the people saw the pillar of cloud poised at the entrance of the Tent, all the people would rise and bow low, each at the entrance of his tent. [11]The LORD would speak to Moses face to face, as one man speaks to another. And he would then return to the camp; but his attendant, Joshua son of Nun, a youth, would not stir out of the Tent.

[12]Moses said to the LORD, "See, You say to me, 'Lead this people forward,' but You have not made known to me whom You will send with me. Further, You have said, 'I

אֲשֶׁר מִחוּץ לַמַּחֲנֶה: [8] וְהָיָה כְּצֵאת מֹשֶׁה אֶל־הָאֹהֶל יָקוּמוּ כָּל־הָעָם וְנִצְּבוּ אִישׁ פֶּתַח אָהֳלוֹ וְהִבִּיטוּ אַחֲרֵי מֹשֶׁה עַד־בֹּאוֹ הָאֹהֱלָה: [9] וְהָיָה כְּבֹא מֹשֶׁה הָאֹהֱלָה יֵרֵד עַמּוּד הֶעָנָן וְעָמַד פֶּתַח הָאֹהֶל וְדִבֶּר עִם־מֹשֶׁה: [10] וְרָאָה כָל־הָעָם אֶת־עַמּוּד הֶעָנָן עֹמֵד פֶּתַח הָאֹהֶל וְקָם כָּל־הָעָם וְהִשְׁתַּחֲווּ אִישׁ פֶּתַח אָהֳלוֹ: [11] וְדִבֶּר יְהוָה אֶל־מֹשֶׁה פָּנִים אֶל־פָּנִים כַּאֲשֶׁר יְדַבֵּר אִישׁ אֶל־רֵעֵהוּ וְשָׁב אֶל־הַמַּחֲנֶה וּמְשָׁרְתוֹ יְהוֹשֻׁעַ בִּן־נוּן נַעַר לֹא יָמִישׁ מִתּוֹךְ הָאֹהֶל:
     ס   שלישי

[12] וַיֹּאמֶר מֹשֶׁה אֶל־יְהוָה רְאֵה אַתָּה אֹמֵר אֵלַי הַעַל אֶת־הָעָם הַזֶּה וְאַתָּה לֹא הוֹדַעְתַּנִי

7. **would take** The verbal forms denote customary and repetitive action, not a one-time occurrence.

the Tent The definite article seems to indicate a well-known specific Tent, although one not hitherto mentioned. It was apparently the locus of Moses' previous dialogues with God.

pitch it Hebrew *natah lo* is literally "pitch it for himself"—for his personal use.

outside the camp, at some distance The description draws attention to the alienation of Israel from God. The camp has become spiritually polluted by the impurity produced by the golden calf affair.

Tent of Meeting See Comment to 27:21. A temporary substitute for the Tabernacle is thus designated.

8. This symbol of alienation was reflective of a heightened mood of contrition and an enhanced respect for Moses.

9. **at the entrance** As distinct from the Tabernacle, in which the Divine Presence is said to rest continuously,[4] and in which God converses with Moses from within the Holy of Holies in its interior,[5] here the locus of communication is at the entrance; God's self-manifestation is intermittent.

10. The sight of the pillar of cloud inspired reverential awe; the people responded with a gesture of homage.

11. **face to face** The same expression is used in Deuteronomy 34:10, whereas in Numbers 12:6–8 it is said that God communicated with Moses "mouth to mouth." This figurative language is intended to convey the preeminence and uniqueness of Moses as a prophetic figure who experiences a special mode of revelation. The experience is personal and direct, not mediated through visions or dreams, and the message is always plain and straightforward, free of cryptic utterances.

Joshua He remained inside the tent and did not share in Moses' revelatory experience.

DIALOGUE WITH GOD (vv. 12–23)

This section illustrates how Moses and God engage in intimate discourse, as verse 11 stated.

have singled you out by name, and you have, indeed, gained My favor.' ¹³Now, if I have truly gained Your favor, pray let me know Your ways, that I may know You and continue in Your favor. Consider, too, that this nation is Your people." ¹⁴And He said, "I will go in the lead and will lighten your burden." ¹⁵And he said to Him, "Unless You go in the lead, do not make us leave this place. ¹⁶For how shall it be known that Your people have gained Your favor unless You go with us, so that we may be distinguished, Your people and I, from every people on the face of the earth?"

¹⁷And the Lord said to Moses, "I will also do this thing that you have asked; for you have truly gained My favor and I have singled you out by name." ¹⁸He said, "Oh, let me behold Your Presence!" ¹⁹And He answered, "I will make

אֵת אֲשֶׁר־תִּשְׁלַח עִמִּי וְאַתָּה אָמַרְתָּ יְדַעְתִּיךָ
בְשֵׁם וְגַם־מָצָאתָ חֵן בְּעֵינָי: 13 וְעַתָּה אִם־נָא
מָצָאתִי חֵן בְּעֵינֶיךָ הוֹדִעֵנִי נָא אֶת־דְּרָכֶךָ
וְאֵדָעֲךָ לְמַעַן אֶמְצָא־חֵן בְּעֵינֶיךָ וּרְאֵה כִּי עַמְּךָ
הַגּוֹי הַזֶּה: 14 וַיֹּאמַר פָּנַי יֵלֵכוּ וַהֲנִחֹתִי לָךְ:
15 וַיֹּאמֶר אֵלָיו אִם־אֵין פָּנֶיךָ הֹלְכִים אַל־
תַּעֲלֵנוּ מִזֶּה: 16 וּבַמֶּה | יִוָּדַע אֵפוֹא כִּי־מָצָאתִי
חֵן בְּעֵינֶיךָ אֲנִי וְעַמֶּךָ הֲלוֹא בְּלֶכְתְּךָ עִמָּנוּ
וְנִפְלִינוּ אֲנִי וְעַמְּךָ מִכָּל־הָעָם אֲשֶׁר עַל־פְּנֵי
הָאֲדָמָה: פ רביעי

17 וַיֹּאמֶר יְהוָה אֶל־מֹשֶׁה גַּם אֶת־הַדָּבָר הַזֶּה
אֲשֶׁר דִּבַּרְתָּ אֶעֱשֶׂה כִּי־מָצָאתָ חֵן בְּעֵינַי וָאֵדָעֲךָ
בְּשֵׁם: 18 וַיֹּאמַר הַרְאֵנִי נָא אֶת־כְּבֹדֶךָ: 19 וַיֹּאמֶר

12. Moses now reverts to the subject matter of 32:34 and 33:1–3—the order to proceed to the promised land without the Tabernacle, the token of God's immediate presence in the camp of Israel. He complains that the aforementioned "angel" is unidentified. Is it to be human or celestial? Is God's name to "be in him," as is promised in 23:21, or not?[6] If Moses enjoys a special intimacy with God, he should be made fully aware of God's intentions in this regard.[7]

I have singled you out by name Literally, "I know you by name." This Hebrew idiom, with God as the subject, is applied to no one else in the Bible. It connotes a close, exclusive, and unique association with God. On the Hebrew stem *y-d-ʿ*, see Comment to 1:8.

you have, indeed, gained My favor The only other biblical personality who enjoys this unequivocal approval is Noah.[8]

13. *let me know Your ways* From God's response to this request, as given in 34:6–7, it is clear that Moses here asks to comprehend God's essential personality, the attributes that guide His actions in His dealings with humankind, the norms by which He operates in His governance of the world.[9] This understanding of what is meant by "the ways of God" is corroborated by Psalm 103:7–8, the earliest extant commentary on this text: "He made known His ways to Moses, / His deeds to the children of Israel, / The Lord is compassionate and gracious, / slow to anger, abounding in steadfast love." Moses' request, like the assertion of Abraham before him—"Shall not the Judge of all the earth deal justly?"[10]—rests on the postulate that God is not capricious but acts according to norms that human beings can try to understand.

this nation Moses stresses that it is the present people of Israel and none other that is God's people, and he wants to extend God's favor to embrace Israel as well as himself.

14. God does not yet relate to Moses' last point but addresses only his personal concerns.

lighten your burden Literally, "I will give you rest," a phrase overwhelmingly found in a context of giving relief from national enemies, especially in relation to the occupation of the land.[11]

15–16. Moses, sensitive to God's omission of any mention of Israel, reacts immediately by stressing the people's interests, thereby affirming once again that he sees his own reputation inextricably bound up with the fate of his people. Note his repetition of "us" and "Your people."

16. *we may be distinguished* Israel's singularity lies in its unique relationship with God.[12]

17. *also . . . this thing* The reference is unclear but seems to be a promise to be present once again in the camp of Israel, that is, to grant permission for the erection of the Tabernacle.

18. *"Oh, let me behold Your Presence!"* Hebrew *kavod* is one of the seminal terms of biblical theology. In the Comment to 16:7 it was explained that it often signifies God's self-mani-

213

all My goodness pass before you, and I will proclaim before
you the name LORD, and the grace that I grant and the
compassion that I show. ²⁰But," He said, "you cannot see
My face, for man may not see Me and live." ²¹And the LORD
said, "See, there is a place near Me. Station yourself on the
rock ²²and, as My Presence passes by, I will put you in a
cleft of the rock and shield you with My hand until I have
passed by. ²³Then I will take My hand away and you will see
My back; but My face must not be seen."

אֲנִי אַעֲבִיר כָּל־טוּבִי עַל־פָּנֶיךָ וְקָרָאתִי בְשֵׁם
יְהוָה לְפָנֶיךָ וְחַנֹּתִי אֶת־אֲשֶׁר אָחֹן וְרִחַמְתִּי אֶת־
אֲשֶׁר אֲרַחֵם: ²⁰ וַיֹּאמֶר לֹא תוּכַל לִרְאֹת אֶת־פָּנָי
כִּי לֹא־יִרְאַנִי הָאָדָם וָחָי: ²¹ וַיֹּאמֶר יְהוָה הִנֵּה
מָקוֹם אִתִּי וְנִצַּבְתָּ עַל־הַצּוּר: ²² וְהָיָה בַּעֲבֹר
כְּבֹדִי וְשַׂמְתִּיךָ בְּנִקְרַת הַצּוּר וְשַׂכֹּתִי כַפִּי עָלֶיךָ
עַד־עָבְרִי: ²³ וַהֲסִרֹתִי אֶת־כַּפִּי וְרָאִיתָ אֶת־אֲחֹרָי
וּפָנַי לֹא יֵרָאוּ: ס   חמישי

festation, some outward, visible sign of His essential presence. At Sinai, the Presence (kavod) of the Lord appeared as a consuming fire on top of the mountain (24:17). Numerous texts use the verb r-'-h, "to see," in conjunction with the kavod.[13] What, then, does Moses request? Maimonides,[14] followed by Radak, understands the phrase figuratively: Moses asks for an intellectual perception of God's essential reality, not simply for what is observable through the senses. Ramban, by contrast, interprets the words literally: Moses actually requests a glimpse of the Divine Presence. In favor of this understanding is the fact that the kavod is generally something visible and usually refers to the supernatural effulgence that registers the intensity of God's immanence. It may be pointed out that every other instance of a visible kavod in the Torah is characterized by three features: (1) It is a mass experience; (2) the kavod is distant from the observers; and (3) God initiates the manifestation and freely chooses the time and place. Here Moses pleads for an exclusively individual experience, one that is close at hand and that occurs in response to his personal request there and then.

19. all My goodness The benevolent attributes that God manifests in His dealings with His creatures. These are detailed in 34:6–7. The theme of divine goodness is frequently featured in the Bible.[15] In classical rabbinic literature tov, "the Good One," and tuvo shel 'olam, "the Goodness of the World," are epithets of God.[16] In Bava Metsia 83a the injunction of Proverbs 2:20 to "follow the way of the good" is interpreted by Rav to mean that one must act with generosity, beyond the requirements of the strict letter of the law. In Mishnah Avot 3:15(19) Rabbi Akiba asserts that "the world is judged by goodness," that is, by divine grace.

In ancient Near Eastern treaties and in several biblical texts,[17] the term tov bears the technical, legal meaning of covenantal friendship, that is, amity established by the conclusion of a pact. In light of this, it is possible that the present verse also contains an intimation of the renewal of the covenant between God and Israel.

proclaim . . . the name LORD The Tetragrammaton: YHVH. As noted in the Comment to 3:13, a name is understood to connote one's character and nature, the totality of personality. Hence, this clause parallels the preceding one and reaffirms God's intention of voluntarily disclosing to Moses His defining characteristics. This is fulfilled in 34:5. Nowhere else in the Bible does this familiar formula appear with God as the subject of the action.

and the grace Literally, "I will grant the grace that I will grant and show the compassion that I will show."[18] The exercise of God's attributes is an act of pure volition on His part. In the religion of Israel there is no magical practice that is automatically effective in influencing divine behavior.

20. Moses' second plea is only partially granted. By virtue of their humanity, human beings (ha-'adam), including Moses, cannot directly and closely observe God's kavod. See Comment to 3:6.

21. on the rock At the top of the mountain (34:2).

22. My Presence passes by Rashbam notes that His action is a feature of covenant-making, as in Genesis 15:17 and Jeremiah 34:18,19, so that the ensuing epiphany, or manifestation of God, would actually be a ceremony that signals the renewal of the covenant. This suggestion is in line with the use of tov in verse 19.

34 The LORD said to Moses: "Carve two tablets of stone like the first, and I will inscribe upon the tablets the words that were on the first tablets, which you shattered. ²Be ready by morning, and in the morning come up to Mount Sinai and present yourself there to Me, on the top of the mountain. ³No one else shall come up with you, and no one else shall be seen anywhere on the mountain; neither shall the flocks and the herds graze at the foot of this mountain."

⁴So Moses carved two tablets of stone, like the first, and early in the morning he went up on Mount Sinai, as the LORD had commanded him, taking the two stone tablets with him. ⁵The LORD came down in a cloud; He stood with

לד ‏1 וַיֹּ֤אמֶר יְהֹוָה֙ אֶל־מֹשֶׁ֔ה פְּסׇל־לְךָ֛ שְׁנֵֽי־
לֻחֹ֥ת אֲבָנִ֖ים כָּרִֽאשֹׁנִ֑ים וְכָתַבְתִּי֙ עַל־הַלֻּחֹ֔ת אֶת־
הַדְּבָרִ֔ים אֲשֶׁ֥ר הָי֛וּ עַל־הַלֻּחֹ֥ת הָרִֽאשֹׁנִ֖ים אֲשֶׁ֥ר
שִׁבַּֽרְתָּ׃ ‏2 וֶהְיֵ֥ה נָכ֖וֹן לַבֹּ֑קֶר וְעָלִ֤יתָ בַבֹּ֙קֶר֙ אֶל־
הַ֣ר סִינַ֔י וְנִצַּבְתָּ֥ לִ֛י שָׁ֖ם עַל־רֹ֥אשׁ הָהָֽר׃ ‏3 וְאִישׁ֙
לֹא־יַעֲלֶ֣ה עִמָּ֔ךְ וְגַם־אִ֥ישׁ אַל־יֵרָ֖א בְּכׇל־הָהָ֑ר גַּם־
הַצֹּ֤אן וְהַבָּקָר֙ אַל־יִרְע֔וּ אֶל־מ֖וּל הָהָ֥ר הַהֽוּא׃
‏4 וַיִּפְסֹ֡ל שְׁנֵֽי־לֻחֹ֨ת אֲבָנִ֜ים כָּרִֽאשֹׁנִ֗ים
וַיַּשְׁכֵּ֨ם מֹשֶׁ֤ה בַבֹּ֙קֶר֙ וַיַּ֙עַל֙ אֶל־הַ֣ר סִינַ֔י
כַּאֲשֶׁ֛ר צִוָּ֥ה יְהֹוָ֖ה אֹת֑וֹ וַיִּקַּ֣ח בְּיָד֔וֹ שְׁנֵ֖י לֻחֹ֥ת

My hand   A poetic term for a screen, most likely a cloud.[19]

23. *My back*   This daring anthropomorphism is conditioned by the contrasting repeated use of *panim*, "face, presence."[20] Here the term means the traces of His presence, the afterglow of His supernatural effulgence.

must not be seen   No human being can ever penetrate the ultimate mystery of God's Being. Only a glimpse of the divine reality is possible, even for Moses.

CHAPTER 34

Renewal of the Covenant   (vv. 1–35)

PREPARATORY MEASURES   (vv. 1–3)

Having been assured of a private manifestation of the Divine Presence, Moses is instructed to prepare for the experience, which actually constitutes the reinstatement of the covenant. This is underscored by several points of contact between this narrative and the account of the original theophany at Sinai: The shattered tablets, which once testified to the reality of the covenant, are to be replaced; the original text incised upon them is to be reproduced; Moses is told to "be ready" by morning just as the people had been ordered to "be ready" for the occasion (19:11,15); access to the mountain is severely restricted in both experiences (34:3; 19:12–13); the Lord again "comes down" upon Sinai (34:5; 19:9,18,20); and the event evokes such fear that the people back away (34:30; 20:15–18).

1. *carve*   The first set is said to have been given to Moses by God.[1]

the words   Identified in verse 28 as the Decalogue. Ibn Ezra suggests that the second set of tablets contained the Deuteronomic version.[2]

3. *No one else*   This time Aaron is excluded—a silent reminder of his role in the breach of the covenant.[3]

GOD'S SELF-DISCLOSURE   (vv. 4–9)

5. *stood . . . proclaimed*   The subject of the two verbs may be either Moses,[4] as verses 2 and 33:21 indicate, or God,[5] as the first clause and 33:19 would suggest. Or perhaps the first verb is governed by Moses and the second by God.

him there, and proclaimed the name LORD. [6]The LORD passed before him and proclaimed: "The LORD! the LORD! a God compassionate and gracious, slow to anger, abounding in kindness and faithfulness, [7]extending kindness to the thousandth generation, forgiving iniquity, transgression, and sin; yet He does not remit all punishment, but visits the iniquity of parents upon children and children's children, upon the third and fourth generations."

אֲבָנִים: 5 וַיֵּרֶד יְהוָה בֶּעָנָן וַיִּתְיַצֵּב עִמּוֹ שָׁם וַיִּקְרָא בְשֵׁם יְהוָה: 6 וַיַּעֲבֹר יְהוָה עַל־פָּנָיו וַיִּקְרָא יְהוָה ׀ יְהוָה אֵל רַחוּם וְחַנּוּן אֶרֶךְ אַפַּיִם וְרַב־חֶסֶד וֶאֱמֶת: 7 נֹצֵר חֶסֶד לָאֲלָפִים נֹשֵׂא עָוֹן וָפֶשַׁע וְחַטָּאָה וְנַקֵּה לֹא יְנַקֶּה פֹּקֵד ׀ עֲוֹן אָבוֹת עַל־בָּנִים וְעַל־בְּנֵי בָנִים עַל־שִׁלֵּשִׁים וְעַל־רִבֵּעִים:

נ' רבתי v. 7.

6-7. These verses constitute the divine response to Moses' two requests—that he "know" God's ways (33:13) and that he "behold" His presence (33:18). God's mysterious passing before Moses answers to the second; the recital of the divine attributes, to the first. Significantly, the description of the theophany lacks a visual element. God's self-disclosure is confined to an oral proclamation of His moral qualities. These are the essence of His character and to "know" them is to achieve a higher conception of Deity.

In Jewish tradition these verses are called the Thirteen Attributes of God (Heb. *shelosh 'esreh middot*).[6] They play a prominent role in the Jewish liturgy, where they are recited aloud in the synagogue on festivals and other holy days (except Sabbaths) when the Ark is opened for the taking out of the Torah scroll in readiness for the appropriate Torah reading. They are also chanted aloud during the Torah readings on fast days and in the Seliḥot—the penitential prayers recited on those occasions as well as during the High Holy Day period. This practice is based on Rabbi Johanan's comment in Rosh Ha-Shanah 17b that God's recital of His moral qualities was intended to set the pattern for Israel's future petitions to God. There is evidence that the liturgical use of these verses preceded Second Temple times and had a long history in Israel, for they are frequently quoted in one form or another in the Bible.[7] Such persistent and widespread popularity could only have derived from the forms of institutional worship.

It should be stressed that the incorporation of the Thirteen Attributes into the liturgy is not to be interpreted as an automatically effective means of attaining forgiveness of sin. Rather, the idea is to inculcate the human imitation of God's moral qualities: compassion, graciousness, forbearance, kindness, fealty, and forgivingness.[8]

6. the LORD! the LORD! The Hebrew text also allows the first YHVH to be taken as the subject of the antecedent verb "proclaimed"; it was so understood by Saadia and Maimonides.[9] Ibn Ezra counters that the repetition of the name in summons or invocation is not uncommon.[10]

compassionate and gracious As opposed to the order in the Decalogue (20:5–6), emphasis and priority here are given to God's magnanimous qualities rather than to His judgmental actions.

kindness and faithfulness Hebrew *ḥesed ve-'emet* appears frequently as a word pair[11] to express a single concept. Each of the components has a wide range of meaning. *Ḥesed* involves acts of beneficence, mutuality, and often also obligations that flow from a legal relationship. See Comment to 15:13. *'Emet*, usually translated "truth," encompasses reliability, durability, and faithfulness. The combination of terms expresses God's absolute and eternal dependability in dispensing His benefactions.

7. extending kindness See Comment to 20:6. The phrase may express either God's continuous and unchanging *ḥesed*[12] or the idea that the merit for the *ḥesed* that people perform endures beyond their own generation.

thousandth generation Hebrew *'alafim*, as in 20:6.

He does not remit Divine forbearance does not mean that sinners can expect wholly to escape the consequences of their misdeeds.[13] Yoma 61a interprets the sentence to mean: "He remits punishment for the penitent, but not for the impenitent." For this reason, the liturgical recitation of the Thirteen Attributes closes with "acquitting" (the penitent) and omits the negative element.

כי תשא

8Moses hastened to bow low to the ground in homage, 9and said, "If I have gained Your favor, O Lord, pray, let the Lord go in our midst, even though this is a stiffnecked people. Pardon our iniquity and our sin, and take us for Your own!"

10He said: I hereby make a covenant. Before all your people I will work such wonders as have not been wrought on all the earth or in any nation; and all the people who are with you shall see how awesome are the LORD's deeds which I will perform for you. 11Mark well what I command you this day. I will drive out before you the Amorites, the Canaanites, the Hittites, the Perizzites, the Hivites, and the Jebusites. 12Beware of making a covenant with the inhabitants of the land against which you are advancing, lest they be a snare in your midst. 13No, you must tear down their altars, smash their pillars, and cut down their sacred posts;

8 וַיְמַהֵר מֹשֶׁה וַיִּקֹּד אַרְצָה וַיִּשְׁתָּחוּ: 9 וַיֹּאמֶר אִם־נָא מָצָאתִי חֵן בְּעֵינֶיךָ אֲדֹנָי יֵלֶךְ־נָא אֲדֹנָי בְּקִרְבֵּנוּ כִּי עַם־קְשֵׁה־עֹרֶף הוּא וְסָלַחְתָּ לַעֲוֺנֵנוּ וּלְחַטָּאתֵנוּ וּנְחַלְתָּנוּ: ששי

10 וַיֹּאמֶר הִנֵּה אָנֹכִי כֹּרֵת בְּרִית נֶגֶד כָּל־עַמְּךָ אֶעֱשֶׂה נִפְלָאֹת אֲשֶׁר לֹא־נִבְרְאוּ בְכָל־הָאָרֶץ וּבְכָל־הַגּוֹיִם וְרָאָה כָל־הָעָם אֲשֶׁר־אַתָּה בְקִרְבּוֹ אֶת־מַעֲשֵׂה יְהֹוָה כִּי־נוֹרָא הוּא אֲשֶׁר אֲנִי עֹשֶׂה עִמָּךְ: 11 שְׁמָר־לְךָ אֵת אֲשֶׁר אָנֹכִי מְצַוְּךָ הַיּוֹם הִנְנִי גֹּרֵשׁ מִפָּנֶיךָ אֶת־הָאֱמֹרִי וְהַכְּנַעֲנִי וְהַחִתִּי וְהַפְּרִזִּי וְהַחִוִּי וְהַיְבוּסִי: 12 הִשָּׁמֶר לְךָ פֶּן־תִּכְרֹת בְּרִית לְיוֹשֵׁב הָאָרֶץ אֲשֶׁר אַתָּה בָּא עָלֶיהָ פֶּן־יִהְיֶה לְמוֹקֵשׁ בְּקִרְבֶּךָ: 13 כִּי אֶת־מִזְבְּחֹתָם תִּתֹּצוּן וְאֶת־מַצֵּבֹתָם תְּשַׁבֵּרוּן וְאֶת־

9. Moses emphasizes God's merciful qualities in asking that the punishment in 33:3 be rescinded.[14]

even though Make allowance for human frailty.[15]

INAUTHENTIC AND AUTHENTIC WORSHIP (vv. 10–26)

This section concentrates on two fundamental issues that flow directly from the apostasy: inauthentic modes of worship (vv. 10–17) and the legitimate festivals and ritual obligations to God (vv. 18–26).

APOSTASY (vv. 10–17)

Mindful of the people's sin, the renewed covenant contains stricter admonitions than those given before (23:23,24) regarding the incursions of foreign cults into the religion of Israel. Pacts with the indigenous peoples of Canaan are prohibited because of their deleterious consequences—religious corruption, intermarriage, and the resultant undermining of national religious integrity. If Israel is to be "distinguished . . . from every people on the face of the earth" (33:16), then it must make itself distinctive by unswerving and exclusive loyalty to its covenantal relationship with God.

10. *wonders* Rashi and Rashbam note that Hebrew *nifla'ot* echoes Moses' *niflinu*, "that we may be distinguished," of 33:16. Bekhor Shor and Ibn Ezra specifically apply the term to the wonder of Moses' radiant face mentioned in verse 29, but it may also relate to the extraordinary events that lie ahead in the course of the wilderness wanderings and the wars of conquest.

13. *sacred posts* Hebrew *'asherim* (sing. *'asherah*) are pagan cultic objects often mentioned in the Bible. They derive their name from the goddess known in Babylon as Ashrat, consort of the god Amurru. She bears the titles "bride of the king of heaven" and "mistress of sexual vigor and rejoicing." In Ugarit she appears as Athirat, consort of Il, who was head of its pantheon, and she is termed "the progenitrix of the gods," "mother of the gods," and "Lady Athirat of the Sea." She was a fertility goddess, and in 2 Kings 23:7 she is associated with sacred prostitution. That text testifies to the assimilation to Canaanite culture on the part of a segment of the Israelite population—a reality demonstrated by an inscription from Kuntillet 'Ajrud in northwestern Sinai that mentions "YHVH and his asherah."

The *'asherim* mentioned in the Bible must have been man-made wooden objects, most likely poles of some kind, that served as the cultic symbols of the goddess. The verbs used for the

¹⁴for you must not worship any other god, because the LORD, whose name is Impassioned, is an impassioned God. ¹⁵You must not make a covenant with the inhabitants of the land, for they will lust after their gods and sacrifice to their gods and invite you, and you will eat of their sacrifices. ¹⁶And when you take wives from among their daughters for your sons, their daughters will lust after their gods and will cause your sons to lust after their gods.

¹⁷You shall not make molten gods for yourselves.

¹⁸You shall observe the Feast of Unleavened Bread—eating unleavened bread for seven days, as I have commanded you—at the set time of the month of Abib, for in the month of Abib you went forth from Egypt.

¹⁹Every first issue of the womb is Mine, from all your livestock that drop a male as firstling, whether cattle or sheep. ²⁰But the firstling of an ass you shall redeem with a

אֲשֵׁרָיו תִּכְרֹתוּן: 14 כִּי לֹא תִשְׁתַּחֲוֶה לְאֵל אַחֵר*
כִּי יְהוָה קַנָּא שְׁמוֹ אֵל קַנָּא הוּא: 15 פֶּן־תִּכְרֹת
בְּרִית לְיוֹשֵׁב הָאָרֶץ וְזָנוּ| אַחֲרֵי אֱלֹהֵיהֶם וְזָבְחוּ
לֵאלֹהֵיהֶם וְקָרָא לְךָ וְאָכַלְתָּ מִזִּבְחוֹ: 16 וְלָקַחְתָּ
מִבְּנֹתָיו לְבָנֶיךָ וְזָנוּ בְנֹתָיו אַחֲרֵי אֱלֹהֵיהֶן וְהִזְנוּ
אֶת־בָּנֶיךָ אַחֲרֵי אֱלֹהֵיהֶן:
17 אֱלֹהֵי מַסֵּכָה לֹא תַעֲשֶׂה־לָּךְ:
18 אֶת־חַג הַמַּצּוֹת תִּשְׁמֹר שִׁבְעַת יָמִים
תֹּאכַל מַצּוֹת אֲשֶׁר צִוִּיתִךָ לְמוֹעֵד חֹדֶשׁ
הָאָבִיב כִּי בְּחֹדֶשׁ הָאָבִיב יָצָאתָ מִמִּצְרָיִם:
19 כָּל־פֶּטֶר רֶחֶם לִי וְכָל־מִקְנְךָ תִּזָּכָר פֶּטֶר
שׁוֹר וָשֶׂה: 20 וּפֶטֶר חֲמוֹר תִּפְדֶּה בְשֶׂה וְאִם־לֹא

ר' רבתי   v. 14.

destruction of these abhorrent objects are frequently those of "cutting down," "lopping off," and "plucking up."[16] It is clear that the adoption of foreign cults involved not only religious but also moral corruption.

14. any other god This Hebrew phrase in the singular—'el 'aher—is unique. Hence, Hebrew 'aher has an enlarged *resh (resh rabbati)* to avoid confusion with the graphically similar *dalet*, which would yield 'ehad, "one." The reverse phenomenon is evident in Deuteronomy 6:4.

Impassioned See Comment to 20:5. The emphasis on this punitive aspect of the divine personality is prompted by the apostasy of the golden calf.

16. lust after The Hebrew stem z-n-h, literally "to engage in prostitution," is often used figuratively to express infidelity to the covenant with God. Its use here may allude to the sexual immorality often associated with pagan cults, and particularly with the popular excesses in connection with the golden calf, as mentioned in 32:6. The story about the apostasy at Baal-peor, as recounted in Numbers 25:1–9, illustrates the pertinence of the admonitions listed in these verses.

17. molten gods The warnings against idolatry in all its forms conclude with this prohibition because the golden calf is frequently so categorized.[17]

FESTIVALS AND RELATED RELIGIOUS OBLIGATIONS (vv. 18–26)

The topics in this section are associated with those of the preceding because the narrative about the golden calf recounts that a "festival of the LORD" was proclaimed and burnt offerings and sacrifices were brought (32:5–6).[18] Similarly, when Jeroboam set up golden calves at Dan and Bethel, he too invented a special festival (1 Kings 12:28–33). Hence the need to recapitulate the list of the legitimate festivals of Israel. These have previously been set forth in 23:12–19.

18. Feast of Unleavened Bread See Comment to 23:15. The list begins with this feast rather than with the Sabbath because the golden calf had been identified with the God of the Exodus and because the religious new year occurs in the spring. See Comment to 12:2.

19–20. The law of the first-born follows since it too, in 13:2,11–15, is grounded in the Exodus. The text presupposes familiarity with that passage. In Deuteronomy 16:1–17, the list of festivals follows the law of the firstlings.

19. drop a male Hebrew *tizzakhar*, a grammatical form of the stem z-kh-r, is not found elsewhere. Also, it is feminine, whereas its subject, *mikneh*, "livestock," is elsewhere always masculine. The Targums render the phrase "all the males of cattle you shall sanctify."

sheep; if you do not redeem it, you must break its neck. And you must redeem every first-born among your sons.

None shall appear before Me empty-handed.

²¹Six days you shall work, but on the seventh day you shall cease from labor; you shall cease from labor even at plowing time and harvest time.

²²You shall observe the Feast of Weeks, of the first fruits of the wheat harvest; and the Feast of Ingathering at the turn of the year. ²³Three times a year all your males shall appear before the Sovereign LORD, the God of Israel. ²⁴I will drive out nations from your path and enlarge your territory; no one will covet your land when you go up to appear before the LORD your God three times a year.

²⁵You shall not offer the blood of My sacrifice with anything leavened; and the sacrifice of the Feast of Passover shall not be left lying until morning.

²⁶The choice first fruits of your soil you shall bring to the house of the LORD your God.

You shall not boil a kid in its mother's milk.

תִּפְדֶּה וַעֲרַפְתּוֹ כֹּל בְּכוֹר בָּנֶיךָ תִּפְדֶּה
וְלֹא־יֵרָאוּ פָנַי רֵיקָם:
²¹ שֵׁשֶׁת יָמִים תַּעֲבֹד וּבַיּוֹם הַשְּׁבִיעִי
תִּשְׁבֹּת בֶּחָרִישׁ וּבַקָּצִיר תִּשְׁבֹּת:
²² וְחַג שָׁבֻעֹת תַּעֲשֶׂה לְךָ בִּכּוּרֵי קְצִיר
חִטִּים וְחַג הָאָסִיף תְּקוּפַת הַשָּׁנָה: ²³ שָׁלֹשׁ
פְּעָמִים בַּשָּׁנָה יֵרָאֶה כָּל־זְכוּרְךָ אֶת־פְּנֵי הָאָדֹן |
יְהוָה אֱלֹהֵי יִשְׂרָאֵל: ²⁴ כִּי־אוֹרִישׁ גּוֹיִם מִפָּנֶיךָ
וְהִרְחַבְתִּי אֶת־גְּבוּלֶךָ וְלֹא־יַחְמֹד אִישׁ אֶת־
אַרְצְךָ בַּעֲלֹתְךָ לֵרָאוֹת אֶת־פְּנֵי יְהוָה אֱלֹהֶיךָ
שָׁלֹשׁ פְּעָמִים בַּשָּׁנָה:
²⁵ לֹא־תִשְׁחַט עַל־חָמֵץ דַּם־זִבְחִי וְלֹא־יָלִין
לַבֹּקֶר זֶבַח חַג הַפָּסַח:
²⁶ רֵאשִׁית בִּכּוּרֵי אַדְמָתְךָ תָּבִיא בֵּית יְהוָה
אֱלֹהֶיךָ
לֹא־תְבַשֵּׁל גְּדִי בַּחֲלֵב אִמּוֹ:   פ   שביעי

---

20. See Comments to 13:13 and 22:29.

None shall appear   See Comment to 23:15. As Rashi notes, this is a separate injunction, unconnected to the law of the first-born. It properly belongs after verse 23.

21. The inclusion of the law of the Sabbath here, after the passover and the first-born, presupposes that the institution of the Sabbath is based on the Exodus, as in Deuteronomy 5:15, and not on Creation, as in Exodus 20:9.

work   The soil.

even at plowing time and harvest time   The busiest times of the agricultural year[19] must give way to the overriding imperative to observe sacred time. This sacrifice becomes a true test of faith.

22. *Feast of Weeks*   See Comment to 23:16.

23. See Comment to 23:17. The present formulation, an expansion of the parallel text, is even further elaborated in Deuteronomy 16:16.

24. Another test of faith. This injunction presupposes the future existence of some central or, at least, regional sanctuary that, for many, will be far from home. It obviously cannot refer to a local shrine. The absence of males on the festivals might tempt an external enemy to time his aggression accordingly. Therefore the people are assured of divine protection on such occasions.

enlarge your territory   Compare Exodus 23:31 and Deuteronomy 12:20.

covet   See Comment to 20:17.

when you go up   The central shrine is assumed to be situated on an elevation.

three times a year   See Comment to 23:17.

25. *the sacrifice of the Feast of Passover*   See Comment to 12:11.

26. See Comment to 23:14 (17).

27And the LORD said to Moses: Write down these commandments, for in accordance with these commandments
I make a covenant with you and with Israel.

28And he was there with the LORD forty days and forty
nights; he ate no bread and drank no water; and he wrote
down on the tablets the terms of the covenant, the Ten
Commandments.

27 וַיֹּ֤אמֶר יְהוָה֙ אֶל־מֹשֶׁ֔ה כְּתָב־לְךָ֖ אֶת־
הַדְּבָרִ֣ים הָאֵ֑לֶּה כִּ֞י עַל־פִּ֣י ׀ הַדְּבָרִ֣ים הָאֵ֗לֶּה כָּרַ֧תִּי
אִתְּךָ֛ בְּרִ֖ית וְאֶת־יִשְׂרָאֵֽל׃
28 וַיְהִי־שָׁ֣ם עִם־יְהוָ֗ה אַרְבָּעִ֥ים יוֹם֙ וְאַרְבָּעִ֣ים
לַ֔יְלָה לֶ֚חֶם לֹ֣א אָכַ֔ל וּמַ֖יִם לֹ֣א שָׁתָ֑ה וַיִּכְתֹּ֣ב עַל־
הַלֻּחֹ֗ת אֵ֚ת דִּבְרֵ֣י הַבְּרִ֔ית עֲשֶׂ֖רֶת הַדְּבָרִֽים׃

EPILOGUE: MOSES REACHES THE PINNACLE OF EMINENCE   (vv. 27–35)

The narrative now reverts to the role and status of Moses, thereby forming a literary framework with
the opening verse of the entire section (32:1). The episode of apostasy began with a disparaging
popular reference to him and closes with an account of his glorification. The key verb *y-d-ʿ*, "know,"
is employed at both the beginning and the end (32:1; 34:29).

27–28.   Apparently, Moses is instructed to write down the commandments contained in
the foregoing, verses 11–26, just as, following the original covenant, he wrote down "all the commands of the LORD" (24:4).

27. in accordance with   Hebrew *ʿal pi*, literally "by the mouth of," is taken by the rabbis
to mean "orally" and to refer to the oral Torah that accompanied the written Torah.[20] Hence, this
oral law is known in Hebrew as the *torah she-be-ʿal peh*. It functions to illuminate obscurities, to
harmonize contradictions, and, in general, to make possible the practical application of the laws of
the written Torah in the everyday life of the people. It has served to make Jewish law responsive to the
needs created by changing social, economic, and cultural conditions.

with you and with Israel   This unexpected order signals the transition to the final episode,
which concentrates on the exaltation of Moses. It reflects his role as the dominant figure in dealing
with the apostasy and in successfully interceding with God on Israel's behalf.

28.   The first half of this verse is the scriptural way of describing Moses' withdrawal into
solitude at the onset of his mystical/spiritual experience on the mountain. In the presence of the
ultimate Source of holiness and in communication with Him, Moses realizes a transformation of his
self. He achieves a state that is beyond the ordinary range of human experience. In this extrasensuous
world he transcends the constraints of time and is released from the demands of his physical being.

This same phenomenon is included in the retrospective summary of the first theophany on Sinai
found in Deuteronomy 9:9,18, although it is omitted in the primary narrative in Exodus 24:18. Its
emphasis here must be taken as another indication that the thrust of this epilogue is to elevate the
status of Moses. It serves as the background for the culminating and extraordinary experience
recounted in the following verses.

forty   A symbolic number in the Bible, often associated with the purging of sin and with
purification.[21]

wrote down   In light of verse 1 and Deuteronomy 10:2,4, it is clear that the subject of the
verb is understood to be God.

the Ten Commandments   Hebrew *ʿaseret ha-devarim*, is also the title given in Deuteronomy 4:13 and 10:4. See introduction to chapter 20.

THE RADIANCE OF MOSES' FACE[22] (vv. 29–35)

Having succeeded in his mission as an intercessor, Moses descends the mountain carrying the two
inscribed tablets that testify to the reality of the renewed covenant between God and Israel.
According to rabbinic tradition, this occurred on the tenth day of the seventh month (*Tishrei*); for
this reason that date was decreed to be the annual Day of Atonement (*Yom Kippur*).[23]

²⁹So Moses came down from Mount Sinai. And as Moses came down from the mountain bearing the two tablets of the Pact, Moses was not aware that the skin of his face was radiant, since he had spoken with Him. ³⁰Aaron and all the Israelites saw that the skin of Moses' face was radiant; and they shrank from coming near him. ³¹But Moses called to them, and Aaron and all the chieftains in the assembly returned to him, and Moses spoke to them. ³²Afterward all the Israelites came near, and he instructed them concerning all that the LORD had imparted to him on Mount Sinai. ³³And when Moses had finished speaking with them, he put a veil over his face.

³⁴Whenever Moses went in before the LORD to speak with Him, he would leave the veil off until he came out; and when he came out and told the Israelites what he had been commanded, ³⁵the Israelites would see how radiant the skin

29 וַיְהִי בְּרֶדֶת מֹשֶׁה מֵהַר סִינַי וּשְׁנֵי לֻחֹת הָעֵדֻת בְּיַד־מֹשֶׁה בְּרִדְתּוֹ מִן־הָהָר וּמֹשֶׁה לֹא־יָדַע כִּי קָרַן עוֹר פָּנָיו בְּדַבְּרוֹ אִתּוֹ: 30 וַיַּרְא אַהֲרֹן וְכָל־בְּנֵי יִשְׂרָאֵל אֶת־מֹשֶׁה וְהִנֵּה קָרַן עוֹר פָּנָיו וַיִּירְאוּ מִגֶּשֶׁת אֵלָיו: 31 וַיִּקְרָא אֲלֵהֶם מֹשֶׁה וַיָּשֻׁבוּ אֵלָיו אַהֲרֹן וְכָל־הַנְּשִׂאִים בָּעֵדָה וַיְדַבֵּר מֹשֶׁה אֲלֵהֶם: 32 וְאַחֲרֵי־כֵן נִגְּשׁוּ כָּל־בְּנֵי יִשְׂרָאֵל וַיְצַוֵּם אֵת כָּל־אֲשֶׁר דִּבֶּר יְהוָה אִתּוֹ בְּהַר סִינָי: מפטיר 33 וַיְכַל מֹשֶׁה מִדַּבֵּר אִתָּם וַיִּתֵּן עַל־פָּנָיו מַסְוֶה: 34 וּבְבֹא מֹשֶׁה לִפְנֵי יְהוָה לְדַבֵּר אִתּוֹ יָסִיר אֶת־הַמַּסְוֶה עַד־צֵאתוֹ וְיָצָא וְדִבֶּר אֶל־בְּנֵי יִשְׂרָאֵל אֵת אֲשֶׁר יְצֻוֶּה: 35 וְרָאוּ

The awe-inspiring radiance emitted by Moses' face may be understood as the afterglow of the refulgent splendor of the Divine Presence. It functions to reaffirm and legitimate the prophet's role as the peerless intimate of God, the sole and singular mediator between God and His people; it also testifies to the restoration of divine favor to Israel. As such, the narrative forms a fitting conclusion to the entire episode of the golden calf. It further serves as an appropriate transition to the last segment of the Book of Exodus—the account of the construction of the mobile Tabernacle that is to symbolize the presence of God in the camp of Israel.

29. tablets of the Pact See Comment to 25:16.

was radiant A unique phenomenon conveyed by a unique Hebrew verb, *karan*. The traditional meaning given here is favored by the context and by Habakkuk 3:4 in which *karnayim*, "rays of light," appears in parallelism with "a brilliant light." This reference relates to God, and numerous biblical passages bear witness to a widespread, poetic notion of God being enveloped in light.[24] Moses' radiance is a reflection of the divine radiance.

Similar imagery was in use in ancient Mesopotamia, where an encompassing, awe-inspiring luminosity known as *melammu* was taken to be a characteristic attribute of divinity.[25] This supernatural radiance was thought to be shared by royalty and was a sign of the king's legitimacy. The present narrative about Moses shows that this notion was not considered to be incompatible with Israelite monotheism, although it appears in the Bible only in connection with Moses.

The peculiar threefold use of *karan* rather than the regular verb '-*w-r* is probably a pointed allusion to the golden calf, for *keren* is the usual word for a horn. It subtly emphasizes that the true mediator between God and Israel was not the fabricated, lifeless image of the horned animal, as the people thought, but the living Moses.

The association of *karan* with *keren* gave rise to the mistaken notion that Moses grew horns—even though the text speaks not of his head but of "the skin of his face." The rendering of *karan* by *cornuta* in the Vulgate translation, based on the commentaries of Jerome (ca. 347–ca. 419), helped foster the error, and a horned Moses later became a familiar figure in art from the eleventh century on.[26] The most famous such portrayal is, of course, Michelangelo's at San Pietro in Vincoli, Rome.

31–35. In the immediate presence of God Moses' radiance is, as it were, recharged. When he mediates the divine word to the people, his radiance authenticates the Source of the message. On neither occasion is a veil[27] appropriate. In his capacity as a private individual, however, Moses veils his face.

The verbal forms used to describe these activities imply repetition of the actions, indicating that from the time that Moses returned to the camp from Mount Sinai until his death his face remained radiant.

of Moses' face was. Moses would then put the veil back over his face until he went in to speak with Him.

VA-YAKHEL

35 Moses then convoked the whole Israelite community and said to them:

These are the things that the Lord has commanded you to do: ²On six days work may be done, but on the seventh day you shall have a sabbath of complete rest, holy to the Lord; whoever does any work on it shall be put to death. ³You shall kindle no fire throughout your settlements on the sabbath day.

⁴Moses said further to the whole community of Israelites:

בְּנֵי־יִשְׂרָאֵל אֶת־פְּנֵי מֹשֶׁה כִּי קָרַן עוֹר פְּנֵי מֹשֶׁה וְהֵשִׁיב מֹשֶׁה אֶת־הַמַּסְוֶה עַל־פָּנָיו עַד־בֹּאוֹ לְדַבֵּר אִתּוֹ: ס

ויקהל

ל"ה וַיַּקְהֵל מֹשֶׁה אֶת־כָּל־עֲדַת בְּנֵי יִשְׂרָאֵל וַיֹּאמֶר אֲלֵהֶם

אֵלֶּה הַדְּבָרִים אֲשֶׁר־צִוָּה יְהוָה לַעֲשֹׂת אֹתָם: ² שֵׁשֶׁת יָמִים תֵּעָשֶׂה מְלָאכָה וּבַיּוֹם הַשְּׁבִיעִי יִהְיֶה לָכֶם קֹדֶשׁ שַׁבַּת שַׁבָּתוֹן לַיהוָה כָּל־הָעֹשֶׂה בוֹ מְלָאכָה יוּמָת: ³ לֹא־תְבַעֲרוּ אֵשׁ בְּכֹל מֹשְׁבֹתֵיכֶם בְּיוֹם הַשַּׁבָּת: פ

⁴ וַיֹּאמֶר מֹשֶׁה אֶל־כָּל־עֲדַת בְּנֵי־יִשְׂרָאֵל לֵאמֹר זֶה הַדָּבָר אֲשֶׁר־צִוָּה יְהוָה לֵאמֹר:

CHAPTER 35

The Construction of the Tabernacle   (35:1–40:38)

THE CONVENING OF THE PEOPLE   (35:1–19)

Va-Yakhel   The renewal of the covenant between God and Israel, as symbolized by the second set of stone tablets, allows the construction of the Tabernacle to proceed. Moses convokes the people to make a public announcement to this effect. Just as the divine instructions about the Tabernacle concluded with the law of the Sabbath rest, so the narrative about its construction commences on the same theme—to the same purpose. See Comment to 31:12–17.

1. According to the Sages, this convocation occurred on the morrow of the Day of Atonement, when Moses descended Mount Sinai bearing the tablets, having obtained divine pardon for Israel.[1]

the whole Israelite community   The construction of the Tabernacle is to be an enterprise of all Israelites.

2–3. The injunction is practically a verbatim repetition of 31:15, with an addition. The manner in which the prohibition against kindling fire on the Sabbath is worded led the rabbis of the Talmud to understand that fire may not be kindled on the Sabbath itself; however, fire lit before the Sabbath and not refueled on the Sabbath is permitted. The Jewish sectarians known as Karaites rejected this interpretation and spent the day in darkness, although some later adherents did accept the rabbinic practice. It was probably to demonstrate opposition to the early Karaite view that the kindling of lights on the eve of Sabbath gradually became obligatory. To this end, the geonim, the post-Talmudic heads of the Babylonian academies, instituted the recital of a blessing over them.[2]

throughout your settlements   Abravanel suggests that the intent of this clause is to apply the prohibition comprehensively—wherever Jews reside.

A CALL FOR CONTRIBUTIONS (vv. 4–19)

4–9. Moses issues a call for donations of materials in accordance with 25:1–9. He specifies the various materials and explains how they are to be used. The actual goal of constructing the

This is what the LORD has commanded: ⁵Take from among you gifts to the LORD; everyone whose heart so moves him shall bring them—gifts for the LORD: gold, silver, and copper; ⁶blue, purple, and crimson yarns, fine linen, and goats' hair; ⁷tanned ram skins, dolphin skins, and acacia wood; ⁸oil for lighting, spices for the anointing oil and for the aromatic incense; ⁹lapis lazuli and other stones for setting, for the ephod and the breastpiece.

¹⁰And let all among you who are skilled come and make all that the LORD has commanded: ¹¹the Tabernacle, its tent and its covering, its clasps and its planks, its bars, its posts, and its sockets; ¹²the ark and its poles, the cover, and the curtain for the screen; ¹³the table, and its poles and all its utensils; and the bread of display; ¹⁴the lampstand for lighting, its furnishings and its lamps, and the oil for lighting; ¹⁵the altar of incense and its poles; the anointing oil and the aromatic incense; and the entrance screen for the entrance of the Tabernacle; ¹⁶the altar of burnt offering, its copper grating, its poles, and all its furnishings; the laver and its stand; ¹⁷the hangings of the enclosure, its posts and its sockets, and the screen for the gate of the court; ¹⁸the pegs for the Tabernacle, the pegs for the enclosure, and their cords; ¹⁹the service vestments for officiating in the sanctuary, the sacral vestments of Aaron the priest and the vestments of his sons for priestly service.

²⁰So the whole community of the Israelites left Moses' presence. ²¹And everyone who excelled in ability and every-

5 קְחוּ מֵאִתְּכֶם תְּרוּמָה לַיהֹוָה כֹּל נְדִיב
לִבּוֹ יְבִיאֶהָ אֵת תְּרוּמַת יְהֹוָה זָהָב וָכֶסֶף וּנְחֹשֶׁת:
6 וּתְכֵלֶת וְאַרְגָּמָן וְתוֹלַעַת שָׁנִי וְשֵׁשׁ וְעִזִּים:
7 וְעֹרֹת אֵילִם מְאׇדָּמִים וְעֹרֹת תְּחָשִׁים וַעֲצֵי
שִׁטִּים: 8 וְשֶׁמֶן לַמָּאוֹר וּבְשָׂמִים לְשֶׁמֶן הַמִּשְׁחָה
וְלִקְטֹרֶת הַסַּמִּים: 9 וְאַבְנֵי־שֹׁהַם וְאַבְנֵי מִלֻּאִים
לָאֵפוֹד וְלַחֹשֶׁן:

10 וְכׇל־חֲכַם־לֵב בָּכֶם יָבֹאוּ וְיַעֲשׂוּ אֵת כׇּל־
אֲשֶׁר צִוָּה יְהֹוָה: 11 אֶת־הַמִּשְׁכָּן אֶת־אׇהֳלוֹ
וְאֶת־מִכְסֵהוּ אֶת־קְרָסָיו וְאֶת־קְרָשָׁיו אֶת־בְּרִיחָו
אֶת־עַמֻּדָיו וְאֶת־אֲדָנָיו: 12 אֶת־הָאָרֹן וְאֶת־בַּדָּיו
אֶת־הַכַּפֹּרֶת וְאֵת פָּרֹכֶת הַמָּסָךְ: 13 אֶת־הַשֻּׁלְחָן
וְאֶת־בַּדָּיו וְאֶת־כׇּל־כֵּלָיו וְאֵת לֶחֶם הַפָּנִים:
14 וְאֶת־מְנֹרַת הַמָּאוֹר וְאֶת־כֵּלֶיהָ וְאֶת־נֵרֹתֶיהָ
וְאֵת שֶׁמֶן הַמָּאוֹר: 15 וְאֶת־מִזְבַּח הַקְּטֹרֶת
וְאֶת־בַּדָּיו וְאֵת שֶׁמֶן הַמִּשְׁחָה וְאֵת קְטֹרֶת
הַסַּמִּים וְאֶת־מָסַךְ הַפֶּתַח לְפֶתַח הַמִּשְׁכָּן:
16 אֵת | מִזְבַּח הָעֹלָה וְאֶת־מִכְבַּר הַנְּחֹשֶׁת
אֲשֶׁר־לוֹ אֶת־בַּדָּיו וְאֶת־כׇּל־כֵּלָיו אֶת־הַכִּיֹּר וְאֶת־
כַּנּוֹ: 17 אֵת קַלְעֵי הֶחָצֵר אֶת־עַמֻּדָיו וְאֶת־אֲדָנֶיהָ
וְאֵת מָסַךְ שַׁעַר הֶחָצֵר: 18 אֶת־יִתְדֹת הַמִּשְׁכָּן
וְאֶת־יִתְדֹת הֶחָצֵר וְאֶת־מֵיתְרֵיהֶם: 19 אֶת־בִּגְדֵי
הַשְּׂרָד לְשָׁרֵת בַּקֹּדֶשׁ אֶת־בִּגְדֵי הַקֹּדֶשׁ
לְאַהֲרֹן הַכֹּהֵן וְאֶת־בִּגְדֵי בָנָיו לְכַהֵן:
20 וַיֵּצְאוּ כׇּל־עֲדַת בְּנֵי־יִשְׂרָאֵל מִלִּפְנֵי מֹשֶׁה:
שני 21 וַיָּבֹאוּ כׇּל־אִישׁ אֲשֶׁר־נְשָׂאוֹ לִבּוֹ וְכֹל

v. 11. בְּרִיחָיו ק'

Tabernacle is not explicitly stated, as in 25:8; it is assumed that the audience is already aware of the project.

12. *the curtain for the screen* The workmanship and function of the curtain, which partitions off the Holy of Holies from the Holy Place, is described in 26:31–33.³ In Numbers 4:5 it is explained that at the breaking of camp during the trek through the wilderness, Aaron and his sons would enter the Tabernacle, remove the screening curtain, and cover the Ark with it.

15. *the entrance screen* The curtain that partitions off the Holy Place (the outer sanctum) from the outer court, as described in 26:36–37.

17. *the screen for the gate of the court* The curtain on the east side, at the entrance from the outer perimeter, as described in 27:9–19, especially verse 16.

THE PEOPLE'S RESPONSE (vv. 20–29)

The people—men and women alike—respond to Moses' call with unstinting generosity, freely contributing their most precious possessions as well as their skilled services.

ויקהל

one whose spirit moved him came, bringing to the LORD his offering for the work of the Tent of Meeting and for all its service and for the sacral vestments. ²²Men and women, all whose hearts moved them, all who would make an elevation offering of gold to the LORD, came bringing brooches, earrings, rings, and pendants—gold objects of all kinds. ²³And everyone who had in his possession blue, purple, and crimson yarns, fine linen, goats' hair, tanned ram skins, and dolphin skins, brought them; ²⁴everyone who would make gifts of silver or copper brought them as gifts for the LORD; and everyone who had in his possession acacia wood for any work of the service brought that. ²⁵And all the skilled women spun with their own hands, and brought what they had spun, in blue, purple, and crimson yarns, and in fine linen. ²⁶And all the women who excelled in that skill spun the goats' hair. ²⁷And the chieftains brought lapis lazuli and other stones for setting, for the ephod and for the breastpiece; ²⁸and spices and oil for lighting, for the anointing oil, and for the aromatic incense. ²⁹Thus the Israelites, all the men and women whose hearts moved them to bring anything for the work that the LORD, through Moses, had commanded to be done, brought it as a freewill offering to the LORD.

³⁰And Moses said to the Israelites: See, the LORD has singled out by name Bezalel, son of Uri son of Hur, of the tribe of Judah. ³¹He has endowed him with a divine spirit of skill, ability, and knowledge in every kind of craft ³²and has inspired him to make designs for work in gold, silver, and copper, ³³to cut stones for setting and to carve wood—to work in every kind of designer's craft—³⁴and to give directions. He and Oholiab son of Ahisamach of the tribe of Dan ³⁵have been endowed with the skill to do any work—

27. The chieftains of the tribes contributed the precious stones on which the names of the tribes are to be incised, in accordance with the instructions of 28:9–12,21,29.

THE MASTER CRAFTSMEN (35:30–36:1)

The people are informed of God's designation of Bezalel and Oholiab as the chief artisans and supervisors of the entire project, as recorded in 31:1–11. Berakhot 55a remarks that this public announcement by Moses is to teach that one must not appoint a communal leader without first consulting the people.

34. *and to give directions* They are endowed with the ability to instruct others, which is a divinely bestowed gift. Ibn Ezra notes that "there are many scholars who are incapable of teaching."

of the carver, the designer, the embroiderer in blue, purple crimson yarns, and in fine linen, and of the weaver— **36** as workers in all crafts and as makers of designs. [1]Let then, Bezalel and Oholiab and all the skilled persons whom the LORD has endowed with skill and ability to perform expertly all the tasks connected with the service of the sanctuary carry out all that the LORD has commanded.

[2]Moses then called Bezalel and Oholiab, and every skilled person whom the LORD had endowed with skill, everyone who excelled in ability, to undertake the task and carry it out. [3]They took over from Moses all the gifts that the Israelites had brought, to carry out the tasks connected with the service of the sanctuary. But when these continued to bring freewill offerings to him morning after morning, [4]all the artisans who were engaged in the tasks of the sanctuary came, each from the task upon which he was engaged, [5]and said to Moses, "The people are bringing more than is needed for the tasks entailed in the work that the LORD has commanded to be done." [6]Moses thereupon had this proclamation made throughout the camp: "Let no man or woman make further effort toward gifts for the sanctuary!" So the people stopped bringing: [7]their efforts had been more than enough for all the tasks to be done.

[8]Then all the skilled among those engaged in the work made the Tabernacle of ten strips of cloth, which they made of fine twisted linen, blue, purple, and crimson yarns; into these they worked a design of cherubim. [9]The length of

לֹ"ו וְעָשָׂה בְצַלְאֵל וְאָהֳלִיאָב וְכֹל ׀ אִישׁ חֲכַם־לֵב אֲשֶׁר נָתַן יְהוָה חָכְמָה וּתְבוּנָה בָּהֵמָּה לָדַעַת לַעֲשֹׂת אֶת־כָּל־מְלֶאכֶת עֲבֹדַת הַקֹּדֶשׁ לְכֹל אֲשֶׁר־צִוָּה יְהוָה: 2 וַיִּקְרָא מֹשֶׁה אֶל־בְּצַלְאֵל וְאֶל־אָהֳלִיאָב וְאֶל כָּל־אִישׁ חֲכַם־לֵב אֲשֶׁר נָתַן יְהוָה חָכְמָה בְּלִבּוֹ כֹּל אֲשֶׁר נְשָׂאוֹ לִבּוֹ לְקָרְבָה אֶל־הַמְּלָאכָה לַעֲשֹׂת אֹתָהּ: 3 וַיִּקְחוּ מִלִּפְנֵי מֹשֶׁה אֵת כָּל־הַתְּרוּמָה אֲשֶׁר הֵבִיאוּ בְּנֵי יִשְׂרָאֵל לִמְלֶאכֶת עֲבֹדַת הַקֹּדֶשׁ לַעֲשֹׂת אֹתָהּ וְהֵם הֵבִיאוּ אֵלָיו עוֹד נְדָבָה בַּבֹּקֶר בַּבֹּקֶר: 4 וַיָּבֹאוּ כָּל־הַחֲכָמִים הָעֹשִׂים אֵת כָּל־מְלֶאכֶת הַקֹּדֶשׁ אִישׁ־אִישׁ מִמְּלַאכְתּוֹ אֲשֶׁר־הֵמָּה עֹשִׂים: 5 וַיֹּאמְרוּ אֶל־מֹשֶׁה לֵּאמֹר מַרְבִּים הָעָם לְהָבִיא מִדֵּי הָעֲבֹדָה לַמְּלָאכָה אֲשֶׁר־צִוָּה יְהוָה לַעֲשֹׂת אֹתָהּ: 6 וַיְצַו מֹשֶׁה וַיַּעֲבִירוּ קוֹל בַּמַּחֲנֶה לֵאמֹר אִישׁ וְאִשָּׁה אַל־יַעֲשׂוּ־עוֹד מְלָאכָה לִתְרוּמַת הַקֹּדֶשׁ וַיִּכָּלֵא הָעָם מֵהָבִיא: 7 וְהַמְּלָאכָה הָיְתָה דַיָּם לְכָל־הַמְּלָאכָה לַעֲשׂוֹת אֹתָהּ וְהוֹתֵר: ס רביעי

8 וַיַּעֲשׂוּ כָל־חֲכַם־לֵב בְּעֹשֵׂי הַמְּלָאכָה אֶת־הַמִּשְׁכָּן עֶשֶׂר יְרִיעֹת שֵׁשׁ מָשְׁזָר וּתְכֵלֶת וְאַרְגָּמָן וְתֹלַעַת שָׁנִי כְּרֻבִים מַעֲשֵׂה חֹשֵׁב עָשָׂה אֹתָם: 9 אֹרֶךְ הַיְרִיעָה הָאַחַת שְׁמֹנֶה וְעֶשְׂרִים

CHAPTER 36   THE OVERABUNDANCE OF DONATIONS (vv. 2–7)

The popular outpouring of donations produced materials far in excess of what was needed, and the people had to be exhorted to contribute no further. See Comment to 12:36.

THE WORK OF CONSTRUCTION (36:8–38:20)

There now follows a lengthy and detailed account of the work. This is really a repetition of the instructions already given, but here the verbs are phrased as completed action, and the various items are listed in a different order.

The organizing principle in the original set of instructions was ideological; here practical considerations are paramount. Whereas the earlier instructions moved from the furnishings to the structure of the Tabernacle, here the sequence is reversed. By presenting the building of the Ark first, the former injunctions highlight the symbol of the covenant as the focal point of the entire enterprise and place it at the apex of a hierarchy of values. From Bezalel's pragmatic perspective, however, priority must be given to the construction of the edifice that is to house the furniture.

In Berakhot 55a, Bezalel is said to question Moses' instruction as follows:

> Moses our teacher, it is universal practice that one first builds a house and then brings in the furnishings; but you say, "Make me an Ark, furnishings, and a tabernacle." Where shall I put the furnishings I am to make? Can it be that the Holy One, blessed be He, said to you,

each cloth was twenty-eight cubits, and the width of each cloth was four cubits, all cloths having the same measurements. [10]They joined five of the cloths to one another, and they joined the other five cloths to one another. [11]They made loops of blue wool on the edge of the outermost cloth of the one set, and did the same on the edge of the outermost cloth of the other set: [12]they made fifty loops on the one cloth, and they made fifty loops on the edge of the end cloth of the other set, the loops being opposite one another. [13]And they made fifty gold clasps and coupled the units to one another with the clasps, so that the Tabernacle became one whole.

[14]They made cloths of goats' hair for a tent over the Tabernacle; they made the cloths eleven in number. [15]The length of each cloth was thirty cubits, and the width of each cloth was four cubits, the eleven cloths having the same measurements. [16]They joined five of the cloths by themselves, and the other six cloths by themselves. [17]They made fifty loops on the edge of the outermost cloth of the one set, and they made fifty loops on the edge of the end cloth of the other set. [18]They made fifty copper clasps to couple the Tent together so that it might become one whole. [19]And they made a covering of tanned ram skins for the Tent, and a covering of dolphin skins above.

[20]They made the planks for the Tabernacle of acacia wood, upright. [21]The length of each plank was ten cubits, the width of each plank a cubit and a half. [22]Each plank had two tenons, parallel to each other; they did the same with all the planks of the Tabernacle. [23]Of the planks of the Tabernacle, they made twenty planks for the south side, [24]making forty silver sockets under the twenty planks, two sockets under one plank for its two tenons and two sockets under each following plank for its two tenons; [25]and for the other side wall of the Tabernacle, the north side, twenty planks, [26]with their forty silver sockets, two sockets under one plank and two sockets under each following plank. [27]And for the rear of the Tabernacle, to the west, they made six planks; [28]and they made two planks for the corners of the Tabernacle at the rear. [29]They matched at the bottom,

בְּאַמָּה וְרֹחַב אַרְבַּע בָּאַמָּה הַיְרִיעָה הָאֶחָת מִדָּה אַחַת לְכָל־הַיְרִיעֹת: [10] וַיְחַבֵּר אֶת־חֲמֵשׁ הַיְרִיעֹת אַחַת אֶל־אֶחָת וְחָמֵשׁ יְרִיעֹת חִבַּר אַחַת אֶל־אֶחָת: [11] וַיַּעַשׂ לֻלְאֹת תְּכֵלֶת עַל שְׂפַת הַיְרִיעָה הָאֶחָת מִקָּצָה בַּמַּחְבָּרֶת כֵּן עָשָׂה בִּשְׂפַת הַיְרִיעָה הַקִּיצוֹנָה בַּמַּחְבֶּרֶת הַשֵּׁנִית: [12] חֲמִשִּׁים לֻלָאֹת עָשָׂה בַּיְרִיעָה הָאֶחָת וַחֲמִשִּׁים לֻלָאֹת עָשָׂה בִּקְצֵה הַיְרִיעָה אֲשֶׁר בַּמַּחְבֶּרֶת הַשֵּׁנִית מַקְבִּילֹת הַלֻּלָאֹת אַחַת אֶל־אֶחָת: [13] וַיַּעַשׂ חֲמִשִּׁים קַרְסֵי זָהָב וַיְחַבֵּר אֶת־הַיְרִיעֹת אַחַת אֶל־אַחַת בַּקְּרָסִים וַיְהִי הַמִּשְׁכָּן אֶחָד: ס

[14] וַיַּעַשׂ יְרִיעֹת עִזִּים לְאֹהֶל עַל־הַמִּשְׁכָּן עַשְׁתֵּי־עֶשְׂרֵה יְרִיעֹת עָשָׂה אֹתָם: [15] אֹרֶךְ הַיְרִיעָה הָאַחַת שְׁלֹשִׁים בָּאַמָּה וְאַרְבַּע אַמּוֹת רֹחַב הַיְרִיעָה הָאֶחָת מִדָּה אַחַת לְעַשְׁתֵּי עֶשְׂרֵה יְרִיעֹת: [16] וַיְחַבֵּר אֶת־חֲמֵשׁ הַיְרִיעֹת לְבָד וְאֶת־שֵׁשׁ הַיְרִיעֹת לְבָד: [17] וַיַּעַשׂ לֻלָאֹת חֲמִשִּׁים עַל שְׂפַת הַיְרִיעָה הַקִּיצֹנָה בַּמַּחְבָּרֶת וַחֲמִשִּׁים לֻלָאֹת עָשָׂה עַל־שְׂפַת הַיְרִיעָה הַחֹבֶרֶת הַשֵּׁנִית: [18] וַיַּעַשׂ קַרְסֵי נְחֹשֶׁת חֲמִשִּׁים לְחַבֵּר אֶת־הָאֹהֶל לִהְיֹת אֶחָד: [19] וַיַּעַשׂ מִכְסֶה לָאֹהֶל עֹרֹת אֵילִם מְאָדָּמִים וּמִכְסֵה עֹרֹת תְּחָשִׁים מִלְמָעְלָה: ס חמישי

[20] וַיַּעַשׂ אֶת־הַקְּרָשִׁים לַמִּשְׁכָּן עֲצֵי שִׁטִּים עֹמְדִים: [21] עֶשֶׂר אַמֹּת אֹרֶךְ הַקָּרֶשׁ וְאַמָּה וַחֲצִי הָאַמָּה רֹחַב הַקֶּרֶשׁ הָאֶחָד: [22] שְׁתֵּי יָדֹת לַקֶּרֶשׁ הָאֶחָד מְשֻׁלָּבֹת אַחַת אֶל־אֶחָת כֵּן עָשָׂה לְכֹל קַרְשֵׁי הַמִּשְׁכָּן: [23] וַיַּעַשׂ אֶת־הַקְּרָשִׁים לַמִּשְׁכָּן עֶשְׂרִים קְרָשִׁים לִפְאַת נֶגֶב תֵּימָנָה: [24] וְאַרְבָּעִים אַדְנֵי־כֶסֶף עָשָׂה תַּחַת עֶשְׂרִים הַקְּרָשִׁים שְׁנֵי אֲדָנִים תַּחַת־הַקֶּרֶשׁ הָאֶחָד לִשְׁתֵּי יְדֹתָיו וּשְׁנֵי אֲדָנִים תַּחַת־הַקֶּרֶשׁ הָאֶחָד לִשְׁתֵּי יְדֹתָיו: [25] וּלְצֶלַע הַמִּשְׁכָּן הַשֵּׁנִית לִפְאַת צָפוֹן עָשָׂה עֶשְׂרִים קְרָשִׁים: [26] וְאַרְבָּעִים אַדְנֵיהֶם כָּסֶף שְׁנֵי אֲדָנִים תַּחַת הַקֶּרֶשׁ הָאֶחָד וּשְׁנֵי אֲדָנִים תַּחַת הַקֶּרֶשׁ הָאֶחָד: [27] וּלְיַרְכְּתֵי הַמִּשְׁכָּן יָמָּה עָשָׂה שִׁשָּׁה קְרָשִׁים: [28] וּשְׁנֵי קְרָשִׁים עָשָׂה לִמְקֻצְעֹת הַמִּשְׁכָּן בַּיַּרְכָתָיִם: [29] וְהָיוּ תוֹאֲמִם

"Make a tabernacle, an Ark, and furnishings."? Moses replied, "Perhaps you were in the shadow of God [Heb. *be-tsel-el*, a play on Bezalel] and you knew!"

Another characteristic of the narrative is the oft-repeated affirmation that everything was executed in precise fulfillment of the divine instructions to Moses.[1]

but terminated as one at the top into one ring; they did so with both of them at the two corners. [30]Thus there were eight planks with their sockets of silver: sixteen sockets, two under each plank.

[31]They made bars of acacia wood, five for the planks of the one side wall of the Tabernacle, [32]five bars for the planks of the other side wall of the Tabernacle, and five bars for the planks of the wall of the Tabernacle at the rear, to the west; [33]they made the center bar to run, halfway up the planks, from end to end. [34]They overlaid the planks with gold, and made their rings of gold, as holders for the bars; and they overlaid the bars with gold.

[35]They made the curtain of blue, purple, and crimson yarns, and fine twisted linen, working into it a design of cherubim. [36]They made for it four posts of acacia wood and overlaid them with gold, with their hooks of gold; and they cast for them four silver sockets.

[37]They made the screen for the entrance of the Tent, of blue, purple, and crimson yarns, and fine twisted linen, done in embroidery; [38]and five posts for it with their hooks. They overlaid their tops and their bands with gold; but the five sockets were of copper.

37 Bezalel made the ark of acacia wood, two and a half cubits long, a cubit and a half wide, and a cubit and a half high. [2]He overlaid it with pure gold, inside and out; and he made a gold molding for it round about. [3]He cast four gold rings for it, for its four feet: two rings on one of its side walls and two rings on the other. [4]He made poles of acacia

CHAPTER 37   THE MANUFACTURE OF THE FURNITURE AND ACCESSORIES (37:1–38:20)

The order of narration reflects descending gradations of holiness: the Ark, which is to be located in the Holy of Holies, comes first, to be followed by the three items that belong in the Holy Place—the table, the menorah, and the altar of incense. The anointing oil and aromatic incense are next because both are needed in the Holy Place. Last are the altar of burnt offering and the laver, both of which are placed in the outer court.

The Ark (vv. 1–9)

1. Bezalel made the ark   This section corresponds to 25:10–21. It is to be noted that there the instruction reads, "They shall make an ark." Ramban suggests that Bezalel personally made the Ark, given its paramount importance, but only directed and supervised the manufacture of the other objects. Moses' statement in Deuteronomy 10:3, "I made an ark," is to be understood in the same way as the phrase "the House which King Solomon built" in referring to the Temple.[1]

wood, overlaid them with gold, ⁵and inserted the poles into the rings on the side walls of the ark for carrying the ark.

⁶He made a cover of pure gold, two and a half cubits long and a cubit and a half wide. ⁷He made two cherubim of gold; he made them of hammered work, at the two ends of the cover: ⁸one cherub at one end and the other cherub at the other end; he made the cherubim of one piece with the cover, at its two ends. ⁹The cherubim had their wings spread out above, shielding the cover with their wings. They faced each other; the faces of the cherubim were turned toward the cover.

¹⁰He made the table of acacia wood, two cubits long, one cubit wide, and a cubit and a half high; ¹¹he overlaid it with pure gold and made a gold molding around it. ¹²He made a rim of a hand's breadth around it and made a gold molding for its rim round about. ¹³He cast four gold rings for it and attached the rings to the four corners at its four legs. ¹⁴The rings were next to the rim, as holders for the poles to carry the table. ¹⁵He made the poles of acacia wood for carrying the table, and overlaid them with gold. ¹⁶The utensils that were to be upon the table—its bowls, ladles, jugs, and jars with which to offer libations—he made of pure gold.

¹⁷He made the lampstand of pure gold. He made the lampstand—its base and its shaft—of hammered work; its cups, calyxes, and petals were of one piece with it. ¹⁸Six branches issued from its sides: three branches from one side of the lampstand, and three branches from the other side of the lampstand. ¹⁹There were three cups shaped like almond-blossoms, each with calyx and petals, on one branch; and there were three cups shaped like almond-blossoms, each with calyx and petals, on the next branch; so for all six branches issuing from the lampstand. ²⁰On the lampstand itself there were four cups shaped like almond-blossoms, each with calyx and petals: ²¹a calyx, of one piece

4 וַיַּעַשׂ בַּדֵּי עֲצֵי שִׁטִּים וַיְצַף אֹתָם זָהָב: 5 וַיָּבֵא אֶת־הַבַּדִּים בַּטַּבָּעֹת עַל צַלְעֹת הָאָרֹן לָשֵׂאת אֶת־הָאָרֹן:

6 וַיַּעַשׂ כַּפֹּרֶת זָהָב טָהוֹר אַמָּתַיִם וָחֵצִי אָרְכָּהּ וְאַמָּה וָחֵצִי רָחְבָּהּ: 7 וַיַּעַשׂ שְׁנֵי כְרֻבִים זָהָב מִקְשָׁה עָשָׂה אֹתָם מִשְּׁנֵי קְצוֹת הַכַּפֹּרֶת: 8 כְּרוּב־אֶחָד מִקָּצָה מִזֶּה וּכְרוּב־אֶחָד מִקָּצָה מִזֶּה מִן־הַכַּפֹּרֶת עָשָׂה אֶת־הַכְּרֻבִים מִשְּׁנֵי קצוותו: 9 וַיִּהְיוּ הַכְּרֻבִים פֹּרְשֵׂי כְנָפַיִם לְמַעְלָה סֹכְכִים בְּכַנְפֵיהֶם עַל־הַכַּפֹּרֶת וּפְנֵיהֶם אִישׁ אֶל־אָחִיו אֶל־הַכַּפֹּרֶת הָיוּ פְּנֵי הַכְּרֻבִים:
פ

10 וַיַּעַשׂ אֶת־הַשֻּׁלְחָן עֲצֵי שִׁטִּים אַמָּתַיִם אָרְכּוֹ וְאַמָּה רָחְבּוֹ וְאַמָּה וָחֵצִי קֹמָתוֹ: 11 וַיְצַף אֹתוֹ זָהָב טָהוֹר וַיַּעַשׂ לוֹ זֵר זָהָב סָבִיב: 12 וַיַּעַשׂ לוֹ מִסְגֶּרֶת טֹפַח סָבִיב וַיַּעַשׂ זֵר־זָהָב לְמִסְגַּרְתּוֹ סָבִיב: 13 וַיִּצֹק לוֹ אַרְבַּע טַבְּעֹת זָהָב וַיִּתֵּן אֶת־הַטַּבָּעֹת עַל אַרְבַּע הַפֵּאֹת אֲשֶׁר לְאַרְבַּע רַגְלָיו: 14 לְעֻמַּת הַמִּסְגֶּרֶת הָיוּ הַטַּבָּעֹת בָּתִּים לַבַּדִּים לָשֵׂאת אֶת־הַשֻּׁלְחָן: 15 וַיַּעַשׂ אֶת־הַבַּדִּים עֲצֵי שִׁטִּים וַיְצַף אֹתָם זָהָב לָשֵׂאת אֶת־הַשֻּׁלְחָן: 16 וַיַּעַשׂ אֶת־הַכֵּלִים אֲשֶׁר עַל־הַשֻּׁלְחָן אֶת־קְעָרֹתָיו וְאֶת־כַּפֹּתָיו וְאֵת מְנַקִּיֹּתָיו וְאֶת־הַקְּשָׂוֹת אֲשֶׁר יֻסַּךְ בָּהֵן זָהָב טָהוֹר: פ

[שלישי כשהן מחוברות]

שׁשׁי

17 וַיַּעַשׂ אֶת־הַמְּנֹרָה זָהָב טָהוֹר מִקְשָׁה עָשָׂה אֶת־הַמְּנֹרָה יְרֵכָהּ וְקָנָהּ גְּבִיעֶיהָ כַּפְתֹּרֶיהָ וּפְרָחֶיהָ מִמֶּנָּה הָיוּ: 18 וְשִׁשָּׁה קָנִים יֹצְאִים מִצִּדֶּיהָ שְׁלֹשָׁה קְנֵי מְנֹרָה מִצִּדָּהּ הָאֶחָד וּשְׁלֹשָׁה קְנֵי מְנֹרָה מִצִּדָּהּ הַשֵּׁנִי: 19 שְׁלֹשָׁה גְבִעִים מְשֻׁקָּדִים בַּקָּנֶה הָאֶחָד כַּפְתֹּר וָפֶרַח וּשְׁלֹשָׁה גְבִעִים מְשֻׁקָּדִים בְּקָנֶה אֶחָד כַּפְתֹּר וָפָרַח כֵּן לְשֵׁשֶׁת הַקָּנִים הַיֹּצְאִים מִן־הַמְּנֹרָה: 20 וּבַמְּנֹרָה אַרְבָּעָה גְבִעִים מְשֻׁקָּדִים כַּפְתֹּרֶיהָ וּפְרָחֶיהָ: 21 וְכַפְתֹּר

קצוֹתָיו ק׳   v. 8.

The Table (vv. 10–16)

This section corresponds to 25:23–30.

The Menorah (vv. 17–24)

This section corresponds to 25:31–40.

with it, under a pair of branches; and a calyx, of one piece with it, under the second pair of branches; and a calyx, of one piece with it, under the last pair of branches; so for all six branches issuing from it. ²²Their calyxes and their stems were of one piece with it, the whole of it a single hammered piece of pure gold. ²³He made its seven lamps, its tongs, and its fire pans of pure gold. ²⁴He made it and all its furnishings out of a talent of pure gold.

²⁵He made the incense altar of acacia wood, a cubit long and a cubit wide—square—and two cubits high; its horns were of one piece with it. ²⁶He overlaid it with pure gold: its top, its sides round about, and its horns; and he made a gold molding for it round about. ²⁷He made two gold rings for it under its molding, on its two walls—on opposite sides—as holders for the poles with which to carry it. ²⁸He made the poles of acacia wood, and overlaid them with gold. ²⁹He prepared the sacred anointing oil and the pure aromatic incense, expertly blended.

38 He made the altar for burnt offering of acacia wood, five cubits long and five cubits wide—square—and three cubits high. ²He made horns for it on its four corners, the horns being of one piece with it; and he overlaid it with copper. ³He made all the utensils of the altar—the pails, the scrapers, the basins, the flesh hooks, and the fire pans; he made all these utensils of copper. ⁴He made for the altar a grating of meshwork in copper, extending below, under its ledge, to its middle. ⁵He cast four rings, at the four corners of the copper grating, as holders for the poles. ⁶He made the poles of acacia wood and overlaid them with copper; ⁷and he inserted the poles into the rings on the side walls of the altar, to carry it by them. He made it hollow, of boards.

The Altar of Incense (vv. 25–28)

This section corresponds to 30:1–10.

The Anointing Oil and Incense (v. 29)

This verse summarizes 30:22–33, 34–37.

CHAPTER 38   *The Altar of Burnt Offering* (vv. 1–7)

This section corresponds to 27:1–8.

תַּחַת שְׁנֵי הַקָּנִים מִמֶּנָּה וְכַפְתֹּר תַּחַת שְׁנֵי הַקָּנִים מִמֶּנָּה וְכַפְתֹּר תַּחַת־שְׁנֵי הַקָּנִים מִמֶּנָּה לְשֵׁשֶׁת הַקָּנִים הַיֹּצְאִים מִמֶּנָּה: 22 כַּפְתֹּרֵיהֶם וּקְנֹתָם מִמֶּנָּה הָיוּ כֻּלָּהּ מִקְשָׁה אַחַת זָהָב טָהוֹר: 23 וַיַּעַשׂ אֶת־נֵרֹתֶיהָ שִׁבְעָה וּמַלְקָחֶיהָ וּמַחְתֹּתֶיהָ זָהָב טָהוֹר: 24 כִּכָּר זָהָב טָהוֹר עָשָׂה אֹתָהּ וְאֵת כָּל־כֵּלֶיהָ: פ

25 וַיַּעַשׂ אֶת־מִזְבַּח הַקְּטֹרֶת עֲצֵי שִׁטִּים אַמָּה אָרְכּוֹ וְאַמָּה רָחְבּוֹ רָבוּעַ וְאַמָּתַיִם קֹמָתוֹ מִמֶּנּוּ הָיוּ קַרְנֹתָיו: 26 וַיְצַף אֹתוֹ זָהָב טָהוֹר אֶת־גַּגּוֹ וְאֶת־קִירֹתָיו סָבִיב וְאֶת־קַרְנֹתָיו וַיַּעַשׂ לוֹ זֵר זָהָב סָבִיב: 27 וּשְׁתֵּי טַבְּעֹת זָהָב עָשָׂה־לוֹ מִתַּחַת לְזֵרוֹ עַל שְׁתֵּי צַלְעֹתָיו עַל שְׁנֵי צִדָּיו לְבָתִּים לְבַדִּים לָשֵׂאת אֹתוֹ בָּהֶם: 28 וַיַּעַשׂ אֶת־הַבַּדִּים עֲצֵי שִׁטִּים וַיְצַף אֹתָם זָהָב: 29 וַיַּעַשׂ אֶת־שֶׁמֶן הַמִּשְׁחָה קֹדֶשׁ וְאֶת־קְטֹרֶת הַסַּמִּים טָהוֹר מַעֲשֵׂה רֹקֵחַ: פ שביעי [רביעי]
[כשהן מחוברות]

לֹ"ח וַיַּעַשׂ אֶת־מִזְבַּח הָעֹלָה עֲצֵי שִׁטִּים חָמֵשׁ אַמּוֹת אָרְכּוֹ וְחָמֵשׁ־אַמּוֹת רָחְבּוֹ רָבוּעַ וְשָׁלֹשׁ אַמּוֹת קֹמָתוֹ: 2 וַיַּעַשׂ קַרְנֹתָיו עַל אַרְבַּע פִּנֹּתָיו מִמֶּנּוּ הָיוּ קַרְנֹתָיו וַיְצַף אֹתוֹ נְחֹשֶׁת: 3 וַיַּעַשׂ אֶת־כָּל־כְּלֵי הַמִּזְבֵּחַ אֶת־הַסִּירֹת וְאֶת־הַיָּעִים וְאֶת־הַמִּזְרָקֹת אֶת־הַמִּזְלָגֹת וְאֶת־הַמַּחְתֹּת כָּל־כֵּלָיו עָשָׂה נְחֹשֶׁת: 4 וַיַּעַשׂ לַמִּזְבֵּחַ מִכְבָּר מַעֲשֵׂה רֶשֶׁת נְחֹשֶׁת תַּחַת כַּרְכֻּבּוֹ מִלְמַטָּה עַד־חֶצְיוֹ: 5 וַיִּצֹק אַרְבַּע טַבָּעֹת בְּאַרְבַּע הַקְּצָוֹת לְמִכְבַּר הַנְּחֹשֶׁת בָּתִּים לַבַּדִּים: 6 וַיַּעַשׂ אֶת־הַבַּדִּים עֲצֵי שִׁטִּים וַיְצַף אֹתָם נְחֹשֶׁת: 7 וַיָּבֵא אֶת־הַבַּדִּים בַּטַּבָּעֹת עַל צַלְעֹת הַמִּזְבֵּחַ לָשֵׂאת אֹתוֹ בָּהֶם נְבוּב לֻחֹת עָשָׂה אֹתוֹ: ס

229

⁸He made the laver of copper and its stand of copper, from the mirrors of the women who performed tasks at the entrance of the Tent of Meeting.

⁹He made the enclosure:

On the south side, a hundred cubits of hangings of fine twisted linen for the enclosure—¹⁰with their twenty posts and their twenty sockets of copper, the hooks and bands of the posts being silver.

¹¹On the north side, a hundred cubits—with their twenty posts and their twenty sockets of copper, the hooks and bands of the posts being silver.

¹²On the west side, fifty cubits of hangings—with their ten posts and their ten sockets, the hooks and bands of the posts being silver.

¹³And on the front side, to the east, fifty cubits: ¹⁴fifteen cubits of hangings on the one flank, with their three posts and their three sockets, ¹⁵and fifteen cubits of hangings on the other flank—on each side of the gate of the enclosure—with their three posts and their three sockets.

¹⁶All the hangings around the enclosure were of fine twisted linen. ¹⁷The sockets for the posts were of copper, the hooks and bands of the posts were of silver, the overlay of their tops was of silver; all the posts of the enclosure were banded with silver.—¹⁸The screen of the gate of the enclo-

ח וַיַּעַשׂ אֵת הַכִּיּוֹר נְחֹשֶׁת וְאֵת כַּנּוֹ נְחֹשֶׁת בְּמַרְאֹת הַצֹּבְאֹת אֲשֶׁר צָבְאוּ פֶּתַח אֹהֶל מוֹעֵד: ס

ט וַיַּעַשׂ אֶת־הֶחָצֵר לִפְאַת ׀ נֶגֶב תֵּימָנָה קַלְעֵי הֶחָצֵר שֵׁשׁ מָשְׁזָר מֵאָה בָּאַמָּה: י עַמּוּדֵיהֶם עֶשְׂרִים וְאַדְנֵיהֶם עֶשְׂרִים נְחֹשֶׁת וָוֵי הָעַמֻּדִים וַחֲשֻׁקֵיהֶם כָּסֶף: יא וְלִפְאַת צָפוֹן מֵאָה בָאַמָּה עַמּוּדֵיהֶם עֶשְׂרִים וְאַדְנֵיהֶם עֶשְׂרִים נְחֹשֶׁת וָוֵי הָעַמּוּדִים וַחֲשֻׁקֵיהֶם כָּסֶף: יב וְלִפְאַת־יָם קְלָעִים חֲמִשִּׁים בָּאַמָּה עַמּוּדֵיהֶם עֲשָׂרָה וְאַדְנֵיהֶם עֲשָׂרָה וָוֵי הָעַמֻּדִים וַחֲשׁוּקֵיהֶם כָּסֶף: יג וְלִפְאַת קֵדְמָה מִזְרָחָה חֲמִשִּׁים אַמָּה: יד קְלָעִים חֲמֵשׁ־עֶשְׂרֵה אַמָּה אֶל־הַכָּתֵף עַמּוּדֵיהֶם שְׁלֹשָׁה וְאַדְנֵיהֶם שְׁלֹשָׁה: טו וְלַכָּתֵף הַשֵּׁנִית מִזֶּה וּמִזֶּה לְשַׁעַר הֶחָצֵר קְלָעִים חֲמֵשׁ עֶשְׂרֵה אַמָּה עַמֻּדֵיהֶם שְׁלֹשָׁה וְאַדְנֵיהֶם שְׁלֹשָׁה: טז כָּל־קַלְעֵי הֶחָצֵר סָבִיב שֵׁשׁ מָשְׁזָר: יז וְהָאֲדָנִים לָעַמֻּדִים נְחֹשֶׁת וָוֵי הָעַמּוּדִים וַחֲשׁוּקֵיהֶם כֶּסֶף וְצִפּוּי רָאשֵׁיהֶם כָּסֶף וְהֵם מְחֻשָּׁקִים כֶּסֶף כֹּל עַמֻּדֵי הֶחָצֵר: מפטיר יח וּמָסַךְ

The Laver (v. 8)

This section summarizes 30:17–21 and provides additional information about the material of which the laver was made and the source of the donation.

8. the mirrors In ancient times mirrors were mainly of the kind held in the hand. They were highly polished disks of molten metal, copper or bronze, and were fitted with handles made of metal, wood, faience, or ivory. Egypt was the manufacturing center of this article of toilet for the entire Near East. One of the letters found at Tell el-Amarna, in Egypt, mentions a dispatch of mirrors from Pharaoh Amenhotep IV (Akhenaten, ca. 1364–1347 B.C.E.) to Burnaburiash, the Kassite king of Babylon.[1] Due to the high cost of metal in Egypt, metal objects were not discarded but were eventually melted down and reused, as here.[2]

the women who performed tasks Hebrew *ha-tsove'ot*. Nothing is known about this class, which is otherwise mentioned only in 1 Samuel 2:22.[3] The Hebrew idiom *tsavo' tsava'* is also used of the Levites and means "qualified to serve in the work force,"[4] so that it is likely that these women performed menial work. None of the evidence supports the notion that they exercised any ritual or cultic function.[5] The idea here is that even these women at the bottom of the occupational and social scale displayed unselfish generosity and sacrificial devotion in donating their valuable bronze mirrors.

the entrance of the Tent of Meeting At this stage, however, the Tent had not yet been erected. Hence, Ramban refers to Moses' private tent situated outside the camp, described in 33:7.[6] More likely, the designation is a retrojection from the later role of these women in performing the lowly tasks in the Tabernacle.

The Enclosure (vv. 9–20)

This section corresponds to 27:9–19. It marks the completion of the report of the construction of the edifice, its furniture, and appurtenances.

sure, done in embroidery, was of blue, purple, and crimson yarns, and fine twisted linen. It was twenty cubits long. Its height—or width—was five cubits, like that of the hangings of the enclosure. [19]The posts were four; their four sockets were of copper, their hooks of silver; and the overlay of their tops was of silver, as were also their bands. —[20]All the pegs of the Tabernacle and of the enclosure round about were of copper.

שַׁעַר הֶחָצֵר מַעֲשֵׂה רֹקֵם תְּכֵלֶת וְאַרְגָּמָן וְתוֹלַעַת שָׁנִי וְשֵׁשׁ מָשְׁזָר וְעֶשְׂרִים אַמָּה אֹרֶךְ וְקוֹמָה בְרֹחַב חָמֵשׁ אַמּוֹת לְעֻמַּת קַלְעֵי הֶחָצֵר: 19 וְעַמֻּדֵיהֶם אַרְבָּעָה וְאַדְנֵיהֶם אַרְבָּעָה נְחֹשֶׁת וָוֵיהֶם כֶּסֶף וְצִפּוּי רָאשֵׁיהֶם וַחֲשֻׁקֵיהֶם כָּסֶף: 20 וְכָל־הַיְתֵדֹת לַמִּשְׁכָּן וְלֶחָצֵר סָבִיב נְחֹשֶׁת: ס

PEKUDEI

[21]These are the records of the Tabernacle, the Tabernacle of the Pact, which were drawn up at Moses' bidding—the work of the Levites under the direction of Ithamar son of Aaron the priest. [22]Now Bezalel, son of Uri son of Hur, of the tribe of Judah, had made all that the LORD had commanded Moses; [23]at his side was Oholiab son of Ahisamach, of the tribe of Dan, carver and designer, and embroiderer in blue, purple, and crimson yarns and in fine linen.

[24]All the gold that was used for the work, in all the work of the sanctuary—the elevation offering of gold—came to 29 talents and 730 shekels by the sanctuary weight. [25]The

פקודי

21 אֵלֶּה פְקוּדֵי הַמִּשְׁכָּן מִשְׁכַּן הָעֵדֻת אֲשֶׁר פֻּקַּד עַל־פִּי מֹשֶׁה עֲבֹדַת הַלְוִיִּם בְּיַד אִיתָמָר בֶּן־אַהֲרֹן הַכֹּהֵן: 22 וּבְצַלְאֵל בֶּן־אוּרִי בֶן־חוּר לְמַטֵּה יְהוּדָה עָשָׂה אֵת כָּל־אֲשֶׁר־צִוָּה יְהוָה אֶת־מֹשֶׁה: 23 וְאִתּוֹ אָהֳלִיאָב בֶּן־אֲחִיסָמָךְ לְמַטֵּה־דָן חָרָשׁ וְחֹשֵׁב וְרֹקֵם בַּתְּכֵלֶת וּבָאַרְגָּמָן וּבְתוֹלַעַת הַשָּׁנִי וּבַשֵּׁשׁ: ס 24 כָּל־הַזָּהָב הֶעָשׂוּי לַמְּלָאכָה בְּכֹל מְלֶאכֶת הַקֹּדֶשׁ וַיְהִי זְהַב הַתְּנוּפָה תֵּשַׁע וְעֶשְׂרִים כִּכָּר וּשְׁבַע מֵאוֹת וּשְׁלֹשִׁים שֶׁקֶל בְּשֶׁקֶל הַקֹּדֶשׁ:

Pekudei

A TALLY OF THE METALS (vv. 21–31)

Moses now orders an inventory of the metals. This is to be undertaken by the Levites[7] under the direction of Ithamar son of Aaron. The tally is prefaced by a restatement of the roles of the two master craftsmen.

The inventory described here is in accord with Egyptian practice. Egyptian art depicting scenes of metalworking regularly features the master weigher weighing the metals on balances and the scribes recording the results in their ledgers before issuing the materials to the artisans.[8]

21. records Rather, "inventory, tally."[9]

Tabernacle of the Pact This rare designation[10] once again emphasizes the emblem of the covenant with God as the focal point of the entire Tabernacle.[11]

Ithamar His birth was recorded in Exodus 6:23,[12] and his nomination to be installed as a priest, in 28:1.[13] Throughout the wilderness wanderings he directed the work of the Levitical clans in connection with the Tabernacle.[14] David is said to have appointed the house of Ithamar as one of the twenty-four priestly courses in charge of the cult. The clan was still in existence in the exilic and early postexilic periods.[15]

23. These qualifications of Oholiab repeat 35:35 and include some additional material as well.

24–30. The metals are listed in descending order of value.

24. talents Hebrew *kikkar* is the largest unit of weight mentioned in the Bible. It was equivalent to 3,000 shekels, as is made clear by the data given in verses 25–26. The same term (pronounced *kakkarum*), having the same equivalence in shekels, is known from Ugarit. In Mesopotamia the talent equaled 3,600 shekels. By one estimate, the *kikkar* would have weighed 34.27 kilograms (75.6 lbs.). The name seems to derive from the rounded shape of the weight.[16] On the shekel, see Comment to 30:13.

silver of those of the community who were recorded came to 100 talents and 1,775 shekels by the sanctuary weight: ²⁶a half-shekel a head, half a shekel by the sanctuary weight, for each one who was entered in the records, from the age of twenty years up, 603,550 men. ²⁷The 100 talents of silver were for casting the sockets of the sanctuary and the sockets for the curtain, 100 sockets to the 100 talents, a talent a socket. ²⁸And of the 1,775 shekels he made hooks for the posts, overlay for their tops, and bands around them.

²⁹The copper from the elevation offering came to 70 talents and 2,400 shekels. ³⁰Of it he made the sockets for the entrance of the Tent of Meeting; the copper altar and its copper grating and all the utensils of the altar; ³¹the sockets of the enclosure round about and the sockets of the gate of the enclosure; and all the pegs of the Tabernacle and all the pegs of the enclosure round about.

39 Of the blue, purple, and crimson yarns they also made the service vestments for officiating in the sanctuary; they made Aaron's sacral vestments—as the LORD had commanded Moses.

²The ephod was made of gold, blue, purple, and crimson yarns, and fine twisted linen. ³They hammered out sheets of gold and cut threads to be worked into designs among the blue, the purple, and the crimson yarns, and the fine linen.

25 וְכֶ֣סֶף פְּקוּדֵ֣י הָעֵדָ֗ה מְאַ֤ת כִּכָּר֙ וְאֶ֔לֶף וּשְׁבַ֤ע מֵאוֹת֙ וַחֲמִשָּׁ֣ה וְשִׁבְעִ֔ים שֶׁ֖קֶל בְּשֶׁ֥קֶל הַקֹּֽדֶשׁ: 26 בֶּ֚קַע לַגֻּלְגֹּ֔לֶת מַחֲצִ֥ית הַשֶּׁ֖קֶל בְּשֶׁ֣קֶל הַקֹּ֑דֶשׁ לְכֹ֨ל הָעֹבֵ֜ר עַל־הַפְּקֻדִ֗ים מִבֶּ֨ן עֶשְׂרִ֤ים שָׁנָה֙ וָמַ֔עְלָה לְשֵׁשׁ־מֵא֥וֹת אֶ֖לֶף וּשְׁלֹ֣שֶׁת אֲלָפִ֑ים וַחֲמֵ֥שׁ מֵא֖וֹת וַחֲמִשִּֽׁים: 27 וַיְהִ֗י מְאַת֙ כִּכַּ֣ר הַכֶּ֔סֶף לָצֶ֗קֶת אֵ֚ת אַדְנֵ֣י הַקֹּ֔דֶשׁ וְאֵ֖ת אַדְנֵ֣י הַפָּרֹ֑כֶת מְאַ֧ת אֲדָנִ֛ים לִמְאַ֥ת הַכִּכָּ֖ר כִּכָּ֥ר לָאָֽדֶן: 28 וְאֶת־הָאֶ֜לֶף וּשְׁבַ֣ע הַמֵּא֗וֹת וַחֲמִשָּׁ֤ה וְשִׁבְעִים֙ עָשָׂ֥ה וָוִ֖ים לָעַמּוּדִ֑ים וְצִפָּ֥ה רָאשֵׁיהֶ֖ם וְחִשַּׁ֥ק אֹתָֽם: 29 וּנְחֹ֥שֶׁת הַתְּנוּפָ֖ה שִׁבְעִ֣ים כִּכָּ֑ר וְאַלְפַּ֛יִם וְאַרְבַּע־מֵא֖וֹת שָֽׁקֶל: 30 וַיַּ֣עַשׂ בָּ֗הּ אֶת־אַדְנֵי֙ פֶּ֚תַח אֹ֣הֶל מוֹעֵ֔ד וְאֵת֙ מִזְבַּ֣ח הַנְּחֹ֔שֶׁת וְאֶת־מִכְבַּ֥ר הַנְּחֹ֖שֶׁת אֲשֶׁר־ל֑וֹ וְאֵ֖ת כָּל־כְּלֵ֥י הַמִּזְבֵּֽחַ: 31 וְאֶת־אַדְנֵ֤י הֶֽחָצֵר֙ סָבִ֔יב וְאֶת־אַדְנֵ֖י שַׁ֣עַר הֶחָצֵ֑ר וְאֵ֨ת כָּל־יִתְדֹ֤ת הַמִּשְׁכָּן֙ וְאֶת־כָּל־יִתְדֹ֥ת הֶחָצֵ֖ר סָבִֽיב:

ל״ט וּמִן־הַתְּכֵ֤לֶת וְהָֽאַרְגָּמָן֙ וְתוֹלַ֣עַת הַשָּׁנִ֔י עָשׂ֥וּ בִגְדֵי־שְׂרָ֖ד לְשָׁרֵ֣ת בַּקֹּ֑דֶשׁ וַיַּעֲשׂ֗וּ אֶת־בִּגְדֵ֤י הַקֹּ֙דֶשׁ֙ אֲשֶׁ֣ר לְאַהֲרֹ֔ן כַּאֲשֶׁ֛ר צִוָּ֥ה יְהוָ֖ה אֶת־מֹשֶֽׁה: פ שני [חמישי כשהן מחוברות] 2 וַיַּ֖עַשׂ אֶת־הָאֵפֹ֑ד זָהָ֗ב תְּכֵ֧לֶת וְאַרְגָּמָ֛ן וְתוֹלַ֥עַת שָׁנִ֖י וְשֵׁ֥שׁ מָשְׁזָֽר: 3 וַֽיְרַקְּע֞וּ אֶת־פַּחֵ֣י הַזָּהָב֮ וְקִצֵּ֣ץ פְּתִילִם֒ לַעֲשׂ֗וֹת בְּת֤וֹךְ הַתְּכֵ֙לֶת֙ וּבְת֣וֹךְ הָֽאַרְגָּמָ֔ן וּבְת֛וֹךְ תּוֹלַ֥עַת הַשָּׁנִ֖י וּבְת֥וֹךְ

26. a half-shekel Hebrew *beka'* as a weight is mentioned elsewhere only in Genesis 24:22. The stem means "to split,"¹⁷ here, in half. Several weights have been found inscribed in paleo-Hebrew script with *beka'* or its abbreviation, *b*. Their average weight is .210 ounces (6.019 gr.).

a head The reference is to the census prescribed in 30:11–16.

CHAPTER 39   THE MAKING OF THE PRIESTLY VESTMENTS   (vv. 1–31)

This section corresponds to chapter 28. It contains some additional information and affirms—seven times in all—that each item was made exactly in accordance with the divine instructions.¹

1.   The omission of the fine linen from the list is especially puzzling since it is included in verses 2, 3, and 5.

3.   The process described here is typically Egyptian. The highly malleable gold was hammered over a stone into a thin sheet from which very narrow strips were cut to make fine gold wire. Gold thread was created by cutting the sheet in spiral form.

⁴They made for it attaching shoulder-pieces; they were attached at its two ends. ⁵The decorated band that was upon it was made like it, of one piece with it; of gold, blue, purple, and crimson yarns, and fine twisted linen—as the LORD had commanded Moses.

⁶They bordered the lazuli stones with frames of gold, engraved with seal engravings of the names of the sons of Israel. ⁷They were set on the shoulder-pieces of the ephod, as stones of remembrance for the Israelites—as the LORD had commanded Moses.

⁸The breastpiece was made in the style of the ephod: of gold, blue, purple, and crimson yarns, and fine twisted linen. ⁹It was square; they made the breastpiece doubled— a span in length and a span in width, doubled. ¹⁰They set in it four rows of stones. The first row was a row of carnelian, chrysolite, and emerald; ¹¹the second row: a turquoise, a sapphire, and an amethyst; ¹²the third row: a jacinth, an agate, and a crystal; ¹³and the fourth row: a beryl, a lapis lazuli, and a jasper. They were encircled in their mountings with frames of gold. ¹⁴The stones corresponded [in number] to the names of the sons of Israel: twelve, corresponding to their names; engraved like seals, each with its name, for the twelve tribes.

¹⁵On the breastpiece they made braided chains of corded work in pure gold. ¹⁶They made two frames of gold and two rings of gold, and fastened the two rings at the two ends of the breastpiece, ¹⁷attaching the two golden cords to the two rings at the ends of the breastpiece. ¹⁸They then fastened the two ends of the cords to the two frames, attaching them to the shoulder-pieces of the ephod, at the front. ¹⁹They made two rings of gold and attached them to the two ends of the breastpiece, at its inner edge, which faced the ephod. ²⁰They made two other rings of gold and fastened them on the front of the ephod, low on the two shoulder-pieces, close to its seam above the decorated band. ²¹The breastpiece was held in place by a cord of blue from its rings to the rings of the ephod, so that the breastpiece rested on the decorated band and did not come loose from the ephod—as the LORD had commanded Moses.

²²The robe for the ephod was made of woven work, of pure blue. ²³The opening of the robe, in the middle of it, was like the opening of a coat of mail, with a binding around the opening, so that it would not tear. ²⁴On the hem of the robe they made pomegranates of blue, purple, and crimson yarns, twisted. ²⁵They also made bells of pure

הַשֵּׁשׁ מַעֲשֵׂה חֹשֵׁב: 4 כְּתֵפֹת עָשׂוּ־לוֹ חֹבְרֹת עַל־שְׁנֵי קְצוֹותָו חֻבָּר: 5 וְחֵשֶׁב אֲפֻדָּתוֹ אֲשֶׁר עָלָיו מִמֶּנּוּ הוּא כְּמַעֲשֵׂהוּ זָהָב תְּכֵלֶת וְאַרְגָּמָן וְתוֹלַעַת שָׁנִי וְשֵׁשׁ מָשְׁזָר כַּאֲשֶׁר צִוָּה יְהֹוָה אֶת־ מֹשֶׁה:

6 וַיַּעֲשׂוּ אֶת־אַבְנֵי הַשֹּׁהַם מֻסַבֹּת מִשְׁבְּצֹת זָהָב מְפֻתָּחֹת פִּתּוּחֵי חוֹתָם עַל־שְׁמוֹת בְּנֵי יִשְׂרָאֵל: 7 וַיָּשֶׂם אֹתָם עַל כִּתְפֹת הָאֵפֹד אַבְנֵי זִכָּרוֹן לִבְנֵי יִשְׂרָאֵל כַּאֲשֶׁר צִוָּה יְהֹוָה אֶת־מֹשֶׁה: פ

8 וַיַּעַשׂ אֶת־הַחֹשֶׁן מַעֲשֵׂה חֹשֵׁב כְּמַעֲשֵׂה אֵפֹד זָהָב תְּכֵלֶת וְאַרְגָּמָן וְתוֹלַעַת שָׁנִי וְשֵׁשׁ מָשְׁזָר: 9 רָבוּעַ הָיָה כָּפוּל עָשׂוּ אֶת־הַחֹשֶׁן זֶרֶת אָרְכּוֹ וְזֶרֶת רָחְבּוֹ כָּפוּל: 10 וַיְמַלְאוּ־בוֹ אַרְבָּעָה טוּרֵי אָבֶן טוּר אֹדֶם פִּטְדָה וּבָרֶקֶת הַטּוּר הָאֶחָד: 11 וְהַטּוּר הַשֵּׁנִי נֹפֶךְ סַפִּיר וְיָהֲלֹם: 12 וְהַטּוּר הַשְּׁלִישִׁי לֶשֶׁם שְׁבוֹ וְאַחְלָמָה: 13 וְהַטּוּר הָרְבִיעִי תַּרְשִׁישׁ שֹׁהַם וְיָשְׁפֵה מוּסַבֹּת מִשְׁבְּצֹת זָהָב בְּמִלֻּאֹתָם: 14 וְהָאֲבָנִים עַל־שְׁמֹת בְּנֵי־יִשְׂרָאֵל הֵנָּה שְׁתֵּים עֶשְׂרֵה עַל־שְׁמֹתָם פִּתּוּחֵי חֹתָם אִישׁ עַל־שְׁמוֹ לִשְׁנֵים עָשָׂר שָׁבֶט:

15 וַיַּעֲשׂוּ עַל־הַחֹשֶׁן שַׁרְשְׁרֹת גַּבְלֻת מַעֲשֵׂה עֲבֹת זָהָב טָהוֹר: 16 וַיַּעֲשׂוּ שְׁתֵּי מִשְׁבְּצֹת זָהָב וּשְׁתֵּי טַבְּעֹת זָהָב וַיִּתְּנוּ אֶת־שְׁתֵּי הַטַּבָּעֹת עַל־ שְׁנֵי קְצוֹת הַחֹשֶׁן: 17 וַיִּתְּנוּ שְׁתֵּי הָעֲבֹתֹת הַזָּהָב עַל־שְׁתֵּי הַטַּבָּעֹת עַל־קְצוֹת הַחֹשֶׁן: 18 וְאֵת שְׁתֵּי קְצוֹת שְׁתֵּי הָעֲבֹתֹת נָתְנוּ עַל־שְׁתֵּי הַמִּשְׁבְּצֹת וַיִּתְּנֻם עַל־כִּתְפֹת הָאֵפֹד אֶל־מוּל פָּנָיו: 19 וַיַּעֲשׂוּ שְׁתֵּי טַבְּעֹת זָהָב וַיָּשִׂימוּ עַל־שְׁנֵי קְצוֹת הַחֹשֶׁן עַל־שְׂפָתוֹ אֲשֶׁר אֶל־עֵבֶר הָאֵפֹד בָּיְתָה: 20 וַיַּעֲשׂוּ שְׁתֵּי טַבְּעֹת זָהָב וַיִּתְּנֻם עַל־ שְׁתֵּי כִּתְפֹת הָאֵפֹד מִלְמַטָּה מִמּוּל פָּנָיו לְעֻמַּת מֶחְבַּרְתּוֹ מִמַּעַל לְחֵשֶׁב הָאֵפֹד: 21 וַיִּרְכְּסוּ אֶת־הַחֹשֶׁן מִטַּבְּעֹתָיו אֶל־טַבְּעֹת הָאֵפֹד בִּפְתִיל תְּכֵלֶת לִהְיֹת עַל־חֵשֶׁב הָאֵפֹד וְלֹא־יִזַּח הַחֹשֶׁן מֵעַל הָאֵפֹד כַּאֲשֶׁר צִוָּה יְהֹוָה אֶת־מֹשֶׁה: שלישי [ששי כשהן מחוברות]

22 וַיַּעַשׂ אֶת־מְעִיל הָאֵפֹד מַעֲשֵׂה אֹרֵג כְּלִיל תְּכֵלֶת: 23 וּפִי־הַמְּעִיל בְּתוֹכוֹ כְּפִי תַחְרָא שָׂפָה לְפִיו סָבִיב לֹא יִקָּרֵעַ: 24 וַיַּעֲשׂוּ עַל־שׁוּלֵי הַמְּעִיל רִמּוֹנֵי תְּכֵלֶת וְאַרְגָּמָן וְתוֹלַעַת שָׁנִי מָשְׁזָר:

gold, and attached the bells between the pomegranates, all around the hem of the robe, between the pomegranates: ²⁶a bell and a pomegranate, a bell and a pomegranate, all around the hem of the robe for officiating in—as the Lᴏʀᴅ had commanded Moses.

²⁷They made the tunics of fine linen, of woven work, for Aaron and his sons; ²⁸and the headdress of fine linen, and the decorated turbans of fine linen, and the linen breeches of fine twisted linen; ²⁹and sashes of fine twisted linen, blue, purple, and crimson yarns, done in embroidery—as the Lᴏʀᴅ had commanded Moses.

³⁰They made the frontlet for the holy diadem of pure gold, and incised upon it the seal inscription: "Holy to the Lᴏʀᴅ." ³¹They attached to it a cord of blue to fix it upon the headdress above—as the Lᴏʀᴅ had commanded Moses.

³²Thus was completed all the work of the Tabernacle of the Tent of Meeting. The Israelites did so; just as the Lᴏʀᴅ had commanded Moses, so they did.

³³Then they brought the Tabernacle to Moses, with the Tent and all its furnishings: its clasps, its planks, its poles, its posts, and its sockets; ³⁴the covering of tanned ram skins, the covering of dolphin skins, and the curtain for the screen; ³⁵the Ark of the Pact and its poles, and the cover; ³⁶the table and all its utensils, and the bread of display; ³⁷the pure lampstand, its lamps—lamps in due order—and all its fittings, and the oil for lighting; ³⁸the altar of gold, the oil for anointing, the aromatic incense, and the screen for the entrance of the Tent; ³⁹the copper altar with its copper grating, its poles and all its utensils, and the laver and its stand; ⁴⁰the hangings of the enclosure, its posts and its sockets, the screen for the gate of the enclosure, its cords and its pegs—all the furnishings for the service of the

[Hebrew text, verses 25–40]

COMPLETION AND INSPECTION (vv. 32–43)

The Tabernacle in all its several parts and with all its appurtenances is completed and brought to Moses for inspection. The text does not record how long the work took nor the dates involved. According to a rabbinic tradition, it was finished on the twenty-fifth day of the ninth month, which is Kislev.² In the time of the Maccabees, the dedication of the new altar in the Temple took place on the same date, commencing the festival of Hanukkah.

32. the Tabernacle of the Tent of Meeting A combination of the two distinct terms for the sanctuary.³ Together they express its dual function as the symbol of the indwelling of the Divine Presence in the camp of Israel and as the site of communication between God and Moses.⁴

234

Tabernacle, the Tent of Meeting; ⁴¹the service vestments for officiating in the sanctuary, the sacral vestments of Aaron the priest, and the vestments of his sons for priestly service. ⁴²Just as the LORD had commanded Moses, so the Israelites had done all the work. ⁴³And when Moses saw that they had performed all the tasks—as the LORD had commanded, so they had done—Moses blessed them.

40 And the LORD spoke to Moses, saying:

²On the first day of the first month you shall set up the Tabernacle of the Tent of Meeting. ³Place there the Ark of the Pact, and screen off the ark with the curtain. ⁴Bring in the table and lay out its due setting; bring in the lampstand and light its lamps; ⁵and place the gold altar of incense before the Ark of the Pact. Then put up the screen for the entrance of the Tabernacle.

⁶You shall place the altar of burnt offering before the entrance of the Tabernacle of the Tent of Meeting. ⁷Place the laver between the Tent of Meeting and the altar, and put water in it. ⁸Set up the enclosure round about, and put in place the screen for the gate of the enclosure.

⁹You shall take the anointing oil and anoint the Tabernacle and all that is in it to consecrate it and all its furnishings, so that it shall be holy. ¹⁰Then anoint the altar

מוֹעֵד: ⁴¹ אֶת־בִּגְדֵי הַשְּׂרָד לְשָׁרֵת בַּקֹּדֶשׁ אֶת־בִּגְדֵי הַקֹּדֶשׁ לְאַהֲרֹן הַכֹּהֵן וְאֶת־בִּגְדֵי בָנָיו לְכַהֵן: ⁴² כְּכֹל אֲשֶׁר־צִוָּה יְהוָה אֶת־מֹשֶׁה כֵּן עָשׂוּ בְּנֵי יִשְׂרָאֵל אֵת כָּל־הָעֲבֹדָה: ⁴³ וַיַּרְא מֹשֶׁה אֶת־כָּל־הַמְּלָאכָה וְהִנֵּה עָשׂוּ אֹתָהּ כַּאֲשֶׁר צִוָּה יְהוָה כֵּן עָשׂוּ וַיְבָרֶךְ אֹתָם מֹשֶׁה: פ חמישי
[שביעי כשהן מחוברות]

מ וַיְדַבֵּר יְהוָה אֶל־מֹשֶׁה לֵּאמֹר: ² בְּיוֹם־הַחֹדֶשׁ הָרִאשׁוֹן בְּאֶחָד לַחֹדֶשׁ תָּקִים אֶת־מִשְׁכַּן אֹהֶל מוֹעֵד: ³ וְשַׂמְתָּ שָׁם אֵת אֲרוֹן הָעֵדוּת וְסַכֹּתָ עַל־הָאָרֹן אֶת־הַפָּרֹכֶת: ⁴ וְהֵבֵאתָ אֶת־הַשֻּׁלְחָן וְעָרַכְתָּ אֶת־עֶרְכּוֹ וְהֵבֵאתָ אֶת־הַמְּנֹרָה וְהַעֲלֵיתָ אֶת־נֵרֹתֶיהָ: ⁵ וְנָתַתָּה אֶת־מִזְבַּח הַזָּהָב לִקְטֹרֶת לִפְנֵי אֲרוֹן הָעֵדֻת וְשַׂמְתָּ אֶת־מָסַךְ הַפֶּתַח לַמִּשְׁכָּן:
⁶ וְנָתַתָּה אֵת מִזְבַּח הָעֹלָה לִפְנֵי פֶּתַח מִשְׁכַּן אֹהֶל־מוֹעֵד: ⁷ וְנָתַתָּ אֶת־הַכִּיֹּר בֵּין־אֹהֶל מוֹעֵד וּבֵין הַמִּזְבֵּחַ וְנָתַתָּ שָׁם מָיִם: ⁸ וְשַׂמְתָּ אֶת־הֶחָצֵר סָבִיב וְנָתַתָּ אֶת־מָסַךְ שַׁעַר הֶחָצֵר:
⁹ וְלָקַחְתָּ אֶת־שֶׁמֶן הַמִּשְׁחָה וּמָשַׁחְתָּ אֶת־הַמִּשְׁכָּן וְאֶת־כָּל־אֲשֶׁר־בּוֹ וְקִדַּשְׁתָּ אֹתוֹ וְאֶת־כָּל־כֵּלָיו וְהָיָה קֹדֶשׁ: ¹⁰ וּמָשַׁחְתָּ אֶת־מִזְבַּח הָעֹלָה

42. the Israelites The entire project is presented from first to last as an enterprise of all the Israelites; compare verse 32.

43. This finale is patterned after the Creation narrative of Genesis, in which the completion of the work evoked divine approbation followed by a blessing.⁵ A rabbinic tradition formulates Moses' blessing as follows: "May the divine spirit rest upon the work of your hands."⁶

CHAPTER 40   ERECTING THE TABERNACLE   (vv. 1–8)

Moses receives divine instructions to set up the Tabernacle and put each item in its assigned place. He personally is charged with this task because the entire enterprise is said to be based on a celestial image or prototype that had been shown to him on Mount Sinai. Hence, he alone possesses a mental picture of the completed whole.¹ Once again, priority is given to the Ark of the Pact. The order of emplacement of the furnishings is from the interior outward, from the most sacred to the less so.

The Tabernacle is to be erected just two weeks short of the first anniversary of the Exodus from Egypt, and exactly nine months since arriving at Sinai.² This is New Year's day, a date which forges another link with the Creation narrative. See the introduction to chapter 25.

3. the curtain See Comment to 26:31–33.

4. lay out its due setting The twelve loaves of the bread of display set out in two rows. See Comment to 25:30.

235

of burnt offering and all its utensils to consecrate the altar, so that the altar shall be most holy. ¹¹And anoint the laver and its stand to consecrate it.

¹²You shall bring Aaron and his sons forward to the entrance of the Tent of Meeting and wash them with the water. ¹³Put the sacral vestments on Aaron, and anoint him and consecrate him, that he may serve Me as priest. ¹⁴Then bring his sons forward, put tunics on them, ¹⁵and anoint them as you have anointed their father, that they may serve Me as priests. This their anointing shall serve them for everlasting priesthood throughout the ages.

¹⁶This Moses did; just as the Lord had commanded him, so he did.

¹⁷In the first month of the second year, on the first of the month, the Tabernacle was set up. ¹⁸Moses set up the Tabernacle, placing its sockets, setting up its planks, inserting its bars, and erecting its posts. ¹⁹He spread the Tent over the Tabernacle, placing the covering of the Tent on top of it—just as the Lord had commanded Moses.

²⁰He took the Pact and placed it in the ark; he fixed the poles to the ark, placed the cover on top of the ark, ²¹and brought the ark inside the Tabernacle. Then he put up the curtain for screening, and screened off the Ark of the Pact—just as the Lord had commanded Moses.

²²He placed the table in the Tent of Meeting, outside the curtain, on the north side of the Tabernacle. ²³Upon it he laid out the setting of bread before the Lord—as the Lord had commanded Moses. ²⁴He placed the lampstand in the Tent of Meeting opposite the table, on the south side of the Tabernacle. ²⁵And he lit the lamps before the Lord—as the Lord had commanded Moses. ²⁶He placed the altar of gold

ANOINTING THE TABERNACLE AND FURNISHINGS (vv. 9–11)

During the next stage every item is anointed with the sacred aromatic anointing oil. See Comment to 30:22–29.

INSTALLING THE PRIESTS (vv. 12–15)

See Comment to 29:1–9.

FULFILLING THE INSTRUCTIONS (vv. 16–33)

16. This Moses did This affirmation applies to all the foregoing instructions. The details are spelled out, item by item, as though to emphasize the point.

236

in the Tent of Meeting, before the curtain. ²⁷On it he burned aromatic incense—as the LORD had commanded Moses.

²⁸Then he put up the screen for the entrance of the Tabernacle. ²⁹At the entrance of the Tabernacle of the Tent of Meeting he placed the altar of burnt offering. On it he offered up the burnt offering and the meal offering—as the LORD had commanded Moses. ³⁰He placed the laver between the Tent of Meeting and the altar, and put water in it for washing. ³¹From it Moses and Aaron and his sons would wash their hands and feet; ³²they washed when they entered the Tent of Meeting and when they approached the altar—as the LORD had commanded Moses. ³³And he set up the enclosure around the Tabernacle and the altar, and put up the screen for the gate of the enclosure.

When Moses had finished the work, ³⁴the cloud covered the Tent of Meeting, and the Presence of the LORD filled the Tabernacle. ³⁵Moses could not enter the Tent of Meeting, because the cloud had settled upon it and the Presence of the LORD filled the Tabernacle. ³⁶When the cloud lifted from the Tabernacle, the Israelites would set out, on their various journeys; ³⁷but if the cloud did not lift, they would not set out until such time as it did lift. ³⁸For over the Tabernacle a cloud of the LORD rested by day, and fire would appear in it by night, in the view of all the house of Israel throughout their journeys.

פקודי

26 וַיָּשֶׂם אֶת־מִזְבַּח הַזָּהָב בְּאֹהֶל מוֹעֵד לִפְנֵי הַפָּרֹכֶת: 27 וַיַּקְטֵר עָלָיו קְטֹרֶת סַמִּים כַּאֲשֶׁר צִוָּה יְהוָה אֶת־מֹשֶׁה: פ שביעי

28 וַיָּשֶׂם אֶת־מָסַךְ הַפֶּתַח לַמִּשְׁכָּן: 29 וְאֵת מִזְבַּח הָעֹלָה שָׂם פֶּתַח מִשְׁכַּן אֹהֶל־מוֹעֵד וַיַּעַל עָלָיו אֶת־הָעֹלָה וְאֶת־הַמִּנְחָה כַּאֲשֶׁר צִוָּה יְהוָה אֶת־מֹשֶׁה: ס 30 וַיָּשֶׂם אֶת־הַכִּיֹּר בֵּין־אֹהֶל מוֹעֵד וּבֵין הַמִּזְבֵּחַ וַיִּתֵּן שָׁמָּה מַיִם לְרָחְצָה: 31 וְרָחֲצוּ מִמֶּנּוּ מֹשֶׁה וְאַהֲרֹן וּבָנָיו אֶת־יְדֵיהֶם וְאֶת־רַגְלֵיהֶם: 32 בְּבֹאָם אֶל־אֹהֶל מוֹעֵד וּבְקָרְבָתָם אֶל־הַמִּזְבֵּחַ יִרְחָצוּ כַּאֲשֶׁר צִוָּה יְהוָה אֶת־מֹשֶׁה: ס 33 וַיָּקֶם אֶת־הֶחָצֵר סָבִיב לַמִּשְׁכָּן וְלַמִּזְבֵּחַ וַיִּתֵּן אֶת־מָסַךְ שַׁעַר הֶחָצֵר וַיְכַל מֹשֶׁה אֶת־הַמְּלָאכָה: פ מפטיר

34 וַיְכַס הֶעָנָן אֶת־אֹהֶל מוֹעֵד וּכְבוֹד יְהוָה מָלֵא אֶת־הַמִּשְׁכָּן: 35 וְלֹא־יָכֹל מֹשֶׁה לָבוֹא אֶל־אֹהֶל מוֹעֵד כִּי־שָׁכַן עָלָיו הֶעָנָן וּכְבוֹד יְהוָה מָלֵא אֶת־הַמִּשְׁכָּן: 36 וּבְהֵעָלוֹת הֶעָנָן מֵעַל הַמִּשְׁכָּן יִסְעוּ בְּנֵי יִשְׂרָאֵל בְּכֹל מַסְעֵיהֶם: 37 וְאִם־לֹא יֵעָלֶה הֶעָנָן וְלֹא יִסְעוּ עַד־יוֹם הֵעָלֹתוֹ: 38 כִּי עֲנַן יְהוָה עַל־הַמִּשְׁכָּן יוֹמָם וְאֵשׁ תִּהְיֶה לַיְלָה בּוֹ לְעֵינֵי כָל־בֵּית־יִשְׂרָאֵל בְּכָל־מַסְעֵיהֶם:

29. he offered up According to Rashi, the subject is Moses; but according to Rashbam, it is Aaron and his sons.

THE APPEARANCE OF THE DIVINE PRESENCE (vv. 34–38)

34. cloud . . . Presence The function of the Tabernacle was to create a portable Sinai, a means by which a continued avenue of communication with God could be maintained. As the people move away from the mount of revelation, they need a visible, tangible symbol of God's ever-abiding Presence in their midst. It is not surprising, then, that the same phenomenon as occurred at Sinai, related in 24:15–17, now repeats itself. It will recur at the dedication of Solomon's Temple, as is narrated in 1 Kings 8:10–11. The cloud is the manifest token of the immediacy of the Divine Presence. (See Comment to 13:1–22.) The Hebrew term *kavod* for God's Presence, also rendered "majesty," actually expresses His intangible immanence. See Comments to 16:7 and 33:18.

35. A similar comment is made in connection with the dedication of Solomon's Temple.³ It is unclear whether entry is literally hindered, or is impermissible, or that he simply dared not enter.

36–38. Henceforth, Israel's wanderings through the wilderness en route to the promised land are determined by the movements of the luminous cloud. This process is repeated in Numbers 9:15–23, and an example is given in 10:11–28.

The Book of Exodus, which opened with a tale of misery and oppression, closes on an auspicious note. Israel is assured that, day and night, the Divine Spirit hovers over it, guiding and controlling its destiny.

חזק
סכום הפסוקים של ספר
אלף ומאתים ותשעה
אֹרֹטֹ
וחציו אלהים לא תקלל
וסדרים ל"ג

תם ונשלם תהלה לאל בורא עולם
חזק חזק ונתחזק

NOTES TO THE COMMENTARY

Chapter 1

U. Cassuto, *A Commentary on the Book of Exodus*, trans. I. Abrahams (Jerusalem: Magnes Press, 1967), 7–16.

1. The books of Leviticus, Numbers, Joshua, Judges, and Samuel also begin this way. The significance of the conjunctive is noted in Exod. R. 30:2 and Lek. Tov 1:4.

2. Gen. 49:3–4; cf. 1 Chron. 5:1.

3. Cf. the seventy progeny of Gideon and Abdon in Judg. 8:30; 9:2; 12:14; and of Ahab in 2 Kings 10:1, 6, 7. The Ugar. pantheon was comprised of seventy members, who are said to have been the sons of the supreme god Il and the mother goddess Ashirat (UT 51.VI.46). An inscription of the eighth century B.C.E. found at Zinjirli in northern Syria mentions "seventy kinsmen of King Panammuwa" (KAI 215, line 3, p. 39).

4. For the phrasing, cf. Judg. 2:10.

5. Gen. 1:28; 9:1.

6. Cf. Gen. 45:10; 46:28,34; 47:1,4,6,27; 50:8; Exod. 8:18; 9:26.

7. Gen. 40:21.

8. Gen. 50:24–25.

9. For this use of *k-w-m* to indicate a significantly new development, especially a discontinuous one, cf. Num. 32:14; Deut. 13:2; 29:21; 34:10; Judg. 2:10; 5:7; 10:1,3; 1 Kings 3:12; 2 Kings 23:25.

10. Gen. 41; 47:13–27.

11. Exod. 1:8; 2:4,14,25; 3:7,19; 4:14; 5:2; 6:3,7; 7:5,17; 8:6,18; 9:14,29,30; 10:2,7,26; 14:4,18. See Comment to Gen. 4:1 in N. Sarna, *The JPS Torah Commentary: Genesis* (Philadelphia: Jewish Publication Society, 1989).

12. E. A. Speiser, "'People' and 'Nation' of Israel," JBL 79 (1960): 157–163; A. M. Good, *The Sheep of His Pasture: A Study of the Hebrew Noun 'Am(m) and Its Semitic Cognates* (Chico, Calif.: Scholars Press, 1986).

13. Cf. Num. 20:20; 31:32; Judg. 5:2; Joel 2:5; Ps. 3:7.

14. Cf. Deut. 7:1 and the reverse order in Deut. 9:14; 26:5.

15. Literally, "should war happen." For the interchange of *k-r-h* and *k-r-'*, cf. Gen. 42:38; 49:1; Lev. 10:19; Deut. 22:6; 2 Sam. 1:6; Dan. 10:14.

16. On the stem *s-b-l*, see M. Held, "The Root *zbl/sbl* in Akkadian, Ugaritic and Biblical Hebrew," JAOS 88 (1968): 90–96. The feminine form occurs again only in Exod. 2:11; 5:4–5; 6:6–7; I. Mendelson, "On Corvée Labour in Ancient Canaan and Israel," BASOR 167 (1962): 31–35.

17. Rashi and Shadal favor the latter; cf. 1 Kings 9:17–18; 12:25.

18. Cf. 1 Kings 9:19; 2 Chron. 8:4, 6; 16:4; 17:12; see H. M. Orlinsky, *Notes on the New Translation of the Torah* (Philadelphia: Jewish Publication Society, 1969), 150.

19. Gen. 46:34; 47:11; cf. LXX to 46:28.

20. Exod. 12:37; Num. 33:3,5.

21. On these cities, see D. B. Redford, "Exodus I:11," VT 13 (1963): 401–418; E. P. Uphill, "Pithom and Raamses: Their Location and Significance," JNES 27 (1968): 291–316; 28 (1969): 15–39; J. Baines and J. Malek, *Atlas of Ancient Egypt* (Oxford: Phaidon, 1980), 177.

22. Cf. Exod. 13:3,14; 20:2; Deut. 5:6; 6:12; 7:8; 8:14; 13:6–11; Josh. 24:17; Judg. 6:8; Jer. 34:13; Mic. 6:4.

23. Gen. 10:24; 11:14.

24. R. Slovenko, "Obstetric science and the development of the psychiatrist in surrogate motherhood," *Journal of Psychiatry and Law* (Winter 1986): 488–489.

25. H. Rand, "Figure-Vases in Ancient Egypt and Hebrew Midwives," IEJ 20 (1970): 209–212.

26. Josephus, Ant. 2.206 (Loeb, p. 253); cf. v. 16; cf. A. Ehrlich, *Randglossen zur Hebräischen Bibel*, vol. 1 (Leipzig: Hinrich, 1908), 262.

27. W. F. Albright, "Northwest Semitic Names in a List of Egyptian Slaves from the Eighteenth Century B.C.," JAOS 74 (1954): 222–233, especially 229, 233.

28. Cf. Gen. 49:21; Ps. 16:6; Job 26:13; Dan. 3:32; 4:24; 6:2.

29. UT 19.2081.

30. So Saadia, Rashi; cf. 1 Sam. 4:19, ANET, p. 381. For *'even* as a possible euphemism for the genitals, see Ehrlich, *Randglossen*, p. 261; M. Tsevat, "Some Biblical Notes," HUCA 24 (1952–53): 110; R. Gordis, *Koheleth: The Man and His World*, 3rd ed. (New York: Schocken, 1968), 230; cf. MdRY to Exod. 15:5, p. 133, Exod. R. 1:18.

31. Cf. Gen. 20:11; 42:18; Lev. 19:14, 32; Deut. 25:18; Job 1:1,8.

32. Cf. 2 Sam. 12:3; Ps. 33:19; Neh. 9:6.

33. Exod. R. 1:19–20. On the verse, see J. C. Exum, "'You Shall Let Every Daughter Live': A Study of Exodus 1:8–2:10," *Semeia* 28 (1983): 63–82.

34. So Ibn Janaḥ, Rashi, Rashbam (cf. his comment to Gen. 18:10), Bekhor Shor, Ramban; cf. Exod. R. 1:20. Frequent in postbiblical Hebrew, *ḥayyah* as a "midwife" may occur in *ka-'et ḥayyah* in Gen. 18:10, 14; 2 Kings 4:16–17. See Comment to Gen. 18:10 in Sarna, *JPS Torah Commentary: Genesis*.

35. So Exod. R. 1:22; cf. Exod. 18:11.

Chapter 2

B. Jacob, "The Childhood and Youth of Moses, the Messenger of God," in *Essays Presented to J. H. Hertz*, ed. I. Epstein et al. (London: Edward Goldston, 1942), 245–259; D. B. Redford, "The Literary Motif of the Exposed Child," *Numen* 14 (1964): 209–228; J. S. Ackerman, "The Literary Context of the Moses Birth Story," in *Literary Interpretations of Biblical Narratives,*, ed. K. R. R. Gos Louis et al. (Nashville: Abingdon, 1974) 74–119.

1. Exod. 6:20; Num. 26:59; cf. 1 Chron. 23:6, 12–13.

2. Cf., e.g., Gen. 24:48; 25:20; 28:6; 36:2; Exod. 6:25; Num. 12:1; Deut. 20:7; 21:11; 22:14; 25:7–8; Judg. 14:2, 3, 8.

3. Gen. 1:4, 10, 12, 18, 21, 25, 31.

4. Sot. 12a, Exod. R. 1:24. For the name, cf., e.g., Zech. 6:10; Neh. 4:1.

5. E.g., Gen. 6:14.

6. A. Lucas, *Ancient Egyptian Materials and Industries*, 4th ed. rev. and enlarged by J. R. Harris (London: Edward Arnold, 1962) 130, 137; cf. Isa. 18:2; Job 8:11.

7. M. Cogan, "A Technical Term for Exposure," JNES 27 (1968): 133–135.

8. Num. 26:59; 1 Chron. 5:29.

9. P. Montet, *Egypt and the Bible*, trans. L. R. Keylock (Philadelphia: Fortress Press, 1968), 80.

10. B. S. Childs, "The Birth of Moses," JBL 84 (1965): 109–122. The laws of Eshnunna (par. 32) deal with the hire of a wet nurse.

11. Sot. 12b, Exod. R. 1:30, so Rashi; the midrash is probably reflected in the Syr. reading *h' lky*.

12. J. G. Griffiths, "The Egyptian Derivation of the Name Moses," JNES 12 (1953): 225–231; ANET, pp. 448, 475; R. de

Vaux, *The Early History of Israel*, trans. D. Smith (Philadelphia: Westminster Press, 1978), 329.

13. For the stem *m-sh-h*, cf. 2 Sam. 22:17 = Ps. 18:17.

14. So Lek. Tov to Exod. 2:10.

15. A. Erman, *Life in Ancient Egypt* (reprint, New York: Dover, 1971), 77, 164, 329f.; R. J. Williams, "Scribal Training in Ancient Egypt," JAOS 92 (1972): 214–221.

16. Exod. R. 1:32.

17. Cf. Exod. 2:12; Exod. 21:12; Lev. 24:21; Deut. 27:24.

18. *Bet ha-midrasch*, ed. by A. Jellinek, Vol. 1 (Jerusalem: Wahrman, 1967), 119; see R. Kimelman, "Torah against Terror," *The Jewish Monthly* (Oct. 1984: 16–22).

19. Exod. R. 1:34; Rashi to Exod. 2:13.

20. Exod. R. 1:35.

21. Num. 31:8; Josh. 13:21.

22. Gen. 25:1–2.

23. Gen. 36:35; Num. 22:4,7; 25:6–7,16; 31:1–12; Josh. 13:21; Judg. 6–8; Isa. 9:3; 10:26; Ps. 83:10.

24. *Ibid.*

25. Cf. Gen. 24:11; 29:2.

26. G. W. Coats, "Moses in Midian," JBL 92 (1973): 3–10.

27. Gen. 24:11, 13; 1 Sam. 9:11.

28. In Gen. 36:4, 10, 13, 17 (cf. 1 Chron. 1:35, 37). Reuel is the name of an Edomite chieftain, and in Num. 2:14, of an Israelite one.

29. So Exod. 3:1; 18:1. It is abbreviated to Jether in 4:18.

30. MdRY *Yitro* 1, p. 189, Sif. Beha'alotkha 78, Targ. Jon. to Exod. 2:18. For the use of "father" and "son" for more remote relationships, cf. Gen. 29:5 with 24:47 and 28:5; in Gen. 46:18 "sons" includes grandchildren and great-grandchildren; in 2 Sam. 19:25 Mephibosheth is called "son of Saul" although he was his grandson (2 Sam. 4:4), while "Jehu son of Nimshi" in 1 Kings 19:16 and 2 Kings 9:20 is actually his grandson (2 Kings 9:2, 14).

31. W. F. Albright, "Jethro, Hobab and Reuel in Early Biblical Tradition with Some Comments on the Origin of 'JE,'" CBQ 25 (1963): 1–11.

32. Gen. 49:3.

33. CAD, s.v. *atru*, p. 501.

34. UT 19.1170–1175 lists several names of this type; cf. 2 Sam. 3:5, Ithream.

35. Cf. Josh. 15:17; 1 Sam. 18:17, 19, 21, 27; 25:44.

36. Exod. 6:1; 11:1; 12:39.

37. Gen. 15:13.

38. ANET, pp. 378–379; M. Weinfeld, *Justice and Righteousness in Israel and the Nations* (Hebrew) (Jerusalem: Magnes Press, 1985), 84.

39. For *z-k-r* as a verb of action, cf. its interchange with *sh-m-r*, "to observe," in Exod. 20:8 and Deut. 5:12, and its use in a parallel construction in Ps. 103:18. For such biblical uses of *z-k-r*, cf. Gen. 8:1; 9:15; 19:29; 30:22; 40:14; Exod. 6:5; 20:18; 32:13; Lev. 26:42, 45; Num. 15:40; Judg. 16:28; 1 Sam. 1:11, 19; Jer. 15:15; 31:20; Ps. 25:6–7; 74:2; 115:12; 136:23–24.

40. Gen. 15; 17:1–8; 26:2–5; 28:13–15; 35:9–13.

Chapter 3

1. For *'aḥar*, "behind," spatially, cf. Exod. 11:5; 2 Sam. 7:8; Isa. 57:8; Ps. 68:26; 78:71; Song 2:9.

2. Heb. *midbar* is derived from the stem *d-v-r*, "to lead sheep to pasture"; so Aram.; cf. Isa. 5:17; Mic. 2:12; cf. *ne'ot midbar*, "wilderness pastures," Jer. 9:9; 23:10; Joel 1:19–20; 2:22; Ps. 65:13.

3. Exod. 33:6; Deut. 1:6; 1 Kings 19:8.

4. Exod. 19:2; Num. 33:14.

5. Critical scholars assign Horeb to E, D, and Sinai to J, P sources.

6. Sif. Deut. 22, p. 33; Exod. R. 2:6. For Horeb as the site of revelation, cf. Deut. 1:6; 4:10, 15; 5:2; 18:16; 28:69; 1 Kings 8:9; Mal. 3:22; 2 Chron. 5:10. In Exod. 33:6; Deut. 9:8; Ps. 106:19, Horeb is the site of the golden calf incident, which occurred while Moses was upon Mount Sinai; so also Exod. 31:18; 32:15; 33:6.

7. See Z. Weisman, "The Mountain of God" (Hebrew), *Tarbiz* 47 (1977–1978), 107–119.

8. Probably, the initial particle *bet* in *be-labbat 'esh* is to be understood as an example of *bet essentiae* conveying the idea of "in the mode of," as in, e.g., Exod. 6:3; 18:4; Ps. 54:6, on which see GKC, sec. 119i.

9. Cf. Gen. 15:17; Exod. 13:21f; 19:18; 24:17; Num. 9:15–16; 14:14; Deut. 1:33; 4:11–12, 24; 9:3; Ezek. 1:4, 13, 27; 8:2; Ps. 78:14; Neh. 9:12, 19.

10. So Lek. Tov to Exod. 3:2. D. N. Freedman, "The Burning Bush," Bib 50 (1969): 245–246.

11. See J. Feliks, *The Plant World of the Bible* (Hebrew) (Ramat Gan: Massada Press, 1968), 110–112; M. Zohary, *Plants of the Bible* (Cambridge: Cambridge University Press, 1982), 140f.

12. Exod. R. 2:1.

13. Gen. 22:11; 46:2; 1 Sam. 3:10.

14. Cf. Gen. 22:1, 7, 11; 27:1; 31:11; 37:13; 46:2; 1 Sam. 3:4, 6, 8, 16; 2 Sam. 1:7; Isa. 52:6; 58:9.

15. Exod. 2:3.

16. Cf. Josh. 5:14. No footwear is mentioned in the prescriptions for priestly attire in Exod. 28, 39 and Lev. 8; cf. Exod. R. 2:13; cf. Sotah 40ᵃ.

17. KAI I, 181.1, p. 33 (ANET, p. 320); KAI 24.1, 9, pp. 4–5 (ANET, pp. 500, 654); KAI 26, I.1, p. 5 (ANET, pp. 499, 653); KAI 13.1, p. 2 (ANET, p. 662); KAI 10.1, p. 2 (ANET, pp. 502, 656); KAI 202.2, p. 37 (ANET, pp. 501, 655); KAI 214.1, p. 38; KAI 216.1, p. 40 (ANET, pp. 501, 655).

18. Gen. 15:7; 17:1; 26:24; 28:13; 35:11; 46:3.

19. Cf. Exod. 6:2; 20:2; Deut. 5:6.

20. Cf. 2 Kings 2:14; 20:5; Isa. 38:5; 2 Chron. 21:12; 34:3.

21. Cf. 2:24. See chap. 2, n. 40.

22. Cf. Gen. 32:31; Judg. 6:22f.; 13:22; 1 Kings 19:13; and cf. also Exod. 20:19; 24:10f.; 33:20.

23. Exod. 33:18.

24. Cf. Gen. 18:21; 19:13; Exod. 22:22–26; Isa. 5:7; Ps. 9:13; Job 19:7; 34:28; Neh. 5:1.

25. Cf. Gen. 11:5, 7; 18:21; Exod. 19:11, 18, 20; 34:5; Num. 11:17, 25; 12:5; 2 Sam. 22:10 = Ps. 18:10; Isa. 31:4; Neh. 9:13.

26. Jer. 11:5 seems to take the phrase as part of the pledges to the patriarchs, but Ezek. 20:5–6 explicitly locates it as given in Egypt to the people. Such texts as Deut. 11:9; 26:15; 31:20; Josh. 5:6; Jer. 32:22 all leave unclear whether the phrase is a quotation or editorial gloss.

27. Cf. The Story of Sinuhe (ANET, p. 19, lines 80 ff.); the Asiatic Campaigns of Thut-Mose III (ANET, pp. 237, 239). See F. C. Fensham, "An Ancient Tradition of the Fertility of Palestine," PEQ 98 (1966): 166–167.

28. Deut. 32:13; Judg. 14:8–9; 1 Sam. 14:25; Ps. 81:17.

29. So Sif. Deut. 297, p. 317, Tosef. Ma'aser Ri'shon 2:2, Tosef. Ter. 9:8, TJ Ter. 11:1 (47d), TJ Bik. 1:3 (63d).

30. For seven peoples, see Deut. 7:1; Josh. 3:10; 24:11; for six, see, e.g., Exod. 3:8, 17; 23:23; 32:2; for five, see Exod. 13:5; 1 Kings 9:20; 2 Chron. 8:7; for three, see Exod. 23:28.

31. 2 Sam. 5:6–10.

32. So U. Cassuto, *A Commentary on the Book of Exodus*, trans. I. Abrahams (Jerusalem: Magnes Press, 1953), comment to Exod. 3:10.

33. Cf. Isa. 6:5; Jer. 1:6; 20:7, 9; Jonah.

34. Cf. Judg. 6:15; 1 Sam. 18:18; 2 Sam. 7:18.

35. Cf. Gen. 26:3; 31:3; Deut. 31:23; Josh. 1:5; 3:7; Judg. 6:16. On the phrase, see Exod. R. 3:5.

36. Cf. Gen. 9:12–13; Judg. 6:14; 1 Sam. 10:1–7; 2 Sam. 2:34; 1 Kings 13:3; 2 Kings 19:29. See F. J. Helfmeyer, TDOT, s.v. *'ot*; M. Fishbane, "The Biblical *'OT*" (Hebrew), Shnaton 1 (1975): 213–234.

37. See H. M. Orlinsky, *Notes on the New Translation of the Torah* (Philadelphia: Jewish Publication Society, 1969), 153; B. S. Childs, *The Book of Exodus* (Philadelphia: Westminster, 1974), at Exod. 3:12.

38. Exod. 4:23; 5:1,3,8,17; 7:16, 26; 8:16, 23; 9:1, 13; 10 passim; 12:31; cf. Lev. 22:33; 25:42.

39. So Rashbam, and cited by Bekhor Shor.

40. Exod. 6:20; Num. 26:59. Num. 13:16 notes that Joshua, born before the Exodus, was originally named Hoshea, which was changed to yehoshua (Joshua) in the wilderness.

41. Cf. Ps. 135:13. For the synonyms *shem* and *zekher*, cf. Isa. 26:8; Prov. 10:7; Job 18:17. For *zekher* as a substitute for "name," cf. Hos. 12:6; Pss. 30:5; 97:12; 102:13.

42. Exod. 3:16,18; 4:29; 12:21; 17:5,6; 18:12; 19:7; 24:1,9,14; Num. 11:16,24,25; 16:25.

43. Cf. Akk. *šibuti*, Heb. *sevah*, "hoary head, old age;" the Greek *gerousia*, "Council of Elders," at Sparta made up of *gerontes*, the Roman *senatus*, and Arab. *sheik*. All are terms that derive from a word indicating advanced age. On this institution, see H. Reviv, *The Elders in Ancient Israel: A Study of a Biblical Institution* (Hebrew) (Jersulem, Magnes Press, 1983).

44. Exod. 3:18; 5:3; 7:16; 9:1, 13; 10:3.

45. See Weisman, "Mountain of God," p. 115.

46. Num. 23:3,4,15,16; Deut. 25:18; 2 Sam. 1:6; cf. Hifil in Gen. 24:12; 27:20. LXX, Sam. Vulg. unnecessarily render as though from the stem *k-r-'*.

47. Gen. 22:4; 31:22; 40:18; 42:17–18; Exod. 15:22; 19:11, 15, 16; Num. 10:33; 19:12, 19; 31:19; 33:8; Josh. 1:11; 2:16, 22; 3:2; 9:16; Judg. 14:19; 19:4; 1 Sam. 9:20; 2 Sam. 20:4; 24:13; 2 Kings 20:5; Hos. 6:2; Jon. 3:3; Esther 4:16; 5:1; 1 Chron. 21:12; 2 Chron. 10:5. The same is featured in Gilgamesh 1.3.48 (ANET, p. 75).

48. Exod. 8:22; cf. Gen. 43:32; 46:34.

49. See Weisman, "Mountain of God," pp. 113–114.

50. K. A. Kitchen, *Ancient Orient and Old Testament* (Downers Grove, Ill.: Intervarsity Press, 1975), 156f.

51. Z. Meshel, "An Exploration of the Journeys of the Israelites in the Wilderness," BA 45 (1982): 20.

52. See J. L. McKenzie, "God and Nature in the Old Testament," CBQ 14 (1952): 139; W. Eichrodt, *Theology of the Old Testament*, Vol. 2 (Philadelphia: Westminster Press, 1967), 162f.; H. Kasher, "Miracles in the Bible," Beth Mikra 104 (1985): 40–58.

53. Gen. 15:14.

54. Exod. 11:2–3; 12:35–36; cf. Ps. 105:37.

55. Philo, *Vita Moses* 1.25 (141), (Loeb 6:341).

56. Sanh. 91a; cf. Exod. R. 1:5.

57. D. Daube, *Studies in Biblical Law* (Cambridge: Cambridge University Press, 1947), 49f., anticipated by R. Hananel and Bahya (to Exod. 11:2).

58. Cf. Josh. 15:18; Judg. 1:14; 5:25; 8:24; 1 Sam. 1:17, 27; 2:20; 1 Kings 2:22; 3:5, 10–11; 10:13; 2 Kings 2:9–10; 4:28; Pss. 2:8; 21:5; 109:10; Prov. 20:4; 30:7.

59. See G. W. Coats, "Despoiling the Egyptians," VT 18 (1968): 450–457; Childs, *Book of Exodus*, pp. 175–177; Y. T. Radday, "The Spoils of Egypt," ASTI 12 (1983): 125–147.

Chapter 4

1. For Heb. *hen* in this Aram. sense, cf. Exod. 8:22; Jer. 2:10; 3:1; Job 13:15; 2 Chron. 7:13; cf. Ezra 5:17.

2. On this subject, see Ibn Ezra's "short commentary" to Exod. 7:9.

3. Cf. Isa. 10:5, 24; 14:5; Jer. 48:17; Ezek. 7:11; 19:11–14; Ps. 110:2.

4. Exod. R. 3:12; cf. Sanh. 97b. In Num. 21:6 snakes come as a punishment for lack of faith.

5. E. V. Hulse, "The Nature of Biblical 'Leprosy' and the Use of Alternative Medical Terms in Modern Translations of the Bible," PEQ 107 (1975): 87–105: J. Preuss, *Biblical and Talmudic Medicine*, trans. and ed. F. Rosner (New York and London: Sanhedrin Press, 1978), 323–339; J. F. A. Sawyer, "A Note on the Etymology of Ṣāraʿat," VT 26 (1976), 241–245.

6. Cf. Num. 12:10; Deut. 24:8–9; 2 Kings 5:26–27; 15:5 = 2 Chron. 26:19.

7. Exod. 7:15–25.

8. See J. H. Tigay, "'Heavy of Mouth' and 'Heavy of Tongue': On Moses' Speech Difficulty," BASOR 231 (1978): 57–67.

9. Exod. 7:7.

10. Cf. Lev. 10:11; Deut. 33:10. So Shadal.

11. Cf. Deut. 15:12; So Kaufmann, *Toledot ha-'Emunah ha-Yisre'elit*, vol. 1 (Tel Aviv: Mosad Bialik, 1966), 175 n. 15.

12. So Exod. R. 4:1; contrast Jacob's departure from Laban, Gen. 31.

13. Cf. Gen. 45:3.

14. MdRY *Yitro* 1, p. 190.

15. So Exod. 17:5. On this topic, see S. Loewenstamm, EB (Hebrew), s.v. *matteh*. Cf. Ibn Ezra's "short commentary" to Exod. 7:9.

16. Targums, so Ibn Ezra.

17. Saadia; cf. 1 Chron. 29:23, "the throne of the LORD."

18. Shadal.

19. Cf. Isa. 10:26 and contrast Isa. 10:24; cf. Mic. 6:9; Hab. 3:9; Ps. 110:2.

20. Exod. R. 27:9, Yal. Num. par. 763, Ps. par. 869, Exod. R. 8:2, Beshallah 26:4; cf. A. Jellinek, *Bet ha-Midrasch*, vol. 1, 3rd ed. (Jerusalem: Wahrmann Books, 1967), 121.

21. See J. H. Hertz, *The Authorized Daily Prayer Book* (London: National Council for Religious Education, 1943), 687.

22. Exod. 7:13, 14, 22; 8:11, 15, 28; 9:7, 34, 35; 13:15.

23. Exod. 4:21; 7:3; 9:12; 10:1, 20, 27; 11:10; 14:4, 8, 17.

24. Cf. Exod. R. 11:7; 13:4. See Maimonides, Hilkhot Teshuvah 5.1–2, 5, 6:1, 3. On the hardening of the heart, see U. Cassuto, *A Commentary on the Book of Exodus* (Jerusalem: Magnes Press, 1967), 55–57; B. S. Childs, *The Book of Exodus* (Philadelphia: Westminster, 1974), 170–175; R. R. Wilson, "The Hardening of Pharaoh's Heart," CBQ 41 (1979): 18–36; W. C. Kaiser, *Toward Old Testament Ethics* (Grand Rapids, Mich.: Zondervan, 1983), 251–256.

25. For the secular use of the formula, cf. Gen. 32:5; 45:9; especially Exod. 5:10.

26. So Exod. 22; 5:1; 7:17, 26; 8:16; 9:1, 13; 10:3; 11:4. See C. Westermann, *Basic Forms of Prophetic Speech*, trans. H. C. White (Philadelphia: Westminster, 1967), 100–115.

27. So Deut. 14:1–2; 32:5–6, 18–20; Isa. 43:6; 45:11; 63:8; Jer. 3:4, 19; Hos. 2:1; 11:1.

28. So Bekhor Shor. The same is also implied in Jer. 2:3; cf. 3:19. Ephraim is described as first-born in Jer. 31:8, cf. v. 19.

29. Exod. 13:1–13; 22:28; 34:19–20.

30. Exod. 13:1–13; 12:28–33.

31. On this episode, see S. Talmon, "The 'Bloody Husband,'" *Eretz-Israel* 3 (1954): 93–96; J. Blau, "Ḥatan Damim," *Tarbiz* 26 (1957): 1–3; B. Childs, *Myth and Reality in the Old Testament* (Naperville: Ill.: A. R. Allenson, 1960), 58–63; idem, *The Book of Exodus* (Philadelphia: Westminster Press, 1975), 103–104; M. H. Segal, "The Religion of Israel before Sinai," JQR 52 (1961): 52–86; H. Kosmala, "The Bloody Husband," VT 12 (1962): 14–28; J. Morgenstern, "The 'Bloody Husband'? (Exodus 4:24–26) Once Again," HUCA 34 (1963): 35–37; S. Loewenstamm, *The Tradition of the Exodus in Its Development* (Hebrew) (Jerusalem: Magnes Press, 1965), 87–88; J. M. Sasson, "Circumcision in the Ancient Near East," JBL 85 (1966): 473–

476; T. C. Mitchell, "The Meaning of *ḤTN* in the Old Testament," VT 19 (1969): 93–112.

32. MdRY Bo' 5, p. 14, Exod. R. 17:3, Targ. Jon. to Exod. 12:13, and Ezek. 16:6.

33. Cf. Gen. 21:4; 34:14; Lev. 12:3; Judg. 14:3.

34. So Gen. 43:30; Zech. 19:9; and in postbiblical Heb., e.g., Mish. Yoma 1:7; cf. the Aram. equivalent in Dan. 2:13.

35. So R. Simeon ben Gamaliel in Ned. 32a; TJ Ned. 3:16 (38b), Exod. R. 5:8; so Targ. Jon., Shadal. Samuel ben Hofni, Saadia, Ramban take the victim to be the second son, Eliezer.

36. Herodotus, Histories 2.37, 104; cf. Jer. 9:24–25; Ezek. 28:10; 31:18; 32:22–30.

37. Cf. Josh. 5:2–3; Ps. 89:44; cf. 2 Sam. 2:16.

38. Cf. Judg. 3:24; 1 Sam. 24:3; 2 Kings 18:27 = Isa. 36:12; 7:20; cf. Deut. 28:57; Ezek. 16:25; Ruth 3:4, 7.

39. Exod. 12:13, 22.

40. Ned. 32a, TJ Ned. 3:14 (38b), TJ Kid. 4:11 (66c); cf. Mish. Nid. 5:3; Sem. 3:1; Ibn Ezra to Exod. 4:25.

41. Cf. Gen. 27:26–27; 29:11, 13; 31:8; especially Exod. 18:7.

42. Cf. Exod. 14:31; 19:9; Ps. 106:12.

Chapter 5

1. Exod. R. 5:17.

2. The original instruction in Exod. 3:18 has "to sacrifice," a nonsignificant variant; cf. 23:14, 18.

3. Exod. 3:11.

4. For the interchange of *k-r-h* and *k-r-'*, see chap. 1, n. 15.

5. Bekhor Shor, Abravanel.

6. Ibn Ezra, Ḥizkuni; cf. Exod. R. 5:19.

7. Cf. Lev. 26:25; Jer. 14:12; 21:7,9; 24:10; 27:8, 13.

8. Rashi, Bekhor Shor, Ibn Ezra.

9. Cf. Gen. 42:6; the Sam. text reads *me'am*, "they are more numerous than the natives of the land."

10. A. Erman, *Life in Ancient Egypt* (1894; reprint, New York: Dover, 1971), 123–124.

11. K. A. Kitchen, "From the Brickfields of Egypt," Tyn Bul 27 (1976): 136–147.

12. M. Weinfeld, "*The Term Šoter, Its Meaning and Functions*" (Hebrew), *Beth Mikra* 71 (1977): 417–420.

13. On brickmaking and the uses of bricks in Egypt, see C. F. Nims, "Bricks without Straw," BA 13 (1950): 22–28; A. Lucas, *Ancient Egyptian Materials and Industries*, 4th ed., rev. and enlarged by J. R. Harris (London: Edward Arnold, 1962), 48–50; A. J. Spenser, *Brick Architecture in Ancient Egypt* (Warminster: Aris and Phillips, 1979).

14. So noted by D. J. McCarthy, "Plagues and Sea of Reeds: Exodus 5–14," JBL 85 (1966): 141.

15. So noted by M. Greenberg, *Understanding Exodus* (New York: Behrman House, 1969), 127–128.

16. Exod. R. 5:23.

17. This English rendering of the difficult *ve-ḥat'at 'ammekha* takes the first word as a noun, a form otherwise unattested. The Sam. tradition also understands it this way but reads *'immekha*, "with you," as does Sym. The LXX and Pesh. read *ve-ḥat'ata*, "you sin against your own people," it being unclear whether the Egyptians or Israelites are intended.

18. Exod. 10:8, 11, 24; 12:31; noted by Greenberg, *Understanding Exodus*.

Chapter 6

1. It should be noted that in Jewish tradition 6:1 completes chap. 5.

2. See Comment to 3:13–14.

3. The preposition *bet* of *'el shaddai* also governs the second clause, as was noted by Judah Halevi (*Kuzari* 2), Ibn Ezra, and Abravanel.

4. Cf. Exod. 7:5; 14:4, 18; 1 Kings 20:13, 28; and frequently in Ezek. (e.g., 6:7; 7:4; 12:15).

5. For El Shaddai in Genesis, cf. also 28:3; 43:14; 48:3. Although Isaac is included here, referring to the divine promises of Gen. 26:3–5, this particular divine name is not used in that text.

6. Cf. Gen. 17:16; 46:4; 1 Sam. 4:17; Jer. 12:6; 31:9; Ezek. 16:52. C. J. Labuschagne, "The Emphasizing Particle *Gam* and Its Connotations," in *Studia Biblia et Semitica* (Wageningen: H. Veenman and Sons, 1966), 193–203.

7. So Exod. R. to 6:6, Rashi, Lek. Tov. Cf. Gen. 4:15; 30:15; Num. 16:11; 20:12; Judg. 8:7; 10:13; 11:18; 1 Sam. 2:27–29; 28:2; 1 Kings 14:10; Jer. 5:2; Ezek. 5:7; 20:27, 30.

8. TJ Pes. 10:1 (37c), Gen. R. 88:4, Exod. R. 6:5.

9. Exod. 21:2–5, 7, 11; Lev. 25:28, 30, 31, 33, 41, 54; Deut. 24:2; Prov. 12:13.

10. Cf. Lev. 25:24–26, 47–49, 51, 54; Jer. 32:6–8; Ruth 2:20; 3:9, 12–13; 4:3–10; cf. Num. 35:19. See TDOT, 2, s.v. *gā'al*. A. R. Johnson, "The Primary Meaning of *g'al*," in (*Congress* Volume) SVT 1 (1953), 67–77.

11. Re the Exodus, cf. Exod. 15:13; Ps. 78:35. The figurative usage is especially prominent in Deutero-Isaiah in reference to the future redemption from exile: 41:14; 43:1–3; 44:23; 48:17; 49:7, 26; 52:3; 54:5; 60:16; cf. also Jer. 31:10.

12. Deut. 4:34; 5:15; 7:19; 9:29; 11:2; 26:8; 2 Kings 17:36; Jer. 32:21; Pss. 77:16; 136:12; Ezek. 20:33, 34. Cf. also 1 Kings 8:42; Isa. 51:9; Jer. 21:5; 27:5; 32:17; Ps. 89:11, 14.

13. Cf. Isa. 50:1; 54:4–7; 62:4–5; Jer. 2:2; 3:1; Ezek. 16; Hos. 2:4–20; 3:1–5.

14. Cf. Gen. 4:19; 6:2; 11:29, and over seventy other biblical occurrences. Akk. *leqû* has a similar usage; (see CAD, s.v. *leqû*).

15. Cf. Lev. 21:3; Num. 30:7; Deut. 24:24; Judg. 14:20; 15:2; 2 Sam. 12:10; Jer. 3:1; Ezek. 16:8; Hos. 3:3; cf. Ruth 1:12–13.

16. Cf. Lev. 11:45; 20:26; 22:33; 25:38; 26:12, 25; Num. 15:41; Deut. 26:17–18; 27:9; 29:12; 2 Sam. 7:24; Jer. 7:23; 11:4; 13:11; 24:7; 30:22, 25; 31:32; Ezek. 11:20; 14:11; 36:28; 37:23.

17. Cf. Ezek. 16:8; Mal. 2:14; Prov. 2:17.

18. So Gen. 14:22; Num. 14:30; Deut. 32:40; Ezek. 20:5, 6, 15, 23, 28, 42; 36:7; 44:12; 47:14; Ps. 106:26; M. R. Lehman, "Biblical Oaths," ZAW 81 (1969): 74–92.

19. Gen. 26:3; 50:24; Exod. 13:5, 11; 33:1; Num. 11:12; 14:16; 32:11; Deut. 1:8, 35; 6:10, 18, 23.

20. Cf. Exod. 7:26; 9:1; 10:1.

21. Gen. R. 92:7 lists ten biblical examples of this logical device.

22. Lev. 26:41; Jer. 6:10; 9:25; Ezek. 44:7,9.

23. U. Cassuto, *A Commentary on the Book of Exodus*, trans. I. Abrahams (Jerusalem; Magnes Press, 1967), 84–88; G. Galil, "Priesthood and Kingship in the Genealogy of the House of Aaron," *Beth Mikra* 100 (1984): 168–172. B. E. Scolnic, *Theme and Context in Biblical Lists* (New York: Jewish Theological Seminary, 1987), 266–300.

24. Exod. 28; Lev. 9; Num. 3:1–10.

25. Num. 1:7; 2:3; 7:12,17; 10:14; Ruth 4:19–20; 1 Chron. 2:10.

26. Exod. 32:26–29; Deut. 10:8.

27. Cf. Gen. 24:3; 38:2; cf. 46:10.

28. LXX reads, "the daughter of his father's brother," i.e., his cousin. This variant exemplifies sensitivity to the tradition about Amran.

29. For the pattern, cf. the biblical names Joab, Joah, Joel, Johanan, Jonathan, Jozadak, Joshaphat.

30. Cf. 1 Chron. 5:27–28.

31. The pertinent sources are 2 Chron. 20:19; Pss. 42; 44–49; 84; 85; 87; 88; 1 Chron. 9:19; 26:1–19.

32. Y. Aharoni, *Arad Inscriptions* (Hebrew) (Jerusalem: Mosad Bialik, 1975), 82, no. 49, line 2.

33. With the first syllable, cf. Potiphar (Gen. 37:36) and Potiphera (Gen. 41:50).

34. W. F. Albright, *Yahweh and the Gods of Canaan* (Garden City, N.Y.: Doubleday, 1968), 165 and n. 34.

35. Cf. Ps. 106:30–31.

36. Cf. Gen. 37:36 and 39:1.

37. Cf. Exod. 7:4; 12:17,41,51; 13:18; Num. 1 passim; 4:23; 8:24.

Chapter 7

R. Alter, *The Art of Biblical Narrative* (New York: Basic Books, 1981), 90–91.

1. So Exod. 3:19; 4:21.

2. Cf. Exod. 5:21–23; 6:9.

3. The Hebrew stem *k-sh-h* with *lev* is used only here in the Exodus narratives; cf. Ps. 95:8.

4. Cf. Exod. 12:41.

5. Cf. Exod. 14:4, 18.

6. For this "fulfillment formula," cf. Gen. 6:22; Exod. 12:28, 50; 39:32, 42–43; 40:16; Num. 1:54; 2:34; 9:5; 17:26; cf. Gen. 50:12; Exod. 27:8; Num. 5:4.

7. So Ps. 90:10; cf. Lek. Tov.

8. Exod. 4:1–9, 30–31.

9. C. J. Labuschagne, "The Emphasizing Particle *Gam* and Its Connotations," in *Studia Biblica et Semitica* (Wageningen: H. Veenman and Sons, 1966), 193–203.

10. Cf. Gen. 41:8, 24; Dan. 2:10, 27. On *ḥartumim*, see T. O. Lambdin, "Egyptian Loan Words in the Old Testament," JAOS 73 (1953): 150 ff.; J. Quaegebur, "On the Egyptian Equivalent of Biblical Hartumim," in *Pharaonic Egypt: The Bible and Christianity*, ed. S. I. Groll (Jerusalem: Magnes Press, 1985), 162–172.

11. Targ. Jon. to Exod. 7:11, Exod. R. 9:4, Men. 85a; cf. Zadokite Fragment 5:18, 2 Tim. 3:8; Pliny, Natural History 30.1,11.

12. Grecized forms of Heb. *yoḥni* and *mamre*.

13. Cf. Num. 22:22.

14. Cf. 1 Sam. 21:10; 1 Kings 19:13; Isa. 25:7; cf. Judg. 4:21; 1 Sam. 18:22; 24:4; Ruth 3:4; 2 Sam. 19:5; Job 15:11. For the expanded form *l-h-t* in vv. 22 and 8:3, cf. *'em/'immahot*; *'avram/'avraham*; *b-w-sh*/Aram. *b-h-t*; *bayit*/ Ugar. *bht, bhtm*; *m-w-l/m-h-l*.

15. L. Keimer, "Histoires de serpents dans L'Égypt ancienne et moderne," MIE, vol. 50 (Cairo: Imprimerie de l'Institut français orientale, 1947); D. P. Mannix, "Magic Unmasked," *Holiday* (Nov. 1960): 32; W. Gibson, *Secrets of Magic: Ancient and Modern* (New York: Grosset and Dunlap, 1967), 13.

16. G. Hort, "The Plagues of Egypt," ZAW 69 (1957): 84–103; and 70 (1958): 48–59; S. E. Loewenstamm, *The Tradition of the Exodus in Its Development* (Hebrew) (Jerusalem: Magnes Press, 1965), 25–79; idem, "The Number of Plagues in Psalm 105," Bib 52 (1971): 34–38; U. Cassuto, *A Commentary on the Book of Exodus*, trans. I. Abrahams (Jerusalem: Magnes Press, 1967), 92–135; B. Margulis, "The Plagues Tradition in Ps. 105," Bib 50 (1969): 491–496; M. Greenberg, *Understanding Exodus* (New York: Behrman House, 1969), 151–192; idem, "The Redaction of the Plague Narrative in Exodus," in *Near Eastern Studies in Honor of W. F. Albright*, ed. H. Goedicke (Baltimore: Johns Hopkins University Press, 1971), 243–252; B. S. Childs, *The Book of Exodus* (Philadelphia: Westminster, 1974), 121–171.

17. This can be calculated from Moses' age given in v. 7 and at his death in his 120th year after forty years in the wilderness. Deut. 34:7; cf. 31:2. Cf. Mish. Eduy. 2:10: "The judgment on the Egyptians lasted twelve months."

18. Z. Zevit, "The Priestly Redaction and Interpretation of the Plagues Narrative in Exodus," JQR 66 (1976): 193–211.

19. The basic threefold division was early recognized in rabbinic literature and expressed through a mnemonic preserved in the Passover Haggadah; cf. Exod. R. 5:6, 8:3, AdRN² 36 (p. 94). The specific characteristics of each triad were noted by medieval Jewish exegetes, e.g., Rashbam to Exod. 7:26, Bekhor Shor to Exod. 8:12 and 9:8, Baḥya to Exod. 10:11, Lek. Tov, pp. 35, 47.

20. Exod. 12:12; Num. 33:4.

21. Exod. 5:2; 7:5, 17; 8:6, 18; 9:14, 16, 29; 14:4, 18.

22. Exod. 4:31; 5:21–23; 6:1, 9. I owe this insight to Professor Marvin Fox.

23. Plagues 4, 5, 7, 9, and 10.

24. Plagues 1, 2, 3, 6, 8.

25. Hort, "Plagues of Egypt," ZAW 69 (1957): 84–103, and 70 (1958): 48–59 is the source of the introductions to the individual plagues explaining their possible natural background.

26. Cf. 2 Kings 3:22; Joel 3:4.

27. Cf. Exod. 12:12; Num. 33:4; cf. Jer. 46:25. So Exod. R. 9:8, Tanḥ. 14, p. 29, Rashi, Lek. Tov.

28. Exod. 1:22; so Exod. R. 9:8.

29. W. Beyerlin, *Near Eastern Texts Relating to the Old Testament*, trans. J. Bowden (Philadelphia: Westminster, 1978), 97–98.

30. ANET, p. 441; M. Lichtheim, *Ancient Egyptian Literature*, vol. 1 (Berkeley: University of California Press, 1973), 151.

31. Lichtheim, *Ancient Egyptian Literature*, vol. 3 (1980), 148.

32. Tanḥ. 14 (p. 29); Lek. Tov.

33. Ibn Ezra, Lek. Tov to 8:6.

34. Cf. Num. 11:5.

35. Cf. Exod. 7:21, 24; Gen. 19:11; Isa. 1:14; Jer. 6:11; 15:6; 20:9; see Rashbam to Gen. 19:11.

36. So Targ. Onk., Exod.R. 9:11, Rashi, Ibn Ezra.

37. So Loewenstamm, *Tradition of the Exodus*, p. 36, n. 37, who cites Ugar. text Anath 3.19–22.

38. So Saadia.

39. Exod. 1:16.

Chapter 8

1. Cf. Judg. 7:2; Isa. 10:15.

2. LXX, Philo, Origen, Vulg. render *kinnim*, as "gnats." Josephus, Ant. 2.14.3 (Loeb, p. 297), Targums, Pesh. have "lice." The form *kinnam*, v. 13, seems to be a feminine collective. The absolute singular form *kinnah* appears in tannaitic Hebrew (Shab. 12a).

3. Cf. Exod. 9:11.

4. For the phrase, cf. Exod. 31:18; Deut. 9:10; Ps. 8:4.

5. Josephus, Ant. 2.14.3 (Loeb, p. 297), Targ. Jon., Exod. R. 11:3 (Rabbi Judah), Rashi, Rashbam, Bekhor Shor, Ramban (to v. 18), Lek. Tov, Shadal, who cites in support Ps. 78:45, which describes the action of the *'arov* as "devouring."

6. Aq., Sym., Exod. R. 11:3 (Rabbi Nehemiah); in Ps. 105:31 *kinnim* in parallel with *'arov* may support "insects."

7. So Gen. 34:2.

8. Gen. 46:28, 34; 47:1, 4, 6, 27, 28, 29; 50:8.

9. So LXX, Vulg., Rashi, Rashbam, Ibn Ezra.

10. Isa. 50:2; Pss. 111:9; 130:7.

11. Cf. Gen. 43:32; 46:34.

12. Cf. Deut. 7:26; 27:15; 2 Kings 23:13; Isa. 41:24; Ezek. 7:20; 11:21; 16:36; 2 Chron. 34:33.

13. Cf. Gen. 16:5; 2 Sam. 24:17; Isa. 45:12.

Chapter 9

1. TDOT, s.v. *yad*, 397; R. Steiglitz, "Ancient Records and the Exodus Plagues," BAR 12 (1987): 47.

2. Heb. *hoyah* is a unique form, either a participle of *h-y-h*, "to be," or of a variant form of *h-v-h*, "to fall," as in Job. 37:6; cf. Arab. *hawa*; and cf. *hovah*, "disaster," in Isa. 47:11; Ezek. 7:26.

Expecially pertinent is Ps. 91:3, *dever havvot*, "destructive pestilence."

3. On the history of the camel, see J. Hawkes and L. Woolley, *Prehistory and the Beginnings of Civilization* (New York: Harper & Row, 1963), 520–521; R. W. Bulliet, *The Camel and the Wheel* (Cambridge: Harvard University Press, 1975), especially 36, 42, 56, 60–67.

4. So in Arab., Aram., Ethiopic, and postbiblical Heb., e.g., *shanah shehunah*, "a year of high temperatures," Yoma 53b, Ta'an. 24b.

5. Cf. Lev. 13:18ff., 39, 42, 57.

6. The stem *s-l-l* means "to raise a mound" as, e.g., for a highway; cf. Isa. 57:14; 62:10. Hence the reflexive could mean "raise yourself as a mound against," that is, create a barrier, obstruct. Exod. R. 12:2 understands, "to treat them as a highway," i.e., to trample on them; hence, probably, Targ. Onk., Rashbam "to trample, suppress." Targ. Jon. has "to be arrogant toward"; cf. Lek. Tov, "to lord it over," treating it as a case of interchange of *resh* and *lamed*; cf. Num. 16:13.

7. Exod. R. 12:3.

8. With *tihalakh*, cf. Exod. 3:19; Num. 22:13; Job 14:20; 34:23; Eccles. 6:8. So Mesha Inscription, line 14. With *mit-lakahat*, cf. Ezek. 1:4, literally "takes itself," i.e., it feeds on itself and requires no fuel.

9. Cf. 1 Kings 8:22, 38, 54; Isa. 1:15.

10. Cf. Mish. Pe'ah 11:7.

11. So observed by Lek. Tov.

12. Men. 70a, Pes. 35a. J. Feliks, *Plant World of the Bible* (Hebrew) (Ramat Gan: Massada, 1976), 149–151; M. Zohary, *Plants of the Bible* (Cambridge: Cambridge University Press, 1982), 75.

13. For the unique *'afilot*, cf. Exod. R. 12:8. The stem is frequently used in rabbinic literature for the late-ripening crops; cf. Mish. Shev. 6:4, MK 6a–b, Ta'an. 3b, 6a.

Chapter 10

1. Cf. Exod. 12:24–27; 13:8, 14; Deut. 4:32; 6:12; 32:7.

2. So Rashi, Ramban. Heb. *hit'allalti* has this meaning in all other biblical usages: Num. 22:29; Judg. 19:25; 1 Sam. 6:6; 31:4; Jer. 38:19; 1 Chron. 10:4. The rendering "I have wrought," supported by Rashbam, Lek. Tov, and Radak, is based on a derivation from *'alilah*, "deed"; cf. 1 Sam. 2:3; Isa. 12:4; Pss. 9:12; 77:13; 78:11; 103:7; 105:1; 1 Chron. 16:8. However, this yields the form *hit'olel*; cf. Ps. 141:4; Lam. 1:12; 2:20; 3:51.

3. Exod. R. 13:5, Rashbam.

4. Targ. Jon., Ramban.

5. Yal. 392; Rashi.

6. See S. Rosenblatt, "A Reference to the Egyptian God Re in the Rabbinic Commentaries of the Old Testament," JBL 60 (1941): 183–185.

7. Cf. Isa. 27:8; Jer. 18:17; Ezek. 17:10; 19:12; 27:26; 42:16; Hos. 13:15; Jonah 4:8; Pss. 48:8; 78:26; Job 27:21; 38:24.

8. See H. Frankfort, *Ancient Egyptian Religion* (reprint, New York: Harper, 1961), 132f.; idem, *Kingship and the Gods* (reprint, Chicago: University of Chicago Press, 1978), 151–159. Cf. Ezek. 32:7–8 in a prophecy against Pharaoh.

9. Following Exod. R. 14:1, the present translation takes Heb. *ve-yamesh* as from *m-sh-sh*, "to touch"; cf. Gen. 27:12, 21, 23. For the Hifil form, cf. Judg. 16:26; Ps. 115:7. Rashi, Rashbam, Bekhor Shor derive from *'-m-sh*, "thick darkness"; cf. Job. 30:3. The existence of such a stem is doubtful.

Chapter 11

1. For the theme of "driving out," cf. Exod. 6:1; 12:31–33, 39; Ps. 105:38.

2. Exod. 10:9. For Heb. *kalah* meaning "altogether, completely," cf. Gen. 18:21.

3. So Exod. 3:21–22; 12:35–36. See G. W. Coats, "Despoiling the Egyptians," VT 18 (1968): 450–457.

4. Cf. Exod. 12:29; Judg. 16:21; Isa. 47:2; Lam. 5:13. Cf. The Instructions of the Vizier Ptah-Hotep (ANET, p. 412): "the maidservants at the grindstone."

5. MdRY Pisha' 13, p. 43; so Rashi.

6. So Rashi.

7. MdRY Pisha' 13, p. 44.

8. Exod. 3:7, 9; 5:15; cf. 2:23.

9. The phrase is probably a proverb, although the exact meaning of *h-r-ts* in this context has not been clarified. Cf. Josh. 10:21. Cf. F. C. Fensham, "The Dog in Ex. XI.7," VT 16 (1966): 504–507.

Chapter 12

On the problems of the chapter, see J. B. Segal, *The Hebrew Passover from Earliest Times to A.D. 70* (London: Oxford University Press, 1970); B. S. Childs, *The Book of Exodus: A Critical Theological Commentary* (Philadelphia: Westminster, 1974), 178–214; B. R. Goldstein and A. Cooper, "The Festivals of Israel and Judah and the Literary History of the Pentateuch," JAOS 110 (1990): 19–31.

1. Exod. 13:4; 23:15; 34:18; Deut. 16:1.

2. 1 Kings 6:1, 37, 38, 8:2. The inscriptions from Arad mention "the month of *tsah*"; cf. Isa. 18:4; Jer. 4:11; see Y. Aharoni, *Arad Inscriptions* (Hebrew) (Jerusalem: Mosad Bialik, 1975), 42.

3. TJ RH 1:2 (56d), Gen. R. 48:9.

4. See J. Milgrom, "Priestly Terminology and the Political and Social Structure of Pre-Monarchic Israel," JQR 69 (1978): 65–81.

5. Lev. 23:27; 25:9–10; Josh. 4:19; cf. Ezek. 20:1.

6. So 2 Chron. 35:7; MdRY Bo' 3–4, p. 12.

7. *Siddur Rashi*, ed. J. Freimann and S. Buber (reprint, New York: Menorah Institute, 1959), 171, par. 352; *Mahzor Vitry*, vol. 1, ed. S. Hurwitz (Nuremberg: Mekize Nirdamim), 222, par. 259.

8. Cf. Josh. 7:14.

9. Deut. 16:1–2; 2 Kings 23:21–23; 2 Chron. 30:1–2, 13–15; 35:1–19.

10. Josephus, Wars 6.9.3 (Loeb, p. 499). So Targ. Jon.

11. Mish. Pes. 5:5, Pes. 64b.

12. The present rendering follows the Masoretic accentuation, which connects the phrase with the preceding. The LXX relates it to the following. Heb. *mikhseh* appears again only in Lev. 27:23; the masculine form *mekhes*, "a levy," appears only in Num. 31:28, 37–41. These terms may well be borrowed from Akk.; cf. Akk. *makāsu*, "to collect a share, etc." CAD, 10.i, p. 127; ii, p. 63f.; see M. de J. Ellis, "Taxation in Ancient Mesopotamia: The History of the Term *miksu*," JCS 26 (1974): 211–250. Rashbam takes the initial *mem* as radical and compares the form with *shikhvah* (Exod. 16:13f.). Hayyuj, Ibn Janah, and Radak derive from *k-s-s*, "to divide, compute." While the following *takhossu* seems to support this, we would expect the geminate verb to yield a noun form *mekhissah*; cf. *megillah*, *mesibbah*, *meshissah*. MdRY Bo' 3, p. 10, and Targ. Onk. render *minyan*.

13. Lev. 1:3; 3:1; 22:19, 21; Deut. 15:21; 17:1; see especially Mal. 1:8.

14. See Shab. 133b.

15. Exod. 22:29; Lev. 22:27. LXX renders the phrase as "a year old."

16. The noun never appears without the preposition. The phrase is a time marker for several daily rituals: the second daily *tamid* offering (Exod. 29:39, 41; Num. 28:4, 8), the lighting of the Tabernacle lamps (Exod. 30:8), and the incense offering

(Exod. 30:8). The quails also arrived in the wilderness at this time (Exod. 16:17). In all but one instance the appropriate time is also variously given as "the evening" (Exod. 27:21; 16:6, 8, 13; Ezra 3:3). In the case of the "griddle cakes of the High Priest," Lev. 6:13 schedules them "in the evening," but rabbinic tradition fixes that term to mean *bein ha-ʿarbayim* (Mish. Men. 4:5). Deut. 16:6 marks the time for the Passover offering as "in the evening at sundown, the time of day when you departed from Egypt." The Targums render *bein ha-ʿarbayim* as though it were identical with the rabbinic term *bein ha-shemashot*, "between the two suns," although the discussion of that phrase in Shab. 34b shows that this is not the case; see the two separate entries in the *Entsyklopaedia Talmudit*, s.v. *bein ha-ʿarbayim* and *bein ha-shemashot*.

17. Mish. Pes. 5:3, MdRY Bo' 5, p. 17; so Sif. 'Emor 9:11 to Lev. 23:5. Both sources cite Jer. 6:4. Mish. Pes. 5:1 and Pes. 58a imply that the slaughtering took place from 2:30 P.M.

18. *Sefer ha-Shorashim*, s.v. *ʿ-r-v*.

19. Josephus, Wars, 6.9.3. (Loeb, p. 499).

20. Gen. 9:4; Lev. 17:11, 14; Deut. 12:23; cf. Ps. 72:14.

21. Deut. 16:7 simply prescribes "cooking," Heb. *b-sh-l*; 2 Chron. 35:13 appears to be a harmonization of this text with Exod. 12:8–9. It is also possible that *b-sh-l* is indeterminate as to the means employed, which is why Exod. 12:9 adds "in water."

22. Cf. Gen. 9:4; Exod. 29:12; Lev. 3:17; 7:26–27; 17:10–14; 19:26; Deut. 15:23; 1 Sam. 14:32–34; Ezek. 33:25.

23. Gen. 19:3; Judg. 6:19–22; 1 Sam. 28:24. It is also an ingredient of various offerings that are unconnected with the Exodus, e.g., in Exod. 29:2, 23; Lev. 2:5; 7:12; 8:2, 26. The etymology of the word is unknown.

24. H. Limet, "The Cuisine of Ancient Sumer," BA 50 (1987): 144, notes that a Sum.-Akk. glossary lists Sum. *ḫi-is-šeš* = Akk. *marrutu*, "bitter lettuce," and Sum. *ḫi-is* = Akk. *ḫassu* "lettuce."

25. Mish. Pes. 10:5.

26. Exod. 23:18; 34:25; Lev. 7:15–16; 8:31–32; 19:5–8; 22:29–30.

27. Mish. Zev. 2:3; cf. Lev. 7:18; 19:7.

28. Deut. 16:3.

29. See N. M. Sarna, *Exploring Exodus* (New York: Schocken, 1986), 86–89, 230 n. 31, 231 n. 33, to which add H. J. Kraus, "Zur Geschichte das Passah-Massot-Festes in Alten Testament," EvT 18 (1958): 47–67; R. de Vaux, *Ancient Israel: Its Life and Institutions* (New York: McGraw-Hill, 1961), 484–495; O. Keel, "Erwägungen zum Sitz im Leben des vormosaischen Pascha und zur Etymologie von *pesaḥ*," ZAW 84 (1972): 414–434.

30. So Targ. Jon. to Exod. 12:11, 13, 27, and Targ. Onk. to vv. 13, 23, 27; MdRY Bo' 7, p. 25 (Rabbi Jonathan); Rashi to v. 13; Saadia to vv. 11, 13, 23, 27; Ibn Janaḥ; Ibn Ezra to v. 1.

31. So Tosef. Sot. 4:5; LXX to vv. 13, 17; Sym.; Targ. Jon. to v. 23; MdRY Beshallaḥ, *petiḥta*, p. 81. This has the contextual support of Isa. 31:5.

32. So Jubilees 49:2–4, LXX to v. 23, Josephus, Ant. 2.14.6 (Loeb, p. 301), Aq. to vv. 11, 27, MdRY Bo' 7, p. 25 (Rabbi Josiah), Rashi, Rashbam, Bekhor Shor, Joseph Kimḥi, Radak. This may have the support of 1 Kings 18:26.

33. Exod. 12:11, 27, 48; Lev. 23:5; Num. 9:10, 14; 28:16; Deut. 16:1, 2; 2 Kings 23:21, 23; 2 Chron. 30:1, 5; 35:1.

34. Cf. Exod. 12:23; 33:22; 34:6; Deut. 9:3; 31:3; 1 Kings 19:11; Ezek. 16:6, 8; Amos 5:17; Job 9:11.

35. Cf. Num. 33:4; Jer. 46:25; Wisd. of Sol. 12:23–27; 16:1–14; Jubilees 48:5.

36. Cf. also Josh. 5:11; 2 Chron. 30:13, 21; 35:17.

37. Cf. Exod. 23:15; 34:18; Lev. 23:6; Deut. 16:3–4, 8.

38. MdRY Bo' 8, p. 27; Pes. 120a.

39. Cf. Mish. Ḥal. 1:1.

40. Cf. Lev. 23:32.

41. Cf. Exod. 34:25; MdRY Bo' 8, p. 28.

42. Cf. Deut. 16:4.

43. MdRY Bo' 8, pp. 26, 29.

44. Ber. 17a; cf. MdRY Beshallaḥ 2, p. 93; Gen. R. 34:12, Yal. Ruth 60. Cf. also Matt. 16:6; Mark 8:15; Luke 12:1; 1 Cor. 5:6ff.; Gal. 5:9; so Plutarch, Quaestiones Romanae 109.

45. Sifra 'Emor 14:4, MK 28a, TJ Bik. 2:1 (64c); cf. Lev. 20:18–20.

46. Mish. Bets. 5:2, Mish. Meg. 1:5, MdRY Bo' 8, p. 31; Sif. Num. 147; Ibn Ezra (cf. Rashbam) notes that in the case of all the festivals the formula for forbidden work is *mele'khet 'avodah* (so Lev. 23:7, 8, 21, 25, 35, 36; Num. 28:18, 25, 26; 29:1, 12, 35), whereas regarding the Sabbath and Yom Kippur the phrasing is simply *kol mela'khah* (so Lev. 16:29; 23:3, 28, 31; Num. 29:7). The present text provides the sole exception, and here preparation of food is expressly exempted.

47. See H. M. Orlinsky, *Notes on the New Translation of the Torah* (Philadelphia: Jewish Publication Society, 1969), 165f.

48. So MdRY Bo' 9 (p. 32), Targums, Pes. 38b; so Rashi, Ibn Ezra, Baḥya.

49. So noted by Ibn Ezra; see GKC, par. 106 n, p. 312f.

50. Sif. Num. 124, Suk. 13a; see Lev. 14:4, 6, 49, 51, 52; Num. 19:6, 18; Ps. 51:9.

51. So MdRY Bo' 11, p. 37, Targ. Onk., Pesh.; cf. Ugar., Phoen. *sp*, Akk. *šappu*. Cf. 2 Sam. 17:28; 1 Kings 7:50; 2 Kings 12:14; Jer. 52:19; Zech. 12:2. For the practice of collecting the blood of sacrifices in basins, cf. Exod. 24:6; 2 Chron. 29:22. The laws regulating sacrifices in Leviticus implicitly assume this practice; cf. Lev. 1:5; 3:2; 4:6, 7. The technical rabbinic term is *kibbul/kabbalat ha-dam*. A. M. Honeyman, "Hebrew *saf*, 'Basin, Goblet,'" JTS 37 (1936): 56–59.

52. Cf. Judg. 19:27; 1 Kings 14:17; 2 Kings 12:10; Isa. 6:4; Jer. 35:4.

53. Cf. Gen. 20:6; 2 Sam. 24:16; Isa. 37:36; cf. Job 1:12; 2:1–6.

54. Cf. Exod. 4:22–23; 11:1–8; 12:12–13.

55. Apparently sensitive to this issue, the Targums followed by Rashi harmonize v. 8 with vv. 34, 39 by connecting Heb. *mish'arot*, "kneading bowls," with the stem *sh-'-r*, understanding it to mean "what remained" of the dough from which the original *matsah* had been baked.

56. Gen. 46:25–26; Exod. 1:5; Deut. 10:22.

57. Num. 1:46–47; 2:32; 26:51; cf. 11:21; 12:37–38. But the number of first-born and Levites as given in Num. 3:39–43; 4:47–48; 26:62 must also be taken into account. A. Lucas, "The Number of Israelites at the Exodus," PEQ 76 (1944): 164–168.

58. So Judg. 6:15; 1 Sam. 10:19 (cf. v. 21); 23:23; Mic. 5:2; and probably also Num. 1:16; Josh. 22:14. See F. Petrie, *Egypt and Israel* (London: Society for Promoting Christian Knowledge, 1911), 40–47.

59. G. E. Mendenhall, "The Census Lists of Numbers 1 and 26," JBL 77 (1958): 52–66. Curiously, numerous texts show that the standard military unit consisted of 600; cf. Judg. 3:31; 18:11, 16, 17; 20:47; 1 Sam. 13:15; 14:2; 23:13; 27:2; 30:9; 2 Sam. 15:18; cf. Pharaoh's 600 charioteers in Exod. 14:7.

60. Cf. 2 Sam. 24:9. See Sarna, *Exploring Exodus*, pp. 94–102.

61. Cf. Targ. Onk. to Num. 11:4 *'eravrevin*. This form seems to reflect a reading in the present text *'eravrav* for *'erev-rav*; so Sam.; cf. reduplicated forms like *'adamdam* and *yerakrak* (Lev. 13:49), *petaltol* (Deut. 32:5), *pekah-ko-aḥ* (Isa. 61:1). Similarly, *kesef sigim* in Prov. 26:23 is most likely *k + safsagim* as in Ugar. *spsg*, "white glaze"; and Isa. 2:20 *laḥpor perot* is to be read as one word *la-ḥprprt*, as indicated by 1/Q/Isa.

62. MdRY Bo' 14, pp. 50–51.

63. Ibid., TJ Meg. 1:9 (71d), Meg. 9a, Tractate Sof. 1:7, ed. Higger, p. 104.

64. The relevant texts are Gen. 12:4; 21:5; 25:26; 47:9: (100–75) = 25 + 60 + 130 = 215 years.

65. See N. M. Sarna, *Understanding Genesis* (New York: Schocken, 1970), 84f.

66. So Rashi, Rashbam, Bekhor Shor.
67. Pes. 109b, RH 11b.
68. Gen. 17:11.
69. Cf. Josh. 5:2–12.
70. Cf. Deut. 15:3; 23:21; Prov. 20:16; 27:13; cf. Neh. 9:2; 13:30.
71. Lev. 22:25; Deut. 14:21; Ezek. 44:7, 9.
72. 1 Kings 8:41–43; cf. Isa. 56:6–7.
73. So Targ. Onk., MdRY Bo' 15, p. 53; Rashi.
74. Cf. Deut. 16:11, 14.
75. See Orlinsky, *Notes*, p. 167, based on Lev. 22:10–12; 25:6, 40. Vv. 44–46 in Exod. 12 prove their non-Israelite affiliation. Lev. 22:10–12 likewise excludes both types from partaking of sacred donations even if they are in the service of a priest.
76. Exod. 20:10; 23:12; Deut. 5:14; Num. 35:13, 15; Josh. 20:9; Deut. 14:29; Lev. 25:6.
77. Lev. 17:8; 22:18; Num. 15:15, 16, 29; Deut. 16:11, 14.
78. Lev. 18:26; 20:2; 24:16; 17:10, 13.
79. Cf. Exod. 12:19; so Num. 9:14.
80. Cf. Lev. 19:34; Num. 15:14–16.
81. MdRY Bo' 15, p. 57.

Chapter 13

1. So Exod. 30:11, 17, 22; 31:1; 40:1; Lev. 5:14, 20; 6:12; 8:1; 14:1; 22:26; 23:26; 24:13; Num. 1:48; 3:5, 11, 44; 4:21; 8:5, 23; 10:1; 13:1; 17:9; 20:7; 25:10, 16; 26:52; 31:1; 34:16.
2. Cf. Exod. 19:10–11, 14–15, 22; 28:3, 41; 29:1, 33, 36, 44; 30:30; 40:13; Lev. 8:12, 30; Num. 11:18; Josh. 3:5; 7:13; 1 Sam. 7:1; 16:5.
3. Exod. 22:28–29; 23:10, 19; Lev. 2:14; Num. 15:19; 18:12–13; especially Deut. 18:4; 26:1–11.
4. So Exod. 13:14; 20:2; Deut. 5:6; 6:12; 7:8; 8:14; 13:6, 11; Josh. 24:17; Judg. 6:8; Jer. 34:13; Mic. 6:4.
5. So in Exod. 3:12.
6. Cf. Lev. 23:6; Deut. 16:8.
7. Cf. Exod. 12:26; 13:14; Deut. 6:20; Josh. 4:6, 21.
8. For the figurative usage, cf. Isa. 49:16; Jer. 17:1; Prov. 1:8–9; 3:1–3; 6:20–21; 7:2–3; Song 8:6.
9. That *yad* may indicate the arm is clear from Gen. 24:22 and Judg. 15:14. The corresponding Akk. *idu* can also convey "arm"; CAD, s.v. *idu*. MdRY Bo' 17, p. 67, cites Judg. 5:26; Isa. 48:13; Ps. 74:11 in support of *yad* meaning the left hand, for in each case it is paralleled by *yemin*, "right hand," taken as contrastive. Men. 37a further cites the unusual orthography of *yadkhah*, "your hand," in Exod. 13:16 as hinting at *yad kehah*, "the weak hand."
10. UT 68:22, 25 in parallel with *qdqd*, "pate."
11. Cf. Deut. 6:7; 11:19; Josh. 1:8; Ps. 1:2.
12. Cf. Num. 27:7, 8; Ezek. 16:21; cf. also 2 Sam. 3:10; Ezek. 20:26, 31. MdRY Bo' 18, p. 70, and so Saadia, Rashi, Rashbam, Bekhor Shor all understand "set apart."
13. Mish. Bek. 2:9, 8:2.
14. Deut. 7:13; 28:4, 18, 51.
15. Cf. Judg. 2:13; 10:6; 1 Sam. 7:4; 12:10; 31:10; 1 Kings 11:5; 2 Kings 23:13.
16. J. Hoftijzer and G. Van der Kooij, *Aramaic Texts from Deir 'Alla* (Leiden: E. J. Brill, 1976), 174, line 16; 273.
17. Cf. Lev. 27:27; Num. 18:15.
18. So Rashi.
19. Mish. Bek. 1:7; cf. Mish. Sot. 9:5. Support for this interpretation of *'arafto* lies in *'oref*, "back of the head"; cf. Jer. 2:27; 18:17; 32:33; 2 Chron. 29:6.
20. Cf. Lev. 27:6; Num. 3:44–51.
21. Cf. Gen. 30:33; Deut. 6:20; Josh. 4:6, 21; 22:24, 27, 28; MdRY Bo' 18, p. 73.
22. So Targ. Jon.
23. Mish. Shab. 6:1, 5.

24. Shab. 57b.
25. Ibid.
26. So Rashi to Shab. 57b.
27. In MK 15a and Ber. 11a *pe'er* is identified with *tefillin*.
28. For divorce, see Deut. 22:19, 29; 24:1, 3, 4; Jer. 3:1; for emancipation of a slave, see Deut. 15:12–13, 18; Jer. 34:9–11, 14–16; cf. Isa. 45:13. See R. de Vaux, *The Early History of Israel* (Philadelphia: Westminster, 1978), 371.
29. Exod. 3:20; 6:1; 11:1.
30. Cf. Pss. 77:21; 78:14.
31. A. H. Gardiner, "The Ancient Military Road Between Egypt and Palestine," JEA 6 (1920): 99–116; Y. Aharoni, *The Land of the Bible: A Historical-Geography*, rev. and enlarged, trans. and ed. A. F. Rainey (Philadelphia: Westminster, 1979), 45–48; B. J. Beitzel, "How to Draw Ancient Highways on Biblical Maps," BR 4 (1988): 37.
32. On the Philistines, see R. Barnett, "The Sea Peoples," in *Cambridge Ancient History*, vol. 2, 3rd ed., ed. I. E. S. Edwards et al. (Cambridge: Cambridge University Press, 1975), 359–378. Several biblical texts preserve a tradition associating the origin of the Philistines with Crete: Deut. 2:23; Jer. 47:4; Ezek. 25:16; Amos 9:7; Zeph. 2:5; cf. also "the Cherethites and Pelethites" in 2 Sam. 8:18; 15:18; 20:7, 23; 1 Kings 1:38, 44; 1 Chron. 18:17. In Gen. 10:13–14 (= 1 Chron. 1:11–12) the Philistines are the off-spring of Mizraim, i.e., Egypt, and are linked with the Caphtorim, i.e., Cretans.
33. Cf. Num. 14:1–4.
34. ANET, pp. 476–478.
35. T. Dothan, "Gaza Sands Yield Lost Outpost of the Egyptian Empire," *National Geographic*, December 1982, 739–768.
36. Num. 33:1–49.
37. T. O. Lambdin, "Egyptian Loan Words in the Old Testament," JAOS 73 (1953): 153.
38. It should be noted, however, that *yam suf* must refer to the Gulf of Akaba in Num. 21:4; Deut. 1:40; 2:1; 1 Kings 9:26; Jer. 49:21. See N. M. Sarna, *Exploring Exodus* (New York: Schocken, 1986), 106–108.
39. Cf. Josh. 1:14; 4:12; Judg. 7:11; so MdRY Beshallaḥ, Petiḥta, p. 77, Exod. R. 20:17, Targ. Onk., Vulg., Rashbam. However, Bekhor Shor cites Gen. 41:34 for a meaning "stocked with food." He points out that the manna did not appear until a month after the Exodus. Radak connects the word with Heb. *ḥomesh*, "the fifth rib," as in 2 Sam. 2:23, and understands, "with swords sheathed at their sides."
40. So Exod. 14:24; 16:10; 19:9, 16; 24:15, 16; 33:9–10; 34:5; 40:34–35; Lev. 16:2, 13; Num. 9:15–16; 11:25; 12:5; 14:14; 17:7; Deut. 4:11; 5:19; 31:15; 1 Kings 8:10–11 = 2 Chron. 5:13–14; Isa. 4:5; Ezek. 1:4; 10:3–4; Pss. 97:2; 99:7. See also Comment to 3:2.
41. So Deut. 1:33; Pss. 78:14; 105:39; Neh. 9:12, 19.
42. So Exod. 40:36–38; Num. 9:17–23.
43. Exod. 14:19–20; Ps. 105:39.
44. God is sometimes portrayed as enveloped in darkness: Exod. 20:18, 21; Deut. 4:11; 5:19; 2 Sam. 22:10; 1 Kings 8:12 = 2 Chron. 6:1; Pss. 18:10; 97:2.

Chapter 14

1. 1 Kings 10:28–29; 11:1, 17–22, 40; 12:2.
2. Josh. 4:22–24; 9:9–11; Isa. 11:15–16; 51:9–11; 63:11–14; Pss. 66:5–6; 77:14–21; 114:3, 53. The exceptions are Josh. 24:5–7; Pss. 78:13; 106:9–12, 22; 136: 9–15. On this subject, see S. E. Loewenstamm, *The Tradition of the Exodus in Its Development* (Hebrew) (Jerusalem: Magnes Press, 1965), chap. 7.
3. A. H. Gardiner, cited in IDB, s.v. Pi-Hahiroth, 3, p. 810.
4. Y. Aharoni, *The Land of the Bible* (Philadelphia: Westminster, 1979), 196.
5. So Targ. Onk., Rashi.

6. The figurative meaning of Heb. *tsafon*, "north," is found in Isa. 14:13; Ezek. 38:6, 15; 39:2; Pss. 48:3; 89:13; Job 26:7.

7. Ugaritic text 9:14, 17.

8. KAI, I, no. 50, lines 2–3; W. F. Albright, "Baal Zaphon," *Festschrift Alfred Bertholet*, ed. W. Baumgartner (Tübingen: Mohr, 1950), 1–14.

9. Cf. Joel 1:18; Esther 3:15; MdRY Beshallah I, p. 84.

10. Cf. Exod. 14:17, 18; Lev. 10:3; Isa. 26:15; Ezek. 28:22; 39:13; Hag. 1:8.

11. Exod. 7:14; 8:11, 28; 9:34; 10:1

12. So Exod. R. 9:6.

13. Exod. 3:18; 5:3; 8:23. "As you said" in 12:31 probably refers to this.

14. Cf. Gen. 46:29; 1 Sam. 6:7; 1 Kings 18:44; 2 Kings 9:21.

15. MdRY Beshallah I, p. 88.

16. Cf. Gen. 33:15; Num. 20:20; 31:32; Josh. 8:1, 3, 11; 10:7; 11:7; Judg. 5:9, 14; 8:5; 1 Sam 11:11; 1 Kings 20:10; 2 Kings 13:7; Pss. 3:7; 18:44.

17. See chap. 12, note 59.

18. Cf. Exod. 15:4; 1 Kings 9:22; 2 Kings 7:2, 17, 19; 9:25; 10:25; 15:25; Ezek. 23:15, 23; 1 Chron. 11:11 (cf. 2 Sam. 23:8); 12:19; 2 Chron. 8:9. MdRY Beshallah I, p. 89, has (1) "a warrior" and (2) "third man in the chariot." See H. J. Cook, "Pekah," VT 14 (1964): 125–126; P. C. Cragie, "An Egyptian Expression in the Song of the Sea," VT 20 (1970): 85; O. Margalith, "The Meaning of the Word *shalish* in the Bible in the Light of Ugaritic TLT," *Beth Mikra* 72 (1977): 68–72; B. A. Mastin, "Was the *šališ* the Third Man in the Chariot?" in *Studies in the Historical Books of the Old Testament*, ed. J. A. Emerton (Leiden: Brill, 1979), 125–154.

19. Cf. Num. 15:30; 33:3; Deut. 32:27; Mic. 5:8; cf. Job 38:15.

20. Cf. Isa. 28:28; Joel 2:4; Hab. 1:8, and possibly also 1 Sam. 8:11 and 1 Kings 5:6; see W. R. Arnold, "The Word *parash* in the Old Testament," JBL 24 (1905): 45–53.

21. LXX, Syr., and Targums have the plural.

22. MdRY Beshallah 2, p. 91, Rashi.

23. MdRY Beshallah 3, p. 97. Exod. R. 21:2, so Ramban, understand that Moses himself engaged in prayer. The Syr. version begins the verse with the phrase, "Moses cried out to the Lord." Cassuto takes *mah* as a negative, like Arab. *ma*'; cf. Song 5:8.

24. The two halves of v. 19 are either a conflation of two textual traditions or the *vav* of *va-yissa*' is explicative, identifying "the angel of God" with "the pillar of cloud"; cf. Gen. 4:4; Exod. 25:12, Isa. 17:8; Pss. 72:12; 74:11.

25. E. A. Speiser, "An Angelic Curse: Exodus 14:20," JAOS 80 (1960): 198–200.

26. So Targums. MdRY Beshallah 4, p. 101; cf. Ps. 139:11–12; Job 37:11; the LXX reads, "the night passed."

27. Judg. 7:19; cf. 1 Sam. 11:11; Isa. 21:11–12; Josephus, Wars 5.12.2 (Loeb, p. 359); Ber. 3b, the view of R. Nathan; Rabbi [Judah] reflects contemporary Roman practice; cf. Matt. 14:25 = Mark 6:48.

28. For the image of God "looking down," i.e., observing the world, cf. Gen. 19:28; Deut. 26:15; Pss. 14:2 = 53:3; 102:20; Lam. 3:50.

29. This translation of Heb. *va-yasar* is found in the LXX, Sam., Pesh, and implies an underlying stem '-s-r, "to tie"; for the elision of the initial *alef* with this verb, cf. *moser*, Isa. 28:22; 52:2; 116:16; *moserah*, Jer. 2:20, etc.; Job 39:5; Nah. 1:13; Pss. 2:3; 107:14; *masoret (ha-berit)*, Ezek. 20:37; cf. *makolet* 1 Kings 5:25. The usual meaning of *va-yasar* is "to remove," i.e., He made the wheels give way.

30. Cf. Deut. 2:4; Amos 5:24; Ps. 74:15; cf. 1 Kings 8:2.

31. So MdRY Beshallah 6, p. 111; cf. Ps. 136:15.

32. For this type of appositional clause, cf. Exod. 27:23; Num. 4:32.

33. Exod. 14:8,16,21,26,27,30,31.

Chapter 15

M. Rozelaar, "The Song of the Sea," VT 2 (1952): 221–228; U. Cassuto, *Commentary on the Book of Exodus* (Hebrew) (Jerusalem, Magnes Press, 1953), 119–128; F. M. Cross and D. N. Freedman, "The Song of Miriam," JNES 14 (1955): 237–250; J. D. W. Watts, "The Song of the Sea. Ex. XV," VT 7 (1957): 371–380; S. E. Loewenstamm, *The Tradition of the Exodus in Its Development* (Hebrew) (Jerusalem: Magnes Press, 1965), 112–118; J. Muilenberg, "A Liturgy of the Triumphs of Yahweh," *Studia Biblical et Semitica* (Wageningen: H. Veenman and Sons, 1966), 233–251; G. W. Coats, "The Song at the Sea," CBQ 31 (1969): 1–17; B. S. Childs, "A Traditio-Historical Study of the Reed Sea Tradition," VT 20 (1970): 406–418; J. Goldin, *The Song at the Sea* (New Haven: Yale University Press, 1971); R. Alter, *The Art of Biblical Poetry* (New York: Basic Books, 1985), 50–54.

1. M. Lichtheim, *Ancient Egyptian Literature*, vol. 2 (Berkeley: University of California Press, 1976), 57–59; ANET, pp. 255–256.

2. Lichtheim, *Ancient Egyptian Literature*, p. 73; ANET, pp. 376–378.

3. Cf. Judg. 5:1.

4. On the use of antiphony in the ancient Near East, see the references in J. L. Kugel, *The Idea of Biblical Poetry* (New Haven, Yale University Press, 1981), 116–119.

5. Philo, Vita Moses 1.32.

6. Mish. Sot. 5:4, Tosef. Sot. 6:2–4, MdRY Beshallah, Shirta 1, p. 119, Sot. 30a, TJ Sot. 5:6 (20c), Exod. R. 23:10.

7. Meg. 16b, TJ Meg. 3:8 (74b), Sof. 12:9.

8. Heb. *'ariah al gabbei levenah u-levenah al gabbei ariah*.

9. See Maimonides, Mishneh Torah, Hilkhot Sefer Torah 8:4.

10. RH 31a.

11. *Mahzor Vitry*, ed. S. Hurwitz (Nuremberg: Mekizei Nirdamim, 1923), par. 265, pp. 226–227.

12. For the imperfect form following '*az*, cf. Num. 21:17; Deut. 4:41; Josh. 8:30; 10:12; 22:1; 1 Kings 3:16; 8:1; 9:11; 11:7; 16:21; 2 Kings 8:22; 12:18; 15:16; 16:5; Ps. 126:2; Job 38:21; 2 Chron. 5:2; 21:10.

13. MdRY Beshallah, Shirta 1, p. 116.

14. Cf. Judg. 5:3; Isa. 5:1; Pss. 13:6; 27:6; 57:8; 59:17; 89:2; 101:1; 104:33; 108:2; 144:9.

15. Cf. Gen. 41:43; Jer. 51:21.

16. Exod. 17:16; Isa. 12:2; Pss. 68:5, 19; 77:12; 89:9; 94:7, 12; 102:19; 105:17, 18; 118:5, 14, 17, 18, 19; 122:4; 130:3; 135:4; 150:6; cf. Song. 8:6.

17. Cf. Arab. *damir*, "brave," Ugar. *dmr*, "a class of troops," Old South Arabic *mdmr*, "strong." This meaning occurs frequently in Semitic proper names; cf. Ugar. *dmrb'l, dmrhd*; Old South Arabic *dmr'l, dmrkrb, dmrmr*; Phoen.-Punic *zmr, Dmr*; West Semitic Mari names *Zimri-abum, Zimri-erah, Zimri-Lim*; North Israelite *B'lzmr* in the Samaria ostraca 112:2–3; biblical Zimran (Gen. 25:2), Zimri (Num. 25:14), Zemirah (1 Chron. 7:8). The same stem is probably behind Gen. 43:11; 2 Sam. 23:1; Isa. 25:5; Ps. 119:54; and Job 35:10. On the above, see N. M. Sarna, "Ezekiel 8:17: A Fresh Examination," HTR 57 (1964): 347–352. R. Zadok, "Some Jews in Babylonian Documents," JQR 74 (1984): 294–297, has noted the Jewish Aramaic name *yhwdmr* in a Neo-Babylonian document and *zmryhw* on a seal from Lower Egypt. On the entire phrase in Exod. 15:2, see U. Cassuto, *Commentary on the Book of Exodus*; S. E. Loewenstamm, "The Lord is My Strength and My Glory," VT 19 (1969): 464–470; J. Blau and J. C. Greenfield, "Ugaritic Glosses," BASOR 200 (1970): 11–12; E. M. Good, "Exodus XV.2," VT 20 (1970): 358–359.

18. Cf. 2 Sam. 10:11; Job 13:16.

19. Cf. Isa. 32:18; 33:20; Jer. 10:25; 23:3; 31:22; 50:7, 19; Ps. 79:7; Prov. 3:33; Job 5:3. For the verbal form, cf. Hab. 2:5. This is

the rendering of Targ. Onk., R. Yose in MdRY Beshallaḥ, Shirta 3, p. 127; cf. Ibn Janaḥ, Ibn Ezra, Baḥya.

20. So LXX, Vulg., Rashbam.

21. MdRY Beshallaḥ, Shirta 1, p. 116.

22. 1 Sam. 18:17; 25:28; cf. Isa. 42:13; Ps. 24:8.

23. Num. 21:14.

24. 1 Sam. 17:47.

25. Zech. 4:6.

26. The phrase, unelaborated, occurs again only in Jer. 33:2 and Amos 5:8; 9:6.

27. The governing verb *yekhasyumu* is doubly archaic in the original third radical *yod* remaining and in the pronominal suffix.

28. Cf. Pss. 77:17; 92:10; 93:3; 94:1.

29. Cf. CAD, s.v. *adàru*, "to fear, be in awe." On the form *ne'edari*, see W. L. Moran, "The Hebrew Language in Its Northwest Semitic Background," in *The Bible and the Ancient Near East*, ed. G. E. Wright (Garden City, N.Y.: Doubleday, 1961), 60.

30. So Ps. 18:16; cf. Hab. 3:8.

31. MdRY Beshallaḥ, Shirta 6, p. 137, Ibn Ezra, Lek. Tov; so Malbim.

32. Cf. Jer. 50:26; Hag. 2:18; Song 7:3; Ruth 3:7; Neh. 13:15 (cf. 3:34); 2 Chron. 31:6, 9.

33. Cf. Exod. 21:14; Josh. 9:4; Prov. 1:4; 8:5, 12.

34. Exod. 1:10, 22, although a different verb is used there; but cf. Prov. 8:12.

35. Cf. Josh. 3:13, 16; Pss. 33:7; 78:13.

36. Cf. Job 10:10.

37. Cf. Judg. 5:27.

38. MdRY Beshallaḥ, Shirta 7, pp. 139f.

39. Cf. Isa. 5:14; Jon. 2:6; Hab. 2:5; Pss. 69:2; 124:4–5; Prov. 23:2; Eccles. 6:2; cf. CAD, s.v. *napištu*.

40. Cf. Josh. 8:7; 15:14; Judg. 1:27, 29.

41. Heb. *n-sh-f* is a variant of *n-sh-v*; cf. Isa. 40:24. The interchange of the labials *b* and *p* is well established; see comment of Ramban to Exod. 15:10; cf. J. C. Greenfield, "Lexicographical Notes I," HUCA 29 (1958): 217–222, especially n. 33.

42. *Metsulah* is formed from *ts-w-l*, not *ts-l-l*; cf. Isa. 44:27, *tsulah*, parallel to *neharot*, "the rivers." In Ps. 68:23 *metsulot* parallels *bashan*, which corresponds to Ugar. *btn*, "serpent, sea dragon."

43. See H. G. May, "Some Cosmic Connotations of *Mayim Rabbim*, 'Many Waters,'" JBL 74 (1955): 9–21.

44. Pss. 35:10; 71:19; 77:14; 89:7–9; 113:5.

45. Cf. 2 Sam. 7:22; 1 Kings 8:23; Jer. 10:6–7; Mic. 7:18; Ps. 86:8.

46. Cf. G. W. Ahlstrom, *Psalm 89* (Lund: Hokan Ohlssons Boktryckeri, 1959), 65; W. G. Lambert, *Babylonian Wisdom Literature* (Oxford: Clarendon Press, 1960), 128, lines 45–46; ANET, pp. 71, 383, 386.

47. Cf. Pss. 82:1; 97:7, 9. The usual expression is *benei 'elim*, *benei (ha-)'elohim*, cf. Gen. 6:1; Pss. 29:1; 89:7; Job 1:6; 2:1; 38:7. For the divine assembly, cf. 1 Kings 22:19–22; Jer. 23:18, 22; Ps. 82:1. It is instructive to compare Ps. 29:1 with its doublets 86:7 and 1 Chron. 16:28; Deut. 32:8 *benei yisrael* appears as *benei el* in Qumran, a reading that underlies the LXX version.

48. So LXX, Syro-Hexapla. *Kodesh* would then be a collective. For *kedoshim* in this sense, cf. Ps. 89:6, 8; Job 5:1; 15:15.

49. So Ramban and Shadal, who cites Ps. 66:5; cf. also Isa. 63:7; Ps. 78:4.

50. So Akk. *erṣetu* (CAD, s.v. *erṣetu*); M. Dahood, *Psalms*, vol. 1 (Garden City, N.Y.: Doubleday, 1966), 106, to Ps. 18:8, for a list of possible biblical examples.

51. R. Alter, *Art of Biblical Poetry*, pp. 53–54.

52. Exod. 20:6; Deut. 5:10; Exod. 34:6; Jer. 32:18. See H.-J. Zobel, TDOT, s.v. *ḥesed*.

53. Cf. Gen. 33:14; Isa. 40:11; 49:10; Ps. 23:2; cf. Arab.

nahala, "to quench thirst," *anhala*, "to water animals"; for the parallel *n-ḥ-h*, *n-h-l*, cf. Ps. 31:4.

54. Cf. 2 Sam. 7:8 = 1 Chron. 17:7; Isa. 65:10; Jer. 23:3; 33:12; 49:20; 50:19, 45; Ezek. 34:14; cf. Zeph. 2:6.

55. Ibn Ezra.

56. Rashbam, Bekhor Shor, Ḥizkuni; cf. Jer. 10:25; 23:3; 31:23.

57. MdRY Beshallaḥ, Shirta 9, p. 146; Targ. Onk., Ramban, Ba'al ha-Turim; cf. 2 Sam. 15:25; Isa. 27:10; Ps. 79:7.

58. For this theme, cf. Num. 22:2–6; Josh. 2:8–11.

59. See Num. 21:24; Deut. 2:19, 37. See Goldin, *Song at the Sea*, pp. 56–57.

60. Cf. *yoshev ha-keruvim*, "Enthroned on the Cherubim," in 1 Sam. 4:4, etc. For *y-sh-v* in this sense, cf. Num. 21:1; 33:40; Amos 1:5, 8; Zech. 9:5–6; Ps. 2:4; Lam. 5:19.

61. Cf. Gen. 36:15–19, 40, 43; cf. also Zech. 9:7; 12:5.

62. Gen. 25:30; 36:1, 8, 9, 19; Num. 20:14–21.

63. So 2 Kings 14:15; Ezek. 17:13; 32:21; cf. Isa. 14:9; 34:6; 60:7; Jer. 50:8. In Ugar. text KRT IV.6–7, "bulls" and "gazelles" stand for noblemen.

64. So MdRY Beshallaḥ, Shirta 9, p. 147; cf. Josh. 2:9, 24 and v. 11; Jer. 49:23; Nah. 1:5; Ps. 75:4.

65. So Targums. For this use of *k-n-h*, cf. Isa. 11:1; Ps. 74:2 (parallel *g-'-l*); Neh. 5:8. See H. M. Orlinsky, *Notes on the New Translation of the Torah* (Philadelphia: Jewish Publication Society, 1969), at Exod. 15:16.

66. This meaning of *k-n-h*, "to produce, create," is found in Gen. 4:1; 14:20, 26; Prov. 8:22. In Ugar. the goddess Ashirat bears the title *qnyt ilm*, "progenitress of the gods," and in an eighth-century B.C.E. Phoenician inscription from Karatepe (KAI 26.A.III.18 = ANET, p. 654) the god Il is called *qn 'rṣ*, "creator of the earth" (cf. also KAI 129.1. See M. Pope, *El in the Ugaritic Texts* (Leiden: Brill, 1955), 49–54; N. C. Habel, "Yahweh: Maker of Heaven and Earth," JBL 91 (1972): 321–337.

67. The Hebrew there is *ha-menuḥah . . . ha-naḥalah*; cf. 1 Kings 8:56, *menuḥah*. The Temple is termed *menuḥah* in Isa. 66:1; Ps. 132:13–14; cf. also 2 Sam. 7:6–11; 1 Kings 5:18–19; 8:16–21.

68. Ugar. Text *'Nt* 3:26–27; 4:63–64: *bqdš bġr nḥlty*, "in the sanctuary, in the mountain of my inheritance." On *sapon*, cf. Ps. 48:3; and see W. F. Albright, *Yahweh and the Gods of Canaan* (Garden City, N.Y.: Doubleday, 1968), 26 n. 59, 45; R. J. Clifford, *The Cosmic Mountain in Canaan and the Old Testament* (Cambridge: Harvard University Press, 1972), 137–139; F. M. Cross and D. N. Freedman, *Studies in Ancient Yahwistic Poetry*, JBL Dissertation Series 21 (Missoula, Mont.: Scholars Press, 1975), 62.

69. F. M. Cross and D. N. Freedman, "The Song of Miriam," JNES 14 (1955): 250. For the present phrase, cf. 1 Kings 8:13, 39, 43, 49; Ps. 33:14; cf. 89:15; 96:2; Isa. 4:5; Dan. 8:11.

70. So Goldin, *Song at the Sea*, p. 45 n. 48.

71. Cf. Exod. 25:8–9, 40; cf. R. Patai, *Man and Temple* (London: Thomas Nelson, 1947), 130–132.

72. See M. Z. Brettler, *God Is King: Understanding an Israelite Metaphor*, JSOTSup 76 (1989).

73. So Ibn Ezra, Baḥya. Rashi (cf. his comment on Git. 90a), Rashbam, and Ramban all connect the verse with the following. The Masoretic division would seem to favor the former.

74. Cf. Jer. 31:3.

75. Judg. 4:4; 2 Kings 22:14; Neh. 6:14. In Isa. 8:3, "the prophetess" is the wife of the prophet.

76. Meg. 14a–b.

77. Gen. 4:22; 28:9; 36:22.

78. See C. H. Gordon, "Fratriarchy in the Old Testament," JBL 54 (1935): 223–231.

79. See C. L. Meyers, "A Terracotta at the Harvard Semitic Museum and Disc-holding Female Figurines Reconsidered," IEJ 37 (1987): 116–122.

80. Pss. 78:11–42; 95:8–11; 106:13–32; Ezek. 20:10–26. G. W. Coats, *Rebellion in the Wilderness* (Nashville, Tenn.: Abingdon Press, 1968), 47–55; S. DeVries, "The Origin of the Murmuring Tradition," JBL 87 (1968): 51–58; B. S. Childs, *The Book of Exodus* (Philadelphia, Westminster, 1974), 254–270.

81. MdRY Beshallah Va-Yissaʿ 1, p. 152; for the verb, cf. Ps. 78:52f.

82. Gen. 16:7; 20:1; 25:18; 1 Sam. 15:7; 27:8.

83. ANET, p. 446.

84. ANET, p. 21.

85. J. Simons, *The Geographical and Topographical Texts of the Old Testament* (Leiden: Brill, 1959), sec. 254, p. 427.

86. For the stem *l-y-n/l-w-n*, "to grumble," cf. Exod. 16:2, 7,8; 17:3; Num. 14:2, 27, 29, 36; 16:11; 17:6, 20, 25; Josh. 9:18.

87. Cf. 2 Kings 2:19, 21. For Heb. *m-t-k* with water, cf. Prov. 9:17.

88. MdRY Beshallah, Va-Yissaʿ 1, p. 156.

89. Ibid., p. 156, Sanh. 56b, Targ. Jon., at Exod. 15:25.

90. Exod. 16:5, 22–30.

91. MdRY Beshallah, Va-Yissaʿ 1, p. 156.

92. Deut. 7:15; 28:27, 60; cf. Amos 4:10.

93. Cf. use of the stem *r-p-ʾ* for making water palatable in 2 Kings 2:21–22; Ezek. 47:8.

94. Simons, *Geographical and Topographical Texts*, sec. 428, pp. 252f.

Chapter 16

1. So Rashbam, Bekhor Shor.

2. Cf. Exod. 14:11–12; Num. 20:3–5.

3. The two objects of the people's craving are again paired in Exod. 16:8, 12 and in Ps. 78:20–29.

4. Exod. 10:24, 26; 12:28; 17:3; 24:3; 34:3.

5. Cf. Isa. 65:24.

6. On this subject, see M. Fishbane, *Biblical Interpretation in Ancient Israel* (Oxford: Clarendon Press, 1985), 326–329.

7. Cf. Deut. 10:12; 11:22; 13:5; 26:19; 28:9. See Sif. 49 to Deut. 1:22; cf. Shab. 133b.

8. Pss. 78:24, 25; 105:40; Neh. 9:15; cf. Wisd. of Sol. 16:20, "angel's food."

9. E.g., Exod. 5:13, 19; Lev. 23:37; 2 Kings 25:30.

10. Cf. the explanation of R. Simeon b. Yoḥai in Yoma 76a.

11. So Rashi.

12. So Rashbam, Ramban.

13. Cf. Gen. 43:16; Josh. 1:11; also Zeph. 1:7; Ps. 78:20; Prov. 6:7. For the syntax, cf. Gen. 47:24; Exod. 33:22; Num. 15:19; 1 Sam. 16:16, 23. For the NJPS rendering, see H. M. Orlinsky, *Notes on the New Translation of the Torah* (Philadelphia: Jewish Publication Society, 1969), 171, at Exod. 16:5.

14. MdRY Beshallah, Va-Yissaʿ 2, p. 162.

15. See L. H. Brockington, "The Presence of God: A Study on the Use of the Term 'Glory of Yahweh,'" Exp Tim 57 (1945): 21–25; B. Levine, *In the Presence of the Lord* (Leiden: Brill, 1974).

16. For the form *naḥnu*, cf. Gen. 42:11; Num. 32:32; Lam. 3:42.

17. Cf. Pss. 8:5; 144:3; Job 7:17.

18. MdRY Beshallah, Va-Yissaʿ 2, p. 162, and 3, p. 163, Yoma 75b.

19. Cf. Exod. 16:33; 27:21; Lev. 6:7; 9:5; 10:1; 16:1; Num. 16:7, 17.

20. On the quail, see J. Feliks, *Ha-Ḥai shel ha-Tanakh* (Tel Aviv: Sinai, 1954), 56; E. Orni and E. Ephrat, *Geography of Israel*, 3rd rev. ed. (Philadelphia: Jewish Publication Society, 1977), 182, 189f., Herodotus, Histories 2.77 mentions quail in his description of the diet of the Egyptians.

21. Cf. Wisd. of Sol. 16:20. Ps. 78:27–31 refer to the incident in Num. 11.

22. For this translation of Heb. *shikhvat ha-tal*, see H. M. Orlinsky, "The Hebrew Root *shakab*," JBL 63 (1944): 36–39.

23. Cf. Gen. 27:28, 39; Deut. 33:13, 28; Hag. 1:10; Zech. 8:12; Prov. 3:20; Dan. 4:12, 20, 30; 5:21.

24. F. S. Bodenheimer, "The Manna of Sinai," BA 10 (1947): 2–6; M. Bates, "Insects in the Diet," *American Scholar* 29 (1959–1960): 46–49; Orni and Ephrat, *Geography of Israel*, p. 186.

25. This rendering of the unique Heb. *meḥuspas* is based on an Arab. cognate, cited by S. R. Driver, *The Book of Exodus* (Cambridge: Cambridge University Press, 1918), at Exod. 16:14.

26. Cf. Ugar. *mn*, Old Canaanite (El Amarna) *mannu*, biblical Aram. *man*, Syr. *manà* for "what."

27. Lev. 23:10, 15; Deut. 24:19; Job 24:10; Ruth 2:7, 15.

28. Ber. 39b; Shab. 117b.

29. Lev. 23:24, 39.

30. Exod. 31:15; 35:2; Lev. 23:3; 16:31; 23:32.

31. Lev. 23:25,36. See J. Milgrom, *Studies in Levitical Terminology*, vol. 2 (Berkeley: University of California Press, 1970), 80–81 n. 297.

32. So Exod. 20:9–11; 23:12; 31:15,17; 34:21; 35:2; Lev. 23:3; Deut. 5:13; cf. also Deut. 16:8; Exod. 24:16; Josh. 6:3–4,14–15. For the syntax *ba-yom . . . bo*, Ibn Ezra compares Gen. 2:17 *mʾets . . . mimennu*.

33. It is hardly likely that the case of the lone wood gatherer of Num. 15:32–36 would have prompted the prophet's tirade.

34. For the reproachful *ʿad ʾanah*, cf. Num. 4:11; Josh. 18:3; Jer. 47:6; Hab. 1:2; Pss. 13:1–2; 6:4; Job 18:2; 19:2.

35. Shab. 10b, Bets. 16a.

36. MdRY Beshallah, Va-Yissaʿ 5, p. 170, Targ. Jon., at Exod 16:29, Mish Er. 5:5, 7. On the interpretation of Jewish sectarians, see L. H. Schiffman, *The Halakhah at Qumran* (Leiden: Brill, 1975), 90–98.

37. See *Entsyklopaedia Talmudit*, s.v. *ein mukdam u-meʾuḥar*. For the second formulation, see Mid. Shoḥer Tov to Ps. 3:2.

38. Josephus, Ant. 3.1, 6 (Loeb 3.28, p. 333).

39. CAD, s.v. *budulḥu*.

40. A similar-sounding *tsapaḥat*, "jar, jug," appears in 1 Sam. 26:11–12,16; 1 Kings 17:12,14,16; 19:6, but no satisfactory connection with *tsapiḥit* has been established. LXX here renders by a term meaning "a cake made with oil and honey." Aq. has "a cake from finest meal," and Targ. Jon. has "a cake baked over a brazier." The stem *ts-p-ḥ* in the Arab. and Ethiopic cognates means "to spread out, extend," but its relevance here is unclear. In Mish. Makhsh. 5:9 *tsapaḥat* occurs in connection with honey, but its meaning is uncertain; see Rashi to Nazir 50a and Maimonides to Mish. Makhsh. 5:9.

41. Cf. Exod. 28:1; 29:30.

42. MdRY Beshallah, Va-Yissaʿ 5, p. 171.

43. Exod. 40:1.

44. Cf. Exod. 25:22.

45. So Exod. 29:40; Lev. 5:11; 14:2; Num. 15:4.

Chapter 17

1. Num. 20:24; Deut. 32:51; Ezek. 47:19; 48:28; Ps. 106:32.

2. Exod. 15:24; 16:2, 8, 9, 11.

3. Exod. 3:1; 1 Kings 19:8.

4. Deut. 8:15; Isa. 48:21; Ps. 78:15, 16, 20; cf. 114:8.

5. Exod. 15:22–25.

6. Gen. 36:9, 12, 16, 20–22.

7. Gen. 14:6; Deut. 2:12, 22.

8. Cf. Num. 24:20.

9. Exod. 33:11; Num. 13:8; 1 Chron. 7:26–27; cf. Num. 1:10; 2:18.

10. Exod. 24:13; 33:11; Num. 11:28; 13:16; 27:15–23.

11. Josephus, Ant. 3.2, 4 (Loeb, p. 235).

12. Exod. 31:12.

13. Num. 27:18; Deut. 34:9.

14. Mish. RH 3:8; cf. MdRY Beshallaḥ 1, Amalek, pp. 179f.

15. Otherwise, Isa. 14:2; Job 14:10; Joel 4:10.

16. The Gk. to 1 Kings 8:13(53) mentions a "Book of the Song," which probably represents a corruption of Heb. *yashar* to *shir*.

17. For this formula, cf. Gen. 26:22; 29:32; Exod. 2:10.

18. The widely accepted scholarly emendation of *kes* to *nes*, "standard," while making good sense, is unsatisfactory in light of the unanimous traditions of the ancient versions that presuppose *kaf* as the initial consonant. Sam. and Syr. read *kisse'*, Vulg. has *solium*, "throne"; and LXX *kruphaia*, "secret," must be based on understanding a Heb. stem *k-s-h*, "to cover up."

19. UT 51.iii 7, 68:10, 1 Aqht 154, 161–162, 168.

20. Judg. 3:12–13; 6:3–6; 7:12; 10:12.

21. 1 Sam. 14:48; 15.

22. 1 Sam. 27:8; 30:18; 2 Sam. 1:1.

23. Esther 3:1; cf. 1 Sam. 15:8.

24. Josephus, Ant. 11.6,5 (Loeb, p. 415).

Chapter 18

W. F. Albright, "Jethro, Hobab and Reuel in Early Hebrew Tradition," CBQ 25 (1963): 1–11; F. C. Fensham, "Did a Treaty Between the Israelites and the Kenites Exist?" BASOR 175 (1964): 51–54; A. Cody, "Exodus 18, 12: Jethro Accepts a Covenant with the Israelites," Bib 175 (1968): 153–156.

1. Cf. Deut. 22:19, 29; 24:1, 3, 4; Isa. 50:1; Jer. 3:1, 8; cf. Mal. 2:16.

2. Gen. 15:2; 1 Chron. 7:8; 15:24; 27:16; 2 Chron. 20:37; Ezra 8:16; 10:18, 23, 31.

3. Cf. Gen. 48:1.

4. Cf. Gen. 48:1–2.

5. So Abimelech with Isaac, Gen. 26:28–29; Rahab with the spies, Josh. 2:9, 11; the Gibeonites with Joshua, Josh. 9:9; King Hiram of Tyre with Solomon, 1 Kings 5:2; 2 Chron. 2:11; and the pagan sailors to Jonah, Jonah 1:16.

6. Exod. 10:28.

7. Cf. Gen. 22:12; Judg. 17:13; 1 Kings 17:24; Ps. 20:7.

8. Cf. Exod. 15:11; Josh. 2:11; 9:9–10; 2 Kings 5:15.

9. So Mekh. Yitro 1, p. 195, Sot. 11a, Targums, Saadia, Lek. Tov, Rashi, Bekhor Shor.

10. Cf. also Josh. 8:30–35; 2 Sam. 3:20–21; Ps. 50:5.

11. Throughout the Bible the order is *'olah* followed by *zevaḥ*; that is, the offering to God precedes that of which the worshiper partakes. The sole exception is 2 Kings 10:24, where, significantly, the reference is to Baal worship.

12. That judges customarily sat while the court was in session is clear from Judg. 4:5; 1 Kings 7:7; Isa. 28:6; Pss. 9:5, 8; 122:5; Prov. 20:8; cf. Ruth 4:2. The references to the divine Judge obviously reflect routine Israelite practice.

13. Cf. Gen. 25:22; 1 Sam. 9:9; 2 Kings 22:18; Jer. 37:7.

14. Cf. Deut. 17:8–9; Isa. 16:5; Ezra 10:16.

15. Cf. below vv. 16, 19; Deut. 1:17; cf. Exod. 21:6; 22:7–8; 2 Chron. 19:6.

16. Cf. Deut. 1:9, 12.

17. Exod. 6:26; 7:4; 12:17, 41, 51; Num. 1:3, 52; 2 passim; 10:13–28; 31:14, 48, 52, 54; 33:1.

18. Cf. 1 Sam. 22:7–8; 2 Sam. 18:1, 4; 2 Chron. 1:2.

19. Cf. 1 Sam. 8:11–12; 29:2.

20. See ANET, p. 568; cf. 1 Kings 21:11; Isa. 32:1; Jer. 26:10–16.

21. So Joshua 7:19–25; 1 Sam. 7:15–17; 8:15; Ps. 72:1–2; cf. 2 Sam. 12:6; 14:4–11; 15:1–6; 1 Kings 3:9–10, 16–28; 7:7; 2 Kings 8:3, 5–6.

Chapter 19

1. Cf. Num. 29:6; 1 Sam. 20 passim; 2 Kings 4:23; Isa. 1:13. This was noted in MdRY, Yitro 1, p. 204, and Shab. 86b.

2. Deut. 32:11; Jer. 48:40; 49:22; Ezek. 17:3, 17.

3. Deut. 32:10–11.

4. Jer. 49:16; Obad. 4; Job 39:27.

5. 2 Sam. 1:23; Jer. 4:13; Lam. 4:19.

6. Deut. 28:49; Isa. 40:31.

7. Cf. Mal. 3:17; Ps. 135:4. On *segullah*, see M. Greenberg, "Hebrew *segullah*: Akkadian *sikiltu*," JAOS 71 (1951): 172–174; M. Held, "A Faithful Lover in an Old Babylonian Dialogue," JCS 15 (1961): 11–12; W. L. Moran, "A Kingdom of Priests" in *The Bible in Current Catholic Thought*, ed. J. McKenzie (New York: Herder & Herder, 1962), 7–20; B. Uffenheimer, *Ancient Prophecy in Israel* (Hebrew) (Jerusalem: Magnes Press, 1973), 86–87; S. E. Loewenstamm, "*'Am segullah*," in *Hebrew Language Studies Presented to Professor Zeev Ben-Hayyim*, ed. M. Bar Asher et al. (Jerusalem: Magnes Press, 1983), 321–328.

8. Cf. BK 87b, BB 52a.

9. Cf. Lev. 11:44–45; 20:7, 26; 21:6; Deut. 6:6; 14:2, 21; 26:19; 28:9.

10. Cf. Exod. 29:1, 4–5; Lev. 8:6; 11:25, 28, 40; 15:5–13; Num. 8:21; 19:21; 31:24.

11. Targ. Jon. to Exod. 19:16, Shab. 86b; Pes. 68b; Yoma 4b; Ta'an. 28b; cf. Tosef. Ar. 1:9.

12. Cf. Gen. 11:5; 18:21; Exod. 3:8; 34:5; Num. 11:17, 25; 12:5; 2 Sam. 22:10 = Ps. 18:10; Isa. 31:4; 63:19; 64:2; Ps. 144:5; Neh. 9:13.

13. Ramban, commentary to Exod. 25:1; introduction to Numbers.

14. Exod. 26:33.

15. Ibid.

16. Exod. 27:9–19; 38:9–20.

17. Exod. 19:22, 24; 24:2, 12–13, 15; cf. 34:2–3.

18. Exod. 19:22; 24:1, 14; cf. Num. 18:1–7.

19. Exod. 27:1–8; 38:1–7; 40:6, 29; cf. 19:12–13, 17, 21; 24:2, 4–5; Deut. 4:11.

20. Exod. 19:12, 21, 23–24; cf. 29:33, 37; 30:29, 33; Lev. 22:10–12; Num. 1:51; 3:10, 38; 4:15, 18–20; 17:5; 18:3, 4, 7.

21. Exod. 19:11, 20; 34:5; cf. Num. 11:17, 25.

22. Exod. 19:3, 20; cf. 25:22; 29:42–43; 30:6; Num. 7:89; 11:17; 17:19.

23. Exod. 19:9, 16, 18; 20:15, 18; 24:15–18; Deut. 4:11; cf. Exod. 40:34–38; Num. 9:15–22.

24. Deut. 33:2–3; Judg. 5:4–5; Isa. 6:3, 4; 29:6–7; 30:30; 42:13, 15; 63:19–64:2; Jer. 10:10, 13; Joel 4:15–16; Mic. 1:3–4; Nah. 1:3–5; Hab. 3:3–4, 6; Zech. 9:14; Pss. 18:8–16; 29; 50:1, 3; 77:17, 19; 97:2–5.

25. Cf. Exod. 13:1–2, 13; 34:20.

26. Cf. 1 Chron. 13:11; 15:13; Ps. 60:3.

Chapter 20

B. Jacob, "The Decalogue," JQR 14 (1923): 141–187; H. H. Rowley, "Moses and the Decalogue," BJRL 34 (1951–1952): 81–118 = *Men of God* (London: Thomas Nelson, 1963), 1–36; D. J. McCarthy, *Treaty and Covenant: A Study in Form in the Ancient Oriental Documents and in the Old Testament* (Rome: Pontifical Biblical Institute, 1963); A. S. Kapelrud, "Some Recent Points of View on the Time and Origin of the Decalogue," ST 18 (1964): 81–90; U. Cassuto, *A Commentary on the Book of Exodus*, trans. I. Abrahams (Jerusalem: Magnes Press, 1967), 235–253; J. J. Stamm and M. E. Andrew, *The Ten Commandments in Recent Research*, SBT 2nd ser. (London: SCM Press, 1967); E. Nielson, *The Ten Commandments in New Perspective*, SBT 2nd ser. (London: SCM Press, 1968); D. R. Hillers, *Covenant: The History of a Biblical*

Idea (Baltimore, Md.: Johns Hopkins University Press, 1969); K. Baltzer, *The Covenant Formulary*, trans. D. E. Green (Philadelphia: Fortress Press, 1971); B. S. Childs, *The Book of Exodus* (Philadelphia: Westminster, 1974), 370–375, 384–439; Ben-Zion Segal, ed., *The Ten Commandments As Reflected in Tradition and Literature Throughout the Ages* (Hebrew) (Jerusalem: Magnes Press, 1985).

1. The modern Heb. singular form *dibbrah* is an erroneous back-formation from *dibberot*. For the feminine plural form of masculine nouns of this type, cf. *kisse'ot* (Ps. 132:5) from *kisse'*, *makkelot* (Zech. 11:7) from *makkel*.

2. Exod. 24:12; 31:18; 32:15; 34:1, 4; Deut. 4:13; 9:10, 11, 15; 10:1–5; 1 Kings 8:9 = 2 Chron. 5:10; cf. Exod. 32:19; 34:28.

3. Deut. 10:5; 31:9, 24–26; 1 Kings 8:9 = 2 Chron. 5:10.

4. ANET, p. 204.

5. ANET, p. 199.

6. MdRY Yitro, ed. Horovitz-Rabin, pp. 233–234; so TJ Shek. 6:1 (49d), Exod. R. 47:6.

7. TJ Shek. 6:1 (49d); TJ Sot. 8:3 (22d).

8. Josephus, Ant. 3.5, 5 (Loeb, p. 361).

9. Ber. 11b; TJ Ber. 1:5 (3c). On this subject, see J. Mann, "Changes in the Divine Service of the Synagogue due to Religious Persecutions," HUCA 4 (1927): 287–294; G. Vermes, "The Decalogue and the Minim," *In Memoriam Paul Kahle*, ed. M. Black and G. Fohrer (Berlin: A. Töpelmann, 1968); Y. Yadin, *Tefillin from Qumran (X Q Phyl 1–4)* (Jerusalem: Israel Exploration Society, 1969); E. E. Urbach, "The Place of the Ten Commandments in Ritual and Prayer," in B. Z. Segal, *Ten Commandments*, pp. 127–145.

10. Mak. 24a; Hor. 8a.

11. The sources are given in Ginzberg, *Legends of the Jews*, vol. 6 (1946), 30–31 n. 181; see also vol. 3, pp. 80–82.

12. Shab. 88b.

13. MdRY Yitro 8, p. 233. On this commandment, see J. Guttman, "The 'Second Commandment' and the Image in Judaism," HUCA 32 (1961): 161–174.

14. Cf. Deut. 24:2, 4; Judg. 14:20; 2 Sam. 12:10; Hos. 3:3; Ruth 1:13.

15. Gen. 17:7; Exod. 6:7; 19:4–6; Lev. 11:45; 22:33; 25:38; 26:12, 45; Num. 15:41; Deut. 26:17–18; 29:12; Jer. 7:23; 11:4; 24:7; 30:22, 25 (31:1); 31:32(33); 32:38; Ezek. 11:20; 14:11; 36:28; 37:23, 27; Hos. 1:9; Zech. 8:8.

16. Cf. Song 8:6.

17. Cf. Num. 25:11, 13; 1 Kings 19:10, 14; 2 Kings 10:16; Joel 2:18; Zech. 1:14; 8:2.

18. Cf. Gen. 37:11; Deut. 29:19; 32:16; Ps. 119:139; Job 5:2.

19. Cf. Gen. 26:14; 30:1; Ps. 37:1; Prov. 3:31.

20. Exod. 20:5; 34:14; Deut. 4:24; 5:9; 6:15. In Josh. 24:19 and Nah. 1:2 the form is *kanno'*.

21. Cf. Prov. 6:34.

22. Cf. Exod. 34:7; Num. 14:18; Jer. 32:18.

23. Jer. 31:29–30.

24. Ezek. 18:1–4, 20.

25. See 2 Kings 14:6.

26. Cf. Gen. 50:23; 2 Kings 10:30; Job 42:16.

27. ANET, pp. 561, 661.

28. Ber. 7a, Sanh. 27b, MdRY, at Exod. 20:5.

29. MdRY, at Exod. 20:6.

30. Cf. Pss. 16:4; 50:16; so Sfire Inscription III:14–16.

31. Cf. Exod. 23:1; Ezek. 13:6–9; Pss. 24:4; 144:8, 11; Job 3:5; and cf. the variant *sheker* in Deut. 5:17 for *shav'* in Exod. 20:13.

32. Cf. 1 Sam. 25:21; Jer. 2:30; 4:30; 6:29; 46:11; Ps. 127:1.

33. Cf. Lev. 19:12.

34. Deut. 6:13; Jer. 4:2; 12:16; Ps. 63:12.

35. On the Sabbath, see N. A. Barack, *A History of the Sabbath* (New York: Jonathan David, 1965); N. E. Andreason, *The Old Testament Sabbath: A Tradition-Historical Approach* (Missoula, Mont.: Scholars Press, 1972); M. Tsevat, "The Basic Meaning of the Sabbath," ZAW 84 (1972): 447–459; A. Toeg,

"Genesis I and the Sabbath" (Hebrew), *Beth Mikra* 50 (1972): 288–296; W. M. Weinfeld, "Sabbath, Temple Building, and the Enthronement of God" (Hebrew), *Beth Mikra* 69 (1977): 188–193; W. Hallo, "New Moons and Sabbaths," HUCA 48 (1977): 1–18; J. Tigay, "Notes on the Development of the Jewish Week," *Eretz-Israel* 14 (1978): 111*–121*.

36. Exod. 16:29.

37. Exod. 34:21.

38. Exod. 35:3.

39. Num. 15:32–36.

40. Isa. 58:13; Amos 8:5; Neh. 10:32; 13:15–18.

41. Jer. 17:21, 24, 27.

42. Neh. 13:15.

43. Exod. 35:2–36:7; cf. 31:1–17; Lev. 19:30; 26:2. See Shab. 49b.

44. BK 2a.

45. Yoma 85a–b.

46. Exod. 22:20; 23:9; Lev. 19:10, 33–34; 23:22; Deut. 10:18–19; 14:29; 16:11, 14; 24:14, 17, 19, 20–22; 26:12–13; 27:19.

47. Cf. Exod. 4:22f.; Jer. 31:20; Hos. 11:1; Mal. 1:6.

48. Cf. Exod. 21:17; Lev. 20:9; Deut. 21:18–21; 27:16 with Lev. 24:10–16, 23; Num. 15:30; 1 Kings 21:10, 13–14.

49. Ezek. 22:7.

50. MdRY Yitro 8, p. 232; cf. Exod. 21:15,17; Lev. 19:3; 20:9; Deut. 21:18–21; 27:16.

51. Cf. Mal. 2:14–16; 3:5; Prov. 2:17.

52. Lev. 20:10; Deut. 22:22; cf. Jer. 29:21–23; Ezek. 16:38. On adultery as the "great sin," see J. J. Rabinowitz, "'The Great Sin' in Ancient Egyptian Marriage Contracts," JNES 18 (1959): 73; W. L. Moran, "The Scandal of the 'Great Sin' at Ugarit," JNES 18 (1959): 280–281.

53. MdRY Yitro 8, p. 232, Sanh. 86a. See B. S. Jackson, *Theft in Early Jewish Law* (New York: Oxford University Press, 1972).

54. Cf. Exod. 21:16; Deut. 24:7.

55. Num. 35:30; Deut. 17:6; 19:15, cf. 1 Kings 21:10; Isa. 8:2.

56. Deut. 13:10; 17:7; 19:16–20.

57. Deut. 6:5; Lev. 19:18; Deut. 10:19; 23:8; Lev. 19:7. B. Jackson, "Liability for Mere Intention in Early Jewish Law," HUCA 42 (1971): 197–225.

58. Cf. Gen. 7:1; 12:17; 18:19; Exod. 2:1; Num. 16:32; Deut. 6:22; 1 Sam. 27:3; 2 Sam. 2:3.

59. Cf. Gen. 32:31; Exod. 33:20; Judg. 6:22–23; 13:22.

60. Cf. Deut. 4:11; 5:19; 2 Sam. 22:10 = Ps. 18:10; 1 Kings 8:12 = 2 Chron. 6:1; Ps. 97:2; Job 22:13; cf. Exod. 40:34–38.

61. Deut. 12:5, 11, 13–14, 17–18, 26; 14:23, 25; 15:20; 16:2, 6, 7, 11, 15, 16; 17:8, 10; 18:6; 26:2; 31:11. Cf. 2 Kings 22:8–23:25.

62. Gen. 8:20.

63. Gen. 12:7, 8; 13:18; 22:9; 26:25; cf. 46:1; 31:46–54; 33:20; 35:1–7.

64. Judg. 6:20–21, 24, 26–28.

65. Judg. 13:19–20.

66. 1 Sam. 6:14–15.

67. Cf. Gen. 28:11; 1 Sam. 7:16; Isa. 26:21; 66:1; Mic. 1:2–3; Ps. 132:5; 1 Chron. 16:27 = Ps. 96:6, *mikdash*.

68. Cf. Isa. 43:26, *hazkireni*, "help me remember."

69. It cannot be denied that a reading *tazkir*, "you utter My name," in place of *'azkir* would be preferable. This is, in fact, the reading of the Pesh. and the Sam. Targ. The comments in Mish. Avot 3:6 = Ber. 6a and Mekh. Yitro 9, p. 243, and the saying of Hillel the Elder in Suk. 53a = R. Eliezer b. Jacob in Mekh. Yitro 9, p. 243—all in connection with this verse—make better sense if a reading *tazkir* is presupposed.

70. Josh. 8:30–31.

71. 1 Kings 6:7.

72. 1 Macc. 4:47.

73. Josephus, Wars 5.5,7 (Loeb, p. 269). Cf. Apion 1.22 (Loeb, p. 243).

74. See ANEP, nos. 597, 600, 603, 605, 619. See A. Sharma, *The Encyclopedia of Religion* (1987), II, s.v. Nudity.

75. Exod. 28:42.
76. Lev. 6:3.
77. Ezek. 43:17; 44:18; cf. Lev. 9:22.
78. Mish. Middot 3:3.

Chapter 21

D. Daube, *Studies in Biblical Law* (Cambridge: Cambridge University Press, 1947); J. A. Thompson, "The Book of the Covenant in the Light of Modern Archaeological Research," Australian Bible Review 2 (1952): 97–107; M. Greenberg, "Some Postulates of Biblical Criminal Law," in *Yehezkel Kaufmann Jubilee Volume*, ed. M. Haran (Jerusalem: Magnes Press, 1960); 5–28; M. Noth, *The Laws in the Pentateuch and Other Studies*, trans. D. R. Ap-Thomas (Edinburgh and London: Oliver & Boyd, 1966), 1–131; U. Cassuto, *A Commentary on the Book of Exodus* (Jerusalem: Magnes Press, 1967), 254–299; A. Alt, "The Origins of Israelite Law," in *Essays on Old Testament History and Religion*, trans. R. A. Wilson (Garden City, N.Y.: Doubleday, 1968), 101–171; S. Paul, *Studies in the Book of the Covenant in the Light of Cuneiform and Biblical Law* (Leiden: Brill, 1970); S. E. Loewenstamm, "Law," in *World History of the Jewish People*, vol. 3, ed. B. Mazar (New Brunswick: Rutgers University Press, 1971), 231–267; Z. Falk, *Hebrew Law in Biblical Times* (Jerusalem: Wahrman, 1964); B. S. Childs, *The Book of Exodus* (Philadelphia: Westminster, 1974), 440–496; B. Jackson, *Essays in Jewish and Comparative Legal History* (Leiden: Brill, 1975); S. Greengus, "Law in the Old Testament," IDBSup (Nashville, Tenn.: Abingdon, 1976), 532–537; H. J. Boecker, *Law and the Administration of Justice in the Old Testament* (Minneapolis, Minn.: Augsburg, 1980); D. Patrick, *Old Testament Law* (Atlanta: John Knox, 1985); R. Westbrook, "Biblical and Cuneiform Law Codes," RB 92 (1985): 247–264; J. H. Walton, *Ancient Israelite Literature in Its Cultural Setting* (Grand Rapids, Mich.: Zondervan, 1989), 69–94.

1. MdRY Mishpatim 1, p. 246; see Comment to Exod. 1:1.
2. Exod. 20:2, 8–11; Deut. 5:6, 12–15.
3. Lev. 25:39–42; Deut. 15:12; Jer. 34:9, 14, 17.
4. Exod. 20:10; 23:12; Deut. 5:14; 16:11–12, 14.
5. Gen. 17:13, 27; Exod. 12:44–45.
6. Exod. 21:20.
7. Exod. 21:26–27.
8. Deut. 23:16–17.
9. 2 Kings 4:1; Isa. 50:1; Amos 2:6–7; 8:6; Neh. 5:4–5; cf. Prov. 2:27. See B. Cohen, "Civil Bondage in Jewish and Roman Law," in *Louis Ginzberg Jubilee Volume* (New York: American Academy for Jewish Research, 1945), 113–132.
10. Hammurabi, par. 117 (ANET, pp. 170–171); Middle Assyrian Laws, par. A.48 (ANET, p. 184).
11. MdRY Mishpatim 1, p. 247; Targums, at Exod. 21:2; cf. Exod. 22:2.
12. Cf. Deut. 15:18; Isa. 16:14.
13. Targ. Jon. 21:7; 22:2; see also Bekhor Shor to 21:6 (*le-'olam*).
14. Cf. Gen. 17:12, 13, 23, 27; Lev. 22:11; Jer. 2:14; cf. Gen. 14:14; 15:3; Eccles. 2:7. Such a bondwoman is called *shifḥah valdanit* in TJ BK 5:6(5a).
15. Cf. Deut. 15:16–17.
16. MdRY Mishpatim 2, n. 252; so Targums. C. H. Gordon, "*Elohim* in Its Reputed Meaning of 'Rulers, Judges,'" JBL 54 (1935): 139–144; Z. W. Falk, "Exodus 22 6," VT 9 (1959): 86–88; F. C. Fensham, "New Light on Exodus 21:6 and 22:7 from the Laws of Eshnunna," JBL 78 (1959): 160–161.
17. ANET, p. 163, par. 37.
18. Cf. Lev. 14:17.
19. Tosef. BK 7:5; cf. MdRY Mishpatim 2, p. 253; TJ Kid. 1:2(59d).

20. MdRY Mishpatim 2, p. 254; Kid. 15b; Targ. Jon., at 21:6. With *le'olam* here, cf. *'eved 'olam* in Deut. 15:17; 1 Sam. 27:12; Job 40:27; cf. *'aḥuzat 'olam* in Lev. 25:46; the phrase *'bd 'lm* in Ugar. KRT 55, 127, 139, 252, 271, 284.
21. MdRY Mishpatim 3, pp. 254–255; Maimonides Mishneh Torah, Hilkhot 'Avadim 4.2,8. With this law, cf. Deut. 21:10–14. See I. Mendelson, "The Conditional Sale into Slavery of Freeborn Daughters in Nuzi and the Law of Ex. 21:7–1," JAOS 55 (1935): 190–195.
22. Cf. Ps. 69:9; Job 19:15.
23. Gen. 25:8, 17; 35:29; 49:33; Num. 20:24; Deut. 32:50; cf. Judg. 2:10; cf. *'am* in such texts as 2 Kings 4:13; Job 18:19, and in such theophoric names as Ben Ammi, Ammiel, Ammihud, Amminadab, Ammishaddai, Eliam, Jereboam.
24. For the stem *b-g-d* as a breach of the marriage bond, cf. Jer. 3:7–8, 20; Mal. 2:14.
25. ANET, p. 160, par. 28; cf. Hammurabi, par. 148 (ANET, p. 172).
26. Cf. Mic. 3:2, 3; Ps. 78:20, 27.
27. Cf. Exod. 22:26; Deut. 22:12; Isa. 50:3; Job 24:7; 26:6; 31:19.
28. MdRY Mishpatim 2, p. 259. Ket. 47b–48a.
29. Cf. Jer. 9:10; 10:22; 49:33; 51:37; Ps. 26:8; 90:1. The verbal form may possibly be found in Isa. 13:22.
30. ANET, p. 413. S. Paul, "Exod. 21:10: A Threefold Maintenance Clause," JNES 28 (1969): 48–51.
31. MdRY Mishpatim 4, p. 261; Sanh. 84b.
32. Num. 35:6, 9–32; Deut. 4:41–43; 19:1–13; cf. Josh. 20:1–9. The institution may well be reflected in Pss. 27 and 61. See M. Greenberg, "The Biblical Conception of Asylum," JBL 78 (1959): 125–132.
33. For *ts-d-h*, cf. Num. 35:20; 1 Sam. 24:12(11). For the varied terminology expressing lack of intention, see Num. 35:11, 22, 23; Deut. 4:42; 19:4, 6; Josh. 20:3, 5.
34. So Gen. 12:6; 13:3; 22:3, 4, 9, 14; 28:11, 17; 32:3, 31; Deut. 12 passim; Josh. 5:9, 15; 1 Sam. 7:16. The term clearly has this meaning in Isa. 26:21; 66:1; Mic. 1:2–3; Ps. 132:5; 1 Chron. 16:27 = Ps. 96:6, "Temple."
35. MdRY Mishpatim 4, p. 263; Sanh. 35b.
36. Cf. Exod. 20:12; 21:17; Lev. 19:3; 20:9; Deut. 21:18–19; 27:16.
37. MdRY Mishpatim 5, p. 265; Sanh. 84b; Mish. Sanh. 11:1.
38. Cf. Deut. 27:16.
39. Gen. 27:12; Deut. 11:26–28; 23:6; 30:1, 19; Josh. 8:34; 24:9–10; Pss. 37:22; 62:5; 109:28; Prov. 30:11; Neh. 13:2.
40. Cf. 1 Sam. 17:43; 2 Kings 2:24; cf. MdRY Mishpatim 5, p. 268, Meg. 15a.
41. Cf. 1 Sam. 2:30; Isa. 8:23.
42. CAD, s.v. *kabātu*, and s.v. qatālu.
43. MdRY Mishpatim 6, p. 270.
44. Ibid. 7, pp. 271f, Targ. Jon.
45. Cf. 2 Sam. 7:14; Isa. 10:5, 24; Prov. 10:13; 13:24; 23:13–14; 26:3.
46. MdRY Mishpatim 7, p. 273.
47. Ibid.; Sanh. 52b.
48. ANET, p. 525, pars. 1–2.
49. ANET, p. 175, pars. 209–214.
50. ANET, pp. 181, 184–185, pars. 21, 50–51.
51. ANET, p. 190, pars. 17–18.
52. Cf. Exod. 2:13; Deut. 25:11; 2 Sam. 14:6.
53. Gen. 25:25; 38:28; cf. Num. 12:12; Job 1:21; 3:11; 38:8.
54. Gen. 42:4, 38; 44:29.
55. MdRY Mishpatim 8, pp. 275–276; so Targums.
56. So LXX. E. A. Speiser, "The Stem PLL in Hebrew," JBL 82 (1963): 301–306.
57. MdRY Mishpatim 8, p. 276.
58. Daube, *Studies in Biblical Law*, pp. 102–153; A. S. Diamond, "An Eye for an Eye," Iraq 19 (1957): 151–155; Cassuto, *Commentary on the Book of Exodus*, pp. 272–278; B. S. Jackson,

"The Problem of Exodus XXI:22–5 (*ius talionis*)," VT 23 (1973): 273–304; Childs, *The Book of Exodus*, pp. 420–474; Boecker, *Law and the Administration of Justice*, pp. 171–175; J. H. Hayes, "Restitution, Forgiveness and the Victim in Old Testament Law," TUSR 2 (1982): 8–13.

59. ANET, pp. 175–176, pars. 196–197, 200, 229–30.

60. ANET, p. 524, pars. 16–17.

61. ANET, p. 163, pars. 42–48.

62. ANET, p. 189, par. 7.

63. ANET, p. 184, par. 50.

64. MdRY Mishpatim 8, pp. 274–278, Mish. BK 8:1, BK 83b–84a.

65. BK 84a–b.

66. MdRY Mishpatim 9, p. 280.

67. Ibid., p. 279; Kid. 25a.

68. MdRY Mishpatim 10, p. 280; Mish. Sanh. 1:4; Tosef. Sanh. 6:18, p. 355. The Sam. Pentateuch here adds "or any animal." See A. van Selms, "The Goring Ox in Babylon and Biblical Law," *AfO* 18 (1969): 321–330; R. Yaron, "The Goring Ox in Near Eastern Laws," in *Jewish Law in Ancient and Modern Israel*, ed. H. H. Cohn (New York: Ktav, 1971): 50–60; J. J. Finkelstein, "The Goring Ox," TLQ, 46 (1973): 169–290.

69. ANET, p. 163, pars. 154–155.

70. ANET, p. 176, pars. 250–252.

71. Cf. Lev. 24:14–16.

72. MdRY Mishpatim 10, p. 284.

73. Ibid., p. 285, Targ. Jon.

74. BK 49b.

75. MdRY Mishpatim 11, p. 289.

76. Ibid. 12, p. 290.

77. Ibid., p. 291. B. S. Jackson, *Theft in Early Jewish Law* (New York: Oxford University Press, 1972).

78. Ibid.

79. ANET, p. 166, par. 8.

80. Ibid., n. 45.

81. ANET, p. 180, pars. 1–5.

Chapter 22

1. Mekh. Mishpatim 13, p. 293.

2. ANET, p. 162, pars. 12–13.

3. ANET, p. 167, pars. 21–22.

4. Cf. Gen. 4:4; Exod. 24:12.

5. So Isa. 3:14; cf. Deut. 13:6; 17:7; 26:13–14. F. C. Fensham, "The Root *b-ʿ-r* in Ugaritic and in Isaiah in the meaning 'to pillage,'" JNSL 9 (1981): 67–69.

6. Tosef. Ket. 12:2; cf. Git. 5:1(46c), BK 6b.

7. Mish. BM 3:1,10,12, Targ. Jon.

8. ANET, p. 163, pars. 36–47.

9. ANET, p. 171, pars. 120,122–136.

10. Cf. Lev. 9:5; Num. 9:6; 15:33; 27:1; 36:1; Deut. 1:17; Josh. 7:14; 17:4; Isa. 41:1,21; 58:2; Mal. 3:5. Y. Hoffman, "The Root QRB as a Legal Term," JNSL 10 (1983): 67–73.

11. Cf. Gen. 33:14; 1 Sam. 15:9; Prov. 24:27; 2 Chron. 17:13.

12. Cf. Exod. 18:16,22,26; 24:14; Deut. 1:17; 15:2; 17:8, 9; 19:4, 15.

13. Cf. 1 Kings 12:19; 2 Kings 1:1; 3:5; 8:20, 22.

14. Cf. Hos. 8:1; Jer. 3:13; 33:8.

15. ANET, p. 177, pars. 266–267.

16. For *sh-v-ḥ* with cattle, cf. Num. 31:26; Amos 4:10; 1 Chron. 5:21; 2 Chron. 4:14.

17. The LXX here reads "God" as in 21:6; 22:7, 8. However, the phrase *shevuʿat YHVH* appears in 2 Sam. 21:7, which refers back to 1 Sam. 20:42, and in 1 Kings 2:43 referring to v. 42; both references prove that an oath by or in the name of YHVH is intended.

18. For the idiom, cf. Gen. 26:28; 2 Sam. 21:7; cf. 1 Sam. 20:42.

19. So BK 106a, Targums, Rashbam, Ibn Ezra. For *l-k-ḥ* in the sense of "accept," cf. Jer. 2:30; Ps. 6:10.

20. Cf. Gen. 31:39.

21. So LXX and the Aram. underlying the conflated Targ. Jon.; so R. Johanan in MdRY Mishpatim 16, p. 303; cf. Vulg. (v. 13).

22. ANET, p. 161, pars. 34–37.

23. ANET, p. 176, pars. 244–249.

24. Pesh. and a recension of the LXX add "an animal"; Targ. Jon. adds "anything," and Vulg., "anything of these."

25. Cf. Mish. BM 8:1.

26. Cf. Lev. 19:13; Job 7:1–2; 14:6.

27. The preposition *bet* meaning "from," as in Ugar., Old South Arab., Phoen. inscriptions, and several biblical texts. See N. M. Sarna, "The Interchange of the Prepositions *beth* and *min* in Biblical Hebrew," JBL 78 (1959): 310–316.

28. BK 45b, BM 93a.

29. Cf. Deut. 22:13–19; Lev. 21:13–15; Ezek. 44:22.

30. 1 Sam. 17:25; 18:20–27; 2 Sam. 3:14.

31. Josh. 15:16–17; Judg. 1:12–13.

32. Gen. 29:15–20, 27–28.

33. A. Cowley, *Aramaic Papyri of the Fifth Century B.C.* (Oxford: Clarendon Press, 1923), 15:4–5, 27; BAP 7:4, 15, 25.

34. So Rashi.

35. So Ramban.

36. Cf. Ps. 21:3; so Ugar. *ʾrs*, Akk. *erēšu*, "to request"; cf. for the phrase, cf. 2 Chron 11:23; cf. CAD, s.v.: *ērišu*, "a bridegroom." See D. Halivni Weiss, "A Note on *ʾasher lo' ʾorosoh*," JBL 81 (1962): 67–69.

37. Cf. Deut. 20:7; 22:23–27; 2 Sam. 3–14.

38. MdRY Mishpatim 17, p. 309; Ket. 10a, 38b.

39. Deut. 18:9–14; 13:13–15; 17:2–4; Lev. 18:22–23.

40. Lev. 19:26, 31; 20:6, 27; Deut. 18:9–14; 1 Sam. 28:3, 7–19, 21; 2 Kings 9:22; 21:6; 23:24; Isa. 3:2–3; 44:25; 47:9–13; Jer. 10:2–3; 27:9; Ezek. 13:3, 6, 7, 9, 17–23; Mic. 5:11; Nah. 3:4; Mal. 3:5; 2 Chron. 33:6.

41. Cf. Deut. 13:9; 20:16.

42. Cf. 1 Sam. 28:7ff.; Ezek. 13:8ff.

43. ANET, pp. 196f., pars. 187f., 199.

44. Cf. Ps. 86:8, *ba-ʾelohim*.

45. Cf. Deut. 13:16–18; Josh. 7:24–25.

46. Exod. 23:9; Lev. 19:33–34; Deut. 10:18–19; 24:14, 17–18; 27:19; Jer. 7:6; 22:3; Zech. 7:9–10. The prophets repeatedly inveighed against their violation: Isa. 1:17, 23; 3:14–15; 10:2; Jer. 5:28; Ezek. 16:49; 18:17; 22:7, 29; Amos 8:4; Mal. 3:5; cf. Pss. 82:3; 94:6.

47. Cf. Deut. 10:18; 2 Sam. 22:28 = Ps. 18:28; Isa. 66:2; Pss. 12:6; 34:7; 35:10; 68:6; 72:2–4, 12–13; 140:13; 146:9.

48. Lev. 19:33–34; Deut. 10:19.

49. Deut. 10:18.

50. Exod. 20:10 = Deut. 5:14; Exod. 23:12; Lev. 19:9–10; 23:22; Num. 35:15; Deut. 14:28–29; 24:19–22; 26:12–13.

51. MdRY Mishpatim 18, p. 311; so Targ. Jon.

52. Cf. Lev. 19:33; 25:14, 17; Deut. 23:17; Jer. 22:3; Ezek. 18:7, 12, 16; 22:7, 29; 45:8; 46:18.

53. MdRY Mishpatim 18, p. 313.

54. In each case the emphatic infinitive absolute appears before the finite verb in a kind of syntactical and exegetical symmetry.

55. 1 Sam. 22:2; 2 Kings 4:1; Isa. 50:2; Jer. 15:10; Ezek. 18:8, 13, 17; 22:12; Amos 2:8; Ps. 109:11; Prov. 28:8; Neh. 5:1–13. See E. Neufeld, "The Prohibition against Loans at Interest in Ancient Hebrew Laws," HUCA 26 (1955): 355–412.

56. MdRY Mishpatim 19, p. 315.

57. So ibid., Rashi, Rashbam.

58. So Deut. 23:20; Ps. 15:15.

59. Lev. 25:36–37; Ezek. 18:8, 13, 17; 22:12.

60. KAI I:36, no. 200.

61. Deut. 24:6, 10–13, 17.

62. Exod. 34:6; Joel 2:13; Jon. 4:2; Pss. 86:15; 103:8; 111:4; 116:5; 145:8; Neh. 9:17, 31; 2 Chron. 30:19.

63. MdRY Mishpatim 19, p. 317, Sanh. 66a.

64. Cf. the same title for the nomadic Ishmaelite and Midianite chiefs in Gen. 17:20; 25:16; Num. 25:14.

65. See Comment to 13:2, 12.

66. MdRY Mishpatim 19, pp. 318f.; cf. Tem. 4a.

67. So Saadia, Ibn Janaḥ, Ibn Ezra, Rashbam, Bekhor Shor, Ramban.

68. MdRY Mishpatim 19, p. 318; cf. Tem. 4a.

69. Mish. Ter. 9:4, Mish. Ḥag. 3:4.

70. See J. Greenfield, "The Small Caves of Qumran," JAOS 89 (1969): 139.

71. Gen. 17:12; Lev. 12:3.

72. *Terefah* is usually paired with *nevelah*, which is an animal that died other than by the prescribed mode of slaughtering; cf. Lev. 7:24; 17:15; 22:8; Ezek. 4:14; 44:31. For the separate prohibition of *nevelah*, see Deut. 14:21.

Chapter 23

1. MdRY Mishpatim 20, p. 321.

2. The present rendering treats the first clause as the counterpart of v. 3 and the second clause as an explanatory expansion of the first. For *rav* as "mighty," cf. Gen. 7:11; Num. 24:7; Ps. 48:3; Job 35:9; 2 Chron. 14:10.

3. Mish. Sanh. 1:6, 4:1, MdRY Mishpatim 20, p. 323.

4. So Shadal.

5. MdRY Mishpatim 20, p. 324.

6. Cf. Deut. 22:4; B.M. 31a–33a. For a different interpretation, see A. Cooper, "The Plain Sense of Exodus 23:5," HUCA 59 (1988): 1–22.

7. Cf. the educated guesses of Rashi, Rashbam, Bekhor Shor (ii), Ibn Ezra (ii), Abravanel; but see Cooper, "Plain Sense of Exodus 23:5."

8. MdRY Mishpatim 20, p. 328, Sanh. 33b.

9. 1 Sam. 8:3; Isa. 1:23; 5:23; 33:15; Ezek. 22:12; Amos 5:12; Mic. 7:3; cf. Pss. 15:5; 26:10.

10. Deut. 10:17; 2 Chron. 19:7.

11. Deut. 27:25.

12. Ket. 105b.

13. Cf. Deut. 1:16; 24:17; 27:19; Mal. 3:5.

14. So Ibn Ezra.

15. Cf. Exod. 34:21; Deut. 5:13–14.

16. The common Heb. verb *sh-m-r*, "be on guard," here takes the preposition *bet*, which lends added force: "guard punctiliously"; cf. 2 Sam. 18:12; 20:10; Jer. 17:21; Mal. 2:15–16.

17. Cf. Ezek. 45:21–25. See B. R. Goldstein and A. Cooper, "The Festivals of Israel and Judah and the Literary History of the Pentateuch," JAOS 110 (1990): 19–31.

18. Cf. Exod. 23:14–15; Lev. 23:42–43; Deut. 16:9–12.

19. Cf. Exod. 12:34, 39; Deut. 16:3.

20. There are reasons to believe that the present Nifal vocalization of the verb *r-'-h* in this context is due to the desire of the scribes to avoid the appearance of anthropomorphism: (1) the consistent use of the syncopated infinitive *lera'ot* for *lehera'ot* in this context in Exod. 34:24; Deut. 31:11; Isa. 1:12 in contrast to the secular full form in 2 Sam. 17:17; 1 Kings 18:2; Ezek. 21:29; (2) the unusual use of the accusative particle *'et* with the Nifal (Exod. 34:23; Deut. 16:16; 1 Sam. 1:22; Ps. 42:3); (3) the use of the same phrase with the Kal form of *r-'-h* for visiting or being admitted to a human presence (Gen. 33:10; 43:3,5; Exod. 10:28,29; 2 Sam. 3:13; 14:24; 28:32; 2 Kings 25:19; Esther 1:14); (4) the actual use of the Kal form in respect of "seeing God" in the Temple in Isa. 38:11; (5) the rabbinic use of *re'iyyah* (Mish Pe'ah 1:1, Mish Ḥag. 1:1) and *re'ayon* (Ḥag. 7a) for a pilgrimage to the Temple indicates an understanding of a Kal form in biblical texts; (6) the corresponding Akk. phrase

amāru panū, "to see personally, to visit" gods or kings, supports a Hebrew Kal form.

21. Cf. Exod. 34:20,23; Deut. 16:16.

22. Exod. 34:22; Deut. 16:10,16; 2 Chron. 8:13.

23. Num. 28:26.

24. Mish. RH 1:2, Song R. 7:4. The antiquity of the name *'atseret* for the festival is proven by Josephus' use of it in Ant. 3.252 (Loeb, p. 438), transliterated *'ασαρθὰ*.

25. Cf. Lev. 23:29; Deut. 16:13; KAI I.34, no. 182.

26. Lev. 23:34,42f.; Deut. 16:13–16; 31:10; Zech. 14:16,18,19; Ezra 3:4; 2 Chron. 8:13.

27. Gen. 33:17; Isa. 1:8; 4:6; Jon. 4:5; Job 27:18; cf. 1 Kings 20:12,16.

28. Lev. 23:43.

29. Lev. 23:34; Num. 29:12ff.; 1 Kings 8:2.

30. 1 Kings 8:3,65; 12:32; Ezek. 45:23,25; Neh. 8:14; 2 Chron. 5:3; 7:8-9.

31. So Exod. 25:12; 34:23; Deut. 16:16; 2 Chron. 8:13; cf. Isa. 26:6; Song 7:2.

32. The unusual Heb. form *zekhurkha* (also Exod. 34:23; Deut. 16:16; 20:13) has not been satisfactorily explained.

33. Cf. Exod. 21:5.

34. Cf. "Sovereign of all the earth" in Josh. 3:11,13; Zech. 4:14; 6:5; Ps. 97:5; "The Sovereign, the LORD of Hosts" in Isa. 1:24; 3:1; 10:16, 33; 19:4; cf. also Deut. 10:17; Pss. 114:7; 136:3.

35. Mish. Pes. 5:4, Tosef. Pes. 3:3, MdRY Mishpatim 20, p. 334.

36. Exod. 12:10; cf. Num. 9:12.

37. Exod. 23:16; 34:22; Lev. 23:17, 20; Num. 28:26.

38. For *re'shit* as "choice, best," cf. Num. 18:12; Deut. 33:21; 1 Sam. 15:21; Ezek. 44:30; Amos 6:6; Prov. 3:9, and probably also Ps. 110:10; Prov. 1:7; 4:7.

39. *Maḥberet Menaḥem*, ed. H. Filipowsky (London: Me'orerei Yeshenim, 1954), 53.

40. *Even Boḥan*, in W. Bacher, *'Otsar ha-Sifrut*, vol. 5 (Cracow: J. Fischer, 1896), 261–262.

41. Cf. Rashi on Deut. 14:22.

42. Maimonides, Guide 3.28.

43. MdRY Mishpatim 20, p. 335, Ḥul. 115b. M. Radin, "The Kid in Its Mother's Milk," AJSL 40 (1923-1924): 213–218; M. Haran, "Seething a Kid in Its Mother's Milk," JJS 30 (1979): 23–25; R. Rather and B. Zuckerman, "A Kid in Milk," HUCA 57 (1986): 15–60.

44. Rashbam, Ibn Ezra, Ramban.

45. Bekhor Shor, Ralbag, Shadal.

46. Sam., LXX, and Vulg. all read *mal'akhiy* as in v. 23.

47. Cf. Gen. 48:16; Exod. 14:19; 32:34; 33:2; Num. 20:16; Judg. 2:1; 2 Sam. 24:1; Isa. 63:9; Dan. 6:23.

48. Josh. 1:18 is not really an exception since Joshua issues commands in the name of God. The "wayward and defiant [*moreh*] son" of Deut. 21:18, 20 may well mean defiant of God.

49. Cf. 1 Kings 12:19; 2 Kings 1:1; 3:5, 7; 8:20, 22.

50. ANET, pp. 200–212.

51. TJ Av. Zar. 4:4 (44a) defines a *matsevah* as a monolith. *Matsevot* are also proscribed in Exod. 34:13; Lev. 26:1; Deut. 7:5; 12:3; 16:21–22; 2 Kings 34:4; Hos. 10:1–2; Mic. 5:12.

52. Cf. Prov. 10:27; Eccles. 7:17.

53. Cf. Exod. 15:16; Josh. 2:9.

54. Cf. Exod. 14:24; Deut. 2:15; 7:23; Josh. 10:10; Judg. 4:15.

55. LXX, Targums, Sot. 36a. See O. Borowski, "The Identity of the Biblical *ṣir'â*," in *The Word of the Lord Shall Go Forth*, ed. C. L. Mayers and M. O'Connor (Philadelphia: ASOR, 1983), 315–319.

56. So Ibn Ezra.

57. Josh. 13:13; 15:63; 16:10; 17:12–13, 16; Judg. 1:19, 21, 27–35; 2:20–23; 3:1–5.

58. David and Solomon asserted political and economic hegemony as far north as the Euphrates (1 Kings 5:1) but did not dispossess the local peoples and settle Israelites in their stead.

59. J. M. Weinstein, "The Egyptian Empire in Palestine: A Reassessment," BASOR 241 (1981): 1–28.

60. Exod. 34:12–16; Deut. 7:2–5; Josh. 23:12–13.

Chapter 24

U. Cassuto, *A Commentary on the Book of Exodus* (Jerusalem: Magnes Press, 1967): 310–316; B. S. Childs, *The Book of Exodus* (Philadelphia: Westminster, 1974), 497–509.

1. Exod. 19:6^2,7,8,9^2,19; 24:3^3,4,7,8,14.

2. Exod. 19:11, 14, 18, 20, 21, 24, 25.

3. Exod. 24:1, 2, 9, 12, 14, 15, 18.

4. Cf. Deut. 31:9–13, 24–26; 2 Kings 22–23; Neh. 8–10.

5. Exod. 20:19 (22); 21:1.

6. Cf. Shab. 88a.

7. Lev. 10:1–3.

8. Exod. 28:1; Lev. 10:12; Num. 3:2–4.

9. Cf. ANET, pp. 483–490; cf. Gen. 27:29; 33:3; 49:8.

10. Ugaritic texts 89.10; 95.5; 2115: rev. 7.

11. PRU 4, pp. 221, 226.

12. Cf. 1 Kings 18:31.

13. Cf. Josh. 4:3, 8–9, 20–24; 1 Kings 18:31; Isa. 19:19–20; cf. Josh. 22:26–29.

14. Ugaritic text 169.12.

15. So Zev. 115b, Targums, Rashi, Rashbam, Bekhor Shor, Ramban; cf. Exod. 13:2, 13, 15; 22:28; 34:20; Num. 3:12–13, 41, 45; 8:18.

16. Cf. Gen. 15:9–10, 17–21; Jer. 34:18f.

17. Lev. 3:17; 7:26–27; 17:10–11, 14; Deut. 12:16, 23; cf. Gen. 9:4–6.

18. Lev. 8:22–23, 30.

19. Y. Aharoni, *Arad Inscriptions* (Jerusalem: Mosad Bialik, 1975), 12, no. 1:10.

20. Akk. *agannu*, Ugar. *'agn*, Aram. *'gn'*, Egyptian *'ikn*.

21. 2 Kings 23:1–3; 22:8; cf. 2 Chron. 34:14–15,29–32.

22. E.g., ANET, p. 205.

23. Maimonides, Guide 1.4.

24. Cf. Ugaritic texts 51. v. 8, 96; 77.21.

25. *ṭhr iqnim* = *zhr 'iqnim*. M.Brettler, *God is King* (Sheffield: JSOT Press, 1989), 83, 184 n. 21 suggests that the image in Exod. 24:10 may have been inspired by the pavings of royal palaces.

26. Cf. Isa. 22:13; Eccles. 3:13.

27. For the tradition of "stone tablets," cf. Exod. 31:18; 34:4; Deut. 4:13; 5:19; 9:9–11; 10:1–3; 1 Kings 8:9.

28. Joshua has the title "attendant" also in 33:11; Num. 11:28; and Josh. 1:1. In Exod. 33:11 he has the added description *na'ar*. The two terms are also combined in 1 Sam. 2:11; 2 Sam. 13:17; 2 Kings 6:15.

29. *sh-k-n* is synonymous with *'-h-l*, "tent," in Num. 24:5; Isa. 54:2; Jer. 30:18; Ps. 78:60; cf. Isa. 13:20; Pss. 15:1; 78:55; Job 11:14; 18:15; 21:28.

30. Cf. Exod. 21:2; Lev. 25:3; Deut. 15:12,18; Jer. 34:14; cf. Judg. 12:7; 1 Kings 16:23; 2 Kings 11:3–4; Prov. 6:16; Job 5:19; 2 Chron. 22:12–23:1.

31. Cf. Ezek. 1 passim.

32. For the phrase, cf. Deut. 4:24; 9:3; Isa. 30:27.

33. Exod. 34:28; Deut. 9:9,11; cf. Deut. 9:8; 10:10.

34. Cf. Gen. 50:3; Num. 13:25; 14:34; 1 Sam. 17:16; Ezek. 4:6; Jon. 3:4.

Chapter 25

A. R. S. Kennedy, "Tabernacle," *Hastings Dictionary of the Bible*, vol. 4 (New York: Charles Scribner's Sons, 1902), 653–668; D. W. Gooding, *The Account of the Tabernacle* (Cambridge: Cambridge University Press, 1959); B. A. Levine, "The Descrip-

tive Tabernacle Texts of the Pentateuch," JAOS 85 (1965): 307–318; M. Haran, *Temples and Temple Service in Ancient Israel* (Oxford: Clarendon Press, 1978); N. M. Sarna, *Exploring Exodus* (New York: Schocken Books, 1987), 190–220.

1. Sarna, *Exploring Exodus*, pp. 196–200.

2. Cf. Exod. 25:9, 40; 27:8; cf. 26:31, 32, 42; 39:1, 5, 7, 21; 40 passim.

3. Sarna, *Exploring Exodus*, pp. 200–203.

4. Exod. 25:1; 30:11, 17, 22, 34; 31:1, 12.

5. Cf. Exod. 29:32 with Gen. 2:1, 3; cf. Exod. 39:43 with Gen. 1:31; cf. 40:33 with Gen. 2:2.

6. Cf. Mish. Kil. 9:1, Yoma 69a; see Haran, *Temples and Temple Service*, pp. 160–162, 211–212.

7. This is clear from the juxtaposition with 24:18 and from 25:9, 40; 26:30; 27:8; and Num. 8:4.

8. See J. Milgrom, EB (Hebrew), s.v. *terumah*.

9. Cf. Deut. 27:5; Josh. 8:31; 1 Kings 6:7.

10. See A. Brenner, *Colour Terms in the Old Testament*, JSOTSup 91st ser. (1982). On dyeing, see R. J. Forbes, *Studies in Ancient Technology*, vol. 4 (1964; reprint, Leiden: Brill); A. Gradwohl, *Die Farben im Alten Testament* (Berlin: Alfred Töpelmann [BZAW 83], 1963).

11. Sif. Deut. 354, ed. Horowitz and Finkelstein (1940; reprint, New York: Jewish Theological Seminary, 1969), Shab. 26a, Men. 42b, 44a.

12. Cf. Judg. 8:26; Jer. 10:9; Ezek. 23:6; Esther 1:6; 8:15; Dan. 5:7, 16, 29. On the subject of the *tekhelet*, see J. Milgrom, *The JPS Torah Commentary: Numbers* (Philadelphia: Jewish Publication Society, 1990), Excursus 38.

13. Cf. Gen. 38:28, 30; Josh. 2:18, 21; 2 Sam. 1:24; Isa. 1:18; Jer. 4:30; Nah. 2:4; Song 4:3; Lam. 4:5.

14. M. Lambdin, "Egyptian Loan Words in the Old Testament," JAOS 73 (1953): 155; A. Hurvitz, "The Usage of *shesh* and *buts* in the Bible and Its Implication for the Date of P," HTR 60 (1967): 117–121.

15. So Exod. 35:26; Num. 31:20.

16. Cf. Gen. 3:21; Lev. 11:32; 13:48; Num. 31:20.

17. Ezek. 16:10, where it refers to the material from which women's sandals were made.

18. The Targums simply rendered the phrase "colored skins." The LXX here translated the term "blue skins," but in Ezek. 16:10 "hyacinth," that is, having that color, which is also the consistent rendering of the Vulg.; cf. Josephus, Ant. 3.6.1 (Loeb, p. 365).

19. Y. Ahitov and H. Tadmor, EB (Hebrew), CAD, s.v. *tahash*; s.v. *dušu*.

20. Cf. Num. 25:1, Shittim; 33:49, Abel-shittim; Judg. 7:22, Beth-shittah; Joel 4:18, Nahal-ha-shittim (NJPS Wadi of the Acacias).

21. Lambdin, "Egyptian Loan Words," p. 154.

22. Exod. 27:20; Lev. 24:2.

23. Gen. 9:27; 35:21–22; Num. 24:2, 5; Judg. 8:11; Pss. 15:1; 78:55; 120:5; Job 11:14; 18:15.

24. Gen. 14:13; 16:12; 25:18; Jer. 25:24; cf. Mic. 4:10; Ps. 78:28; Song 1:8.

25. Num. 16:24, 27; 24:2, 5; 2 Sam. 7:6; Isa. 54:2; Jer. 30:18; Job 21:28.

26. E.g., Num. 9:15; 17:22–23; 18:2; cf. 2 Chron. 24:6.

27. Exod. 28:43; 30:20; 40:32.

28. Exod. 25:40; 26:30; 27:8; Num. 8:4. Heb. *tavnit*, "pattern," usually refers to the imitative reproduction of a material entity that exists in reality; cf. Deut. 4:16–18; Josh. 22:28; 2 Kings 16:10; Isa. 44:13; Ezek. 8:3, 10; 10:8; Pss. 106:20; 144:12. But *tavnit* here could be understood as an archetypal model; see V. Hurowitz, "The Priestly Account of Building the Tabernacle," JAOS 105 (1985): 22 n. 4.

29. The admonition appears four times: 25:9, 40; 26:30; 27:8.

30. Cf. Deut. 3:11.

31. Yoma 72b.

32. TJ Shek. 6:1 (49d).

33. So for the table, 25:24, 37:11–12; the altar of incense, 30:3–4; 37:26–27. The origin of Heb. *zer* is uncertain.

34. Heb. *pa'am*. Cf. Judg. 5:28; Isa. 26:6 parallel with *regel*; Pss. 17:5; 57:7; 58:11; 74:3; 85:14; 140:5; Prov. 29:5; Song 7:2. Cf. the synonymous variants *shalosh pe'amim* in Exod. 23:17; 34:23–24; Deut. 16:16 with *shalosh regalim* in Exod. 23:14; cf. Num. 22:28, 32, 33.

35. So only Exod. 37:3 and 1 Kings 7:30.

36. Exod. 31:18; 32:15; 34:29.

37. Deut. 9:9, 11, 15.

38. Cf. Akk. *adû* for the stipulations of a vassal treaty; see CAD, s.v. *adû*. In Old Aram. *'dy'* (pl. *adaya'a*), see KAI 222.I, A 7. A twelfth-century B.C.E. Egyptian text features the same word as a borrowing from Canaanite; see K. H. Kitchen, *Ancient Orient and the Old Testament* (Downers Grove, Ill.: Intervarsity Press, 1975), 108. The Ark is sometimes called "the Ark of the Covenant" (Heb. *'aron ha-berit*; Num. 10:33; 14:44; Deut. 31:9, 25, 26; Josh. 3:3, 6, 8) and sometimes "the Ark of the Pact" (Heb. *'aron ha-'edut*; Exod. 25:22; 26:33–34; 39:35; 40:3, 5, 21).

39. ANET, p. 205.

40. R. de Vaux, *Ancient Israel* (New York: McGraw-Hill, 1961), 301.

41. T. G. Allen, "Types of Rubrics in the Egyptian Book of the Dead," JAOS 56 (1936): 151, sec. 20.

42. To bow down at God's footstool, mentioned in Pss. 99:5; 132:7, certainly refers to the Holy of Holies. Lam. 2:1 is an instance of synecdoche. See J. Morgenstern, "The Ark, the Ephod and the Tent of Meeting," HUCA 17 (1942–1943): 153–266, and 18 (1944): 1–52; G. von Rad, "The Tent and the Ark," in *The Problem of the Hexateuch and Other Essays* (Edinburgh: Oliver & Boyd, 1966), 103–124; G. H. Davies, "The Ark of the Covenant," ASTI 5 (1967): 30–47; R. de Vaux, "Ark of Covenant and Tent of Reunion," in *The Bible and the Ancient Near East* (Garden City, N.Y.: Doubleday, 1971), 136–151.

43. According to Suk. 4b–5a, it was one "handbreadth," i.e., a span, thick.

44. J. M. Grintz, "Early Terms in the Priestly Torah" (Hebrew), *Leshonenu* 40 (1975–1976): 5–32, proposes an Egyptian etymology.

45. Exod. 31:7; 35:12; 39:5.

46. 1 Sam. 4:4; 2 Sam. 6:2 = 1 Chron. 13:6; 2 Kings 19:15 = Isa. 37:16; Pss. 80:2; 99:1.

47. 2 Sam. 22:11; Ps. 18:11.

48. CAD, s.v. *kuribu*.

49. See W. F. Albright, "What Were the Cherubim?" BA 1 (1938): 1–3; M. Haran, "The Ark and the Cherubim: Their Symbolic Significance in Biblical Ritual," IEJ 9 (1959): 30–38, 89–94.

50. So Exod. 29:42–43; 30:6, 36; Num. 7:89; 17:19.

51. Cf. Exod. 27:21; 28:43; 29 passim.

52. Exod. 39:32; 40:2, 6, 29; cf. 39:40.

53. Exod. 26:35; 40:22.

54. Men. 96b. The sages differ as to the place of the frame.

55. Josephus, Ant. 3.6.6 (Loeb, p. 381).

56. So Rashi.

57. Sifra 'Emor 18:4.

58. 1 Kings 7:28–36; 2 Kings 16:17.

59. Cf. Ps. 18:46.

60. Num. 3:31; 4:12, 15; 2 Chron. 24:14.

61. Men. 94a, 97a, 99b; cf. Mish. Men. 11:1.

62. Cf. Akk.; CAD, s.v. *kappu*, "a bowl."

63. Mish. Men. 11:5.

64. Ugar. *qš*, parallel with *ks*, "cup," in texts 51.IV.45 and Anat V.41 appears to be the cognate of Heb. *kisvah*. 1 Chron. 28:17 mentions *kesavot* in the list of the gold vessels of the Temple. Tosef. Zev. 1:12 mentions *kasva'* (or *kisva'*) as a libational vessel. Suk. 48b cites a statement that there were two libational vessels (Heb. *kisva'ot*), one for water and one for wine. In Sanh. 81b *kasvah* is defined as a "service vessel."

65. Exod. 37:16; Num. 4:7; Jer. 52:19.

66. Cf. Gen. R. 79:6, 91:5.

67. Josephus, Ant. 3.10.7 (Loeb, p. 441), 6.6.6 (Loeb, p. 38); cf. Mish. Men. 5:17.

68. Cf. Exod. 24:4; 28:9–10. Twelve loaves of bread placed on a sacrificial table before Ishtar are mentioned in Mesopotamian sources; see CAD, s.v. *akalu* (1, i, p. 244, 7).

69. Lev. 24:6–8.

70. 1 Chron. 9:32; 23:29; Neh. 10:34; cf. 2 Chron. 13:11 with Exod. 40:23.

71. Num. 4:7.

72. On the menorah, see L. Yarden, *The Tree of Light: A Study of the Menorah, the Seven-Branched Lampstand* (Ithaca, N.Y.: Cornell University Press, 1971); C. L. Meyers, *The Tabernacle Menorah: A Synthetic Study of a Symbol from the Biblical Cult*, ASOR Dissertation Series no. 2 (Missoula, Mont.: Scholars Press, 1976); E. R. Goodenough, "The Menorah among the Jews of the Roman World," HUCA 23 (1950–1951): 449–492.

73. Exod. 26:35; 40:24.

74. Men. 29b.

75. Traditions about the dimensions of the menorah are preserved in Men. 28b and in the tannaitic work *Baraita di-Melekhet ha-Mishkan*, ed. J. Jellinek, *Beit Ha-Midrasch*, vol. 3 (1938; reprint, Jerusalem: Warhmann Books, 1967), xxix–xxx, 144–154. They probably, however, refer to that of Herod's Temple. The height of the central shaft is given as 18 handbreadths or 3 cubits (i.e., ca. 4.5 ft.).

76. 1 Kings 7:49 = 2 Chron. 4:20; cf. Jer. 52:19.

77. AHW, s.v. *ḫurasu sagru*; cf. CAD, s.v. *sekerû*, "to heat, to treat gold in a certain way."

78. See R. J. Forbes, *Studies in Ancient Technology*, vol. 8 (Leiden: E. J. Brill, 1971), 172; Meyers, *Tabernacle Menorah*, pp. 26–31, 41–43.

79. Gen. 41:5, 22; 2 Kings 18:21; Isa. 19:6; 36:6; Ezek. 29:6–7.

80. L. Koehler, "Hebräische Etymologien," JBL 59 (1940): 36.

81. Gen. 44:2, 12, 16, 17; cf. *giv'ol*, derived from it, in Exod. 9:31. Interestingly, a talmudic tradition preserved in Men. 28a likens the "cups" to "the goblets of the Alexandrians" of Egypt.

82. Meyers, *Tabernacle Menorah*, pp. 182–184.

83. Exod. 27:20–21; 35:14; 39:37; cf. 2 Chron. 13:11 and Rashbam to v. 31.

84. Exod. 27:21; 30:7–8; Lev. 24:1–4.

85. Exod. 31:8; 39:35–37.

86. Cf. Jer. 1:11–12; 31:26–27; Ps. 127:1; Prov. 8:34; cf. Eccles. 12:5.

87. Pss. 36:10; 44:4; 49:20; 56:14; Job 3:16, 20; 33:28, 30; cf. Ps. 58:8; Eccles. 6:4; 11:7.

88. Isa. 2:5; 10:17; 60:1–2, 19–20; Mic. 7:8; Pss. 27:1; 43:3.

89. RH 24a–b, Av. Zar. 43a, Men. 28b; Maimonides, Hilkhot Beit ha-Beḥirah 7.10.

90. E. R. Goodenough, "Menorah among the Jews of Roman World"; idem, *Jewish Symbols in the Greco-Roman Period*, vol. 4 (New York: Bollingen Foundation, 1954), 71–77; D. Barag, "The Menorah in the Roman and Byzantine Periods: A Messianic Symbol," *Bulletin of the Anglo-Israel Archaeological Society* (1985–1986), pp. 44–47.

91. Meyers, *Tabernacle Menorah*, pp. 20–22.

92. Gen. 10:14 = 1 Chron. 1:12; Deut. 2:23; Jer. 47:4.

93. So LXX, Targums, Vulg., Pesh.

94. 1 Kings 7:19, 22; cf. v. 26; 2 Chron. 4:5.

95. This issue is debated in Men. 88b–89a.

96. So Rashbam, Bekhor Shor.

97. So Rashi, Radak.

98. Cf. Isa. 6:6.

99. For the verbal form, cf. Isa. 30:14; Prov. 6:27; 25:22; for the noun, cf. Lev. 10:1; 16:12; Num. 16:6, 17, 18; 17:2, 3, 4.

Chapter 26

1. So 2 Sam. 7:2; 1 Chron. 17:1; cf. Isa. 54:2; Jer. 4:20; 10:20; 49:29; Hab. 3:7; Song 1:5.
2. Yoma 71b–72a.
3. Exod. 26:31; 28:6, 15; 36:8, 35; 39:3.
4. See Rashi to Yoma 72b, Maimonides, Hilkhot Kelei ha-Mikdash 8.15.
5. R. J. Forbes, *Studies in Ancient Technology*, vol. 4 (Leiden: E. J. Brill, 1964), 211.
6. Both the sing. form and the stem are uncertain. Arab. *lawa'*, "to twine, twist, wind," and Akk. *lamû/lawû*, "to enwrap" (CAD, s.v. *lamû* 7), may be cognates; cf. Heb. *livyah*, "a wreath, coronet," in Prov. 1:9; 4:9.
7. Cf. the verbal form in Isa. 46:1–2, "to bow, bend down."
8. Cf. Jer. 49:7; Ezek. 17:6; 23:15; Amos 6:4,7.
9. Josephus, Ant. 3.6.3 (Loeb, p. 371).
10. UT 49.I.7; 51.IV.24; 129.5, 2 Aqht VI.49; cf. 67.VI.2; *'nt* ix.III.23.
11. So A. R. S. Kennedy, "Tabernacle," in *A Dictionary of the Bible*, ed. J. Hastings, vol. 4 (New York: Charles Scribner's Sons, 1902), 659–661; R. E. Friedman, "The Tabernacle in the Temple," BA 43 (1980): 241–247; F. M. Cross, "The Priestly Tabernacle in the Light of Recent Research," in *Temples and High Places in Biblical Times*, ed. A. Biran (Jerusalem: HUC-JIR, 1981), 170.
12. M. Haran, "The Priestly Image of the Tabernacle," HUCA 36 (1965): 192 and n. 2; idem, *Temples and Temple-Service in Ancient Israel* (Oxford: Clarendon Press, 1978), 150–151 and n. 2.
13. It should be noted that outside the Tabernacle context, *keresh* appears only in Ezek. 27:6, where it seems to indicate the deck of a ship for which a primary meaning of "planks" would be most appropriate. In the Ugar. passages, the context gives no clue as to its precise signification.
14. So Rashi, Rashbam, Bekhor Shor, Hizkuni.
15. In 1 Kings 10:19 the same word means the arms of a throne; in 1 Kings 7:32 it means an "axletree"; and in 1 Kings 7:35f. it apparently means "sides."
16. In rabbinic Heb. *shelivah* is the rung of a ladder; so Shab. 60a, Er. 77b, Mak. 7b. In later Heb. *shalav* is so used; hence the derived meaning "parallel."
17. So Exod. 27:9; 36:23; 38:9; Ezek. 47:19; 48:28; cf. the paired terms for eastward in Exod. 27:13; 38:13; Num. 2:3; 34:15; Josh. 19:12.
18. Other than in Song 5:15 and Job 38:6, the word is exclusive to the Tabernacle context.
19. Cf. "the remotest parts of the north" and its equivalents in Isa. 14:13; Ezek. 38:6, 15; 39:2; Ps. 48:3; "the ends, or the remotest parts, of the earth" in Jer. 6:22; 25:32; 31:7; 50:41.
20. Neh. 3:24 and 2 Chron. 26:9 show that the *miktsoa'* and the corner (*pinnah*) were not identical. Exod. 26:24; 36:28; Ezek. 41:22; 46:21–22; Neh. 3:19, 20, 24, 25; 2 Chron. 26:9 all have *miktsoa'* or *miktsoa'*. Exod. 26:23; 36:28 read *mekutsa'ot*, whereas Ezek. 46:22 has *mehuktsa'ot*. A different stem seems to be behind Lev. 14:41; Isa. 44:13.
21. Cf. Deut. 3:5; Judg. 16:3; 1 Sam. 23:7.
22. Exod. 35:12; 39:34; 40:21; Num. 4:5.
23. Lev. 24:3.
24. Lev. 4:6.
25. AHW, s.v. *parakku, paraku*.
26. So *Baraita di-Melekhet ha-Mishkan*, ed. A. Jellinek (Jerusalem: Wahrman, 1967), chap. 4, p. 147.
27. Shulkhan Arukh, Orah Hayyim sec. 154.3.
28. Rashbam comments, "like a fork."
29. Heb. *masakh* derives from the stem *s-kh-kh*, "to screen, close off cover"; cf. Exod. 25:20; 33:22; 37:9; 40:21; Ps. 91:4; Job 3:23; 38:8; Lam. 3:44.

Chapter 27

1. Exod. 30:28; 31:9; 35:16; 38:1; 40:6, 10, 29; Lev. 4:7, 10, 18, 25, 30, 34; 1 Chron. 6:34; 16:40; 21:26, 29; 2 Chron. 29:18.
2. Exod. 29:38–43; Num. 28–29.
3. Exod. 38:30; 39:39; 1 Kings 8:64; 2 Kings 16:15; 2 Chron. 1:6; 4:1; 7:7; Ezek. 9:2.
4. Mish. Yoma 5:5, 6; Mish. Zev. 4:1, 4; 5:1, 2; Mish. Men. 4:1.
5. Exod. 17:15; 24:4; cf. 32:5.
6. Y. Aharoni, "Arad: Its Inscriptions and Temple," BA 31 (1968): 19, 25.
7. Exod. 30:1–2; Ezek. 43:15.
8. A. Biran, "An Israelite Horned Altar at Dan," BA 37 (1974): 106–107; Y. Aharoni, "The Horned Altar of Beer-sheba," BA 37 (1974): 1–6; cf. editor's note, BARev 1 (1975): 1–8.
9. Exod. 29:12; Lev. 4:7, 18, 25, 30, 34; 8:15; 9:9; 16:18; cf. Ezek. 43:20.
10. Cf. 1 Sam. 2:10; 2 Sam. 22:3; Ezek. 29:21; Amos 6:13; Pss. 18:3; 89:18, 25; 92:11; 132:17; 148:14; Lam. 2:17. For the lopping off of the horns as the opposite, cf. Jer. 48:25; Ps. 75:11; Lam. 2:3; cf. Amos 3:14.
11. They are mentioned frequently in connection with the altar appurtenances: Exod. 38:3; 1 Kings 7:45; 2 Kings 25:14; Jer. 52:18f.; Zech. 14:20; 2 Chron. 4:11, 16; 35:13. Why they are omitted from the list of Num. 4:14 is unclear.
12. So Rashbam. The verbal form is found in Isa. 28:17, where it means "to sweep away"; see Targ. Onk. here to Exod. 27:3, and cf. *magrefita'* from *g-r-f*, "to sweep away," as in Judg. 5:21. The *ya'eh* is listed in Exod. 38:3; Num. 4:14; 1 Kings 7:40, 45; 2 Kings 25:14; Jer. 52:18; 2 Chron. 4:11, 16.
13. The *mizrak* is mentioned in Exod. 38:3; Num. 4:14; 7:13 and passim; 1 Kings 7:40, 45, 50; 2 Kings 12:14; 25:15; Jer. 52:18, 19; Zech. 9:15; 14:20; Neh. 7:70; 1 Chron. 28:17; 2 Chron. 4:8, 11, 22.
14. Lev. 17:11–12, 14; Deut. 12:23.
15. Gen. 9:4; Lev. 3:17; 7:26–27; 17:10–12; 19:26; Deut. 12:16, 23–15; 15:23; cf. 1 Sam. 14:32–34; Ezek. 33:25.
16. The flesh hooks are mentioned in Exod. 38:3; Num. 4:14; 1 Sam. 2:13, 14; 1 Chron. 28:17; 2 Chron. 4:16.
17. Cf. Isa. 30:14; Prov. 6:27; 25:22. The fire pans are frequently mentioned: Exod. 38:3; Lev. 10:1; 16:12; 17:11; Num. 4:9, 14; 16:6, 17, 18; 17:2, 3, 4; 1 Kings 7:50; 2 Kings 25:15; Jer. 52:19; 2 Chron. 4:22.
18. Mish. Shek. 8:8, TJ Shek. 8:6 (51b), Zev. 62a.
19. Zev. 53a.
20. R. J. Forbes, *Studies in Ancient Technology*, vol. 4 (Leiden: E. J. Brill, 1964), 175–192, 225f., 228.
21. Exod. 35:18; 38:20, 31; 39:40.
22. Cf. Exod. 28:1, 3; 30:23; 31:13; Num. 1:50.
23. Sifra Tsav 1:1; so Rashbam, Ibn Ezra.
24. See Mish. Men. 8:4, Men. 86a; so Rashi, Rashbam; cf. Exod. 30:34; Lev. 24:7.
25. Cf. Exod. 30:7–8.
26. Josephus, Against Apion 1.22 (Loeb, p. 243).
27. Shab. 22b.
28. On this issue, see M. Haran, *Temples and Temple-Service in Ancient Israel* (Oxford: Clarendon Press, 1976), 209 n. 6; B. Levine, "The Descriptive Tabernacle Texts of the Pentateuch," JAOS 85 (1965): 311–312.

Chapter 28

1. Cf. Josh. 5:15, Shek. 5a, Exod. R. 2:13; cf. Mish. Yoma 1:7.
2. Mish. Yoma 3:4, 6; 7:3, 4.
3. Ben Sira 45:6–13.
4. Josephus, Ant. 4.1–7 (Loeb, pp. 387–407).
5. Especially tractate Yoma.
6. So Exod. 29:1, 4ff.; 40:12, 14; Lev. 8:2, 6, 13, 21.

7. For the technical meaning of the phrase "bring forward" in a cultic context, cf. Num. 3:6; 8:9–10; 16:9–10.

8. So noted by Lek. Tov.

9. Lev. 10:1–2.

10. Num. 3:1–4.

11. Num. 20:25–28; Deut. 10:6; cf. Num. 25:13.

12. Exod. 38:21.

13. 1 Sam. 14:3; 1 Chron. 24:3; cf. Ezra 8:2.

14. So frequently; cf. Exod. 28:4; 29:29; 31:10; 35:19, 21; 39:1, 41; 40:13; Lev. 16:4, 32.

15. So Bekhor Shor, Ibn Ezra (i).

16. So Ibn Ezra (ii); cf. Ezek. 44:19.

17. Exod. 35:19; 39:1, 41.

18. Mish. Zev. 14:10; cf. Exod. 28:35, 43; 29:29–30; 35:19; 39:1, 41; Ezek. 44:27; cf. also Num. 3:31; 4:12.

19. Sefer ha-Mitsvot 33.

20. Gen. 41:38–39; Exod. 31:1–5; 35:25, 31; 2 Sam. 14:2; Jer. 9:16–17; 10:9; Ezek. 27:8; Dan. 5:14.

21. Cf. Exod. 36:3–6.

22. UT 1152.3, in an inventory of an estate, and UT 67.1.5, 31, where the contexts do not allow exact definition. The *ipd* fetched a high price of twenty-five shekels. See R. R. Stieglitz, "Commodity Prices at Ugarit," JAOS 99 (1979): 19.

23. CAD, s.v. *epattu*; cf. Syr. *pedta*, "priestly garment."

24. Judg. 17:3–5; 18:14, 17–20; Hos. 3:4; on the teraphim, cf. 1 Sam. 15:23; 2 Kings 23:24.

25. Judg. 8:24–27.

26. 1 Sam. 2:28; 14:3; 22:18; 23:6.

27. 1 Sam. 2:18; 2 Sam. 6:14; cf. 1 Chron. 15:27.

28. 1 Sam. 23:9–11; 30:7–8; cf. the use of teraphim for a similar purpose in Ezek. 21:26; Zech. 10:2; and probably also in Gen. 31:19; 34–35.

29. Josephus, Ant. 3.7, 5 (Loeb, p. 393); So LXX.

30. Cf., e.g., Exod. 29:9; Lev. 8:13; Num. 22:21; cf. *keves* in Lev. 4:22 = *kesev* in Lev. 3:7; *simlah* in Deut. 10:18 = *salmah* in Exod. 22:8.

31. Maimonides, Hilkhot Kelei ha-Mikdash 9.9.

32. Written *yehosef*.

33. T. O. Lambdin, "Egyptian Loan Words in the Old Testament," JAOS 73 (1953): 151.

34. For Heb. *mishpat* in this sense, cf. Prov. 16:33. On the Urim and Thummim, see R. de Vaux, *Ancient Israel* (London: McGraw-Hill, 1961), 349–353; E. Robertson, "The Urim and Thummim: What Were They?" VT 14 (1964): 67–74; E. Lipinski, "Urim and Thummim," VT 20 (1970): 495–496.

35. Isa. 23:18; 33:6; Jer. 20:5; Ezek. 22:25; Prov. 15:6; 27:24.

36. So EB (Hebrew), s.v. *hoshen ha-mishpat*.

37. So Tosef. Kelim BM 6:12.

38. Lambdin, "Egyptian Loan Words," p. 149.

39. Exod. 24:10; Isa. 54:11; Ezek. 1:26; 10:1; 28:13; Job 28:6, 16; Song 5:14; Lam. 4:7.

40. Ezek. 1:16; 10:9; 28:13; Song 5:14; Dan. 10:6.

41. Gen. 2:12; Exod. 25:7; 28:9, 20; 35:9, 27; 39:6, 13; Job 28:16; 1 Chron. 29:2.

42. See U. Cassuto, *A Commentary on the Book of Exodus* (Jerusalem: Magnes Press, 1967), at Exod. 28:17–19.

43. Maimonides, Hilkhot Kelei ha-Mikdash 9.7.

44. Ibid. has the variant *shivtei yah*.

45. AHW, s.v. *rakasu*; Ugar. *'nt*: pl.x: 10, 23, in parallel with *'sr*, "to tie"; cf. Ps. 31:21. It is hard to find a connection with *rekhasim*, "ridges," in Isa. 40:4.

46. So noted by Ramban.

47. Lev. 16:8; Josh. 18:6, 8, 10; Isa. 34:17; Joel 4:3; Obad. 11; Jon. 1:7; Nah. 3:10; Ps. 22:19; Prov. 1:14; 16:33; 18:18; Esther 3:7; 9:24; Neh. 10:35; 11:1; 1 Chron. 24:5, 31; 25:8; 26:13, 14; cf. also the use of the verb *l-k-d* in Josh. 7:14–18; 1 Sam. 10:20f.; 14:41f.

48. Josephus, Ant. 3.7, 9 (Loeb, p. 421).

49. See Sot. 48b, TJ Sot. 9:14 (24b); contrast Mish. Yoma 7:5.

50. See Maimonides, Hilkhot Kelei ha-Mikdash 10.10.

51. So Josephus, Ant. 3.7.4 (Loeb, p. 391); Wars 5.5, 7 (Loeb, p. 271); cf. Ramban to v. 31.

52. Cf. the governing verb *'-t-h* in 1 Sam. 28:14; Isa. 59:17; 61:10; Ps. 109:29, as noted by Ramban.

53. Cf. 1 Sam. 15:27; 24:4, 11 (Saul); 18:4 (Jonathan); 28:14 (Samuel); 2 Sam. 13:18 (daughters of royalty); Job 1:20; 2:12 (Job and his friends); Ezek. 26:16 (kings on their thrones); Ezra 9:3, 5 (Ezra); cf. 1 Chron. 15:27 (David).

54. So Rashbam. for Heb. *kalil* governing a noun, cf. Judg. 20:40; Ezek. 28:12.

55. Cf. Y. Yadin, *The Art of Warfare in Biblical Lands*, vol. 1 (New York: McGraw-Hill, 1963), 84. *Tahra'* may be derived from Egyptian *dhr*, "hide of an animal," although this is doubted by Lambdin, "Egyptian Loan Words," p. 155. See also N. H. Tur-Sinai, *Ha-Lashon ve-ha-Sefer* (Jerusalem: Mosad Bialik, 1959), 219–223.

56. So Isa. 6:1; Jer. 13:22, 26; Nah. 3:5; Lam. 1:9.

57. Cf. Num. 13:23 and 20:5.

58. 1 Kings 7:18, 20, 42; Jer. 52:22–23; 2 Chron. 3:16; 4:13.

59. Ben Sira 45:9 also mentions the pomegranates of the High Priest's attire but offers no explanation for them.

60. Song 4:3, 13; 6:7, 11; 7:13; 8:2.

61. Mish. Zev. 2:1, Zev. 17b.

62. Cf. Exod. 28:43; 30:21; Lev. 8:35; 10:7; 16:13.

63. Num. 17:23; 1 Kings 6:18, 29, 32, 35; Isa. 28:1; 40:6, 7, 8; Job 14:2; Ps. 103:15.

64. Isa. 28:1; cf. Ezek. 21:31.

65. Both *tsits* and *nezer* appear together in Exod. 39:30; Lev. 8:9.

66. 2 Sam. 1:10; 2 Kings 11:12; 2 Chron. 23:1; Pss. 89:40; 132:18; cf. Zech. 9:16.

67. A. De Buck, "La Fleur au Front du Grand-Prêtre," OTS 9 (1951): 18–29.

68. Lev. 21:6; Num. 16:5, 7; cf. Num. 6:8; 2 Kings 4:9.

69. Shab. 63b; Suk. 5a.

70. Aristeas, sec. 98; Josephus, Wars 5.5, 7 (Loeb, p. 263) and Ant. 3.7, 6 (Loeb, p. 401). Cf. Maimonides, Hilkhot Kelei ha-Mikdash 9.1.

71. Ezek. 21:31, parallel with *'atarah*, "crown." In Isa. 62:3 *tsanif*, derived from the same stem as *mitsnefet*, is combined with *melukhah*, "royalty," whereas in Zech. 3:5 this is part of the regalia of the High Priest. In Isa. 3:23 *tsenifot* appears in an inventory of the luxurious finery owned by the wealthy women of Jerusalem. The primary meaning of the stem *ts-n-f* seems to be "to twist, wind," and appears in this sense in Lev. 16:4; Isa. 22:18.

72. Exod. 34:2; Lev. 10:17; Num. 14:18; Hos. 14:3; Mic. 7:18; Pss. 32:5; 85:3.

73. Exod. 28:43; Lev. 5:1, 17; 7:18 and so overwhelmingly in biblical texts.

74. Cf. Ugar. *ktn*, UT 19.1324; Akk. *kitinnu* and *kutānū* may be connected, see CAD, s.v. *kutānu*; F. C. Fensham, "A Cappadocian Parallel to Hebrew *kutonet*," VT 10 (1960): 196.

75. Cf. Lev. 8:7. Gen. 3:21, *kotnot 'or*, can be translated "garments for the skin."

76. Cf. Exod. 28:20. The term is used both of gold settings for gems—in Exod. 28:11,13f,20; 39:6,13,16; Ps. 45:14—and as a type of weave, as here. The term still seems to have been in use in tannaitic times; see M. Jastrow, *Dictionary* (New York and Berlin: Choreb, 1926), 1,516.

77. Josephus, Ant. 3.7, 2 (Loeb, p. 389).

78. Josephus, Wars, 5.5, 7 (Loeb. p. 273).

79. Josephus, Ant. 3.7, 6 (Loeb, pp. 391, 399).

80. T. O. Lambdin, "Egyptian Loan Words in the Old Testament," JAOS 73 (1953): 146, suggests that *'avnet* may be an Egyptian borrowing into Heb.

81. Maimonides, Hilkhot Kelei ha-Mikdash 8.19.

82. Josephus, Ant. 3.7, 2 (Loeb, pp. 389f.), reports a width of four fingerbreadths.

83. Mish. Yoma 7:5 uses *mitsnefet* for both. Jth. 4:15 likewise has the same Gk. word, *kidaris*, "miter," for both. In Exod. 39:28 the headwear of the ordinary priests is called *pa'arei migba'ot*. In Isa. 3:20 *pe'erim* are included in the inventory of the luxurious finery of the rich women of Jerusalem. In Ezek. 24:17; 44:18 the headdress of the priest is called *pe'er*, which apparently means "a turban." Isa. 61:3, 10 shows that the *pe'er* was not exclusive to the priesthood.

84. Josephus, Ant. 3.7, 3 (Loeb, p. 391).

85. Exod. 29:21; 30:30; 40:13, 15; Lev. 7:35f.; 8:30.

86. Exod. 29:7; Lev. 8:12; 21:10; cf. Ps. 133:2.

87. Exod. 30:26–29; 40:9–11.

88. Lev. 21:10; Num. 3:3; Judg. 17:5, 12; 1 Kings 13:33; 2 Chron. 13:9.

89. Rashi draws an analogy from contemporary practice in French ruling circles.

90. In Ezek. 43:26 it is used of consecrating an altar.

91. Exod. 39:28; Lev. 6:4; 16:4; Ezek. 44:18.

Chapter 29

1. I have greatly benefited from the exposition of this chapter by B. A. Levine in his commentary to Lev. 8–9. *The JPS Torah Commentary: Leviticus* (Philadelphia: Jewish Publication Society, 1989).

2. This refers back to Exod. 28:40–43.

3. For the anomalous imperative form, cf. Ezek. 37:16; Prov. 20:16.

4. Mish. Men. 7:1.

5. Cf. Lev. 8:3.

6. Targ. Jon.

7. See Exod. 28:42; Lev. 6:3; 16:4.

8. Lev. 4:3, 15, 16; 6:15. See Targums to these passages. The exception is Num. 3:3 in the plural. Cf. Ps. 133:2.

9. Exod. 28:41; 30:30; 40:14–15; Lev. 7:35–36; 10:7; Num. 3:3.

10. On this issue, see B. A. Levine, "The Descriptive Tabernacle Texts of the Pentateuch," JAOS 85 (1965): 307–318.

11. See H. M. Orlinsky, *Notes on the New Translation of the Torah* (Philadelphia: Jewish Publication Society, 1969), 192. It should be noted that the narrative in Lev. 8 separates the two investitures.

12. So Exod. 29:10, 15, 19. On the rite of *semikhah*, see J. S. Licht, EB (Hebrew), s.v. semikhah; R. Peter, "L'imposition des mains dans l'Ancien Testament," VT 27 (1977): 48–55; D. P. Wright, "The Gesture of the Hand Placement in the Hebrew Bible and in Hittite Literature," JAOS 106 (1986): 433–446.

13. Mish. Men. 9:7–8, Sifra 'Aḥarei Mot, parshata 4:4; Men. 92a–93b.

14. Lev. 24:14; Num. 8:10; 27:18, 23; Deut. 34:9. Note that although the singular form appears in the instruction of Num. 27:18, the account of its fulfillment in v. 23 has the plural.

15. Ibid.

16. The exceptions are Exod. 29:10, 15, 19; Lev. 4:15; 8:13, 18, 22; 16:21; Num. 8:12; 2 Chron. 29:23.

17. Mish. Men. 9:8, Men. 93b, Sifra 'Aḥarei Mot. Note that Targ. Jon. to Lev. 1:4 specifies the use of the right hand only.

18. S. I. Levin and E. A. Boyden, *The Kosher Code of the Orthodox Jew* (Minneapolis: University of Minnesota Press, 1940), 100; ANEP, no. 594, and n. 321; A. Leo Oppenheim, *Ancient Mesopotamia* (Chicago and London: University of Chicago Press, 1964), 213; J. Preuss, *Biblical and Talmudic Medicine*, trans. and ed. F. Rosner (New York and London: Sanhedrin Press, 1978), 96–97.

19. See Rashi to 29:16.

20. See the author's Comment to Gen. 8:21 in this series (*The JPS Torah Commentary: Genesis* [Philadelphia: Jewish Publication Society, 1989]). Texts such as Lev. 26:31 and Amos 5:21 express the rejection of sacrifice by the negative form of the idiom. Its original, literal implication of sacrifice as a means of sustaining the god, which it had in the ancient Near East, has, of course, been lost in the Hebrew Bible; cf. Ps. 51:18–19.

21. UT 19.117; cf. the Hebrew proper names *yeho'ash*, *yo'shiyahu*.

22. See B. A. Levine, *JPS Torah Commentary: Leviticus*, pp. 14–15.

23. Cf. Exod. 29:27 and Lev. 7:32f.

24. On the *tenufah*, see J. Milgrom, "The Alleged Wave-Offering in Israel and in the Ancient Near East," IEJ 22 (1972): 35–38; idem, *The JPS Torah Commentary: Numbers* (Philadelphia: Jewish Publication Society, 1990), 425f. For the stem *n-w-f* in the sense of "lifting," cf. Exod. 20:22; Deut. 23:26; 27:5; Isa. 10:15; 19:16; Zech. 2:13.

25. Lev. 7:34; cf. 8:29.

26. Cf. Lev. 6:9, 19.

27. See M. Haran, "The Priestly Image of the Tabernacle," HUCA 36 (1965): 216ff.; idem, *Temples and Temple-Service in Ancient Israel* (Oxford: Clarendon Press, 1978), 174ff. For the Kal verbal form of the stem *k-d-sh* in the meaning "to be/ become holy," cf. Exod. 30:29; Lev. 6:11, 20; Num. 17:3; Deut. 22:9; 1 Sam. 21:6; Hag. 2:12. B. A. Levine in his Commentary to Lev. 6:11 renders, "Anyone who is to touch these must be in a holy state" (*JPS Torah Commentary: Leviticus*). He notes that Hag 2:11–12 seems to deny the theory of contagious holiness. On that passage, see the discussion of C. L. Meyers and E. M. Meyers, *Haggai, Zechariah 1–8* (Garden City, N.Y.: Doubleday, 1987), 55–56, which notes that indirect contact is the issue there. Still, by the theory of contagious holiness, the garment should have become sacred, and in turn it would have imparted holiness to the other items.

28. So Meg. Ta'an., scholium.

29. T. O. Lambdin, "Egyptian Loan Words in the Old Testament," JAOS 73 (1953): 148; J. M. Grintz, "Early Terms in the Priestly Torah" (Hebrew), *Leshonenu* 39 (1974–1975): 15–17, 181.

30. For the phrase, cf. Gen. 17:8; Lev. 26:12; Jer. 7:23; 31:33 (32); Ezek. 37:27.

Chapter 30

G. W. Van Beek, "Frankincense and Myrrh in Ancient South Arabia," JAOS 78 (1958): 141–152; idem, "Frankincense and Myrrh," BA 23 (1960): 70–95; N. Glueck, "Incense Altars," in *Translating and Understanding the Old Testament*, ed. H. T. Frank (Nashville, Tenn.: Abingdon, 1970), 325–329; M. Haran, *Temples and Temple-Service in Ancient Israel* (Oxford: Clarendon Press, 1978), 208, 230–245.

1. Exod. 40:34–36; Lev. 9:23.

2. The same occurred at the inauguration of Solomon's Temple; see 1 Kings 8:10; 2 Chron. 5:14.

3. The same Heb. word (*le-doroteikhem*) is used in both passages.

4. Exod. 39:38; 40:5, 26; Num. 4:11; cf. 1 Kings 7:48; 2 Chron. 4:19.

5. Exod. 30:27; 31:8; 35:15; 37:25; Lev. 4:7; 1 Chron. 6:34; 2 Chron. 26:16, 19.

6. E.g., Yoma 59a, Shevu. 10b.

7. Exod. 27:1–8.

8. Exod. 25:11, 24.

9. Exod. 25:12–15, 26–28; 27:4, 6–7.

10. So Ibn Janaḥ, Abravanel.

11. Maimonides, Guide 3.45–46. Note that Akk. *qutaru* means "a fumigant"; CAD, s.v. *qutaru*.

12. For the differences of opinion as to the precise meaning of Heb. *heitiv* here, see *Entsyklopaedia Talmudit* (Jerusalem: 1957), s.v. *hatavat nerot*, vol. 8, cols. 743–753.

13. See E. A. Speiser, "Census and Ritual Expiation in Mari and Israel," BASOR 149 (1958): 17–25; J. Liver, "The Ransom of Half Shekel" (Hebrew), in *Yehezkel Kaufmann Jubilee Volume*, ed. M. Haran (Jerusalem: Magnes Press, 1960), 54–67; J. Liver, "The Half-Shekel Offering," HTR 56 (1963): 173–198; A. Ben-David, "The Talmud Was Right! The Weight of the Biblical Shekel," PEQ 100 (1968): 145–147.

14. Num. 1:2, cf. v. 49; Josh. 8:10; Judg. 7:3; 20:14f.; 1 Sam. 11:8; 15:4; 2 Sam. 18:1; 24 (1 Chron. 21); 1 Kings 20:15, 27f.; 2 Kings 3:6. The controlling verb is usually *p-k-d*.

15. Cf. 2 Chron. 24:4–10, although Liver, "Ransom of Half Shekel," disputes the identity of *mase'at mosheh* with the half-shekel of this passage. Shek. 4b understands Exod. 30:12–13 to be an annual obligation.

16. Josephus, Ant. 18.9.1 (Loeb, p. 181).

17. These are detailed in Mish. Shek. 4.

18. Josephus, Wars, 7.6.6. (Loeb, pp. 567f.).

19. Mish. Shek. 1:1, 3:1.

20. Num. 1:2, 49; 4:2, 22; 31:26,49. Akkadian *našû reš* can also mean "to muster, summon"; see CAD, s.v. *našû-reš*, 107–108.

21. Cf. Ps. 49:8–9; Prov. 6:35; 13:8; Job 33:24.

22. Lev. 27:32; Jer. 33:13; Ezek. 20:37.

23. Ibn Janaḥ understands *pekudim* as though it were *pokedim*, "the census takers." Ibn Ezra treats "pass" figuratively: those who have passed (i.e., who have reached) the age of recruitment.

24. Gen. 23:16; 2 Sam. 14:26; 2 Kings 15:20; Jer. 32:9; Zech. 11:12f.

25. So, e.g., Exod. 38:24–26; Lev. 5:15; 27:3, 25.

26. Gen. 23:16.

27. 2 Sam. 14:26.

28. R. B. Scott, "Weights and Measures of the Bible," BA 22 (1959): 22–40; idem, "The Scale-Weights from Ophel," PEQ 97 (1965): 128–139; Y. Aharoni, "The Use of Hieratic Numerals in Hebrew Ostraca and the Shekel Weights," BASOR 184 (1966): 13–19; V. I. Kerkhof, "An Inscribed Stone Weight From Shechem," BASOR 184 (1966): 20–21.

29. G. Barkay, "Iron Age Gerah Weights" (Hebrew), *Eretz-Israel* 18 (1981): 288–296.

30. E.g., Num. 1:3.

31. See Ibn Ezra's comment to Exod. 30:12.

32. Exod. 35:27.

33. So U. Cassuto, *A Commentary on the Book of Exodus* (Jerusalem: Magnes, 1967), 396.

34. Van Beek, "Frankincense and Myrrh in Ancient South Arabia"; idem, "Frankincense and Myrrh."

35. The syntax with the reversed order of words in Heb. *besamim ro'sh* is unusual, but it is paralleled in Ps. 141:5, *shemen ro'sh*, "choice oil." For *ro'sh* in the sense of "choicest," cf. Ezek. 27:22; Ps. 137:6; Song 4:14; cf. also *re'shit* in the same sense in Exod. 23:19 and Amos 6:6.

36. On myrrh, see U. Feldman, *The Plants of the Bible* (Hebrew) (Tel Aviv: Dvir, 1957), 231; J. Feliks, *The Plant World of the Bible* (Hebrew) (Ramat Gan: Massada, 1968), 252; M. Zohary, *Plants of the Bible* (Cambridge: Cambridge University Press, 1982), 200. Song 5:5, 13, "flowing myrrh," refers to the fluid form; Song 1:13, to the coagulated kind. Heb. *deror* is connected with Arab. *dur*, "pearls."

37. Aromatic cinnamon is clearly intended also in Prov. 7:17; Song 4:14.

38. Isa. 43:24; Jer. 6:20; Ezek. 27:19; Song 4:14.

39. Only also Ezek. 27:19 and not translated in the Targum. LXX there has "cassia."

40. Only Ps. 45:9, *ketsi'ah*; cf. Job 42:14.

41. 1 Sam. 8:13; Neh. 3:8.

42. Cf. Exod. 40:9–11; Lev. 8:10–11; Num. 7:1.

43. Mish. Shek. 5:1, Tosef. Shek. 2:6, TJ Shek. 5:6 (48b), Mish. Yoma 3:11, Tosef. Yom ha-Kippurim 2:6–7, TJ Yoma 3:11 (40b); cf. Mish. Yoma 1:5; Mish. Tam. 1:1, Yoma 38a.

44. See Y. Feliks, *Mishnah Tractate Shevi'it* (Hebrew) (Jerusalem: Mass, 1987), 182–183.

45. Ibid., pp. 183f.; Ms. Anne Nunes of Houston, Tex., in a private communication, points out that the malodorous substance ambergris is often used as an ingredient in the manufacture of perfume, with the same effect.

46. Ker. 6b.

47. Van Beek, "Frankincense and Myrrh," pp. 71f., 82f.; Feliks, *Plant World of the Bible*, p. 260; Zohary, *Plants of the Bible*, p. 197.

48. V. Hurowitz, "Salted Incense: Exodus 30, 35," Bib. 68 (1987): 178–194.

Chapter 31

1. For the idiom, cf. Josh. 21:9; Isa. 43:1; 45:3–4; 1 Chron. 6:50.

2. For *tsel* in this sense, cf. Gen. 19:8; Ps. 91:1. The element appears as a component of Akk. personal names, such as Ina-silli-Bel, Ina-silli-Nabû, "in the protection of Bel/Nabu." Y. Aharoni, *Arad Inscriptions* (Hebrew) (Jerusalem: Mosad Bialik, 1975), 82, 84, points to *benei bzl* in the guild list of inscription no. 49.1, which name he identifies as an abbreviation of Bezalel. The name also appears in the clan of Caleb in the genealogy of 1 Chron. 2:20, and in Ezra 10:30 among the returnees from the Babylonian exile.

3. For these names, cf. 1 Kings 4:19; 1 Chron. 6:9; 2 Sam. 11:3; Ezra 10:24.

4. Exod. 17:10, 12; 24:14. In 1 Chron. 2:19f. there is, listed in the genealogy of Caleb, a Judahite named Hur whose son is Uri and whose grandson is Bezalel; those are the same names respectively as those of Bezalel's family.

5. Names composed of *'ohel*, "tent, tent-shrine," are widespread in the regions of Phoenicia and southern Arabia; cf. Edomite *Oholibamah*, Gen. 36:2, etc.; Phoen. *'hlb'l*, *'hlmlk*; Sabean *'hl'l*, *'hl'ttr*; Thamudi *'hln*. For word play on the name Oholiab, see M. Garsiel, *Midrashic Name Derivations in the Bible* (Hebrew) (Ramat Gan: Revivim, 1987), 142f. Cf. also Ezek. 23:4, Oholah, Oholibah.

6. Ber. 55a.

7. Heb. *'aron la-'edut* is unique. The form may anticipate v. 18.

8. On *bigdei serad*, see M. Haran, *Temples and Temple-Service in Ancient Israel* (Oxford: Clarendon Press, 1978), 172–173.

9. Exod. 35:19; 39:1, 41. The jarring *vav* before *'et bigdei ha-kodesh* in the present verse may well be explanatory, as in Gen. 4:4, *u-me-helbehen*; Exod. 25:12, *u-shetei*; 28:23, *ve-natatta*, etc. M. Held, "A Difficult Biblical Expression and Its Parallel in Ugaritic" (Hebrew), *Eretz-Israel* 3 (1954): 101–103, claims to have found *serad* in Ugar. text KT 76.81 as a dialectic variant of Heb. *sharet*.

10. Cf. Gen. 9:3–4.

11. So Ezek. 20:12, 20.

12. Cf. Exod. 23:12.

13. Johs. Pedersen, *Israel: Its Life and Culture* (London and Copenhagen: Oxford University Press, 1926), I & II, pp. 99–181.

14. On this notion, cf. Exod. 24:12; 32:16; 34:1; Deut. 9:10.

Chapter 32

1. Lewy, "The Story of the Golden Calf Reanalysed," VT 9 (1959): 318–322; F. C. Fensham, "The Burning of the Golden

Calf and Ugarit," IEJ 16 (1966): 191–193; M. Aberbach and L. Smolar, "Aaron, Jeroboam, and the Golden Calves," JBL 86 (1967): 129–140; S. E. Loewenstamm, "The Making and Destruction of the Golden Calf," Bib 48 (1967): 481–490; idem, "A Rejoinder," Bib 56 (1975): 330–343; J. M. Sasson, "Bovine Symbolism in the Exodus Narrative," VT 18 (1968): 380–387; L. G. Perdue, "The Making and Destruction of the Golden Calf: A Reply," Bib 54 (1973): 237–246; J. Faur, "The Biblical Idea of Idolatry," JQR 69 (1978): 1–15; H. C. Brichto, "The Worship of the Golden Calf: A Literary Analysis of a Fable on Idolatry," HUCA 54 (1983): 1–44.

1. Cf. Deut. 5:20–24.
2. Num. 16:3; 17:2; 20:2; Ezek. 38:7.
3. Cf. the use of 'elohim in Gen. 31:30, 32, also termed terafim, Gen. 31:19, 34, 35.
4. Cf. 1 Sam. 10:27; 21:16; 25:21; 2 Sam. 13:17.
5. Cf. Gen. 2:8; 1 Kings 7:15.
6. Cf. Deut. 14:25; 2 Kings 5:23; 12:11; Ezek. 5:3.
7. Isa. 8:1.
8. Exod. 32:4, 8; Deut. 9:12, 16; Ps. 106:19; Neh. 9:18.
9. Isa. 3:22.
10. So Rashi, Rashbam, Bekhor Shor.
11. Judg. 8:25.
12. Cf. the rabbinic term makkeh be-patish in Shab. 75b, literally "striking with a hammer," as a generalized rubric for various types of labors as well as figuratively for any act that completes a piece of work, suggested by Professor Marvin Fox orally.
13. Cf. Isa. 30:22; 40:19; Hos. 8:6, cf. Hos. 8:4; Hab. 2:19.
14. Cf. ANEP, nos. 470–474, 479, 486, 522, 525–526, 531, 534, 537, 830, 835.
15. Gen. 20:13, hit'u; Deut. 5:23; 1 Sam. 17:26, 36; Jer. 10:10; 23:36, 'elohim ḥayyim; Josh. 24:19, 'elohim kedoshim.
16. Cf. Hos. 1:9.
17. Exod. 3:7, 10; 5:1; 7:4, 16, 26; 8:16–19; 9:1, 13, 17; 10:3, 4; 22:24.
18. So Shadal.
19. Ber. 32a, Exod. R. 42:10.
29. Num. 11:2; 12:13; 14:13–20; 16:22; 21:7.
21. 1 Sam. 7:8–9; 12:19, 23.
22. Amos 7:2, 15.
23. Jer. 7:16; 37:3; 42:2–4.
24. Gen. 12:2; 18:18, 46:3.
25. E.g., Exod. 7:5; 8:6, 18; 9:29.
26. Num. 14:15–16; Deut. 9:28; 32:26–27; Isa. 48:9, 11; 66:5; Jer. 14:7, 21; Ezek. 20:9, 14, 22, 44; Joel 2:17; Ps. 106:8; cf. Pss. 79:10; 115:2.
27. Ps. 106:23; cf. Num. 11:2; 14:20; 21:7.
28. Maimonides, Guide 1.66.
29. The stem ḥ-r-t may be an Aramaized form of ḥ-r-sh, "to cut in," so Jer. 17:1, or it may be a metathesized form of ḥ-t-r, "to dig, bore through"; cf. Exod. 22:1; Ezek. 8:8; Job 24:16.
30. Cf. Isa. 27:2; Ps. 88:1.
31. Deut. 9:17 has "before your eyes."
32. UT 49.II.31–36, ANET, p. 140.
33. Cf. the description in 2 Kings 23:15 of Josiah's destruction of Jeroboam's altar and Asherah at Bethel; cf. 2 Chron. 15:16.
34. The injunction of Deut. 7:25 shows that the verb s-r-f, "to burn," is not inappropriate for the destruction of a metal idol.
35. So Rashi, Rashbam, Ibn Ezra, Ramban, and others.
36. Cf. Exod. 34:16; Num. 15:39; Jer. 3:1–5, 8; 5:7–9; Ezek. 16; 23:27; Hos. 2. The marital bond is defined as a berit, "covenant," in Prov. 2:17 and Mal. 2:14.
37. Cf. Exod. 32:21, 30, 31; 2 Kings 17:21.
38. However, Rashbam and Bekhor Shor point to Isa. 54:16 and Prov. 25:4 as proof that the verb y-ts-' is a technical metallurgical term.

39. For the stem p-r-', cf. Prov. 1:25; 13:18; 15:32; 29:18.
40. Num. 1:48–54; 2:17; 16:9.
41. Num. 3:40–51.
42. Gen. 50:17; Ps. 118:25; Dan. 9:4; Neh. 1:5; cf. the confession of the High Priest in the Second Temple as given in Mish. Yoma 4:2.
43. Cf. 1 Sam. 12:14f.; Ps. 27:13.
44. Cf. Isa. 4:3; Jer. 22:30; Ezek. 13:9.
45. Cf. Num. 1; Ezra 2:62 = Neh. 7:7, 64.
46. Cf. Ezek. 2:9–10; Zech. 5:1–4; Pss. 40:8; 139:16.
47. Cf. Isa. 65:6; Jer. 1:1, 13; Pss. 51:3; 109:14; Neh. 13:14; Dan. 7:10; Mish. Avot 2:1.
48. Maimonides, Guide 2.47.
49. So Rashbam, Ramban; cf. Ber. 32a. On the phenomenon in the ancient Near East, see S. Paul, "Heavenly Tablets and the Book of Life," JANES 5 (1973): 345–353.

Chapter 33

1. Tanḥ. Ki Tissa' 26, Rashi.
2. LXX manuscripts here read "My angel."
3. Cf. Exod. 25:8.
4. Exod. 40:38.
5. Exod. 25:8, 22; 30:6.
6. So Ibn Ezra.
7. Cf. Amos 3:7. J. Muilenberg, "The Intercession of the Covenant Mediator (Exodus 33:1a, 12–17)," in Words and Meanings, ed. P. R. Ackroyd and B. Lindars (Cambridge: Cambridge University Press, 1968), 159–181.
8. Cf. Gen. 6:8.
9. So Maimonides, Guide 1.54.
10. Gen. 18:25.
11. Deut. 3:20; 12:10; 25:19; Josh. 1:13, 15; 21:42; 22:4; 23:1; 2 Sam. 7:1–11; 1 Kings 5:18; 1 Chron. 22:9(8), 18(17); 23:25; 2 Chron. 14:5,6; 15:15; 20:30.
12. For the idea of Israel's chosenness, cf. Exod. 19:5; Lev. 20:24, 26; Num. 23:9; Deut. 7:6–8; 14:2; 26:18; Amos 3:2; Ps. 135:4.
13. Exod. 16:7, 10; 24:17; Lev. 9:6, 23; Num. 14:22; 16:19; 17:7; 20:6; Isa. 35:12; 59:19; 60:2; 62:2; 66:18, 19; Ezek. 3:23; Ps. 102:17; 1 Chron. 16:24; 2 Chron. 7:3.
14. Maimonides, Guide 1.4, 64.
15. Cf. Jer. 33:1; Hos. 8:7; Pss. 86:5; 106 passim; 145:9; and cf. the personal name tobijah (Tobias).
16. A. Marmorstein, The Old Rabbinic Doctrine of God, vol. I (Oxford University Press: 1927), 85f., no. 43.
17. Cf. Gen. 32:10, 13; Deut. 23:7; Josh. 24:20; 1 Sam. 25:30; 2 Sam. 2:6; 7:28; Jer. 18:10; 33:9, 14; M. Fox, "ṬÔB as Covenant Terminology," BASOR 209 (1973): 41–42; TDOT, s.v. ṬÔB, pp. 311, 314.
18. For this idem per idem construction, cf. Exod. 3:14; 4:13; 16:23; 1 Sam. 23:13; 2 Sam. 15:20; 2 Kings 8:1.
19. Cf. Exod. 34:5; Lam. 3:44; So Saadia, Bekhor Shor, Radak.
20. Exod. 33:11, 14, 15, 20, 23.

Chapter 34

1. Exod. 24:12; 31:18.
2. Deut. 5:6–18.
3. So Ibn Ezra, Ramban; contrast Exod. 19:24.
4. So Targ. Jon.
5. So Rashbam, Ibn Ezra, Ramban.
6. For the several different ways of calculating the thirteen, see S. D. Luzzatto, Commentary to the Pentateuch (Hebrew) (Tel Aviv: Devir 1965), 386–387; cf. Mid. Pss., Ps. 93 (ed. S. Buber), 416. See also Tosafot to RH 17b.

7. Num. 14:18; Jer. 32:18; Joel 2:13; Jon. 4:2; Nah. 1:3; Pss. 86:15; 103:8; 145:8; Neh. 9:17; cf. also Pss. 111:4; 112:4; 116:5; Neh. 9:31; 2 Chron. 30:9.

8. Sif. to Deut. 10:12; 11:22, ed. Horovitz-Finkelstein, p. 114, par. 49.

9. *Teshuvot ha-Rambam*, ed. J. Blau (Jerusalem: 1957), 505–507; Maimonides cites gaonic support; cf. Maimonides, Guide 1.21. This finds justification in Num. 14:18.

10. Cf. Gen. 22:11; 46:2; Exod. 3:4; 1 Sam. 3:10. LXX has the repetition also in 1 Sam. 3:4, 6.

11. Cf. Gen. 24:27, 49; 32:11; 47:29; Josh. 2:14; 2 Sam. 2:6; 15:20; Pss. 25:10; 40:11; 57:4; 61:8; 85:11; 86:5; 89:15; 103:8; 115:1; 138:2; 145:8; Prov. 3:3; 14:22; 16:6; 20:28.

12. So Ibn Ezra; cf. Deut. 7:9; 1 Kings 8:23 = 2 Chron. 6:14; Dan. 9:4; Neh. 1:5; 9:32.

13. Cf. Jer. 30:11.

14. So Rashbam, Bekhor Shor.

15. Cf. Gen. 8:21.

16. Exod. 34:13; Deut. 7:5; Judg. 6:25, 26, 28, 30; 2 Kings 18:4; 23:14; Mic. 5:13; 2 Chron. 14:2; 31:1; cf. Deut. 16:21. On 'Asherah, see "Asherah in the Hebrew Bible and Northwest Semitic Literature," John Day, JBL 105 (1986): 385–408.

17. Exod. 32:4, 8; Deut. 9:12, 16; Ps. 106:19; Neh. 9:18; cf. 2 Kings 17:16.

18. So Bekhor Shor.

19. For these terms as indicative of agricultural activity in general, cf. Gen. 45:6; 1 Sam. 8:12.

20. TJ Pe'ah 2:6 (17a), TJ Meg. 4:1 (74d), Git. 60b.

21. Cf. Gen. 7:4, 12, 17; 18:6; 50:3; Num. 13:25; 14:33; Josh. 5:6; 1 Kings 19:8; Ezek. 4:6; 29:11–13; Ps. 95:10. For the tradition of Moses' forty days on Sinai, cf. Exod. 24:18; Deut. 9:9, 11, 18, 25; 10:10.

22. On this topic, see J. Morgenstern, "Moses with the Shining Face," HUCA 2 (1925): 1–27; M. Haran, "The Shining of Moses' Face: A Case Study in Biblical and Ancient Near Eastern Iconography," in *In The Shelter of Elyon: Essays on Ancient Palestinian Life and Literature in Honor of G. W. Ahlstrom*, ed. W. B. Barrick and J. R. Spencer (Sheffield: JSOT Press, 1984), 159–173. (Note that an unfortunate typographical error has crept in on p. 167, tenth line up.)

23. Ta'an. 30b, BB 121a; SOR 6, ed. B. Ratner, p. 29.

24. Cf. Num. 6:25; Isa. 2:5; Ezek. 1:27–28; Pss. 4:7; 31:17; 36:10; 44:4; 67:2; 80:20; 89:16; 104:2; 118:27; 119:135; Job 29:3.

25. A. L. Oppenheim, "Akkadian *pul(u)ḫtu* and *mellamu*," JAOS 63 (1943): 31–34.

26. R. Mellinkoff, *The Horned Moses in Medieval Art and Thought* (Berkeley: University of California Press, 1970).

27. The unique noun *masveh* is probably derived from the stem *s-v-h*, which is behind Gen. 49:11, *sutoh*, "his garment," a word attested in the Phoen. Kilamua (KAI 24.8) and Batnoam (KAI 11) inscriptions, and in Punic (KAI 76 A24.8) as well as in Mish. Kel. 16:7. *Masveh* itself occurs in Tosef. Kel., BB 1.7, and most likely also in Er. 22a.

Chapter 35

1. *Seder Olam*, ed. B. Ratner (reprint, New York: Talmudical Research Institute, 1966), chap. 6, pp. 27–31.

2. B. Lewin, *Otzar Ha-Geonim*, Tractate Shabbat (Haifa: N. Wahtaftig Press, 1930), 27f., pars. 83–85.

3. The same phrase is used in Exod. 39:34; 40:21; Num. 4:5.

Chapter 36

1. Exod. 36:1, 5; 38:22; 39 passim; 40 passim.

Chapter 37

1. 1 Kings 6:2; cf. v. 4.

Chapter 38

1. J. A. Knudtzon, *Die El-Amarna-Tafeln* (Reprint Aalen: O. Zeller, 1964) 14, col. 2, 1.75.

2. T. G. H. James, *An Introduction to Ancient Egypt* (New York: Farrar, Straus, Giroux, 1979), 224–225; for such mirrors, see ANEP, nos. 71, 78, 632.

3. The verse is missing from LXX B and from the Hebrew text of 4QSamᵃ.

4. Num. 4:23; 8:24; see J. Milgrom, *The JPS Torah Commentary: Numbers* (Philadelphia: Jewish Publication Society, 1990), Comment to Num. 4:23.

5. Cf. R. de Vaux, *Ancient Israel: Its Life and Institutions* (New York, McGraw-Hill, 1961), 296, 383.

6. So Bahya; U. Cassuto, *A Commentary on the Book of Exodus* (Jerusalem: Magnes Press, 1967), at 38:8.

7. On Heb. *'avodah* in this context, see Milgrom, *JPS Commentary: Numbers*, Excursus 6.

8. For an excellent example, see ANEP, no. 133.

9. So Rashbam; cf. the use of the stem *p-k-d* in Exod. 30:12; Num. 1:44; 3:39; 4:37; 41, 45, 46, 49.

10. Only also Num. 1:50, 53; 10:11.

11. Cf. "Tent of the Pact" in Num. 9:15; 17:22, 23; 18:2; 2 Chron. 24:6; "Ark of the Pact" in Exod. 25:22; 26:34; 30:6, 26; 39:35; 40:3, 21; Num. 4:5; 7:89; Josh. 4:16; "tablets of the Pact" in Exod. 31:18; 32:15; 34:29; "curtain of the Pact" in Lev. 24:3; and simply "the Pact," using the abstract for the concrete, in Exod. 16:34; 25:16, 21; 27:21; 30:6, 36; 31:7; 40:20; Lev. 16:13; Num. 17:19, 25. On *'edut*, see Comment to 16:34.

12. So Num. 26:60; 1 Chron. 5:29.

13. Cf. Num. 3:2, 4; 1 Chron. 24:1–2.

14. Num. 4:28.

15. Ezra 8:2; 1 Chron. 24:3.

16. Cf. *kikkar lehem*, "a loaf of bread," in Exod. 29:23; 1 Sam. 2:36; *kikkar ha-yarden*, "the plain of the Jordan," in Gen. 13:10–11.

17. Cf. Isa. 63:12; Ps. 78:13; Neh. 9:11 used regarding the sea; Isa. 48:21; Eccles. 10:9 regarding wood.

Chapter 39

1. Exod. 39:1, 5, 7, 21, 26, 29, 31.

2. So Exod. 40:1, 6, 29; 1 Chron. 6:17.

3. See Comment to 25:8.

4. *Pesikta Rabbati*, ed. M. Friedmann (Vienna: Friedmann, 1880), chap. 6, p. 24a.

5. Gen. 1:31; 2:3.

6. *Seder Olam*, ed. B. Ratner (reprint, New York: Talmudical Research Institute, 1966), chap. 6, p. 30; Tosef. Men. 7:8, ed. M. S. Zuckermandel (reprint, Jerusalem: Wahrmann, 1968), 522.

Chapter 40

1. Cf. Exod. 25:9, 40; 27:8; Num. 8:4.

2. Exod. 19:1.

3. 1 Kings 8:10–11; 2 Chron. 7:2. Ezek. 43:4–6 seems to convey the same experience.

EXCURSUSES

The Hebrews 1:15

The designation "Hebrew(s)," *'ivri(m)*, is found approximately thirty times in the Hebrew Bible. It can only derive from an original *'iver* or *'ever*, and its form permits a connotation that is either geographic or gentilic—that is, having an ethnic denotation like *kena'ani*, "Canaanite," or *mo'abi*, "Moabite." The former possibility is based on the use of *'ever*, meaning "the region beyond," as used in Genesis 50:10 and Numbers 21:13, so that *'ivri* is "the man from the other side." Such an understanding might be reflected in Joshua 24:2: "In olden times, your forefathers—Terah, father of Abraham and father of Nahor—lived beyond the Euphrates." The Septuagint rendered *'ivri* in Genesis 14:13 as *ho perátes*, "the one from beyond," or "the wanderer." Opposed to the geographic interpretation is the associated "Mamre the Amorite" in that verse. This and the vast majority of citations weight the balance heavily in favor of the ethnic nature of the term.

Biblical references to "Hebrews" are concentrated within three contexts. The first is the cycle of Joseph stories,[1] always having to do with relationships with Egyptians. The second cluster appears in the early chapters of Exodus,[2] in which, again without exception, "Hebrew" contrasts with "Egyptian." The third collection is in the Book of Samuel,[3] in which the term is invariably in opposition to "Philistines." The only other narrative usage is in Jonah 1:9, also in a non-Israelite ambience. It will be noted that, apart from this last source, which is most likely a conscious archaism, all citations are pre-Davidic; all refer only to Israelites (including 1 Sam. 13:3,7; 14:21) in contrast to other peoples.

Apart from a narrative context, there is the sociolegal term "Hebrew slave," *'eved 'ivri*, in Exodus 21:3 and Deuteronomy 15:12. This, too, means an Israelite, as is proven by the descriptive "your fellow" (*'ahikha*) in Deuteronomy 15:12 and by Jeremiah 34:9,14.

The foregoing data overwhelmingly support the view that *'ivri* is an ethnic term. The alternative geographic explanation is, moreover, discounted by the fact that Abram's family back home in Mesopotamia, "beyond the River," is not called "Hebrew" but "Aramean" (Gen. 25:20).

There are, however, several curious aspects of the biblical employment of the word "Hebrew." Of the three patriarchs, why does Abram alone bear this epithet, and why only in Genesis 14:13? Why are the other peoples who are related to Israel and also descended from Eber, grandson of Noah, called "sons of Eber" in Genesis 10:21 but never "Hebrews"? And why is the description reserved exclusively for the descendants of Abraham through the line of Isaac and Jacob but not used of the lines of Ishmael or Esau? Not all of these questions can be satisfactorily resolved in the present state of our knowledge, but the possible relationship of the Hebrews to a well-documented Near Eastern phenomenon needs to be examined because this latter has often been adduced as evidence to provide a solution.

From the beginning of the second millennium B.C.E. through the twelfth century B.C.E., cuneiform tablets from Sumer, Babylon, Upper Mesopotamia, Anatolia, and the Syrian-Canaanite area, as well as hieroglyphic texts from Egypt, register the presence of

groups of people variously referred to as SA.GAZ, *ḥapiru*, *ʿpr(m)*, and *ʿpr(w)*. The meaning of these terms has long been the subject of scholarly debate, but each term is concerned with the same class of people. SA.GAZ is a Sumerian ideograph that is read in Akkadian as *šaggašu* and to which the scribes often attached the gloss *ḥabbātu*. *Šaggašu* in Akkadian means "killer, aggressor, violent person." In West Semitic languages the same stem denotes "to be restless, ill at ease." *Ḥabbātu* means "a robber" as well as "a migrant," but *ʿpr*, which must be West Semitic, is as yet of uncertain meaning.

The people referred to by these terms are distinguished not only by extensive geographic distribution but also by considerable ethnic and linguistic diversity. Everywhere, they constitute a recognizable subservient social class, essentially an urban element. They are rootless aliens, deprived of legal rights, who often hire themselves out as professional soldiers of fortune or as slaves. Within the Egyptian sphere of influence, where authority was weak and centralized control was lax, this group exhibited independence and aggressive behavior and appeared as a socially disruptive element. The phenomenon as a whole seems to be the product of the convulsions that afflicted the Near East in the course of the second millennium B.C.E. By the end of the period, conditions became more stabilized, and the ʿApiru (*ḥapiru*) disappeared from history.

Were the Hebrews part of the ʿApiru? Various lines of evidence converge to reject the likelihood. First, there is no doubt that *ʿapiru*, an adjective, is the correct form of the name, as Egyptian and Ugaritic texts show, and the differences in the vowels and middle consonant between it and *ʿivri*, a gentilic, cannot easily be reconciled. Further, the *ʿapiru* are a social entity, not an ethnic group like the Hebrews. They possess nothing remotely resembling the Israelite tribal system. Extrabiblical sources of the second millennium B.C.E. do not identify *ʿapiru* with Israel, and where Israel is mentioned, it is not identified as belonging to the *ʿapiru*. If Abram is an *ʿapiru*, it is surprising that he enlists the support of Amorites in Genesis 14, rather than call upon his fellow *ʿapiru* for help. Even more persuasive is a comparison between the descriptions of the *ʿapiru* in Canaan, given in the El-Amarna letters (14th c. B.C.E.) and the activities of the invading Israelites under Joshua. The *ʿapiru* are never portrayed as being invaders from without, as are the Israelites; they often collaborate with the local Canaanite rulers, absorb local elements into their ranks, and defy Egyptian suzerainty over the land. The Israelites, on the other hand, are implacably hostile to the Canaanites, and Egypt never appears as a factor in the Israelite wars of conquest. Significantly, the term "Hebrews" is never featured in Joshua or Judges, which report on the Israelite wars of conquest and settlement in the land—precisely those books in which they would be expected to appear, were they to be identified with the aggressive *ʿapiru*.

The true origin of the term "Hebrew" is still to be determined. Perhaps it came to be used of social elements marginal to a society. If it was a self-designation for the people in the formative period of Israelite history, it would explain why it was used exclusively of Israel. At any rate, the term fell into disuse with the founding of the monarchy and was revived in much later times.

EXCURSUS 2
The Abandoned Hero Motif   2:3

The story of the baby Moses placed in a basket and abandoned to the River Nile has attracted the attention of scholars, especially folklorists, because it appears to conform to a widespread motif that is characteristic of tales about the birth of heroes.

A well-known example is the nativity of Oedipus in Greek mythology. Laius, his father, had received an unfavorable oracle from Apollo; therefore, when a son was born to him, he handed him over to a shepherd to be exposed on Mount Cithaeron. Disregarding instructions, the shepherd entrusted Oedipus to another shepherd, who, in turn, gave him to Polybus, King of Corinth. The monarch and his wife reared Oedipus as though he were their own son.

Another example of the same genre is the story of the birth of Heracles (Hercules). He was abandoned by his mother Alcmene but was found by Athena, who handed him over to Hera. She, unaware of the baby's parentage, gave him to his own mother.

A third instance from classical literature is the famous tale of Romulus and Remus, the mythical founders of the city of Rome. The twins were born to Rhea Sylvia, a princess and Vestal Virgin, who had been violated by Mars. Amulius, younger brother of her father Numitor, deposed the king and ordered the infants to be thrown into the River Tiber. However, the chest in which they were placed washed ashore; the twins were found and suckled by a she-wolf until their discovery by Faustulus, the royal herdsman. He and his wife brought up Romulus and Remus as their own sons.

The identical motif occurs in the biographies of two Near Eastern heroes. One concerns the birth legend of Sargon of Accad, the great empire builder of Mesopotamia. Purporting to be autobiographical, the cuneiform text claims that he was the love child of a high priestess of noble descent, the father being unknown. Disclosure of his mother's indiscretion would have entailed the loss of her office, for which childlessness was an indispensable precondition. Accordingly, Sargon's mother placed him in a basket of reeds, which she caulked with bitumen, and abandoned him to the River Euphrates. Carried downstream, the infant was discovered and saved by Akki the water drawer, who adopted him. Later in life, Sargon was favored by the goddess Ishtar and seized the throne of Akkad, which he held for fifty-five years.

The other Near Eastern example of this popular theme pertains to Cyrus, son of Cambyses, founder of the Achaemenid Persian empire. His grandfather Astyages, king of the Medes, experienced two dreams that were interpreted to mean that his newly born grandson Cyrus would one day usurp his throne. He therefore ordered his trusted servant Harpagus to murder the infant. Forebearing to commit the deed himself, the man summoned a herdsman named Mithradates, handed him the baby, and commanded him to leave him to die on a mountain range. The herdsman, however, took the infant home, only to discover that his wife had just given birth to a stillborn baby. The couple substituted Cyrus for the dead infant, whose body they left on the hills instead. Ten years later, by a quirk of fate, Cyrus's true identity was uncovered.

A close examination of the account of the birth of Moses clearly demonstrates striking differences that distinguish it from the foregoing examples. Other than the life-threatening exposure of the infant, all the significant details of the Torah's narrative are antithetical to

the conventional characteristics of the literary genre that has to do with the birth legends of heroes. First of all, a singular feature in the biography of Moses is the absence of a divine announcement foretelling his birth. There are no prophecies about his destiny or fate, no omens of future greatness, and no supernatural phenomena appear in connection with the event. The absence of these items conspicuously distinguishes the biblical narrative from the popular biographies of heroes.

There are many other considerations as well. The baby Moses is neither the issue of an illicit relationship nor the child of nobility or royalty. There is no parental or grandfatherly hostility to the newly born. The mother desperately makes every effort to retain her offspring at home as long as possible, and she cedes him to the river only to circumvent the pharaoh's decree of genocide. Even then, she does not assign the task to someone else but carefully and tenderly puts the baby in a well-caulked basket that she places among the clumps of reeds by the river bank so that it would not float away and would be spotted by the princess. She also takes measures to make sure that she keeps track of developments. Again, the finder in the Exodus story is not the usual person of humble birth but the daughter of royalty, who at once recognizes the Hebrew identity of the infant.

EXCURSUS 3
"God of the Father"   3:6

A distinctive and characteristic feature of the Book of Genesis is the frequent use of a certain type of divine epithet that is made up of the phrase "God is my/your/his father,"[1] often with "Abraham" or "Isaac"[2] or both names[3] added in apposition to "father." In some instances, God is further identified as YHVH.[4] This designation appears once again in Exodus 3:6 in God's self-manifestation to Moses, where it is intended to emphasize continuity. The God who speaks at the Burning Bush is the selfsame One who spoke to the patriarchs. Thereafter in the Torah the epithet becomes "God of your/their fathers," the plural referring to the entire people of Israel.[5]

The epithet "God of the father" is not unique to the Bible. It is, in fact, documented over a wide area of the ancient Near East over a long period of time, from the nineteenth century B.C.E. on. In these texts the "god of the father(s)" sometimes appears anonymously, sometimes with an accompanying personal name. For example, we find "Ashur, god of my father," "Ashur and Amurrum, the gods of our father," "Shamash, the god of my father," "Ilaprat, god of your father," an oath "by the name of the god of my father," an appeal to the king "by the name of (the god) Adad, lord of Aleppo, and the god of your father."

The connotation of this divine epithet is a special, personal relationship between the individual and his god, who is his patron and protector. This designation is particularly appropriate in the patriarchal narratives, since they revolve around the lives of individuals. It is highly significant that it is never used in reference to Abraham's father. This is to be explained by the tradition, preserved in Joshua 24:2, that Terah was an idolator. It indicates that the advent of Abraham constituted a new stage in the history of religion. Similarly, the change from the singular to the plural form, "fathers," following the commissioning of Moses, registers a further development.

EXCURSUS 4
'El Shaddai   6:3

This is the most common of the several divine names constructed with an initial *'el* element. Like *'el 'elyon*, it could be a fusion of an initially independent element *shaddai*, with *'el*, or the compound could be original. One way or the other, the distribution of *shaddai* both with and without the accompanying *'el* is highly instructive. This divine name appears nine times in the Torah, of which three are in poetic texts.[1] All but two of the Bible's other thirty-nine usages are likewise poetic (Prophets, Psalms, and Job). The prose exceptions (Ruth 1:20–21) are more apparent than real, since the Book of Ruth possesses a poetic substratum and frequently displays archaisms.

These statistics have an important bearing on the question of the antiquity of usage. The overwhelming appearance in poetic contexts points a priori to a venerable tradition, for Hebrew poetry tends to preserve or consciously to employ early forms of speech. The remarkably high incidence of *shaddai* in Job is of particular importance in light of that book's patriarchal setting. All the true prose usages are concentrated within the Genesis narratives,[2] a fact that is in perfect harmony with Exodus 6:3: "I appeared to Abraham, Isaac, and Jacob as El Shaddai," a tradition explicitly assigning the divine name to the pre-Mosaic age. Significantly, of the vast store of biblical personal names, only three are constructed with the element *shaddai*. These are Shedeur (= ? *shaddai-ur*), Zurishaddai, and Ammishaddai—all appearing solely in the lists of Numbers 1–2. Each is the father of a tribal representative at the time of the Exodus. In other words, the divine name Shaddai lost its vitality in Israel with the advent of Moses and was preserved only as a literary relic in poetic compositions. Interestingly, the personal name *shaddai-'ammi*—that is, the biblical Ammishaddai with its two components inverted—has turned up in a hieroglyphic sepulchral inscription as the name of a petty official in fourteenth-century B.C.E. Egypt. Since it cannot be explained as Egyptian, and because it is written in the syllabic orthography often reserved for foreign words, there is every reason to believe that the name belongs to a Western Semite in Egyptian employ. It is indeed known that Semites served the Egyptian bureaucracy in the fourteenth and thirteenth centuries B.C.E. There is thus additional evidence of the use of *shaddai* in pre-Mosaic times.

The great antiquity of the name and its obsolescence in Israel in the Mosaic period explain why there are no consistent traditions as to its meaning and why the ancient versions have no uniform rendering. The Septuagint variously has "God," "Lord," "All-powerful," and "The Heavenly One," among others, as well as the transliteration *shaddai*. The Vulgate has "Omnipotens," whence the English tradition "Almighty." The Syriac has "The Strong One," "God," and "The Highest," as well as *shaddai*. The Greek rendering *hikanós*, "He that is Sufficient," found in the versions of Aquila, Symmachus, and Theodotian, reflects a rabbinic suggestion explaining the name as a combination of the relative particle *sha* with *dai*, meaning "sufficiency" (Gen. R. 46:2). The modern conjecture that has gained widest currency connects shaddai with Akkadian *šadu*, "a mountain," often used as a divine (and royal) epithet. The name would originally have meant, "The One of the Mountain," probably referring to a cosmic mount or corresponding to the divine epithet "The Rock."

Notwithstanding the various conjectures, the original meaning of the divine name *shaddai* still eludes us.

Tefillin 13:9,16

Exodus 13:9 states as follows: "And this shall be as a sign (Hebrew, *'ot*) on your hand and as a reminder (Hebrew, *zikkaron*) on your forehead." The same is repeated in verse 16 with a variant term: "And it shall be as a sign upon your hand and as a symbol (Hebrew, *totafot*) on your forehead."

The terms "sign," "reminder," and "symbol" evoke some material object that serves to jog the memory, but they do not in themselves require a literal meaning for these verses. Rashbam actually considered the "deep, straightforward meaning" of the verses to be metaphorical. He adduced, in support, Song of Songs 8:6: "Let me be a seal upon your heart, / Like a seal upon your arm." Abraham Ibn Ezra mentions, but rejects, this figurative interpretation, which its proponents bolstered by citing additional biblical sources such as "For they are a graceful wreath upon your head, / A necklace about your throat" (Prov. 1:9). "Let fidelity and steadfastness not leave you; / Bind them about your throat, / Write them on the tablet of your mind" (*ibid.* 3:3). "Tie them over your heart always; / Bind them around your throat" (*ibid.* 6:21). Other texts of the same order are Proverbs 7:3 as well as Jeremiah 17:1 and 31:32.

Apparently, both the Samaritans and the medieval Jewish sect of Karaites also took the instructions of Exodus 13:9,16 metaphorically, for they do not have tefillin. Traditional rabbinic exegesis, however, interpreted Exodus 13:9,16 literally as enjoining the wearing of tefillin. This understanding is upheld by two other texts in the Torah that reiterate the precept. Deuteronomy 6:8, which is part of the section that has traditionally become known as the Shema, states: "Bind them [i.e., God's teachings, v.6] as a sign on your hand, and let them serve as a symbol on your forehead." A literal meaning is here favored by the immediately adjacent verse: "Inscribe them on the doorpost of your house and on your gates." The other text is Deuteronomy 11:18, which is part of the second paragraph of the Shemaʿ in the Jewish prayer book: "Therefore, impress these My words upon your very heart; bind them as a sign on your hand, and let them serve as a symbol on your forehead."

The tefillin comprise two small, cubelike, blackened leather capsules that are called in Hebrew *battim* (sing. *bayit*, lit. "house"). One is placed on the arm and one on the forehead, preparatory to the morning prayers. Because the singular form is *tefillah*,[1] which is also the Hebrew word for "prayer," a widespread explanation for the term "tefillin" is "objects worn during prayer." It has been argued that this is not entirely satisfactory because in tannaitic times it was the custom among many to wear the tefillin all day long. Still, the designation could have derived from their being first put on for morning worship. Another possible derivation is from the biblical Hebrew stem *p-l-l* in the sense of "to intercede."[2] That is, the tefillin, with their expressed purpose of reminding the worshipper of God's teachings and commandments, perform indirectly a propitiatory and expiatory function.

The English rendering for tefillin is usually "phylacteries." This is an unfortunate misnomer. It is based upon the Greek term used in the Christian Bible.[3] The Greek noun *phylakterion* derives from a stem that means "to protect, guard," the noun form indicating "a safeguard, amulet." It is quite possible that at the lowest popular level the tefillin were regarded as being charged with magical power, able to protect the wearer from malignant

influences. Such a misconception may have arisen from the similarity in shape of tefillin to amulets in the ancient world,[4] and from the fact that the preferred area of the body for the wearing of amulets was the forehead and often the arm as well, as Song of Songs 8:6 shows. Also, inscribed amulets were frequently stored in small leather cases.

Ancient popular misinterpretation notwithstanding, and despite the widespread use of the designation "phylacteries," the tefillin have nothing to do with amulets. Their contents carry neither incantations nor petitions—standard items in all such paraphernalia. Rather, the biblical passages inscribed within the capsules express fundamental doctrines of Judaism. They proclaim the existence and unity of God, the call for the loving surrender of the mind and will to His demands, the charge to make God's teachings the constant subject of study and to ensure the education of the young, faith in divine righteousness with its corollaries that society is built on moral foundations, that there is reward for virtue and punishment for evil, and finally, and above all, that the experience of the Exodus is of transcendent importance in the religion of Israel.

Aside from the contents of the tefillin, which in themselves preclude any phylacteric function, there is also the confounding fact that halakhic requirements exempt from the obligation to wear tefillin precisely those who, in the popular mind, would be expected to be most in need of protection from baneful influences—namely, minors, slaves, women, those who labor under certain sicknesses, and pall-bearers.[5] Moreover, it is in places such as the cemetery and toilet, where, in the pagan world, people were thought to be most vulnerable to evil spirits, that Jewish law forbids the wearing of tefillin.

The biblical sources are silent on the implementation of the command. It is only from the Second Temple period that the evidence is forthcoming. The Sadducean faction that departed in so many ways from Pharasaic interpretation of Scripture, adhered to this command. Since that party was formed about the year 200 B.C.E., it must have already enjoyed a venerable past by then. The earliest post-biblical literary source to comment upon the tefillin is the Hellenistic-Jewish propagandist work known as *The Epistle of Aristeas*,[6] composed about 170 B.C.E.; however, it mentions only the hand tefillah. From the last years of the Second Temple we have the testimony of the Jewish historian, Josephus, who records both the hand and head tefillin.[7] In addition, rabbinic sources mention the existence of tefillin that originated two generations before Hillel and Shammai,[8] that is, to about 70 B.C.E., and also a pair that had belonged to Simeon ben Shetah,[9] of the same century.

The aforementioned literary traditions about the use of the tefillin have been abundantly reinforced in recent years by the finds from the region of Qumran in the Judean wilderness near the northwestern shore of the Dead Sea.[10] Here was uncovered the headquarters of a sectarian Jewish community that occupied the site from about 135 B.C.E. to about 68 C.E. Among the hoard of manuscripts and numerous objects found in the nearby caves were many fragments of tefillin, including the capsule of a head tefillin that still contained its four inscribed slips. Other fragments have been found in the Wadi Muraba'at region in the Judean wilderness, about twelve miles southwest of Qumran. During the first and second centuries C.E., this site served as a refuge for Jewish soldiers who fought against Rome.

The widespread use of tefillin in this period contrasts with the surprising silence of the Mishnah, edited ca. 200 C.E., about their makeup and contents. Maimonides suggests that it is because the public was so thoroughly familiar with the rules that it was not necessary to specify them.[11] Be that as it may, the details are discussed at length in the Talmud, tractate Menahot 34a–37b.

As stated above, the tefillin are cube-shaped, although the height need not be the same as the equal length and breadth. The capsule for the arm is hollow and contains a single slip of rolled or folded parchment, called *klaf* in Hebrew, on which are inscribed all four relevant biblical passages in the same script as used for writing a scroll of the Torah: Exodus 13:1–10, 11–16, Deuteronomy 6:4–9 and 11:13–21. For the head tefillah, these passages are transcribed onto separate slips, and each is inserted into one of the four compartments into which the capsule is divided. The order of the passages was a matter of dispute in talmudic times[12] and was still an issue in the eleventh and twelfth centuries between Rashi (1040–1105) and his grandson Rabbenu Tam (1096–1171). The view of Rashi became universally accepted in the Jewish world. It is now clear that both systems existed in the time of the Second Temple, as the finds from Qumran prove.[13]

As to the makeup of the tefillin, the two capsules rest on a wider, square base of thick leather known in the Talmud by its Aramaic name, *titora'*. This has a hollow projection at the back, called *ma'abarta'*. Through it the strap (in Hebrew *retsua'*) is passed. Both capsules and straps are made from the hide of a ritually clean (kosher) animal. They must be especially prepared for their sacred purpose. The entire tefillah is sewn together with twelve stitches, using tendon thread derived from a kosher animal.

The two straps, which are blackened on their visible side, are made from a single piece of leather. They hold the tefillin in place on the arm and forehead. The strap for the hand tefillah needs to be long enough to be wound seven times around the arm, three times around the hand, and three times around the middle finger. The strap for the head tefillah must reach to the navel on the right side and the chest on the left; or, according to another ruling, that on the right should reach down as far as the genitalia and that on the left to the navel.

The hand tefillah is put on first, following the order of mention in the passages in the Torah. Its proper position is on the left arm (unless the wearer is left-handed), directly on the biceps, slightly inclined toward the heart, thus symbolizing the literary image "Impress these My words upon your very heart" (Deut. 11:18). The strap is tied in the form of a noose and is knotted so as to form the Hebrew letter *yod* at the end of the side nearest the heart. The winding round the hand shapes the letter *shin*, and that round the finger, the letter *dalet*, so that in combination they make up the divine name *shaddai*, "Almighty."

The proper place for the head tefillah is at the high point in the center of the forehead at the edge of the hair line, "between the eyes." The knot of the encircling strap lies on the nape just where the skull ends. The Hebrew letter *shin*, probably standing for *shaddai* or *shema'*, is embossed on both sides of the head capsule. That on the right is the standard form with three upright strokes, but that on the left side has four such strokes. The meaning of this unusual shape is uncertain. An interesting hypothesis is that it arose to indicate that the tefillin so marked are normative, having four, not five, compartments. The extra parchment slip would have contained the Decalogue, which was recited daily at the morning service in the Temple,[14] but which practice was discontinued in the face of sectarian polemics.[15] It is theorized that the Decalogue also once had a place in the tefillin and was removed at the same time and for the same reason.[16] Mishnah Sanhedrin 11:3 refers to those who claim that there should be five compartments in the head tefillah, and similar references are to be found elsewhere in Rabbinic literature.[17] The findings at Qumran provide evidence of the early existence of tefillin containing the Decalogue. The Church Father Jerome (347–420 C.E.) reported that the tefillin contained the Decalogue.[18] He apparently saw a sectarian pair.

Tefillin are not worn on Sabbaths and scriptural festival days, nor are they worn at night; hence, this precept falls within the category of "time-conditioned performative *mitzvot*." According to rabbinic halakhah, women are exempt from all such obligations and, therefore, are not duty-bound to wear tefillin.[19] Nevertheless, rabbinic sources mention that Michal, daughter of King Saul, did assume the obligation to put on tefillin, and the sages of the day did not object.[20] The Code of Rabbi Aaron ben Jacob ha-Kohen of Lunel (ca. 1330–1360), called *Orhot Ḥayyim*,[21] quotes Rabbi Solomon ben Abraham Adret (Rashba, ca. 1235–ca. 1300) to the effect that women are permitted to recite the benedictions even over performative, time-bound precepts.[22] Rabbenu Jacob b. Meir Tam (ca. 1100–1171), grandson of Rashi, made a similar ruling,[23] thus allowing women to wear tefillin. However, these views did not become the norm.

EXCURSUS 6

Biblical and Ancient Near Eastern Law [1] (21:1–22:16)

If, as the Rabbis frequently stated, God employed the everyday language of human beings in order to communicate His will,[2] then there is no section of the Torah in which this principle is more patently manifest than in the collections of legal ordinances. Extant corpora of laws, records of court proceedings, and judicial decisions provide ample evidence to prove that in its external form, in legal draftsmanship, in its terminology and phraseology, the Torah followed long-established, widespread, standardized patterns of Mesopotamian law.

Documents from the practice of law run into the many tens of thousands, uncovered at several widely dispersed sites in the Near East. Collections of laws recovered number no more than six.

Two such collections have survived in the non-Semitic Sumerian language spoken in southern Mesopotamia during the third and early second millenniums B.C.E., written in cuneiform script. The older one is that of King Ur-Nammu[3] of the city-state of Ur, founder of the Third Dynasty of that city in the twenty-first century B.C.E. The original has not been found, only a fragmentary copy from Nippur, a city about one hundred miles (ca. 160 km.) south of Baghdad. This has been supplemented by two broken tablets from Ur itself, both of which are much older. The extant materials preserve the prologue to the collection, together with twenty-nine stipulations, probably less than half of the original number. The prologue refers to "principles of equity and truth" and describes social abuses that the king sought to correct in order "to establish equity in the land" by standardizing weights and measures and by protecting the orphan, the widow, and the poor. The stipulations cover sexual offenses, support of divorcées, false accusations, the return of runaway slaves, bodily injuries, the case of an arrogant slave-woman, perjured testimony, and encroachment of another's private property. The laws are formulated in "casuistic" style; that is to say, they are conditional, the opening statement beginning with "if" followed by the hypothetical, concrete case, and the concluding statement giving the prescribed penalty.

The second Sumerian collection of laws comes from Lipit-Ishtar,[4] king of the city of Isin, in central lower Mesopotamia, in the nineteenth century B.C.E. Although an Amorite, he wrote his laws in Sumerian. There may once have existed also an Akkadian version, now lost. The laws, of which about thirty-eight remain, are estimated to have originally num-

bered about two hundred. They are framed by a prologue and an epilogue. In the former, the king writes that his god had commissioned him "to establish justice in the land" and "to promote the welfare" of his people. In the latter, he declares that he has restored domestic tranquility and established righteousness and truth. The extant laws, which belong to the concluding part of the corpus, deal with a variety of civil cases: the hiring of a boat, horticulture, the institution of slavery, house ownership, family laws such as marriage, divorce, polygamy, inheritance, and responsibility for injury to a rented animal. In these laws too, the casuistic formulation is the rule.

The other law collections from Mesopotamia are all written in Akkadian. The earliest in this language derives from the city of Eshnunna,[5] situated about twenty-six miles (42 km.) northeast of Baghdad, on a tributary of the Tigris River. Its author is unknown, and its date is uncertain. The laws, some sixty in all, are preserved on two tablets, neither being complete. These were copied in the time of a contemporary of Hammurabi, but the original is believed to be considerably older. Neither prologue nor epilogue, if there were any, has been preserved. The legislation concerns the prices of various commodities, the cost of hiring a wagon and a boat, negligence on the part of the hirer, the wages of laborers, as well as laws pertaining to marriage, loans, slavery, property, personal injury, a goring ox, a vicious dog, and divorce. As before, the casuistic formulation is predominant. A peculiarity is that the application of the laws may vary according to the social status of the persons involved.

Mesopotamian jurisprudence reached its zenith in the seventeenth or eighteenth century B.C.E., with the promulgation of Hammurabi's great collection.[6] These were inscribed on an eight-foot-high black diorite stele that was originally placed in the temple of Esagila in Babylon. In the early part of the twelfth century B.C.E. it was looted by the Elamite king Shutruk-Nah-hunite and carried off to Susa (Hebrew, *shushan*), capital of his kingdom, where French excavators discovered it in 1902. It now resides in the Louvre in Paris.

The upper front part of the stele bears a relief that features King Hammurabi standing before a seated deity, either the sun god Shamash or the chief god of Babylon, Marduk. The scene is often misinterpreted in popular books as Hammurabi receiving the laws from the god, but it is nothing of the kind. The god is really investing the king with the ring and the staff, which are the symbols of sovereignty. He thereby endows him with the authority, and perhaps also the wisdom, to promulgate the laws. The text makes it perfectly clear that Hammurabi himself is the sole source of the legislation.

Written in cuneiformed Akkadian in fifty-one columns, the stele now contains what is calculated to be two hundred and eighty-two legal paragraphs. About thirty-five to forty paragraphs were erased by the Elamite king; a few of these have been restored from other tablets. An extensive literary prologue and a lengthy epilogue frame the legal section. The prologue abounds in lofty sentiments about the purpose of the legislation, which is to further public welfare, to promote the cause of justice, to protect the interests of the weak, and to ensure the rule of law. The epilogue repeats these noble ideals and adds that the statutes are there so that anyone may know the law in case of need and that a future ruler may be guided by Hammurabi's ordinances. It closes with a series of blessings invoked on him who is faithful to the laws and heaps fearful curses on him who is perfidious. Both prologue and epilogue are unabashedly replete with Hammurabi's copious and effusive self-praise and with massive hyperbole extolling his own greatness and mighty deeds.

The corpus of the laws, mostly styled casuistically, includes a large variety of legal

topics. The first forty-one paragraphs deal mainly with matters of public order; the rest belong overwhelmingly to the domain of private law, matters that affect the individual citizen. Distinctive features of the laws are the extraordinarily large numbers of capital offenses (some thirty in all), the penal mutilation of the body, vicarious punishment, the principle of talion, or legal retaliation in kind, intense concern with the protection of private property, and an innovative approach to several areas of private wrong that are now recognized as issues of public welfare to be regulated by the state. Finally, as in the laws of Eshnunna, those of Hammurabi reflect a stratified society; as mentioned above, the penalties and judgments may vary according to the social standing of the litigants.

Considerably different from the collections hitherto described is the body of legislation that has come to be known as the Middle Assyrian Laws.[7] Uncovered at the ancient city of Asshur on the Tigris River, about two hundred and fifty miles (563 km.) north of Babylon, the several clay tablets on which these are inscribed come from the twelfth century B.C.E., but the legislation itself may well go back three centuries earlier. Although they conform to the casuistic pattern, the legal formulations and terminology as well as the prescribed penalties suggest influences, presently unknown, other than the standard Mesopotamian traditions. One hundred and sixteen paragraphs are preserved in full or partial form. An extraordinarily large number deal with matters relating to the status of women and to family law. Peculiarly characteristic of these Assyrian laws are the savagery and severity of the punishments they mete out: numerous instances of the death penalty, even for offenses against property; mutilation of the body; flogging, even to the infliction of one hundred lashes; pouring pitch over the head; tearing out the eyes; subjection to the water ordeal; forced labor; and the exaction of grievously heavy fines. There are also instances of multiple punishments imposed for a single offense.

Greatly under the influence of Mesopotamian legal traditions but deriving from quite a different cultural and linguistic milieu and geographic region are two hundred Hittite laws[8] that have survived from the Old Hittite kingdom in Asia Minor, now central Turkey. The extant tablets date from about 1250 B.C.E., but they go back to a much larger corpus of laws, apparently promulgated or collected for the use of jurists about five centuries earlier. A unique feature of this compilation is the clear references to earlier laws that have been revised. Capital punishment has been restricted to but a few offenses and has been replaced by restitution. The casuistic style is extensively employed.

At this point it should be emphasized that none of the collections discussed can be considered to be codes in the usually understood sense of the term. First, one and all, they omit important spheres of legal practice, and none comes close to being a comprehensive regulation of the citizens' lives. Second, not one of the compilations decrees that it is henceforth to be binding on judges and magistrates. Third, none is ever invoked as the basis of a legal decision in all the thousands of extant documents from the actual practice of law in the courts. For these reasons, the various collections are to be regarded as recording emendations and additions to bodies of existing unwritten common law that are seen to be in need of reform. This conclusion applies equally to the corpus of laws embedded in the Torah. It is silent on matters of commercial law, on such indispensable practices as sales and contracts, the transfer of ownership, the legalization of marriage, the regulation of professions, and on most aspects of inheritance. Clearly, there existed in Israel a body of unwritten common law, orally transmitted from generation to generation, knowledge of which is assumed. What is prescribed in the Torah is a series of innovations to existing laws.

It should be further underlined that the review of the legal corpora of the ancient Near

East given above unquestionably establishes that when the people of Israel first appeared on the scene of history, their world was already heir to a widely diffused common legal culture of long standing. No wonder, then, that Israelite laws exhibit so many points of contact with the earlier collections. Like them, the Torah expresses itself in terms of concrete, real-life cases, and, like them, the underlying legal principles are not abstractly stated but are to be deduced from the resolutions of those cases.

Another feature that is common to both ancient Near Eastern law collections and their Torah counterpart is the difficulty in uncovering the organizing principle that determines the arrangement and sequence of legal topics, although some progress has been made in this regard in recent years.[9]

The affinities and analogues that abound between the Israelite and the other Near Eastern law collections tend to obscure the fundamental distinctions that exist between the two, a subject that must now be addressed. First and foremost is the essential fact that biblical law is the expression of the covenant between God and Israel. Several important consequences flow from this. The legal sections of the Torah cohere with the Exodus narratives and cannot be separated from them without losing their integrity and identity. Their sole source and sanction is Divine will, not the wisdom and power of a human monarch. As imperatives of a transcendent, sovereign God who freely entered into a covenanted relationship with His people, the laws are eternally binding on both the individual and society as a whole. Hence the public nature of the law. There can be no monopoly on the knowledge of the law, and the study of it is a religious obligation. Further, there can be no differentiation between the branches of public and private law and between both of them and religion and morality. All topics that fall under any of these rubrics are equally binding. Law is not severed from morality and religion. As to the substance of the law, the Torah allows of no vicarious punishments, no multiple penalties, and, apart from the special category of the slave, demands equal justice for all, irrespective of social status. Finally, whereas the Near Eastern laws place great stress on the importance of property, the Torah's value system favors the paramount sacredness of human life.[10]

NOTES TO THE EXCURSUSES

Excursus 1

M. Greenberg, *The Hab/piru* (New Haven: American Oriental Society, 1955); W. F. Albright, "Abram the Hebrew," *BASOR* 163 (1961): 34–54; N. P. Lemche, "The Hebrew Slave," *VT* 25 (1975): 136–142; M. B. Rowton, "Dimorphic Structure and the Problem of the *'Apiru-'Ibrim*," *JNES* 35 (1976): 13–20; R. de Vaux, *The Early History of Israel* (Philadelphia; Westminster, 1976), 209–216; E. Lipiński, "L'esclave hébreu," *VT* 25 (1976): 120–126; O. Loretz, *Habiru-Hebräer, Eine sozio-linguistische Studie über die Herkunft des Gentiliziums 'ibri vom Appellativum ḫabiru* (BZAW, 160) (Berlin: Walter De Gruyter, 1984).

1. Gen. 39:14, 17; 40:15; 41:12; 43:32.
2. Exod. 1:15,16,19; 2:6,7,11,13; 5:3; 7:16; 9:1,13; 10:3.
3. 1 Sam. 4:6,9; 13:3,7,19; 14:11,21; 29:3.

Excursus 2

B. Jacob, "The Childhood and Youth of Moses, the Messenger of God," in *Essays Presented to J. H. Hertz*, ed., I. Epstein, *et al.* (London: Edward Goldston, 1942), 245–259; O. Rank, *The Myth of the Birth of the Hero*, ed. P. Freund (New York: Vintage Books, 1959); B. S. Childs, "The Birth of Moses," *JBL* 84 (1965): 109–122; D. B. Redford, "The Literary Motif of the Exposed Child," *Numen* 14 (1967): 209–218; Th. H. Gaster, *Myth, Legend and Custom in the Old Testament* (New York: Harper, 1975), I, para. 78; B. Lewis, *The Sargon Legend*, Cambridge: ASOR (Diss. Series No. 4), 1980.

Excursus 3

J. P. Hyatt, "Yahweh as the God of My Father," *VT* 5 (1955): 130–136; M. Haran, "The Religion of the Patriarchs," *ASTI* 4 (1965): 51–52; A. Alt, "The God of the Fathers," in *Essays on Old Testament History and Religion*, trans. R. A. Wilson (Garden City, N.Y.: Doubleday, 1967), 3–100; F. M. Cross, *Canaanite Myth and Hebrew Epic* (Cambridge: Harvard University Press, 1973), 4–43.

1. Gen. 31:5, 46:3; 31:29; 46:1.
2. Gen. 24:12; 46:1.
3. Gen. 28:13; 32:10
4. Gen. 24:12,27,42,48; 28:13; 32:10.
5. Exod. 3:15,16; 4:5.

Excursus 4

W. F. Albright, *Yahweh and the Gods of Canaan* (Garden City, N.Y.: Doubleday, 1968), 108,188–189; F. M. Cross, *Canaanite Myth and Hebrew Epic* (Cambridge: Harvard University Press, 1973), 52–60.

1. Gen. 49:25; Num. 24:4,16.
2. Gen. 17:1; 28:3; 35:11; 43:14.

Excursus 5

A. Haberman, "The Tefillin in Antiquity," *Eretz-Israel* 3 (1954): 174–177; S. Goren, *Mahanayim* 62 (1961): 5–14; Y. Yadin,

Tefillin from Qumran. Jerusalem: Israel Exploration Society, 1969; M. Meiselman, *Jewish Women in Jewish Law* (New York: Ktav, 1978), 147–151; O. Keel, "Zeichen der Verbundunheit," *Orbis Biblicus et Orientalis*, 38 (1981): 159–240; J. Tigay, "Tefillin," *Encyclopaedia Mikrait* (Jerusalem: Mosad Bialik, 1982), 8:883–895.

1. M. Men. 4:1; M. Mik. 10:3; cf. *tehillim*—sing., *tehillah*.
2. Cf. Ezek. 16:52; Ps. 106:30. Less convincing is the attempt to find an Akkadian origin—E. A. Speiser, "Palil and its Congeners," in *Studies in Honor of Benno Landsberger* (Chicago: Chicago University Press, 1965), 389–393.
3. Mtt. 23:5.
4. Cf. Targ. to Song of Songs 8:3.
5. Eruv. 96a.
6. *Aristeas to Philocrates*, ed. M. Hadas (New York: Harper, 1957), 163, par. 159.
7. Josephus, Ant. 4.8.113 (Loeb 4.213, p. 579).
8. MdRY Bo' 17, p. 69; cf. TJ Eruv 10:1 (26a).
9. TJ Hag. 2:2 (77d).
10. Yadin, op. cit.
11. Commentary to M. Men. 4:1.
12. Men. 34b–35a.
13. Yadin, op. cit.: 11–15.
14. M. Tamid 5:1.
15. Ber. 12a.
16. J. Mann, "Changes in the Divine Service of the Synagogue Due to Religious Persecution," *HUCA* 4 (1927): 288–299; E. E. Urbach, "The Place of the Ten Commandments in Ritual and Prayer," in *The Ten Commandments*, ed. B. Z. Segal (Jerusalem: Magnes, 1985), 127–145.
17. Sifrei, Deut. *va-'ethanan* 34(6), 35(8), ed. L. Finkelstein (New York: Jewish Theological Seminary, 1969), 60–61, 63–64; Sanh. 89a.
18. Commentary to Mtt. 23:6 in J. P. Migne, *Patrologia Latina* (Turnholti, Belgium: Typographi Brepols, 1963), vol. 26, col. 174.
19. Ber. 20b; TJ Ber. 3:3(6b); Eruv. 96a; M. Kid. 1:7; Kid. 34a–35b; cf. Targ. Jon. to Deut. 22:5.
20. MdRY Bo' 17, p. 68; Eruv. 96a. Contrast TJ Eruv. 10:1 (26a).
21. *Orhot Hayyim*. Florence, 1750, I "tefillin," No. 3.
22. Cited by Tosafot in RH 33a (top). See also Responsa of Rashba, 1:123; *The Novellae of R. Solomon b. Adret on the Treatise Rosh Hashanah*, ed. H. Z. Dimitrovsky (New York: Alexander Kohut Memorial Foundation, 1961), 185–186.
23. Tosafot, RH 33a.

Excursus 6

1. See bibliography above to Chap. 21.
2. This principle, *dibberah torah kileshon benei 'adam*, is registered in Sifrei 112:11; Yev. 71a, Ket. 67b; Ned. 3a–b; Git. 41b; Kid. 17b; BM 31b, 94b; Sanh. 56a, 64b, 85b, 90b; Mak. 12a; Av. Zar. 27a; Zev. 108b; Bek. 31b; Arak. 31a; Ker. 11a; Nid. 32b, 44a.
3. ANET, 523–525.
4. ANET, 159–161.
5. ANET, 161–163.
6. ANET, 163–180.
7. ANET, 180–188.
8. ANET, 188–197.

9. H. Petschow, "Zur Systematik und Gesetzestechnick im Codex Hammurabi," ZA 57 (1965): 146–172; B. Eichler, "Literary Structure in the Laws of Eshnunna" in *Language, Literature and History: Philological and Historical Studies Presented to Erica Reiner*, ed. F. Rochberg-Halton (New Haven: American Oriental Society, 1987), 71–84; S. A. Kaufman, "The Structure of the Deuteronomic Law," Maarav 1/2 (1978–1979): 105–158.

10. On this topic, see M. Greenberg, "Some Postulates of Biblical Criminal Law," *Yehezkel Kaufmann Jubilee Volume*, ed. M. Haran (Jerusalem: Magnes Press, 1960), 5–28; *idem*, "More Reflections on Biblical Criminal Law," in *Studies in Bible*, ed. S. Japhet (Jerusalem: Magnes Press, 1986), 1–17.